UCD
A National Idea

UCD
A National Idea

The History of University College, Dublin

Donal McCartney

Gill & Macmillan

Gill & Macmillan Ltd
Goldenbridge
Dublin 8
with associated companies throughout the world

www.gillmacmillan.ie

0 7171 2336 7

Print origination by
O'K Graphic Design, Dublin

Index by Helen Litton

Printed by ColourBooks Ltd, Dublin

1 3 5 4 2

This book is typeset in 10/13 pt Stempel Garamond

Dedication
To all who in their various ways have been part of the history of UCD

'I look towards a land both old
and young; old in its Christianity,
young in the promise of its future ...
I contemplate a people which
has had a long night,
and will have an inevitable day.
I am turning my eyes towards
A hundred years to come, and I
dimly see the island I am gazing on,
become the road of passage and union
between two hemispheres,
and the centre of the world ...
The capital of that prosperous and
hopeful land is situate in a beautiful
bay and near a romantic region; and
in it I see a flourishing University,
which for a while had to struggle
with fortune, but which, when its first
founders and servants were dead
and gone, had successes far
exceeding their anxieties.'

John Henry Newman, 1854

'... What are the needs of Ireland? I claim that the peculiar circumstances of Ireland demand an extremely democratic university ...

... I hold and maintain that if we are to reconquer this land for ourselves, it is to the brains of the children of the people we must look for the means to conquer it. I hold this, that on the day on which the portals of a great and richly endowed institution are thrown wide open to the children of the poorest in this country the greatest blow will have been struck that ever has been to emancipate our people from slavery.

The next demand I should be disposed to make for that university is that it should be given from the start the priceless gift of a free academic life and self-government, ensuring that it will be a genuine expression of national intellect and national ideals, and will form a genuine intellectual centre for the Irish race.

... What I have proposed is this—to look for students, not amongst the classes, but the masses of the country ... If they only get the chance, believe me they will carry the name and fame of this city and of Ireland to the uttermost ends of the earth. What we want to have in Ireland is a National institution which will represent the ideals of our people, which will be an intellectual centre not only for our race at home but for our race throughout the world ...'

John Dillon MP, 1904

Contents

Foreword

D onal McCartney's splendid history of University College Dublin traces its developments from its origins as the Catholic University to its position as the largest and most diverse university institution in the country. The vicissitudes through which it passed are reflected in the changes in nomenclature which accompanied them. The Catholic University became, in 1882, University College Dublin, a college of the Catholic University, with its degrees conferred by the recently established Royal University of Ireland. When it became a constituent college of the National University of Ireland in 1908, it retained the title University College Dublin, but for many years after was known colloquially as 'National' to distinguish it from the rival Dublin institution at Trinity College. That appellation also reflected its status as a national institution which was recognised at the outset by the decision to have its eight local authority representatives elected by a national body, the General Council of County Councils, rather than by province or individual county. In the absence of any national legislature, the General Council was the body most representative of the country as a whole. It was only in the sixties that 'UCD' replaced 'National' as the usual description. When the Universities Act 1997 conferred the official designation of National University of Ireland, Dublin, the Governing Authority opted to retain the more established description. Thus the institution was formally, if cumbersomely, entitled University College, Dublin, National University of Ireland, Dublin, leading one observer to suggest that the university's soccer club now had a longer name than any other soccer club in the world!

The Catholic University had suffered from the handicap that its degrees were not recognised by the state, and it was no accident that the one section of the university that did flourish was its medical school at Cecilia Street because its graduates were granted a licence to practise, mainly through the Royal College of Surgeons in Ireland. Newman himself was less preoccupied with examinations and degree results and his observations still have a relevance today when there are debates about the merits of the 'virtual university'. He wrote that if asked to choose between a university that merely concentrated on examinations and degree results and one which had no professors or examinations at all, but merely brought a number of young men together for three or four years, he would undoubtedly opt for the latter.

'When a multitude of young men, keen, open-hearted, sympathetic and observant, as young men are, come together and freely mix with each other, they are sure to learn one from another, even if there be no one to teach them; the conversation of all is a series of lectures to each, and they gain for themselves new ideas and views, fresh matter of thought, and distinct principles for judging and acting, day by day.'

After 1908 it was possible for students at University College, Dublin, men and women, both to enjoy the advantages delineated by Newman and also to take the degrees of the National University of Ireland.

The history deals preponderantly with the period 1908–72 and with the four presidencies of Denis Coffey (1908–40), Arthur Conway (1940–47), Michael Tierney (1947–64) and Jeremiah Hogan (1964–72). Denis Coffey had been Dean of the Catholic University School prior to his appointment by the government as president. Reputed to know the history of every student in the college, an extravagant claim even if numbers were then much smaller, Coffey guided the institution through its early very difficult years and by the close of his lengthy term had firmly established UCD in the public mind as the principal university institution in the country. His successor as president, Arthur Conway, inherited a growing financial crisis and the pressure of increasing student numbers. The coincidence of his presidency with the Second World War added to the difficulties of achieving the necessary physical expansion, and his best efforts to expand in the Earlsfort Terrace area were ultimately frustrated.

There is not doubt that the dominant figure of the era was Conway's successor, Michael Tierney, a surprise choice as president in 1947. Having finished only third with four votes at the Governing Body, he decisively reversed this result at the NUI Senate. In the immediate aftermath of the election the shrewd James Meenan confided to his diary.

'T. may be very good president. He will have a long run of seventeen years. He has an academic mind and is interested in the College. He will be very sound on Irish. But I don't know that he is very good at handling students and I think he feels that their proper kind of life should be copied from a seminary. He is also quicker in action than in judgment. There may be trouble over things as a result. But he has moral courage—as was shown in the censorship debates—and a lot can be forgiven for that.'

This was a percipient judgment. There were to be troubles with both students and staff arising, in part at least, from the perception that the President acted as a benevolent (or not so benevolent) despot. Clashes with students in the Literary and Historical Society punctuated his term of office and disputes over staff appointments led to the Visitation of 1960. Yet what might be seen as faults in one context could appear as virtues in another. And the President's 'moral courage' and single-mindedness were nowhere better displayed than in his ultimately successful campaign to move the university to Belfield.

As early as 1949 Michael Tierney had purchased the property then known as Whiteoaks to become the official residence of the President under the new title of University Lodge. He took up residence there in 1952 as an act of faith in the future. In the previous year the Governing Body had unanimously resolved to move to the new site. However, a long and arduous battle had to be fought before that resolution could become reality, and in that battle Michael Tierney was the key figure. The author observes, 'Without his tenacity and the steel in the fibre of his character, Belfield might never have materialised'. After the Dáil's final approval of the transfer to Belfield in 1960, Professor Robin Dudley Edwards justifiably termed him 'the second founder of UCD'.

Jeremiah Hogan's presidency saw the implementation of the building plans devised under his predecessor. But his term of office also saw, perhaps in part as a reaction to the Tierney regime, growing student discontent which, fanned by international examples, produced the 'Gentle Revolution' of 1968–9. Though it provided an opportunity, as one participant put it, for 'a short frolic on the world stage', the heady excitement it generated produced little enough in the way of results.

The other main issue of Hogan's presidency, the projected merger with Trinity College Dublin also promised much more than it achieved. Pharmacy and dentistry went to Trinity, and veterinary medicine came to UCD with a promise to transfer the faculty from the unsatisfactory Ballsbridge site to the main Belfield campus. Another commitment was made in 1969 when the then Minister for Education informed the SRC that the Student's Union Building would be constructed by August 1971. Work will begin this summer (of 1999) on both the veterinary faculty and the Student Centre!

The book closes with an epilogue briefly tracing the main developments since 1972. A longer perspective will be required before an assessment of those years can be made. But a large gap in the history of higher education in Ireland has now been filled. This chronicle of the fortune's of Ireland's premier university—a national reality, no longer an idea—deserves and will attract a wide readership. The book matches the eminence of its subject, and is a major contribution both to the history of university education and the study of modern Ireland.

Art Cosgrove BA PhD
President
University College Dublin
June 1999

Preface

*H*istories of educational institutions are normally published to celebrate centenaries or other jubilee occasions. This book can offer no such justification. It might be argued that since classes in the Dublin college of the National University of Ireland commenced on 2 November 1909 we are in 1999 commemorating our ninetieth birthday. Sophistical apologies of the sort are hardly necessary. For long the largest third-level institution in the country, UCD has supplied graduates in their thousands to every corner of Ireland and all over the world. The need for a history of a national institution of such significance has been long felt. Despite some notable contributions to special aspects of its history, no full-length survey exists.

The history of a university institution may take several forms, each of them with its own validity. Michael Tierney once wrote: 'With an institution so Irish as the College has been and is, it is probably inevitable that some day someone will write its history in a series of anecdotes.' (*Struggle with Fortune*, p. 231.) Although 'characters' abounded and have become the stuff of College folklore, the present volume makes no attempt to fulfil Tierney's prophecy.

Another legitimate form which a history of the College might have taken would have been a reconstruction from the students' point of view of what life was like during their time there. It would be too much to hope that all would have remembered it with Newman as 'the shrine of our best affections, the bosom of our fondest recollections, a spell upon our after life ...' (*Historical Sketches*, 1891 edition, iii, 215.) Most, however, would appreciate the point in a remark by Professor Arthur Clery: 'To the student of a college there never was a time like his time there, or any colleagues like his old friends and enemies.' (*National Student*, i, no 2, new series, June 1930, p. 100.) Colourful as the recollections of the different generations of students would undoubtedly have been, it was not the prime aim of this book.

When I first began to plan this work, I considered incorporating a survey of the major advances contributed successively by members of the various Faculties and departments. I soon realised that any worthwhile academic history of the kind, given the complexity and diversity of the many specialisms involved, was well beyond my modest understanding or training and was probably best left to a team of specialists. I could not so much as begin to appreciate the significance of the research which had earned international reputations even for the earliest generation of UCD's academics: for A.W. Conway on quaternions; McClelland and his students on the equilibrium of ionisation in the atmosphere; Hugh Ryan on flavanoids; Bergin on Celtic philology; Mac Neill on Ogham inscriptions. The equally exotic and numerous specialist studies of the more recent scholars likewise retained their mysteries for me. Apart from the advances in Arts and Science, an academic history of the College would also have to take into account the varieties of progress that had been made by the professional and more utilitarian Faculties of Agriculture, Veterinary, Engineering and Architecture, Commerce, Law and Medicine. I hope I will not be too harshly judged by colleagues disappointed that more attention had not been given to the origins and development of their own particular Faculty.

I considered myself better qualified to examine the general historical framework within which the routine business of the College operated, the students studied and played, the 'characters' conducted themselves and the research work prospered. This resulted in the concentration of my efforts on the broader canvas of the inter-relationship between Church, State and College. In doing so I had come to appreciate another comment by Michael Tierney: '... the story of the development of Newman's Catholic University into the modern University College, Dublin, is one of the most complex and fascinating chapters in the history of modern Ireland. At every stage the work of the College has been intimately linked with the slow but inexorable recovery of the national strength.' (*Struggle with Fortune*, p. 237.)

While it was hoped that the Catholic University of Ireland might become the intellectual headquarters for English-speaking Catholics from all over the world, it was established primarily as a national institution for the benefit of the religious majority in Ireland. Even its very English first Rector had insisted that among its other objectives the practical end of a university training 'aims at ... purifying the national taste'. (Newman, *The Idea of a University*, Discourse vii, 10.) And in his address to the evening classes he declared: 'You are born for Ireland; and, in your advancement, Ireland is advanced.'

As a constituent college of the National University of Ireland, UCD was always intended by its founders to be a great national institution—but one that had its doors and windows open to the world of scholars and scholarship. It is in that sense that even before its formal establishment, UCD has always been a national idea—'national' but not in any narrow, exclusive meaning of the word. Its national character, closely integrated with its Catholic ethos, pre-dated the intense political and cultural nationalism of the early twentieth century; and it was to survive the later loosening of the bonds with the Church and merge quite smoothly into that European community being moulded in the last quarter of the twentieth century.

Important as he undoubtedly was, Newman was by no means the sole contributor to UCD's rich inheritance. The Faculties of Engineering, Science, Agriculture, Veterinary and Medicine owed much to the College of Science, the Albert College, the Veterinary College, the Dublin schools of Medicine and to the great traditions stretching back behind these to the Royal Dublin Society, the Royal Irish Academy and the Museum of Irish Industry. Newman himself had drawn upon these native sources for many of his original staff. It was, however, the Newman tradition in its powerful flow that swept along the contributions from these other streams which, mingling together, gave UCD its individual colour and character.

'Our university is destined for great things,' wrote Newman at the commencement of his enterprise in Ireland (*Historical Sketches*, London, 1891, iii, 146). It was that conviction which remained an inspiration and sustained UCD through the most difficult periods of its history.

I remain acutely aware of my sins of omission, and of how much has yet to be researched and written in order to do full justice to the massive contribution which University College has made to society and scholarship. I draw comfort from another Newman aphorism—'No man is given to see his work through; ... others are destined to complete what he began'. (*Essays: Critical and Historical*, London, 1891, ii, 317.) My hope is that others will be stimulated into providing further accounts of the multi-faceted history of our College.

Donal McCartney
Professor Emeritus of Modern Irish History
UCD
July 1999

Acknowledgments

M ost of my research for this volume was undertaken in UCD's own archives. When I began my work the relevant sources had not yet been professionally catalogued. I must express my gratitude, therefore, to Breidge Doherty for the thoroughness with which she assisted in rooting out and listing the required material. I am indebted to the personnel of UCD's Archives Department: Kerry Holland, Seamus Helferty, Jennifer O'Reilly, Donal Dunne, Ciaran Trace and more recently Rena Lohan, the College Archivist. I also acknowledge the assistance of the UCD Librarian, Sean Phillips, and his staff; David Sheehy of the Dublin Diocesan Archives; the staffs of the National Archives, National Library and National University of Ireland. Joyce Padbury and Ronnie Hayes of the President's office were helpful at all times. Many in UCD—far too numerous to list—answered my questions or volunteered information, advice or goading. I am most deeply indebted to Louise Richardson who in addition to her other administrative work made sense of my handwriting, followed complicated additions and deletions, offered intelligent comments and ultimately transferred the apparent chaos to a clean computer print-out. A very sincere word of thanks must go to Louis Mc Redmond who read my early drafts, offered acute observations and many valuable suggestions and assisted with great generosity in all aspects of the final production. My thanks also to Deirdre Greenan and the highly efficient staff of Gill & Macmillan, and to Michael Gill for his patience and encouragement and the personal interest he took in the project. As first editor of the resurrected student magazine, *St Stephen's*, in 1960 he had written: 'We look to the future with confidence because of pride in the traditions of the past'. That confidence and pride have never left him.

Credit for the illustrations must go to UCD's Audio Visual Centre— especially Mitchell Sheridan and Margaret Delaney; to Ruth Ferguson, Curator of Newman House; to Peter Costello, Professor Caoimhin Breathnach and the Michael Tierney and Michael Hayes family collections. Materials from the Curran collection are published by permission of University College, Dublin Library. I wish to thank Veronica Meenan and Ruth Dudley Edwards for permission to quote from their fathers' papers.

It was President Tom Murphy who first suggested to me that I should consider undertaking this work. I can only regret that President Murphy did not live to see my tardy effort to repay his faith in me. President Paddy Masterson continued to apply every gentle encouragement and support. My former history colleague, Dr Art Cosgrove, now President of UCD, facilitated in various ways the final appearance of the book. Although asked by the College authorities to write a history of UCD and given free access to the relevant records, I was left to treat the subject entirely in my own way. No doubt the book could have benefited from President Cosgrove's experienced editorial eye, but he did not see the volume until it had been completed. I am, therefore, all the more grateful for his foreword.

Finally, my thanks to my wife, Peig, for having shared me so generously with UCD, and for all the help, love and understanding which she has given over the years. It was Peig who suggested the dedication.

Abbreviations

AC	Academic Council
ASA	Academic Staff Association
AW	*John Henry Newman: Autobiographical Writings*, ed. Henry Tristram (London and New York, 1956)
CSO	Central Statistics Office
CUI	Catholic University of Ireland
DCU	Dublin City University
DDA	Dublin Diocesan Archives
DNB	*Dictionary of National Biography*
EHR	*English Historical Review*
GB	Governing Body
IFUT	Irish Federation of University Teachers
L&H	Literary and Historical Society
LD	*The Letters and Diaries of John Henry Newman*, ed. Charles Stephen Dessain *et al.* (Oxford and London, 1961–77)
MS	Manuscript
NA	National Archives of Ireland
NLI	National Library of Ireland
NUI	National University of Ireland
QUI	Queen's University of Ireland
RUI	Royal University of Ireland
SCM	Students' Christian Movement
SDA	Students for Democratic Action
SRC	Students' Representative Council
TCD	Trinity College, Dublin
UCC	University College, Cork
UCD	University College, Dublin
UCG	University College, Galway
USI	Union of Students Ireland

1

Antecedents

*Let us set up our own University: let us only set it up, and it will teach
the world its value by the fact of its existence.*
                    J. H. Newman, *Historical Sketches*, iii, 58–9.

THE CATHOLIC UNIVERSITY OF IRELAND

The two principal and recurring issues in Irish politics in the nineteenth
century were repeal of the Act of Union and reform of the land system. Next
in order of importance, at least as far as the Catholic bishops were concerned,
was education, of which the university question formed a crucial part.

For two-and-a-half centuries after its foundation in 1592 by Queen
Elizabeth I, Trinity College—sole college of the University of Dublin—was
the only university institution in Ireland. From the beginning, college statutes
made it obligatory for all students to attend the Anglican services in the
college chapel. Religious tests and anti-papal oaths were imposed on provost,
fellows and scholars and on all who wished to obtain a degree. So, for most of
its first two hundred years, Trinity College was in effect an exclusively
Protestant institution.

The Catholic Relief Act (1793) enabled Catholics to enter Trinity and
obtain a degree without violating their conscience. They were still, however,
debarred by religious tests from becoming scholars or fellows and from
holding office. An Act of 1873 removed all religious tests; but in spite of this,
Trinity's ethos and management continued to be Protestant and unionist. The
provost was always a Church of Ireland clergyman during the hundred years
preceding the appointment of a lay provost in the early twentieth century.
Three hundred years after its foundation one of its distinguished graduates,
Judge Webb, declared in 1891 that 'their university was founded by
Protestants, for Protestants and in the Protestant interest … and Protestant
might it ever more remain.'[1] Another distinguished graduate, Lord Justice
Fitzgibbon, speaking on the same occasion, agreed and said it was the proud
boast of the church to which he belonged that every bishop on its bench but
one was a graduate of the University of Dublin.

Following the Catholic Emancipation movement and the progress of civil and religious freedom in the early nineteenth century, both Catholics and Protestant dissenters began to look for equality of treatment in the field of higher education, which hitherto had been an Anglican monopoly. In the eighteen-forties Sir Robert Peel made the first of many attempts on the part of the British government to solve the Irish university problem. Peel's government sought a solution partly to remedy the sectarian situation and partly to answer the slowly growing demand from Catholics and dissenters but also in the hope of detaching the Catholic bishops and middle class from supporting O'Connell's repeal agitation.

The soundings Peel made about the possibility of creating new colleges within the University of Dublin were strongly repulsed by Trinity and its friends. He decided instead in 1845 to establish 'Queen's Colleges' in Belfast, Cork, and Galway. This was intended to be a conciliatory measure for those Catholics and dissenters who were unwilling or unable to attend Trinity. A Queen's University was incorporated in 1850 for the purpose of regulating courses and conferring degrees on graduates of the three colleges.

The colleges were to be strictly undenominational: that is, no religious tests could be applied, and public funds could not be used for any theological teaching. But if Trinity was deemed by the Catholic bishops to be too Protestant, many of them felt that the Queen's Colleges were too irreligious. Though some bishops were prepared to give the Queen's Colleges a chance to prove themselves, and a few were to remain, at least privately, convinced of their value—despite repeated censures with which they themselves were associated as members of the hierarchy—the weight of opinion among Catholic leaders, both lay and ecclesiastical, was strongly opposed to what O'Connell and others called a 'gigantic scheme of Godless education.'[2] This soon became the official position of the hierarchy. It was based on the grounds that, in the first place, the scheme did not give Catholics equality, since religious teaching and catechetical instruction, which Protestants received officially in Trinity, was prohibited in the Queen's Colleges. But the main objection raised by the bishops was that these colleges were dangerous to faith and morals. 'Mixed' education, whereby people of different religions were educated alongside each other and in a secularist atmosphere, was objected to in principle by the Catholic Church. Three papal rescripts—1847, 1848, and 1850—condemned Peel's colleges, and at the National Synod of Thurles in 1850 the condemnation was formally promulgated by the bishops.

The Synod of Thurles, as a result of repeated urgings from Rome, resolved to adopt a recommendation that a Catholic University of Ireland be established, taking as a model the Catholic University of Louvain. A Catholic University

Committee was appointed, consisting of the four archbishops, four bishops representing each of the provinces, and eight priests and eight laymen co-opted by the episcopal members.

John Henry Newman, who had been one of the leaders of the Oxford Movement, which had sought reform of the Church of England, had become by this time the most famous convert to Catholicism. He was requested by Archbishop Cullen to advise on the setting up of a university, and in November 1851 he was formally invited to become its first rector.[3] In the Rotunda, Dublin, on five consecutive Monday afternoons during May and June 1852 he delivered in part those lectures that, when published, became famous as the 'Discourses' of his well-known and important book *The Idea of a University*.

Before Newman had ever set foot in Ireland the Catholic University Committee had begun its search for a site for the university, with Thurles and Dublin the chief contenders for the honour. St Patrick's College, Thurles, which had housed the National Synod, had the advantage of a fine ready-to-use building. But Dr Cullen had come around to the idea that on practical grounds Dublin had far more to offer.

On his first visit to Ireland, Newman travelled to Thurles in early October 1851 to meet fellow-members of a three-man sub-committee that had been requested to draw up a report on the organisation of the university. Newman's rejection of Thurles was quite decisive. From there he wrote on 30 October to a friend in England: *'Entre nous* this would never do for a site —a large building but on a forlorn waste, without a tree, in a forlorn country and a squalid town.'[4] Later he was to add: 'How could we have had a medical school in a country village like Thurles.'[5]

The search then switched to Dublin. Various proposals were explored. Archbishop John MacHale was for spending the £30,000 that had been collected in the first year 'on some one imposing building which should lodge the whole university, after the model of Trinity College.'[6] Newman and Cullen were agreed that the university should begin modestly; and Newman favoured the idea of a number of houses, which in time could become halls and colleges of the university, on the model of Oxford. At a meeting of the Catholic University Committee in July 1852 Dr Cullen was requested to inquire into the feasibility of acquiring houses 'in a desirable position of the city for our first essay.'[7]

A short time later a fine Georgian house, number 86 St Stephen's Green, became available. This had been built in 1765–66 by Richard Chapell Whaley, whose anti-Catholic activities during the era of the Penal Laws had earned him the nickname 'Burn-Chapel' Whaley; it was also said that he had sworn that no papist would ever cross his threshold. The house was bought in February 1853 at a cost of £3,500 'as the most eligible position to be had in Dublin to make a commencement of the Catholic University of Ireland.'[8]

Charles Bianconi, the wealthy founder of a large-scale coach service and a member of the Catholic University Committee, acted as the agent through whom the purchase was made. Given the popery scare in Britain that had led to the introduction of the Ecclesiastical Titles Bill (1851) the preceding year, it was discreet and publicly inoffensive to Ascendancy sensitivities to have Bianconi make the transaction and then transfer the deeds to the trusteeship of the archbishops.

Not until February 1854 was Newman able to make a detailed inspection of the premises. He noted in his 'University Journal' that he 'went over the house … marking out the alterations in order to turn it into rooms. It will make 17 (single) rooms in two upper stories.'[9] A few days later, on 17 February, he reported that he had 'thrown lawyers, architects, painters, paperers, and upholsterers into the University House with a view of preparing for our Autumn opening.'[10]

However architecturally imposing and splendid as a Georgian house, '86' left much to be desired as a university. Compared with the 'spaciousness of the handsomely housed' Trinity College and the Queen's Colleges it was a gloomy and miserable enough receptacle for Newman's great dream of a Catholic university that was to be the intellectual headquarters of the English-speaking world.

In the meantime Newman had also been busy recruiting a staff for the university. His aim was to appoint as professors Catholics whose names were widely known and whose eminence in their various departments would draw public attention to the university, whether or not there were any students for the subjects they taught. The idea was that these men would advertise the institution by giving a short series of public lectures. Appointments such as those of Eugene O'Curry (chair of archaeology and Irish history), John O'Hagan (political economy), Aubrey de Vere (political and social science), Denis Florence McCarthy (poetry), T. W. Allies (philosophy of history), Terence Flanagan (civil engineering), Rev. Patrick Leahy (holy scripture), Rev. Edward O'Reilly SJ (dogmatic theology) and J. H. Pollen, the architect of the University Church (fine arts), may have seemed like no more than intellectual window-dressing had they not also contributed inaugural public lectures. Allies gave an inaugural lecture but apparently nothing else. McCarthy gave only a few lectures. These professors were more akin to what would now be described as honorary or research professors.

Newman's expectation that they would also publish while professors of the university was fulfilled in Eugene O'Curry's *Lectures on the Manuscript Materials of Ancient Irish History* and *The Manners and Customs of the Ancient Irish* and in J. B. Robertson's *Lectures on Some Subjects of Modern History and Biography Delivered at the Catholic University of Ireland, 1860–1864.* The 'dozen lectures' that de Vere gave were afterwards published in substance as *Essays, Chiefly Literary and Ethical* (1889). *Atlantis* (1858–1870), a literary and scientific journal, was also founded by Newman for the purpose of advertising the work of these professors of the university.

The routine slog of teaching courses and preparing students for examinations was done by such men as Robert Ornsby in Latin, James Stewart in Greek, Edward Butler in mathematics, Dr David Dunne in logic, Signor Marani in Italian and Spanish, Peter Renouf in French, Henry Hennessy in mathematical physics, James Robertson in history and geography, and later Thomas Arnold in English literature and W. K. Sullivan in chemistry, especially for the medical students.

STUDENTS OF THE CATHOLIC UNIVERSITY

The Catholic University opened its doors on the feast of St Malachy, 3 November 1854. On that day the names of seventeen students were entered on the register; the first name entered was that of Daniel O'Connell, grandson of the Liberator. The following Sunday, to a grand total of four officers and fifteen students, Newman gave an address entitled 'What are we here for?' Conscious of the small numbers with which they were beginning their great endeavour, he prophesied that when they were old they would look back with great pride and pleasure to St Malachy's Day, 1854. He ended his address by reminding his audience of the words attributed by Shakespeare to King Henry V before the battle of Agincourt: 'We few, we happy few, we band of brothers.'

Newman was a great believer in the idea that his students should stay in independent, self-supporting halls or colleges in small groups under a dean and private tutors. Each house was to have its own chapel and common table. With this purpose in mind the university opened with three houses: 86 St Stephen's Green, which was known as St Patrick's or University House, under the care of Rev. Dr Michael Flannery; 16 Harcourt Street, known as St Lawrence's, under the care of Rev. Dr James Quinn, who also had his school there; and Newman's own house, 6 Harcourt Street, known as St Mary's, under Newman's personal supervision.

It is usual to think of Newman of the Dublin years as the grand philosopher of a liberal university education; the theorist who delivered the famous lectures on the idea of a university; the author of the *University Sketches* on the origins and development of universities, in which he provided a practical illustration of what his *Idea of a University* had only dealt with in the abstract and which were first published in the *Catholic University Gazette,* edited by Newman, to provide information about the proceedings of the Catholic University. It is usual to think of him as the deliverer of the inaugural and other addresses to the Faculty of Arts, to the School of Medicine, and to the evening students; the preacher of sermons in the University Church, published as *Sermons Preached on Various Occasions* (1857); the defender of the Catholic University in articles published in several journals; and the writer of the annual reports of the rector and the drafter of structures, rules and regulations for the new institution, published in *My Campaign in Ireland.* All these things he did, and did admirably and elegantly; but there was another, more prosaic and practical side to his Dublin career. For at times Newman was obliged to behave more like the harassed housemaster in a boarding school than as the rector of a new university.

Of the eight original students in Newman's own house, two were Irish, two English, two Scottish, and two French. Among them were a French viscount, an Irish baronet (Sir Reginald Barnewall), the son of a French countess, the grandson of a Scottish marquis, and the son of an English lord. The rector felt that this was a good start and one that should raise the tone and image of the university and attract others. Later were added to his care two Belgian princes and a Polish count.

The one native-born middle-class Irishman to be admitted to Newman's house was the sixteen-year-old only son of a solicitor from Limerick by the name of O'Shea. 'That O'Shea', as Newman called the inmate of his front drawing-room, lasted for half a year only, but half way through that period he was causing the rector much trouble. 'My youths, all through that O'Shea, or rather in the person of O'Shea, are giving me trouble—and I don't know how I possibly can stand another year. I think he must go at the end of the session.'[11] The troublesome student left and went to Trinity instead, but his mischief-making was far from over. It might be said that the rector had unerringly recognised the boy who was to be father to the man: for as Newman lay dying in August 1890 his former student, Captain William O'Shea, was at the centre of the divorce scandal that was to destroy the political career of Charles Stewart Parnell.

The non-Irish students were attracted because of Newman's reputation. Many of them were the sons of friends who had been influenced by the Oxford Movement; a number followed him directly from the Birmingham Oratory School. Some of his professors and benefactors were converts. To that degree the Catholic University was, if not a product, at least an extension of the Oxford Movement.

The great majority of the students did not have the privilege of living in the rector's house, and Newman was from time to time to be agreeably surprised at the calibre of the Irish students who lived in the other houses. And well he might, for among the prizemen, during and after Newman's time, were William Walsh, afterwards Archbishop of Dublin and first Chancellor of the National University of Ireland; Patrick O'Donnell, who, as Bishop of Raphoe, serving on the Governing Body of UCD, was another link between the Catholic University and University College; H. H. O'Rourke-McDermott, afterwards Attorney-General for Ireland under Gladstone; John Dillon, who as a parliamentarian played a big part in the university legislation of 1908 that established the NUI; and James Lynam Molloy, afterwards the composer of many popular songs, including 'Bantry Bay', 'The Kerry Dances', and 'Love's Old Sweet Song'. Molloy was the only student who was threatened with rustication by Newman, for absconding one night from University House and attending an evening party without leave. Newman, however, accepted the pleas of Molloy's mother and allowed him to continue his studies. And so, of the Irish students who caused Newman most trouble, one was afterwards to be condemned also by generations of nationalists for the role he played in Irish politics, while the other was to be loved and admired for the pleasure his songs have given down the years.

The Catholic University Medical School was opened in 1855 in Cecilia Street. No more than a stone's throw from the front gates of Trinity College, the Medical School symbolised the emergence of Catholic Ireland. Newman claimed that before he established the Medical School, out of 111 doctors in situations of authority in Dublin's five medical schools and hospitals, 12 were Catholic and 99 Protestant.[12] The Medical School was the Catholic University's great success story: by the end of the century it had become the largest medical school in the country. After 1908 it became the Medical Faculty of UCD.

Newman's own beautiful University Church was opened in 1856 beside 86. Apart from religious services it was used also for public university functions and occasions such as the opening of academic sessions and the making of awards.

Newman's numerous publications,[13] the fruit of his association with the Catholic University, together with his voluminous correspondence, present the image of a most intelligent and dedicated man attending meticulously to every detail of the work of the Catholic University.[14] One of his students has given us a vivid glimpse of the rector on his daily journey from his home to the university: 'His was a striking figure as he walked with short, rapid steps from Harcourt St. to the Green, tenuous and angular, his head bent forward, his ascetic features shrouded in meditation, and his keen eyes looking neither to the right nor the left, but introspectively, as it were, with a contemplativeness far removed from things of the thoroughfare.'[15]

A friend, Aubrey de Vere, confessed that he was pained to find a man of Newman's intellectual achievements spending his precious time carving meat for some thirty hungry students, or listening for hours to visitors who came to recommend a new organist. The humble labours to which Newman subjected himself, no less than the enduring products of his intellect, were all undertaken for the benefit of the Catholic University. Such tireless effort deserved far greater success than Newman himself in his modesty ever felt he had achieved.

EARLY DIFFICULTIES

The sense of failure that haunted Newman for some time after his resignation in 1858 had much to do with the frustration he had experienced during his seven years as rector. Despite his great hopes and personal commitment, the university had not turned out to be the intellectual headquarters for Catholics of the English-speaking world. Only a handful of the sons of fellow-converts and friends in Britain followed Newman to Dublin, and this source dried up with Newman's departure. The Catholic University became instead an institution for Irish Catholics; and this development, though it pleased some of its Irish friends, was not the aim of its first rector or indeed of Cullen and his Catholic University Committee.

In the twenty-five years from 1854 to 1879 the grand total of full-time students—excluding evening, affiliated and medical students—was 521, or an average yearly intake of about twenty.[16] Newman's expectation that it would attract large numbers from throughout the English-speaking world never materialised. Only twenty-four Irish-born students educated in England registered for the Catholic University. Some twenty-two British-born and British-educated were registered; other foreign students numbered perhaps no more than fifteen, about half of whom were attracted to Dublin during Newman's time. It was over-optimistic ever to think that American students would flock to Dublin during the nineteenth century. Even as an Irish institution, however, it failed to emulate the success of one of its faculties, the Medical School.

For Newman in the thick of the experiment the frustrations were too easily personalised. The controlling power in the university was Paul Cullen, Archbishop of Dublin. When he returned to Ireland as Rome's Apostolic Delegate he had already spent thirty years—most of his life up to that time—in Rome. By temperament, tradition and training he was very different from the English convert whom he had invited to be rector. The two men who should have been co-operating most closely in the enterprise were temperamentally incompatible. Archbishop MacHale of Tuam, who distrusted Cullen's centralising policies and his control of the university, was as a result rude to Newman, disliked his appointment of Englishmen to some of the professorships, and made matters difficult for him.

Apart from these two powerful figures on the ecclesiastical scene, Newman said he experienced nothing but kindness from the Irish bishops. This also meant, however, that some were only lukewarm towards the university enterprise, or even apathetic, as in the conditions of post-Famine Ireland it was hardly a social or religious priority with many of them.

Newman claimed never to be able to understand the Irish or the Ireland of his day. He later admitted that he knew nothing of the men with whom he had to work and was perplexed by his ignorance of whom to trust and whom to choose. He was right when he said that Dr Cullen himself was 'a stranger to Ireland'[17] and that he did not know Ireland well.[18] But what made matters more difficult for Newman was that he had to rely to a considerable extent on Anglo-Irish and English friends, who may not have been the best to keep him informed of Irish affairs.

Personal factors, much as they may have added by the end of his rectorship to Newman's sense of frustration, were less important than the material conditions, which greatly hampered the progress of the Catholic University. There had been no urgent or pressing demand for the university from public opinion at the moment when it was launched; it was supported in large measure as a counter to the Queen's Colleges. The number of Catholic secondary schools producing qualified potential entrants to the university was still, in the eighteen-fifties, quite small. The Jesuit Vice-Provincial had warned Newman that 'the class of youths did not exist in Ireland who would come to the university.' In the circumstances, therefore, it made sense to look outside Ireland for the students; but it was hardly realistic to expect that they would come in numbers large enough to compensate for the absence of Irish entrants.

The Catholic University also suffered from the handicap that, unlike Trinity and the Queen's Colleges, its degrees were not recognised by the state, nor did it receive any state funding. The British government, which had just provided the Queen's Colleges, was understandably reluctant to give a charter or funds to an institution that the bishops had founded in opposition to the government's own scheme.

In the meantime the Irish masses recovering from the disasters of the Famine had not much interest in the Catholic University. They would generously make their contributions at the annual collection in the churches for as long as they were asked to do so by their bishops and priests; but those students and parents who were more anxious for a state-recognised degree than for the ideal of a Catholic university education looked beyond Newman's institution for their satisfaction. So, while some middle-class Catholics went to Trinity for their degrees, and Anglo-Irish gentry sent their sons to the English universities, and English Catholics (especially after Newman's time) were not attracted to Dublin, a number of Catholics in the provinces found the Queen's Colleges more attractive than the Catholic University.

An interesting reason for the failure of the Catholic University to draw larger numbers of Irish students was advanced by a committee of the Senate of the university in a report of July 1859. This committee comprised seven of the university's leading professors, six of whom were Irish. Their report stated that one of the great obstacles encountered at the outset was the 'general tone and habits of mind' of a great portion of the educated laity of Ireland, which were not likely to render them favourably disposed towards an institution professing to be founded on an exclusively Catholic basis. Because of the political circumstances and the subordinate position held by Catholics, and their long struggle against an unjust exclusiveness, the idea of a Catholic university was not likely to be apprehended by them but was seen by many 'to wear an aspect of narrowness and want of enlightenment.' It was conceded by the committee that only time and the progress of truth could remove such impressions.[19]

Newman himself was noted for his strong commitment to the laity—the church would look foolish without them, he said. He insisted that a university was not a convent or a seminary: it was to prepare men of the world for the world. Nevertheless, given the control of the university by the bishops, he was aware that some of the laity were suspicious that it might easily become a clerical college. There is a certain irony in this, as one of the reasons the Catholic University did not attract greater numbers than it did was precisely that the large number of seminarians were only too well catered for in Maynooth and the various other diocesan seminaries throughout the country. Though modelled on the Catholic University of Louvain, it never attracted ecclesiastical students in the way the Belgian college did; and whereas Church of Ireland ministers received their training in the Theological Faculty of Trinity College, the Catholic bishops never used the Catholic University in the same manner.

The Catholic University Medical School prospered largely because it adapted its courses to those of the chartered medical licensing bodies, from which it formally sought recognition, and students who passed the examinations were granted a licence to practise, mainly through the Royal College of Surgeons in Ireland.

The university's Liberal Arts School, despite the rector's reputation and some good professors, did not attract the numbers that were expected, and the projected faculties of theology, engineering and law, despite the initial establishment of some chairs in these areas, never got off the ground.

In each successive phase of UCD's evolution the name of the illustrious first rector was never to be forgotten; and the college's indebtedness to Newman has often been gratefully and proudly recalled. In his own lifetime a group of former students assured him some twenty years after his resignation that his name would ever be mentioned with veneration and love in the institution for which he had laboured. On the physical side he left behind him the home of his labours, the fine eighteenth-century house in St Stephen's Green. Newman House has been the cradle of University College and its heart's core throughout every phase of its development. Newman also left the University Church, largely designed by himself, which he considered the most beautiful in Ireland or Britain, as a memorial of his presence among us. It symbolised for him the indissoluble union of philosophy with religion. He wanted, as he said, 'the intellectual layman to be religious and the devout ecclesiastic to be intellectual.'[20]

Newman's legacy, therefore, also included an insistence on the importance of the role the laity must play in the management and teaching of the university. His emphasis on this point was one of the principal causes of friction between himself and Archbishop Cullen: they differed, for example, on the need to have a Finance Committee of the university in the charge of laymen. Newman's experiment had shown in practice that laity and clergy could work harmoniously together in the best interests of university education and scholarship without the one usurping the legitimate functions of the other. It was a lesson not lost on successive generations of those Catholic laymen who interested themselves in the university question and its settlement, despite the sectarian fears (unfounded, as it transpired) that were still being expressed as late as 1908 in Parliament that the bishops and Maynooth would control the National University, then being established.

In his publications, Newman bequeathed a philosophy of university education that is as valid today as it was when first written and that may be profitably studied by administrators, academics and students alike. In that philosophy he provided a definition and a defence of liberal, as distinct from professional, education and emphasised the significance of arts in the life of the university.

It is a fairly common mistake to think that what Newman advocated was merely a sort of non-useful education in the classics and other liberal arts for gentlemen of leisure. This error arises out of a superficial acquaintance with his defence of a liberal education in *The Idea of a University*. But all his activities in connection with the university in Dublin, as well as his plans for its progress, proclaimed his recognition of the need also for professional schools in the university. Not alone did he establish the successful Catholic University Medical School, propose a faculty of law and appoint a professor of engineering but he further stressed the necessity of creating 'a school of useful arts, developing and applying the material resources of Ireland: that is, comprising the professorships of engineering, mining, agriculture etc.'

In his approach to university education Newman strove for a proper balance between utilitarian and liberal objectives. He not only sought to preserve what was best in the older university courses but was also eager to have his university respond to the needs and the developments and ever-widening field of knowledge of his own time. He knew the value of an education in the classics; but any notions that his university was therefore hampered by, or restricted to, a classical education are very wide of the mark. Newman founded in the Catholic University a chair of poetry and one of the first chairs of English literature in Ireland or Britain. His university was also in the forefront of European academic advancement, with chairs of political and social science, political economy, and geography. It was this sensitivity that led him to found the first chair of archaeology and Irish history in Ireland. The appointment of Eugene O'Curry to this chair, Newman's own attendance at O'Curry's lectures and the arrangement made by him for the publication of the lectures firmly established a tradition of commitment to Irish studies that has been maintained in each successive phase of the university's evolution.

Newman recognised the benefits that a university could bestow on the community in which it was situated by initiating a series of public lectures to be delivered by the professors of the Catholic University. Before any other university college in the country he launched a system of evening lectures for students who were employed during the day.

In one of his best-remembered passages, Newman held forth a challenge and a prophecy for Ireland as well as for his university:

> I look towards a land both old and young; old in its Christianity, young in the promise of its future ... I contemplate a people which has had a long night, and will have an inevitable day. I am turning my eyes towards a hundred years to come, and I dimly see the island I am gazing on become the road of passage and union between two hemispheres, and the centre of the world ... The capital of that prosperous and hopeful land is situate in a beautiful bay and near a romantic region; and in it I see a flourishing University, which for a while had to struggle with fortune, but which, when its first founders and servants were dead and gone, had successes far exceeding their anxieties.[21]

In all he has bequeathed, whether by way of the buildings in St Stephen's Green in which he laboured or the ideas incorporated in his legacy, or the vision he handed on, or the challenges he posed, Newman has for ever left UCD in particular, and university education in general, in his debt.

The Catholic University of Ireland was unique not only in having as its first president a person who became a candidate for sainthood but also in being the only university institution in Ireland or Britain financed by the pennies of the poor.

Newman had resigned in November 1858, but it was not until April 1861 that a new rector, Monsignor Bartholomew Woodlock, was appointed as his successor. Dr Woodlock, ordained in Rome, had been involved in the foundation of All Hallows Missionary College, Drumcondra, in 1842 and had been since 1854 its third president when he was appointed Rector of the Catholic University. He served as rector until he became Bishop of Ardagh and Clonmacnoise in 1879.[22]

Compared with John Henry Newman, Woodlock may not have seemed the most inspiring of rectors. Nevertheless, though confronted by grave obstacles, he attempted bold initiatives, was a dedicated and competent administrator, was more acceptable to Cullen and MacHale than Newman was to either, and raised fewer apprehensions among the bishops generally than did the convert English intellectual.

Woodlock's first great venture was the attempt to provide a new and worthy building for the university. On his proposal, a site of thirty-four acres (equal to that on which Trinity College stood) at Clonliffe West, part of the estate of the late Earl of Blessington, was bought for the university, and a building fund was opened. The bishops agreed that when completed the new structure could cost £150,000 but that the initial portion should be no more than £20,000. The well-known architect James Joseph McCarthy, whose commissions had included many churches throughout Ireland, was appointed to draw up the plans. These envisaged a grandiose building in the Italianate style.[23] The foundation stone was laid with grand ceremonial in 1862, but the scheme collapsed when expansion of the railway system on the north side of Dublin so interfered with the site as to make it inappropriate for the university. Legal difficulties and protracted court cases caused considerable expense before the Clonliffe West site was eventually surrendered to the trustees of the Blessington estate in 1870.

The costly failure of Woodlock's ambitious project made him turn his attention to more modest expansion plans in the St Stephen's Green area. In 1865 the lease on number 87, which Newman had acquired for student accommodation on a short term, was extended for five hundred years. Also in 1865 two houses, numbers 85 and 82, were bought for the university. Number 85, dating from about 1738, when it was designed by Richard Castle, and the most richly decorated with plasterwork of all the university's houses, was acquired after the death of its last private owner, Mr Justice Nicholas Ball, for £3,400. Number 82 was bought for £1,200.

A decade later, in 1876, number 84 was bought, for £1,760, and the building of the Aula Maxima, on the site of the two stables between numbers 84 and 85, was begun. The contract for the Aula Max was for £2,420, which was paid for largely by Cardinal Cullen. Shortly after Woodlock's resignation in 1879 number 83, for which he had been negotiating, was acquired. This gave the university possession of all the houses from number 82 to 87, including the University Church and the Aula Max—in all a frontage of 250 feet. Though hardly compensating for the demise of his grand scheme for the transfer of the university to Clonliffe West, the acquisition of the contiguous houses in St Stephen's Green provided Woodlock with some consolation.

Another of Woodlock's grand designs that floundered was the plan to establish Catholic University intermediate schools in different parts of the country. The idea was that these schools would be under the control and direction of the university, to which they would serve as feeders. The first opened in Waterford in 1862 under a headmaster, an Oxford convert, who had been recommended by Newman; it was surrendered to the diocese in 1868. St Flannan's Catholic University School in Ennis also lasted only a short while. The third, the Catholic University School in Dublin, survived in name, but only after it had been taken over by the Marist Fathers. The deteriorating financial circumstances of the university itself had made it necessary to surrender all three schools, by which time they had cost the university close on three thousand pounds.

Woodlock had somewhat better success with the system of affiliated schools, where pupils were encouraged to take the matriculation of the university, though this too had become ineffective by 1868. From 1873 students in affiliated colleges were permitted to prepare in their own colleges for all Catholic University examinations, except the final for degrees. Though this arrangement inflated the numbers for propaganda purposes, the other side of the coin was that it had been made necessary by the small numbers actually registered for and attending the lectures in the St Stephen's Green institution. The affiliation idea laid the ground for the constitutional change, put into operation in the early eighteen-eighties, whereby the Catholic University was no longer just St Stephen's Green and Cecilia Street but comprised a certain number of other colleges around the country.

An attempt to establish a school of agriculture connected with the university was fated to last only a couple of years. The Benedictines, who had bought a 1,300-acre farm at Leopardstown, County Dublin, were persuaded by Woodlock and Cullen to open St Benedict's Agricultural College in 1875. Encumbered, however, by enormous financial difficulties, the Benedictines had to sell their property at Leopardstown, which eventually became the Leopardstown racecourse.

From the start, the financial circumstances of the Catholic University were precarious. The lack of sufficient income badly hampered all Woodlock's major ventures. Given the difficulties of maintaining enthusiasm in the parishes for the annual collection, there was some justification for Bishop Dorrian's comment on the university that 'extravagance has been its ruling passion ... Nothing but a waste of money meets you in its early history. And if it is to go on there must be more economy or it will fall with and by the acts of its own friends.'[24]

Great fluctuations occurred in the amounts realised in the annual collections. These produced sums ranging from £1,000 to £2,000 annually in Dublin, but between May 1854 and October 1859 the diocese of Galway collected only £1, from 'a parishioner of the Isles of Arran'[25]—which was gratuitous, since the Aran Islands are in the diocese of Tuam. Tuam itself contributed nothing between 1859 and 1879, because of MacHale's opposition. The annual total raised varied from £4,000 to £9,600 and rarely met the running costs. The university avoided bankruptcy only by drastic economy measures, such as not filling vacant chairs or reducing salaries. Some well-known professors appointed by Newman—Renouf, Sullivan, and Thomas Arnold—resigned to go to better-paid posts.

Paralleling the financial difficulties, and contributing to them, was the paucity of students attracted to the arts and science faculties in St Stephen's Green. The rector drew a veil over the reality by including evening students and those in affiliated colleges to inflate the size of the total student body. A realistic picture of the situation emerges from the number of students registered for the first time in each calendar year. During Newman's time (1854–58) this had ranged from 24 to 30. The number of actual (as opposed to affiliated) students during Woodlock's rectorship (1861–1879) ranged erratically from 36 in 1862 to 3 in 1879.

Judged by several criteria, the Catholic University probably reached the nadir of its existence in 1872/73. With scarcely any professors or students, the public perception was that the university was 'shut-up'.[26] This too was the opinion of the professor of chemistry, W. K. Sullivan, who wrote to an MP: 'The University is all but defunct.'[27] Sullivan, one of the country's leading scientists, then resigned on being appointed President of Queen's College, Cork. His acceptance of the presidency of one of the condemned non-denominational colleges was regarded by Woodlock as a body-blow to the Catholic University.

With such difficulties and obstacles preventing the progress of the St Stephen's Green institution, the thought of closing it down occasionally presented itself. But the arguments against such drastic action were always too powerful. Whenever it appeared that the experiment might have to be abandoned, a fresh ray of hope and a renewed determination kept it alive as the flagship of the Catholic demand for fair play and equality of treatment in higher education. It was as if the bishops had hearkened to Newman's exhortation, 'Therefore, I say, let us set up our University: let us only set it up, and it will teach the world its value by the fact of its existence … Shall it be said in future times, that the work needed nought but good and gallant hearts, and found them not?'[28]

The bishops could not afford to let its abandonment be seen as the surrender of principle to the non-denominational Queen's Colleges. Besides, the School of Medicine, despite an unsatisfactory building and poor facilities, continued to prosper and earned the admiration of the bishops, who were proud of its achievements. Its flourishing state, resulting from the recognition given to it by the licensing bodies, also owed much to the high calibre of the professors first recruited by Newman, who continued to occupy their chairs for long after his departure—men such as Andrew Ellis FRCSI, a former President of the College of Surgeons, Thomas Hayden FRCSI, later Vice-President of the College of Physicians, Robert Cryan, holding qualifications from both the College of Surgeons and the College of Physicians, Robert D. Lyons, with qualifications from Trinity College, the College of Surgeons, and the College of Physicians—all of whom were leading consultants and lecturers in the Dublin medical world.

To the more optimistic also during the eighteen-sixties and seventies it looked as if the government might be persuaded into granting the Catholic University the elusive charter or some other concession. Each time hopes were to be dashed; but Woodlock and certain Irish MPs persisted in lobbying the governments of the day. In the hope of mollifying anti-clerical feeling among the legislators, Woodlock proposed admitting laymen to the governing body of the university, from which they had been excluded since the departure of Newman, when a solely episcopal board replaced the partly lay University Committee. Cullen and MacHale now resisted Woodlock's proposal, thereby effectively killing it. Newman wrote to Woodlock: 'They won't further the University till they trust lay Catholics more.'[29]

Successive governments nonetheless brought forward proposals to meet the Catholic grievance. In 1866 the Russell administration attempted to incorporate the Catholic University as a college of the Queen's University, without endowment but providing access to its degrees; a legal challenge by Queen's graduates put a stop to this move. The Disraeli government in 1868 envisaged a Catholic University, initially without endowment but serving Catholics as Trinity served Protestants; this fell through when the bishops insisted on having exclusive control in matters of faith and morals, which could have involved a veto on texts to be used by the students and the right to have professors dismissed for behaviour of which the bishops disapproved.

The bishops, however, let it be known that they would accept a single 'National University' with one or more Catholic colleges enjoying the same privileges as other colleges of whatever denomination. Alternatively, they would accept a reconstituted University of Dublin to include a second college 'in every respect equal to Trinity College and conducted on purely Catholic principles.' The Gladstone government responded in 1873 with a Bill that would have abolished the Queen's University and reconstituted the

University of Dublin so as to comprise all the colleges in Ireland, including those of the Catholic University—but still without endowment for the latter. The government fell following defeat of the measure in Parliament.

The University Education (Ireland) Bill (1879), brought in by Disraeli's government and leading to the establishment of the Royal University of Ireland, ended that phase (1854–1879) in the history of the Catholic University during which it could not confer degrees, in the absence of state recognition. The Royal University, incorporated by charter in 1880, was a non-teaching, degree-awarding institution on the model of the University of London. Students from any of the existing colleges, or indeed by private study, could take its examinations. Fellows were appointed to set the courses for degrees and act as examiners, and this system allowed the state to endow indirectly the Catholic University, since half of all the fellows appointed were to be drawn from its staff. To avail itself of these circumstances the Catholic University was reorganised in 1882, when a number of seminaries and other educational establishments under religious orders were added to the Medical School and the St Stephen's Green institution as constituent colleges. The St Stephen's Green institution was renamed University College. Its management was transferred to the Jesuits in 1883; and it was soon thereafter revitalised.

UNIVERSITY COLLEGE AND THE ROYAL UNIVERSITY

After the resignation of Woodlock, Monsignor Henry Neville, Dean of Cork, was appointed Rector of the Catholic University in September 1879. The appointment of a rector who was also a parish priest in Cork was in itself an unconscious admission of the Catholic University's state of inanition. Dr Neville's regular commuting between Cork and Dublin earned him the nickname 'Monsignor Often-Back' among his handful of students.[30]

The Intermediate Education Act (1878), by introducing the system of payment by results, had given a boost to the Catholic secondary schools. It was widely felt that some such indirect endowment would provide a life-line for the Catholic University. Along with others, Monsignor Neville concentrated much of his efforts on securing such a benefit. The fellowship and prize scheme of the Royal University ensured this indirect endowment.

The boost given to the Catholic secondary schools and the prospects of even greater success encouraged some of the leading schools of the religious teaching orders to establish university departments of their own to prepare their students for the examinations of the Royal University. The Catholic University would have to compete not only with the Queen's Colleges but also with the university departments of the successful and ambitious secondary colleges; and to judge by the matriculation results issued in early 1882, the St Stephen's Green institution was simply not in the same league as Blackrock College or the Jesuits' Tullabeg College at Rahan, near Tullamore, County Offaly.

The bishops also had in mind the advantage, from the point of view of public perception, of grouping a number of these Catholic colleges together, whose accumulated examination results would offset the results from the combined Queen's Colleges. Accordingly, in October 1882 the bishops, developing a scheme proposed by Woodlock, modified the constitution of the Catholic University so as to include a number of institutions. In 1876 St Patrick's College, Maynooth, had already been added to the Medical School and St Stephen's Green as a constituent college of the Catholic University. Now, in October 1882 and January 1883, Blackrock College, Carlow College, Clonliffe College, Terenure College, the Jesuit College in Temple Street and St. Kyran's, Kilkenny, also became constituent colleges.

Up to 1882 the institution in St Stephen's Green had been called the Catholic University. Under the new constitution of the Catholic University the St Stephen's Green constituent now became University College, and it opened for the session 1882/83 under new management. Rev. John Egan, a professor of English, afterwards Bishop of Waterford, was appointed president. Dean Neville resigned as rector in January 1883, and Dr Gerald Molloy, who had been vice-rector since 1873 and professor of natural philosophy, was appointed his successor.

The creation of the office of president, as distinct from rector, emphasised the fact that St Stephen's Green was no longer the Catholic University but merely a college of the university. It was realised, however, that what was required to make it viable was more than a change of status. For some time many associated with the college had held that it should be handed over to the Jesuits, who were the foremost teaching order in the country, if it were to succeed. In October 1883 Father William Delany SJ signed an agreement with the episcopal trustees of the Catholic University to lease numbers 84 and 85, the two top storeys of number 86 and the Aula Maxima and to undertake the management of the institution 'to be called University College.'[31]

The Jesuits took possession of the buildings and other property in November 1883. This marked the end of the Catholic University as a teaching institution, though it continued to have a nominal existence. With the well-known educationalist Father Delany as President of University College, and the degrees of the Royal University open to all, there began a new and brighter phase in the history of higher education for Catholics.[32]

University College was for Father Delany not just another educational undertaking. Consciously following in the footsteps of Newman, he dreamt of his college becoming 'a great national home of learning and religion ... a centre of civilisation,' renewing the glories of Ireland's golden age.[33] The reality was often quite different. The Catholic University premises that had been leased to the Jesuits was described by the Provincial of the society as 'a dingy old barrack that would require a vast outlay, the floors all rotten, dosed; the woodwork, window-sashes, crumbling with powder.'[34]

The new managers, without the financial assistance of the annual parish collections, which had been discontinued, were responsible for the upkeep of the buildings. The space allocated in the lease was limited to three houses and the Aula Max. Under the agreement the tenant of number 84 became the tenant of the lessees, so that that house was not available. Number 85, though less spacious than 86, had a few large rooms that could serve as lecture halls. Since the University Church had not been part of the agreement, and since the bishops were not willing to allow the Aula Max to be used as a church, one of these larger rooms in 85 had to serve as a chapel. The biological and anatomical museums and medical library were to be removed to the Aula Max. The larger rooms in 86 were on the first floor, but this, as well as the ground floor, had been retained for the use of the rector of the phantom Catholic University. Casey, the eminent professor of mathematics, was once asked: 'What is the difference between University College and the Catholic University—seeing that both are in the same building, together with the president of one and the rector of the other?' He replied: 'If you take University College from the Catholic University, the remainder is Dr Molloy.'[35]

The two upper storeys of 86 consisted mainly of bedrooms, and these had to serve as classrooms as well as living quarters for the resident students and Jesuit staff. To ease pressure, the Jesuits rented from the rector the hallway and one room on the ground floor.

Academic equipment was also in short supply. Before the transfer of University College to the Jesuits, the Catholic University library, with the exception of the medical volumes, had been removed to Clonliffe College. Archbishop Murray's library had been acquired for the Catholic University in its first year of operation: no doubt the bishops felt that the diocesan seminary was the more appropriate place for this and similar collections. Father Denis Murphy SJ, the bursar and librarian of University College (he also helped with courses in archaeology, Irish and history), exclaimed: 'I have not a penny in my burse nor a book in my library.' Some of the professors had been inherited from Newman's time and were well past their best—hence Father Delany's anxiety to have all the fellowships of the Royal University that were earmarked for Catholics assigned to University College and not dispersed among the other colleges of the Catholic University. He also needed, for the financial support of his college, to have a number of these fellowships assigned to Jesuits on his staff. The case of the poet Gerard Manley Hopkins illustrates the risks that had to be taken in the pursuit of this policy.

When Father Delany was looking for staff among Jesuits abroad, he was informed by a Jesuit in Italy that Father G. M. Hopkins of the English province might be available. He was very clever, had obtained first-class honours in classics at Oxford and taught well, but without achieving much success: 'his mind runs in eccentric ways.' The English provincial, to whom Delany applied for staff, replied that six of the seven he had asked for were the cream of the province and could not be spared; the seventh, Hopkins, was a possibility. He was a clever scholar, but, the provincial added, 'I should be doing you no kindness in sending you a man so eccentric. I am trying him this year in coaching B.A.s at Stoneyhurst, but with fear and trembling.'[36]

As part of the policy of concentrating all the Catholic fellows in University College, Father Delany submitted Hopkins's name to the Senate in January 1884. In recognition of the success of Blackrock College, three members of the Senate—Cardinal McCabe, Dr Walsh, President of Maynooth, and Bishop Woodlock—supported the nomination of Blackrock's president, Father Reffé, for the fellowship. But Hopkins was awarded it on a vote of 21 to 3.[37]

The salary attached to Hopkins's fellowship was welcome; but Hopkins's contribution to the examination results of the students was not so certain. Indeed, his contribution to University College in general was mainly posthumous and of the intangible kind. Alongside Newman and Joyce, he provided the institution with its greatest claim to literary renown; but as a teacher grinding pupils for examinations in a highly competitive atmosphere he was less than effective. So scrupulous was he about the system whereby fellows were also the examiners of students, including their own, that he undertook at the beginning of each year not to teach anything that would be on the examination papers. It was said that his lectures were attended only by those who loved learning for its own sake, or those who merely wanted to know what could be safely omitted from their pre-examination preparation. On one occasion this least practical of teachers wanted to illustrate as practically as he could the death of the Trojan hero Hector. A colleague, attracted to the classroom by the uproar, found Hopkins on his back on the floor being dragged around the table by a student. The unhappy fellow of the Royal University died of typhoid fever in 1889, contracted, it was thought, as a result of the poor plumbing in 86.

A more prolonged result of the fellowship row was the friction it introduced into the relationship between Father Delany, the most successful administrator of a Catholic university institution, and Dr Walsh, Archbishop of Dublin from 1885 and the leading champion of the rights of Catholics in higher education; up to that point Walsh had been one of Delany's staunchest allies. It was a tension that obtruded from time to time until the university settlement of 1908.

The archbishop and the Jesuit in fact always acted towards each other with diplomacy and respect. But while Delany and his college became the greatest beneficiaries of the Royal University system, Walsh remained its most outspoken critic. Noone used Newman's writings on the superiority of a teaching university over a merely examining board, such as the Royal University, more effectively than Walsh.[38] An ambitious Delany, pushing hard the interests of his own college, was suspected of having less concern for the other Catholic colleges and for the general solution. Walsh objected to any plan that might seem to be an attempt to buy off Catholic opposition with an endowed Catholic college within the Royal system. The archbishop was ready to rap the Jesuit across the knuckles for what was described as any 'unauthorised interference with the conduct of negotiations' connected with Catholic university education. He was opposed to the policy of 'killing Home Rule with kindness' as applied to the university question. The President of University College had a more pragmatic approach.

The fundamental cause of the differences between these two leading advocates of university education for Catholics lay in how each saw the best solution: Walsh preferred a college for Catholics alongside Trinity in the University of Dublin and equal to Trinity in every way; Delany preferred a settlement outside of Trinity and the University of Dublin. Temperamental differences increased estrangement. Walsh was an outspoken nationalist whose appointment as archbishop the British had opposed and who was deeply involved in the political questions of the day. Delany was more of a whig, more ready to seek accommodation with the government and anxious to steer clear of divisive political issues.

Despite all the drawbacks and the conflicts, there was no mistaking the successful progress of University College under Delany's vigorous administration. He was president from 1883 to 1888 and again from 1897 to 1909. By the end of his first year the college boasted that it had a hundred students—in stark contrast to the last years before the Jesuits took it over. During the session 1901/02, 181 students attended one or more courses of lectures in arts. Of these, probably not more than eight intended to proceed to become clergymen—a much smaller number than was to be found in Trinity College. This was Delany's refutation of the allegation that a Catholic university college was necessarily sectarian and possessed the character of a seminary.[39]

From the beginning of the Royal University the students of University College were already well ahead of the students of the Queen's Colleges in Cork and Galway in examination results; by the middle of the eighteen-nineties they had outdistanced Belfast. The impressive statistics of the achievements of University College students in the Royal University examinations were constantly advertised by Father Delany in his public pronouncements, his writings, and his evidence before the Robertson Commission. It was claimed by the Jesuits[40] that the list of first-class distinctions in arts showed the following totals for the sixteen years 1894–1909:

University College, Dublin	702
Queen's College, Belfast	330
Queen's College, Galway	130
Queen's College, Cork	26

The total number of distinctions (including first-class) was:

University College, Dublin	1,364
Queen's College, Belfast	917
Queen's College, Galway	362
Queen's College, Cork	98

By 1907 a similar claim was made in Parliament by Tom Kettle MP (himself one of the most brilliant graduates of University College): that 'in every year and every examination for at least the last five years ... the single unendowed University [college] had secured more first-class honours and distinctions of every kind than the three Queen's Colleges put together.'[41]

On this policy of advertising success in examinations Archbishop Walsh and Father Delany were at one. The archbishop emphasised the successes of the Catholic colleges generally, and more especially those of Blackrock College and the Medical School (of whose board he was chairman). The whole point behind this kind of propaganda was to make the case that Catholics, under great handicaps, financial and other, deserved a university worthy of their achievements. Newman had urged the setting up of the Catholic University on the grounds that 'it will teach the world its value by the fact of its existence.'[42] The patent success of Delany's college was that it took Newman's exhortation one step closer towards the ultimate goal. Asked to tell in a few words what he conceived to be the relationship between University College and Trinity College, J. P. Mahaffy is reported to have replied: 'Illegitimate sister—begotten by vowed celibates.'[43] The witticism was, in its own way, an acknowledgment of the academic status that had been achieved under Jesuit management.

Because of the successes in examinations and the importance attached to them, some critics thought of University College as a grind-school. Such a description was very wide of the mark. Delany himself, in evidence before the Royal Commission, said he thoroughly agreed with Newman that for many the social life of the college was of more importance for their education than the lectures of the classroom; he added that he valued a man much more who had a collegiate training than the man who had simply passed the examination.

The president encouraged several student societies and clubs. The Literary and Historical Society (the 'L&H'), originating in Newman's time, was resuscitated during Delany's presidency. It was the college's premier debating society, in which many who became household names in independent Ireland first attracted attention.[44] It was during Delany's time too that the student magazine *St Stephen's* (1901–06) carried the work of many of the same students.

The academics too had their journal. The *Lyceum* (1887–1894), a monthly literary magazine and review, was founded by two brothers, Fathers Tom and Peter Finlay. They were assisted by William Magennis. The *Lyceum* was replaced by the *New Ireland Review* (1894–1911), which in turn was replaced by the still surviving *Studies.* Though contributions to the *Lyceum* and the *New Ireland Review* were not restricted to the academics of University College, a large number of the articles were the work of the staff and former students.

The golden age of University College under the Jesuits coincided with Delany's last period of office, 1897–1909. During this time the names associated with the college as students, academics or both included James Joyce, Tom Kettle, Francis Skeffington (later Sheehy Skeffington), Francis Cruise O'Brien, Arthur Clery, William Magennis, John Marcus O'Sullivan, Thomas Bodkin, Father Tom Finlay SJ, Patrick Pearse, Hugh Kennedy (first Chief Justice of the Irish Free State), Éamon de Valera, Eoin MacNeill, Alfred O'Rahilly, Hanna Sheehy, Mary Hayden, Agnes O'Farrelly, Pat McCartan, T. F. O'Rahilly, Michael Hayes, J. A. Costello, Patrick McGilligan and others who were later prominent in the war of independence and in the new Ireland. Behind the shabby exterior of the St Stephen's Green houses, a brilliant intellectual life had come into being.

Given such talent and the revolutionary fervour in the contemporary political and cultural life of the country, there was bound to be some student unrest. In keeping with the nationalist and reformist mood of the country, the students between 1900 and 1907 became increasingly critical of the educational and political status quo. Loyalist speeches by the Earl of Meath, Chancellor of the Royal University, and the playing of 'God Save the King' at the conferring ceremonies in Earlsfort Terrace, which were attended by unionist and nationalist students alike, led to rowdy interruptions and the singing of 'God Save Ireland'. From 1903, though police were now in attendance, the protests became stormier. At the 1905 ceremony the organ gallery was occupied to prevent the playing of the anthem. The Gaelic League congratulated the student protesters; they also received support from the *Leader,* from Griffith's *United Irishman,* and from the *Irish Catholic.* At the inaugural meeting of the L&H the protests continued.

Father Delany, owing to his dual role as senator and president, was placed in a deeply embarrassing situation by these protests. In 1906 steps were taken to control admission to the conferring ceremony. The students demonstrated outside Earlsfort Terrace and then withdrew to St Stephen's Green, where Father Delany, aided by the presence of the police, refused to allow them access to the college for their protest meeting, whereupon the students marched down Grafton Street and held their protest at the Medical School in Cecilia Street. There Father Delany was censured for allegedly allying himself with the police and the Ascendancy party for the purpose of preventing the free expression of nationalist views. This resolution was supported by Sheehy Skeffington, a graduate and former registrar of the college, and by Francis Cruise O'Brien, now identified as the leader of the student protest.

O'Brien was both editor of *St Stephen's* and auditor of the L&H. When the L&H endorsed the action of the students in censuring Delany, the college responded by rusticating O'Brien. The president had already (in November 1905) censored a report in *St Stephen's* for its criticism of the Senate of the RUI. Because of the magazine's continued outspokenness against these senators, *St Stephen's* was suppressed at about the same time as O'Brien's rustication. O'Brien's attempt to continue as auditor led to a split in the L&H and to further newspaper controversy. His labelling of Father Delany as 'a decaying old Whig' tended to stick.

In his first period as president, 1883–88, Father Delany had felt himself subjected to Archbishop Walsh's 'vigilant hostility'. His last years, between 1900 and 1908, were clouded by student unrest led by three of his brightest students—the famous future brothers-in-law Kettle, Sheehy Skeffington, and Cruise O'Brien.

Delany's row with the students may have left bitter feelings but could not obliterate his contribution to the higher education of Catholics and the role he continued to play in helping to bring about the establishment of the National University of Ireland. A close parallel can be drawn between Delany's and a later presidency of University College. Father Delany's notable achievements for his college were to be obscured for some because of matters of discipline, leading to rows with the L&H and the banning of student publications. In this he was to have much in common with Michael Tierney, another great presidential achiever who was also to be subjected to much student criticism.

2

The New College

It's something new in universities ... It may be a bit shoddy, but we might make something of it.
                              Eimar O'Duffy, *The Wasted Island*, p. 111

B y the beginning of the twentieth century the need for reform and for a comprehensive inquiry into the condition and needs of university education had become widely recognised. The Catholic bishops had continued to press their case for an acceptable and adequate system for Catholics; a similar demand had been made in a 'Declaration of the Catholic Laity of Ireland' in 1897. The Senate of the Royal University adopted a resolution on 21 February 1901 calling for a royal commission 'to report as to the means by which University education in Ireland might receive greater extension and be more efficiently conducted than at present.'

The Royal Commission on University Education in Ireland (known from the name of its chairman as the Robertson Commission) advised in 1903 that the Royal University be converted into a federal teaching university, its constituent colleges being the existing Queen's Colleges in Belfast, Cork and Galway together with a new college for Catholics to be established in Dublin.[1]

A lukewarm reception by the bishops, Presbyterian resistance in the North and sundry reservations by most members of the commission inhibited legislative action on the Robertson Report. Alternative proposals were put forward by the Conservative Chief Secretary for Ireland, George Wyndham, by the Earl of Dunraven, and by a group of junior fellows of Trinity College; but the definitive move came with the appointment in June 1906 by Wyndham's Liberal successor, James Bryce, of the Royal Commission on Trinity College, Dublin, and the University of Dublin. This commission, chaired by Sir Edward Fry, was specifically charged with advising on the steps that might be taken to increase the 'usefulness to the country' of Trinity College and the University of Dublin.[2] In strongly worded arguments the bishops, the Irish Party and the Gaelic League, among others, alleged that the

Protestant and British ethos of Trinity left it alien to the sentiments of Irish Catholics, though the possibility was not altogether ruled out of founding a second college within the University of Dublin, side by side with Trinity, to be conducted on Catholic principles.

As the debate developed, a shift of emphasis emerged in public opinion, with demand strengthening for a *national* university, reflective of nationalist cultural attitudes, rather than an arrangement suitable merely from a Catholic viewpoint. This, combined with vociferous opposition from a 'hands off Trinity' campaign mounted from within the University of Dublin and by a number of academics and Protestant churchmen in Britain as well as Ireland, ensured that the Fry Commission was more helpful for the evidence it elicited than for its recommendations. The members of the commission, as it happened, differed among themselves over whether a solution lay in creating a new institution or in incorporating a number of colleges within the University of Dublin, as Bryce—pre-empting the commission—had already decided should be done.

Augustine Birrell replaced Bryce as Chief Secretary in 1907. Acting with pragmatic diplomacy, he revoked his predecessor's decision, assured the University of Dublin that it would not be interfered with, and set about devising a system that would attract the broadest possible support. He consulted widely, not least with Archbishop Walsh and other members of the hierarchy, as well as John Dillon of the Irish Party and its leader, John Redmond. The outcome was the Irish Universities Bill (1908). This would leave the University of Dublin and Trinity College untouched, elevate Queen's College, Belfast, to the status of a university in its own right, and create a National University consisting of three constituent colleges: the Queen's Colleges in Cork and Galway and a new college in Dublin (the nucleus of which, in practice, would be the exiting University College and the Medical School). They were to be undenominational: all religious tests would be debarred by law in the new universities and their colleges, and no public money could be spent on building or maintaining a church or other place of religious observance or in providing any theological or religious teaching. In its final form the Bill also provided that every professor, on entering office, would sign a declaration pledging 'respectful treatment of the religious opinions of any of his class.'

Each university would be governed by a Senate, at first nominated for five years and thereafter elected from panels representing the colleges and the graduates in convocation, together with some *ex officio* officers, government nominees, and co-opted members. The Governing Bodies of the colleges at Dublin, Cork and Galway, at first nominated for three years, would afterwards for the most part be elected from panels, one of which would provide representation by local authorities (both as a democratic element and to encourage the granting of county council scholarships). Apart from the constituent colleges, the universities were to be permitted to affiliate institutions capable of giving university training—such as St Patrick's College, Maynooth, and Magee College, Derry. Women were to be 'equally eligible with men' for all privileges of the new universities.

Some northern unionists and British Nonconformists resisted the Bill for conceding too much to Catholic wishes. The Catholic bishops in fact accepted it without especial enthusiasm but also without overt opposition, except for Bishop Edward O'Dwyer of Limerick, who felt it did not give them enough.

Irish Party support, as well as majority backing from both the Conservatives and the Liberals, enabled Birrell to steer the measure skilfully through Parliament, and it became law as the Irish Universities Act on 1 August 1908. This was the statute that brought into being the National University of Ireland, with its administrative centre in Dublin and its constituent University Colleges (as they were now termed) in Dublin, Cork, and Galway. It signalled also the demise of the Royal University and with it the Jesuit-run University College. The premises in St Stephen's Green, however, were to be the first home of the new University College when it enrolled its first student in the following year, appropriately a young Jesuit scholastic, yet to be ordained. His name was Aubrey Gwynn and in time he would confer distinction on the college during his tenure of the chair of mediaeval history.

Between the passing of the Act and the inauguration of the college much had had to be put in hand. Notwithstanding his admiration for Father Delany, Birrell was already determined that the first head of the Dublin institution should be a layman. At the urging of John Dillon the government therefore appointed the Dean of the Catholic University Medical School, Dr Denis J. Coffey (1865–1945), to be President of UCD. It was an appropriate appointment, even if not arrived at by the elective procedure used for all later presidents. Coffey was a graduate of the Royal University, had studied under leading physiologists in various Continental cities, became a lecturer in Cecilia Street in 1893, professor of physiology in 1897, and dean in 1905. He had given evidence before the Robertson Commission and had been a member of the Fry Commission. The Cecilia Street school was itself to become the UCD Medical Faculty.

The most immediate of all influences shaping UCD was the Dublin Commission, a body established under the Irish Universities Act to frame the statutes for the university having its seat in Dublin—the NUI—and for each of its constituent colleges, to decide what academic and other offices should be created, and to make the first appointments. Its members were the presidents of the three colleges (Windle of Cork, Anderson of Galway, Coffey of Dublin), Henry Jackson (professor of Greek at Cambridge), Sir John Rhys (professor of Celtic at Oxford), Archbishop Walsh, two Irish

Party MPs (Stephen Gwynn and John Pius Boland), and a distinguished soldier and author (General Sir William Francis Butler) who was also a commissioner for national education. Its chairman was the Lord Chief Baron, Christopher Palles, a Catholic jurist who had a long record of involvement in efforts to secure improvements in the educational system. It was a group responsive to nationalist and Catholic wishes but marked as well by an objectivity that came from the broad and varied experience on which so many of its members could draw. It understood equally the tradition of liberal education derived from Newman and a particularly Irish utilitarian need identified by the Robertson and Fry Commissions for training in commerce, engineering, agriculture, and other avocations.

In its allocation of academic positions under Statute I, the Dublin Commission established thirty-six chairs (twenty-six of them full-time) at UCD and fifteen lectureships (five full-time). A bird's eye view of the provisions made by the Dublin Commission indicates the range of disciplines covered. In the humanities, Celtic studies was the greatest beneficiary, with four full-time chairs and two part-time lectureships. Chairs were provided in subjects under the traditional headings of classics, modern languages, English, political economy, and mathematics. Three chairs were founded in philosophy and one each in education, history, and national economics. Outside the humanities there were full-time chairs in civil engineering, mathematical physics, experimental physics, chemistry, geology and zoology. Architecture and commerce each received part-time chairs and law no fewer than three. There were lectureships in botany, pure mathematics and physics. Three full-time chairs and five part-time chairs went to medicine.

While this represented a substantial improvement in the number of positions and the spread of subjects offered by comparison with the Royal fellowships at the former University College, the commission nonetheless felt obliged to say that technological subjects and agriculture, which they considered essential, were omitted only because they were already being taught at the College of Science. For the same reason it had not provided for mechanical engineering or applied science. It was a matter of making the best use of the limited funds available. The College of Science, the commission felt, might be recognised as a college of the university, or at least the university might agree to accept its courses of study.

The chairs and lectureships were widely advertised, though the commission was somewhat restricted in whom it might appoint, since the Act specified that officers of the Royal University would be offered 'so far as practicable and expedient' equivalent offices in the new university. Of the fifteen fellows attached to the Jesuit college, eleven were nominated to full-time professorships and one to a full-time lectureship; another (J. W. Bacon) was appointed Secretary and Bursar and granted £500 compensation, since he was not appointed to an equivalent office (the chair of English).

The non-fellows who were successful emerged from strong competition; some unsuccessful candidates were at least as interesting as those who got the posts. Éamon de Valera was one of the nineteen who applied for the chair of education, which in the event went to Timothy Corcoran SJ. Patrick Pearse sought the lectureship in Irish, describing himself as '30 years of age ... of good physique ... a total abstainer and a non-smoker.' His testimonial from Douglas Hyde (who himself got the chair of Modern Irish) said that Pearse had 'probably edited more Irish matter than any other person living'; but he also wrote on behalf of the successful candidate, Agnes O'Farrelly, asserting that 'there is no other candidate that I know of who would fill the post more suitably.'

The lectureship in Irish history went to Mary Hayden, rather than to Edmund Curtis; while of four brothers-in-law from a well-known political and intellectual dynasty who applied for various posts—Francis Cruise O'Brien, Francis Sheehy Skeffington, Richard Sheehy, and Tom Kettle MP—only Kettle was successful: he became professor of national economics. His rival for the chair, Robert Donovan, got English instead, as a result of which J. W. Bacon received his financial compensation and appointment as Secretary.

Behind such pillar-to-post decisions lay much discreet lobbying by Father Delany and others, but there is no evidence that the members of the commission chose otherwise than on the merits as they assessed them. One appointment only was to be the subject of public controversy. Maria Degani, a native of Trieste, then under Austrian rule, sought the lectureship in German but was made lecturer in Italian and Spanish instead. Highly critical comments appeared in newspapers and elsewhere, but no impropriety was discovered in what admittedly seemed a bizarre decision.

The calibre of the staff in UCD's early years would show that, in general, the commission chose wisely, not least indeed in those cases where it offered alternatives to candidates whose first applications had been for different posts. It was thus that John Marcus O'Sullivan, with his Heidelberg doctorate in philosophy, became an outstanding professor of history instead of logic and psychology. Another imaginative stroke by the commission was in the area of Celtic studies. It had advertised a single chair in Celtic archaeology and early Irish history. R. A. S. Macalister, a leading authority on the archaeology of the Middle East as well as of Ireland, applied, as did Eoin MacNeill. The commission had the good sense to divide the subject into two separate chairs and thereby secure the services of both scholars.

In fields of such abundant talent some candidates, quite possibly worthy if judged in isolation, stood little chance—not even the one who sent a testimonial from the President of Mexico. And the members of the commission would have been less than human if they did not feel a little sad in turning down the application for the chair of Latin received from a Church of Ireland clergyman. He was not in the way of obtaining testimonials, he said, but in their place he enclosed some sets of Latin verse as 'a test of my ability.' Among these were pieces entitled 'To my cat stalking a robin', 'A croquet tournament', 'To Sir Hiram Maxim, designer of aeroplanes', and 'An inspiration for the Olympic Games, London, 1908'. He must have given pleasure to Latinists on the commission, such as the archbishop and the Chief Baron, not to mention John Pius Boland, who had competed successfully in tennis at the first revived Olympics in Athens in 1896.

UCD was not being established *de novo*. Both the Act and the intention behind it had to take account of the constraints imposed by existing institutions and by the political and social circumstances of the time. When, therefore, UCD opened its doors in its new career as a constituent college of the NUI its character had already been genetically determined, to a considerable extent, by powerful institutional precedents and moulded by contemporary ideological influences.

Chronologically, the earliest of the institutions to have a direct influence on UCD were the Queen's Colleges. The undenominational principles of the Queen's Colleges, including the prohibition on the use of public funds to provide courses in theology, survived to become part of UCD's statutory framework; and the pledge that professors signed on appointment retained in part the same form of words as that used in 1845.

The Catholic University, with Newman as rector, was in the long run a much more powerful and direct influence on UCD than were the legalities of Peel's 'godless colleges'. The intellectual and personal links with the Catholic University through its successor, the Jesuits' University College, were consciously fostered by UCD, which regarded the CUI as its parent and itself as the inheritor of the Newman legacy. Even the physical links between UCD and the Catholic University were pronounced, as UCD retained the use of the buildings in St Stephen's Green and inherited the Catholic University School of Medicine in Cecilia Street.

Another of the formative institutional influences on UCD was the Royal University, a distinctive feature of which was its system of fellowships, whereby the fellows determined the courses, set the examinations, and were the chief examiners. These fellows were paid by the state. The Jesuit college and the Catholic University Medical School achieved outstanding success in the examinations of the RUI in competition with the Queen's Colleges. Fifteen of the twenty-nine fellows of the RUI were attached to University College, and three of the eight medical fellows taught in the Catholic

University Medical School, thus allowing for the indirect endowment of Catholic university education. (The fifteen fellows were paid a salary of £400 each; less was paid to the medical fellows.)

When the National University of Ireland was established, therefore, the whole examination ethos, the subject matter of the courses, the examiners of the RUI, the Jesuit influence, the very buildings of the Jesuit college in St Stephen's Green, the Catholic Medical School in Cecilia Street and (as will be seen) the RUI buildings in Earlsfort Terrace, and the professors and students of the Jesuit college, together with the Medical School—all were transformed smoothly into the new University College. The remarkable success of UCD students in the NUI examinations (especially in the early years of the travelling studentships) was a continuation of Father Delany's achievements and those of the Catholic University School of Medicine, in competition with the Queen's Colleges.

EARLY ETHOS

Apart from the institutional precedents, significant ideological forces also combined to shape the new UCD. One of these was the 'red-brick' university movement in England, which had resulted in the foundation of a number of civic, utilitarian, regional, non-residential universities, flourishing from the eighteen-eighties. The principle behind this movement was that, unlike the older universities of Oxford, Cambridge and TCD, which traditionally had educated through the humanities the sons of the landed and governing classes for politics, the church and the army, these new universities of the middle class would provide a more pragmatic training for the industrial, commercial, professional and social needs of the local community; and as a guarantee of this they would have on their governing bodies representatives of the local civic authority. One of the criticisms made of Newman's idea of a university education was that it was too liberal and not utilitarian enough for the practical needs of an undeveloped Ireland emerging from the Famine. A regular criticism of Trinity was that it served neither the practical needs of the country nor the cultural needs of the nation. When the Dublin Commission, charged with the business of setting up the NUI, began its task it determined therefore to establish in UCD pragmatic departments such as commerce, education, agriculture, applied science (technology), engineering, architecture and veterinary medicine—though not all of these turned out to be feasible at the outset.

Because of the particular circumstances of university education in Ireland, the regional emphasis was less pronounced in UCD's case than in that of Belfast, Cork or Galway. From the beginning, therefore, UCD tended to be a national institution for the Catholics of Ireland. A major, if not *the* major, component of UCD's ethos at its foundation was Catholicism. The bishops, on practical grounds, had long given up the hope that any British government would consent to the establishment and financing of a Catholic university so designated. British politicians, for their part, had come to recognise that if a university was set up to satisfy the demands of the Catholic majority, the predominant element in that university was bound to be Catholic. Beginning with the stalemate positions of 1845, the bishops and the government had slowly but gradually, over sixty years, made concessions and moved closer to an accommodation. In a statement of 1897 the bishops declared that they were prepared to accept that there would be no religious tests, that there would be no state funding of theology, and that clergy did not have to be a majority on the Governing Body.

Since 1899 Arthur Balfour, the Conservative leader, had supported the idea of *de facto* if not *de jure* denominational universities for Belfast and Dublin. When Birrell introduced the 1908 scheme he insisted that he was not establishing denominational universities, though account would have to be taken of the religious environment in which they were being situated and the people they were intended to serve. This balancing act of what one might call an undenominational Catholic college had the full backing of the Irish Party and its leading spokesmen, who were anxious to distinguish between a Catholic university and a university for Catholics.

Because of the balancing process between the bishops and the government, the University College in Dublin that emerged from the legislation was essentially the result of a compromise. It was recognised by the supporters of the 1908 scheme that the predominating atmosphere was bound to be Catholic but that in law it must be undenominational. Apart from the undenominational principles written into the Act, no bishops were to be appointed to the Governing Body *ex officio*; and UCD was not to begin with a Catholic clergyman as its first president.

In the words of Tim Healy, 'the Bill is nobody's ideal.'[3] Extremists on both sides among its opponents had a field day in ransacking the vocabulary of denunciation. Among the Catholics its most extreme opponents included Bishop O'Dwyer of Limerick and Father Peter Finlay SJ.[4] According to O'Dwyer (in Birrell's colourful paraphrase) it was a Nonconformist university, planned by a Nonconformist Chief Secretary, who was palming off on the Irish people a rank, denominational institution of a Nonconformist character.[5] And because it was to be non-residential, the bishop described it as a lodging-house university built on Nonconformist principles. Irish Catholics, wrote Father Finlay, were to be saddled with a university that no-one in Ireland wanted, except the friends of Trinity and a small group of Dublin's medical men. Cardinal Logue's first reaction was to label it 'godless';

though 'a pagan bantling had been dropped in the midst of us,' he prayed later that 'please God if we can, we will baptise it and make it Christian.'[6] The more moderate position of Archbishop Walsh and of Dr Delany, both of whom had been consulted by Birrell at every stage of the Bill's progress, helped to carry the day with the majority of the bishops, though without any show of enthusiasm.

The 1908 Act, after all, had shed none of the undenominational principles of the condemned Queen's Colleges. The bishops' acceptance of the Act therefore requires some explanation. The difference was that the Catholic atmosphere of the college was guaranteed at the start through its government, its academic staff, and its body of students. Though bishops had no right *ex officio* to a seat on the Senate or the Governing Body, the government nominated, among other clergy, two archbishops to the first Senate and two bishops to the first Governing Body.

The University Colleges of Cork and Galway were silently surrendered to the Catholics. As in 1970, when, with the proposed merger of Trinity and UCD, the bishops dropped the ban on Trinity, so in 1908, when the Queen's Colleges in Cork and Galway were merged with UCD in the federal NUI, the condemnation of Cork and Galway as 'godless' and not suitable for Catholics was quietly dropped from the bishops' pronouncements. Archbishop Walsh was elected unanimously by the Senate to be the first Chancellor of the NUI; and, as we have seen, the Dean of the Catholic University Medical School, Dr Denis Coffey, was appointed first President of UCD.

Of the twenty-six full-time professors who were appointed, all but seven had been connected with the Jesuit college, where the Catholic ethos had been consciously strong. Six of the twenty-six were priests, including four Jesuits. Of the ten part-time professors appointed under Statute I (five in medicine, three in law, one in architecture, and one in commerce), all but three had been connected with the Catholic University Medical School or the Jesuits' University College.

As for the students, the bulk of them simply transferred from the CU Medical School and the Jesuit college and the two women's university colleges, Eccles Street and Loreto College, St Stephen's Green. A large proportion came from the seminaries of Clonliffe and All Hallows and other religious houses and convents. The great majority of first-year entrants came from the Catholic secondary schools, headed by Clongowes Wood, Belvedere, Castleknock, and Blackrock.

So, whether from the point of view of staff, or students, or buildings, or ethos generally, the strong lines of continuity between the new UCD and the Jesuit college, Cecilia Street and the Catholic University were unmistakable and undeniable. And all of this soon became publicly evident in the confraternities, sodalities, deans of residence and annual retreats and the 'Red Mass' at the opening of the academic year.

Another of the powerful ideological influences contributing to the ethos of UCD was nationalism, both cultural and political. The name National University of Ireland was itself significant. It was a title that was assumed and appropriated by consensus rather than consciously chosen; and what was intended to constitute and vitalise a major part of its ethos had to be secured and proclaimed in its title.

The term 'National University' had recurred continuously during the debates on the university question and was given currency in many of the schemes proposed between 1870 and 1908. When it became clear that Trinity's refusal to co-operate in a 'National University' was final and that it had excluded itself from the idea, the title was claimed enthusiastically for the one possible alternative, which would also be politically and culturally national in the sense that Trinity did not wish to be. This was clearly the sense in which a National University was advocated by John Dillon in his celebrated address of December 1904 entitled 'The urgent need of a National University for Ireland, and how best to construct it'. Dillon's address did much to send into general circulation the term 'National University'. It was taken up enthusiastically by Patrick Pearse in the pages of the influential Gaelic League journal, *An Claidheamh Soluis*; and it was in widespread use in the deliberations and discussions about a new university in the four years immediately preceding 1908.

Following the lead of its Welsh model, the University of Wales, it could have been called simply the University of Ireland. But to remind everyone of its purpose and direction the loaded, emphatic epithet 'National' was prefixed. The National University of Ireland had emerged from the wrecks of three nineteenth-century universities—Queen's, Catholic, and Royal—with all the political implications involved in the change of title.

Outside the unionist Ascendancy it had been generally accepted that Trinity had not served the needs—the spiritual, cultural, material or political needs—of the Irish people. But a nationalist Ireland demanded a national university. John Dillon had insisted that the new university was to be an intellectual centre for nationalist Ireland; Douglas Hyde and Patrick Pearse had said that what was needed was an intellectual headquarters for the Gael. Not only did the establishment of UCD reflect this nationalist opinion but as soon as it was established as the metropolitan college of the National University it aimed at providing leadership for nationalist Ireland.

The staff of the Jesuit college always had its fair sprinkling of English Jesuits—Gerard Manley Hopkins, Father Darlington (the dean) and Father

H. Browne (professor of Greek). Father Delany himself was regarded as an old whig. When the history of the Jesuit college was being published in 1930 a wag suggested that instead of its rather curious title, *A Page of Irish History,* a more apt one would be *Whigs on the Green.*

With the transformation from Jesuit to undenominational college, the political colour of UCD also changed to a deeper shade of green. In the new college, Denis Coffey, the president, and Arthur Conway, the registrar, and most of the other professors were staunch home rulers. Coffey, after all, owed his appointment as president largely to the influence of John Dillon. By 1916 a number of the junior staff (Michael Hayes, Thomas MacDonagh, Liam Ó Briain) and a number of their students had joined the Irish Volunteers and had participated in the Rising. In the contest for the NUI parliamentary seat during the 1918 general election MacNeill, the Sinn Féin candidate, overwhelmed Arthur Conway, the Home Rule candidate. After 1922 UCD's politics were predominantly of the pro-Treaty, Cumann na nGaedheal or Fine Gael variety.

In the cultural sphere the college was distinctly national, with a renowned Celtic Faculty that included Macalister in Celtic archaeology, MacNeill in early Irish history, Hyde and Agnes O'Farrelly in Modern Irish, Bergin in Old Irish, Lloyd-Jones in Welsh and Mary Hayden in modern Irish history. It was not without reason that for long after its establishment UCD was known colloquially as the 'National'—sometimes much to the chagrin of its provincial sisters at Cork and Galway but quite understandable given its cultural and political rivalry with Trinity.

To ensure that the new institution should be a 'genuine expression of national intellect and national ideals' it also had to be, in John Dillon's phrase, an 'extremely *democratic* university.'[7] It must be under what Kettle called 'popular control'. Therefore the Governing Body, it was concluded, should be effectively representative of the various public authorities. The Chief Secretary and the Irish Party were in favour of strong representation from the county councils on the Governing Body of the colleges.

The Local Government Act (1898), which established the county councils, had taken the control of local government out of the hands of the Ascendancy landlords and handed it over to the nationalists. Many of those elected as county councillors were strongly involved in the Irish Party organisation, the United Irish League, at local level. Success in county council elections and experience in local government affairs would in time become the launching-ground for a career in national politics. By 1908 the county councils, now ten years old, were in the first flush of political enthusiasm. They were seen as marking a sweeping victory for democracy over the Ascendancy. When, therefore, nationalists both inside and outside Parliament were insisting that any new university should be democratic as well as nationalist, they naturally thought of county council representation on the Governing Body.

In his evidence before the Robertson Commission in 1902 the President of the Gaelic League, Douglas Hyde, had stated that the league desired that 'the popular element, either through itself or the county councils,' should be represented on the governing body of any new university.[8] Patrick Pearse, in an editorial in *An Claidheamh Soluis* early in 1904, wrote that a very obvious way in which popular opinion might find expression on such governing bodies would be through representatives nominated by the county councils and county borough (city) councils.[9] Not surprisingly, therefore, *An Claidheamh Soluis* strongly endorsed John Dillon's address to the Catholic Graduates' Association in which he stated that one of the essentials of the new university was that it should be extremely democratic.[10] The idea of county council representation was welcomed by Father Delany, Bishop O'Dwyer, and others.

Against the idea of a strong local government representation, and in response to Birrell's initial memorandum on the matter, Archbishop Walsh had recommended that to avoid 'jobbery' the composition of UCD's Governing Body should be as 'purely academic' as possible.[11] In the House of Commons Professor Butcher, Philip Magnus, Arthur Balfour and the Ulster Unionists voiced strong opposition to this aspect of Birrell's proposal. The question at issue was not whether there should be any civic representation on the Governing Bodies but whether the panel was being given undue influence: it was the size of the proposed county council representation that gave rise to much criticism.

In reply to the critics, Birrell said he had sufficient confidence in the good sense of the county councillors to imagine that they would not interfere in the election of professors of Greek or of philosophy. If they did not interfere, replied the critics, it would be the very first instance in which county councillors had refrained from exercising their patronage: county councillors, they said, would canvass for the election of professors of literature just as they did for the appointment of a charwoman or a gate porter in the local government system. Balfour said he would not call a university democratically governed if it was governed by county councils: he regarded *that* as the worst possible form of university government; a university was democratically governed when it was governed by its own graduates.

Some of the strongest criticism came, understandably enough, from those in the House of Lords who had landed interests in Ireland. Since the 1898 Act they had been displaced in local government by the new county council democracy. These landlords had reason for believing that county councils had become agents of the Home Rule party, and they feared that the new seats of learning would be turned into political machines. They argued that county councillors in such numbers would introduce not so much local as parochial interests and that all sorts of jobbery would ensue.

By the time the Bill appeared in Parliament in its final form, UCD was to have a Governing Body of thirty-four members, of whom ten were local authority representatives (eight elected by the General Council of County Councils, one elected by Dublin County Council, and the Lord Mayor of Dublin *ex officio*). This meant that the local authority representation was the largest electoral panel of the Governing Body. So while the clergy had no more entitlement to a seat on the Governing Body than the fact that they were not legally debarred, county councillors were guaranteed a significant influence by legislation.

The outcome for Dublin had owed much to the influence of the situation in Cork. Butcher's proposal was that the civic authorities would be adequately represented by the Lord Mayor and one other person from the relevant local council. Rejecting this, the Chief Secretary said he had himself gone carefully into the matter with the MP for Cork (William O'Brien) and the president of the Cork college (Dr Windle). They attached the greatest importance to the co-operation not only of the Lord Mayor but also of the Mayors of Limerick and Waterford and the chairman or other person representing the county councils of Munster. They wanted the people of the province to feel that they had a voice in the representation. The fortunes of the Galway college, he said, largely depended on being able to enlist the interest of the people of Connacht. The number of local authority representatives on the Governing Bodies of the three colleges had been made 'after elaborate consultation and enormous correspondence.'

Speaking for the government in the House of Lords, the Earl of Crewe reminded members that the Queen's Colleges at Cork and Galway (unlike Belfast) had not aroused local support. In reconstituting these colleges in a new university, the idea of the government, he said, 'was that they rouse the greatest possible degree of local interest.' He acknowledged that they were not to be endowed on a scale that was intended to make them independent of local support. Therefore, to secure that local support it certainly did seem very important to the government that a large element representing the different neighbourhoods should be placed on the Governing Bodies. This too was an acknowledgment that the needs of the colleges at Cork and Galway were to influence the composition of the Governing Body at Dublin.

After the preliminary draft of the articles for a Charter for the Dublin college was laid on the table of the House of Commons, the Catholic Graduates' Association had criticised it, not because eight county councillors were to serve on its Governing Body but because six of them were to be from Leinster and two from Ulster. In a memorandum issued after their meeting of

13 May 1908 they stated that such a mode of representation 'might fairly be taken to imply an intention to stereotype the metropolitan college as a provincial in the place of a national institution ... This would indicate that the metropolitan foundation must not pretend to be a national institution, but is devised merely to meet the needs of a section of the country.'[12] This would condemn the new college to 'perpetual provincialism', whereas the demand hitherto in the name of equality with Trinity College and other non-Catholic institutions has been for 'a great college in Dublin equal at least to Trinity College, with the Queen's Colleges adapted to their environment.' The Catholic Graduates' Association went on to claim that 'the General Council of County Councils, if it is to be accorded representation at all, should elect its representatives irrespective of provinces.' Copies of this memorandum, demanding for the new college in Dublin 'the status of a national institution,' were sent to the secretaries of the Standing Committee of the Irish Bishops, the Archbishop of Dublin, the Chief Secretary, John Redmond, John Dillon, and the nationalist members of the Standing Committee, who were examining the Bill in Parliament.

The pressure from both inside and outside Parliament worked, for when the Charter was finally agreed it was simply to state that eight members of the Governing Body of UCD were to be elected by members of the General Council of County Councils, and no restriction by province or county or even membership of a county council was imposed. By contrast, the individual county councils in Munster and Connacht elected one member each to the Governing Bodies of Cork and Galway.

Concluding the debate on this issue, the Chief Secretary said that the number of local representatives on the Governing Bodies was not to be regarded as final but could be left to experiment, and after a few years some reductions might be made in the numbers.[13] Since the composition of the Governing Bodies was written into the charters of the colleges, and since it became notoriously difficult to change these charters, the county council representation remained as if the arrangement had been engraved in stone. County councillors *have* played a role in appointments—in the election of presidents and registrars and of academic staff. It was naïve of Birrell to argue that they would not. Those who benefited by their votes talked about the common sense, practicality, political clout, shrewdness and business acumen they brought to their task. Losers in these contests were understandably less enthusiastic. Writing in the nineteen-fifties, Professor Thomas Dillon of UCG remarked that since the establishment of the Local Appointments Commission in 1926, the only appointments that county councillors still had a vote on were those of rate collectors and university professors.[14] They have long since lost the power to appoint rate collectors; they continued to exercise, and relish, the right to vote on university appointments.

Why was University College made part of a federal system and not established as a separate and independent university in 1908? After all, Trinity was to remain outside any federal scheme and to remain, as always, the only college of the University of Dublin. And Queen's College in Belfast was raised to the status of an independent university by the same Act that joined Dublin with Cork and Galway as constituent colleges of the NUI.

It should be noted that all the attempted solutions, from Peel's efforts in 1845 down to Birrell's Act in 1908, had one thing in common. Whether it was a variation of the extended University of Dublin scheme or of the Royal University scheme, federation was involved. It was always assumed, no matter which scheme was being seriously considered or discussed, that University College, Dublin, would be part of the federation and not an independent university.

Acknowledging the weaknesses of federalism, the Chief Secretary assured Parliament that this federal NUI was not intended to be permanent. He said he would prefer if Cork and Galway were strong enough to run universities of their own; he hoped that Cork would soon be in a position to become the independent university of Munster that its spokesmen were demanding. The implication was that the two former Queen's Colleges needed the infusion of strength that Dublin would bring to them. Oddly, there was no serious discussion whether UCD deserved to be given independent university status: its main role in the federation seemed to be to bolster up a weak Cork and an even weaker Galway.

From the point of view of size alone, UCD stood next to Trinity College and above all other university institutions in the land. And with UCD from 1908 guaranteed state funding, its numbers could be expected to expand rapidly, which is exactly what happened. It was soon to overtake Trinity to become by far the country's biggest university institution.

Before 1908 a campaign had been launched to turn Queen's College, Cork, into an independent university. During the debate on the Irish Universities Bill, William O'Brien (MP for Cork), reluctantly accepted Birrell's argument that 'some federation is unfortunately necessary.' It was acknowledged that the trend in England was to defederalise; Manchester, Liverpool and Leeds, which had been constituents of Victoria University, had recently been turned into independent institutions. But the model for the NUI was not the defunct Victoria University but the University of Wales (1893), which had its constituent colleges at Aberystwyth, Cardiff, and Bangor.

Apart from size, another anomaly was that UCD was clearly regarded during the debate as a national institution in the geographical sense. Cork and Galway, on the other hand, were looked upon as being provincial. The distinction, as we have seen, was emphasised in the election of the county councillors on UCD's Governing Body from a national panel while in Cork and Galway the county councillors were elected from a provincial panel.

What the NUI federal arrangement had done was to marry UCD, with all its Catholic University, Cardinal Newman and Jesuit traditions, to two Queen's Colleges, with a very different, undenominational tradition and officially frowned upon by the bishops from 1845 until 1908. The effect of this marriage of convenience, however, was that UCD and the two former Queen's Colleges drew much closer. UCD's Catholicism was minimised, at least in law, while Cork and Galway became more Catholic, at least in practice. Within a short period a similar Catholic ethos became common to the three constituent colleges.

A somewhat similar fusion was taking place in the sphere of political and cultural nationalism. All presidential and professorial appointments in the Queen's Colleges down to 1908 were made by the British government. The result was that Cork and Galway had a fair number of British academics on their staff who were unionist in outlook. In contrast, UCD was strongly nationalist in both the political and the cultural sense. One far-reaching outcome of this was that so-called compulsory Irish for matriculation was imposed by the nationalist UCD representatives on the NUI Senate, in the face of strong opposition from some Cork and Galway senators.

Again, within a short few years of the marriage, the political and cultural philosophies of Sinn Féin and the Gaelic League also came to dominate in Cork and in Galway. And all three colleges could boast that they were truly national in spirit as well as in name.

The common national spirit and the common Catholic ethos made generally for a happy relationship and a healthy rivalry between the metropolitan UCD and its provincial sisters, at least during the first forty years of the NUI. There were occasional tensions and hiccups, but during this period Cork was the only one seriously to seek separation and independence. In 1919 the authorities in Cork, under their president, Sir Bertram Windle, applied to Dublin Castle for a new charter of independence as the University of Munster. Apart from internal Cork resistance, led by Alfred O'Rahilly, strong opposition was mounted in the Senate of the NUI, where the UCD members in particular opposed the splintering of the NUI with all the power of a well-organised majority. It was reported to Dr Windle that the president of UCD, Dr Coffey, was 'bitterly—savagely opposed.'[15] And UCD's Governing Body passed a resolution declaring that it was 'unanimously opposed' to the break-up of the NUI. In 1919, therefore, UCD had played a leading role in defending the NUI federation and in keeping Cork within that federation. Thirty years later there was to be something of a reversal of roles when UCD wanted to leave the NUI and strong opposition came from its sister in Cork.

Having its links with the University Colleges of Cork and Galway

John Henry Newman in the 1850s, first Rector of the Catholic University of Ireland.

	CHRISTIAN AND SURNAME, at full length.	AGE next Birth Day.	BIRTH PLACE.	FATHER'S CHRISTIAN AND SURNAME, at full length.
1	Daniel O'Connell	16	Paris	John O'Connell
2	John Henry Bracken	20	Wexford	James Henry Bracken
3	Patrick Conolly	20	Monaghan	
4	Patrick Fitzgerald Galway	17	Dublin	Michael Galway
5	Patrick Mc Mullan	18		Daniel Mc Mullan
6	Jerome Eaton Mc Swiney	16	Clonmel Co. Tipperary	Peter Mc Swiney
7	Bernard John Meagan	18	Cork	
8	James Murphy	17	Middleton	James Murphy
9	Francis Ansell	17	Dublin	Francis Ansell
10	Thomas Butler	17	Dublin	Richard Butler
11	Alfred J. Byrne	18	Dublin	John Byrne
12	John Thomas Doyle	16	Portsmouth	Christopher Doyle
13	Patrick Gorman	16		
14	Andrew Washington Linnian	18	Dublin	James William Linnian
15	Thomas Meaunsell	15	Dublin	John Meaunsell
16	Henry O'Neil		Bodenstown Clane	
17	Francis Tobin	15	Dublin	Patrick Tobin
18	Venite Louis de Vaulchier	18	Besançon France	Louis de Vaulchier

Section from first page of the Register of the Catholic University of Ireland. Note the first name is Daniel O'Connell, grandson of the Liberator.

The Seal of the Catholic University School of Medicine.

Dr Bartholomew Woodlock, Rector of the Catholic University of Ireland (1861–79), Bishop of Ardagh and Clonmacnoise (1879–94), who commissioned McCarthy's project below.

THE CATHOLIC UNIVERSITY OF IRELAND. DUBLIN.

1862.

Design for the Catholic University of Ireland by James Joseph McCarthy, 1862. Only the foundation stone was laid at the site in Drumcondra.

The calibre of Father Delany's University College can be gauged from this group of students and staff photographed about 1901.

Standing (*from left*): Father George O'Neill, S.J., Fellow of the Royal University, who would become Professor of English at UCD after the establishment of the National University and later a famous preacher in Australia; James Joyce, destined to be 'the only author in the English language more written about than Shakespeare'; John Marcus O'Sullivan, a future Professor of History at UCD and Minister for Education; Bob Kinahan, later an eminent K.C.; Séamus Clandillon, who would be Ireland's first Director of Broadcasting; Patrick Semple, Professor of Latin at UCD from 1909 to 1947. Seated centre row (*from left*): George Clancy, who as Mayor of Limerick would be murdered by the Black-and-Tans; Father Edmund Hogan, S.J., Fellow of the Royal University and a leading authority on the Irish language; Edouard Cadic, later Professor of French at UCD; Father Joseph Darlington, S.J. (Father Delany's assistant). Front row (*from left*): Felix Hackett, future Professor of Physics at UCD and President of the Royal Dublin Society; Séamus O'Kelly, a Gaelic scholar who became a medical doctor and Lecturer in Obstetrics at UCD; Michael Lennon, who became well known both as a District Justice and as a critic of James Joyce; and Con Curran, renowned authority on the architecture of Dublin.

Caption from McRedmond, *To the Greater Glory*, Dublin 1991

The exclusive Cui Bono club was originally intended to discuss questions of literature, art and drama. Among the notable persons in this photograph were three future professors, two judges and two cabinet members.

Back row (*from left*): Vincent Clarke, Felix Hackett, Tom Kettle. Seated (*from left*): William Dawson, J.M. O'Sullivan, Hugh Kennedy, Charles McGarry, James Murnaghan, C.P. Curran.

Minutes of the meeting of the L&H, 20 January 1900, at which James Joyce read his paper on 'Drama and Life'.

Newman House, 85 & 86 St Stephen's Green.

Professor Edouard Cadic, Professor of French in the Jesuit University College (1894–1909) and in University College, Dublin (1909–14). The drawing was by the student, Thomas Bodkin, afterwards Curator of the National Gallery of Ireland.

Father William Delany, S.J., President of University College (1883–88; 1897–1909).

The Dublin Commissioners who drew up the first statutes for the National University and its Colleges and made the first appointments.
Back row (*from left*): Stephen Gwynn, John P. Boland, Alexander Anderson, Bertram C.A. Windle, Denis J. Coffey. Front row (*from left*): Gen. Sir William F. Butler, Most Rev. William J. Walsh, Rt. Hon. Christopher Palles, Sir John Rhys, Henry Jackson.

The Royal University of Ireland as it was in the 1880s and 1890s on Earlsfort Terrace, later adapted as the home of UCD from 1909.

The formal reception of Mr de Valera as Chancellor of the National University of Ireland took place in UCD on 19 November 1921. The Chancellor is seen here with members of the Committee of Convocation.

Seated (*from left*): Mary Kate Ryan (Mrs S.T. O'Ceallaigh), Assistant in French; Rev. Timothy Corcoran, S.J., Professor of Education; The Chancellor, Eamon de Valera; Dr Michael Cox, Chairman of Convocation; Arthur E. Clery, Professor of the Law of Property and Contracts. Standing (*from left*): James Creed Meredith, K.C., Judge of Dáil Éireann High Court; Patrick McGilligan, Assistant in Latin; Louise Gavan Duffy, Assistant in Education; Ian Bloomer, Demonstrator in Engineering; William J. Williams, Lecturer in Education, Royal College of Science; Mary Macken, Professor of German; Michael Hayes, Assistant in French; Michael Rynne, President of the Students' Representative Council.

MSc graduates in 1917 Standing (*from left*): George Hanlon, Tony Glover, (Unknown), (Unknown), Philip Connell. Seated (*from left*): Edward J. Conway, Phyllis Ryan, Roy Geary, James Drumm. Conway became Professor of Biochemistry and Pharmacology 1931–64; Phyllis Ryan (later Mrs Sean T. O'Ceallaigh) became State Chemist; Roy Geary became head of the Central Statistics Office; James Drumm invented the Drumm battery.

probably fed UCD's opinion of itself as a national institution. UCD seemed content with its constituent status, at least down to the nineteen-fifties, when Michael Tierney argued that his college was hampered and constrained by the federal system. And since the report of the Commission on Higher Education in 1967 the whole idea of defederalisation and the creation of independent universities had been constantly debated.

Under the Universities Act (1997) the constituent colleges of the NUI have been raised in status and established as independent but constituent universities of the NUI. The Act was very much a compromise between those who advocated outright independence and those who wished to retain some form of federation.

The institution that was founded by the 1908 Act may not have been—as Pearse noted at the time, and as Michael Tierney often reiterated afterwards— the university that an independent Ireland might have given itself. Clearly it was not all that the bishops wanted. It was rather the Liberal government's compromise solution. But it did receive some strong support from the Irish Party, and it answered the wishes of Father Delany and others for an institution completely separate from Trinity, though it also imposed the joint education of men and women that Father Delany disapproved of but that Mary Hayden, Agnes O'Farrelly and others demanded.

Without the constraints of its conflicting institutional precedents and ideologies it is conceivable that UCD might have served the nation better. But, despite its hybrid origins, it was indeed to serve the country well. Its ethos accounted for that. Remarkably, its charter and original statutes survived without major amendment for ninety years. Archbishop Walsh and others took the line that they should make the most of a far from ideal solution. They would have agreed with the character in George Eliot's *Middlemarch* who said: 'Instead of preaching against humbug *outside* the walls, it might be better to set up a disinfecting apparatus *within.*' It was the ethos, the *genius loci* that Newman often wrote about as essential to a university, that provided the disinfectant.

UCD was the response to certain needs in Irish society. There was, first of all, a sixty-year-old demand for a university institution that would be acceptable to the religious majority and that would place Catholics on a footing of equality with the hitherto privileged minority. Secondly, there was a demand for a university that would be openly and frankly national—from both the political and the cultural point of view. Thirdly, there was a demand for a university that would be democratic. And fourthly, there was a demand for a university that would be clearly utilitarian and modern and would contribute to the economic growth of Ireland in agriculture, industry and commerce and in the training of teachers and clergy and other professions, capable of playing a significant role in raising the tone of the whole of Irish society and in preparation for self-government, which could not be for long denied.

The college that was established in 1908, specifically to meet these demands, incorporated characteristics that were Catholic, national, democratic, and utilitarian. And UCD would continue for a long time after its foundation to exhibit these qualities and to live by them. The later history of UCD would show in its progress how these characteristics influenced the life of the college and its members, and also the lives of the community beyond its walls, and how these qualities were themselves modified by the circumstances and aspirations of a changing society.

DR COFFEY'S PRESIDENCY

Far from being a 'weak and second-rate' individual, as some had expected, Dr Denis Coffey, during all his more than thirty years in the presidency, was seen by informed observers, such as Professor Mary Macken and Professor John Marcus O'Sullivan, as 'a great Irishman'. They lauded him for what they saw as excellent qualities displayed in office during very difficult circumstances.[16] One of the most noted characteristics of his presidency on which several commentators were agreed was his personal interest in and knowledge of the students.

William Doolin, professor of the history of medicine at UCD, who had been a student of Coffey's in the early years of the century, recorded that in Cecilia Street he was

> the most approachable member of the staff, who was never at a loss for any student's name or record, so that to the general body he was known as 'the students' professor' … He was the busiest personality in our cramped community, often lecturing twice and three times a day in addition to constant laboratory work; he never seemed to leave the premises, yet always could find time to attend or take the chair at committee meetings concerning the welfare or the recreations of the youth in the School. He was quite the most selfless individual whom we had ever met … Outside the class-room, he taught us more: from his richly stored mind, well-informed on all subjects—history, classics, philosophy, travel—we learned, almost unconsciously, that the future of Ireland—our future—was the subject nearest to his heart, and that the scientific education of Irish youth was essential to her—and our—progress and prosperity.[17]

This unique relationship with the students he carried with him into the presidency. Professor Macken wrote: 'He knew every student, not only their college, but their school records ... Men returning to College after a period of absence glowed with pleasure when Dr Coffey not only identified them at once but could tell them a good deal about themselves.'

Professor O'Sullivan confirmed this remarkable aspect of Coffey's regime:

> We should have regarded the stories of his knowledge of all those who passed through the College as legendary, did we not have daily evidence of its reality. His brain ... seemed to be a living compendious dossier of all students past and present. He made it his business to know something about every one of them; to know them all by appearance and name, from what part of the country they came, their family circumstances, their history; their proposed career and numerous other details ... He was always accessible to them.

These accounts of the extent of Dr Coffey's personal knowledge of his students can only seem greatly exaggerated to a later generation. The professor of English, Jeremiah Hogan, might be excused on grounds of poetic licence for also asserting without qualification that Coffey 'knew every one of them and never forgot them. He was like a remote ancestor to them all, or an old Irish genealogist; he considered each individual in the light of his family name and district, and looked for hereditary and traditional qualities.'[18]

The extravagant claim lost nothing in the retelling. Thomas Dillon (a student, then a junior member of staff, and later professor of chemistry at UCG) wrote of Coffey's 'personal knowledge of every student in the College, and of how he was or was not progressing, and frequently of his ancestry. He would recognise a student and give an account of his career often years after he had left the College.'[19]

Given that UCD in Coffey's time was scattered between Earlsfort Terrace, Cecilia Street, the College of Science in Merrion Street and Albert College in Glasnevin, and that the number of students in Coffey's last year was almost 2,400, the claim by so many respectable witnesses that he knew *every* student is rather startling.

Coffey was only beginning on his third year as president when Michael Tierney entered UCD as a student in 1911. Later as a junior member of staff, and then, from 1923, as one of the college's most prominent professors, Tierney's association with Coffey stretched over thirty years (since Coffey continued to attend meetings of the Governing Body until his death in 1945)—long enough to allow him to observe his predecessor at close quarters. Slightly more restrained than his colleagues, Tierney stated: 'Even at the end of his term of office, when numbers were beginning to be overwhelming, he was still reputed to know the history of every student.'[20] The word 'reputed' makes the assertion less extravagant while at the same time emphasising Coffey's legendary knowledge of his students.

Coffey's knowledge of and interest in the students' welfare was emulated only by another medical, Dr Tom Murphy, who during his presidency was reputed to know the names of every member of the staff of the much larger college of the nineteen-seventies and eighties. And in each case it certainly added much to the spirit of collegiality.

The students had great affection and reverence for Dr Coffey, though in Hogan's view it could not be said that he exactly put them at their ease. By all accounts he gave the impression of being shy, reserved, austere, and dignified. One student remembered him during the early years of his presidency as 'tense and nervous, a vaguely ecclesiastical personality somewhat suggestive of the seminary.'[21] But he also displayed what Mary Macken called 'extraordinarily human kindliness'. A 'never-ending sympathy', according to Michael Tierney, was one of his outstanding qualities. One example of Coffey's legendary sympathy with his students, noted by Tierney, was his capacity to assist borderline students at meetings of the Examination Board, 'often under peculiar circumstances and in devious ways,' while retaining 'a very effective, if quiet, dignity of manner.'

There was a reverse side to all this. Dillon remarked that Coffey often irritated staff and students by wanting to do everything himself. Even the Calendars, said Mary Macken, were the work of his own hand. O'Sullivan spoke of his 'failure to delegate enough' and said that he allowed nothing to get out of his hands. Hogan agreed: 'Dr Coffey kept things to himself and made the government of the College mysterious to an extent beyond anything required.'

Because he delegated so little, Coffey's administration suffered much; and it was soon overtaken by the sheer growth of the college. Michael Tierney has remarked on how much of the business of the faculties Coffey kept in his own hands. The earliest minute books of the faculties recording the briefest of transactions at infrequent meetings are eloquent testimony to the accuracy of Tierney's criticism. It was only under Coffey's successor, Dr Conway, that, as Tierney said, the academic balance was restored, 'which after thirty years of almost one-man rule had come to be badly needed.'[22] And it was only under Conway's successor in the registrarship that that office became more important than Dr Coffey had ever allowed it to be.

In matters of college business, wrote Tierney, 'he relied heavily on patience, and the proceedings at meetings over which he presided were apt to be devious. The complaint was often humorously made that he got important matters through under the heading of "Other Business".' Within a single paragraph Tierney applied the word 'devious' twice to Coffey's style of conducting meetings. The younger man's impatience with the ageing president as administrator is barely concealed in these comments.

Professor Jeremiah Hogan was more tolerant: he sought to explain

Coffey's peculiar methods but stopped short of apologising for them. According to Hogan, he

> rejected common efficiency and ordinary business methods; he did not answer letters as they came, if at all; it was difficult to see him, though he was always in the College, and when you saw him he would talk about anything but the business you came upon. He had what seemed a morbid dislike of having people ask for things or make suggestions, appearing to regard all propositions as *prima facie* dangerous or unnecessary. Yet he neglected nothing; the unanswered letters were not forgotten, the suggestions that nettled him sometimes became his own line of action, and the requests he would not allow to be worded were sometimes granted later on, unasked. He wanted time, and he was ready to pay a lot for it, in efficiency and in his own comfort.[23]

Despite her obvious affection for him, Mary Macken had to admit: 'I would not say he was "efficient" in the American sense of the word; he even rejected aids to efficiency.' No-one, she said, ever saw him rush or allow himself to be rushed. He did not use a telephone. He disliked cars, and his horse-drawn cab, in which he travelled to and from the college, became famous. It was admitted, as Macken put it, that he was 'no wizard of finance.' And Hogan described him as a man who had little personal interest in money, and perhaps no great skill in dealing with it. Yet this was perhaps the greatest battle he had to fight, and he had to devote thirty years to tugging together ends that could not meet.[24] A man who habitually avoided the strong word, by 1920/21 he was describing the financial position as 'intolerable'. In the forties his successor was trying to focus attention on the almost desperate financial straits in which the college found itself.

There were to be no inspirational speeches from Coffey. His 'interests did not lie in the fashioning of words,' as Macken said. Because of his low voice he was not, in Tierney's opinion, an effective speaker, though his sincerity and warmth had their own kind of eloquence. He left behind him no remarkable memoranda or statement of policy. But he did have a shrewdness that he used to great effect when the political and military storms lashed his college between 1916 and 1922 and those in responsible positions had to tread warily. Considering the involvement of a number of his professors in the first Free State government, his tact and patience were also required on the change of government in 1932. It could be said that he managed to insist on the principle that the college was a national institution above party politics.

One is tempted to think that the college could have done better under a more imaginative, energetic or forceful first president. But then one has to recall that the infant institution was dogged by adverse circumstance throughout Coffey's regime: the lack of finance for building and expansion, the First World War, the Easter Rising and the Anglo-Irish war of 1916–1921, the Civil War, the problems of the Free State, the economic weaknesses of the twenties and thirties, and the Second World War. A more dynamic or ideal-istic person might have found the circumstances utterly frustrating. The times probably required a president who was cautious, prudent, and pragmatic, and these virtues Coffey possessed in abundance. Despite his administrative foibles he was held in great affection by the staff. And if he was unlucky in the times that were in it, his good fortune lay in the calibre of the staff and students with whom he had to work.

Coffey had begun with thirty-six chairs and fifteen lectureships. When he retired, another twenty or so had been added to each category, and a comparatively large number of assistants had also been added to the teaching team. He took a keen interest in the selection of staff to fill the vacancies that occurred, and in this it was believed that his judgment was usually sound. To encourage graduates to devote themselves to advanced work, he held that staff should normally be recruited from UCD's own graduates. But he also sought to encourage those graduates to do a period of research work abroad. The second generation of professors would include many who had taken advanced degrees in universities outside Ireland.

Student numbers increased nearly five-fold during Coffey's term of office. Though it was severely under-financed and under-provided with space and facilities, Coffey believed it was his duty somehow to fit these students into University College. Denied a university education for so long, Irish Catholics were entitled to it. The progress and welfare of the country demanded it. And so, under Coffey, the country began to be permeated with the doctors, lawyers, teachers, engineers, higher civil servants, scientists and others who had graduated from UCD.

Taking all the circumstances into account, teaching had to be the priority. But Coffey had at least always remained aware of the need for research in a university institution. Indeed, first-class work in research did take place during his time, especially in Celtic studies and in science.

A devout Catholic, in 1902 Coffey had advocated in his evidence before the Robertson Commission the foundation of a Catholic university, under clerical or lay control. As president, he fostered in its several manifestations the Catholic life of the college. He played a leading layman's role in and associated his college with the public celebrations of the Catholic Emancipation Centenary in 1929 and the Eucharistic Congress in 1932. A committed nationalist, he had been active in the Gaelic League and was an intimate friend of the Irish Party leader, John Dillon. Coffey's nationalism and his Catholicism were both admirably suited to the ethos of the new college.

The years of Dr Coffey's presidency had seen a new building in Earlsfort

Terrace (however inadequate the incomplete structure turned out to be); a massive increase in student numbers; a more modest increase in teaching staff; the addition of the College of Science and Albert Agricultural College in 1926; and the transfer of the Medical School in 1931 to an additional new building in Earlsfort Terrace. He had such developments to look back on when he retired. He could also be proud that a college, however starved of resources, had been firmly established in the public mind as the principal university institution in the country.

SCHOOLS AND HOME RESIDENCE

The last examinations of the Royal University of Ireland were held in September and October 1909, and the 'old Royal', as it was later affectionately called by many, was officially dissolved on 31 October. In his first report as president, Dr Coffey was able to boast that, following the dissolution of the Royal University, University College, Dublin, entered on its career as a teaching institution on Tuesday 2 November 1909 without the loss of a single working day (Monday 1 November was All Saints' Day).[25] This was fifty-five years, almost to the day, after the Catholic University of Ireland had begun its classes under Newman on 3 November 1854. In October, immediately preceding the opening of the session, the Dublin Commission had made appointments to thirty-three professorships and nine lectureships, and the remaining vacancies were filled during the session. Sixteen demonstrators and assistants and six student demonstrators were appointed by the Governing Body to assist in teaching during the first session.

The number of students attending UCD in its first year of operation was 530. A large proportion of that number were already attending the Medical School in Cecilia Street and second and third-year arts and science in the Jesuit college in St Stephen's Green. These were now transferred to the books of the new college. So, for those students already launched on their university studies, the official beginning of teaching in UCD meant no more in practice than a paper transfer from the abolished Royal to the new National. The medical students remained in Cecilia Street for most of their classes. Arts, law and commerce were still restricted to 86 St Stephen's Green until the new college should be built. The library, such as it was, was also in St Stephen's Green, in the Aula Maxima, though the National Library, as in Joyce's time, was to remain a sort of extension of UCD for the more eager students. The laboratories in Earlsfort Terrace, which had previously been used for examinations of the Royal University, were made available by the Senate of the NUI to UCD for engineering, physics, chemistry, geology, and physiology.

A register of 1909/10 listed the schools attended by 370 of the students.

The principal ones were:

Cecilia Street	121
University College	51
Clongowes Wood	26
Holy Cross (Clonliffe)	19
Belvedere	14
Castleknock	13
Blackrock	11
Loreto	10
St Mary's, Dundalk	10
Eccles Street	9
O'Connell CBS	9

Several other schools throughout the country contributed students in fewer numbers. Many listed under Cecilia Street and University College would have received their secondary education in Clongowes Wood, Belvedere, Castleknock, or Blackrock. These were the same schools that had already been among the principal feeders of the Catholic University. While it cannot be claimed that the schools attended were listed with anything like complete accuracy, or with any consistency of method, the list does give a fair indication of the schools from which UCD's first students were drawn.

The list for the college's second year of operation confirms the general trend. The total number of students in 1910/11 was 695. For 571 of these the name of the school attended was given; with only the exceptional one from abroad, these had come from between seventy and eighty different schools all over Ireland. Such numbers represented from the beginning a widespread vote of confidence in the new college. If we exclude those students listed under UCD (mainly those in medicine from second year upwards) the order reads:

All Hallows	43
Holy Cross (Clonliffe)	37
Clongowes Wood	35
Eccles Street	22
Castleknock	21
Blackrock	19
Loreto	17
Belvedere	16
Terenure	13

Building on the success of Cecilia Street, the Medical Faculty for many years outnumbered each of the others, its closest contender being Arts. The proportion of the student body in Medicine was:

1909–10	59%
1911–16	31–37%
1916–23	40–49%

Medicine took second place behind Arts in the years 1911–16 but re-established its primacy between 1916 and 1923. The last year in which Medicine was the largest faculty was 1922/23, after which Arts (including philosophy and Celtic studies) established itself firmly as the largest—a position it was to maintain from then onwards.

Since the students of All Hallows and Clonliffe College were registered virtually without exception in the Faculty of Arts, almost 30 per cent of all arts students in 1910/11 were seminarians from these two colleges alone.[26] During the first fifty years of UCD's existence the number of seminarians and other religious continued to be a feature of the college. Seminarians from Clonliffe, missionaries in the making from All Hallows, Jesuit aspirants from Rathfarnham and members of the Holy Ghost congregation from Blackrock converged daily on Earlsfort Terrace on their bicycles, like so many army squadrons. At lunchtime they occupied a whole section of an overcrowded restaurant, and one of their number, acting as quartermaster, signed the lunch book on behalf of his colleagues. Since the clerics were uniformed—black suit, white shirt and black tie or Roman collar—they appeared to be even more numerous than they were, and this impression was augmented by the presence of an increasing number of nuns filling the front rows of the lecture room, maintaining a regulated custody of the eyes and keeping ever busy with note-taking. Despite their numbers, no tension was detected between religious and lay. The presence of so many religious was accepted as part of the natural order of things then existing in Ireland.

With the number of lay students—especially women—increasing almost annually, the ratio of religious to lay in the student body correspondingly decreased over the years. In the early sixties, after the Second Vatican Council, the black clerical suits were gradually replaced by anoraks, jumpers, and jeans, becoming ever lighter in colour; and with the decline in vocations this once very noticeable cohort was submerged in the general body of students.[27] Gone were the days when a contributor to the *National Student* could ask: 'Remove the Medical School from University College and what have you left? A miniature Maynooth with a handful of lay students.'[28]

As a student in UCD between 1916 and 1919, the future novelist Kate O'Brien remembered pushing her way into some debate or lecture in 86 St Stephen's Green 'through an excessive crowd of beetle-black, scrubby-faced boys from All Hallows, and having to crush against the hieratic touch-me-not robes of young daughters of St. Louis.' A friend looking around at this 'black and rosary-beaded mob' remarked: 'Newman said that a university is neither a convent nor a seminary.' Yet O'Brien had to admit that, though appearances were against it, the 'rough-and-tumble place was *not* a convent or a seminary':

it was, she said, 'a seemingly ill-directed, or if you like non-directed, place of learning—but it was open.' Between the 'four old houses' in St Stephen's Green and 'the hideous tin huts' in the back garden she found that there was 'learning and eccentricity about,' so that whoever wanted 'could run free and wild enough into at least the first sweet shallows of the humanistic studies.'[29]

Engineering came next in numbers after medicine and arts in those early years, though it was occasionally surpassed by law (because of the numbers of non-matriculated students taking legal studies). In the first couple of years students in the Science Faculty were not enumerated separately in the president's report but were included in the numbers taking arts. That is not to say that science was insignificant—on the contrary: large numbers doing medicine had to take courses in physics, chemistry, zoology and botany, and these and other science subjects were also taken by students registered in engineering and arts. It was not until 1918/19 that the Faculty of Science (as distinct from students in other faculties taking science subjects) had overtaken both Engineering and Law to become the third-largest faculty in the college. By then also Commerce had overtaken Law; by 1921/22 it had overtaken Engineering and by the mid-twenties it had even overtaken Science as the third-largest faculty. While Arts maintained its primacy in the number of students, the order of the other faculties varied depending on job opportunities and economic conditions in the country.

From the beginning, those attending UCD had come from every county in Ireland. Since UCD was non-residential, and Dublin and its neighbourhood was well supplied with secondary schools, one would have expected that a very large proportion of UCD students would have come from homes in or near the populous capital city. It is mildly surprising, therefore, to find that in the great majority of cases in the years before 1960 the domiciliary origins of full-time students were outside Dublin city and county. For reasons that include the comparative growth of Dublin, the flight from the land, and increasing prosperity, which opened up university education in the first instance to greater numbers within easy reach of UCD, the proportion of students from the city and the surrounding area steadily expanded during the fifties. It was only in the nineties that the proportion dropped again with any consistency to slightly below the 50 per cent mark. This decrease was no doubt related to the bigger number of students coming to UCD from abroad, to the increased availability of third-level education in other institutions in the city, and to the spread of the country's increasing prosperity to provincial Ireland. The proportion of students from homes within a radius of approximately thirty miles of Dublin was:

1920/21	28%
1950/51	32%
1958/59	52%
1990s	slightly under 50%

Over the decades, however, the great majority of students continued to be drawn from the Catholic middle class. Their parents were doctors, engineers, civil servants, teachers, bank officials, shopkeepers, publicans, and farmers; they had been to the 'best' Catholic secondary schools. The sons and daughters of the working class—the skilled and semi-skilled manual workers, shop assistants, transport and factory workers, labourers—were always scarce enough in the lecture halls and college clubs and societies; and of those who did make it to the university, some perhaps felt awkward in the presence of those from the more expensive schools. Between 1964/65 and 1978/79 the socio-economic background of entrants was as follows:[30]

Middle class (as defined by CSO)	
(c. 25% of population)	70–75%
Farming (c. 26% of population)	13–15%
Working class (c. 45% of population)	11–16%

COUNTY COUNCIL SCHOLARSHIPS

Students from the working class and lower middle class and from small farming and shopkeeping backgrounds were in college largely because of the system of county council and city council scholarships. Section 10 (2) of the Irish Universities Act (1908) had empowered any local rating authority to award scholarships tenable in any university in Ireland, provided these scholarships would not be conditional on any religious qualification or be devoted to any religious purpose. It was clear from the involvement of county councillors on the Governing Bodies of the constituent colleges of the National University, and from the debates in Parliament in 1908, that these scholarships were intended to provide an additional source of income for the colleges. Most of the assisted students in UCD were in fact the beneficiaries of these scholarships.

1910/11	4
1911/12	34
1918/19	272
mid-1920s	200+
1926–29	<200
1931/32	124
1956/57	271
1958/59	215
1962/63	277
1967/68	605

(Though the number of scholarships more than doubled in the sixties, so too did the total number of students—from 4,768 in 1959/60 to 10,253 in 1969/70.)

At first, special examinations set by the college were held to determine the county council scholarship awards; later the Leaving Certificate was prescribed as the test whereby candidates were placed in order of merit. (By special arrangement between UCD and Donegal County Council, only candidates for the County Donegal scholarships continued to take a test set by the college.) The scholarship-holders undoubtedly raised academic standards, and many of these students later became well-known academics and professionals.

By no means all holders of scholarships came from the working class. This was partly because comparatively few children from this class then completed secondary education, and many of those who did were eager to accept the jobs for which a Leaving Certificate qualified them. One can only conclude that the scholarships were availed of mainly by families of the middle and lower middle class, who traditionally placed great emphasis on the education of their children. This was made possible by a certain flexibility attached to the interpretation of the 1908 Act, which referred to students 'who satisfy the council that they ... are in need of assistance.'

This interpretation is confirmed by the comparatively large number of scholarship-holders who were in the Medical Faculty. County council scholarships for the year 1918/19 were distributed between faculties as follows:

Medicine	104
Arts	65
Engineering	38
Commerce	36
Science	29
Total	272

In this year 47 per cent of the total number of students were in medicine, 34 per cent in arts.

Most of the county council schemes provided scholarships for three or at most four years at the university. One would have expected, therefore, that the winners would have chosen courses such as arts, commerce, science, and engineering, which could have been completed within that time. Yet what is surprising is the large number of scholarship-holders who chose medicine. Given the length of time it took to qualify in medicine, and the additional cost of expensive textbooks and equipment, few from the working class would have been able to afford to take this subject.

The numbers in medicine had perhaps something to do with the contemporary social syndrome of having a priest and a doctor in the family. As expressed by a character in Eimar O'Duffy's *The Wasted Island* (1919) (p. 132):

This stunt of making every available man a doctor is going to be the ruin of this unfortunate country ... in Ireland every farmer and businessman puts one son into the Church, another into medicine and hands the farm or the business over to the third—usually the fool of the family.

The regulations attaching to the scholarship schemes varied greatly from county to county and from time to time. In the original schemes, outlined for example in the UCD Calendar for 1913, Dublin City Council—offering by far the greatest number (24)—Dublin County Council (6) and Wicklow County Council (3) specified UCD as the college at which their scholarships were tenable; Waterford City Council specified UCC or UCD; most of the others stated that their scholarships could be held in any of the constituent colleges of the National University. UCC, UCG and Queen's, Belfast, were specified in the schemes of their home counties and cities.

The Irish Universities Act (1908) had empowered county councils and city councils to assist any students at any university in Ireland. The interpretation given to this—perhaps not unreasonably—was that the universities that were intended by the framers of the Act were those that the Act itself had founded. This had been the general practice down to the early fifties, when the authorities of Trinity College inaugurated a campaign to induce county councils to allow their scholarships to be tenable also at Trinity.[31] The phrase 'any university in Ireland' was seized on to claim that Trinity was unfairly treated and that its exclusion from any of the county council schemes constituted an injustice to Irish citizens who were not Catholics. Certain county councils proceeded to alter their schemes to include Trinity; but the UCD authorities protested, and most of those councils that had changed reverted to their original schemes.

It was the reversion of Dublin County Council to the original policy (with a proviso that in special circumstances allowed an extension to any university) that sparked off controversy in the press, in which the college authorities defended their action. Dr Roger McHugh, a member of the Governing Body, publicly described the newspaper correspondence as 'an unseemly wrangle'; this provoked Dr Tierney into presenting a memo to the Governing Body in which he defended UCD's position on the scholarships and castigated McHugh for placing himself among the critics of the college. Tierney asserted that any unseemliness 'was altogether on the side of those responsible for the attempt to rob the college of part of its meagre if indirect endowment.'[32]

The 'unseemly wrangle' was undoubtedly a consideration when the question of financial assistance for students seeking access to third-level education was examined by the Commission on Higher Education. The commission's report in 1967 recommended in place of the county council scholarships a comprehensive national scheme, on the British model, financed and administered by the Department of Education, based on a revised method of measuring a family's income and providing a system of graded awards, ranging from the tuition fees to a maintenance grant plus fees.[33] A version of this recommendation was brought into operation shortly thereafter, and county council scholarships began to be phased out. By 1973/74 the number of higher education grants and county council scholarships came to 1,997, of which the higher education grants formed the great majority. A note in the statistics section of the president's report for 1973/74 (p. 204) states that only two of the thirty-one local authorities were at that date still involved with the payment of university scholarships.

STUDENT SOCIETIES

Outside the classes, the library, and the laboratories, student interests were well catered for in clubs and societies inherited from the Jesuit college and Cecilia Street, and many new ones were added. The first of the UCD Calendars (1910/11) listed the L&H and the Scientific, Gaelic, Classical and French Societies; while Football, Hurling and Boxing Clubs were represented in the Athletic Union. Clubs and societies for all seasons and for the most esoteric purposes proliferated over the years. Down to about 1970 the Calendars could still find space for the names of the officers and committees of some thirty-six societies and nineteen clubs; but the sheer number made it necessary for the Calendar of 1980/81 to exclude the lists, with the statement that there were over a hundred societies and clubs, which catered for the varied interests of the students and about which information could be obtained from the Students' Services offices.[34]

It was in these societies and clubs, and indeed in the general companion-ship that mere presence in the university provided, that the greatest impact was made on successive waves of students. This aspect of university life was the one most easily recalled in later life—almost apologetically, for the graduate sometimes felt an obligation to try to recall any intellectual influence that a lecturer might have had. These graduates had probably never known that the camaraderie of university life that they had enjoyed was precisely what the founding father, Newman, had emphasised as the most beneficial aspect of life in the university. He had written that if he had to choose between a university that merely concentrated on examinations and degree results and

> a University which had no professors or examinations at all, but merely brought a number of young men together for three or four years, and then sent them away ... if I must determine which of the two courses was the more successful in training, moulding, enlarging the mind, which sent out men the more fitted for their secular duties, which produced better public men, men of the world, men whose names would descend to posterity, I have no hesitation in giving the preference

to that University which did nothing, over that which exacted of its members an acquaintance with every science under the sun ... When a multitude of young men, keen, open-hearted, sympathetic and observant, as young men are, come together and freely mix with each other, they are sure to learn one from another, even if there be no one to teach them; the conversation of all is a series of lectures to each, and they gain for themselves new ideas and views, fresh matter of thought, and distinct principles for judging and acting, day by day.[35]

For the inspired few in any year there would be the wonderment of crossing intellectual frontiers; and for most there would be at least some academic growth and development.

The Literary and Historical Society, the college's premier debating society, proudly traces its foundation back to Newman.[36] Its survival through the vicissitudes of three successive universities—Catholic, Royal, and National— not only mirrors the developments in higher education for Catholics but indeed also reflects in its proceedings the emerging independence of the Irish state. In a prefatory note to its *Centenary History,* Michael Tierney wrote that he found himself continually displaying the old Physics Theatre in 86 St Stephen's Green 'as the room where most of the renowned politicians and public speakers of modern Ireland received their early training in the indispensable arts of oratory, persuasion and the management of men.'[37]

The L&H has been for many an important formative influence. In the early years of the new college it was dominated by the students of the Law and Medical Faculties, many of whom, as in the last years of the Jesuit college, were also Clongownians. In later years it appeared to be dominated by names that afterwards were the most prominent in the legal profession. If over the years the L&H provided the first stamping ground for future lawyers and politicians, it also attracted its share of the non-inhibited. Many had come from secondary schools where debating skills had already been encouraged; students from the Christian Brothers' schools, whether from shyness or some other cause, seemed to be slower to become involved in the oratorical and other antics of the society. Guest speakers and visiting chairmen were often former members of the L&H or notabilities from the worlds of politics and law.

Tierney was also impressed, however, by the 'long, sad list of the numerous brilliant young people for whom the bright promise that they gave in the Literary and Historical was almost the whole of their achievement.'[38] Yet one has only to dip into the pages of the *Centenary History,* containing the recollections of some thirty former members, to get some inkling of the *joie de vivre* the L&H gave not only to those who had since made their mark in the world as lawyers, academics or writers but to the many hundreds who had been content to be merely audience and spectators at L&H meetings.

A great variety of talents was also attracted into other activities. The studious attended the reading of papers at those societies devoted to their particular academic disciplines, while the budding lawyers began the practice of forensic skills at the L&H; the politically ambitious were initiated into the art of manipulating votes at elections to the Students' Representative Council and other bodies; the sportsmen and sportswomen had their grounds at Belfield; the literary-minded wrote for the student magazines; and from the late twenties and early thirties the Dramatic Society began to cater for those with acting and creative writing skills.

The flamboyance and undergraduate exuberance at student 'rags' and sometimes at meetings of the L&H, the supremely confident philosophical, literary, political and religious discussions, the drinking bouts and other excitements of students making their first entrance to the adult world, and the irreverence towards teachers and college authorities—all evoked or described by Joyce in *Stephen Hero* and *Portrait of the Artist*—were intensely relived by each generation of UCD's students, as if their particular experience of these matters were somehow unique.

STUDENT MAGAZINES

St Stephen's

The first generation of students in UCD inherited from their predecessors in the Jesuit college the determination to run a students' magazine worthy of their ambitions for themselves, the college and the nation. *St Stephen's,* conducted by the students of the Jesuit college, flourished from June 1901 to June 1906. For a student magazine it maintained a standard that was remarkably high and only rarely equalled by later student productions.

The philosophy that inspired *St Stephen's* was a blend of the assertive Catholicism of the time, the Irish-Irelandism of the *Leader,* the nationalist aspirations of the Home Rule movement, the self-respect and self-reliance of Sinn Féinism, and the revivalism of the Gaelic League.

That the students were themselves very conscious of their inheritance was exhibited in an editorial that urged readers never to forget that they had a university 'with no money, no charter, no accommodation, no external pomp or show, but with a glorious history, a glorious tradition, and a glorious ideal.' The new university, when they got it, would be a continuation, a development, and not an absolute starting point. 'The University for which we stand is ... the old Catholic University of Ireland—the University of Newman, of O'Curry, and of so many distinguished and patriot Irishmen of modern times.'[39]

St Stephen's was edited successively by Hugh Kennedy (later Chief

Justice), Felix Hackett (later professor of physics), T. M. Kettle (later professor of national economics), Con Curran (later Registrar of the Supreme Court), John Kennedy (brother of Hugh), and Francis Cruise O'Brien (later leader-writer on the *Freeman's Journal* and *Irish Independent*). Other student contributors included Arthur Clery (later a professor of law), who, under the pseudonym 'Chanel', wrote many of the wittiest pieces; Thomas Bodkin (later Director of the National Gallery), who provided many of the illustrations; James Murnaghan (later a Supreme Court judge); and John Marcus O'Sullivan (later professor of history and Minister for Education).

In the light of later careers and developments, what *St Stephen's* rejected has for some assumed more significance than what it published. Sheehy Skeffington's article advocating equal rights for women in university education was turned down by the Jesuit adviser; so too was James Joyce's 'The Day of the Rabblement', 'partly because of its tendencies—but also on the ground that it was too flimsy for publication!'[40] *St Stephen's,* however, made amends to Joyce by publishing in its issue of May 1902 the paper on James Clarence Mangan he had read to the L&H and that the *Freeman's Journal* said was 'generally agreed to have been the best paper ever read before the Society.'[41]

Eventually, *St Stephen's* sadly succumbed to the recurring rows between the editor, Cruise O'Brien, and Father Delany or, in the words of the Jesuit history of the college, 'was put an end to by a ruthless act of authority.'[42] It was replaced by the short-lived *Hermes,* many of whose poems, essays and illustrations were the work of its editor, Thomas Bodkin. But this was more of a literary than a college journal.

The National Student

Though in all the practicalities attending it the transfer from the Jesuit college and the Catholic University Medical School to the new university was so smooth that it was hardly noticeable, for the students who transferred as well as the newcomers it had in abstract terms all the enchantment and anticipation of a new dawn. Some of this excitement was captured by Eimar O'Duffy in his semi-autobiographical novel *The Wasted Island* (1919).[43] In the novel, one student educated by the Jesuits in England tells another that his father was not prepared to send him to Oxford but wanted him to go to Trinity. The Clongowes-educated student, who has just obtained the Matriculation of the NUI, replies: 'Look here, why not strike out a new line entirely and come to the National? It's something new in universities ... Trinity's just a second-rate Oxford ... The National's new. It may be a bit shoddy, but we might make something of it.'[44] What followed had to do with the impact the revolutionary turmoil of the years from 1910 to 1923 had on that generation of UCD students.

The idealism of that first wave of entrants to the new University College was palpable in the pages of a new journal. Students who had been involved in the last hectic years of unrest in the Jesuit college lost no time in launching the *National Student,* 'conducted by the students of University College Dublin' and intended to be published in five issues every session. It made its first appearance in May 1910. Its editor was Michael McGilligan,[45] the manager was J. J. O'Connell,[46] and it included on its editorial staff P. J. Little.[47] Little had been manager of the suppressed *St Stephen's,* and McGilligan too had counted himself a supporter of Cruise O'Brien (auditor of the L&H and last editor of *St Stephen's*) in his rows with the president, Dr Delany.[48] O'Connell belonged to the group opposed to Cruise O'Brien's holding of the L&H meetings outside college.[49]

The deep sense of responsibility shown in *St Stephen's* was also exhibited in the *National Student.* The university question, which had been so much the concern of *St Stephen's,* had been settled by the 1908 Act, but the new university was going to be made live up to its promise by the *National Student.* And while politics in the party sense had left the contributions to *St Stephen's* largely untouched, the *National Student* could not escape the explosive political circumstances that surrounded it. University College, in the eyes of the *National Student,* would have to justify itself and apply itself to the promotion and building of a new, independent Irish state.

Its first editorial described the journal as 'a student organ, fearless and vigorous in expressing the views of the student body on any question that may concern them.' It had been brought out 'to show that, among the students at least there is some stir of youth and intellectual life.' It promised that 'the tone of the magazine will be national' and insisted that the good will of the nation should be secured by the university at the outset by complying with the national demand on essential Irish for the Matriculation. The students, it announced, had already taken up their position; 'they see that if the University is not an engine of national culture, it has no reason for existence.'[50]

The first article following the editorial was entitled 'The mission of the new university to the nation', by J. J. O'Connell. The title was itself an indication of the sense of high purpose that inspired that first generation of UCD students. The new university, O'Connell argued, should do more than merely mark a stage: it should initiate a new development in national life and direct its energies towards the regeneration of the country. It should be the centre of cultural nationalism and, following the example of the German universities, should ensure that every student should be proud of being Irish. 'The establishment of the national language as a *sine qua non* in the National University is an absolutely essential part of its mission.' And 'where else is Ireland to seek her future leaders except in that University?'[51]

The same febrile spirit of nationalism infused much of the writing in the *National Student* in the years of heightened political activity. The idealism and high hopes of the time were captured in a college song, written by Professor George Sigerson and published in the *National Student*: the chorus ended with the line, 'And the bright Dawn light before us.'[52]

From 1915, however, the *National Student* began to appear only irregularly, burdened by debt and alleged student indifference. The SRC took it over until quarrels with its editorial staff brought about the magazine's temporary demise. It came back in 1923 with a directive that in each issue 'there should be one article on a serious subject.'[53] It was not seen again until 1930, when it reappeared under the control of the L&H. The SRC reacted by issuing *Comhthrom Féinne*, journal of the newly founded Cumann na Mac Léinn (Students' Union). This journal operated from May 1931 to May 1935 when the two publications were merged under both names and SRC direction. Twice (February and March 1943) using the single title, *Comhthrom Féinne*, it published issues entirely in Irish. The *National Student: Comhthrom Féinne* petered out in the early 1950s, by which time it had become more and more a literary journal and a launching-pad for young poets.

The Student

By 1954 the need was felt for another attempt 'to provide the College with some sort of literary magazine.' The editorial acknowledged that in recent years some of the more intense efforts of the *National Student* had not been acceptable to the readers and had met with 'scant success.' The name was changed to the *Student,* which was welcomed by Michael Tierney, because of the confusion that had existed in the minds of people between the National University and University College.

There is much that was pertinent in the remarks of the president on the occasion of the launch of the *Student*. The success of the students' magazine, he said, seemed to stand in inverse ratio to the number of students in the college. Probably the best journal ever produced by the students had been *St Stephen's,* however slightly Victorian, not to say prim, it might have seemed to the more recent reader. And *St Stephen's* had flourished at a time when the number of students, between St Stephen's Green and Cecilia Street, was hardly a tenth of what it was in 1954. Its successor, the *National Student,* under editors such as Michael McGilligan and Eimar O'Duffy, had also shown a brilliance rare enough in student publications. Tierney, however, declared that he had not found much to admire for the past thirty years in either the *National Student* or its temporary alias, *Comhthrom Féinne*.

This criticism may have been too extreme. *Comhthrom Féinne* had published the early writing of Brian O'Nolan (then using the pseudonym

'Brother Barnabas'), Cyril Cusack, John D. Sheridan, Roger McHugh, Charles Donnelly, Niall Sheridan, and Donagh MacDonagh. (O'Nolan's wit, especially in his career as 'Myles na gCopaleen', did not appeal to everyone in his alma mater. A biographical note in the *Centenary History* notes that he 'has written much ephemeral material in English and Irish,' whereas a note on Ulick O'Connor describes O'Connor as 'a contributor to newspapers and periodicals.') Tierney was also somewhat unfair to the more recent contributors to the *National Student,* which between 1948 and 1951 contained the names of such aspiring poets and writers as Pearse Hutchinson, Thomas Kinsella, John Jordan, John Montague, Ulick O'Connor, Desmond Fennell, Carroll O'Connor (later an American television actor), Michael Gorman, Seán White and Máirín O'Farrell.

Some truth, however, attaches to Tierney's observation that there was 'a feeling among students at large that the *National Student* was the property and the particular concern of a narrow class of students with "literary aspirations"' and that 'it was given over to the effusions of young men who seemed to imagine themselves called to fill the strange role of recapitulating the not very desirable or comfortable career of the late James Joyce.' Tierney wondered how many pages that had appeared over the last ten years had been devoted to the esoteric description of the lamentable early experience of young men finding out for the first time what it was like to drink too much stout. Perhaps, he conceded, it was dignifying these efforts too much to fancy that the imitation of Joyce played any part in their production. He admitted that there was a place for every kind of writing but suggested that in their college magazine the chief place should be reserved for plain, honest-to-goodness journalism, with straightforward reporting and discussion.[54]

During the mid-fifties and early sixties the *Student* continued very much in the literary mould, with such contributors as Thomas Kilroy, Thomas McIntyre, James Liddy, Peadar Mac Maghnais, Augustine Martin, Des Keogh, Basil Payne, Macdara Woods, and Paul Durcan. And Tierney was to ban the *Student* because of a story written by Peter Donnelly.[55]

Ironically, it was only as Tierney retired from office that the journalistic type of student publication that he had advocated, notably *Awake* and *Campus,* began creating the critical atmosphere surrounding the emergence of the student troubles of the late sixties.

St Stephen's again

The problem of producing the *Student* had, in the words of its editorial of January 1961, 'become more difficult this year.'[56] The reason for the difficulty was the existence of another two rivals. *Awake,* a fortnightly, was covering the day-to-day activities of the college—sporting, social, and intellectual. And a new journal, *St Stephen's,* consciously borrowing its name from that with which Joyce had been associated, appeared for the first time in the Trinity term of 1960. Its theme, as proclaimed on its cover, was 'literature and opinions'. While it wished well to the two other undergraduate publications in their particular tasks, it felt that the good, serious writing that it aimed at could not be framed with the 'light-hearted gleanings' and 'witty banter' found in the others.[57] The second issue reaffirmed the commitment to 'serious student expression' and paid tribute to the memory of Joyce—'the most outstanding person that has passed through the College in all its history.'[58]

In pursuit of seriousness, St Stephen's, in contrast to the Student, carried long editorials. These were exhortations to thoughtful people to put behind them the 'parochial' horizons of the age of nationalism and insularity and to become 'European', with all the intellectual and moral dilemmas that would entail. Those associated with the journal hoped to extend and communicate their own awareness of creativity beyond the university to the whole Irish scene. The 'traditional, jansenistic perversion of Catholicism and an inherent moral immaturity'[59] had to be swept aside in the age of the Second Vatican Council. The future of Catholicism in Ireland seemed 'more promising and exciting than at any time during the last few centuries.'[60] Liberalisation and a greater freedom of speech were called for. As if to emphasise the point, St Stephen's carried in the same issue an article by Patrick Walshe (later to be the Irish ambassador successively to Argentina and Spain) on 'The Irish Rosary',[61] the general thrust and argument of which, it claimed, no undergraduate magazine in the college had published at least for some time. The article described the Rosary as having become 'the greatest cliché of our faith,' the beads as a 'crude, old-fashioned stop-watch,' and the 'Rosary priest', Father Peyton, as the 'rabble-rousing ralliest [sic] ... continuing his work on behalf of ersatz religion.' The fact that the article was written in the hope 'that the decisions of the Council may go some part of the way towards lifting this new penal darkness from our Faith' did not prevent it from causing shock and offence to the college authorities.

An editorial in the next issue maintained the attack on Irish Catholicism as it existed and called for the substitution of orthodox Catholicism, which, it acknowledged, would require 'nothing less than a new army of evangelists.'[62] Rahner, Kung and Gregory Baum had replaced Camus, Lawrence and Henry Miller as intellectual heroes for the editor of St Stephen's.

In the early sixties the state of religion in Irish society had come under close scrutiny in periodicals and on television. The editorials in St Stephen's between 1960 and 1963, especially under the editorship of Liam Hourican, had been obsessed with the topic. By 1963 it had been exhausted, and from 1964 literature reasserted itself as the primary concern of the journal—not that the commitment to literary creativity had ever been lost.

Indeed, throughout the sixties the college seemed to have become (once again) the nursery for a nation of minor poets. Every issue of the *Student,* as well as *St Stephen's,* published several poems. 'Every year', declared a *St Stephen's* editorial, 'there is enough verse submitted to fill at least two issues of the magazine,'[63] much of it, the editor said, not much inferior to what was published. It was written covertly, almost with a sense that a habit of suspicious eccentricity was being indulged by a subterranean circle of undergraduates, who frequently did not know one another. A poetry workshop in the college could be the ideal solution. Four years later, by which time the poetry workshop had come into existence, the same claim about being able to fill more than two issues with poetry was again made by *St Stephen's.*[64] This time, not only were most of the contributors unknown to the editor but, he added, they 'remain unknown even when they are published.'

Many of these aspiring poets of the college magazines of the sixties were never to be heard of again—at least not as poets. But the outpourings of the more prolific, which were published in both *St Stephen's* and the *Student,* appeared over names that continued to make a mark in the world of poetry: James Liddy, Macdara Woods, James McAuley, Paul Durcan, Michael Hartnett, Richard Ryan and Aidan Mathews.

When *St Stephen's* began publication in 1960 there were only two other student publications in the college. By 1966, according to *St Stephen's,* a total of fourteen magazines and newspapers appeared regularly. Some of these (for example *Retrospect,* papers read at the history students' congress) appeared no more than once a year. *Campus,* in newspaper format—the training ground for a generation that would make its way into radio, television, and newspaper journalism—came to play an influential role in the heralding of the student revolt of the late sixties.[65]

Over the years the objectives and aspirations of students changed from those of Joyce and the pre-independence generation, but the basic idealism, freshness and enthusiasms remained to form one of the most attractive features of college life. By no means all students became involved in the societies, clubs, and magazines: it was a combination of experiences that made their all too few years in college memorable. Besides the clubs and societies and the friends that had been made there was the unflagging talk over endless cups of coffee in the restaurants, both inside and outside college. Stronger beverages were consumed in the Leeson Street pubs—O'Dwyer's, Hourican's and Hartigan's. Among these the medical students and the Rugby Club had their own favourite bar. The historians and their honorary colleagues were known to adjourn occasionally to Hartigan's snug. While the social life could be enjoyed to the full, there would always be for some the excitement of new intellectual worlds being opened up in lecture, tutorial, library, or laboratory.

SERVANTS OF THE COLLEGE

For many of the pre-Belfield generations some of the pleasantest memories were of those loyal, indispensable 'servants' of what might otherwise have been seen as an overcrowded, coldly managed, impersonal institution. These included the women in the restaurant known to generations by their first name; the women in the front or main office, typified for many by the kindly face of Hilda O'Brien; the chaplains who had befriended students in trouble; Miss Greene, who had inherited her post as Lady Dean from her mother and served in that capacity from 1932 to 1970; and perhaps most beloved of all, the head porter, Paddy Keogh. What Nuala O'Faolain wrote of her student days in UCD would have echoed in the minds of many: 'But I was also shaped by UCD, especially the women who ran the front office. I loved the place. I love the memory of Earlsfort Terrace.'[66] It was her impression also that Paddy Keogh organised the lectures.

Hilda O'Brien was the first woman appointed to what was known for years before the move to Belfield as 'the College office'. When she began in 1918 she acted as secretary to all the officers of the college. Resigning on her marriage in 1937, she returned after the death of her husband in 1954 and took charge of the office of the Secretary. Until her retirement in 1969 varied problems of students and staff were brought to her for solution.

Norah Greene returned to the college in 1932 to act as Officer of Residence for women students. Apart from this role, with the task of finding acceptable lodgings for an ever-increasing number of women students (there were 600 when she began and nearly 3,500 in her last year), she was president of many women's sports clubs. She attended their games and travelled constantly with the teams.

Paddy Keogh had joined the college as a boy porter in 1916 and retired as head porter fifty-five years later in 1971. He began his work when the college was still in 86 St Stephen's Green, worked in Earlsfort Terrace and Merrion Street, and helped in the transition to Belfield. Appointed head porter in 1947, he was the most widely known person in the college. Stories and legends grew up around him. He delighted numerous classes when he came to explain why a lecture was being cancelled. He once told a first-year philosophy class: 'Due to the exigencies of the circumstances and the unfortunate inclemency of the elements this morning, the course of metaphysical and philosophical instruction on man's potentiality will not be ...' Three rows of clerics at the front of the classroom were said to be busily scribbling down his words in their notebooks.[67] It was said that Paddy could have lectured equally well on English literature and economic theory. He himself liked to tell the story of how on one occasion an American academic came to visit Dr Macalister, the professor of archaeology. The professor was not available, but in the course of conversation Paddy, who used to show the lantern-slides in the professor's classes, gave an erudite archaeological exegesis, at the end of which he was warmly thanked and asked: 'Dr ... er, to whom have I had the honour of speaking?' When Paddy explained that he was merely the porter, the visiting academic went away wondering that if UCD porters were so learned, what must the professors be like!

Paddy, who looked after all the organisational details, was asked by a new student where to find his class. Paddy proceeded to speak in Latin before replying that the course prescribed under the particular section of the regulations was to be found in the Physics Theatre, and then sent the student on his way with *'Ite in pacem.'*[68] It was said of him that while others taught their specialisms, Paddy was the one who 'taught us all nice manners.' His kindness, courtesy and tact were a feature of college life during the half century of his association with it. When he retired, the college marked its appreciation by conferring on him an MA, *honoris causa*.

THE ORIGINAL STAFF: SCHOLARSHIP AND RESEARCH

One might have expected that the first generation of professors in UCD would have been teachers, perhaps even scholars, but not researchers. This was certainly true of Patrick Semple (Latin), William Magennis (metaphysics), John Marcus O'Sullivan (history), Henry C. McWeeney (mathematics) and Édouard Cadic (French). It was true also of Robert Donovan (English literature), Arthur Clery (law) and Tom Kettle (national economics) — scholars and gentlemen all, but hardly researchers in their own fields in any modern meaning of the term. It is not at all surprising that those who had been associated with St Stephen's Green and Cecilia Street should have been better known as teachers than as researchers. After all, the RUI had required its fellows specifically to teach, to set courses of study for the Royal University examinations, and to examine. Research was not so much as mentioned among the duties of fellows; whereas Statute I of UCD had specified that 'every full-time professor shall, so far as is compatible with the other duties of his chair, devote himself to research and the advancement of knowledge.' The phrase 'so far as is compatible with the other duties of his chair' could be, and was, interpreted as relegating research to a secondary role among the duties of full-time professors. Nowhere was that phrase defined. What can be asserted without question is that the Statutes did not oblige any academic to publish; teaching, on the other hand, was very definitely obligatory.

The Royal University, to which the foundation professors belonged, had been very much an examining body. These men had been conditioned to think and act in terms of examination marks, of results and prizes. Both the Jesuit college and the Medical School were proud of their examination achievements, and Archbishop Walsh and Father Delany on every possible public occasion boasted of the number of Catholic University students who took the prizes ahead of the Queen's Colleges of Belfast, Cork, and Galway. And it *was* a remarkable achievement as far as examination results went.

The whole ethos of the Jesuit college and of its infant successor was one of teaching and examining rather than research. The surprise is that not only were these first professors good teachers who got results but that so many of them were also scholars, even if they were not quite involved in original specialist research. It has also to be remembered, in defence of their lack of specialist publications, that areas in the humanities such as history, political economy, national economics and English literature had not yet developed into the specialisms they have since become. A trained philosopher held the chair of history; a Jesuit who had first taught classics and then philosophy held the chair of political economy; a member of Parliament held the chair of national economics; and a journalist held the chair of English.

The harsh judgment, therefore, that has been passed on William Magennis by MacDowell and Webb in their history of Trinity sprang from an unfortunately limited understanding. It could be — if one wanted to be derogatory (but unhistorical and anachronistic) — extended to many of his colleagues from the old Royal University who occupied the foundation chairs in UCD. MacDowell and Webb wrote of Magennis: 'Though he extolled so forcibly the "philosophical system" in University College as immeasurably superior to the merely historical teaching of the subject in Trinity, one searches library catalogues in vain for any contributions which he made to the "system" during his tenure of the chair of Metaphysics for over thirty years.'[69] It is true that Magennis published no monograph on philosophy; this does not mean that he and his colleagues in UCD did not write. Far from it: they published a great deal, especially in the scholarly journals and reviews — but not, it has to be conceded, in what might be looked upon as their own narrowly specialist fields.

The teaching given by these gentlemen-scholars was never narrow, and not always restricted to the subject professed. What was said of Thomas MacDonagh's lectures on English literature by a student could have applied to the lectures of other members of the early staff: they were 'never relevant and invariably interesting.'[70] A student of Kettle's, George O'Brien, has recounted how the few students of national economics used to go with Kettle to St Stephen's Green and listen to him discourse learnedly on all sorts of topics.[71] O'Brien may have heard very little economic theory from Kettle, but, he said, 'I learned a great deal about history and literature.'

What was said of the Athenians could have been applied to many of these colourful literary scholars who occupied the first chairs at UCD: 'Such a people were in a true sense born teachers, and merely to live among them was a cultivation of mind.'[72] An academic system, said Newman, without the personal influence of teachers on pupils is an Arctic winter; it will create an ice-bound, petrified, cast-iron university, and nothing else. They also held with Newman that 'the True and the Serviceable as well as the Beautiful should be made the aim of the academic intellect and the business of a University.'[73]

These professors had campaigned for a university that would serve Irish society as, they alleged, Trinity did not. They saw themselves in the role of nation-builders, and one of their chief duties was to devote themselves to the new state, which they served as ministers and TDs and senators and members of numerous committees. Time given to research in their various ivory towers would have been regarded by them as selfish and self-indulgent when the young state had need of all the intellectual talent and energy it could command from an institution founded on such ideals of service to the nation.

Nevertheless, some of the science professors—less colourful, perhaps, than those of the humanities—were top-rank researchers in their appropriate fields: John McClelland (physics), Hugh Ryan (chemistry), Arthur Conway (mathematical physics). All three established departments and contributed much to the tradition of original research in the college.

McClelland, having graduated from the Royal University, had devoted four years to research in the Cavendish Laboratory, Cambridge, as one of the original group of external research students serving their apprenticeship under the famous physicist Thomson. This laboratory, under Thomson and Rutherford in the early decades of the twentieth century, was the mecca for students from all over the world. McClelland's first important research paper was jointly written with Thomson. His later papers were all written in collaboration with his research students. These included Felix Hackett, J. J. Nolan, J. J. Dowling, P. J. Nolan, and J. J. McHenry, all of whom became professors, and Henry Kennedy. McClelland and his students were very much involved in the so-called 'new physics' of the day; some of the original work of the UCD Physics Department was selected for reproduction in the prestigious journals *Nature* and *Le Radium*.

When supplying a testimonial for Conway for the chair of mathematical physics in UCD in 1909, the Astronomer-Royal, Sir Edmund Whittaker FRS, wrote that he did so with great diffidence, 'lest the writing of a testimonial should be taken to imply on the part of the writer an assumption of superiority, which in this case would be totally unwarranted. But it is surely unnecessary to say more than that Professor Conway's researches have made his name honoured in every Academy in Europe.'[74] More than forty years later, when writing an obituary for Conway, Whittaker recalled:

> With Conway and McClelland the maths and physics school of University College came to be recognised as one of high distinction. On the other hand the splendid succession of great mathematical physicists in T.C.D. which had begun seventy-eight years before with Hamilton,

came to an end with the death of FitzGerald in 1901, and in the early years of the new century University College actually outshone the older foundation.[75]

McClelland was elected a fellow of the Royal Society in 1909 and Conway in 1915. As long as McClelland lived 'he and Conway exerted a powerful intellectual stimulus on each other.'[76] Some students of quaternions regarded Conway as 'the world's greatest authority on the subject,' and Whittaker said that 'by general consent' Conway was 'the most distinguished Irish Catholic man of science of his generation.'[77] Among the academic honours bestowed on him were honorary degrees from the Royal University, University of Dublin and University of St Andrews. He was made an honorary fellow of Corpus Christi College, Oxford, and in 1939 he was elected to fill the vacancy created by the death of Rutherford as one of the seventy members of the Pontifical Academy of Sciences.

One would have expected a scholar of Conway's standing to do everything in his power as President of UCD from 1940 to 1947 to foster research and publication among the academic staff. But the period of office of one of the finest scholars in the history of the college happened to coincide with the Second World War, years of special difficulty. Student numbers were expanding rapidly, from 2,400 at the start of the war to 3,300 at the end; accommodation had been strained to its limits; and there were serious financial difficulties. One slight indication of Conway's support for scholarship within the college and an intimation of what might have been in better times was the appearance of a new section in the annual reports of the president devoted to the academic publications of the staff.

Hugh Ryan, the first holder of the chair of chemistry, had studied for two years at the University of Berlin under the renowned Emil Fischer. Ryan was described as 'combining in the happiest manner Celtic imagination and Teutonic industry.'[78] A bibliography of research papers, formidable both for their quality and their quantity, ensured that he was at the top of the list of chemists in Ireland. Among his collaborators in some of these publications were his students Thomas Dillon (who became professor in UCG) , T. J. Nolan (who succeeded him in 1932 at UCD) and Joseph Algar (who was appointed to the chair of organic chemistry in UCD in 1937).

One faculty in the humanities also consisted of professors who by any standards then or since were top-rank researchers as well as scholars who had gained international recognition and status. These were the intellectual giants in the Faculty of Celtic Studies: Macalister in Celtic archaeology, MacNeill in early Irish history, Hyde in Modern Irish, Bergin in Early Irish, and Lloyd-Jones in Welsh, 'all of them scholars of such distinction that from the beginning the College was recognised as the chief centre of Celtic Studies in the learned world.'[79] There were leading individual Celticists in other university institutions; but what other university in Ireland or abroad could boast of a faculty or school of Celtic studies of comparable strength and prestige? That four of them (MacNeill was the exception) happened also to be Protestants was a healthy indication that the undenominationalism of the Charters and Statutes was operating smoothly. Sadly, MacDowell and Webb permitted themselves a blinkered comment when they wrote: 'There were a few Protestant professors, mainly in peripheral subjects.'[80] Archaeology, early Irish history and Irish language and literature are most certainly not peripheral, that is, outside of a certain academic tradition, even then antiquated and now happily very much a thing of the past.

R. A. S. Macalister (1870–1950) was the son of a professor of anatomy in Trinity who had transferred to the chair in Cambridge. Following graduation in Cambridge he joined an archaeological expedition to Palestine and in time took charge of the excavations at Gezer and published several reports, while continuing to write on Irish antiquities. Because of his excavations in Palestine he already had an enviable international reputation among orientalists when he was appointed to the chair in UCD. Leading professors of archaeology in Cambridge, Beirut and Freiburg sang his praises. Back in Dublin, as Professor Frank Mitchell of Trinity has said, 'he threw himself vigorously into every facet of archaeological activity.'[81] He was the first of UCD's professors to become President of the Royal Irish Academy (1926–1931) and was conferred with honorary degrees by several universities. He held the chair until 1943, and 'throughout that long period he was teaching, organising, excavating and writing vigorously.'[82] His literary output was prodigious; his excavation methods may have been amateurish when compared with the more sophisticated techniques of his successor, Seán P. Ó Ríordáin, but he established a proud tradition of Celtic archaeology in UCD.

Osborn Bergin (1873–1950), when he was appointed to the chair of Early Irish, may have been less widely known than Macalister, Hyde, or MacNeill, but by the time he resigned his chair in 1940 his impact may have been even more notable than that of his colleagues. He had studied under Zimmer in the University of Berlin and under Thurneyssen in the University of Freiburg. He held the chair in UCD until 1940, when he resigned to become the first Director of the School of Celtic Studies in the Dublin Institute for Advanced Studies. As a teacher he was noted for his love of precision. Professors Frank Shaw, Gerard Murphy and Dan Binchy were among his students. Binchy said of him that as a teacher he had succeeded in establishing a standard of Celtic scholarship in Dublin that could challenge comparison with the most famous Continental centres and drew students to UCD from abroad. In an obituary in the *Irish Times* on 7 October 1950 Binchy wrote:

It is a measure of his achievement that virtually all the Celtic chairs in existence today should be held by former pupils of his—not merely at home in the two universities and the Dublin Institute but also in Oxford, Harvard, Edinburgh, Liverpool, Zurich, Amsterdam and the Scandinavian countries. The death of Bergin marked the close of what might be called 'the heroic age of Celtic Studies.'

Given the standing of McClelland, Conway, and Ryan, it is hardly surprising that their departments in the Science Faculty should have been flagships of postgraduate studies in UCD. The research schools they established were so firmly and successfully founded that they continued to grow and gather momentum long after the founders were dead.

Physics got off to the faster start and stayed numerically ahead of Chemistry until 1915. From then on Hugh Ryan's men and women in Chemistry easily became the biggest of the postgraduate research schools, not only in Science but in the college. By 1928 the score was Chemistry, 66 postgraduates, Physics, 26, with the other areas of science well behind.

From the training these young researchers received in these postgraduate schools in the Faculty of Science a number went on to establish reputations in extended or related fields of research. Among these were Roy Geary, who subsequently took charge of the Central Statistics Office; E. J. Conway, who later established the very successful School of Biochemistry and Pharmacology in UCD; J. J. Drumm, who became famous for a while in applied science for the Drumm battery train; Thomas McLoughlin, who was to be managing director of the Shannon Electrical Scheme; and Michael Hogan, who was to be of considerable importance in the Engineering School and in the building projects that resulted in Belfield.

When we turn to postgraduate research in the Faculty of Arts during this same period of the first two decades of UCD's existence we are faced with a few surprises. Some departments that one might not have expected much of by way of research were in fact acquitting themselves comparatively well; others, with well-known scholars leading them, were performing poorly.

If we take the MA by dissertation as the basic standard of research, we find that in the first twenty years the two leading research departments in Arts were English (20) and Economics (19), followed by Celtic Studies (16), Classics (15), and Philosophy (12). Given the fact that English had far more undergraduate students than any other department except for Modern Irish, this was not very surprising. What is interesting is that the professor of English, Robert Donovan, was not a research man in the way that, say, the professor of Modern Irish, Douglas Hyde, was. Yet Modern Irish, with more students in these early decades of the college than any other department, had a relatively poor record in MA students. It produced in fact less than half (9) the number produced in English. And the quality of those emerging with the MA in English was impressive—Thomas MacDonagh, Austin Clarke, Jeremiah Hogan.

The very successful start in postgraduate work in economics is perhaps even more surprising than in the case of English. Here the professor was Father Tom Finlay (political economy). The quality of the students who graduated with the MA in economics may be gauged by naming some of those who were afterwards in the public eye as economic and social policy-makers: J. J. McElligott, Secretary of the Department of Finance; Father Edward Coyne SJ of the Commission on Vocational Organisation (1943); T. J. Kiernan, who had a brief spell as an academic economist in Cork before becoming Director of Radio Éireann and a distinguished diplomat and author.

Research in the area of Celtic studies was one of the great success stories of the young UCD. With a relatively small number of undergraduates compared with the bigger departments, many of the MA graduates were to make reputations for themselves in Celtic studies: Paul Walsh and Éamonn O'Toole (1914), T. F. O'Rahilly (1916), Kate Mulchrone and Cecilia O'Rahilly (1917), John Ryan (1918), Tarlach Ó Raifeartaigh (1926), Frank Shaw (1931), Dan Binchy (1920), James Delargy (1923) and Myles Dillon (1923).

By contrast, the History Faculty, compared with its later successes, was a very slow starter. A Board for Post-Graduate Studies in History was set up, but it never met. Modern Irish history under Mary Hayden could boast only of three MAs; modern history under John Marcus O'Sullivan had only two— no more than Semitic languages; but, most amazing of all, early Irish history under MacNeill, one of the biggest names ever in the area, had only one MA (William G. O'Loughlin, 1916). MacNeill's contribution was in the Celtic studies degree. A printed list of his published writings alone runs to over twenty-three pages.[83]

One of the reasons for the poor showing of history in postgraduate research was no doubt in part related to the fact that MacNeill and John Marcus O'Sullivan were otherwise engaged as ministers in the Free State government in the nineteen-twenties. Besides, O'Sullivan had been trained as a philosopher. And Mary Hayden, despite her undoubted talents, was not involved in modern historical research in the same way as the young scholar whom she defeated for the post in 1909 was—Edmund Curtis, afterwards professor in Trinity.

One of the most successful schemes initiated for postgraduate studies was the NUI Travelling Studentship. The number awarded annually was comparatively small—an average of a little over three a year during the first twenty years (1910–1929). They were, therefore, very competitive and highly prestigious. UCD's record of success in the travelling studentships was quite impressive and was perhaps a direct continuation of the proud tradition of first places, prizes and honours won by the Jesuit college and Cecilia Street in the RUI examinations.

It is not altogether surprising, therefore, that in the first six years of the travelling studentship (1910–15) sixteen of the seventeen awarded, and seven of the nine prizes for reaching the required standard, were won by UCD postgraduates. In the first forty years UCD students won 74 per cent of the travelling studentships awarded. Even more impressive than the bare percentages are the names of those who won the coveted awards. They are the ones who succeeded to the chairs of the first generation of professors. Every leading research centre on the Continent, and some in the United States and Canada, was visited by one or other of these wandering scholars from UCD, and they brought back with them contacts that were invaluable for the promotion of scholarship. Dr Mahaffy, Provost of Trinity College, once said that James Joyce was the living proof of his conviction that it was wrong to provide a separate university for the 'aborigines' of the country, who, like corner-boys, spent their time spitting into the Liffey. The achievements of those early students of UCD must have gone some way towards calming Mahaffy's ghost.

The original staff of UCD constituted a good mix of successful teachers, reputable scholars and researchers skilled in the best modern methods and trained in the best schools and leading laboratories of their day. The students were fresh and eager and ready to respond to challenge, and among them was some first-class talent.

3

Women in UCD

A struggle within a struggle.
Mary Macken in *Struggle with Fortune*

ADMISSION TO UNIVERSITY COLLEGE, 1883–1901

The Royal University was the first university in Ireland to make its degrees available to women (women had been admitted to London University in 1878). The charter of the Royal University (May 1880) specifically stated that the university had power to confer degrees 'upon every person, male or female,' who qualified according to the regulations. Women, therefore, were admitted by right and not on sufferance.

Once women could get degrees from the Royal University, separate university departments to prepare them for the university courses and examinations began to appear. Alexandra College, established in Dublin as a Church of Ireland secondary school in 1866, was among the first to provide education of a university type. Success in the examinations of the Royal University and increasing numbers encouraged both the Dominican and the Loreto sisters, following the example set by the colleges for boys, to found separate university departments in their schools. In 1886 the Dominicans established a University College, afterwards called St Mary's, in Donnybrook, where their elementary and secondary schools already existed (this college later moved to Eccles Street). The Loreto nuns established Loreto College in St Stephen's Green in 1893 for the matriculated students from Loreto secondary schools.

As intermediate education was endowed by the state, it became a serious grievance that the women's colleges were not also subsidised while they had to compete with the endowed Queen's Colleges as well as with the partially and indirectly endowed Jesuit University College, where the men were prepared for university examinations. It was a further grievance that the fellows who determined the courses, gave the lectures and other teaching, set the examinations and examined the candidates were fellows of the Royal University, attached to the Queen's Colleges and University College.

The non-endowment of the women's colleges, with the consequent lack of laboratories and library facilities and of the most highly qualified lecturers and the fellowship system, created demands for the reform of university education so as to guarantee equality of opportunity for women. Whereas at first the demand was for endowment for the women's colleges, gradually there grew a demand for co-education as the best way to guarantee equality.

Petitions and protests by and on behalf of the women students had partial success, but the admission of women successively to the Queen's Colleges in Belfast, Cork and Galway during the eighteen-eighties and also to the Royal College of Surgeons served only to emphasise the disadvantages of the RUI undergraduates in Dublin. Father Delany allowed his professors and lecturers to give classes for women in accommodation made available by the Royal University in Earlsfort Terrace. This proved to be a patchy and short-lived solution. Some professors—the Abbé Polin (French)[1] and Father T. A. Finlay SJ (philosophy)—undertook the additional work load with enthusiasm; others refused, or charged excessive fees. The scheme lapsed after a few years, though some University College staff continued to give lectures in the women's colleges.

When Dr Delany returned in 1897 for a second term as president of the college the agitation for the admission of women to full participation in university education had gained momentum. He responded by arranging what were called public lectures, which anyone who paid the fees could attend. These dealt with courses from second arts upwards; they were of no avail for women students studying for first arts. The scheme began in 1898/99 by allowing women to attend lectures on the English course; by 1901/02 the syllabus also included history, political economy, logic, mental science, French, Irish, and postgraduate French and German. To ensure that women did not penetrate into the inner sanctum, these lectures were not given in the small classrooms of number 86 but in the Aula Maxima alongside University House. Where small classes were sometimes required, an area at the back of the hall was screened off while a larger class was conducted from the platform in the front.

The women who availed themselves of these lectures came mainly from St Mary's and Loreto and from the nearby Alexandra College in Earlsfort Terrace. In 1901 the college register, for the first time, listed some nineteen women as students of University College, including Agnes O'Farrelly and Joanna (Hanna) Sheehy.

THE ROBERTSON COMMISSION

The Royal Commission on University Education in Ireland (1901–03) was a landmark in the history of higher education for women. It acknowledged the problem and investigated it thoroughly. The members of the commission questioned closely officials and administrators who had an influence in and control over higher education; and they allowed the leading advocates and practitioners of the higher education of women to present their case before them. At the end of the inquiry the commission provided in its final report what amounted to a charter of rights for women in university education.

The first sittings of the commission dealt mainly with the requirements of the Catholic population generally with regard to university education. This was of course the great issue of the day. Some witnesses, like the spokesman for Loreto College (James Macken), saw the issue of the higher education of women as essentially a part of the broader question of provision for the higher education of the Catholic body.[2] Most of the women witnesses, however, regarded university education for women as a priority in its own right.

In summary, the evidence presented emphasised the restrictions that operated with regard to women in higher education, drew attention to their grievances, turned the spotlight on Trinity for its complete exclusion of women, complained of the half-measures adopted by University College, urged reforms within the Royal University, and demanded state endowment for the women's colleges. These witnesses argued their case on the grounds of social and educational needs, as well as simple justice. It was held that the whole of society would benefit from the extension of higher education to women; that there would be fewer 'distressed ladies' if university education had been open to them; that the number of women seeking degrees was rapidly increasing and that women with degrees were needed in the schools; and that blatant discrimination against women existed in that women's colleges, unlike men's, were not subsidised by public funds, nor did they have as teachers the fellows of the RUI, nor were women who were more highly qualified than men (as in the particular case of Mary Hayden) appointed to these fellowships. And they supported their claim to equality of treatment with evidence taken from abroad, including from colleges in Britain, where higher education had been extended to women.

The practitioners and advocates of higher education for women were not only united in their general demands but were also persuasive in their argument. However, a division emerged over the question whether women should receive their university education separately in state-endowed women's colleges or in mixed classes in the Queen's Colleges and a proposed new college in Dublin. Fairly predictably, the principals of the successfully established women's colleges—Miss White of Alexandra, Miss Byers of Victoria College, Belfast, and the spokesman for Loreto—favoured separate university education in the women's colleges and argued that the numbers showed that that was what the students themselves and their parents wanted. Among the members of the commission it was clear from the remarks of

Bishop Healy that he too favoured separate education. Mary Hayden, however, though officially representing St Mary's, was steadfast in her opposition to the segregation of men and women in university education. And the organisations to which she actively belonged—the Central Association of Irish Schoolmistresses and the Irish Association of Women Graduates and Candidate Graduates—gave forceful evidence in favour of the education of men and women together in the same university classes.

Though influential witnesses, including the President of University College, the Provost of Trinity College and such members of the commission as Bishop Healy gave their support to the idea of endowed separate colleges for women, other witnesses, including Monsignor Molloy, Rector of the Catholic University, and members of the commission such as Professor Butcher and Judge Madden, seemed more sympathetic to the idea of co-education.

The final report of the commission came out decisively in favour of co-education. Noting the alternative proposals—endowed separate colleges for women, or students of both sexes receiving their education together—the commission reported that the case could not be more clearly or succinctly stated than in the recommendations of the Association of Women Graduates, with whose views the commission was in general accord. The women graduates had recommended that 'all degrees, honours, prizes, privileges and appointments of the University be open to women equally with men'; that all lectures be open to women; that attendance at recognised lectures be necessary for graduation; and that lectures delivered exclusively for women not be recognised. The commission incorporated these recommendations in the report and recommended that existing women's colleges in Dublin and Belfast might serve as halls of residence.

ADMISSION TO UNIVERSITY COLLEGE, 1904–08

Trinity College admitted women in January 1904. This threw into greater relief the grievances of Catholic women undergraduates living in the vicinity of Dublin, distanced from the Queen's Colleges and advised by their bishops not to attend Trinity. A comment that Dr Delany had made earlier was taken by some of the women activists to imply that University College would admit women when Trinity did so. In 1904, therefore, a memorial was submitted to University College by the Association of Women Graduates, which was now leading the campaign to make sure that all the advantages of university education should be open to women equally with men and that all university lectures should be open to women students. In support of this request, Francis Sheehy Skeffington, Registrar of University College (1901–04), organised forty-four signatures from male graduates, including fellows of the Royal University, among whom were Denis Coffey, future President of

UCD, and the future professors George Sigerson and Patrick Semple. Dr Delany admonished his registrar for publicly advocating what was contrary to college policy. Skeffington, though denying that any policy had been formulated by the college authorities, resigned in order to be free to continue his advocacy on behalf of the women. The women's petition was turned down by Delany and the Academic Council, on the grounds of lack of facilities.

Though the Royal Commission on Trinity College, Dublin, and the University of Dublin (the Fry Commission) was restricted to consideration of the role of Trinity, witnesses managed to raise again the whole issue of the higher education of women. In her evidence before this commission, Agnes O'Farrelly, one of the two representatives of the Association of Women Graduates, complained that there were about 120 lectures a week in University College that women were not allowed to attend. (There were twenty public lectures on the timetable open to them.) They could not therefore take a full course in arts in the college in Dublin to which the fifteen fellows were attached. Yet these women had to compete for honours and prizes with men students who had the full teaching of the fellows and examiners.[3] The representatives of the women graduates once again made it clear that what they desired was co-education. When asked whether, in the case of a large number of parents preferring that their daughters should be educated in women's colleges rather than in mixed colleges, she would object to their having the benefit of the lectures, Miss Hanan, the other representative of the women graduates, replied: 'I think the cleavage would be most unfortunate.'[4]

Despite the arguments put forward by the representatives of the women graduates, and the recommendation of the Robertson Commission a few years earlier, the Fry Commission came down in favour of maintaining separate women's colleges. In its report it stated that 'there is no doubt in our minds that there exist many parents in and about Dublin who prefer for their girls an education in colleges exclusively for women to co-education in mixed classes ...'[5] It went on in effect to recommend that Trinity should regard Alexandra College as a recognised college of the University of Dublin.

The report of the Fry Commission was an encouragement to women principals and others who had a vested interest in the women's colleges, and to clergy and others who preferred separate universities for men and women. We can accept that Dr Delany was sincere when he stated before the Robertson Commission: 'I am a strong advocate for the higher education of women.'[6] He was pleased too that women came to University College because, when compared with other institutions, they saw it as offering competent teachers.[7] On grounds of expediency he had shown himself willing, in spite of serious accommodation problems, to ease the women's grievances by gradually introducing remedial measures. Faced with mounting pressure from within as well as from outside the college, he had shown some flexibility. About a year after the Fry Commission, temporary structures behind 86 provided University College with garden classrooms, otherwise known as 'Father Finlay's tin university'.[8] When these were in operation women were admitted to greater participation in the college during its last two years under Jesuit management.

Yet on all issues relating to the treatment and protection of the 'gentler sex', Dr Delany was very much a Victorian moralist. His attitudes were by no means confined to Catholic clergymen: it was because the Provost of Trinity, Dr Salmon, shared these views that he had proposed as the solution a separate university for women. It was an era when the rules of social behaviour were easily confused with the commandments of morality. Champions of co-education shared many of its opponents' assumptions about the proper comportment that should regulate relations between the sexes. On this Mary Hayden was no different from Father Delany when she reported to Mother Patrick the 'most objectionable habit' of one former Dominican girl of 'gossiping for ever so long with usually about half a dozen young men' in the porch of the National Library. To do the girl justice, however, she admitted that it was never with one young man only. Still, she complained, 'it looks very badly. I rarely go there that I don't see her.'[9]

Towards the end of 1907 the L&H amended its constitution in order to admit women to membership; but Dr Delany refused to sanction this change in the society's rules. A deputation that waited on him in February 1908 to put the views of the society reported that

> the President proceeded to point out the great dangers which would result from the ladies being out late at night and having to cross the city on their return home. He also pointed to the gravity of the position of the male students, whose morality might be jeopardised through intercourse with the lady students in the Literary and Historical Society, as well as the possibility of undesirable or unhappy marriages which such an arrangement would bring about.[10]

The evidence would seem to suggest that Father Delany's ideal solution for the problem of university education for women would have been separate and endowed women's colleges. He wrote to Archbishop Walsh shortly after the introduction of the Irish Universities Bill in 1908:

> That women are to receive university education I think we must accept, but it is another question whether they are to sit in the same class-rooms and be associated with men students throughout the university course.
>
> I have to confess that we are not at all satisfied here that it is in the interest of the educational formation of either the men or the women students that there should be such co-education. Our experience here

goes to show that the work of a co-educative system tends to diminish refinement amongst the women students and to lessen markedly in the men students the love of courtesy and consideration for women. Of course there are other and nearer considerations into which I need not enter. In America where this co-education grew up and flourished, there are already grave doubts about the wisdom of maintaining it. It is important now, before committing ourselves finally to it here, to weigh the matter duly and make up our minds. What makes it urgent is the consideration that if there is not to be co-education it would be necessary to make suitable provision for the separate education of women—which would of course entail additional expense ...[11]

Since its foundation in 1902, the Association of Women Graduates had been consistent in its demand that women be admitted equally with men to all the benefits and privileges of university education. The Robertson Commission in 1902 had recommended the acceptance of this demand.[12] Again, in their statement to the Fry Commission of 1906–07 the association, reiterating the point it had made in a memorial to the Chief Secretary in 1904, had requested

that in laying down any scheme for Irish University education as a whole, your Commission will recommend that no charter or endowment be given to any university or university college which will not give to women-students the same teaching, degrees, honours and prizes as are open to men students.[13]

When it looked as if the government was about to introduce a university settlement in 1907, the women graduates wrote to the Permanent Under-Secretary of State for Ireland, Sir Antony MacDonnell, soliciting his support for their cause while asserting that 'the Association has no reason to fear that there will be any curtailment of the privileges already enjoyed by women students.'[14] They were referring to the position already won in Trinity and the Queen's Colleges; but they earnestly asked that in any further development and in the framing of any new scheme the government would secure for women students equal privileges with men with regard to lectures, degrees, offices, and direct representation on the governing body.[15]

Given that the Royal University, the Queen's Colleges, the Catholic University Medical School, Trinity College and (since about 1906) the Jesuits' University College had all opened their doors to women students, there was simply no way that a Liberal government in 1908—already under pressure from a swelling suffragist agitation—was going to propose, or Irish Party MPs support, a Bill that would exclude women students from the new universities. It was not surprising, therefore, that the Irish Universities Act

(1908) should state (in its first schedule) that on the 35-member Senate of the NUI four members would be nominated by the king, 'of whom one at least shall be a woman.' The Charters and Statutes of the university and its colleges confirmed that 'women shall be eligible equally with men to be members of the University or of any authority of the University, and to hold any office or enjoy any advantage of the University.'[16]

There was an element of historic justice in the nomination of Mary Hayden as the first women to serve on the Senate of the NUI. She had seemed to be ever poised for battle on behalf of women's rights. A colleague remembered her with her cropped hair (as a student she had it cropped to save time and, finding it convenient, she retained it in that style), her shortened skirt, her Gladstone bag, and her father's watch and chain at her waist.[17] She loved to cycle and used her bicycle while on a holiday in Connemara with Patrick Pearse. She loved travel and added Modern Greek to her languages during a prolonged stay in Athens in 1896. She was the first woman scholar of the RUI (in 1883) and the first woman to win a junior fellowship (in 1895).

In 1900/01 Mary Hayden became the focus of a *cause célèbre* when Father Delany twice blocked her efforts to secure a senior fellowship in English at University College. Among several explanations he gave, perhaps the one most indicative of his attitude was that he did not feel himself authorised 'to introduce so strange a novelty in a Catholic university college' as appointing a woman to lecture to 'large classes of young men.' He observed also (this was in 1902) that 'Trinity College has persistently excluded ladies altogether.'[18] Not surprisingly, Mary Hayden could not be counted among the admirers of the man she spoke of sardonically as 'Sweet William'![19]

Hayden was a founder-member of the Irish Association of Women Graduates and Candidate Graduates, which did so much for the emancipation of women in university education, and later became president of one of its successors, the National University Women Graduates' Association. Moderate and reasonable, she was no amazon. She founded St Joan's Club (named after Joan of Arc), which helped to feed and clothe the children of the poor. Her nomination to join thirty-nine men on the first Senate, and, with her friend and fellow-fighter Agnes O'Farrelly, her nomination to the first Governing Body of UCD, where they joined twenty-eight men, might now be seen by some as mere tokenism. But the Irish Universities Act was, in its own time, a bill of rights for women, legally guaranteeing their equality with men in university education. It removed the last of the restrictions regarding Convocation and the senior fellowship and membership of the Senate that had been associated with the Royal University. Women graduates now had the right to vote in the Convocation elections to the Senate and the Governing Body, to stand in these elections, and to hold the highest offices in the university. Mary Hayden herself soon became lecturer in Irish history at UCD and subsequently professor of modern Irish history.

For people like Dr Delany, worried about the social and moral dangers lurking in co-education, the last line of defence was the hope that the Senate of the NUI would recognise the Catholic women's colleges as affiliated institutions of the university. Nor did the colleges themselves waste much time in seeking that recognition. But by now Delany was no longer President of University College, and the question of the recognition of the women's colleges was a matter for the Governing Body of UCD and the Senate of the National University.

WOMEN IN THE NEW COLLEGE

Ironically, the Irish Universities Act, which conferred on women equality with men in all matters relating to university education, also brought into question the very existence of the women's colleges. The Act laid down that only students of the three constituent colleges of the NUI, or others that might be granted 'recognised college' status by the NUI, could sit for degree examinations of the university. The question then was, would the Senate, which was prepared to recognise Maynooth, also grant recognition to the women's colleges?

When introducing his Bill, Birrell said he had done his best to make the regulations governing recognition as strict as possible, so as to exclude institutions that could not be said to be doing university work. On this point the Chief Secretary had the full encouragement of Archbishop Walsh.[20] Birrell had explained in Parliament: 'Unless you have a severely restricted right of affiliation your University may become a sort of conglomeration of secondary schools and that is a thing to be avoided.'[21]

Stringent conditions for recognition were subsequently incorporated in the Act and Statutes. These laid down that recognition could be granted provided, among other things, 'the college does not prepare students for Intermediate, or other school examinations or does not give education of an Intermediate or Secondary kind.' It was also required that the Senate be satisfied of the applicant college's financial position, the academic status both of its teachers and its teaching, and the admission standards set for its students.[22]

An application received by the Senate had to be referred to the Governing Body of the relevant constituent college. If the Governing Body consented to recognition, its report and the application had then to be laid before the General Board of Studies, which in turn could obtain further reports from the faculties concerned. The Senate was also entitled to depute an inspection of the college that sought recognition, and to take the report of such inspection and of the General Board of Studies into consideration. Recognition could be withdrawn by the Senate at any time.

Following the establishment of the NUI, Loreto, St Mary's and Mount Anville Sacred Heart convent, Dundrum, applied variously for recognition of their approved courses of study or recognition of the colleges themselves. The Senate referred consideration to the Governing Body of UCD, which was soon inundated with petitions, memorials and letters for and against the women's colleges. The Association of Women Graduates, the Teachers' Guild of Great Britain and Ireland and others opposed recognition, which they felt would undermine the standards of the constituent colleges to which women now enjoyed the right of entry. On the other hand, the clerical members of the Governing Body favoured recognition and, when that failed to win majority support, proposed recognition for the purposes of first arts. This also was voted down, and the possibility of recognising either Loreto or St Mary's (Mount Anville having withdrawn), or a single college formed *ad hoc* from the two of them, faded away when the Dominicans and Loreto Sisters proved unable to agree with one another. Eventually a revived proposal to recognise Loreto for first arts courses won the approval of the Governing Body, only to run aground on legal advice obtained by the Senate that Loreto College was too closely associated with the same order's secondary school to satisfy the requirements of the Act. The same reasoning defeated a further application from St Mary's. The struggle for the women's colleges ended in December 1912 when the Senate informed both Loreto and St Mary's that legal difficulties made their recognition impossible.

The case for the recognition of two women's colleges had become difficult to sustain. The two in question were strikingly similar: run by orders of nuns, tied to secondary schools, offering the same limited range of courses, with small numbers of students at university level, and dependent largely on part-time academic staff. The justification for maintaining both was clearly open to criticism; the fact that neither was prepared to give way before the other and amalgamate resources only strengthened the resolve of those whose attitude in any case was 'a curse on both your houses.' At an earlier period all the fellowships of the Royal University had been bestowed on the Jesuit University College, to the exclusion of Blackrock and others. If this precedent set by the men's colleges were to be followed, a women's college should not be allowed to dissipate the resources that could be concentrated in UCD. The rationalisation argument was on the side of a single, integrated institution capable of maintaining high standards and catering for both men and women.

One of the problems facing the religious who ran the Catholic women's colleges was the need for nuns themselves to have access to higher education. This was one of the arguments advanced by Father Peter Finlay SJ against the abolition of the status of extern students in the Irish Universities Bill when he asserted that nuns 'could not, under any circumstances, assist at College lectures.'[23] During the debate in Parliament on the Bill, C. J. O'Donnell had mentioned the possibility that nuns might find themselves virtually excluded from university education unless some provision were made for extern degrees.[24] Since nuns had not been exposed to mixed education, the non-recognition of Loreto and St Mary's posed particular problems for them. In an attempt to find a solution, Father Timothy Corcoran, professor of education in UCD, as late as September 1914 drew up a proposal for a Women's Department, which would provide separate lectures for women within UCD in subjects where the numbers made it feasible. Nothing came of this, and from the early twenties nuns from religious communities all over the country began to occupy the front rows at lectures and were provided with their own reading rooms.

NUMBERS AND PROPORTIONS

The refusal to give Loreto and St Mary's the status of recognised college meant that women students came instead to University College. The proportion steadily increased until the mid-thirties, when it reached as high as 36 per cent. A decrease followed, and over the next thirty years the proportion remained below 29 per cent. This almost static figure no doubt reflected the general attitude towards women in de Valera's Ireland, where the Constitution saw women's place as in the home. In 1964/65 the proportion began to rise again, going over 40 per cent for the first time in 1977/78.

From the start, women had entered certain faculties and were not to be found at all in others. The proportion, though fluctuating, was always high in arts. The developing area of social science attracted many women after the early sixties, and by 1987/88 women accounted for 64 per cent of arts students—or, to state it in different terms, out of a total of 4,300 students in arts, women outnumbered men by over 1,200.

Since the first of their sex were admitted to Cecilia Street in the eighteen-nineties, women students were always to be found in the Medical School. Their numbers increased in the early years of UCD, until by 1919/20 they numbered one in six of the medical students. The twenties saw a dramatic decline in the total number in medicine, with an even greater drop in the proportion of women, which by 1931/32 stood at one in ten. In addition to the country's social and economic circumstances, this probably had to do with changes in the regulations for entry to medicine and a perception that Ireland was producing too many doctors. When the trend reversed, the ratio of women to men steadily improved, until by 1987/88 more than half the students in medicine were women.

In science and commerce women were well represented up to mid-century, when men began to predominate, as they had in the beginning. Agriculture and engineering were male bastions until the sixties, since when women, tentatively at the outset, have become more evident. From an early date, however, a sprinkling of women had been present in architecture.

The proportion of women students in the college generally and in the various faculties by the mid-nineties might be expressed in the following table for the year 1994/95:

Arts	66%
Medicine	64%
Law	55%
Science	52%
Veterinary medicine	42%
Commerce	39%
Agriculture	37%
Engineering and architecture	22%
Total percentage of women	53%

An institution that had begun as a totally male preserve at the time of Newman's Catholic University, and had tentatively admitted women at the turn of the century to the Jesuit college, was eventually in the nineteen-nineties to have more women than men among its students.[25]

WOMEN ACADEMICS

The ratio of women to men among the academic staff had started out on a promising note. The original appointment of senior (statutory) staff under Statutes I and II had provided for the establishment of forty-five professorships and six statutory lectureships. Three women were among the professors appointed, and one woman among the lecturers. All the senior appointments were in the Faculty of Arts: Professor Mary Hayden (modern Irish history), Professor Mary Macken (German), Professor Maria Degani (Italian and Spanish) and Agnes O'Farrelly (lecturer in Irish language). Among the junior staff, Mary K. Ryan was appointed an assistant in French. She was promoted to a statutory lectureship in 1926, and Agnes O'Farrelly became professor of modern Irish poetry in 1932.

The total of four women professors and one statutory lecturer was a high water mark for women in senior posts. With the death of Mary O'Kelly (née Ryan) in 1934 and the retirement of both Hayden and Degani in 1938, only two women (Macken and O'Farrelly) occupied senior posts. This situation began to improve somewhat with the appointment to statutory lectureships of Sheila Power (mathematical physics), Carmel Humphries (zoology) and Phyllis Clinch (botany) in the late forties; and though Macken retired in 1949 she was replaced by Kathleen Cunningham (the solitary woman professor between 1949 and 1957). In 1960/61 only two women — Cunningham

(German) and Humphries (zoology, appointed to the chair in 1957)—were among the increasing number of professors. Ten years later (1970/71) there were three women professors—Humphries, Clinch, and Eva Philbin (organic chemistry)—and one associate professor—Sheila Tinney (née Power)—but there were no women among the statutory lecturers. In 1980/81, though six women were now statutory lecturers, not a solitary woman sat among the professors, associate professors, deans and heads of departments on the Academic Council of 141 members. As far as senior academic positions were concerned, women had reached their lowest point. Since the eighties, because of an awareness of this situation and because of the increasing number of women in the junior academic ranks, matters could only improve.

Until the early eighties, such senior posts as women did occupy had all been in the faculties of Arts and Science. They were just beginning to make a tiny inroad in Medicine. A small but increasing number had also made an entry into the other faculties as assistants. Until the nineties women were to remain entirely absent—even at junior staff level—from the Departments of Engineering.

The deterioration that had taken place in the position of women as senior academics, compared with the promise of the early years, no more than reflected the status of women generally in contemporary society. The pre-1908 campaign for equality for women in higher education and the suffragist and feminist movements, not to mention the political role women had played up to the establishment of an Irish state, seemed to have run out of steam in post-independence Ireland. Whatever other benefits may have resulted from the non-recognition by the NUI of the existing women's colleges, their total disappearance from the university scene may well have affected the presence of women in academic life. After all, the first women to be appointed to senior posts, and for long the only ones (Mary Hayden, Mary Macken, and Agnes O'Farrelly), had all been lecturers in the women's colleges. And the paucity of role models for women students could well have been an unconscious consequence of the extinction of these institutions.

Various other factors were also at work militating against the emergence of women as professors. The numbers for whom motherhood was a full-time occupation, and the numbers then entering convents, severely limited the supply of qualified women for the academic world as well as for all other areas of business and the professions. And the thinking behind the ban on the employment of married women in the public service and teaching, which lasted in the case of teachers from 1933 to 1958, was bound to be extended also to the university. It should also be noted that, though the number of women undergraduates was increasing, this increase was not reflected proportionately in the number of women staying on for postgraduate studies.

4

Teething Problems, 1909–1926

You are born for Ireland; and in your advancement Ireland is advanced.
J. H. Newman, 'Discipline of Mind', an address to the evening classes.

A SITE FOR UCD

When introducing the Irish Universities Bill (1908), Birrell had stated that the government would give £150,000 as a maximum for building and equipping the new college and the new university at Dublin. With this figure—which it would have to share with the NUI—as its financial limit, the Governing Body of UCD had to decide how and where the college would be housed. It set up a Sites (later Sites and Buildings) Committee, which considered sites as far apart as Marino on the north side of Dublin, Elm Park in Mount Merrion to the south, and Kilmainham to the west. It concluded that the former exhibition buildings in Earlsfort Terrace, most recently the premises of the Royal University, offered the only practicable solution.

It had been intended that the somewhat run-down premises in Earlsfort Terrace, including medical and scientific laboratories, would provide temporary accommodation both for UCD and the NUI. The Governing Body and the NUI Senate came to an agreement whereby the NUI received £40,000 from the grant to find itself a new home, in return for which it vacated Earlsfort Terrace. Accordingly, when UCD opened in November 1909 it consisted physically of a dilapidated property in Earlsfort Terrace and, by a rental arrangement with the bishops, the Georgian houses of the former University College in St Stephen's Green and the Medical School in Cecilia Street. Curiously, it also bought fifty tons of coal that had been left behind by the Jesuits. And it had the right to draw down £110,000, being what was left of the grant, to develop Earlsfort Terrace into an appropriate and permanent college structure.

EARLSFORT TERRACE

The Governing Body's General Purposes Committee was now requested to prepare a report on the new buildings required and the best means of obtaining plans for them, and this report was presented at a special meeting of the Governing Body. Here was the opportunity that had been awaited and longed for since the middle of the nineteenth century, not only by Catholic and nationalist Ireland but by all who sought fair play and equality in university education. The Robertson Commission (1903) had declared that

> unless what is done is done on an adequate and impressive scale it need not be done at all. It is necessary that in the dignity of the buildings ... and the equipment of the establishment, the institution should command respect and inspire enthusiasm.[1]

A couple of years later, in a note appended to the Fry Report, Baron Palles, Dr Coffey and Dr Hyde, quoting that statement, added:

> Were there any marked difference between the dignity of the buildings of Trinity College and those of the new College, it would serve to prevent the Roman Catholics of Ireland being convinced that the principle of equality upon which, and upon which only, they have throughout insisted had not been admitted and acted upon. Were this so, a sense of the long-felt injustice would continue. The feeling of unrest would not be laid—a sense of inferiority would exist in those connected with the new College, and thus the consummation so devoutly to be wished for, a final settlement, would not have been reached.[2]

The Governing Body, however, went about its task in a businesslike way and without any oratorical flourishes or trumpeting of the occasion. The minutes of the meeting were low-key: it was decided 'that it is desirable to proceed on the basis of plans for a complete College even though it may not be possible to provide the whole building at first.'[3] The characteristically low tone of Dr Coffey's speaking voice, his great patience and quiet determination, can be sensed in this simple sentence.

Two determinants were to be kept in view: the probable increase in numbers of students for some years to come and, on the other hand, the limitation in financial resources in the parliamentary grant and, inferentially, in respect of any grants in the future. With this framework in mind, a detailed scheme was drawn up for a complete college, keeping as closely as possible to the standards found suitable in other university colleges.

The scheme outlined the entire structure that would be desirable if the resources were available; and it was agreed that as much of the scheme as the present resources permitted should be carried into effect. Since it was essential that the architectural character of the college buildings as a whole be maintained in their integrity, it was agreed to appoint an assessor, an architect of eminence, to advise on all questions relating to the scheme and to act as arbitrator in a competition for suitable plans. Open competition for the best architectural plans was to be limited to practising architects living in Ireland.

Since the site in the college's possession fell short of the dimensions proposed in the scheme, an approach was to be made to Lord Iveagh (Edward Guinness), the gardens of whose residence in St Stephen's Green adjoined the property (and who, coincidentally and rather embarrassingly, was Chancellor of the University of Dublin), requesting him to facilitate UCD in respect of an extension to the site.

In the light of a reply early in 1909 by Lord Iveagh's agents that he was not willing to dispose of any part of his grounds, the likelihood of his having changed his mind in the intervening two years was perhaps not very high. The president's letter (24 April 1911) informed him that the Royal University site was 'the only one available in Dublin' and that the Governing Body, having under consideration general plans for the erection of a new college on the site, found that 'a moderate extension of the available space would prove of the greatest utility in permitting the necessary buildings to be raised without inconvenient crowding or great elevation.' Since all the college buildings were to be erected in Earlsfort Terrace, he wrote, 'a very limited addition at any part of the area would have an exceptional value,' if this could be done without disturbing the general arrangement of Lord Iveagh's gardens and grounds.

A memorandum annexed to the letter gave an account of the general circumstances of the college and dealt more especially with the site and buildings problem. In it Dr Coffey explained that UCD was 'the institution in which the whole teaching work of the National University in Dublin is conducted.' By virtue of its endowment, the number of its teaching staff (about fifty professors and lecturers), and the number of its students (about seven hundred), it was the principal college of the University. Classes were conducted in temporary premises in different parts of the city in buildings formerly occupied by the Catholic University; but the Royal University in Earlsfort Terrace was to be 'the permanent site' of the college. It would be necessary (1) to remove part of the present buildings and to modify another part, since they had never been intended for the business of a teaching institution and because of their dilapidated state, and (2) to erect new laboratories so that a suitable type of collegiate structure on modern lines might be provided. Even at the estimated 150,000 square feet, the new non-residential college would fall far short of the size and extent of similar institutions among the recently established universities and colleges in England. The college could indeed be erected on the available site, but only in a very much restricted manner. Any extension of the site, no matter how limited, would be a matter of the greatest advantage to the college and would especially facilitate the preparation of architectural plans before the work of construction was undertaken.

Lord Iveagh's letter opened by saying that he need hardly say that he had 'no wish to part with any portion, however small,' of his Dublin property; and in any case there were difficulties in the way, since he was merely a tenant for life, and the rights of others would have to be considered. However, he had carefully read the letter and the memo, he said, and if the difficulties to which he referred could be overcome, and if satisfactory terms and conditions could be agreed between him and UCD, he would be prepared to consider whether he could facilitate the college by disposing of a portion of his land, namely a piece that cut into the university property in the Hatch Street frontage measuring about 87 feet by 116 feet, and a portion of his riding-school at the other (St Stephen's Green) end measuring about 270 feet by 39 feet—an area of nearly half an acre. In fairness to UCD, himself and his successors he wanted it clearly understood that this concession should be looked upon as final, and it should not be followed by any further application for an extension of boundaries.

The Governing Body accepted the offer and the conditions attached and in a resolution that was passed unanimously tendered 'our heartiest thanks to his Lordship for his generous proposal.'[4] In another resolution it put on record 'that we convey our sincere thanks to the Hon. Mr. Justice Barton for his valuable co-operation in the negotiations with Lord Iveagh, and for his many services to the College.'[5]

In his reply to the Governing Body's resolution, Lord Iveagh said he was anxious to bring forward a point that was inadvertently omitted from his earlier letter and that he hoped would not prove an obstacle. He wished to preserve for himself and his successors the privacy and amenities of his gardens. He would be obliged, therefore, if it could be arranged that the windows of living-rooms would not open on that side of the college buildings facing his gardens, though he had no objection to roof-lights and large windows of halls, laboratories and lecture-rooms, so long as they offered nothing unsightly. He had no doubt that his architect would be allowed see the designs for the elevation of the new buildings facing the gardens and that the Governing Body would be prepared to consider any reasonable objection he might raise.

In a second letter he asked that his gift of ground to the college be associated with the names of his two old and valued friends, Monsignor Molloy and Father Healy, and said that he would be gratified if the Governing Body would permit this association to be permanently recorded in the form of a memorial tablet to be placed in the new buildings. The

Governing Body accepted the suggestions with regard to the windows of living rooms and accepted 'with pleasure' the proposal with regard to the memorial tablet.

The marble plaque with the Guinness coat of arms at the top was subsequently placed in the wall outside the Council Chamber on the first floor. The inscription reads:

> A portion of the ground whereon this college stands was the gift A.D. MDCCCCXI of Edward Cecil First Earl of Iveagh, K.P., F.R.S., LL.D, M.A. In accordance with the wish of the donor the gift here commemorated is associated with the name of his old and valued friends—the late Right Revd. Monsignor Gerald Molloy LL.D. Rector of the Catholic University of Ireland and the late Revd. James Healy, Parish Priest of Little Bray.

Underneath the inscription is a smaller reproduction of the coat of arms of the college.[6]

One of the proposed conditions of the transfer of the property was that no building exceeding 40 feet in height should be erected on the site then occupied by the riding-school. As a result of further negotiations, the restriction on height was agreed at 60 feet. This restriction was to protect Lord Iveagh's right to light on a tennis court adjoining the riding-school, close to the junction of Earlsfort Terrace and St Stephen's Green, and a palm house at the north end of the riding-school site and adjoining what is now Iveagh Gardens. The last clause in the schedule prohibited the college from opening windows of living-rooms looking out on Lord Iveagh's grounds.

The readiness of Lord Iveagh to compromise on the height was not the end of his generosity to the college. The head landlord of the Hatch Street portion of the grounds, Hely-Hutchinson, was unwilling to make any concessions in waiving the covenant against conducting a school or college on this property without the payment of £100. This sum, together with the costs of the transaction to Hely-Hutchinson's solicitors and the stamp duty on the deeds, Lord Iveagh paid.

In his final letter to the president (10 November 1911) Lord Iveagh took the opportunity of saying how pleased he was that the conveyance had been completed and how much he had appreciated the good will with which his suggestions and conditions had been met by everyone connected with the college. The college, however, had even greater reason than he had to be appreciative of the outcome of the negotiations. It could be argued, perhaps, that among the motivations behind Lord Iveagh's gift was that of self-interest. If he had refused the extension, it is likely that UCD would have been left with no alternative but to compensate for the space by way of elevation, and clearly Lord Iveagh was anxious to protect the privacy of his tennis courts and gardens. To take legal action against the new college for the Catholic Irish in order to ensure his privacy would not have been at all popular. He wanted to be on good terms with his neighbours. It is equally clear, however, that his gift was also motivated by genuine friendship with two deceased Catholic priests—Monsignor Molloy and Father Healy—and with Mr Justice Barton, who did so much to persuade Lord Iveagh of the justice of UCD's request. One should not overlook, above all, the generosity of spirit with which he responded to what was admittedly the well-reasoned case presented in Dr Coffey's letter and memorandum.

But whichever motivation stood highest with him, it has to be admitted that, when this Chancellor of the University of Dublin decided to part with ground he had no wish to surrender, he did so with a becoming graciousness. He deserves to be remembered among the college's most generous benefactors at a time when UCD was struggling to establish a suitable home for itself.

Plans

UCD now had a site of about five-and-a-half acres (modest enough by contemporary university standards); a maximum building grant of £110,000 (already being necessarily depleted by the costs of organising and advertising a competition for the designs for the new buildings); some temporary accommodation in St Stephen's Green and Cecilia Street rented from the bishops; the inadequate structures in Earlsfort Terrace inherited from the Royal University; and the urgent need to complete the new college.

The architect-assessor appointed to advise on all questions relating to the building scheme and to act as arbitrator in the competition for suitable designs was Henry T. Hare of London, honorary secretary of the Royal Institute of British Architects. Early in 1912 he inspected the site and prepared a draft of the proposed conditions for the architectural competition. Hitherto the question of buildings had been dealt with by the Sites Committee, which searched specifically for a suitable site, or by the General Purposes Committee, which reported on the building requirements, or by the Special Committee, which dealt with the acquisition of Lord Iveagh's grounds. A Buildings Committee was now (26 February 1912) appointed to deal with all questions relating to the proposed new buildings, and from then onwards it became a permanent feature of the college's administrative structure. This and the Finance Committee have been ever since the two principal committees of the Governing Body.

On 21 May 1912 the Governing Body invited architects to submit designs for the new building not later than 30 September. The competition was limited to architects 'living and practising in Ireland,' and despite a request from the Irish Institute of Architects that it should also be confined to those who were members of recognised architectural bodies, it was decided not to place any further limitations on the eligibility of competitors. Twenty-two designs were carefully examined by the assessor, who informed the Buildings Committee that the design submitted by R. M. Butler best fulfilled the conditions and requirements, and he was formally appointed architect on 28 October 1912. Cash prizes were awarded to the designs placed second and third, and an exhibition of the designs submitted was held in Earlsfort Terrace.

The plans for the college proposed a quadrangle. The front, facing east along Earlsfort Terrace, would contain Arts, Commerce, and Administration; the north wing would house Science; the south wing, along Hatch Street, would provide for Medicine; the west wing, backing on to the Iveagh Gardens, would accommodate Engineering, Architecture and departments of Science and Medicine not assigned to the north and south wings; and a central block would enclose the Library and Aula Maxima. The whole was intended to accommodate a thousand students comfortably.

Before any construction had got under way certain modifications in the winning design were approved. The most substantial of these involved the Physics and Chemistry Theatres, among the most striking features of the college. This modification provided a central projection on the façade of the north wing, which allowed for an increase in the height of the ceilings of the two theatres. The south wing was to be treated similarly when the time came.

The order of the earliest stages was: (a) the removal of the Royal University front; (b) the building of the north wing; and (c) the building of the front as far as the southern termination of the portico of the Royal University. The time required for these three stages was estimated as two-and-half years. Assuming that the work of construction would begin in June 1914, it was expected that the north wing and about two-thirds of the front section (including the main entrance and that half of the front nearest the north wing) would be complete by about December 1916. The subsequent removal of the old RUI science laboratories in order to complete the front, and the erection of the south wing, thereby completing three sides of the quadrangle, was calculated to take a further one-and-a-half or two years. All of this, it was estimated, would exhaust the financial resources available under the parliamentary building grant.

The work of clearing the ground given by Lord Iveagh was begun. Lord Iveagh proposed that he would remove at his own expense the boundary wall adjoining Hatch Street; the college would remove the riding-school wall; and Lord Iveagh would pay half the cost of erecting a new boundary wall between the two properties. Meanwhile there was the pressing question of the accommodation of increasing numbers of students. It was agreed that it was desirable that Physiology and Anatomy be transferred from Cecilia Street as soon as possible to temporary accommodation in or near Earlsfort Terrace, without having to wait until the medical wing was complete in, at the earliest, four years' time. A permanent site for a students' union building (including a gymnasium) was also in question.

With a view to acquiring temporary accommodation for these medical departments and a permanent site for the students' union, an approach was made to the owners of the American Roller Rink, which stood as next-door neighbour on the southern corner of the junction of Hatch Street and Earlsfort Terrace (the site occupied later by Crawford's Garage before the present office block was built there). The sum of £2,500 was offered to the owners for the rink, and declined. The rejection was an inauspicious sign. The word 'permanent' in reference to the Earlsfort Terrace site had been used regularly—and with conviction—by Coffey in his statements and correspondence during these early years. The refusal to sell the rink to the college in May 1913 was an omen of the trauma that UCD was to undergo in later decades in the attempt to expand its premises in the Earlsfort Terrace area.

However urgent the accommodation needs, the completion of a building such as that proposed would take time. When the architectural drawings were revised and the quantities estimated, and Treasury approval granted after lengthy correspondence about the details, advertisements were placed in the newspapers inviting tenders for the building work. Twelve were received, from as far apart as Belfast and Waterford. They ranged between almost £112,000 and £127,000, which put them all above the maximum grant available—and this maximum had to include building, professional fees, fittings, and scientific equipment. The contract was awarded to the Dublin firm of G. and T. Crampton, subject to the limitation of the contract to £90,000 or thereabouts for a smaller portion of the whole of the work tendered for by the omission of such part of the proposed scheme as would bring the total expenditure within the limits of the parliamentary grant.

The work began, and so, almost immediately, did a formidable array of problems. Flooding delayed the supply of limestone from Stradbally quarry; costs mounted when unforeseen work arose because an underground passage was discovered, which had to be filled in and buttressed; a strike by Crampton's labourers in 1916 hampered construction more effectively than the Rising, with which it coincided; and, above all, prices rocketed as a consequence of the Great War, then in progress. By February 1917 about half the proposed building (the north wing for Physics and Chemistry and the front for Arts and Administration) were nearing completion, at a cost of £118,000. The college had about £6,000 in hand to meet the deficit of £8,000 over the grant. Even after scaling down a number of elements contracted for, much remained to be done, but an application by the president for an additional grant of £50,000 was turned down. The growth in the number of students, which had more than doubled since 1909, meant a higher return from fees, and for running costs there was still the unincreased annual endowment of £32,000, none of which offered any surplus to help cover the builders' increasing charges. An overdraft met some pressing needs while also, of course, adding to the debt.

When the erection of the proposed quadrangle was suspended (permanently, as it transpired), the front and the wing that had been completed had already cost almost £150,000. In his statement on the financial needs of the college made to the Governing Body on 20 July 1920 the president showed that the cost of the buildings was now almost £153,000; the debt outstanding to the contractors, architect and bank amounted to almost £37,000; and the amount required to complete the railings and furnishings and to provide the planned Medical and Engineering buildings, the Library and Hall would be an additional £150,000.

Meanwhile the old luncheon-room had been fitted out to alleviate the requirements of the Engineering Department. The facilities for the Medical Faculty were such that Convocation had forwarded to the Governing Body a resolution 'that Convocation desires to draw the attention of the Governing Body of U.C.D. to the urgent need of proper equipment and decent housing of the Medical Faculty in U.C.D.' It must have been surprising to some, and rankled with others among the medical staff, that the most successful school of the old Catholic University found itself in the matter of facilities in such poor circumstances in the new college and particularly under the presidency of a former Dean of the Medical School. On the other hand, it could be said to underline the objectivity of Dr Coffey that he had not been seen to favour his old faculty at the expense of Arts, Science and Administration in the building priorities of the new college.

By the non-completion of the original plans, the students' facilities had also been seriously restricted. A letter was read at the meeting of the Governing Body on 2 December 1920 from the Students' Representative Council conveying a resolution demanding the establishment of 'the long-promised students' Union.' And Professor Corcoran complained that no heating of the theatres and class-rooms had been provided from October to December 1920. The 'extremely mild' weather for the greater part of the term was matched only by the mildness of the reply from Dr Coffey, who admitted, however, that there were three weeks of severe weather during which 'heating would have been necessary.'

If a certain frustration was seen to be creeping in among academic staff and students alike because of the aborted building plans, the Governing Body too was experiencing some frustration and embarrassment at not being in a position to pay off its debt to the contractor for what had been built and fitted out. More than a year and a half after the architect had certified the completion of the revised contract, on 21 December 1920, the Governing Body was impressing on the government 'the urgency of a settlement of the debt contracted by the erection of the college buildings, and particularly the immediate necessity for paying the sum still due to the Contractors, Messrs. G. & T. Crampton.'

Almost two months later, on 15 February 1921, the president reported that he had received urgent requests from Crampton for a settlement of the account and that he had informed them of the efforts being made by the college to induce the government to discharge the debt on the buildings arising out of the circumstances of the war. The government replied, however, that,

> in view of the previous explicit warnings that any increase in cost involved in the completion and equipment of the college buildings, over and above the statutory grant under the Irish Universities Act, 1908, would have to be met by the college out of its own resources, the Lords Commissioners of His Majesty's Treasury are unable to contemplate making any grant to the College specifically in respect of the buildings.[7]

Financial problems had beset several universities in Britain as a result of the war. The standstill in the salaries of academic staff was one source of widespread discontent and had led to the establishment of the Association of University Teachers in these colleges. In UCD the Association complained in a memorandum to the Governing Body that during 'three years when other bodies administering public monies had granted substantial increases to their staffs, no allowance whatever had been paid to any employee of the College above the rank of Porter.'[8]

In comparison with other universities and colleges in Ireland and Britain, UCD's financial problems were exacerbated by the building debt. To relieve the financial burdens, the government had established the University Grants Committee, and it was to this body that it referred UCD's request. The committee recommended that £20,000 be paid to UCD as a non-recurrent grant for the year 1920/21 'to assist the authorities in meeting expenditure on the most urgent needs of the current academic session.' The Governing Body protested against the inadequacy of the grant, and a special meeting was called to consider its allocation. The Association of University Teachers could not admit that building debts and bank overdrafts should rank equally with the 'just and moderate' claims of the staff and protested 'most vehemently' against the policy of trying to meet what was 'in reality a war debt' out of revenues that elsewhere were generally used for promoting educational ends. Despite the wishes of the president, the Governing Body assigned £13,000 out of the £20,000 grant for the payment of the staff and £7,000 'to the other urgent needs of the College.'[9] A further resolution assigned £5,000 out of the £7,000 to Crampton and the other £2,000 to the electrical contractors. Further accommodation from the bank was therefore needed for the overdraft, and this was granted.

In these circumstances, the question of completing the old front wall and removing a wooden paling at Earlsfort Terrace had to be postponed.[10] After a meeting between representatives of UCD and the bishops, the proposal to buy the St Stephen's Green premises was likewise deferred, and it was agreed that the best course was to renew the lease. (Cecilia Street was costing the college £200 a year and St Stephen's Green £515 a year in rents alone, thereby adding to an expenditure that it was felt could be eliminated by a more adequate building in Earlsfort Terrace.) Notice was given of a motion before the Governing Body 'that the Governing Body regrets its inability to provide seating, a fire, and lavatory accommodation' in the professors' room; and the president undertook to see that as far as it was possible any cause for complaint in these matters would be removed. The old Convocation Hall had to be heated and in part repainted and used as an additional reading-room for the Library. When Agnes O'Farrelly called the attention of the Governing Body to the 'uninhabitable state of the Students' Rooms at Earlsfort Terrace,' a sub-committee of the women members of the Governing Body (Agnes O'Farrelly, Mary Hayden, and Mary K. O'Kelly) was formed 'for advising on the decoration and furnishing of the Students' Rooms; limit of expenditure, £150.'[11] And the president had to report that his appeal to the University Grants Committee for a special grant for 1921/22 was met with the reply that the committee was unable to make further grants to universities and colleges.

But UCD's plight did receive a sympathetic hearing by the hard-pressed Provisional Government, which had only come into existence in January 1922. A letter dated 1 August 1922 (a few days before the deaths of Arthur Griffith, President of Dáil Éireann, and of Michael Collins, President of the Provisional Government) was received by Dr Coffey from the secretary of the Ministry of Finance of the Provisional Government. It read:

I am directed by the Minister of Finance to inform you that he has had under consideration representations made to him as to the financial position of U.C.D., particularly in regard to the building debt, and I am to state that, after careful review of the whole position, the Minister is willing to sanction a special non-recurrent grant of £10,000 provided that an undertaking is given on behalf of the College that the whole of this amount will be applied in discharge of outstanding accounts in respect of buildings.

Payment of amount in question will be immediately on receipt of an undertaking to this effect.[12]

The undertaking was speedily given, and out of this £10,000 the Governing Body resolved to pay to Crampton the outstanding £8,623 and to the architect the remaining £1,376. With this settlement of the accounts of the contractor and architect, an important phase in the saga of Earlsfort Terrace had been ended. Henceforth it would be a matter of dealing with the bank regarding the overdraft that had arisen because of the building costs, and of trying to persuade the new government of the Irish Free State to meet the building and financial requirements of the college.

It has sometimes been said that the College of Science in Merrion Street, built in the early years of the twentieth century, was the last major building project of the British administration in Ireland.[13] But UCD in Earlsfort Terrace was later still and, like the country itself, was left truncated by the British as they withdrew in 1922 from the greater portion of Ireland with the establishment of the Irish Free State. The aborted building in Earlsfort Terrace stood as the symbol of thwarted dreams. The final attempt in a series made by British governments since the eighteen-forties to solve the Irish university question, despite its great promise, had not gone far enough. And from the point of view of the young and enthusiastic University College, the crushing blow to its building programme was a major frustration. It was not without its own symbolism that the Treaty debates of what had been an outlawed Dáil Éireann should have taken place in the Council Chamber of the unfinished Earlsfort Terrace building.

A hard-pressed UCD, using the old buildings of the Royal University of Ireland before the new building was begun, had found it necessary to exclude all non-college functions from its premises. The Great Hall, in which the annual examinations and conferrings of the Royal University had been held, was not in constant use. But Dublin, which at the turn of the century seemed to be experiencing something of a golden age in the enjoyment of music, benefited from the availability of the Great Hall. It had been used regularly for concerts of the Royal Irish Academy of Music, the Dublin Oratorio and Choral Society, the Dublin Orchestral Society, and the Amateur Operatic Society. Nellie Melba and John McCormack were among the celebrated artists who had performed in the hall. The fanciful and superstitious might have said that in revenge for the muse of music being expelled from the temporary habitat in the old dilapidated Exhibition Hall in which she had found shelter, the gods, led by Mars and Vulcan, had conspired against UCD and let loose on Earlsfort Terrace the price inflation of the First World War, the natural disaster of the flooding of the limestone quarry, the trade union strike of the builders' employees, and the civil commotion of the Easter Rising and the 'Troubles'—all of which hampered the building of the college.

Staff and students alike had reason to regret the non-completion of the building along the lines of the original plans. There was of course a certain Victorian touch about plans that showed the 'female students' entrance' at the St Stephen's Green end and the 'male students' entrance' at the far end of the building at Hatch Street. In addition there was what was described— ambiguously enough—as a 'female dissecting room' in the Anatomy Block. Nevertheless, the tiling and plasterwork in the interior, and the Stradbally limestone and granite and Albert Power sculpture on the exterior, made it a pity that more of the building was not completed. It was in appearance more attractive than its academic models, the 'red-brick' university buildings of the industrial cities of the north of England.

While the college was still in the process of construction and hopes were still high that money would be forthcoming to complete them, and before the war had had its most disastrous effects on the building programme, the president in his report for 1916/17 claimed with much justification that 'the buildings, now so far advanced, are, in general opinion, such as to make a noble addition to the architecture of Dublin.' With regard to the cost, internal arrangements, structure and character of the buildings he felt that it would be difficult to surpass them and that they compared favourably 'with the best modern institutions.'

Dr Coffey's matter-of-fact, dull or businesslike presidential reports over the thirty years of his presidency rarely indulged in flights of literary charm. On this occasion he allowed himself a nod in this general direction.

> The growth of the College is a striking testimony to the part we are called upon to take in Irish University education. We all look forward with profound interest to the entry of the whole College into the beautiful building which will be its permanent home. We shall then begin to realise adequately the magnificent organisation which the College represents for the encouragement of learning and for the worthy development of our talented Irish youth. Not today nor in the immediate future can all of its possibilities come into view, but we shall, I think, have the conviction that the future of the College will not be unworthy of the great and generous sacrifices, made during two generations in the past, to which it owes its foundation.[14]

It would be an inaccuracy, based on what was later known to be the financial consequences of the prolonged world war, to suggest that this statement had in it something of the nature of whistling past the cemetery. The same report, however, more than hints that increasing costs and the ever-widening gap between resources and expenditure were beginning to cause anxiety. At the end of another disastrous year of war, hints of trouble ahead were no longer appropriate, and they were replaced with cries of urgency. The president was still claiming that many had said 'that our new buildings form a worthy addition to the noble buildings of Dublin.' They were rapidly approaching completion, according to the revised and restricted plan, and 'in a few months the College should be able to take possession of the whole.' He concluded:

> The application, as we have seen, was to no avail, and the College in Earlsfort Terrace was never to be finished. There it stood, new and impressive enough so far as it went, but incomplete; proud and ambitious but somewhat thwarted and maimed as it began its career. The front along Earlsfort Terrace and the North Wing looking towards Stephen's Green presented a façade of clean limestone and stout columns, concealing, however, the derelict Great Hall that lay behind the main entrance and the vacant spaces (except for temporary dumps) where the south wing and the back should have been completing the collegiate quadrangle ...[15]

However much it had been promising to do so in the early years, UCD in its unfinished state found itself unable to shed its 'temporary' rented premises in St Stephen's Green and Cecilia Street. Arising phoenix-like out of the ashes of the Royal University buildings in Earlsfort Terrace, UCD was unable to shake off the roots of its origins, which clung to it physically and infused into the new college the spirit of its Catholic University, Royal University and Jesuit college ancestry.

POLITICAL TROUBLES

Eight of the nine members of the Fry Commission had recommended in 1907 that a new college in Dublin, acceptable to Catholics, be established and endowed. S. B. Kelleher FTCD alone dissented: he wrote that the establishment of a college for Catholics must result in 'grave danger, at no distant date, to the peace of the country.'[16] This appeared to have in it the germ of prophecy in the revolutionary circumstances that meantime had arisen. Between 1909 and 1916 most of the staff and students of the college, like the majority in Ireland, supported no more than the constitutional objective of Home Rule. At the Home Rule demonstration of 31 March 1912 members of the Governing Body, professors and students spoke from the 'University platform', proving, as the *National Student* claimed, that University College 'was really part of the national life' and that nothing that concerned Ireland's affairs was alien to its sympathy.[17]

There was an atmosphere of anticipation, in which students expected to be called upon to play a leading part in the moulding of the new state. The *National Student* commented that the Law School swarmed with students who 'are expected by their parents to become lawyers, and by themselves to become cabinet ministers.'[18] The witticism could not hide the seriousness of purpose in that journal's editorials. Militant opposition to Home Rule and the formation of the Ulster Volunteer Force in 1913 led to the creation of the Irish Volunteers following an article, 'The north began', in *An Claidheamh Soluis* (1 November 1913), by Professor Eoin MacNeill. The Irish Volunteers were formed at a public meeting in the Rotunda attended by thousands and presided over by the UCD professor.

A newspaper report claimed that 'a large body of students — 350 of them — marched to the meeting in processional order from the National University and attracted a good deal of attention.'[19] If this report was not an exaggeration it was a remarkable show of solidarity, given that it represented half the total of male students, 690, then registered as students of the college. The *National Student,* indeed, agreeing with the figure, claimed that it was practically every male student not restricted by special circumstances (clerical students, for example, were confined to their seminaries).[20] In an editorial, 'Arms and the man', the students' journal welcomed the formation of the Volunteers, saw the movement as deepening 'our ideas of nationality', recognised the armed man as standing at the base of citizenship, and asserted that the discipline of arms was the resource of every people and every freeman 'when its and his rights and liberties are threatened.'[21]

The immediate outcome fell short of the promise. A company of 'about forty members' was formed in the college, but it had a short life.

UCD AND THE GREAT WAR

On the outbreak of the First World War, John Redmond had called on the Volunteers to join 'wherever the firing-line extends, in defence of right, of freedom and of religion.' In the split that ensued between Redmond and MacNeill, the majority supported Redmond. The college company disbanded; those who stayed with MacNeill joined their local companies, but in all 'less than two dozen students and about half a dozen junior members of the academic staff supported the Volunteers led by MacNeill.'[22]

The college authorities and almost all the senior staff were Home Rulers who were grateful to Redmond, Dillon and the Irish Party for the Irish Universities Act. It was not surprising, therefore, that the college generally was prepared to assist in the war effort. A scheme was recommended by the Academic Council for the establishment in the college of an Officers' Training Corps and the appointment of a Military Education Committee, consisting of the president, the registrar, the deans, and five professors. This scheme was approved and adopted by the Governing Body.[23]

In his correspondence with Major-General Friend, officer in command of troops in Ireland, Dr Coffey pointed out that, excluding women and ecclesiastical students, the available body was about five hundred, half of whom were medicals; that large halls were available in the college for drilling, and one for miniature rifle practice; that the athletic grounds at Terenure consisted of eighteen acres and a good pavilion; that some staff and students were already receiving elementary training in other contingents; that from inquiries already made more than 120 students were prepared to join the Officers' Training Corps if established; and that well-balanced units of infantry, engineering and medicals could be provided. In reply, the Irish Command requested from the president the names and qualifications of the men who might be recommended for commissions if the corps were established. Among others, the president recommended Professors Edward McLaughlin (anatomy), Bayley Butler (botany), and Pierce Purcell (engineering). The War Office, however, informed Friend that the UCD proposal could not be sanctioned, because the review of the Officers' Training Corps had been postponed for the duration of the war.

When the new Lord Lieutenant, Lord Wimborne, was appointed in 1915 a special meeting of the Governing Body unanimously passed a resolution to present him with an address of welcome. It declared:

> In union with the spirit which has animated the universities of the Empire, many members of the College, graduates and students, have volunteered for active service. Their devotion will always entitle them to an honoured place in the records of the College ...[24]

The first of the professors to be granted leave of absence was Tom Kettle (national economics). This was granted on terms similar to those for other universities in Ireland and Britain.[25] Professor Oldham (commerce) was appointed to act as temporary professor of national economics and to be paid one guinea (£1.05) per lecture and £10 for examination work, these fees to be deducted from Professor Kettle's salary.[26] Professor Bayley Butler, Professor Collingwood (physiology) and Dr Crofton of the Medical School were given leave of absence to accept temporary commissions in the Royal Army Medical Corps.[27]

The professorial staff was affected in other ways also by the war. Interviews arranged for six candidates for the vacant chair of French had to be postponed, because it was considered impractical to interview the best of these, who were of French birth. Mary K. Ryan, an assistant, was appointed to act as temporary professor.

Rev. Professor Henry Bewerunge had been appointed to the chair of music in February 1914. After the outbreak of the war the president reported to the Governing Body that the professor was unable to return to Ireland, and temporary arrangements had to be made for the carrying out of his duties.[28] When he had not returned by February 1915 it was decided to refer to the law officers of the Crown whether Bewerunge was still a professor of the college, having regard to his position as a German subject. As a result of the legal opinion obtained the Governing Body passed a resolution that, Professor Bewerunge having failed to discharge his duties since July 1914, and the Governing Body having had no communication from him, his chair was vacant.[29]

The support that recruitment and the war effort received from the college authorities and from most of the senior staff was given in the genuine belief that it was in the best interests of Ireland. This support from a nationalist UCD was very different in kind from that which emanated from a unionist TCD, where the emphasis was on the interests of the United Kingdom and the Empire. There was also that minority among the staff of UCD, represented by Professor Eoin MacNeill and Thomas MacDonagh, an assistant in English and big in the councils of MacNeill's Volunteers, that the place of the Volunteers was in Ireland and not in France. Nor did the official stance of the college authorities and the senior staff percolate all the way down to the students. The editorials in the *National Student* show that the young intellectuals who ran that journal were more of MacNeill's and MacDonagh's way of thinking. And they were quick to point out the fundamental differences between UCD and Trinity students in their different attitudes to the war.

The *National Student* understood that there were about a thousand men on the books of Trinity College and that already by November 1914 between three and four hundred had joined the British army and a large number of others had applied for commissions. The total number available for military service in UCD was under 550; the number that had joined the British army by November was anywhere between fifty and a hundred. The *National Student* drew the conclusion that the essential difference between the attitude of Trinity and UCD students was that the Trinity man who did not make some attempt to go to war must have some reason preventing him, whereas with UCD the men who had gone were exceptional. The journal expressed its opposition to further recruitment, on the grounds that 'Ireland has already paid more that she can afford to lose, unless she will invite her own destruction.'[30]

It was claimed that by the end of 1916 about 450 members of UCD staff, graduates and students had volunteered.[31] Nearly 870 students left Trinity to join the forces; the number of students fell from over 1,250 in 1914 to scarcely over 700 in the last year or two of the war.[32] This is understandable, especially given the number of students in Trinity from Britain. By comparison, the number of men students alone in UCD increased from 726 in 1914 to 886 in 1918 and to 1,051 in 1919.

The British authorities were not satisfied with UCD's efforts; and Sir

Matthew Nathan, the Under-Secretary for Ireland, complained to Dr Coffey in November 1915 about the anti-enlistment propaganda in the college. If for no other reason, Coffey had to remember that it was the government that provided the building fund and the annual endowment. He told Nathan that he did not believe the anti-recruitment campaign would influence many, since the present generation of students happened to be 'very lethargic'. Nevertheless he would endeavour to counteract the propaganda by speaking in the first instance to the chaplains who visited the students in their lodgings. Nathan enquired especially about MacNeill and MacDonagh and the leading part they were playing in the Irish Volunteers. According to Nathan's memorandum of the interview, Dr Coffey 'referred as usual to Professor MacNeill as being full of chimeras and an unpractical man. Professor MacDonagh was the more dangerous of the two. He would try to make an opportunity of talking with them.'[33]

While resistance to recruitment was becoming more vocal in the country generally as the war progressed, the college authorities continued to lend their official support to the British war effort. There had been, of course, much sympathy for 'little Belgium', which had fallen to the Germans early in the war. Convocation of the NUI resolved that facilities be offered by the university to the students of Louvain and other Belgian universities whose studies had been interrupted by the war, and that if possible temporary posts be offered to some of Louvain's professors. Responding to this, the Academic Council recommended that Belgian students in Dublin be permitted to attend courses in UCD without payment of fees, and if such students were in a position to do tutorial work they should be given the opportunity of doing so. Travelling expenses from Paris to Dublin, as well as a fee, were also to be paid to a Louvain professor of French literature to deliver a course of lectures during Trinity term, 1915.[34]

The provision of courses for wounded officers, requested by the government, was sanctioned.[35] Arrangements were also made at the end of the war, at the request of the commander in chief in Ireland, for an Army Education Scheme, whereby about fifty military personnel would be given courses in science subjects and for whom the army would pay the fees. By this time, however, there was a voice on the Governing Body registering dissent— Father Tim Corcoran.[36]

The commanding officer of the US Army students in British universities thanked the college on behalf of the Americans who had attended courses at the end of the war in UCD.[37]

Like all other institutions, UCD suffered its share of war casualties. The college was particularly saddened by the death of Professor T. M. Kettle, killed in action on 9 September 1916, 'whose eminent ability and public services were at once a distinction to the College of which he was a beloved member, and to the Irish Nation of which he was a most faithful son.'[38] In his report for 1917/18 the president wrote: 'The College will I have no doubt, give suitable permanent expression to its appreciation of the memory of those who had made the great sacrifice. I hope that a place may be found in our new buildings for a memorial to those who, as we knew them, had the promise of high careers and included not a few of exceptional distinction. They are all gallant, good, true-hearted Irishmen.'[39]

UCD AND THE 1916 RISING

If the new building in Earlsfort Terrace was not to have its 1914–18 war memorial, the explanation is to be found in the events of Easter week, 1916, and its aftermath. UCD, like everywhere else, was taken unawares by the Rising, though some of its staff and students were deeply involved. Thomas MacDonagh, one of the signatories of the Proclamation of the Republic and the officer in charge of the occupation of Jacob's factory, was executed for his part in the insurrection. MacNeill, Chief of Staff of the Irish Volunteers, who had countermanded the general mobilisation on Easter Sunday but had lost control over those who marched out on Monday, was arrested, court-martialled, found guilty of inciting to rebellion, and sentenced to penal servitude for life.

A number of the junior staff and students participated in the Rising in one way or another. These included Michael Hayes (French), who served under MacDonagh in Jacob's; Liam Ó Briain (French), who joined with the Citizen Army in St Stephen's Green and the College of Surgeons; Louise Gavan Duffy (education), a founder-member of Cumann na mBan, who was in the GPO during Easter Week; James Ryan (a fifth-year medical student), who was in charge of the temporary hospital inside the GPO; and Joseph Sweeney (an engineering student), who was also in the GPO.[40]

Following the suppression of the Rising, the Chief Secretary, Birrell, in his letter of resignation informed the Prime Minister, Asquith: 'A great band of prisoners has been made today, and I hear that some of the instigators and inspirers of this mad revolt are taken. A great many *young* fools from the National *University!* are amongst them.' The underlining of 'University', followed by the exclamation mark, revealed the deep irony of the predicament in which Birrell found himself. He whose hard work and tactful negotiations had bestowed the great blessing of the National University on Ireland had been brought down by the youth of that university and had seen his ambition of being the last Chief Secretary of Ireland in ruins like the GPO.

That there were 'a great many' from University College was, however, an exaggeration. Of course he probably included among the 'instigators and inspirers' the commander in chief, Pearse, whose associations with the Jesuit college as a part-time lecturer and with the Cumann Gaelach of the new college as a guest speaker had been close. Pearse had lectured for a short period about 1908 on the literature of the Fianna to a small class, which included Michael Hayes and Liam Ó Briain. Other UCD people, such as Joseph Sweeney, had been to his school, St Enda's, and Louise Gavan Duffy had taught in his school for girls, Scoil Íde. Besides the commander in chief, two other commanding officers had strong UCD connections, MacDonagh and de Valera—a former postgraduate student.

Whatever the strength of UCD's involvement in the Rising, it was an embarrassment for the college authorities. In the president's report for that year there was scant reference to what a later author called *Six Days to Shake an Empire*.[41] Sandwiched between a reference to the 'highly important' work of completing the pension scheme and a long account of the college war list arising out of 'the convulsions of the Great War, in which the interests of Ireland and the Empire are so much involved' and in which not fewer than 450 past and present students had enlisted 'for noble service,' was the single sentence: 'There occurred during the session the sad and tragic events of the rebellion in Dublin.'[42]

One source of embarrassment was the legal position of Professor MacNeill. In accordance with the Irish Universities Act, all the professorships and statutory lectureships were to become vacant from 31 October 1916, seven years after the dissolution of the Royal University. In what was largely a matter of routine, it had been announced that retiring professors and lecturers would be eligible for reappointment. When the Governing Body met to consider the reappointments, MacNeill was on trial, and it was decided to postpone consideration of his chair of early (including mediaeval) Irish history. It was also decided to take legal opinion on the question of the payment of salary to members of the staff under arrest. At the next meeting of the Governing Body the president reported the opinion of counsel, which was that under the Forfeiture Act (1870) MacNeill's office was to be treated as vacant, and that no salary was payable from the date of his conviction, 23 May 1916. It was arranged that Professor Macalister (archaeology) and Professor Hayden (modern Irish history) would between them lecture on the course formerly given by MacNeill. The remuneration that MacNeill's two colleagues received for undertaking his lectures they offered to share with his wife, but, though touched by their kindness, she did not accept the offer.

After his release in June 1917, and since all civil disabilities ceased to operate against him, MacNeill applied for reappointment. The Governing Body in November 1917 decided to postpone advertising the vacancy for three months. The *National Student* believed that the decision to postpone was made for political reasons and in the hope that the Irish Convention, then meeting, would solve the problem of Anglo-Irish relations. The postponement was lambasted in a well-written editorial.[43] MacNeill—the only applicant—was formally recommended for reappointment 'without further delay of any kind' with the unanimous support of the Faculties of

Arts and Celtic Studies. The report from these faculties quoted the testimony of Osborn Bergin, who said of one publication by MacNeill that it was 'the finest example ever published of an exhaustive and critical study of one of the sources of Irish history.' Robin Flower of University College, London, was quoted as describing MacNeill as 'the most original and stimulating of living Irish scholars.' The Academic Council also unanimously recommended MacNeill. The county councils of Cork and Tipperary (North) also wrote to the Governing Body advocating MacNeill's appointment.

One member of the Governing Body, Charles O'Connor, Master of the Rolls, still saw legal problems with the payment of MacNeill's salary until this was cleared up for him by Dublin Castle. Eventually MacNeill was reappointed in December 1918, the appointment to date retrospectively to May of that year.[44]

In what she called that 'cold and bitter autumn of 1916,' Kate O'Brien came up to University College as a student. She wrote: 'The world was deep in miserable war, and Dublin itself a bleeding, smoking theatre of tragedy, was to bleed much yet awhile with the rest of Ireland.'[45] And she realised that 'the deaths and mad faith of a handful' were deeply affecting the political mood of the country. 'University College was involved, impassioned; and in the ensuing years of violence it is probable that most of its students and many of its younger teachers felt themselves as closely united with the proclamation of Easter Monday as did the hundred or so lonely men who had heard it read in the Post Office.'[46] She was aware that among her friends in college there were some who 'held their lives ready for Ireland at all hours.' Nor did she think that 'the groves of Arcady or Academe would half as well have suited our collective temperament as did ruined Dublin.'[47]

The college, like the country, was experiencing a swing of mood in favour of the 1916 men. The *National Student,* which before the Rising had boasted of its Home Rule politics and disclaimed any separatist views, now carried criticisms of Redmond and tributes to the 1916 martyrs. 'Some memories of Thomas MacDonagh', written by 'D.R.' (Desmond Ryan), appeared in December 1917. The same writer had an article in praise of 'The man called Pearse' in the June 1917 number. A review article dealing with *The Story of a Success* by Patrick Pearse and edited by Desmond Ryan pointed out that Pearse was a graduate of the old Royal University, and Desmond Ryan a recent graduate of UCD. The review by 'E.' (Eimar O'Duffy?) concluded that 'one could do no better than to steep oneself in the ideals of Pearse.'[48] By December 1918 the *National Student* was discussing the 'advantages which will accrue to the University from the establishment of an Irish Republic.'[49]

That the college, like the majority of voters, had swung its allegiance to

Sinn Féin and away from the Home Rulers of the Irish Party was shown in the 1918 general election.

THE 'TROUBLES' AND CIVIL WAR

In the National University of Ireland constituency, Professor MacNeill, standing for Sinn Féin, received 1,644 votes, twice the number cast for the Registrar of UCD, Professor Arthur Conway, standing for Redmond's Irish Party, who polled 813 votes. The writing was on the wall. A group of speakers from the L&H, at the request of Min Ryan,[50] acting on behalf of Sinn Féin's director of elections, went electioneering for de Valera in East Mayo, where he defeated John Dillon, again by almost two to one.

Only two months before the Easter Rising, Kevin O'Higgins, then a law student, had proposed in a speech of great intensity at the L&H 'that constitutional agitation has been a failure in Ireland.' In the election of 1918 he too, as the Sinn Féin candidate for Queen's County (now Laois), had received twice the number of votes of his Irish Party opponent. Other victorious Sinn Féin candidates with UCD connections included Richard Mulcahy (Clontarf), Joseph Sweeney (Donegal West), Pat McCartan (King's County, now Offaly), and James Ryan (Wexford)—the list does not pretend to be comprehensive.

Soon after the establishment of Dáil Éireann in January 1919, the 'Troubles' or Anglo-Irish war involved the country in turmoil. Over the next couple of years, until the Truce in July 1921, 86 St Stephen's Green and Earlsfort Terrace were on a number of occasions raided and searched by British forces, while staff and students were jailed or 'on the run'. After his involvement in the Rising, Richard Mulcahy became a medical student in 1917 and Chief of Staff of the Volunteers in 1918. All through the worst phases of the war he operated from an office in the Chemistry corridor of Earlsfort Terrace—a fact that was known to students and porters and to Hugh Ryan, the professor of chemistry, but not, apparently, to British intelligence.[51] An article in the *National Student* of March 1919 called on the students and the SRC to defy the forces of West Britonism in the university.[52] This was regarded as an 'open manifesto of rebellion.'[53] The SRC co-opted 'a representative of the IRA from each Faculty.'[54]

Kevin Barry, an eighteen-year-old medical student, was captured after he had taken part in an ambush in Dublin in which a young soldier was killed, and he was hanged on 1 November 1920. His execution—the first since May 1916—had a profound effect, nowhere more than among his fellow-students. Celia Shaw wrote in her diary that terrible stories were current about how he was 'being tortured in Mountjoy to make him reveal the names of his companions.' She continued: 'I never experienced anything like the surging fury which the news produced in everyone.' They all went to Mountjoy on the day before the execution, where they knelt and prayed. A priest brought out Barry's last message to the students—'an exhortation to fight for the cause for which he was dying.'[55] 'No country ever mourned or mourned more deeply, even in times apparently dedicated to death and mourning,' wrote another contemporary.[56] And another student claimed that Kevin Barry's execution did more than any other event 'towards influencing students in the direction of the republican idea' and produced 'a wave of intense anti-English feeling.'[57]

On the day after the execution the college was raided and searched. A 'Sinn Féin flag' was flying at half mast over the building. On her way down from the Library, Celia Shaw and her companions were crowded into the Geological laboratory and threatened, and the men students were searched. 'They made Coffey deliver up the Register of the College and so they had all the names and addresses. I believe there was a great shuffling of digs that night. We heard Dick Mulcahy had been in the College that morning but we never could verify that.'[58]

The SRC produced a memoriam card, the Irish version of which was supplied by Douglas Hyde. A resolution of the Governing Body, proposed by MacNeill and seconded by Agnes O'Farrelly, sympathised with the Barry family and said that the Governing Body 'desires in union with the Irish nation, to express its appreciation of the courage and dignity with which Mr. Barry met his untimely death.'[59] At the same meeting MacNeill asked for an account of the raid by the military on the college the day after Kevin Barry's execution. The president reported that there had been no damage to property and that the military had acted courteously.

Later, in 1936, a stained-glass window in Kevin Barry's memory, the work of Richard J. King, was given a place of honour in the Council Chamber.

On 'Bloody Sunday', 21 November 1920, eleven British intelligence agents were killed by Collins's Squad. Later that day the Black and Tans in reprisal fired into a crowd in Croke Park, killing twelve and wounding sixty, and three Republican prisoners were shot in Dublin Castle. 'College life', wrote Celia Shaw, 'became unbearable.'[60] Students were charmed at 'the hair breadth escape of Dick Mulcahy' when Michael Hayes's house was raided. Students were afraid to speak openly; they were credibly informed that speeches made at the L&H were reported to the Castle; some were arrested in the street or at home; and they were warned about a person in the women's reading-room who was always seen with a newspaper but never joined in the conversation.

On the day of the funeral of the British officers, aeroplanes circled low over the city and dropped 'threatening notices'. Orders were given to all public establishments to close for a fixed time. When students turned up for their lectures they discovered a notice saying that the college would not be open that day. Dr Coffey was in London; an official letter had arrived from the Castle, and it was thought that it was the order to close.

Another student called it 'a reign of terror'.[61] The curfew, which in November was from 10 p.m., was extended in February and March 1921 from 9 p.m. to 5 a.m. It seriously restricted the life of the college. The Library closed at 5 p.m.

In the troubled years between 1914 and 1924 no inaugurals of the L&H were held. Yet, as Celia Shaw recorded, 'the L&H drags apace to the sound of bombing and firing.'[62] Reporting another raid in February 1921, she wrote:

> We were [seated] at Pol. Econ. [political economy] listening to the boring lectures of Fr. Finlay, I thought I heard lorries outside but wasn't quite sure whether they stopped or not. Two minutes later we heard the clanking of armed men on the stone corridor. The door was opened and an insolent looking officer said without a word of apology 'keep your places for the present.' Till 1 o'clock we were kept in that appalling room and every place was thoroughly searched. We had two lady searchers in the room off Bacon's office, dreadful women they were.[63]

At the next meeting of the Governing Body, Professor Sigerson gave notice of a motion that the Governing Body 'protested against the unprovoked and repeated interruptions' and the personal searches, including searches of women professors and students by the ordinary female searchers of criminals, and appealed to all universities to support the solemn protest.[64] When this motion did not appear on the agenda of the next meeting, Cathal Brugha asked for the reason, and the president said that he was personally responsible. Brugha gave notice that he would propose the original Sigerson motion, and another motion to establish a sub-committee to examine the powers of the president so far as they related to procedures.

When after three months the sub-committee had not met, Patrick McGilligan asked for an explanation. The president said it was because of the pressure of work in preparing the college accounts, but it would report to the next meeting. Brugha withdrew the motion about the military raids. The sub-committee recommended a compromise to the effect that a motion given by any member of the Governing Body be taken, provided that it be within the powers and functions of the Governing Body, as defined in the Charter and Statutes. The propriety of any such motion was to be decided by a vote of the members.

It had all the ingredients of a good old row between incensed nationalists trying to clip the wings of a cautious president and a president who was trying to keep political tension out of meetings of the Governing Body at a critical and emotional time for the college.[65] In the meantime arrangements had to be made for lectures to be given by colleagues in the absence of jailed members of the teaching staff: MacNeill, Michael Hayes, and Eileen McGrane (later Eileen McCarvill). The new professor of French, Roger Chauviré, had been assisting the Paris office of Sinn Féin, under Seán T. O'Kelly's direction, with propagandist literature.[66] The execution of an engineering student, Frank Flood, for participation in an ambush was the occasion of a vote of sympathy at the Governing Body, similar in terms to that recorded for Kevin Barry.[67]

Even the students, however, had some realisation of the difficulties in which Dr Coffey and the college authorities found themselves. It was appreciated that the president had a 'prime responsibility' to prevent publicity for the students' actions or their views on current events provoking the British authorities into closing the college. A member of the L&H during those troubled years was later to testify that the situation had called for all the president's legendary gifts of compromise, and that in this respect it was Dr Coffey's 'finest hour'.[68] When the Truce was signed and a settlement of Anglo-Irish relations was being negotiated, one can sense Dr Coffey's relief in his report for 1920/21. 'We look forward with confidence to the new era about to open for our country and to that interest in Irish education which will aim at full and adequate achievement in all the activities of our national life.'[69]

Between 1909 and 1921 the Governing Body had adhered rigidly to its rule of confining the use of its grounds and buildings exclusively to the students of the college. Requests from several outside bodies had been refused. However, after the signing of the Treaty in December 1921, Dáil Éireann's request for the use of the Earlsfort Terrace building for the Treaty debates was granted. The significance of the event and the high drama of the occasion were scarcely captured in the minutes of the Governing Body, which made the concession:

> The president reported that he had granted the use of portion of the College buildings for the important meeting of Dáil Éireann now being held, and that he had instructed the servants in the College Lunch Room to provide tea for the members and officers of the Dáil. The action of the president was approved. It was decided to pay the women attendants in the lunch Room £2 each and the College porters £1 each for extra work in connection with these meetings.[70]

Oscar Wilde's cynic might say that this was UCD's contribution to the establishment of the Irish Free State.

How the students received the news of the Treaty was recorded by Celia Shaw.

> We heard tonight Ireland is a Free State and every English soldier is to be out of Ireland in six months — we cheered ... there is an oath though

subtly worded ... the irreconcilables say we're sold ... Dev's proclamation causes a panic ... Opinion pretty evenly divided ... Dev is making impassioned speeches but talking too much ... Dev seems to us illogical ... Mick [Collins] is talking too much, Harry Boland is malicious so is C. Brugha. Mary McSweeney took our breath away—the unbalanced feminine ... Cathal Brugha's speech disgusting, personal abuse is so weak for an argument.[71]

There were Treatyites and anti-Treatyites among students and staff, though the former, as in the rest of the country, were in the majority. Yet the Governing Body tried to maintain a balance, especially when civil war led to the death of individuals connected with the college. A vote of sympathy with the relatives of the republican Cathal Brugha, a former member of the Governing Body, proposed by Father Tim Corcoran and seconded by Professor Sigerson, was carried unanimously.[72] Celia Shaw wrote: 'Cathal Brugha dead ... he certainly did his best for Ireland ... it was a tremendous pity he was so bitter, and to think he met his death at the hands of Irishmen is awful.'[73]

From the start the *National Student* had proclaimed its nationalism and had issued strong comments on the political issues of the day. The split in nationalist ranks in the Civil War made it change its policy; an editorial in March 1923 explained why:

We have completely excluded politics from these columns. The fact that both the country and the College are so greatly divided in political thought renders it impossible to publish a Student on any but non-political lines ... In times of national stress a flippant periodical is a relief to the mind ...[74]

The First World War, the Rising, the Anglo-Irish War and the Civil War had exacted a heavy toll on the young college: in individuals who had been killed or whose studies were interrupted; in the buildings that had been left unfinished; in the financial resources that had been scarce and diverted elsewhere. Yet during this same turbulent decade, from 1914 to 1924, the college had experienced a remarkable expansion in numbers:

1909/10	530
1916/17	1,017
1923/24	1,232

Academic work had continued to flourish, and the foundations were laid with the students of that time for some notable achievements in the future: Dan Binchy and Myles Dillon in Celtic studies; Michael Tierney in classics; Aubrey Gwynn, Denis Gwynn and James Hogan in history; Kate O'Brien in literature; P. J. Nolan in physics; George O'Brien in economics. In the end there would be much pride in the significant role the college had played in the emergence of modern Ireland. Among the students who passed through the college in those troubled years many were to become household names in the new state: J. A. Costello, Kevin O'Higgins, Patrick Hogan, Patrick McGilligan, James Dillon, Seán MacBride, P. J. Little, Ernie O'Malley, Todd Andrews. In the first ranks of the civil service would be their college contemporaries: Joseph Brennan, J. J. McElligott (Finance); Thomas Coyne (Justice); and perhaps most prominently in the diplomatic service: Joseph Walsh, Dan Binchy, Leo McCauley, Michael Rynne, Joseph Hearne. Finally, though by no means exhaustively, the leading names in the judiciary of the new state read like a roll-call of the L&H of those years: Cahir Davitt, Dermot F. Gleeson, Cecil Lavery, Conor Maguire, John O'Byrne.

All in all, and despite the drawbacks of a troubled decade, it was a record of which any institution might have felt proud.

5

Expansion

The College of Science and Albert College

UCD graduates and staff involved in government were largely responsible for a major development in 1926, when the University Education (Agriculture and Dairy Science) Act transferred the Royal College of Science in Merrion Street and Albert Agricultural College in Glasnevin to UCD.

These nineteenth-century institutions had been established to promote technical instruction for teachers, engineers and others through improvements in agricultural and industrial practices. The two colleges worked closely together, especially in disciplines related to agriculture, on which they shared lectures and staff. On the establishment of the Irish Free State both became the responsibility of the Department of Agriculture. The concern of the Free State government for agricultural development would in any case have stimulated official interest in the role of these bodies; but the need for speedy decisions arose from the seizure of premises in the same complex as the College of Science to serve as government and departmental offices (the entire complex would become Government Buildings in the nineteen-eighties). Security during the Civil War required the evacuation of the college for a time, and Dr Coffey managed to find space for its activities in Newman House. Trinity College also offered refuge, no doubt sensing (like UCD) that new arrangements were likely to be made that would involve one or other university; but this invitation was not taken up.

On the logic that all educational institutions should come under the purview of the same department, the two technical colleges were committed to the care of the Department of Education by the Ministers and Secretaries Act (1924); and on the further logic that the duplication of technical training was wasteful and inefficient they were duly given to UCD by the Act of 1926 (with dairy science being hived off for the benefit of UCC after some defensive protests by the students and mutterings of discontent from Trinity).

The transfer had been effected largely through the work of Professor MacNeill, Minister for Education, and Patrick Hogan, Minister for Agriculture, assisted in the Dáil debates by John Marcus O'Sullivan (who succeeded MacNeill as minister in 1925), Patrick McGilligan and William Magennis—politicians all closely associated with UCD.

Objectively speaking, however, the move made much sense, given the commitment of the new university to utilitarian as well as liberal disciplines, not to mention the pressing accommodation and financial needs of UCD. The Merrion Street premises, to which the College of Science had returned, eased the accommodation problem, providing space and facilities for large segments of the Engineering and Science faculties. The merger also gave UCD a considerable number of additional staff: three professors from the College of Science (botany, pure and applied mathematics, and physical and electrical engineering) and two from Albert College (plant diseases and forestry), as well as lecturers and support staff. Their expertise made possible the expansion of the curriculum in the relevant faculties, and the creation of the entirely new Faculty of General Agriculture.

These practical matters were also to prove the catalyst for a remarkable academic controversy that in time would lead to tensions within the NUI and UCD alike touching the future site and status of the Dublin college.

ACQUIRING A SPORTS FIELD

It was nothing more than the need to find playing-fields for its students that led UCD to acquire its first piece of land on the Stillorgan Road, then virtual countryside south of Dublin. In that sense it could be said that the college followed the sports flag out to Belfield.

One of the drawbacks of a city-centre college was that its facilities for outdoor games were severely cramped. These restrictions the college in Earlsfort Terrace had inherited, like so much else, from the Jesuit college and the Medical School in Cecilia Street. Unlike Trinity, which had its own sports ground within the college, these two remnants of the Catholic University had to rely on rented grounds, which were often a good distance from the city.

The Medical School and UCD authorities resorted to a variety of stop-gap devices to meet the problem. At first they depended for facilities on the hospitality of various Dublin clubs. Early in the eighteen-eighties the college sub-let from Belvedere College its grounds near Milltown Park. In the nineties the Medical School rented a ground in Sandymount, which was also used by the college. In the early years of the twentieth century there was a return to the Milltown Park facilities, then known as the Cowper Road ground. Croydon Park in Fairview was rented from 1900 by the Medical School, and this was regarded as being better than anything previously held.

The Governing Body of the new UCD continued as tenants of Croydon

Park from November 1909 without entering into any new agreement with the landlord, Mr O'Byrne. The tenancy was from year to year, expiring on 31 March each year. Meanwhile the college had been unsuccessfully trying to buy its own athletic ground. In November 1912 the solicitor for the landlord informed the college that the premises at Croydon Park had been sold. In 1913 the Governing Body approved the lease of eighteen acres at Terenure, the property of Maurice Flood, for twenty-one years at £120 a year; and an estimate for a temporary pavilion and for preparing the various grounds was accepted.

Officially named University Park, Terenure, this became the base of the UCD sports clubs between 1913 and 1934. Despite several offers from UCD during this time, the landlord refused to sell the site; nevertheless an extensive development programme was undertaken in order to provide UCD with up-to-date sports facilities. Over a thousand pounds was expended in 1914 on the construction of a pavilion. And the money invested in the facilities seemed to have been worth while, judging from the successes that attended the UCD clubs. The Irish Inter-University Championships began in 1912, and 148 individual championships were awarded in the various track and field events between 1912 and 1931. Of these UCD won 72, with the University of Dublin its nearest rival with 42.[1]

The development of University Park continued throughout the twenties, and as late as 1932 permission had been granted to UCD's Rugby Club to rent an additional playing field at Terenure. However, in November 1931 the son of the original owner informed the college that he would not grant a renewal when the lease expired on 29 September 1934. The Governing Body, therefore, on the proposal of the president, decided on 21 November 1933 to appoint a Grounds Committee, with power to negotiate the purchase of suitable grounds. Prophetically, as it were, under this same item on the agenda—'Provision of athletic grounds'—it was also decided to submit to the government the needs of the college for additional buildings because of the increase in the number of students.

The Grounds Committee had completed its work within a mere four days. An extraordinary meeting of the Governing Body was held on 25 November 1933 'to consider and to authorise, if so decided, the purchase of Athletic Grounds.'

> The President stated that the Grounds committee had inspected various properties for sale in the neighbourhood of Dublin with a view to their suitability as possible athletic grounds for the College, and had recommended the acquisition of 'Belfield', on the Stillorgan Road, as the best of all the available sites in respect of the proximity to the city, extent of grounds, and general suitability for the purpose of playing

fields. This property contained a fine residence, walled gardens, with greenhouses, five grass tennis courts, and about 44 acres of fairly level land easily adaptable to the requirements of football and hurling grounds. The price asked for the property was £8,000.

The Governing Body resolved to buy Belfield and to open a special 'grounds account' with the National Bank that, as agreed with the bank, might be overdrawn by £11,000 for the purpose of buying and equipping Belfield. An agreement between the college authorities and Frieda Bernard for the purchase of Belfield was signed on 21 December 1933.

Belfield was the first of about a dozen neighbouring villas and estates on Stillorgan Road to be acquired by UCD, most of them between 1949 and 1958. They were gentlemen's residences of the late eighteenth and early nineteenth centuries. Belfield (originally Bellefield) had been completed in 1801 for Ambrose Moore. It was bought in the early nineteenth century by a member of the well-known banking and parliamentary family of La Touche; after the death of Peter Digges La Touche it was put up for sale in 1820.[2] During the rest of the nineteenth century it was owned by a legal family named Wallace.

Another legal family, named Lynch, owned Belfield between 1901 and 1933, when it was bought by UCD. John Patrick Lynch (1858–1920) was the second son of Stanislaus Lynch, a Chief Examiner of Titles in the Irish Land Commission. He was educated at Clongowes Wood, became head of the legal firm of O'Keeffe and Lynch, Cork and Dublin, consul for Bolivia, and commissioner for deeds for New York. His residence before he moved to Belfield was, by an odd coincidence, in Earlsfort Terrace—number 1. He married an American woman, Frieda Ottmann of New York, in 1896, and they had three daughters. He received a knighthood in 1911, and when he died in 1920 his widow inherited Belfield. She had apparently remarried by 1924 and, as Frieda Bernard, sold the property to UCD in 1933.

The second daughter of Lynch and his wife married Robert A. Maguire, who under the pen-name Michael Taaffe wrote his reminiscences of his early life as *Those Days Are Gone Away* (1959), in one chapter of which he describes life in Belfield. (The house is called Belrose in the book, and the names of Lynch, his wife and daughters are also thinly disguised.) He mentions the children playing in a field in which there was a holy well. Many years later, when the property had been sold to UCD, Maguire revisited Belfield and wrote: 'In the Holy Well field, its undulations ironed flat by engineering students, white posts of some athletic import sprouted. Over behind Dawson's lodge there were more white posts, thrusting upwards into the haze of autumn.'[3]

At a bus stop outside the college in the spring of 1971 'a strange old woman with a slightly posh accent' gave Dáithí Ó hÓgáin of the UCD

Department of Irish Folklore the following account of what is 'perhaps the only piece of collected folklore relating to the place.'

> The lord of Belfield had a daughter who was a beautiful girl with flowing blonde hair. She fell in love with an army officer who was stationed in Dublin at that time. They were engaged to be married, but duty called the officer away to war. He was years away and finally he wrote to her saying that he would be back in Dublin on an appointed day. A few days before the time came, however, one of her servants reported to her that her fiancé had been noticed lodging in the Shelbourne Hotel. She thought that he had arrived early so as to make a surprise appearance in Belfield and, thrilled by what she imagined was his kind intention, she herself determined to outdo him. She therefore went immediately to surprise him at the Shelbourne but to her great disappointment found him lodged there with a wife and young family. So great was her disconsolation that her health began to fail from that day onwards. Doctors failed to restore her, and she deteriorated until finally she died. Her ghost is still seen walking up and down the laneway at Belfield House crying aloud in her sorrow. She is the White Lady of Belfield.[4]

The work of the Grounds Committee resulted in what was arguably the most important purchase in UCD's history. There is no indication that anybody on the Governing Body then contemplated the possibility of transferring UCD to Belfield. However, the speed with which it was approved and agreed is an indication of how necessary and valuable the property was in the eyes of the college authorities. Given the fact that as early as 1910 a college committee had concluded that a site to the south of the city would be most suitable for UCD's development, and given the growing realisation that expansion would be necessary to meet the pressing demands of increasing student numbers, it is not improbable that some speculation about Belfield's worth for the future may have crossed some minds. Certainly in the years that followed, optimism and a sense of potential were to surround the Belfield site. And it is possibly not altogether without significance that present at the meeting of the Governing Body that made the decision to buy the property was Michael Tierney, who, from almost the beginning of his Presidency in the late nineteen-forties, was more than any other person determined to transfer UCD in its entirety to Belfield.

In the years immediately following the acquisition of Belfield, reconstruction, expenditure on specialist equipment and maintenance, together with alterations at Earlsfort Terrace, Merrion Street, St Stephen's Green and Glasnevin, accounted for much of the financial outlay of UCD. But the most significant physical developments were connected with Belfield itself. To meet the expense of the newly acquired grounds, the Governing Body decided on 19 July 1934 to increase the college fees from £2 7s to £3 8s. Five shillings of this was to be set aside for the purposes of a students' union building (a question that regularly recurred since 1909 and was still not satisfactorily solved ninety years later). This increase, the president later told the Governing Body (12 March 1935), was felt to be a hardship by students from religious houses, who were precluded in practice from using the athletic grounds, and it was decided to grant them a rebate of ten shillings.

By November 1935 it was estimated that a further comparatively large sum of £8,000 had been spent on the development of facilities at Belfield. (This included, in round figures, £3,000 for laying out the grounds, £3,000 for buildings—repairs, alterations, dining-rooms, toilets, etc.—and £2,000 for extras.) The professor of engineering (1909–1953), Pierce Purcell, drew up the plans for the sports grounds, and the professor of architecture, R. M. Butler, was associated with him. It was then decided to lay down five hard courts for tennis, at a further cost of £650. Part of the residuary estate of Professor Arthur Clery was devoted to the construction of these tennis courts. In his will Clery had already given a bequest of £1,400 to the Boat Club (Governing Body, 23 March 1934). The residuary estate of £1,906 was perhaps the most generous donation UCD had received from any former professor. Part of it was devoted to a memorial stone over Clery's grave in Dean's Grange cemetery; to a tablet to his memory in the boathouse at Islandbridge (now in Newman House); and to a special prize for the Law School. It was Professor Timothy Corcoran (like Clery, Father Corcoran gave active encouragement to the sports clubs of the college) who made the suggestion, adopted by the Governing Body on 31 March 1936, that since Clery had taken such interest in the Tennis Club it would only be appropriate to devote part of the inheritance to the new courts. They were in fact named in honour of Arthur Clery.

A committee was appointed to manage the house and grounds at Belfield; a steward who should live in the house was employed; and the maintenance of the valuable facilities continued to be a significant charge on the college's finances. The impact on UCD's already weakened financial position was immense; by October 1949 the capital cost of the athletic grounds was £20,344.

A CITY-CENTRE COLLEGE?

Denis Coffey's successor in the presidency (1940–47), Dr Arthur Conway, had inherited a growing financial crisis and the pressure of increasing student numbers. In 1929/30 there were 1,520 students in buildings that had to house 2,398 by 1939/40 and 3,362 by 1946/47. That his presidency also coincided with the Second World War added to the difficulties of embarking on any programme of much-needed physical expansion.

When in the spring of 1939 it became known that Lord Iveagh intended to dispose of Iveagh House (80 St Stephen's Green) and gardens, the college immediately became interested in the possibility of acquiring this very desirable property, which lay between its own houses in St Stephen's Green and the Earlsfort Terrace buildings. A deputation waited on the Taoiseach, Éamon de Valera, and put forward the need for new buildings. Among the points raised was the argument that the transfer of the Engineering and Science Departments from the College of Science in Merrion Street would free valuable space suitable for Government offices. After Lord Iveagh's house and gardens had been presented to the state, Dr Conway, within months of taking office, had conversations and correspondence with de Valera—his former pupil—about the uses that could be made of Lord Iveagh's gift.

In a letter to Conway, de Valera submitted certain proposals to be put before the Governing Body. (1) The Government would be prepared to make a grant to UCD for the building and equipment of a new Engineering or Science Building on a site at the Hatch Street side of the grounds acquired from Lord Iveagh; on the completion of the new building, the existing lease of the College of Science in Merrion Street would be terminated. (2) The Government would also be prepared to enter into an agreement for a lease to the college of the riding-school and covered court section of Lord Iveagh's property alongside the college in Earlsfort Terrace, reserving to the state a right of way for traffic to the rear of Iveagh House. (3) The Government would be prepared to make an arrangement by which the college would have the use of the grounds, other than the small enclosed garden at the rear of Iveagh House. It was understood, the Taoiseach's letter said, that the college authorities wished to be allowed a passage through the gardens from the premises at Earlsfort Terrace to 86 St Stephen's Green.[5]

It took until September 1941, however, for the legal formalities to be completed, when Iveagh Gardens was made over by licence by the Government for the use of UCD. This meant the acquisition of eight very valuable acres at the rear of both Earlsfort Terrace and St Stephen's Green, in return for which UCD agreed to certain conditions with regard to the maintenance of the property and also agreed to undertake certain alterations, including the rebuilding of a boundary wall and the removal of buildings then standing in the gardens of 82 and 83 St Stephen's Green, to facilitate the plans of the Department of Finance in the area.

It was estimated that the annual expenditure by UCD on the gardens, including rent, rates, and the wages of three men for maintenance, would amount to approximately £654. A brief formal opening of the gardens by the

Taoiseach was arranged for 6 October 1941.[6] The making available of Iveagh Gardens to UCD reopened the possibility of expansion in the area and of a solution to its ever-increasing accommodation problems and paved the way for what was to be the last serious attempt by the college to establish itself on its city-centre site.

Between December 1940 and November 1942 the question of new buildings for both Engineering and Science on the portion of the Iveagh Gardens along the Hatch Street side was discussed and examined, and block plans were prepared. A great amount of activity was engaged in, and much work went into memos and plans drawn up by the professors of architecture and engineering. Professor Butler (architecture) prepared the sketch plans for the removal of the Merrion Street departments to the site along Hatch Street. Other studies by Butler related to the possible building of a Library and School of Architecture on the site of the riding-school and a Medical School along Hatch Street. These plans were ultimately dropped, because the Hatch Street site was found to be inadequate for the purpose. In the autumn of 1942 confidential inquiries were also made about the possibility of acquiring either Crawford's Garage or other property, including the adjoining Church of St Matthias on the south side of Lower Hatch Street, or the laundry on the Harcourt Street corner. The price asked for the garage, however—£30,000— was considered too high, and the other property was not available. Butler had included these sites in one of his sketch plans, and the Town Planning Department had informed UCD that if the properties were acquired it would be possible to close Hatch Street as a public thoroughfare.

But the search continued, and the removal of the Engineering and Science Departments from Merrion Street was again contemplated by the Government in 1944; the Office of Public Works and the college had agreed on the amount of space to be vacated and replaced elsewhere. Before anything more was done about this proposal (which would recur until the Engineering School finally moved to Belfield in 1989), the conflicting accommodation interests of UCD and the civil service now also emerged in the area of the Iveagh Gardens.

In January 1945 the Department of Finance began to consider the possibility of building a department restaurant at the back of Iveagh House, where the tennis courts were. UCD, encouraged by de Valera's sympathy, had come to regard the whole area as a potential site for development. In May 1945 it was thought that if Iveagh Gardens (and the riding-school) were put at the disposal of the college for building instead of for 'pleasure grounds' only, as specified in the licence of transfer, it might be possible to use the extended Earlsfort Terrace site for all the buildings needed for the college's development.

A comprehensive survey of all possible sites in the Earlsfort Terrace area was made to see in what direction the college might be extended. Dr Conway wrote to the Taoiseach on 6 September expressing a hope that the tennis courts behind Iveagh House might be acquired for the building of a new School of Architecture—the facilities in the old Exhibition Building being considered hopelessly inadequate. The Office of Public Works responded with a request that a fifteen-year guarantee against a further extension of UCD's interests in the direction of Iveagh House be required from the college.[7] This emphasised the conflicting interests that would hamper every attempt to achieve a solution to UCD's accommodation problems through a major programme of development around Earlsfort Terrace.

Time passed. Further plans were drawn up by Professor Joseph Downes (architecture), further difficulties were encountered, and eventually it was decided that the School of Architecture could be placed in the gardens of numbers 83–86 St Stephen's Green, where earlier there had been old class-rooms. This was put before the archbishops, as trustees of the Catholic University of Ireland, and in March 1947 Dr John Charles McQuaid informed the president that they were prepared to grant the college a 100-year lease of the site for the purposes of a School of Architecture. Following this indication of continuing good will towards the college by the archbishops, the position that had been reached by April 1947 with regard to sites was as follows: (1) The college was allowed to build on Iveagh Gardens, subject to certain stipulations made by Lord Iveagh. (2) A building could be placed in the gardens of 82–86 St Stephen's Green. (3) It was understood that the college could occupy the site of the tennis court, subject to maintaining an access road to the stables.

It was felt that these sites would suffice to provide buildings for the college on the scale suggested in the Statutory Officers' Report of 1946.[8] As part of the hectic planning for the proposed new buildings, Professors Downes and Hogan (engineering) were sent to Switzerland, Denmark and Sweden to visit new university buildings.

Unfortunately, within a month of permission being given by the archbishops, the Office of Public Works raised new objections: a high building on the site 'might affect the amount of sunlight falling on, and possibly the privacy of, the garden allocated to the Department of External Affairs at the rear of Iveagh House.'[9] The plan with regard to Architecture was in effect abandoned. The construction by the Office of Public Works of a Civil Service Club in the area of the riding-school and tennis court made it impossible to house the projected new college on the Iveagh Gardens site.

Efforts were made to buy Mespil House and gardens in Mespil Road, a short distance from Earlsfort Terrace, for Engineering and Architecture, thereby relieving the pressure on the Earlsfort Terrace site. This fell through because a state body offered a better price.[10] Early in 1946 a two-acre site,

'The Laurels', in Peter's Place, between the railway and Harcourt Terrace, came on the market. Dr Conway went at once to seek the Taoiseach's permission to buy this property, and a general discussion on sites ensued, in which Professor Purcell took part.[11] When during this discussion it was made known that compulsory purchase powers, whether for Harcourt Terrace or for property around Iveagh Gardens, were not to be made available, it was realised that even a scattered central city site for UCD seemed to be no longer feasible. Despite de Valera's evident good will towards the college's building projects between 1940 and 1947, difficulties with the Office of Public Works and the Departments of Finance and External Affairs, and competition from state and private business interests for expensive property in the city, defeated UCD's best efforts to expand in the Earlsfort Terrace area. But it was not for want of trying on the part of UCD.

The assertion that UCD moved to Belfield because Archbishop McQuaid wished it to be safely distanced from the contamination of neighbouring Trinity College has no supporting evidence. On the contrary, if this had been his purpose he would hardly have granted permission for the projected Architecture buildings on the gardens of the Catholic University houses in St Stephen's Green.

Given all the successive frustrations, it was not to be wondered at that the college authorities began to despair of ever developing the city-centre college; nor was it any wonder that they began to think instead of a suburban site as the only solution to the increasingly acute accommodation problems.

LOOKING ELSEWHERE

Dr Conway presided over his last Governing Body meeting in June 1947 and retired on 2 October. Michael Tierney was appointed president from 30 October and took the chair at his first Governing Body meeting on 18 November. At that meeting a resolution was passed to affix the seal of the college to an agreement to buy from the trustees the Roebuck lands of the Little Sisters of the Poor (to be added to the Belfield sports grounds).

This was an augury of his presidency. Tierney would be intimately involved in UCD's fever of purchasing, involving a number of villas and a couple of hundred acres, in the neighbourhood of Belfield over the seventeen years of his presidency. Belfield and Tierney became almost synonymous. In his very decisive way he came to the conclusion that, after the unsuccessful efforts made between 1940 and 1947, any further attempt to house an expanding UCD at the Earlsfort Terrace site was not realistic. He then conceived the scheme of a new UCD on a suburban site; and he pursued this objective with all the skill and single-mindedness that he possessed in abundance. Only his hero, Newman, had taken up the 'struggle with fortune' with as much determination. Newman's vision of a university college of which the nation could be proud had eluded realisation for a century; it became Tierney's burning ambition to fulfil Newman's dream.

In his first week in office Tierney was briefed by Professor Michael Hogan of the Buildings Committee, who sent him (6 November 1947) a long memo that had been prepared in April. Hogan had discussed his memo with Professor Purcell and Professor Downes, who were in general agreement with its contents. It dealt with the history of the various discussions that had been held since the spring of 1939 and sketched out the points that would have to be considered when arranging the design and construction of the buildings on the proposed Earlsfort Terrace and Iveagh Gardens site, as still proposed in April 1947.

Tierney soon concluded that unless there was some change in Government policy that would allow for a better use of the Iveagh Gardens and Earlsfort Terrace site, the college must look elsewhere. But before he finally turned his eyes away from Earlsfort Terrace he was to experience for himself the frustrations of trying to acquire satisfactory sites in the vicinity.

It was arranged that the Taoiseach would meet a deputation from UCD led by Dr Tierney on 14 January 1948 regarding the possibility of the purchase by UCD of Mespil House and its five-and-a-half acres. At this meeting Tierney handed over a memo that outlined the attempts by the college to acquire this property.[12] It was felt that the site would accommodate the Merrion Street departments (Engineering and Science) and leave enough room for all the rest on the Earlsfort Terrace and Iveagh Gardens site. It claimed that in 1946, when Mespil House came on the market, the Department of Finance had agreed to the college expending £15,000 with a view to acquiring it, but this offer was refused. (It appears that Conway was prepared to pledge £5,000 of his own money to make up the deficit.)[13] The property was then bought for £18,000 by Irish Estates Ltd, a subsidiary of a company owned by Irish Assurance Company Ltd, which in turn was controlled by the state. Since Irish Estates Ltd had invested in the property with the intention of developing the site for building, UCD remained interested in the possibility of leasing a hostel for students there. Shortly after Tierney had become president it was rumoured that difficulties regarding the building programme had arisen for Irish Estates Ltd and that the company might consider disposing of the site, or some portion of it. It did not seem too late for the property to go to UCD. The house and grounds would seem to be both large enough and near enough to meet pretty fully, in addition to the Iveagh Gardens, all the college's requirements for a long time to come.

At the meeting de Valera said he would consider whether anything could be done to acquire Mespil House. Tierney also referred to Tullamaine Lodge, adjoining Mespil House, to the property of Wesley College in St Stephen's Green, and to Ardmore on Stillorgan Road, adjacent to Belfield, which had been acquired by the Department of Posts and Telegraphs and where the college would like to acquire about three-quarters of an acre.

In response to Tierney's inquiries the Taoiseach was informed that there was no truth in statements that Irish Estates Ltd had experienced difficulties in its plans for the development of the Mespil House site. The Office of Public Works also told him that Ardmore had been approved by the architects for the purposes of broadcasting studios. Having regard to the difficulty experienced in finding a suitable site, in view of the special characteristics required, the Office of Public Works could not recommend a diversion of Ardmore to any other purpose.

The Taoiseach then instructed the secretary of his department, Muiris Ó Muimhneacháin, to inform the President of UCD of the position of Mespil House, Tullamaine Lodge, and Ardmore. Ó Muimhneacháin's memo (26 January 1948) of this meeting reveals that Tierney was considering making a direct approach to Irish Estates Ltd but was not confident that it was likely to lead to any useful result. Only pressure from the Government would be effective. Then Tierney, in his forthright way, went on to complain bitterly that when there had seemed to be a chance of securing a suitable site, some Government department or state-sponsored organisation stepped in—as in Iveagh House, Mespil House and Ardmore. The college, he said, was tied 'hand and foot' by financial restrictions, which did not appear to apply to departments and state bodies. The existing college accommodation, particularly for the Schools of Architecture and Engineering, was a national disgrace.

He also referred to the site behind Iveagh House, which it was proposed to use for the purposes of a canteen for civil servants, and to the difficulties that had obstructed the plans for a School of Architecture at the rear of 86. The object of the college was to concentrate its buildings. If the difficulties about the Iveagh Gardens site had not arisen it would have become possible for UCD to vacate the College of Science buildings in Merrion Street, which would then be available for Government use. A canteen there would have been more convenient for civil servants. If the college proceeded with its building plans on the Iveagh Gardens site, as modified by difficulties put in its way by Government departments, there was the danger that in fifteen years' time they would find themselves as badly off as ever in the matter of accommodation.

This memo also reported that Tierney had asked for state assistance with regard to purchases in the Stillorgan Road area, and had urged that in view of the problems at Earlsfort Terrace 'some decision should be taken ... even if the removal of the entire College to another site should be involved.'[14]

It was understood that the President of UCD in this meeting with the secretary of the Government openly mooted the plan for a new site at

Stillorgan Road.[15] Tierney had now begun what was to be the long and persistent task of educating the Government and the public into acceptance of the Belfield project. From the outset of his presidency, Michael Tierney was the driving force behind all that followed.

A SUBURBAN UCD?

Though the importance of the role of the president can hardly be exaggerated, the decision to begin planning the move of UCD from the city centre was by no means taken by Michael Tierney in isolation. He was nudged forward and encouraged in this decision by some very influential people.

On 16 February 1948 Professor Downes sent a memo, headed 'Some notes on the present position', to the president and his colleagues, Professors Purcell and Hogan.[16] The professor of architecture began by saying that the position with regard to the proposed new buildings had reached the point where a broader view of the whole problem was called for. Despite earlier expectations, he said, circumstances had eventually made the Iveagh Gardens impossible as a site for a complete group of college buildings. For reasons of expediency and for the sake of keeping the college within the city, the policy had been adopted of saving as much as possible of the original Iveagh Gardens scheme and of spreading the remainder on isolated sites elsewhere. But having regard to very limited financial resources and statutory powers, the college might never acquire these sites. If it could be said that the extra sites would be available in the near future, the issue would be a simple one between a properly co-ordinated, decentralised college in the centre of the city and a fully centralised group of buildings on a suburban site. The 'wait-and-see' policy that had been pursued for some time would only leave the college falling between two stools.

Downes argued that UCD should definitely turn its attention to the possibility of transferring all college activities to some less central and less difficult site. In making this proposal he was not unaware of the advantages of a city-centre site. But from his own experience and from what he knew of the planning of university buildings, especially in Sweden, he thought that the advantages of moving to a non-central site, where all the work of the college could be concentrated, were not fully appreciated.

Downes then outlined for Tierney what he considered to be the advantages of the more open site of adequate dimensions, which would allow for liberal planning. With considerable logic, this rather 'quiet and unassuming man'[17] argued that architectural harmony in the grouping of buildings, landscaping and the planting of trees, and a sense of unity, could be more readily achieved on a larger suburban site, where the sports grounds could also be incorporated in the main scheme. Space would also be available for residential accommodation (Newman's ideas about the importance of residential colleges was bound to carry weight with Tierney), or at least there would be much less difficulty in acquiring nearby hostel sites than was the case with regard to the Earlsfort Terrace site. Under the present arrangements, students in certain faculties attended classes in various widely separated departments of the college: architectural students attended at Earlsfort Terrace, Merrion Street, and the College of Art in Kildare Street, and a good deal of time was lost in travelling. On a unified site the co-ordination of teaching facilities would be possible, and its advantages would merit a good deal of consideration. The cost of a suburban site, he pointed out, would be much less than the cost of providing the extra sites that would be required if UCD were to remain in the city. There was also the time element, which was becoming increasingly important. They had already seen how little could be achieved in the Earlsfort Terrace area over a number of years. Sites immediately outside the city were now obtainable—but in another ten years most of them would have been developed as residential areas.

Certain advantages of Earlsfort Terrace's central site might be admitted, but some of these, Downes felt, had been exaggerated. One point concerned distance. But if the new site were to be Belfield, the additional time for students living on the city's north side should not be more than ten minutes— less if special transport were available. Hostels too might reduce the numbers living a distance from the college. Another point raised dealt with the accessibility of the teaching hospitals. But this overlooked the fact that some at least would eventually be transferred to suburban sites: St Vincent's in a few years time would be at nearby Elm Park.

Finally, lest his views were thought to be based on theory rather than on practice, Downes argued that he had experienced for himself two technical institutes of university rank in Sweden, at Stockholm and Göteborg, both established in non-urban sites, which had permitted large-scale planning, which in turn had been based on current practice in North and South America. He added that the suggestion that UCD should be placed on one large suburban site was not new: everyone concerned with its building problem had considered it from time to time, but for the last year or two they had lost sight of its significance. His memo ended: 'Having regard to the position in which we now find ourselves, a position which I think may not unfairly be described as "drift", I submit that the whole position should now be seriously re-examined from every possible angle.'[18]

Ever-expanding student numbers, coupled with the increasing costs of acquiring suitable sites close to Earlsfort Terrace, also raised the issue of the provision of additional university hostels, precisely at the moment when Professor Downes was urging Tierney to consider the advantages of moving out of the city altogether. Traditionally, university hostels had been a matter for the religious orders and church authorities, and Michael Tierney had no intention of disturbing this arrangement.

Providing sites for student hostels had been a consideration in all UCD's negotiations with the Government over the possibility of acquiring suitable sites in Peter's Place or Mespil House in the last months of Conway's presidency and the early months of Tierney's. Shortly after his election, Tierney sought the advice of Archbishop McQuaid concerning the provision of university hostels. In reply, Dr McQuaid explained that the problem had engaged his attention for years, and particularly in the last two years (1946–48). Religious institutes were required by Canon law to obtain the archbishop's sanction for the siting of their hostels and invariably consulted him about the best position. Weeks earlier he had sanctioned the establishment of another such hostel for women students, and at least three other religious institutes were in communication with him about the building of other hostels for women students. He regretted that there was one aspect of this progress that was not so encouraging, and he was gravely hampered in giving them practical advice. The outlay in establishing a hostel was considerable, but he did not feel justified in sanctioning the purchase and equipment of a hostel in proximity to University College, since

> there seems no guarantee possible, up to the present moment, that University College will, or even can continue to exist in its present position. And in this context, may I recall the time spent by me on arranging for the site of a Faculty of Architecture, only to learn months afterwards that the project had been abandoned. I would then, with respect, suggest that it is impossible for me to treat with Religious Institutes, willing and able to establish hostels, in a definitive and satisfactory manner, until the problem of the extension of University College has been, once and for all, decided.

He went on to explain that for the moment he had asked one institute to desist from its purpose, 'in the fear that University College may be found to be so cramped in its actual position, as to necessitate a total transfer to an extra-city site.' He ended with the following carefully worded sentence, which must have strengthened Tierney's determination to move from Earlsfort Terrace, or removed any wavering doubts he might still have had about the advisability of the move: 'If then I may be allowed to give any advice, and you have several times invited me to state my opinion, I would respectfully suggest that the University authorities boldly face a definitive decision concerning the site of University College, in relation to its ultimate development.'[19] He renewed his assurance that he would use every endeavour to assist the president in providing proper residential accommodation for men and women students.

A short time later, on 6 November 1951, Tierney admitted to the

Governing Body that it was his discussion with the archbishop regarding the establishment of hostels under religious orders, and the considerations arising out of it, that 'finally convinced me that a move away from our present site was inevitable.' Belfield, where the college already possessed valuable property, and in whose vicinity there still seemed to be a good deal of undeveloped land available, 'almost suggested itself.'

THE MAKING OF A PRESIDENT, 1947

Michael Tierney had not been expected to become president. When Dr Conway retired in 1947 it was assumed by many that he would be succeeded by the registrar, without any contest, as Conway had succeeded Coffey. The registrar (1940–1952) was J. J. Nolan, professor of experimental physics (1920–1952), a highly respected physicist, secretary of the Royal Irish Academy (1923–1949) and later its president (1949–1952). It was said of him that he brought to the post of secretary of the academy 'great initiative and drive and was such an efficient secretary that his election to the office of president was for some years deliberately deferred.'[20]

There were those in UCD, like Monsignor P. J. Boylan, who privately expressed their opposition to Nolan as president; and there were others, like George O'Brien, who, although they supported Nolan, were gloomy at the prospect of his presidency, on the grounds that he was not an inspiring candidate, that his health was not good, and that Louis Roche (French) and Paddy Donovan (English) were pushing him and themselves too hard and might alienate voters.[21] Then the co-option in March 1947 of Roche and Donovan to the Governing Body, at the expense of Pierce Purcell and Paddy McGilligan, left Nolan beaming but others more apprehensive, especially when shortly afterwards Nolan made it known to George O'Brien (himself being talked about as a possible registrar) that he would push Roche for the registrarship.

Opposition to the idea of Roche—who had made powerful enemies—as registrar began to grow. Tierney, on behalf of John Marcus O'Sullivan, Jeremiah Hogan, Pierce Purcell and Aubrey Gwynn, told George O'Brien that they were not prepared to put up with both Nolan as president and Roche as registrar, with Donovan completing the triumvirate. They asked O'Brien to consider his candidacy for the registrarship. When O'Brien wanted it to be a full-time position they began to look elsewhere, and there was a rumour that Tierney would be put forward in opposition to Roche.

By the end of August it was confirmed that Senator H. L. Barniville, professor of surgery in the Mater Hospital, would stand for the presidency. He was regarded as a strong candidate and likely to do well when it came to the vote in the NUI Senate. It was now being said that Nolan had brought the contest on himself by letting it be understood that he wished Roche to succeed him in the registrarship. Nolan would have been accepted, if with murmurings, but few could stomach a Nolan-Roche regime. Nolan, it was thought, could still save the day if he were prepared to do a deal with Tierney over the registrarship and support either Tierney or O'Brien for that position. Paddy Donovan then wrote to Nolan to say that in view of Barniville's great kindnesses to him he had no option but to withdraw his support. The Barniville campaign was gathering momentum, but there was also strong opposition, on the grounds that as a surgeon working in the Mater he had less interest in the college and its buildings problem. And he was thought to be unwell, with eye trouble.

For the last couple of years of his seven years as president, Conway was seen to be inert and his term of office in many ways disappointing. With anxiety growing over the prospect of a Nolan-Roche regime or, alternatively, a Barniville presidency, some began to feel that what was badly needed was vigorous leadership, which they were unlikely to get from either Nolan or Barniville. A number of these academics now put their support behind Michael Tierney as the best prospect. Alfred O'Rahilly, President of UCC, was clearly well disposed towards Tierney, though six weeks before the Governing Body was to hold the election meeting, on 16 October, he admonished him: 'You are pretty late in the field.'[22]

In the meantime, during the last two weeks of September, George O'Brien and others who had given their support to Nolan were very confident, since, as they saw it, the old guard on the Governing Body was also committed to Nolan. However, early in October the Nolanites were talking about a crisis in the presidential position as a result of a change of opinion, they said, in the highest quarters. The crisis turned out to be caused not by the intervention of church or state but by something just as racy of the soil. That well-known political and academic family, the O'Malleys of Galway, were supposed to have canvassed heavily for Barniville, in the expectation, it was said, that a highly qualified O'Malley would succeed to the vacancy on the Mater staff. The family's connection with another well-known political family, the Ryans, would be used to wean the support of the county councillors on the Governing Body away from Nolan. A substantial showing in the Governing Body vote was thought to be all that was needed to give Barniville the edge in the Senate. Nolan's supporters were now wondering whether a word from de Valera would put the county councillors back where they belonged, since de Valera did not like interference in university matters by anyone but himself.[23]

When the Governing Body met on 16 October to record its members' preferences on the names to be forwarded to the Senate of the NUI, three people had intimated their wish to be considered. As there was no precedent for a contest in UCD for the filling of the office, the acting president, James N. Meenan, proposed, after consultation with Professor M. J. Ryan SC, that the Governing Body proceed as in the case of the appointment to a statutory office of professor or lecturer. This was agreed, and the candidates were proposed and seconded as follows:

— Professor J. J. Nolan: proposed by Professor George O'Brien (economics) and seconded by Professor Joseph Doyle (botany);
— Professor Michael Tierney: proposed by Professor Jeremiah Hogan (English) and seconded by John Marcus O'Sullivan (history);
— Professor H. L. Barniville: proposed by Professor Cormac Ó Cadhlaigh (Irish) and seconded by Patrick Donovan (English).

The result of the first or straw vote was:

Barniville	8
Nolan	14
Tierney	6

The result of the second vote was:

Barniville	9
Nolan	15
Tierney	4

Representations to the Senate were made accordingly.

Nolan's camp considered the result reasonably decisive but felt it could have been better, in view of Barniville's supposed strength in canvassing the Senate. As the critical date of the meeting of the Senate approached— 30 October—it was complained that Nolan was listening to Roche and not taking the advice of others, who were urging him to canvass the Senate also. These advisers began to feel that if elected he might not be responsive to his friends' advice.

With only four votes in his favour at the Governing Body, Tierney was in a weak position. A letter from Dr O'Donovan, professor of medicine in UCC, who was a member of the Senate, reminded Tierney of an attitude that was fairly widespread among the Senate members. O'Donovan wrote: 'In matters concerning the other colleges I have always felt that the Senate members should be guided by the decisions of the college concerned, and I will follow that practice here, since it seems to me the most equitable one.'[24]

Even among Tierney's friends on the Senate the tendency to accept the strong preference of a particular college prevailed. O'Rahilly wrote to Tierney: 'You must have been very disappointed at the result. Outsiders like myself are in an extremely awkward position. In general we do not like to butt in against any clear decision of a college. This courtesy is not always extended to us by the Dublin representatives at the Senate. Nevertheless I feel in a difficult position and I must talk to my colleagues.'[25]

Tierney certainly had his work cut out for him at the Senate, but he also had old and influential political allies at work for him in both Cork and Galway. James Hogan, professor of history in UCC, had been, with Tierney, a leading advocate of the corporate state in the nineteen-thirties and one of the foremost intellectuals in Fine Gael. Hogan wrote to his friend:

> I was very disappointed that you did not get a few more votes at the Governing Body, but was relieved at your confidence in the Senate. You can count absolutely on me and I think O'Rahilly and Harry Atkins [Registrar of UCC]. Both tell me they are voting for you. But this is between ourselves. The most terrific pressure has been brought to bear on us. From one side of my family I have been asked to vote for Barniville and from the other for Nolan ... I have not approached the other Cork Senators. It would be rather tricky, and I thought it better to leave it to O'Rahilly to exercise his influence discreetly. [26]

From Galway, Liam Ó Briain, professor of romance languages, wrote: 'At first sight undeniably, 4 votes makes a bad impression and you are now racing against a handicap. But what you said clears up a great deal.'[27] Apparently Tierney had made the point that none of the outsiders on the Governing Body—the county councillors, Lord Mayor, and Government nominees— had voted for him. So, despite the connections between prominent UCD academics and Fine Gael, the college's Governing Body did not vote for Tierney. It was hardly likely that Fianna Fáil councillors or Government nominees would have voted for someone so strongly Fine Gael as Tierney was. In approaching members of the Senate for their vote he was able to turn his poor showing at the Governing Body into something of a virtue. His four votes, he claimed, had come from academics only. He also pointed out that Nolan would have no-one from UCD to propose and second him at the Senate.

Liam Ó Briain showed Tierney's letter to Professor Mitchell, the Registrar of UCG, who had already told Nolan that a lot would depend on what UCD wanted and believed it was all over as a result of the Governing Body's endorsement of Nolan. By the time Ó Briain was finished with Mitchell, the Galway registrar was thinking differently. He decided to check on the number of academic members on the Governing Body and the number of 'medical courtesy votes'. Fifteen academics had voted; four of these voted for Tierney, leaving eleven academics, of whom two were medicals. Eleven academic votes were divided, therefore, between Nolan and Barniville. This kind of calculation gave Tierney a relatively more respectable support among UCD's academics, and the support of John Marcus O'Sullivan especially counted for much.

'I think in the end Mitchell will vote for you alright,' Ó Briain wrote reassuringly to Tierney.[28] He added that the President of UCG, Pádraig de

Brún, would be discreet and leave it to Professor Power (mathematics), also a UCG Senate member, to work on Mitchell. Ó Briain criticised Agnes O'Farrelly and Cormac Ó Cadhlaigh, both of UCD's Irish Department, for giving their votes to Barniville at the Governing Body meeting, since Tierney among the candidates had the greatest proficiency in Irish and the most interest in Irish scholarship, apart from being the son-in-law of Eoin MacNeill, founder of the Gaelic League. He put O'Farrelly's vote down to pure snobbery, and wondered whether Ó Cadhlaigh considered Barniville more orthodox Fine Gael than Tierney. Ó Briain in conclusion complimented Tierney: 'You are obviously still stout of heart and in the thick of the fray. I do hope you get it. Really these mathematicians are becoming like the alien house-buyers—grabbing everything.'[29] This was clearly a reference to the fact that the President of UCG, Pádraig de Brún (who had defeated Ó Briain for the presidency), the President of UCC, Alfred O'Rahilly, the Registrar of UCC, Henry St John Atkins, and the outgoing President of UCD, Arthur Conway, were all mathematicians, and the Registrars of UCG and UCD were both scientists.

The contest was not without its lighter moments. Rev. T. Fahy, professor of ancient classics in UCG, wrote to Tierney offering him certain bits of advice on the canvass and telling him that he would get the former President of UCG, Father Hynes (whom Tierney had been assured was in his camp), to make sure that a certain Galway member of the Senate turned up for the election meeting. The only problem was that Father Fahy put his letter addressed 'Dear Michael' into an envelope addressed to J. J. Nolan. Nolan had the grace to forward it to his rival with a covering note, which read: 'Dear Tierney, The enclosed arrived this morning addressed to me … It is quite possible that you have received its counterpart.'

At the Senate meeting on 30 October 1947 the result of the first vote was:

Barniville	9
Nolan	9
Tierney	11

It was then decided to take a vote as between Barniville and Nolan, the result of which was:

Barniville	18
Nolan	11

Apparently only two of Tierney's supporters voted for Nolan, and nine voted for Barniville. This was seen as a plan by Tierney's backers to get Nolan out of the race. The result of the final vote was:

Barniville	11
Tierney	18[30]

Again it would seem that only two of Nolan's original votes went to Barniville and seven went to the benefit of Tierney. Meenan wrote in his diary: 'So Pierce Purcell [a member of the Senate] who is the organiser has brought the outsider home on the rails.'[31]

There was a good deal of sympathy for Nolan, who it was felt might well have prayed to be saved from his friends. In general, however, the result was hailed in UCD as a victory for the academic side over the college politicians. In the stunned professors' room everybody was trying to calculate what the new regime would mean for themselves and for others. It was assumed, correctly, that Pierce Purcell and Jeremiah Hogan would become influential members of the 'kitchen cabinet'. Séamus Tierney would succeed to the vacant chair of Greek. And Robin Dudley Edwards got the reversion of the judging of the *Sunday Independent* crosswords, with its fee of £400–£500, from which Tierney had resigned.

The irrepressible Liam Ó Briain of Galway wrote: 'Whoopee! That was a famous victory! ... To tell you the truth I would have privately given three to one against you yesterday, in spite of your optimism. With your victory ... the nation is on the march again.' And he ended with a word of advice: 'Give up all that reactionary, whiggish old attitude of yours about teaching through Irish!'[32]

Myles Dillon, who affected a very poor opinion of his alma mater (which he once described to the author as 'the technical school around the corner'), wrote to his friend: 'I read with delight and some surprise of your election. There is hope for University College after all. I had thought your fitness for the position would have been enough to deprive you of the appointment.'[33]

Another friend, Michael Duignan, professor of archaeology in UCG, was shaving when his wife reported the newspaper account of Tierney's triumph. He claimed that he took the stairs three at a time and sent up such a cheer that it was still echoing in the neighbourhood. Tierney and his wife would introduce 'that warm humanity which has been lacking in the College for the whole of its forty years.' He was also pleased that Tierney had before him 'a term of office long enough to steer the College on to the right road at last. Your election will prove a turning point in the history of the College, and inevitably therefore in the country too.'[34]

Tierney was prepared to acknowledge that James Hogan of UCC had made a special contribution to his success. But Hogan put it down to the consensus that saw in Tierney the calibre of a president. Tierney must have appreciated in particular the comment in one letter of congratulation: 'I think the great Newman will be well pleased with his successor.' The same well-wisher recognised that the problems and responsibilities were, if anything, greater than 'when the great Cardinal embarked on his task of founding the University.'[35]

The election of 1947 was the first occasion on which there had been a contest for the presidency of UCD. The public interest in the result was amazing. Letters of congratulation poured in from all over the country, not only from fellow-academics, former colleagues and churchmen but also from people who might have been expected to be restrained in their enthusiasm. Mrs James Carty felt that he had the qualities to make an excellent president, despite the fact that he and she wore different coloured shirts since the split in 1922. A letter from the Registrar of Trinity College, Dr Kenneth Bailey, said: 'Your appointment gives particular pleasure to all who believe in friendly co-operation between T.C.D. and U.C.D., and you will always have a warm welcome here.' Many former pupils congratulated him. 'Boy, am I pleased!' wrote Dr Richard Hayes of the National Library.

Genuine hope was expressed by many of his numerous well-wishers that a new era had dawned for UCD. After forty years of an administration headed by a medical man and a scientist there was a sincere welcome for an arts man, a classicist, 'a man of culture' who was also well versed in Irish studies, history and education and who was widely respected for his writings. 'It is time', wrote one correspondent, 'the Faculty of Arts took that primacy it is entitled to in secular learning.' Mrs Walter Starkie felt that he was 'the only person who could bring back the scholarly tradition of the humanities to education here.' Other correspondents remarked on the versatility of his scholarly interests, his 'vision, energy and first-class ability—not to mention toleration of the other person's opinion.' One former student, Tom Donnelly, writing from the Law Library, said that his election pleased 'all of us who deplored the apathetic, yet increasingly "illiberal" drift of College policy,' and he described Tierney's appointment as 'the long-overdue triumph of dynamic liberalism in university education.'[36]

A more cautious and perspicacious comment was expressed by the shrewd James Meenan of the Economics Department, writing in his diary:

> T. may be a very good President. He will have a long run of 17 years. He has an academic mind and is interested in the College. He will be very sound on Irish. But I don't know that he is very good at handling students and I think he feels that their proper kind of life should be copied from a seminary. He is also quicker in action than in judgement. There may be trouble over things as a result. But he has moral courage—as was shown in the censorship debates—and a lot can be forgiven for that.[37]

A history of UCD can be written without naming chapters after the individual presidents who guided its development. If there is an exception to this it is for the seventeen years from 1947 to 1964, which might justly be described as the Tierney era. No other president had so forceful a personality; no other stamped his personality so clearly on his period of office. It was to become UCD's age of benevolent despotism—with some emphasising the benevolence and others the despotism, as they saw it.

In either case the excitement of the era was palpable. Student numbers more than doubled, the academic staff expanded, and new departments and specialisms were developed during his presidency. But the stirrings in the college also exploded into the public arena, with court cases, a visitation, criticisms in the press and in the Dáil and Seanad, and committees of inquiry. Inside and outside college there emerged pro-Tierney and anti-Tierney camps. Friends claimed that no president before him had improved administration or devolved government more than Tierney did; critics claimed that no other president had been so autocratic. No other president was ever so politically identifiable; none had so deep a scholarly involvement in areas outside his own specialism and in all of which he was a prolific and eloquent commentator; no President of UCD expressed himself more strongly in his opposition to Trinity College; no other president had so deep a sense of UCD's history and of its role in the development of Irish society.

Tierney was only a short time in office when he determined that UCD should move out to a suburban site worthy of the premier role the college had to play in Irish society, and by 1949 he had made the first of many purchases of estates on the Stillorgan Road at Mount Merrion for this purpose. The hugely ambitious plan would require for its realisation all the character, vision, energy and ability that were imputed to the new president.

But the robustness that was necessary in the interests of the Mount Merrion plan in his dealings with politicians and civil servants was quite excessive when applied to students. Already by 1949 Tierney had begun creating for himself those difficulties with students that would also be a feature of his regime. In January 1949 he had banned a proposed debate at the L&H.[38] This was only the first of the many rows he would have with the society and of the adverse public criticisms to which he would expose himself as a result. By November 1949 he would find himself involved in a wrangle with the Irish-language lobby. A quarrel had arisen out of a request to have entrance scholarship examination papers in all subjects set in Irish. In the course of the dispute Tierney had refused permission for the sale of the magazine *Comhar* in the main hall of the college. For the rest of his period in office he would find Irish-language enthusiasts among his severest critics. And while he was receiving it hot and heavy from this quarter he was simultaneously censoring the *National Student* in what was to be the first of many conflicts with the magazine.

THE SLANDER CASE

The incident that caused perhaps most public interest was the legal action for slander brought against the president by one of his students. Walter Kirkwood Hackett, a mature student of thirty-one, had served in the RAF during the Second World War and had been awarded the Distinguished Flying Cross. In his second-year architectural examination in June 1948 he had failed one subject (archaeology) and also failed the supplemental in autumn. The British Ministry of Education, from which he had a grant, was informed that he would not be allowed to proceed until he had completed the second-year requirements, and that the paying order received from the ministry was being held. The student requested the paying order, and a college clerk had mistakenly made over the draft (£124 6s 8d), out of which the student paid fees for the third-year course. When the mistake was discovered, the college requested the return of the paying order, but it had already been lodged in a bank. The student was summoned to an interview with the president, during which it was alleged that Tierney aggressively walked up and down and shouted, 'Don't you realise that you have obtained this cheque by false pretences?' The student sued Tierney for slander. Tierney denied any aggressive behaviour, denied speaking the words, and pleaded that if he did speak them it was on a legally privileged occasion.

The court action received a great deal of publicity in the press.[39] In the High Court Mr Justice Martin Maguire ruled that the occasion was privileged, and the question before the jury was whether the words alleged, if true, were spoken maliciously. His summing up seemed to favour Tierney's version; despite this, the jury found that the words complained of had been spoken maliciously, and judgment was given for £750 against Tierney, with costs.

Many were astounded at the jury's verdict. Within the college it was seen as a terrible slap in the face for the president. The jury had not believed him on his oath. It was felt that it was bound to weaken his position; that the college could become ungovernable; and that it would have a calamitous effect on the way the public would regard the management of UCD.

From friends and people unknown to him outside the college came several messages of support and sympathy. They expressed shock, horror, astonishment and indignation at the 'absurd', 'perverse' verdict, which was described as a travesty of justice. They approved of his attitude and assured him that their confidence in him had not been shaken. They regretted the agony of mind and the ordeal to which he had been submitted, the insults offered to him, and the 'nauseating' publicity. Clergy (including Archbishop Walsh of Tuam and Dr Dunne of Dublin), nuns, teachers and others involved in all levels of education or with responsibility for youth expressed a fellow-feeling with him and their sense of outrage and distress that he had been made suffer for a whole army of people endeavouring without fear or malice to exercise authority.

The critical issue for many of his correspondents was what they saw as this undermining of authority. The jury's verdict was regarded as an ominous declaration against legitimate authoritarianism. One said that people in authority now would need to be crooks to deal with the present generation and that the less a person did, the better he would be thanked. It was felt that in these 'ruthless, turbulent and standardless times' people in positions like that held by Tierney certainly had an unenviable task. Some wondered whether the world had begun to spin in the opposite direction when the President of UCD could be dragged into the courts over so trivial a matter. Others (including Alfred O'Rahilly) offered to assist him with any personal costs to which he might be liable.

Tierney was encouraged not to let the injustice divert him from the good work he was doing nor be deterred in his efforts to raise the whole standard of UCD. He also received some sound advice. Kevin O'Shiel of the Land Commission said that the president of so large a college with multitudinous important duties should have an officer of discipline to deal with such annoying and, on the whole, minor matters of student behaviour.

Though an appeal to the Supreme Court proved successful, the cost to the reputation of both president and college had been considerable. Legal costs had come to over two thousand pounds; but the damage done to the good name of the president could not be so easily calculated.

THE BANNED DEBATE ON THE COMMUNIST MANIFESTO

On Friday 14 January 1949 the registrar's office drew the attention of the president to a notice announcing an L&H debate to be held on the following day, Saturday 15 January, on the motion 'that the ideals of the Communist Manifesto are worthy of humanity.' Dr Owen Sheehy Skeffington of Trinity was to open the debate. Dr Tierney sent for the auditor, Patrick O'Kelly, and told him the motion could not be debated.[40]

According to the auditor, the president stated that under no circumstances was Dr Sheehy Skeffington to be permitted to speak to the society. When Sheehy Skeffington was informed of this he stated that he would if necessary make a statement in the public press. The president saw the auditor again the following day (Saturday) with Professor M. J. Ryan (law), who was the senior treasurer of the society. At this meeting the auditor informed the president of Dr Sheehy Skeffington's statement. The president reiterated his ban on Sheehy Skeffington and told the auditor that if the matter went to the press the society would suffer, and further that if this matter were raised during private business, or if the matter arranged for debate was discussed, the society would suffer.[41] He advised the auditor to hold instead an impromptu debate.

That evening at the L&H—with Dr Sheehy Skeffington present—the auditor gave an account of the interviews with Dr Tierney and defied the president's ruling by allowing discussion. A number of former auditors had been invited to the meeting. A stalwart of the society, William Kingston, introduced the motion 'that the L&H Society having always preserved the right of debate on all subjects whatever to its members, has never recognised any superior authority in the matter of selection of subjects for debate; and that therefore the members of the Society do approve and applaud the decision of the Auditor and Committee to debate publicly in the Society the motion "That the ideals of the Communist Manifesto are unworthy of Humanity".' The motion was seconded by another L&H stalwart, Séamus Sorohan. Apparently it was felt that one of the reasons for the president's objection to the motion was that in its original form it was too positive in relation to communism, hence the alteration in the wording from 'worthy' to 'unworthy'. This clever avoidance of the letter of the ruling was hardly likely to mollify the president.

Among recent ex-auditors who spoke for the motion were Kevin Burke, Frank Martin and Éamon Walsh. Two who had been defeated for the auditorship at different times, Niall McCarthy and Michael McDevitt, also spoke in favour, as did P. J. Connolly, shortly to be elected auditor. Many of these were later to become prominent in the legal profession.[42] Those who spoke against the motion included Desmond Fennell, the future journalist, and a former auditor, Vincent Grogan, later head of the Knights of St Columbanus. It was reported that another former auditor, Arthur Cox, the well-known solicitor, tendered his advice.

A vote on the motion, which might have resulted in an even more serious confrontation with the college authorities, was not taken. The reason for this was reported in the minutes:

> The entrance at this stage of the proceedings of Mr. Ulick O'Connor and his subsequent and customary disturbing influence together with his complete lack of regard for the seriousness of the occasion resulted in a statement made by the Auditor to the effect that Mr. O'Connor was suspended for the remainder of the session ... The Auditor continued by saying that the conduct of the majority of the Society towards Mr. O'Connor and their obvious and total lack of responsibility was felt by him to be sufficient reason for his withholding the vote on such a serious motion as he felt they were incompetent to judge the important issues in question.[43]

Under the heading 'Discussion banned by university', the *Irish Times* reported on 17 January that Dr Sheehy Skeffington, who was to have spoken in favour of the original motion on the Communist Manifesto, and the Earl of Wicklow, who was to have been the chairman, and other prominent persons attended for a debate that was not allowed to take place by order of the

President of UCD. Dr Tierney told the *Irish Times* that he could not discuss with the press the reasons that led him to inform the society that the meeting was not to be held, beyond saying that he had not authorised the subject for debate. Neither would he discuss whether the meeting was banned because of the subject. Dr Sheehy Skeffington said that he had first been told that he was banned as a speaker but that the meeting would go ahead; later he was told that the meeting was cancelled but that the students intended to hold it anyway, discuss the subject, and allow him to speak. C. J. Gore Grimes, secretary of the Irish Association for Civil Liberties, said he was surprised that the students were not permitted to discuss any particular subject inside the walls of the college and that he had attended the meeting because it appeared to him that the question of civil liberty was involved.

Over the next ten days or so the *Irish Times* published a spate of letters on the subject, fulfilling a function for which the paper had already become remarkable in intellectual and educated circles in providing a forum for a sometimes lengthy, informative and stimulating debate on a controversial issue. The first of the letters was from the novelist Kate O'Brien, who said she was embarrassed and shocked as a graduate of UCD by the news that the president had banned the debate. 'I protest against this arbitrary and unjustifiable gesture of intolerance. Firstly, the action in itself, the interference with the students' rights to have academic discussion, horrifies me. Secondly, it is appalling that a distinguished member of the staff of our sister university should be made to feel himself so definitely *persona non grata* in ours.'

This drew a predictable right-wing response. A correspondent who signed himself Seán Murphy could indeed have been any one of several hundred Catholic Actionists who were constantly on the alert in the face of the much-feared threat of post-war communism and 'the materialistic and secularistic civilisation that surrounds us.' For years, he pointed out, the church had been pouring out warnings and impressing on Catholics the urgency of the situation, so that no-one would be ignorant of the fact that atheistic communism was the greatest evil and danger to Christianity that had arisen for centuries and that with it there could be no compromise. UCD was by no means considered ideal but it was seen as a college for the education of Catholics, one in which the propagation of communism through student debating societies had no place.[44]

However, a greater number of correspondents represented the voice of a more liberal Catholicism. One of these was the Earl of Wicklow, who pleaded for a free discussion.[45] F. X. Rooney, an activist in the society since 1944 who had recently been called to the bar, asserted that until Michael Tierney assumed office the students of UCD were always permitted to discuss political questions, including communism, in their various societies without let or hindrance. Besides, the Communist Manifesto was a document that all students of legal and political science were recommended by their professor to study, and properly so, since an understanding of communism and its errors could only be obtained by a close examination of the philosophy of its founders.[46] The point that the Communist Manifesto was not unknown to students of legal and political science in UCD (and, he might have added, to history students also) was a timely one, for other correspondents made charges about 'the present lack of intellectual freedom' in the college and its transformation into 'an intellectual nursery'.

One notable feature of the controversy in the *Irish Times* was that all the correspondents—with the exception of Sheehy Skeffington—agreed with Michael Tierney that communism was the great enemy. The only argument among them was about the method of defeating it—whether by a free discussion or by blocking every opportunity communism might have of propagating itself.

Tierney's action in vetoing the debate had the blessing of contemporary right-wing elements among Catholics, which were probably more an embarrassment than a support to him. It was, after all, the era of such fringe Catholic activist organisations as Maria Duce, which put forward the claim that the state should formally recognise the Catholic Church as the one true church.[47] The one correspondent in the *Irish Times* who supported Tierney's action might well have been a Maria Duce member. He agreed that Catholic students should not be kept ignorant of communism and other errors but said that they should learn about them from Catholic teachers; spokesmen for communism should not be allowed to propagate its doctrines in UCD.[48] An adversary of Christianity should not be encouraged to argue his position: this was called 'dallying with temptation,' it led to casualties every day, and it was absolutely forbidden.

These arguments, though put forward by only a single correspondent in the newspaper controversy, help to place Tierney's vetoing of the debate in the context of Irish Catholic obsessions of the time. All correspondents—both those for and against Tierney's action—assumed that the reason for his banning the debate was his hostility towards communism and his determination to protect the Catholic students of his institution from its errors. It is at least as likely, however, that his objection was rather to the guest speaker than to the debate itself. Noel Browne has alleged that when Seán MacBride accused him in 1951 of having communist sympathies it was on the basis of a Special Branch file that listed meetings he had had with Sheehy Skeffington, who had earlier been expelled from the Labour Party for his liberal views.[49] Sheehy Skeffington was not merely an individual with strong left-wing views (though also anti-Stalinist) but, what some people would say was almost as bad in Tierney's eyes, was a lecturer in Trinity College. The attendance by Catholics at Trinity was being strongly condemned in these years in Archbishop McQuaid's Lenten pastorals. In the circumstances, for Tierney to allow Sheehy Skeffington, of all TCD teachers, to address Catholic students in UCD on the Communist Manifesto would have been seen as a direct insult to the archbishop.

This aspect of the situation in which Dr Tierney found himself, though overlooked or unstated by other correspondents, was not entirely lost on Sheehy Skeffington himself. Several of the letter-writers had pointed out that UCD was not specifically a Catholic institution but an interdenominational one, proclaimed by Archbishop McQuaid in his Lenten pastorals only as 'sufficiently safe' for Catholics to attend. With tongue in cheek, Sheehy Skeffington argued that recent events had now shown that the measures taken to keep UCD 'sufficiently safe' for Catholic students had not afforded enough protection. Lay supervisors, with the best will in the world, were not sufficiently vigilant: therefore it would be quite understandable if Professor Tierney, in accordance with the expressed views of the archbishop, were to resign to make way for a clerical president and the reorganisation of the system on which the college was now run, and to set right a state of affairs that had been frequently, expressly and publicly condemned by the church authorities.[50]

Not content with this sarcasm at the expense of both the President of UCD and the archbishop, Sheehy Skeffington extended his attack to the church generally. He asserted that the church and Stalinist Russia had the same attitude of mind: both held that free discussion of unorthodox or heretical ideas only weakened one's faith and must therefore be prevented. It was precisely this kind of fearless generalisation that Tierney as an individual and as president found offensive in the banned speaker.

While the debate still raged in the *Irish Times,* the auditor of the L&H had another interview with the president. According to the auditor's report to a meeting of the L&H, Tierney informed him that no subject could be discussed without the approval of the president; that no visiting chairman could be invited without the approval of the president; and that no former auditor or vice-president of the society could be invited to discuss any matter whatever without the approval of the president. As a result of these instructions, the auditor told the meeting that he did not intend to have any public debates unless they met with the approval of the president. Furthermore, he would not allow any discussion of the matter at that meeting.

At the next meeting of the Governing Body the president made a statement about the L&H affair and the recent newspaper publicity. He explained that there were long-standing rules that subjects for debate by college societies must be submitted to the president and that no outside speakers might be invited into the college without his prior sanction. He proposed, he said, to have these rules incorporated in the General Regulations for the next session. The Governing Body approved the action taken by the president.[51] The UCD Calendar in the years before Tierney became president had a section entitled 'General regulations for students of the college'. These eleven general regulations for 1946/47 now increased in number to eighteen for 1949/50, and the heading 'General regulations' was changed, significantly, to 'Discipline'. Under this new heading, regulation no. 14 (later numbered 13) was a direct result of the banned L&H debate on the Communist Manifesto. It reads: 'All social and other functions in the College are held by permission of the President and under such conditions as he may prescribe. No person not a member of the College may be invited to take part in or be present at any meeting of a College Society without the permission of the President.'

This Tierney regulation continued to be published in the UCD Calendar forty years later, though in the interval it has perhaps become a dead letter. It was very characteristic not only of its author but also of its time. It was accepted in 1949 demurely by students and Governing Body alike. Ten years later, in 1959/60, during another confrontation between the L&H and Dr Tierney, the students were noticeably more defiant and were talking about legal action against the president. Ten years later still, during the student revolt of 1969, the banning of a debate on the Communist Manifesto would have been inconceivable, so much had the ethos of the era of censorship and of authoritarian rule been transformed in Irish society generally.

TIERNEY AND NEWMAN

One of Michael Tierney's virtues was a vivid consciousness of Ireland's debt to Cardinal Newman; but the perception of his own role as successor to Newman was to lead him into bitter controversy with academic colleagues.

The transfer of the College of Science and Albert Agricultural College to UCD in 1926 had given a strong boost to the utilitarian aspects of the college's mission. Shortly after the transfer a philosophical rationale for this strengthened utilitarianism was supplied by Father Tim Corcoran SJ, the professor of education. Corcoran's book *Newman's Theory of Education* (1929), 'printed for academic use in the Department of Education, University College, Dublin,' advocated the utilitarian, technical and professional aspects of university education while vigorously attacking what in his view was Newman's wrong-headed attempt to impose on post-Famine Ireland a gentleman's liberal education imported from a decadent Oxford.[52]

The first major reaction in UCD to Corcoran's assessment of Newman came with Roger McHugh's *Newman on University Education* (1944), though it did not specify Corcoran by name. McHugh's modest volume made a generation of UCD students of English aware of the largeness of mind of the English cardinal and the magnitude of the country's debt to him.

A year after the publication of McHugh's book there came from Michael Tierney a barrage directly aimed at Corcoran, with no quarter given and a deliberate rebuilding of the pedestal that Corcoran had attacked and the re-garlanding of Newman as hero of the Irish university story. Tierney, who seemed to thrive on argument, gathered together, influenced and led a group of UCD and other academics who perhaps on their own would not have taken on Corcoran but who were prepared to join behind Tierney in an attack on the former professor. Tierney, the professor of Greek, with a lively interest in Plato and other classical and modern theories of education, was concerned to do justice and more than justice to Newman.

If Corcoran conducted a personal crusade against Newman, Tierney carried out not only a personal crusade but an institutional or UCD campaign to glorify him. The Tierney campaign in time brought its own reaction, or at the least spent itself, but it lasted throughout Tierney's period of dominance in UCD. It was perhaps no coincidence that Newman was dropped from English courses in the mid-sixties after Tierney had retired from the presidency and a new professor of English literature, Denis Donoghue, who belonged to a younger generation, was appointed in 1966.

The suggestion in the nineteen-seventies, during the discussions on independent university status, that UCD be named Newman University did not win favour with a younger generation of academics. It was perhaps not unrelated to Tierney's public enthusiasm that they wanted to give an overworked Newman a much-earned rest.

In *A Tribute to Newman* (1945), edited by Tierney, the president said that the original intention was that the volume should be 'an exclusively Irish tribute to the great English Cardinal, whose contact with Ireland was so critical a moment in his own life and work, and had such an influence on Irish higher education.' Of the thirteen chapters, eleven were contributed by Irish scholars, including from UCD Jeremiah Hogan, Roger McHugh, and Aubrey Gwynn, and some former students of the college, including Fergal McGrath, Con Curran, and Tom Wall. The chief object of the book, said Tierney, was to show 'that educated Irishmen are fully conscious of the debt which Ireland in particular owes to Newman, and to arouse among Irish Catholics, at home and abroad, a closer and better informed interest in his life and teaching.'[53]

Tierney's own essay was a stirring and hard-hitting defence of Newman against Corcoran's criticisms and is peppered throughout with admiration for Newman. Tierney was very conscious of the impact Corcoran's assessment of Newman had made both in Ireland and abroad. Both McHugh and, to an even greater extent, Tierney were aware of the book *J. H. Newman: Éducateur* by Fernande Tardivel (Paris, 1937). Readers would find in that book, said Tierney, a fully documented refutation of Corcoran's 'strange charges'; but, he went on, 'the Irish reader of this cool, objective and well-informed French critic' must be saddened to meet on her second page the judgment that in Ireland Newman was studied 'against the grain' and to know that one of her reasons for writing in French was to avoid appearing to provoke controversy with exponents of wrong-headed Irish views. The force of Tardivel's contradiction of Corcoran was an argument to the effect that nowhere was Newman more gravely misunderstood or studied 'against the grain' than in Ireland, and Tierney understood this as specifically the case in the Education Department of UCD, where Corcoran, as professor for thirty-three years, had mis-instructed some 2,600 future secondary teachers about Newman's philosophy of university education. 'It is regrettably the case', wrote Tierney, 'that the sole considerable work on Newman done in Ireland in many years was of a nature to justify such strictures, and still more regrettable that this work was reinforced by lectures of considerable authority and power delivered to several generations of students of educational theory in the college where Newman's name should be most especially honoured.' Too many Irish students, of whom Newman spoke with such hope and eloquence, wrote Tierney, had been taught to decry and dismiss his teaching. They had been indoctrinated with the belief that his philosophy of liberal education was to be summarily rejected.

According to Tierney, Tardivel had most clearly demonstrated the unity of Newman's doctrine and had fully answered Corcoran's indictments of Newman's source as a degenerate Oxford and his allegations that the university was for English gentry paid for by the Irish peasantry, that he had pursued a philosophy of severance by separating education from religion, and that the changes made in the London edition of the *Discourses* were for sinister reasons.

Tierney fully agreed with Tardivel's contradiction of Corcoran and supported it in his own characteristically strong language. He referred to Corcoran's 'misguided zeal,' 'considerable misrepresentation,' 'obscurantism,' and 'theological imperialism.' And Corcoran's arguments were dismissed as being 'peculiar and perverse,' 'grotesquely unfair,' 'wrong-headed,' 'regrettable,' 'disconcerting and painful,' 'much confused,' 'an absurdity,' and 'a one-sided study.' Yet leaving aside the epithets of denunciation, Tierney's essay was a tour de force, coherently and convincingly argued, with each of Corcoran's charges against Newman examined and contradicted.

The UCD protagonists held diametrically opposed views of Newman's philosophy of university education, because the professor of education was essentially a utilitarian and the professor of Greek very much a champion of Newman's idea of liberal education. Tierney denied Corcoran's claim that an exclusive emphasis on technical and professional training was the Christian and European tradition; and he rejected as 'utterly wide of the mark' Corcoran's statement that 'the professional schools should be the major factors and specific outlets of academic discipline in study and in skilled scientific training.' Tierney held that liberal arts 'must and can become the living centre of the modern university' and that the true home of the intellectual culture provided by the university is its Faculty of Arts.

The debate between Tierney and Corcoran, featuring Newman at its centre and raising the whole question of UCD's philosophy of education, was a sign of healthy intellectual life in the college at a period when the problems of gross overcrowding, lack of proper facilities and woefully inadequate funding occupied the minds of its administrators. Tierney's defence of Newman and his ideas about the centrality of the humanities in university education was quite significant for UCD's development. The rehabilitation of Newman in UCD was given additional prestige by the fact that Tierney became president two years after his *Tribute to Newman* had been published, and that his presidency was followed by that of Jeremiah Hogan, professor of English (1934–1964), registrar (1952–1964), a published admirer of Newman and an articulate cohort in Tierney's 'Irish phalanx'.

The spirited defence of his hero in *A Tribute to Newman* was merely the beginning of Tierney's long and sustained campaign of praise for Newman's ideas. In 1952, when he had been president for five years, he brought out an edition of Newman's *University Sketches,* which had originally been published in the *Catholic University Gazette* and were for Tierney the 'most readable, perhaps, of all his writings on university education.'[54]

The high point in Tierney's celebration of Newman took place two years later, in 1954, the centenary of the opening of the Catholic University of Ireland, with radio talks, public celebrations hosted by UCD, and the publication of a volume of essays, *Struggle with Fortune,* edited by Tierney for the occasion. The centenary celebrations provided a splendid opportunity for Tierney, Hogan and their friends to pay further tribute to the man they were by now claiming as the founder of UCD. It was the year that completed what might be called the 'Newmanising' of UCD.

The celebrations, which began on Sunday 18 July, lasted for six days. Sixty-five universities, mainly on the Continent and in North America, sent delegates; congratulatory addresses were received from a further twenty-five. When the final preparations were being made the roof of the Aula Maxima in Newman House burned down overnight, and it seemed impossible that the necessary repairs could be made in time. 'But Dr. Tierney's courage and perseverance were unshaken,' and the problem was overcome.[55]

It had been intended that the celebrations would open with High Mass in University Church, at which Archbishop John Charles McQuaid was to preside, but because of the success that attended the president's campaign a Votive Mass was held instead in the much larger St Andrew's Church, Westland Row, at which Cardinal D'Alton presided and Archbishop

McQuaid preached the sermon. The Apostolic Nuncio and 'rows of bishops in their purple filled the wide sanctuary.'[56] The attendance included the President of Ireland, Seán T. Ó Ceallaigh, the Taoiseach, J. A. Costello, other members of the Government, the Lord Mayor of Dublin, the Chief Justice and other judges, members of the diplomatic corps, and representatives of cultural and educational bodies. 'A phalanx of delegates in their academic robes ... contributed a mosaic of colour and costume.'[57]

The following day the presentation of the addresses took place in the Aula Maxima, Newman House, with the Archbishop of Dublin in his capacity as Rector of the Catholic University in the chair. The Catholic University had never been abolished. It survived, and still survives (though more as a legal fiction), in the person of its rector, the Archbishop of Dublin, and in the trustees of the Catholic University Medical School, which awards prizes to medical students in UCD. This very faint or tentative existence of the Catholic University made it all the easier to claim a significant lifeline between UCD and Newman's university. Of course it also tended further to emphasise the Catholic ethos of UCD.

In the afternoon nine hundred guests were present at a garden party held, significantly, in the gardens of Belfield, where they were received by the president of the college. The garden party in such a setting was a clever piece of symbolism, linking the brave projected college site, long before it had got to the drawing-board, with its misty origins in Newman and the Catholic University. Further events that week included a conferring of honorary degrees on eighteen foreign scholars (eleven of them Catholic churchmen), receptions by the President of Ireland and the Minister for Education, an archaeological expedition to the Boyne Valley, and a centenary banquet in the Gresham Hotel. The ceremonies were closed on Friday 23 July by the Archbishop of Dublin with Benediction and Te Deum in University Church.

The centenary celebration was the most splendid public occasion in the history of the college. It emphasised certain things: it gave public recognition to UCD's claim to direct lineal descent from the Catholic University and to its claim to Newman as founder of the college; it was a public proclamation of the Catholic nature and ethos of UCD, as envisaged by Dr Tierney and the registrar, Jeremiah Hogan; and its organisation and significance were personal successes for Michael Tierney.

More emphatically than anyone else, Tierney saw UCD as coming in direct succession from the Catholic University, and he saw Newman as the founder of UCD; but these claims had been presented in a more tentative way and in more qualified language in *A Tribute to Newman*. In Tierney's own essay the Faculty of Medicine was seen as the one sure link between the institutions, and he was careful to acknowledge the real difference that also existed. 'In spite of many changes, hazards and imperfections, the University College of today with all its difference in character is the living and flourishing witness to the achievement of Newman.' And he referred, rather modestly, to 'the College which can claim some share of his tradition.' By 1954, however, when Tierney edited *Struggle with Fortune* and was president of the college, the claims on Newman and on the Catholic University had become markedly stronger and more purposeful. No-one was more convinced or now claimed more eloquently, or frequently, that Newman was the 'founder' of UCD and that the college was 'the harvest of Newman's sowing.' The radio talks given in April and May 1954 by Jeremiah Hogan, C. P. Curran and Tierney himself to celebrate the centenary of the Catholic University were designed to show, in Tierney's words, 'the story of the development of Newman's Catholic University into the modern University College, Dublin.'

It was in the centenary publications and speeches, however, that the claims on Newman and the Catholic University reached a crescendo. The booklet recording the celebrations asserted: 'University College derives by an unbroken line from the institution opened one hundred years ago ... As the principal seat of higher education for Irish Catholics it has, despite its change of title, maintained a strong and vivid sense of its original function and status.'[58] In his address of welcome to the delegates Tierney claimed that UCD had 'in fact reached its centenary.' He admitted that having 'undergone so many Protean transformations and so many rejuvenations' on the way it was 'in some danger of being unrecognisable to its oldest friends.' But any doubts on this point he was determined to remove, for he did not hesitate to appropriate Newman as 'our first Rector and founder.' Through 'our founder', he said, UCD had been given a 'feeling of proud communion with the great European and world-wide fellowship of science and learning' and could lay claim to a 'humble kinship' with two noble centres of liberal culture: Newman's beloved Oxford, and Louvain, on which the Catholic University had been modelled. This tradition of intellectual and spiritual contact had made UCD 'one of Ireland's largest windows to the world.'

The President of UCD made it clear that it was 'to commemorate our origin' that the Catholic University centenary celebrations were organised. And he stressed that although UCD shared with Maynooth, UCC and UCG one household and a common family in the National University of Ireland, nevertheless 'our origin' was very different and quite distinct. It could also be understood that by stressing UCD's relations with Maynooth, which 'have always been closest and most vital' and which he hoped would 'continue to be of the greatest profit and value to both sides,' Tierney was distancing himself further from Cork and Galway, which had their roots in Peel's non-denominational Queen's Colleges.[59]

This important address was the culmination and essence of the message Michael Tierney had been shaping in his pronouncements over the previous decade. It could be seen as a proposed new charter of independence for the college—a charter that emphasised its descent from Newman and the Catholic University, which proclaimed its Catholic ethos, treasured its links with Maynooth, and made a statement about its separateness from Cork, Galway, and the National University of Ireland. What was perhaps even more remarkable was the general acceptance by leaders of church and state of Tierney's vision of UCD. It was a measure of the success of his claims that Archbishop McQuaid especially—who was extremely jealous of his title of Rector of the Catholic University, proclaimed annually in the *Catholic Directory*, and whose Lenten pastorals did not regard the undenominational colleges of the NUI as ideal but to be tolerated only as less dangerous to the faith and morals of Catholic students than Trinity—was prepared to go along to a considerable extent with Tierney's claims. Though McQuaid used the same terms as Tierney to describe Newman as 'founder and first Rector,' he was referring to the Catholic University, while the president was referring to UCD. Nevertheless, the archbishop was prepared to recognise UCD's rights of succession. In his sermon, preached at the opening Votive Mass, he said: 'Today we can salute in University College, Dublin, successor of the Newman College, an assembly of learned professors, a throng of eager students, loyal in thought and living to the Faith of Jesus Christ.'[60]

If the Rector of the Catholic University went a considerable distance with Tierney, so too did Éamon de Valera, Chancellor of the National University of Ireland. While being careful to stop short of fully endorsing Tierney, he admitted to a certain justification in UCD's claims. Welcoming the visitors, he said that the aim of those who had founded the Catholic University 'was being realised in the University of which UCD was the leading constituent and the chief connecting link with the foundation of a hundred years ago.'[61] These public admissions of both McQuaid and de Valera represented an extensive victory for Tierney's claims and objectives.

Some of the celebratory addresses received on the occasion (which were later exhibited publicly in UCD) also showed the extent to which Tierney had been successful in linking UCD to its beginnings in the Catholic University. Even Rome officially seemed to recognise the connection, since the papal blessing was conferred on the Archbishop of Dublin, the president, professors and students, thereby associating the Rector of the Catholic University with the personnel of UCD. This kind of confusion helped to blur what differences there were between the two institutions and underlined instead the connections. To that extent, Tierney's initiatives had been quite successful.

The more vividly UCD's connections with the Catholic University were emphasised in these centenary celebrations, the more apparent became the Catholic ethos of this constituent college of a university that was legally undenominational. The celebrations had opened and closed with all the solemnity of a great religious occasion. The cardinal, Apostolic Nuncio, archbishops, bishops and other ecclesiastical dignitaries from Ireland and abroad graced the events of the week; the majority of the recipients of honorary degrees were also leading churchmen. And, as if these signs and symbols were not sufficient, the speeches—especially those made by the laymen—left nobody in any doubt about UCD's Catholic spirit. De Valera said that the primary aim of those who had founded the Catholic University was to provide an institution where the teaching would be informed and inspired by the Catholic conception of life; this was being fulfilled in UCD. Jeremiah Hogan, the registrar, praised the bishops for having shouldered many tasks beyond their religious functions when there was as yet no-one else to take up those tasks. And, speaking for those who were in control of the college in 1954, he said that they 'did not want to alter their filial relations to the Irish Hierarchy.' 'We venture to hope', he added, 'that their successors and our successors may meet in the same harmony to celebrate the academic occasions of the future.'[62]

The praising of bishops for operating outside their strictly religious functions, the glorification of the 'filial' relationship between academics and the hierarchy and the expression of the hope that such harmony between laity and clergy in UCD would continue were phrases that if employed by anyone in authority in UCD a couple of decades later would be the cause of much embarrassment. But in the atmosphere of Catholicism that pervaded public life in the nineteen-fifties, and given the large number of priests on UCD's teaching staff, the many seminarians and nuns who made up the classes (especially in arts), such language and sentiments were not at all surprising. If there was any criticism of the centenary celebrations at the time it was not because of the Catholic ethos of UCD that they proclaimed: rather was it more on grounds of jealousy that UCD should be so successfully and publicly appropriating to itself the Catholic University and Newman; for UCC, under the Presidency of Alfred O'Rahilly, and especially in its extramural sociology courses, took its Catholic missionary role at least as seriously as did UCD.

Another triumph that the centenary commemoration achieved for Tierney was the linking of Belfield with the Catholic University and Newman. This involved more than just the garden party. He openly admitted that part of the purpose of the celebrations had been to bring home to the public and to those abroad something of the truth about the history and status of UCD as successor to Newman's Catholic University. It was clearly important to him that the proposed new structures at Belfield should be understood historically in the context of Newman's legacy.

While the winning of the public acceptance of Tierney's version of the history of UCD was to him and his staff a matter of great significance, a further task awaited them. For forty-six years, as he pointed out, UCD's numbers had always outrun its resources. Thanks to the generosity of successive governments they had now acquired a substantial estate on which to build worthily a new college. This was something to which the Taoiseach, John A. Costello, referred when proposing a toast to the college at the centenary banquet in the Gresham Hotel. The poor thing that had been founded in 1908, he said, had been moulded and fashioned by Irish men and women to their own circumstances and their own purposes. They had every right to be proud of University College, and he hoped that the new college to be built at Stillorgan Road would be worthy of this great nation. Replying to the toast, Dr Tierney said that for this task they would need the active support of their graduates, the people, and the Government.

The celebrations, as planned by the president, with all their implications, had gone a considerable way towards proclaiming UCD's historical significance and its origins in the Catholic University. The commemoration ceremonies, of which the president had been chief organiser and in which he had played a leading role, together with the books on Newman and on the history of the college that he had edited, amounted to a great personal success for him. They were, however, only the beginning of his presidential objectives. There still lay ahead of him the building of the new college. In his reply to the Taoiseach's toast he had already deftly associated the future Belfield site with the Catholic University and with the Newman tradition; but, looking beyond the physical erection of the new college, he held up an academic ideal for it, asserting that 'it was in the devotion to Newman's ideals and in the determination to deepen and develop their knowledge of his teaching that lay the greatest hope and promise for the future of the institution.'[63]

Of Tierney's own personal devotion to Newman the educator there had never been any doubt. In the great debate that had begun with defending Newman against Father Corcoran, Tierney to all appearances had had a massive victory. In this he had had the support of such Newman scholars as Father Fergal McGrath and Roger McHugh. And the co-operation of other colleagues and the backing of his point of view that he had first received from them in his *Tribute to Newman* had culminated in what amounted to the public and international recognition of his position by church and state in the grand climax of the Catholic University centenary celebrations.

The centenary commemoration ended with the publication of *Struggle with Fortune*, edited by the president of the college. It was a miscellaneous collection of essays tracing the history of the institution in its various transformations during a hundred years of existence. The title came from

Newman's own prophetic sentence: 'I see a flourishing university, which for a while had to struggle with fortune, but which, when its first founders were dead and gone, had successes far exceeding their anxieties.'

Any notions that might have existed that the inheritance claims made by UCD's authorities during the Catholic University centenary were merely the rhetoric produced by the occasion were soon dispelled by the carefully chosen words of most of the president's collaborators. Father Aubrey Gwynn, appropriately, stressed the Jesuit connection, Professor William Doolin the link through the Medical School, Professor Mary Macken the role of women as fighters for equality in one college and beneficiaries of that struggle in its successor. Likewise Professor Gerard Murphy on Celtic Studies and James Meenan on the student body handled their particular subjects as one seamless web from Newman's time to Tierney's. Professor George O'Brien said that University College's 'new beginning in 1909 should be described as a reincarnation rather than a birth,' because 'we derive our tradition from the Catholic liberal outlook of Newman.'

A different note was struck by the youngest of the contributors, Professor T. Desmond Williams. His links with the institution were almost entirely with its most recent or Earlsfort Terrace days. He wrote: 'It is true that University College goes back to Newman's University; that connection, however, though it may be strong, can only be described as indirect.'[64] He pointed out how times had greatly changed since the days of Newman: that UCD was unlike the Catholic University in that by law it was undenominational and that it was established for the people rather than for an elite drawn from a traditional aristocracy; that special consideration had therefore to be given to the professional and vocational aspects of education rather than to any exclusively humanistic training after the fashion of the Oxford ideal that Newman brought with him to Ireland; and that it had a 'red-brick' character, so distrusted by Newman. And he drew attention to the fact that 'in the parliamentary debates on the Irish Universities Bill, for example, almost no reference was made to Newman's university ideal, and therefore it is only natural that neither in the intentions of its founders, nor in the historical results, is it very easy to trace a direct, comprehensive connection between Newman's ideal of a University and the reality of University College, Dublin.'[65]

In some of these comments, especially in those about Newman's elitism and Oxford ideal, Williams was sailing close to the views of Father Corcoran that had been so vigorously rejected by Tierney. But this young professor of modern history was by nature, as well as experience in the British Foreign Office following his Cambridge days, adept at the understatement, the hint, the tight-rope expression, and the qualifying phrase. He could placate Tierney with an implied criticism of Corcoran by writing that 'Newman has been unfairly and ungraciously criticised for his alleged intention of creating in Ireland a university for British (including Irish) Catholic "gentlemen".'[66] He could further placate the president with the characteristically balancing verdict that UCD was 'in the process of creating a tradition not inconsistent with the Newman ideal, though it certainly does not coincide entirely with it,'[67] and also that 'it is only in recent times that its governing authorities have tried to capture the vision, which Newman so often called for, of ever-increasing promise and influence.'[68]

The Williams essay attempted a compromise between Tierney's more extreme claims on Newman as founder and inspirer of UCD's ideals and Corcoran's rejection of Newman because of his alleged intention of creating a university for 'gentlemen' modelled on the aristocratic Oxford of his time. But the literary balancing act by Williams provided an opening for those outside the college who resented Tierney's claims and who feared even more keenly their implications for other third-level institutions.

CRITICISMS OF TIERNEY'S APPROPRIATION OF NEWMAN

It may well have been that the bigger the leap forward contemplated by Tierney for UCD, the more anxiously he looked backwards to maintain the link with Newman. Criticism of Tierney's appropriation of Newman and the Catholic University, however, came, perhaps not unexpectedly, from UCC but most unexpectedly indeed from two UCC professors in particular: Denis Gwynn, research professor of modern Irish history, and James Hogan, professor of history. Both historians, graduates of UCD, were personal friends of Tierney and his allies in national and university politics. Hogan had been Tierney's great champion and confidant at the time of Tierney's election to the presidency, and Tierney had been ready to reciprocate with his support had Hogan been a candidate for UCC seven years later. From July to November 1954 the two UCC friends had corresponded confidentially with Tierney about the vacant presidency in Cork, discussed intimately with him the merits and chances of the different candidates, and thanked him for his interest. Both had participated prominently in the centenary celebrations.

Tierney, understandably, was surprised and deeply hurt by their joint article, 'Some afterthoughts on the Newman centenary', which appeared as the first article in the second issue of *University Review* in the autumn of 1954. They must have been composing this article at the very time that they were corresponding in confidence with Tierney about the presidential vacancy in Cork, which could only have made it seem all the more ungracious to their recent host. It may very well have been one of the reasons why Tierney confided to Myles Dillon, one of the unsuccessful candidates for the UCC presidency, that he was better out of it.[69]

The Gwynn and Hogan article opened flatteringly enough by saying: 'The whole country, and especially the National University, is deeply indebted to Dr. Michael Tierney for his enterprise and perseverance in organising the centenary celebrations ...' But it went on immediately to point out that people were inevitably puzzled about how UCD could possibly be celebrating its own centenary, and how Newman's short-lived university could become the subject of such celebrations long after it had ceased to function. This confusion, the article alleged, was reflected in some of the addresses of congratulation, which referred mistakenly to 'Dublin University', while others 'appeared to assume that Newman's Catholic University is still being carried on as he intended it. Some misapprehensions were to be expected, and the prospect might well have intimidated a less vigorous personality than Dr. Tierney.'

The two UCC professors acknowledged that there had always been 'a clear connection with the Newman tradition; and Dr. Tierney himself has done much to strengthen and revive it since he became President of U.C.D.'[70] They stated that 'the direct links which connect University College, Dublin, with Newman and his university, have been very properly stressed and published.'[71] And they repeated with emphasis: 'Undoubtedly U.C.D. can claim much more than a direct inheritance of the buildings which Newman acquired and of the living tradition handed on from him and his disciples ...'[72] The essays in *Struggle with Fortune* 'are designed to show the direct connection between Newman's Catholic University and the present U.C.D. as its successor.'[73]

Introducing a more controversial note, they wrote: 'How far Newman's ideals and plans are in fact reflected in the modern evolution of U.C.D. is more debatable than some of these writers would admit.'[74] Then they latched on to the essay by Professor Williams, whom they described as writing 'in a more restrained tone than some of the contributors,'[75] and used him as a stick with which to beat the Tierney thesis. They quoted fairly extensively from the Williams essay to underline the points that, they said, he had 'candidly' made illustrating the differences between Newman's university and the modern UCD. By selecting the comments of one of UCD's own professors they were cleverly questioning Tierney's thesis of direct descent while at first appearing to accept it, at least superficially. They then made the case against UCD's appropriation of Newman for itself alone and displayed, perhaps, a certain jealousy in this regard. Rather extravagantly, they asserted: 'Among the bishops particularly ... it is extremely doubtful whether Dublin's claim to inherit the whole of Newman's legacy to Ireland would be accepted.'[76] They felt that Tierney underrated the claims and the traditions of the other colleges within the NUI. Using Newman against Tierney, they argued that the smaller colleges in Galway and Cork, 'with their more self-contained academic life, and their overwhelmingly Catholic surroundings, come much closer to

Newman's ideals' than UCD could possibly be.[77] 'Certainly his inspiration was never meant to be appropriated by one institution.'[78] This citing of Newman against his own thesis must have been particularly galling to Tierney.

The projected move to Belfield, in the opinion of Gwynn and Hogan, could have very harmful implications for Cork and Galway, so much so that they were prepared to strike what they themselves recognised might be a 'needlessly alarmist' note. Tierney, they said, attached such importance to Newman's idea of a residential college 'that he urges that the whole college should be moved out of the city into its southern suburbs, where he advocates that a new university with many residential houses should be built.'[79] Williams in his essay had noted how the request by UCD for much more ambitious financial assistance had coincided with the advent of Costello's Government in 1948, and there was raised the new and revolutionary proposal of virtually a new college to be erected outside the city area; this in turn had stimulated speculation on the future relations of such a college with the other constituent members of the National University. The Gwynn-Hogan article noted that at the centenary banquet John A. Costello, now in his second period of office as Taoiseach, had made statements that, while reflecting his personal gratitude as an eminent former student of UCD, could not fail to arouse serious misgivings among the other colleges of the NUI.

The UCC professors stated that in the Republic nobody could count on a university endowment on anything approaching the scale available to Queen's University, Belfast, or the provincial British universities. This being the case, they feared that 'the enrichment in numbers and resources of University College, Dublin, raised, let us suppose, to the status of an independent university, and possessed of all the advantages of metropolitan position and prestige, could hardly fail to result in a proportionate decline and impoverishment for the provincial universities.' The argument, they felt, was all for several small or medium-sized university colleges, instead of a few overgrown ones. It would be fatally easy, they claimed, striking at Tierney, to have a miscellaneous expansion that in the end would leave not so much a university as a polytechnic, while on the other hand 'Newman ... would have found much to please him in the size and atmosphere of the provincial colleges of Cork and Galway.'[80]

They were strongly opposed to any move there might be towards the dissolution of the NUI federal system. The Williams essay had said that the proposal to build a new UCD outside the city had stimulated speculation about its future relations with Cork and Galway. Tierney's own essay had stated that only the loyalty and good will of the three colleges towards each other had been able to postpone a breakdown, which seemed to him to be 'eventually inevitable.'[81] In the eyes of the Cork professors this was warning enough of Tierney's intentions, which they greatly disliked and feared. 'So long as the provincial colleges share in the federal unity, they share in the benefits—not least in matters of finance—accruing to its strongest member by virtue of its position of vantage in Dublin in proximity to the government of the country.'[82] And they added that 'the dissolution of the National University as a federal body carries a real danger to the well-being, even the existence, of the provincial university colleges.'

The working of the federal system for nearly fifty years must have proved satisfactory enough, they claimed, given the absence of any serious agitation. (Here, it should be pointed out, they conveniently overlooked the attempts in 1919 by Professor Windle to have UCC made an independent University of Munster.) Among the advantages they claimed for the federal system was the fact that the existence of the NUI Senate had enabled the colleges to make their appointments and to plan their curriculums with freedom from interference both from local bodies and the state. If, then, dissolution was in contemplation by the UCD authorities, no time should be lost in examining the implication of such a policy for the whole university.[83]

This touched a very raw nerve in Dr Tierney. Only a year earlier he had reacted bitterly to the very same points of criticism from the *Irish Independent*.[84] The paper had protested that the community should not be committed to the Stillorgan Road site, which it considered unsuitable, without a comprehensive public inquiry into the whole question of higher education; that a veil of secrecy had been drawn around the whole project by people who were acting undemocratically; and that the new buildings should not be erected without reference to the NUI. In a public controversy with the editor, Tierney had stated that the cause of higher education was not served by the paper's charges or suggestions, which seemed to indicate a determination on its part to put obstacles at all costs in the way of a decision about the future of UCD. What Tierney in that newspaper controversy could ascribe to the ignorance of the *Irish Independent's* editor he now found hurtful and altogether intolerable from old friends and eminent colleagues in UCC, writing deliberately and extensively in a scholarly journal. The ultimate argument in the *University Review* article was that in the centenary celebrations large questions about the future of UCD and NUI had been raised, casting inevitably a shadow of future dissension that it would be foolish to ignore.

TIERNEY REACTS

It must have appeared to Tierney that what his Cork friends were selfishly advocating was the blocking of the projected move to Belfield, the financial and academic curtailment of UCD, and the use of the NUI as a strait-jacket for the purpose of constricting its growth and development. He must have seen it as a deliberate attempt to spike his guns and to frustrate his plans for his college: it was a more authoritative reiteration from within the university community of points of opposition raised in the press. He would have suspected also that the opponents of his scheme within UCD had hired very weighty voices from among Tierney's own most eminent friends to defeat his plans. He was all the more annoyed because the Senate of the NUI, of which he, as President of UCD, was a member *ex officio,* was financing the Graduates' Association of the NUI, of which the *University Review* was the official organ. And, as he saw it, in only the second issue of this journal a serious attack had been launched on the policies of the Governing Body of UCD.

The first object of the recently founded Graduates' Association of the NUI was 'to foster a corporate spirit among the graduates of the University.' This could have been seen by Tierney as intended to defend the NUI against any possible dissolution that might be sought by the UCD authorities in favour of the college's independent university status in its projected new site. The association's second aim was 'to advance learning, scholarship and research.' In pursuit of these aims the association had launched a series of lectures on subjects of university and scholarly interest, published the *University Review,* and intended establishing a donation fund.

The respectability of the association was beyond question. The President of Ireland, Seán T. Ó Ceallaigh, had consented to be its first patron. The president of the association was Mr Justice Cahir Davitt; the chairman and one of its leading spirits was Professor E. J. Conway FRS; the editorial board at the time of the row with Tierney was E. J. Conway, Patrick Lynch, Roger McHugh, John O'Meara and T. Desmond Williams, all of UCD, James Hogan of UCC, Rev P. J. McLaughlin of Maynooth, and Judge Cearbhall Ó Dálaigh; the trustees were Ó Dálaigh, Williams, and Alexis FitzGerald; and the committee members included Henry St John Atkins (registrar and, in November 1954, newly elected President of UCC), Thomas Dillon (UCG), Séamus Wilmot (Registrar of the NUI), and Tom O'Rourke (clerk of Convocation). The Association's address was Newman House; all three colleges submitted university news to the journal, in which UCC and UCG also advertised. Significantly, however, neither the President nor Registrar of UCD was involved in the business of the association or of *University Review.* According to John O'Meara, Tierney was 'hostile' to the association from the start, refused the chairmanship of the Dublin branch, and attempted to persuade some members of the editorial board to withdraw their support.[85]

At the time of the publication of the offending article the Finance Committee of the Senate had under consideration the possibility or desirability of a journal to be published by the university. When the Finance Committee met on 9 December 1954 it was divided on the question of renewing the grant to the Graduates' Association, and since a number of members were absent because of the weather, the issue was left to the meeting of the Senate on the following day. Each member of the Senate had received a copy of the issue of *University Review* containing the Gwynn-Hogan article.

After the matter was discussed, the President of UCD proposed and the registrar, Jeremiah Hogan, seconded the motion 'that an annual grant to the Graduates' Association of the NUI be discontinued.' Given the number of leading names involved in one way or another with the association, it was evident that Tierney was taking on a task from which a man of less combative disposition would have shrunk. But it was a new Senate since October, whose membership included a number of Tierney's close associates from UCD: Jeremiah Hogan, his brother, Michael Hogan (very much involved in the plans for Belfield), Aubrey Gwynn, Monsignor John Horgan, T. S. Wheeler, Monsignor Boylan, Senator Barniville, Senator Michael Hayes, George O'Brien, Dr James O'Connor. Most of these would have supported Tierney's resolution. But ranged against him on this issue were Senate members who saw great merit in what the Graduates' Association and its *University Review* were attempting and were themselves active participants in the pursuit of its objectives.

James Hogan, joint author of the offending article, spoke against Tierney's resolution. The Presidents of UCC and UCG proposed a compromise formula, as did two leading personalities in the Graduates' Association, E. J. Conway and Roger McHugh, but without success. Tierney's motion was put and carried by twelve votes to eleven.[86]

The split in the Senate of the NUI could hardly have been more dramatic. The fact that as many as five members appear to have abstained from the final vote was only one indication of the tension that was felt at the meeting. One of those who abstained was James Meenan, professor of economics in UCD. Something of the dilemma, the strain and the anxieties that the controversy created for those caught between warring camps were plainly evident in the letter Meenan sent to Tierney two days after the meeting.

> I abstained from the final vote in the Senate on Friday and I feel that it is due to you to say why. I had, of course, at no time any intention of differing from you on the merits or demerits of the article—and its offence was made worse by Hogan's defence. But I had the greatest possible reluctance to cutting off the grant to the Association so long as people like Davitt and O'Daly and O'Rourke were associated with it. I have known these people all my life in College and I know them to be disinterested. I did not wish to censure them, or to see them possibly forced out of the Association and displaced by less disinterested people.[87]

This reflected what Meenan had confided to his diary. There he said he could not have voted against the president, especially after James Hogan had spoken (as he thought) maliciously. But he was damned if he was going to go against the 'good crowd' in the association, in which he included Tom O'Rourke, Cahir Davitt, and his colleagues in the UCD Economics Department, Alexis FitzGerald and Paddy Lynch. After graphically describing the atmosphere at the controversial Senate meeting, where Tierney repulsed every compromise suggested, Meenan went on to note the reaction to the withdrawal of the grant. Within the association, he thought, 'they won't all take it lying down.' O'Rourke was furious. The judges, Davitt and Ó Dálaigh, regarded the Senate decision as an insult and intended to keep the association going; while Meenan sympathised with them, he noted that they had conspicuously failed to make any gesture off their own bat about the offending article.

Meanwhile the president and the college were becoming dangerously isolated. Monsignor Horgan, who had been pressuring O'Brien and Meenan to support the president before the vote, alleging that Conway and the Graduates' Association would take control of the college if he were beaten, now buttonholed Meenan in an effort to save Lynch and FitzGerald from the burning, to which Meenan replied that it had not been made any easier by slapping them in the face. The president himself regarded Meenan more in sorrow than in anger but was very annoyed with Lynch. It was being said that he had resolved to resign if defeated in the Senate.

Moderates like O'Brien and Meenan were anxious that the row would not be resumed at the next Senate meeting. When it met on 13 January the Standing Committee had hammered out a compromise: the Graduates' Association was to get £500, and nothing for the future. When the Chancellor put this before the Senate it was accepted, with a great sense of relief all round. The last word in Meenan's diary on the subject was notably that Horgan and Jeremiah Hogan on one side and Desmond Williams on the other had come out of it very badly and he felt it would be remembered against them.[88]

The Senate row was significant, and its repercussions spread out in ever-widening circles. It exhibited Tierney's fearlessness, or bull-headedness—depending on one's point of view—and his sheer determination to take on and overcome any opposition to his Belfield plans. A man with less backbone might have been tempted to bend with the storm and seek some kind of accommodation with his formidable opponents. He took a jaundiced view of the Graduates' Association, seeing it as a weapon manufactured by his opponents in UCD to negative his policies and to involve elements in UCC and UCG against him. The association had worthy objectives and a respectable membership, who were not in it simply to oppose and criticise

Tierney; but, as he saw it, if not founded directly to oppose his policies it had been hijacked from the start by his critics.

If he took the opposition too personally, there were times when he might have felt justified in his stance. At one of the annual dinners of the Graduates' Association a guest, the Provost of Trinity College, Dr McConnell, who had greatly enjoyed the hospitality, used the occasion to launch an attack on the President of UCD. Even some of Tierney's UCD opponents regarded the attack as being totally out of place. It did nothing to help the association's image with Tierney and his friends.

Tierney's action in the Senate in withdrawing financial support from the Graduates' Association was followed by denying it facilities in Newman House, withholding any advertising from UCD in the *University Review,* and letting it be known to academic staff that their membership of the association did not necessarily please him. The row in the long run, together with other factors, did not help the association, for by 1960 it was struggling to attract membership. Though the Graduates' Association became defunct, the *University Review* (later *Irish University Review*) survived as an important journal of Irish studies.

Immediately, however, Tierney's displeasure with the association served only to strengthen the resolve of his arch-critics. E. J. Conway, chairman of the Graduates' Association, successfully sought election to the Governing Body in December 1955. Here he was joined by other activists—Roger McHugh, Lorna Reynolds, and John O'Meara—who formed the opposition party to Tierney on the Governing Body and from whom he had not heard the last word.

The internal politics of what was developing into a bitter struggle between the Tierney and anti-Tierney camps within UCD was one consequence of the quarrel with the Graduates' Association. The participation of what Tierney referred to as 'elements in UCC and UCG' on the side of his critics did not make for smooth relations between Tierney's administration and those of the two sister colleges. Consultation and co-operation between administrations in the constituent colleges were strained, or at least not very enthusiastic in the circumstances. The opposition to, or jealousy of, UCD that he felt to be present in the Senate of the NUI was very probably one of the reasons why he proceeded in the matter of lectureships and professorships in the college without reference to the Senate, which was to lead to a visitation.

The row that had surfaced in the Senate confirmed Tierney in his view that the NUI had become more of an obstacle than a help to UCD's development. The notion that UCD should 'go it alone' had become more firmly embedded in his mind following his experience with the Graduates' Association; the climax would come a few years later with his submission to the Commission on Higher Education in favour of UCD's independent status as a separate university.

6

Church and College

The Catholic ethos of the Jesuit college in St Stephen's Green, like so much else from that institution, was bequeathed to the new University College, Dublin. Despite the undenominationalism laid down in the Irish Universities Act, and despite a rigid adherence to that principle on the part of the college authorities, the mind and character of the college from the outset was permeated by Catholicism.

The college that was established in 1908 was, *mutatis mutandis,* not at all unlike the Trinity College described by the Chief Secretary, Arthur Balfour, in 1889 when he said: 'If not by its constitution, at all events by its composition, Trinity College is now what it has always been, a Protestant institution by its religious flavour and complexion.'[1] He had spoken with a note of stark realism when he reminded his Scottish unionist supporters that 'undenominational' education in any sense in which they might use the epithet was all but unknown in Ireland, and in this, Queen's College, Belfast, was not so very different from Trinity College, Dublin. 'Undenominationalism' in Ireland, he asserted, did not ignore the existence of various denominations.[2] When, therefore, a later Chief Secretary, George Wyndham, proposed a solution in 1903 it was also according to the Balfour formula, that the new college would only be Catholic in the sense that Trinity College was Protestant. And it was on this assumption that all serious schemes proposed between 1903 and 1908 had been discussed.

Michael Tierney, as late as the nineteen-fifties, could point to the ways in which Trinity persisted in being more Protestant than UCD was Catholic. TCD had no Catholic on its Board—the Government had nominated a Protestant clergyman to UCD; TCD rarely had a Catholic professor on its staff—UCD had a number of Protestant professors; TCD had its School of Divinity and its chapel—UCD was forbidden to spend public money on theology or on the erection and maintenance of a church building.

Among the thirty people nominated under the Act to serve for three years on the first Governing Body there were two bishops (O'Donnell of Raphoe, who held the title of Rector of the phantom Catholic University of Ireland, and Foley of Kildare and Leighlin); the President of St Patrick's College, Maynooth (Monsignor Daniel Mannix); and the President of the Jesuit college (Rev. William Delany SJ), then coming to the end of its existence and being subsumed into the new UCD.

During the decades preceding the establishment of the National University of Ireland, spokesmen for the bishops had made it clear that they had no wish to control, nor did they demand to have a majority of representatives on, the Governing Bodies of any university institution that the state might establish. It was the British Liberal government that gave this relatively strong clerical representation to UCD's first Governing Body. Thereafter the Governing Body was to consist of thirty-four people, of whom four were to be nominated by the state. Among its four nominees the British government continued to include one bishop (Foley), down to the formation of the fourth Governing Body in 1920. The second bishop (O'Donnell) was among the eight representatives elected by the members of the General Council of County Councils for the period 1913–16. He was co-opted for the third Governing Body (1916–19) but was defeated in the voting for co-option for the fourth Governing Body in 1920. Since 1923, with the coming into office of the fifth Governing Body, no bishop has served on the Governing Body of UCD; bishops continued to serve, however, down to the nineties on the Governing Bodies of UCC and UCG.

The governments of independent Ireland between 1923 and 1976 nominated a leading ecclesiastic (usually a monsignor of the Dublin diocese) to UCD's Governing Body instead of a bishop; in 1976 and thereafter no senior clergyman was nominated, though in the mid-eighties the Government appointed a religious from a teaching order.

The nomination of a woman occasionally lapsed, but from 1959 it has been normal for the Government to include a woman with political affiliations and since 1970 the president of the Students' Council: these practices have tended to squeeze out the clergy by limiting the Government's unqualified freedom of choice to two nominees. Clerics could, of course, be chosen by one or other of the panels of electors, and in fact over the years between one and four were usually found serving on the Governing Body. Since 1982 none has been elected, and since 1988 none appointed. Clerical presence on the Governing Body has therefore disappeared entirely.

Given the origins of UCD and its roots in the Catholic University and the Jesuit college, it was not surprising that in its early years it should contain a good number of clerics on its academic staff. Of the original appointments in 1909/10 to thirty-six professorships and fifteen lectureships that were established by Statute I of UCD, five (four chairs and one lectureship) went to Jesuits[3] and three (two chairs and one lectureship) went to secular clergy.[4] The presence of clerics on the staff was even more weighty if we remember that of the twenty-six chairs that were full-time (the ten part-time professorships were largely in medicine and law) clerics held six, as well as one of the five lectureships initially designated as full-time—a total of seven out of thirty-one full-time academic posts. All of these were in the Faculty of Arts.

Four of the Jesuits initially appointed to UCD (the exception being Corcoran) had been fellows of the Royal University. In proportion to the rest of an expanding academic staff, however, the number of Jesuits soon declined, through retirement or resignation: Browne in 1922, O'Neill in 1923, Finlay in 1930, Corcoran in 1942, and Egan in 1946. In each case the replacement was a lay person. The Society of Jesus, however, continued its association with UCD with the appointment of such scholars as Aubrey Gwynn (mediaeval history, retired 1962), John Ryan (early, including mediaeval, Irish history, retired 1964), Frank Shaw (early Irish language and literature, died 1970), Seán Ó Catháin (education, retired 1973), and John Moore (botany, resigned 1983). Since Father Moore's resignation no Jesuit has held a chair in the college. Father Martin Brennan retired in 1980 from a college lectureship in botany, and Father Michael Paul Gallagher resigned in 1991 from a college lectureship in English. UCD then briefly had no member of the Jesuit order on its teaching staff until the appointment of Father David Tuohy to a college lectureship in education in 1993.

The Jesuit connection with UCD had been long and honourable. Even the name University College had been inherited from the institution placed under Jesuit management in 1883, and the premises in St Stephen's Green that had housed the Jesuit college also served as UCD's original home. The transformation of the Jesuit college into UCD provided also the core of the first academic staff and the nucleus of the original student body. Secondary schools managed by the Jesuits continued for many years to be among the principal suppliers of undergraduates, and many a Clongowes or Belvedere boy became a distinguished professor in UCD. It was in the Jesuit journals— notably *Studies,* since 1912—that many UCD academics published their articles.

The Jesuit teachers on the staff since 1909 could hardly be described, either collectively or individually, as in any way aggressively clerical or evangelical. In college they conducted themselves as academics, not as pastors—and this would have to be said of all, or nearly all, the priest-academics who taught in the college over the years. Bishop O'Dwyer, speaking on behalf of his fellow-bishops, had told the Robertson Commission in 1901 that they would never dream of asking a professor of history or of science to falsify his own judgment or to suppress the facts of history or science. They wanted the professor in any projected university for Catholics to profess his subject absolutely honestly and truthfully and as he knew it and found it. They expected such a professor to work out his subject as best he could for the instruction of his pupils and without restrictions by the ecclesiastical authorities. 'We want the full and free air and light of this time of the world to play into that university as well as they do into any university that is in existence.'[5]

It was very much in the spirit of that statement that those UCD professors who also happened to be priests carried out their functions. Their influence was scholarly, or of that intangible kind that all good and respected teachers exercise on their students. Exceptionally among the Jesuits, Professor Corcoran may have had an influence wider than the simply scholarly. Because he helped the government plan the curriculum for the schools, and because he trained so many of the secondary teachers of the fledgling state, he had an impact on generations of pupils who personally had never sat in his classes. But that kind of social influence came from his position as professor of education and not from his vocation as a priest or as an anonymous contributor in the polemical *Catholic Bulletin*.

The bishops had always been adamant that priesthood was not an automatic barrier to a professorship—not indeed that the point was ever an issue in UCD, but in dealing with a Liberal government committed to the principle of undenominationalism, and in warding off the anti-clericalism and anti-Catholicism of certain radicals, non-conformists and bigots, the bishops felt that this was a matter that demanded frank and bold assertion. As the bishops acknowledged, anti-clericalism of this type was alien to Irish Catholicism.[6] They had a point too when they stated in 1897 that the projected university that would be acceptable to Catholics would be likely to have a large proportion of seminarians and religious among its students.

Nor were applicants for academic posts ever excluded from appointments in UCD merely on the grounds that they were priests. Like much else that was inherited from the Jesuit college in St Stephen's Green, there would have been agreement in UCD with Father Delany's statement to the Robertson Commission in 1901 that 'I do not believe that a clergyman should be shut out because he comes as a clergyman.'[7] It was taken for granted that being priests did not prevent men from behaving as scholars. And in a country where the religious controlled and permeated the schools, priests on the academic staff of the university were seen to be a natural and logical extension into tertiary education of the culture prevailing at the secondary level. Ever since the days of Newman, clergy and laity had worked easily and even amicably together. When Newman was made a cardinal in 1879 a congratulatory address from former students of the Catholic University stated that, thanks to him, the Irish people had now realised what a true university should be and what inestimable benefits a national Catholic university could confer upon Ireland. 'You have shown that education is a field in which both clergy and laity can work together, harmoniously and without jealousy, for a common object, and in which both have duties, and both have rights, and in establishing this, you, as it appears to us, have rendered valuable assistance to the Catholic Church in her great struggle for freedom of education throughout the world.'[8]

The Academic Council consisted of the president, the professors, and such lecturers of the college as might be co-opted—normally those with responsibility for areas where there were no professors. As the body with ultimate responsibility for all academic affairs it managed the curriculum and related matters and regulated the discipline of the students. It was, therefore, one of the most important bodies in UCD.

When Father Conor Ward retired from the chair of sociology in September 1991 the Academic Council of UCD was for the first time in its history without a cleric among its members. What was perhaps even more significant was that areas where they had once been dominant—philosophy (or metaphysics, as it had been called down to 1990), politics, psychology, and sociology—had all been taken over by lay professors. The laicisation of UCD was all but complete.

The decline and fall of the clerical profile in UCD, however dramatic in statistical terms, was scarcely noticed. There were never any clerical professors in medicine, law, commerce, engineering, architecture, agriculture or veterinary medicine and only very rarely in science. Their disappearance from the staff excited little or no interest, or even awareness, outside the Faculty of Arts.

STUDENTS AND THE CATHOLIC ETHOS

The Catholic ethos of the college was also evident among the students. Seminarians and other religious made up a sizable proportion of the student body, especially in arts and to a lesser extent in science, from 1909 at least down to the move to Belfield in the nineteen-sixties. In the larger classes in arts the front rows of the lecture-rooms were occupied by nuns with downcast eyes and in full religious habits. To these had to be added the generous sprinkling of seminarians occupying the rest of the lecture-room. Clerical black was often the dominant colour of the garb facing lecturers in the arts area. This was especially so in such subjects as philosophy, where the lecturer himself was also likely to be dressed in a clerical outfit and almost the entire class made up of students from the seminaries. These seminarians were also a feature of the city's traffic as they cycled in a snake-like procession from Clonliffe College to Earlsfort Terrace in their daily quest for a university education.

Apart from this physical reminder in UCD that Ireland was overwhelmingly a Catholic country, many of the lay students lived in the several hostels around the city that were managed by the teaching orders of priests and nuns. In a non-residential UCD these hostels, while providing an environment meant to be conducive to study, were also intended as places where the spiritual and moral welfare of the students would be safeguarded. Part of the pastoral work of the deans of residence was visiting the even greater proportion of students living in lodgings; and this aspect of the work of the deans was carried out dutifully and earnestly, if also unobtrusively and sensitively.

The following extracts from 'Rules of Discipline' reflect the Catholic Church's puritanical preoccupation with sexual mores and the public warnings issued by ecclesiastics about the moral dangers of 'company-keeping' and modern dancing.

16. Students are strictly forbidden to give, or to attend, in any lodgings occupied by students, any entertainment to which it is proposed to invite men and women students.

17. Except in case of permission obtained for a College Society, students are strictly forbidden to organise dances or other entertainments for men and women students conjointly.

18. Women undergraduates not residing with their parents are required to obtain the permission of their officers of residence before accepting invitations to dances or similar entertainments.

And rule no. 19 was to the effect that men and women students were not permitted to reside in the same lodging-house except in the case of members of the same family or in cases approved by the officers of residence. The UCD Calendars of this period stated:

> Every student must enter under an Officer of Residence, who is charged with the supervision of his conduct outside the College premises, and in particular with the supervision of the boarding-houses recognised as suitable by the College. No student may occupy any boarding-house except with the approval of his Officer of Residence.[9]

It could be argued that the students were avowedly even more Catholic than the academics. *Comhthrom Féinne*, the official organ of the Students' Union during the early thirties, was conducted by a committee appointed by the Students' Representative Council.[10] Once edited by Brian O'Nolan (alias Myles na gCopaleen, alias Flann O'Brien), it was hardly the publication where one would have expected to find earnest articles by eager young Catholic Actionists. And yet an editorial in December 1934 pointed out that although the membership of the college, both students and staff, was overwhelmingly Catholic, the title and constitution of UCD remained undenominational fourteen years after the establishment of self-government.[11] It asserted that no provision was made for the higher religious education of lay Catholics, and that only for the efforts of the deans of residence and the chaplains the students would be little better off than in a non-Catholic university. Therefore it was the duty of the students to organise and agitate for a Catholic University of Ireland, whose banner would be *Pro fide, pro patria.*

Another article in the same issue, written by an active member of the Pro Fide Society, called for a Catholic intellectual movement in Ireland and regretted that some modern Irish writers had been affected by the intrusion of non-Christian ideas.[12] It described how all Catholic activities among the students were united and co-ordinated under the name and direction of Pro Fide. These co-ordinated aspects of Catholic Action included a study circle, special social science lectures, the Missionary Society, founded to support the foreign missions, the St Vincent de Paul Society, which had an impressive eighty-one members, the Sodality of the Sacred Heart, and the Choral Society for the performance of church music. It was intended that the spiritual director of Pro Fide should send a quarterly report of all Catholic activities in the college to the hierarchy for their consideration.

The religious zeal of the students burst into a remarkable display in March 1936 when crucifixes mysteriously appeared on the walls of the classrooms throughout the college and in the main hall. They were placed at such a height that they could not be removed without some difficulty. It came as a surprise to many to learn that the crucifixes had been positioned surreptitiously and not as a result of official action. Members of the academic staff were angered by the event, and feelings ran high. Michael Tierney, professor of Greek and a member of the Governing Body, was heard by his friend Father Aubrey Gwynn to declare that no man had a right to say whether he was or was not as good a Catholic as others, and that the choice of a crucifix as an emblem was no more than an accident—the essential fact being the lack of discipline on the part of the students. Gwynn argued that talk such as Tierney's could only do harm; that there were two sides to the question; that Tierney's Catholicism was a question that did not arise; that far from the crucifixes being merely an emblem of the students' indiscipline, the incident had raised the whole question of the desirability of having a religious emblem in the college, which indeed many favoured. He reminded Tierney of a point that

Tierney himself would make much of in his argument for a Catholic university in the nineteen-fifties, namely that the 1908 Act and Charters had been imposed by an English Nonconformist Liberal government. It seemed perfectly natural to Gwynn that a younger generation should be impatient with the restrictions then imposed.[13]

Though the students responsible for placing the crucifixes had found to some degree an apologist in Father Gwynn, the mood of the Academic Council was much less tolerant. At the meeting of 26 March 1936 it was decided to call a special meeting 'to consider irregular acts against discipline on the part of some students in regard to religious emblems.'[14] Four days later, when this special meeting convened, the Academic Council had before it a letter to the president, Dr Coffey, dated 29 March, signed by Pierce Kent, president of the SRC, and Niall Brunicardi, two of the leaders in the crucifix incident, saying that the religious emblems unlawfully erected had been removed as an act of reparation and in token of obedience to the college authorities, the students having come to realise that disobedience to lawful authority was 'a serious fault which the Church unreservedly condemns as gravely immoral.'[15] The Academic Council considered this letter to be satisfactory. It seemed that the affair was closed, and the walls of the college were 'restored to their non-sectarian nudity.'[16]

The president of the SRC, however, went on to publish an article entitled 'In hoc signo vinces' in the *National Student* that asserted that the students had never dreamt that the professors, who, at least occasionally and in full regalia, proclaimed their faith in the divinity of Christ and of his church, would insist on the removal of the crucifixes. But the 'credulous students' had soon found themselves, like Nicodemus, having to take Christ down 'in deference to the wounded susceptibilities of a Catholic body.'

The Academic Council was, predictably, once more incensed. It arraigned the SRC president before a disciplinary committee, where he defended the article by claiming that it stated nothing untrue. Students had often noticed, he said, that while professors attended the October Red Mass (for the opening of the academic year) they rarely attended other student Masses or college religious ceremonies. The Academic Council's unanimous response was to censure Kent, demand the publication of an apology in the *National Student,* and direct the SRC to exclude from the journal all articles dealing with personalities in connection with religious practices.[17] The apology duly appeared, and there the incident appears to have ended, despite veiled references in a later editorial to 'rigorous censorship' and the stifling of originality.[18]

It cannot be read into the affair of the crucifixes that the college authorities were anti-religious, or aggressively non-sectarian, or even resolutely undenominational. The issue was more simply a matter of discipline in the first instance, and outrage at the imputations that the Academic Council as a body was weak on good Catholic practice. In that same summer of 1936 the Governing Body voted a grant of £60 to defray the expenses of delegates to the Pax Romana Congress at Salzburg.[19] The principal activities of the UCD branch of the association included lectures and discussions on topics of interest to Catholic students; and as membership was open to all students of the college, it could not be alleged that public money was being spent for denominational purposes. Likewise the Governing Body was prepared to give special consideration to students who were seminarians and other religious.[20]

If the students in 1936 seemed more right-wing than the authorities and the academics, then this situation had been reversed by 1966. The contrast could not have been starker. The factors responsible for this reversal of roles and for the change of attitude on the part of religious-minded students no doubt include the reaction there had been to Michael Tierney's paternalistic regime; the increasing tolerance and ecumenism that affected church attitudes in the wake of the Vatican Council; the growing liberalisation of Irish society; the gradual move towards more freedom and fewer restrictions in the university; and the early warning breezes of the students' revolutionary storms that would beset universities all over the world a couple of years later.

The establishment of a branch of the Student Christian Movement in UCD at the beginning of the 1966/67 session was one indication of the change that had taken place. It was stated that by Michaelmas term the SCM, an ecumenical organisation open to members of every church, had 242 branches in colleges of higher education in Britain and Ireland. In Ireland these included Queen's University and Stranmillis (Church of Ireland) Teachers' Training College, Belfast; Magee College, Derry; and Trinity College, Dublin. John Feeney, a left-wing Catholic, was prominent among those who, in his words, 'decided to tread where most angels would not even dream of' when he set up the SCM branch in UCD.[21]

An application to establish the branch was made to the registrar, Dr Tom Murphy, at the beginning of the term. According to Feeney, the venture foundered in the registrar's office when he 'demanded that they get the permission of the Head Chaplain, i.e. the Archbishop, first.' 'All this,' said Feeney, 'happened in a non-sectarian University to a group whose committee had ten Catholics on it out of twelve, including originally a Christian Brother.' The students decided to go ahead in a hall beside Newman House, thanks to the generosity of such people as Lionel Booth TD, who had contributed £5 to the society. The branch planned meetings that would be addressed by Dr Simms, Church of Ireland Archbishop of Dublin, and the Chief Rabbi, Isaac Cohen.

Just as the right-wing Catholic students in 1936 had the support of the *National Student,* so now, thirty years later, the left-wing students were given the full backing of the students' paper *Campus*. In an editorial entitled 'Freedom of speech', *Campus* asserted that the application for recognition of the SCM had been refused 'by the University Chaplains representing the views of the Archbishop of Dublin.' It was alleged that the members of the SCM were warned not to inform the press of the registrar's decision, for fear that 'those against it would use it to the detriment of the College.' The laying down of the law was less distasteful to *Campus* than the 'odious manner in which it was brought into force.' The fear of free speech, haughty presumption and dogmatic conservatism, said the editorial, were evident in the SCM episode. The complete contrast with the mentality of those who edited the *National Student* of 1936 was emphasised in the following paragraph in *Campus* in 1966:

> The predominance of one religion in this country together with the considerable influence of the local Archbishop, has corrupted the non-denominational charter of the National University to an extent where it can no longer be considered anything other than a de facto Catholic University. In such a context, not only can it be seen why a liberal group like the SCM cannot be tolerated but also that its members are threatened.[22]

The college authorities, of course, saw the episode in an entirely different light and pointed to 'serious mis-statements' both in Feeney's account and in the editorial. According to the registrar, the application for recognition of the SCM had not been refused. While it was under consideration—but assuming there would be a refusal—the students had gone ahead and established the movement outside the college without permission. Permission had not been refused by the Archbishop of Dublin, who had indicated to the students that the question of recognition was primarily one for the college authorities. Feeney, as one of the students who brought copies of the correspondence with the archbishop to the registrar, had to have been aware of the facts. Permission to establish a branch of the SCM was still under consideration and might have been granted in the normal way.[23] The president had taken the precaution of asking the registrar to prepare a draft letter to the editors of the newspapers outlining the authorities' version of the affair, in case the papers published extracts from the *Campus* version.[24]

THE CHANGING STUDENT PROFILE

That UCD was a college acceptable to Catholics was demonstrated in the overwhelming proportion of its students who belonged to the Catholic Church. The number of students entered on the register for the first session of 1909/10 was 474.[25] The religious denomination, where given, was: Roman Catholic, 405; Church of Ireland, 6; Presbyterian, 2; Jewish, 2. In the case of

Extra curricular activities in the College between the wars. The Dramsoc (*above*) playing *The Importance of Being Earnest*: Roger McHugh as Canon Chasuble and Cyril Cusack as Jack Worthing (bending over table). James Meenan and Robin Dudley Edwards in fancy dress, perhaps for the Student's Rag, c. 1930 (*left*). Sean Lavan (UCD) defeating J.W. Rinkel, the Cambridge President and champion of Gt. Britain in the 440 yards flat in 1926 (*below*).

The Catholic and National Ethos. Earlsfort Terrace *en fête* for the Eucharistic Congress in 1932 (*above*) and President Coffey reviews the College OTC in 1931 (*below*).

Eoin MacNeill, Professor of Early (including Medieval) Irish History (1909–41).

Douglas Hyde, Professor of Modern Irish Language and Literature (1909–31).

Mary Macken, Professor of German (1911–49).

Robert Donovan, Professor of English Literature (1910–34).

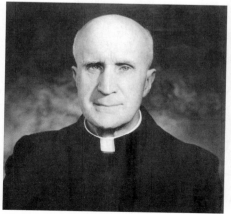

Monsignor John D. Horgan, Professor of Metaphysics (1942–71).

Mary T. Hayden, Professor of Modern Irish History (1911–38).

Two aspects of the pre-War College:
(*Above*) The 'Red Mass' procession from Newman House to University Church:
(*from left*) Professor Mary Macken, Michael Hayes, Michael Tierney and John Marcus
O'Sullivan (smiling), c. 1933/4. (*Below*) Cartoon by Brian O'Nolan (Myles na
gCopaleen) 'perhaps recalling the blatherers of the L&H' (Costello & Van de Kamp,
Flann O'Brien, London, 1987).

ÐACTRA AN FIR ÓLTA

ÞRIAN UA NUALLÁIN DO CEAP

President Tierney and friends: with Archbishop McQuaid (*above*) and Provost
McConnell of Trinity College (*below*).

College buildings. (*Above*) Earlsfort Terrace now shared with the National Concert Hall. (*Left*) The College of Science Merrion Street before its restoration as part of Government Buildings. (*Opposite, above*) The Veterinary College, Ballsbridge. (*Opposite, below*) Albert Agricultural College, Glasnevin.

Denis J. Coffey, President of UCD (1908–40).
From the portrait by Sir William Orpen

Arthur W. Conway, President of UCD (1940-1947).
From the portrait by Leo Whelan, RHA

Jeremiah J. Hogan, President of UCD (1964–72).
From the portrait by David Hone, RHA

Michael Tierney, President of UCD (1947–64).
From the portrait by Séan O'Sullivan

fifty-nine students no details about religion were registered. These were not to be taken as people who on principle refused to state their religious persuasion, for in practically all fifty-nine cases only the name, without any further details of address, parents, school attended, etc., was given on the register. For example, no details beyond their names were entered for the eighteen students in law and the six students in engineering. Of those, then, whose religion was given, 98 per cent were Catholics. An even more telling detail is the fact that of the known non-Catholic students, three out of the six Church of Ireland students were in medicine, as were the two Jews and the two Presbyterians. The other three Church of Ireland students were in arts.

The religious affiliations of the students hardly changed over the first fifty years, for in 1960/61, 97 per cent were still Catholics.[26] What was changing, however, was the proportion of clerical students to lay, and the proportion of those living in hostels under the supervision of religious. The numbers of clerical students, religious sisters and religious brothers were as follows:

Mid-1960s	700 (12%)
By 1980	100 (1%)
1990	65 (0.6%)

By 1990 the rarity would have been a person dressed in religious garb. The fall in vocations greatly affected the number of clergy and nuns in UCD. The college had been truly laicised in its students as well as in its staff.

The steady decline in the number of students living in hostels run by religious also reflected the retracting role that religious were playing in Irish society. As a proportion of the student body, these were:

1930	18%
1990	1.5%

Hand in hand with this secularisation in the residence of students there occurred a change in student life-styles. For a period—during the late fifties—the proportion of students living in lodgings was slightly greater than the figure classified as living at home. But this trend was quickly reversed from the sixties onwards. The proportion of full-time students in lodgings was:

1930/31	28%
1955/56	41%
1960/61	41%
From 1970s	24% to 9%
By 1990/91	7.5%

The proportion of students living at home was:

1930	38%
1955/56	38%
1960/61	38%
From 1970s	>50%
By 1990/91	59%

This increase corresponded to the growth of the city, the increasing numbers availing themselves of higher education, and the easier access to Dublin from nearby counties.

Flat-dwellers were not a category that merited inclusion in the first fifty years of the annual president's report. The first mention of students resident in flats is for the session 1969/70, when they made up 9 per cent of the student body. This assertion of an independent life-style coincided with the emergence of the student revolutionaries. By 1980/81, 25 per cent of students were living in flats; by 1990/91 the figure was 28 per cent, which made it the second-largest category after that of home residence.

Although, therefore, the vast majority of UCD's students between 1909 and 1990 had remained Catholics, there had gradually occurred subtle changes in the student profile reflecting developments that had taken place in society as a whole. Developments within the Catholic Church from the sixties—the papacy of John XXIII (1958–1963), the Vatican Council (1962–65), the abandonment of the index of prohibited books (1966), liberation theology, the ecumenical movement, the fall in the number of vocations, and liberalisation and secularisation in general—were bound to affect the younger generation, who could adapt more easily to change. All these modifications, together with the impact of the worldwide student revolution movements and the more local cause of alterations in residential habits, resulted in the emergence of a student profile by the sixties that was very different from that of its predecessor of the thirties.

If, therefore, students in the thirties appeared to be more right-wing than the authorities and the academic staff in their attitude to Catholicism, the students of the sixties had become more deliberately left-wing. And although the revolutionary fever soon subsided and students since the seventies became more concerned about employment than revolution, the militant Catholicism of the students of the thirties had disappeared.

The annual 'Red Mass'—the Votive Mass for the opening of the university year in October—had been a splendid occasion, with large numbers of students walking in procession into Newman's University Church, followed by the staff in their academic gowns, the clerical celebrants, and the archbishop, who presided from his throne in the sanctuary. An invited and invariably distinguished churchman preached the sermon, often dwelling on the need for a vigorous Catholic lay movement and the formation of educated men and women imbued with papal teaching and able to meet the menace of communism. Sometimes there were references to the misuse of advances in technology. Commenting on the Red Mass in his diary in October 1940, James Meenan wrote: 'Sermon by Bishop of Derry—remarkably good if with the usual tilts at science which seem to be common form. Pity that we don't keep up with the times—or rather that our church doesn't.'[27]

After the move to Belfield, however, the Red Mass lost much of its splendour; the attendance of the academic staff became comparatively sparse; the more isolated temporary church in Belfield did not attract the public's attention. What was in a sense a final flourish of this tradition took place in Belfield in 1973, when Dermot Ryan, sometime professor of eastern languages and by then successor to John Charles McQuaid as Archbishop of Dublin, presided at the Mass. The sermon was preached by James Kavanagh, auxiliary bishop of Dublin, who had been until that very year professor of social science. The closeness of relations between the church and the college was further emphasised in the fact that the lessons at the Mass were read by the President of UCD, Dr Thomas Murphy, and the president of the Students' Representative Council, Adrian Hardiman. And in his sermon Bishop Kavanagh stressed the need for a faculty of theology in UCD. 'Such a university as ours, which owes its origin to John Henry Newman, can hardly consider itself a true son of Newman without the presence of a faculty of Theology. Such a faculty would benefit not only the university but theology itself.'[28]

THEOLOGY IN UCD

Under the terms of the 1908 Act and Charters it was permissible to establish a lectureship or professorship in theology in the National University, provided no part of the cost came out of public funds. In December 1912 an indenture made between the four archbishops and the NUI established a part-time chair in theology, to be based in UCD. The hierarchy would nominate the holder, subject to confirmation by the Senate of the NUI.[29] No faculty of theology was set up, as the professor was required simply to give such lectures as might be agreed with the president. From 1925 money prizes totalling £50 were awarded by the bishops on the results of an examination for a certificate 'in the matter treated each year.' The first professor was Father Peter Finlay SJ. Father John Hannon SJ succeeded him in 1924 and began the practice of publishing his weekly lecture in the *Irish Catholic*.

When Father Hannon resigned in 1938 the archbishops replaced the one chair with three: dogmatic theology, moral theology, and biblical theology. The weekly lecture could be given by any one of the appointees, who at various times included such well-known Maynooth professors as Dr Edward Kissane, Dr P. F. Cremin, Dr Patrick Hamell, and Dr Kevin McNamara (later

Archbishop of Dublin). The examinations were not unduly onerous, and in 1959 Archbishop McQuaid found 'scant respect for the existing certificate in theology.'[30] At the time of the proposed merger with TCD, however, Rev. Professor Dermot Ryan of UCD welcomed the prospect of 'Schools of Divinity or Theology' in the new university and suggested ways in which this might be brought about.[31]

A decline set in in the nineteen-seventies, when reference to the chairs was dropped from the UCD Calendar. By the end of the decade no more remained than a series of lectures on a specific theological subject, open to the public. Theology in UCD now enjoyed the status of a free adult extra-mural course. Over the following decades it never appeared on the list of priorities when the establishment of new chairs or departments was under consideration, and no encouragement to promote it came from Dr Ryan, by now Archbishop of Dublin.

Progress was made in a more specific area in 1959 when Archbishop McQuaid proposed a diploma course in catechetical pedagogy to be taken at UCD by aspirant teachers. The president, Michael Tierney, agreed in principle but felt it necessary to be circumspect in the arrangements made, in order to minimise NUI involvement and to avoid having to assign the course to any college faculty; both he and the archbishop had by this time attracted criticism over a variety of issues and had no wish to offer hostages to fortune. In the event it took several years before a lectureship in catechetics, endowed by the archbishop, was established, strictly for teachers or trainee teachers of religion. A lecturer (Father Seán Ó Cuív) and four assistants were approved by the Governing Body. Nine students were conferred with the diploma in 1966; by 1970 the number was twenty-seven and by 1986 as many as thirty-five. Father Dónal Murray, later an auxiliary bishop of Dublin before becoming Bishop of Limerick, succeeded Father Ó Cuív in 1973.

THE ACADEMIC STAFF AND THE CATHOLIC ETHOS

With the return of the Liberals to government in 1905, Home Rule had seemed to be no more than a question of time. Pronouncements by the bishops illustrated profusely how the leaders of the Catholic Church in Ireland looked forward to the establishment of a native legislature under which a Catholic moral ethos might be promoted in Irish society. The setting up of the National University of Ireland in 1908, which established 'home government' in university education for Catholics, was looked upon by clergy and laity alike as a great opportunity for advancing the Catholic moral ethos in higher education.

The emergence of the Irish Free State coincided with the publication of Pope Pius XI's Encyclical on Catholic Action in 1922, which inaugurated the participation of the laity in the hierarchical apostolate for the purpose of restoring a society animated by the Christian spirit and of permeating public life with Catholic doctrine and morals.

Following independence there was a blossoming of organisations and of individual effort committed to Catholic Action.[32] Some prominent UCD academics became closely associated with various strands of this crusade. The headline was set by the college authorities. The president, Dr Coffey, was one of the leading laymen serving on the committee established by the hierarchy in 1928 to commemorate the centenary of Catholic Emancipation. The registrar, Professor Arthur Conway, was a prominent shareholder and chairman of the board of the *Standard,* the Catholic newspaper, when it was founded in the late twenties. Others, like John Marcus O'Sullivan (history), Arthur Clery (law) and William Magennis (metaphysics), had already been deeply involved in Catholic societies and publications since their time in the Jesuit University College.

The apostolate of the printed word was considered to be of vital importance, and intellectuals were expected to play their part in this aspect of Catholic Action. The series of papal pronouncements beginning with Pope Pius IX's *Syllabus of Errors* (1864) and continuing with Pope Leo XIII's *Rerum Novarum* (1891) and Pope Pius XI's *Quadragesimo Anno* (1931) had singled out and condemned the political and social evils of the modern world. Academics in the principal university college for Catholics in Ireland, especially those intellectuals who wrote commentaries on the political and social questions of the day, took seriously their vocation to save Ireland especially, but also to help to save the world, from what were seen to be the prevailing evils and errors of modern times.

Among the UCD professors who were the most prominent crusaders against the alleged false gods and philosophies of the day was John Marcus O'Sullivan, professor of history (1910–1948) and Minister for Education (1926–1932). O'Sullivan was a prolific contributor to Catholic publications such as *Studies,* the *Irish Ecclesiastical Record,* the *Irish Rosary,* the *Irish Catholic,* and the booklets of the Catholic Truth Society. He wrote and lectured extensively on subjects that were then of huge importance to the church: communism, Russia, Luther, contemporary ideologies, the French Revolution, Spain, Africa, South America, fascism, ethics, and 'state worship'. Though he pleaded for tolerance and prudence by Catholics in the circumstances of the modern world, he also asserted that indifferentism and neutrality were repugnant to the whole spirit of Catholicism. Whether as Government minister or university professor, O'Sullivan's personal commitment to 'whole-hearted acceptance of all the Church's teaching' and his belief that 'there must be propaganda for the truth' inspired his writing.[33]

A series of four articles by O'Sullivan in the *Irish Ecclesiastical Record* was entitled 'Perversion of values: reflections on some ideologies of to-day and yesterday'.[34] This series had all the solemnity of a lay encyclical on the topsy-turvy values of the political, social and economic systems and philosophies of modern times. The distinct and alarming possibility of the collapse of centuries-old European civilisation was to be ascribed to the disruption of the mediaeval system and those doctrines and ideas that since the beginning of modern history had worked for the exclusion of religion and moral considerations from one sphere after another of public and private life. The prevailing perversion of values meant the materialistic dominating over the spiritual, and in the process the state had become the object of supreme worship.

O'Sullivan argued that if Christianity was to be once more a success in the political field its spirit must permeate the lives of the people in their social activity. He had no ready-made political system to offer as the solution; but if Europe was to regain its role, then the people's allegiance must be won back to the living Christian faith. This was all in keeping with Pope Pius XI's encyclical on Catholic Action, just as O'Sullivan's identification of the evils of contemporary society owed much to the encyclicals of Pius IX, Leo XIII, and Pius XI.

Closely related to the apostolate of the printed word was the issue of 'evil literature'. With many others, Professor O'Sullivan argued that 'it is the Church's duty to protest when evil literature threatens to undermine morality.' But he qualified this by saying that if repressive measures were to be taken, their nature was not to be a matter of mere abstract formulation but of sound judgment and prudence.[35] When the Minister for Justice appointed a Committee of Enquiry on Evil Literature in 1926, it was O'Sullivan's colleague Robert Donovan, professor of English literature in UCD, who was appointed chairman. The report of this committee prepared the way for the Censorship Act (1929), one of the most characteristic pieces of legislation passed by the Free State to protect the traditional moral values of Irish society. It set up a Censorship Board to consider complaints whether a book or a periodical was 'indecent or obscene' or advocated 'the unnatural prevention of conception' and to report to the minister, who was empowered to issue an order prohibiting the sale and distribution of publications so considered.

The Censorship Board appointed by the minister consisted of five people, among whom UCD academics were prominent between 1930 and 1950. Canon (later Monsignor) P. J. Boylan (eastern languages) chaired the board from 1930 to 1942. Professor Donovan served with him from 1932 until his death in 1934, when he was replaced by Professor William Magennis (metaphysics), who served as a member from 1934 to his death in 1946. As chairman of the board from 1942, Magennis, also a member of Seanad Éireann, became the best-known defender and spokesman of the Censorship

Board. Between 1936 and 1942 four of the five members of the board were UCD academics: Boylan, Magennis, Coffey and Williams (education). Between 1950 and 1954 there was no UCD academic on the board, until Jeremiah Hogan between 1954 and 1957 served as a member of the Appeal Board, established by the Act of 1946.

On the other hand, another UCD professor, Michael Tierney, had been one of the moderating and even liberal influences during the discussions in the Dáil on the Censorship Bill in 1928 and subsequently in the Seanad debate in 1942 on the operation of the Censorship Act. He could justly claim that he stood 'in a sort of stepfatherly relation to the Censorship of Publications Act.'[36] A great many of the more operative phrases and a good many of the sentences in the Act were inserted by way of amendments with which Tierney's name had been associated; the Act as it finally emerged represented very largely the result of efforts on his part to amend what he considered in its original form to be unreasonable and rather wild. It was recognised that his contribution had led to the prohibition of newspapers and journals that devoted an undue proportion of space to sensational crime.[37] Not surprisingly, the professor of Greek had also been in part responsible for that section in the Act that stated that when considering a complaint referred to them the board should have regard to the 'literary, artistic, scientific or historic merit or importance and the general tenor of the book' that was the subject of the complaint; the language in which the book was produced; the nature and extent of the circulation it was intended to have; and the class of reader it was likely to have.[38]

Professor Tierney's involvement in the censorship controversy and its consequences illustrates well some of the narrower aspects of public opinion in Catholic Ireland in the early decades of the independent state. The Tierney and censorship affair also illustrates the context of the Catholic ethos in which UCD academics had to operate. No-one would ever accuse Professor Tierney of not being a good Catholic: indeed he was himself a Catholic Actionist; but clearly even Michael Tierney was not Catholic enough for some. His important contribution to the Dáil debate on the Censorship Bill and his amendments were severely criticised in a Catholic Truth Society circular, in the *Standard* and the *Universe,* and by the more conservative Catholic lobby, who, in the words of one critic, 'would rather a thousand times see Ireland ignorant but clean.'[39] The role he had played in the censorship controversy probably contributed to the loss of his Dáil seat for the NUI constituency in the 1932 general election.

From 1938 to 1944 Tierney was a member and vice-chairman of Seanad Éireann, elected for the NUI constituency. The role of independent senator admirably suited his temperament and provided him with a forum for advocating his views in the legislature. Tierney believed that the Censorship

Board had done a great deal of valuable work in keeping out literature that ninety-nine people out of a hundred would agree was, to a very great extent, undesirable and worthless; but he thought that the Censorship Board in discharging its functions had been too conscientious. Censorship, he asserted, did as much harm by excess as by defect in its operation. In the debate in the Seanad in 1942 he proposed the creation of an Appeal Board, which in fact was established by an Act four years later.

Besides providing Catholics with a philosophical response to the identified errors of the modern world, the papal encyclicals also contributed in part to that romantic nostalgia for the Catholic Middle Ages or the 'Age of Faith' then very much in vogue among Catholic intellectuals on the Continent. G. K. Chesterton, Hilaire Belloc and Christopher Dawson, among others, popularised the idea among English readers.

In the battle between zealous mediaevalists assigning responsibility to the Reformation for the sins of capitalism and industrialism and equally zealous Protestants ascribing modern progress to the same Reformation, UCD's intellectuals were enthusiasts in the camp of the mediaevalists. It is important to note here that one is not referring to mediaeval scholars as such—of whom UCD had its generous share in such figures as Eoin MacNeill (early Irish history), Osborn Bergin (Old Irish) and Aubrey Gwynn (mediaeval history)—but to those who looked back to the Age of Faith as a golden age and advocated mediaeval remedies for the ills of modern society. This view formed part of the intellectual framework within which the college operated.

Belloc and Chesterton had their admirers in UCD. Among these were Arthur Clery[40] and George O'Brien. 'As an undergraduate [1910–13] I had been a great "Chester-Belloc",' wrote O'Brien, professor of the national economics of Ireland (1926–1961).[41] More remarkable even than O'Brien's pioneering work in Irish economic history[42] were his two books on European topics. His *Essay on Medieval Economic Teaching* (1920) was cited by R. H. Tawney as among the then few treatments in English of the relations between religion and economics.[43] *An Essay on the Economic Effects of the Reformation* (1923) was also highly thought of at the time. These two books show that O'Brien was quite familiar with the work of the Continental and English scholars in this field.

Max Weber was among those eminent scholars on the Continent who were already stressing the connection between Protestantism and capitalism. Tawney, most notably, advanced the study of this relationship for English readers. This aspect of the work of Weber and Tawney and the other Continental and English scholars strongly appealed to O'Brien, who gave the thesis his own Catholic emphasis.[44] The juxtaposition of O'Brien's personal

Catholicism with his professionalism as a political economist gave his writing a richness and his thought its own dynamic sophistication, which raised him above the mere partisan.

Though O'Brien in his economic view of the world has to be described as a 'Catholic mediaevalist', he stopped short of advocating any detailed political system as a solution to the problems of modern society. His biographer has stated: 'He could never bring himself to be much interested in schemes of social regeneration, whether they were Marxist or Papal.'[45] Much the same might be said of John Marcus O'Sullivan, who was, however, decidedly more 'papal' than O'Brien. But, like O'Brien, O'Sullivan too was more concerned with philosophical principle than with the details of any particular scheme for remedying the ills of society.

If John Marcus O'Sullivan stayed on the high moral and philosophical ground and offered no immediate remedy beyond the re-evangelising of Europe, others in UCD strongly advocated the corporatism proposed in Pope Pius XI's *Quadragesimo Anno* (1931). The corporatists regarded the corporate character of the mediaeval guild as the model for the political and economic reform of modern society. In the sphere of government and politics they proposed a system based on the vocational group or corporate body, rather than on the geographical constituency.

One of the leading Irish exponents of the corporative system was Michael Tierney. Supported by his friend Professor James Hogan of UCC, he was prepared to offer concrete proposals for the application of corporatism to the political situation of the nineteen-thirties. He believed, with *Quadragesimo Anno,* that the aim of social legislation must be 'the re-establishment of vocational groups' or, as he himself put it, 'the mediaeval system brought up to date.' Like other champions of this system in Ireland, Tierney was careful to distinguish between corporatism as advocated by Pope Pius XI and the corporate states established under fascism in Italy and Germany. In this he was at one with his friend and colleague Professor Daniel Binchy (law), who wrote a well-informed, perceptive and widely acclaimed book on fascist Italy[46] and, during a spell as Irish minister to the Germany of the Weimar Republic, recorded his contempt for the opportunism of Hitler in his pursuit of power.[47]

Tierney and Binchy, as members of a government commission in 1936, were among those who most strongly urged the establishment of a senate elected from vocational panels, so that its composition would be as different from the Dáil as possible. The Seanad that emerged from the Constitution of 1937 made grand overtures to vocationalism, in that the electoral panels were in name based on vocational groupings; in practice, however, politicians in the

Dáil and local government made up the electorate in these panels, and senators elected under this system tended to be chosen for their party allegiance rather than for any vocational representation.

WORKERS' EDUCATION

By the time Tierney had become President of UCD in 1947, corporatism had lost its appeal and much of its momentum. Yet one of Tierney's early acts in his presidency was to appoint Father Edward Coyne SJ, a fellow-campaigner in the cause of vocationalism, as director of UCD's Board of Extra-Mural Studies in 1948 for the provision of adult and workers' education.

Interest in adult and continuing education was largely an outgrowth of the campaign to bring the social encyclicals into the offices, workshops and fields of Ireland. In UCC Alfred O'Rahilly had pioneered university extension courses to make trade unionists and others familiar with papal teaching on the social and economic issues of the day. The Jesuits at a General Congregation in Rome in September 1946 had taken the decision to become involved in the teaching of social study courses to adults. In Ireland the society set up a committee (which included Father Coyne) to implement this decision, and it was recommended that a Catholic Workers' College be founded. Father Coyne was requested by the provincial, with the enthusiastic approval of Archbishop McQuaid, to organise this. Alfred O'Rahilly urged his Jesuit friends that the Workers' College should be linked with UCD, and he intervened with Michael Tierney in favour of such a development; but given Tierney's well-known independent temperament, O'Rahilly was careful to avoid creating the appearance that UCC was interfering in UCD, and he warned his Jesuit contacts not to mention 'me or Cork.'[48]

Tierney was at first wary about committing UCD to these extension courses. He would always remain anxious that resources available for full-time degree courses not be attenuated. He believed, for example, that the part-time pass degree (evening) was of doubtful value and insisted that it should not reduce the standard and quality of the BA.[49] He felt that the Commerce Faculty and the Education Department might have been better left outside of the university altogether. The education of lawyers, he held, should be firmly based in the humanities. Professional training within the Faculty of Arts never appealed to him; and he did not hold therefore with the idea that the university should provide direct professional training for trade unionists or others. The fact that the President of UCC had become embroiled in a public row between the two divisions of the trade union movement at the time—the Irish Trades Union Congress and the Congress of Irish Unions, each with its own educational programme—only increased Tierney's caution. And to add to all of this, an early experiment at providing continuing education for trade unionists by UCD had only recently failed.

At the request of the ITUC and the Labour Party, Professor George O'Brien had organised a course in economics and social science for the session 1945/46, and a nominal fee was paid to the lecturers.[50] This came to an abrupt end the following year. In a letter to the trade union organisers' meeting in February 1947 O'Brien stated: 'The lectures have been almost a complete failure, the attendance has steadily dropped down to seven or eight and the present method of providing adult education should be discontinued.' He added that he was willing to give any help he could if invited by the president of the college to assist in preparing a new scheme.[51]

The ITUC then decided to set up its own People's College, along the lines of the Workers' Educational Association in Britain, and talks were held with TCD and UCD in the hope that these colleges would co-operate and provide some of the lecturers. UCD's Academic Council appointed a committee to meet delegates of the Irish Workers' Educational Association. The terms of reference given to this committee indicated UCD's extreme caution. These insisted that 'this must be a matter purely for the College with no part in Inter-University organisation in Dublin ...' And the committee was also to keep in mind the question 'to what extent is the WEA representative of all Trade Unions in Ireland?'[52] In the course of the meeting Dr Tierney explained that the workers' education was not the business of a university; and he stated that there could be no question of UCD appointing members to any joint committee with TCD.[53]

Tierney always wanted UCD to be in charge of anything done in its name, and he decided that a system of continuing education should be established independently. O'Brien had agreed to provide lectures for the People's College but, feeling that his first loyalty was to UCD, found it impossible to continue his association. It made sense to Father Coyne of the Catholic Workers' College and to his friend Michael Tierney that they should co-operate. And although the Catholic Workers' College continued its own constitutional existence, it was in effect incorporated in UCD by the appointment of Father Coyne as director of extra-mural studies in UCD. He was to take charge, in consultation with the president and registrar, of workers' educational courses. These were to be held in the college or elsewhere in the city, and the president reported that 'the College would give all the help it could.'[54]

The People's College was left without any official links with the universities and without any university recognition for its courses. It found itself attacked by the Catholic right—in particular by the *Standard* and by Alfred O'Rahilly—and suspected of communist links and of intending to inoculate workers with Marx's alien philosophy. Trade unionists were all the more pleasantly surprised, therefore, when they were approached and their co-operation sought by the director of UCD's Extension Courses Department. The work intended to be carried out by the People's College, as well as by the Catholic Worker's College—what might loosely be called the left and right wings of the workers' educational movement—was to a large extent absorbed by UCD's extra-mural department.

The Extension Courses Department was established in October 1948, and Father Coyne was entrusted with its organisation. Immediately he set to work making contact with the two rival trade union congresses and with some thirty or thirty-five union officials. The outcome of his negotiations was encouraging. One congress and seven unions agreed to endow the lectureships, and eighteen unions promised to grant over a hundred scholarships, equivalent to two-thirds of the tuition fee. The programme was described as 'classes suitable for members of Trade Unions and leading to a College Diploma in Social and Economic Science.'[55] Applications were received from 384 people for the course that opened on 17 January 1949. Eventually 271 were enrolled, and there was a regular attendance of about 260.

The students attended for two hours on three nights a week. In the first term they had six subjects: social theory and ethics (Dr Lucey of Maynooth, soon to be appointed Bishop of Cork), political theory and institutions (Arthur Cox), economics (J. P. MacHale), accountancy (C. P. Martin of Aer Lingus), Irish culture (Seán O'Sullivan on folklore and Professor Seán P. Ó Ríordáin on archaeology), and a tutorial class (Father Coyne on the conduct of meetings and Gabriel Fallon on public speaking). In the second term the archaeology course included a field tour of the Boyne Valley. The Irish culture course included traditional music and was conducted by Dónal O'Sullivan, John F. Larchet and Michael O'Higgins and was regarded as a notable success. In the second term 260 students were enrolled, with an average attendance of 225. The Government agreed to a grant of £809 towards the development of adult education in UCD.[56]

What began almost as a side-show to the university's main business — accurately conveyed in the terms 'extra-mural' and 'extension' lectures — soon became a significant contribution by UCD to the community, and it fitted very much into the tradition of Newman's evening classes for 'the young men of Dublin' and those engaged in various employments during the day.[57] Alfred O'Rahilly explained how the programme worked in Cork with the assistance of the vocational teachers, adding: 'A priest, nominated by the bishop, teaches sociology.' The advantage of co-operation with the vocational education committees, he stated bluntly, was that 'we are able to have a Catholic Course and yet to use State finances.'[58]

Father Coyne looked to see how far the Cork course could be adapted by UCD to meet the needs of provincial towns. He wrote: 'I know that Alfred wants to concentrate almost entirely on Sociology and the history of Trade Unionism. Our course is a little wider.'[59] He agreed rather with Tierney: 'we ought to have less accountancy etc.'[60]

It would seem that it was largely as a result of a lecture given by O'Rahilly in Carlow and Kilkenny on the need for adult education that Bishop Keogh of Kildare and Leighlin and Bishop Collier of Ossory decided to start a workers' course in these towns. Father Robert Prendergast of Carlow College and Father Peter Birch (afterwards Bishop of Ossory) were appointed the organisers of these courses in Carlow and Kilkenny, respectively; they applied to UCD's Extension Courses Department to be recognised as centres preparing students for the diploma, and were accepted. Following Carlow and Kilkenny, the social and economic studies course was conducted in a number of other centres in Leinster. Wexford, Mullingar, Drogheda, Dundalk, Tullamore, Naas, Portlaoise, Athlone, Edenderry and Tullow were all involved at one time or another.[61] A visitation of provincial centres in the session 1952/53 by Dublin lecturers claimed that the standard of intelligence was higher on average than that of the Dublin students. Their average age was twenty-four, and most of them had the Leaving Certificate. The unions were well represented at all centres except Naas, where the students were all members of the local Young Farmers' Club.[62]

Of the 122 students from the original group who sat for the final diploma examination in 1951, two years after enrolling in the course, 109 qualified. The diplomas were awarded at a public ceremony attended by Monsignor O'Reilly, representing the archbishop, and by the Taoiseach and other members of the Government. Emphasising the fuss that was made of these courses was the fact that the Minister for Education, Seán Moylan, was present at the award ceremony the following year. It was taken that 'the widespread demand for the courses is a clear indication of a national need which the College is happy to assist in meeting.'[63]

From the start of the extra-mural programme the influence of Tierney's concern for the humanities was apparent. Not only was there on offer a two-year diploma in social and economic studies but there was also, beginning in 1949/50 (in the Dublin centre only), a two-year diploma in liberal arts, embracing Greek, Roman and Celtic civilisations, English literature, history, and the fine arts.

By the mid-fifties it was clear that more students were being attracted to the liberal arts course than to that in social and economic studies. On the other hand, a much smaller proportion of those who registered for liberal arts sat for the examinations. In 1958/59 the Extra-Mural Board offered a total of fourteen courses in Dublin, which catered for adults wishing to attend individual lecture courses without taking examinations. These 'occasional' students immediately outnumbered those registered for the diplomas: in that first session, of the 149 who enrolled, 81 (54 per cent) signed on as non-examination students. The non-diploma courses proved so attractive that in 1960 the board took the decision to suspend examinations for the diplomas in Dublin except for those already enrolled. The diploma courses were, however, continued in the other centres.

Over the next couple of decades the number of extra-mural courses offered in Dublin, and the number of students availing themselves of them, greatly increased. One side benefit that these courses bestowed on the ordinary undergraduates of the college was the creation of a fund to aid students in need of financial assistance. The nucleus of that fund was formed by setting aside contributions from the surplus in the extra-mural income.[64]

	Courses offered	Number of students
1958/59	14	149
1968/69	25	2,048
1975/76	57	5,469
1976/77	61	5,650
1977/78	67	5,710
1978/79	69	4,955
1988/89	80	2,638
1992/93	245	2,621

So what began with the purpose of arming trade unionists with a knowledge of the social encyclicals to fend off communism soon became a liberal, aesthetic education for adults without reference to any earlier educational experience on their part. Courses were specifically designed 'to cater for the varying backgrounds of an adult audience.'[65] Record enrolments were taken as evidence of the ever-increasing demand for this type of education.

The extra-mural courses taken by students who wanted to employ their leisure to the best advantage had become an established characteristic of UCD's service to the community. Universities had come into existence under the motherly wing of the mediaeval church and in time became great secular institutions. In somewhat similar fashion, the extra-mural movement grew out of the concern that Catholic Actionists expressed for the propagation of the social encyclicals and the need they felt to oppose the threat of communism. In Dublin any confessional origins were soon absorbed into a more secular, or at least cultural, concern for the extension of education to a wider community beyond the normal university undergraduate.

Given so much commitment to Catholic Action on the part of the academic staff, it was hardly surprising that Michael Tierney in 1940 could claim that the university—a 'pagan bantling' with its dominant secularist framework transplanted to Ireland in 1908—'has become more and more Catholic as time has passed.'[66]

Tierney was by no means alone in holding this view of the college. Its religious ethos was justly characterised by one of John Marcus O'Sullivan's brightest students and his successor, Professor T. Desmond Williams. In the chapter he wrote for *Struggle with Fortune* in 1954, Williams claimed that the criticism made of the National University at its inception by Cardinal Logue and a few bishops to the effect that it was not Catholic enough was answered by the later history of the university. He wrote of UCD:

> Its atmosphere has been Catholic but not clerical, scientific but not secular. The provisions made for the religious life of its members have been extensive and pervasive, and they have fostered therefore a Catholic spirituality which has been voluntary and natural rather than imposed and external. There is no single instance of action or of work undertaken by the college to which the religious authorities have taken exception; and the system as a whole has afforded excellent opportunity for intellectual co-operation between the laity and the clergy. The relations between the clerical and lay members of the staff can thus develop in academic matters on the basis of equal and independent partnership. If that co-operation has not as yet resulted in the establishment of a flourishing Catholic intellectual tradition which could claim comparison with some of the older Catholic colleges on the Continent, the fault does not lie with the legal system.[67]

The degree of commitment by the academics to the Catholic ethos varied from John Marcus O'Sullivan's extensive promotion of Catholic apologetics to George O'Brien's dissatisfaction with the capitalist and socialist economic dogmas of the day. It is important to stress that there is no evidence that any of these academics allowed their 'Catholic' opinions to intrude on their university teaching for evangelistic or proselytising purposes. Similarly, the relatively liberal views of Michael Tierney or the narrower views of William Magennis on censorship did not divert these teachers from their professional tasks. Notwithstanding the pervasive Catholic ethos and its almost 100 per cent Catholic student population and the significant sprinkling of Catholic Actionists on its staff, UCD was seen to keep within the undenominational limits of its Charter.

THE BISHOPS AND THE COLLEGE

The establishment of a university acceptable to Irish Catholics was the *fons et origo* of the NUI; hence the involvement of the bishops in the negotiations that preceded the passing of the Act of 1908. They acted in effect as patrons of all its colleges in the years that followed, a connection in part invited by the colleges themselves, especially in mid-century, when the church's influence was at its most pervasive. In these years the President of UCG, Monsignor Pádraig de Brún, was a cleric, and the President of UCC, Alfred O'Rahilly, was a leading Catholic controversialist and apologist. And of course there was Michael Tierney at UCD, with his strong convictions about the Catholic ethos of his college.

In fact the bishops' relationship with UCD was particularly intimate. They had leased the houses in St Stephen's Green and the Medical School building to the new institution, lent it the Catholic University Library, which had been transferred successively to Clonliffe and Maynooth, donated Chief Baron Palles's law library to the college, given permission for an architectural school to be built on their property in the forties for no additional rent, and were indeed to present gratis the famous and valuable houses of the Catholic University at 85 and 86 St Stephen's Green to UCD in the nineteen-eighties. Apart from these practical matters, the bishops had a long-standing view, not to be abandoned until 1970, about the unsuitability of Trinity College for Catholics: this was a question primarily of relevance within the NUI to UCD and within the hierarchy to the Archbishop of Dublin. Regarding Trinity, Dr Tierney concurred emphatically with the bishops and especially with his friend Archbishop McQuaid.

It would be disingenuous to suppose that, together with the other presidents, Tierney did not also observe the weight carried by the bishops' attitudes on political issues in the clericalised society of the day. The bishops would clearly be valuable allies for any college needing to pressure the government into conceding its wishes. The bishops, for their part, would not be reluctant allies for institutions, in practice if not in law, charged with the higher education of Catholic students. Against this background, when the four presidents of the NUI colleges (Maynooth included) asked the bishops in 1950 to set up a committee with which the presidents could discuss matters of common concern, the proposal met a positive and warm response. At their meeting of 10 October 1950 the bishops appointed a committee composed of the four archbishops and the Bishops of Galway and Limerick, with the Archbishop of Armagh as chairman. (The Bishop of Cork was added to the committee when Dr Lucey succeeded the aged Dr Coholan in 1952.) Tierney was requested to draw up, in consultation with the other presidents, an agenda for the meeting and to develop the points on which discussion was invited.[68]

The dominant role Michael Tierney now played as organiser and driving force was emphasised in correspondence between O'Rahilly and himself in the two weeks preceding the first meeting. He sent O'Rahilly a copy of a memorandum he had drawn up setting out the position of UCD, which might serve as a basis for preliminary discussion.[69] O'Rahilly was glad that Tierney's memo should be thoroughly discussed, though he did not agree with its main thrust—the scrapping of the NUI Charters and the establishment of independent universities in place of constituent colleges. Monsignor de Brún prepared a brief second memorandum, which raised the question of philosophy for lay students.

The Tierney and de Brún memoranda made up the agenda for the first meeting between the presidents and the bishops' committee, which took place in the Bishops' Room in Newman House on 17 January 1951, with Tierney acting as host. The President of St Patrick's College, Maynooth, had not been included; the Bishop of Limerick was unable to attend; and the President of UCG was not listed among those present.

'Memorandum on University Question. No. 1. Jan. 1951', which the President of UCD submitted to the meeting with the bishops' committee, was a historic document.[70] It revealed Michael Tierney's objective: to turn UCD into a Catholic and independent university playing a leading role among the Catholic universities of the English-speaking world. He aimed to bring to a flourishing reality Newman's grand mid-nineteenth-century ideal.

The 1908 Act, he argued, was an unsatisfactory answer to the needs of Irish Catholics, having been given by an English Parliament and Liberal government a character similar to that of the secular provincial universities of Britain. The bishops had been able to say no more of the NUI colleges than that they were 'sufficiently safe in regard to faith and morals.' They should in fact be 'not only negatively safe but capable of making positive contributions towards the growth and preservation of a fully Catholic society.' The NUI should be broken up and its colleges re-established as independent universities (UCD, he memorably wrote, was already 'a university masquerading as a college'). These new universities should be 'frankly Catholic' and be organised into halls of residence under the discipline of the religious orders, subject to the general control of the university. The universities themselves should maintain the principle of control by the Catholic laity, which had worked so admirably during the previous forty years. Their Governing Bodies should be composed of representatives of the Government, the hierarchy, and the academic staff. The representatives of the academic staff, as being responsible for the day-to-day working of the universities, should, however, be the majority. The proposed new universities would be chartered bodies, protected from the casual or ill-considered interference by the state. They should have full power, under the authority of the hierarchy, to set up faculties of philosophy, sociology and canon law. In such a reorganisation, he concluded, Trinity College should be left to serve the Protestant community.

What support within the college Tierney might have found for the proposal to turn UCD into a Catholic university, in name as well as ethos, can only be guessed at. Certainly, notwithstanding the confessional ambience of the era, many would have opposed any move to Catholicise UCD officially had Tierney put it forward publicly. It would have been altogether divisive.

But it was not the suggestion of establishing formally Catholic universities on which Tierney's grand scheme foundered: it was rather on his necessary preliminary proposal, the abolition of the NUI. Alfred O'Rahilly, of course, wanted his college to be at least every bit as Catholic as Tierney's UCD; but he took a view of the 1908 Act very different from that of Tierney.

On several occasions O'Rahilly had expressed the belief that the 1908 settlement for the university education of Catholics was 'a much more favourable scheme than we could obtain today even from our own Government and Legislature.'[71] He feared that if the 1908 Charters were abandoned and the Dáil asked to bring in an amending Act, the university question would be thrown open; 'certain elements will become vociferous— anti-clericals, friends of Trinity College, so-called liberals etc.'; there would be a widespread desire to restrict university autonomy; and an attempt would be made to impose 'neutrality' in matters religious on the colleges. Certain supporters of Irish, he said, would have no scruple in advocating new state restrictions. The outcome would be fraught with grave risks as regards Catholic interests and academic autonomy. He urged that prelates and Catholic academics should hold firmly to the 1908 Act and Charters as a final settlement of Catholic claims.

O'Rahilly held that it was inaccurate and unfair to blame the lack of philosophy and theology for lay students in the NUI colleges on their Charters. People (by implication, people like Michael Tierney) had got into the habit of reading into these documents a neutral secularism that was not in fact contained in them. The remedy, he argued, was not in breaking up the NUI but in using the actual powers permitted under the 1908 Charters to give an integral Catholic university education. This remedy was in the hands of the colleges themselves. Hence the importance of agreement on a common policy for the colleges in such areas as philosophy, sociology, apologetics, and theology, which O'Rahilly then proceeded to outline.

The difference between Tierney and O'Rahilly was essentially that the President of UCD would make the colleges Catholic by amending the 1908 Act and Charters, whereas the President of UCC would do so by providing courses in philosophy and theology for lay students.

How were the bishops to react? The meeting had taken place not because the bishops had pressed for it but on the initiative of the college presidents. There is no evidence that the bishops were stirring up a campaign for the formal establishment of a Catholic university in place of the NUI. But if even

O'Rahilly, the foremost controversialist and apologist among the Catholic laity, was opposed to Tierney's arguments about the breaking up of the NUI in order to replace it with a Catholic university, what chance would the proposal have of winning the backing of the politicians and the public? The bishops had no wish to have to arbitrate between two such staunch Catholics; and they realised that without agreement between Cork and Dublin, the idea of a Catholic university was simply going nowhere.

The two opposing points of view had been aired at the first meeting between the bishops' committee and the presidents of the colleges; and though there had been, according to Tierney, 'such an interesting discussion,'[72] no decision had been taken and the two friends had agreed to differ, apparently in the most amicable spirit. The three presidents were to have further discussions, with a view to trying to arrive at agreement; the bishops were to discuss the question among themselves and examine what means might be adopted to remedy any defects in the 1908 Act and Charters. Tierney commented: 'The prospects of getting much further do not seem too good, but we shall see.'[73]

And there the matter lay until three months later, when a rather bitter private row blew up between the presidents of UCD and UCC over the issue. It resulted from an address by Tierney that O'Rahilly chose to see as part of a UCD campaign to obtain independent status from the rest of the NUI. A sequence of angry private letters flew between the two presidents, which revealed little more than the strength of their rival convictions on the future of the university, their pugnacity, and their over-sensitivity in protecting their colleges. It showed them to be two academics who could never resist a challenge or a controversy and who, when they were not involved in intellectual jousts or arguments with students, staff, Government, or spokesmen for other institutions, religions or philosophies, kept themselves in practice by carrying on private arguments. There were, as the saying goes, two of them in it.

One year after their controversy the two presidents restated, for the benefit of the bishops, their positions on the 1908 Act and Charters, but this time without any of the personal abuse that had marked their earlier private correspondence.

O'Rahilly believed that the 1908 Act should be taken as a foundation on which to build. Tierney's argument was that before doing so it should be thoroughly examined in the light of forty years' experience. He did not suggest that a simple or easy answer was available to the problem of what form university education for Catholics should take; but he proposed that the hierarchy and the authorities of the colleges make a study of the problem as a whole and work out something in the nature of a long-term solution that could be applied whenever the favourable moment happened to present itself.

The whole emphasis in Tierney's second memo had now switched from the ideal of a Catholic university to the need for an independent UCD. He argued that the three constituent colleges differed widely from each other in their needs, and thereby in the outlook that these needs dictated. What might be a comfortable situation as seen from Cork took on a very difference aspect as seen from Dublin.

Strong reasons existed for a reconsideration at least of the constitution of UCD. With the enormous growth in its numbers, from 530 in 1909 to over three thousand since the mid-forties, the government of the college had assumed an aspect completely different from anything in the minds of those who had formulated its Charter. It had at least a thousand students more than Trinity. The present position in Dublin, Tierney wrote, might be roughly described by saying that while Trinity was a college masquerading as a university, UCD was a university masquerading as a college.

The salient feature in the higher educational landscape as seen from Dublin was the growing competition with Trinity College, which in its constitution, site and buildings had many advantages over UCD. By its Charter it found itself in a much freer position in many respects than UCD, which was hampered by its federal nature and by other defects imposed by the 1908 settlement. Trinity was governed by a small and intelligently selected academic body, which could meet frequently and act with decision. By contrast, the Governing Body of UCD was large and unwieldy and could only meet at long intervals. Tierney then revealed, in outspoken language, what he thought of the nature of his own Governing Body. In purporting to give the body a 'representative' character, the Act of 1908 had included an external element of county councillors and others that constituted nearly a third of its numbers, as well as a number elected by the graduates. 'By an unfortunate and unforeseen development it can happen that these non-academic members of the Governing Body are people who not only have no conception of the nature of a University or of the type of education it gives, but who are for one reason or another bitterly hostile to the college itself and to its work.' The system of appointments was an outcome of the character of the Governing Body. The higher sense of responsibility consistently shown by the Senate of the NUI in this matter had been due to its more academic nature.

These were but a few of the more evident disabilities suffered by the college as a result of the rigidity of its Charter, aggravated by its own extraordinary growth. Reform in the status and constitution of UCD was necessary to give the college its rightful place as a great university for Catholics. In this task, Tierney argued, the assistance of the hierarchy was absolutely essential. The method and occasion for carrying out the reforms, he concluded, might well be left to later consideration.

The emphasis in Tierney's first memo had been on scrapping the 1908 Act and Charters and establishing instead a Catholic university. After O'Rahilly's disagreement with him, the emphasis in Tierney's second memo was placed instead on the creation of an independent UCD. One is left, therefore, with the question whether a Catholic university or an independent UCD serving the needs of Catholic students was his priority. Probably the latter—or, expressed differently, his long-term ideal was a Catholic university, but the more immediate and more tangible objective was an independent UCD.

When O'Rahilly had retired from UCC and had come to live in Dublin, he too was able to view UCD's problem, and especially the rivalry with TCD, more sympathetically from Tierney's standpoint.

TRINITY COLLEGE

The other important issue discussed at the first meeting between the bishops and the presidents was that of relations between University College and Trinity College. Michael Tierney pointed out that a good deal of competition existed between the two colleges, and he claimed that the situation had been made worse by the action of two successive Governments in awarding grants to Trinity out of public funds. Trinity College, he said, had a very strong Protestant tradition, and any suggestion, such as was frequently made, of amalgamation between UCD and TCD was bound to founder on this fact. There was a real danger that, almost by inadvertence, a situation might be created in which University College might find itself in an inferior position, even with regard to Catholic students, to Trinity College. It was a fact, he argued, that the requirement of compulsory Irish, for example, had produced almost as its sole effect a regular annual flow of Catholic students to Trinity.

The Archbishop of Dublin remarked that at present about 120 students a year from different parts of Ireland had to be given permission to enter Trinity because of certain courses that were available to them there and that were either not available in University College or were available only on disadvantageous terms compared with Trinity. He instanced in particular courses for diplomas in social science and public administration. These diplomas were in many cases practically a necessity to students of small means, who could pursue their studies for them only at evening classes. The classes available in University College were at unsuitable hours, and the fees were considerably higher than at Trinity. (This was a reference to the fact that at that time some of the lectures for these diplomas were only available during the day.)

Tierney in reply was defensive. He did not think it likely that Trinity would offer courses accompanied by free teas, but it was an extreme illustration of the competition for students. He nevertheless undertook to have the matter re-examined and set right as far as possible.[74]

Serious as the epistolary row and their persistent divisions over the future of the NUI had been, Tierney and O'Rahilly were both such battle-hardened controversialists that these differences did not interfere with their co-operation on other issues, where they shared much in common and where they still felt that the bishops' committee could be useful. One such issue was the practice by which the state made appointments to posts in teaching hospitals and in the Veterinary College that were also chairs in colleges of the NUI: this was seen by the presidents as state interference in the autonomy of the university. And with regard to the hospitals, any appearance that the state might be interfering unduly in questions of health so soon after the bitter controversy over the Mother and Child Scheme was bound to seem more urgent to the bishops than the speculative differences between O'Rahilly and Tierney over the 1908 Act and Charters.

A second meeting with the bishops' committee took place on 23 January 1952, and Tierney sent a brief summary of what had been agreed to the Archbishop of Armagh, who had been absent through illness. The points of agreement between presidents and bishops included:

1. That the Senate should approach the Government, privately in the first instance, with regard to the scheme for Maternity Hospitals in Cork and Galway, pointing out the Catholic principles involved in this question and its bearing on University autonomy and on University facilities for Medical Teaching both in Cork and in Galway ... The University should acquaint the Standing Committee of the Bishops with the results of this action so that the Bishops can consider their own attitude to the question.

2. The Senate should also consider the principles involved in the petition made last year by Trinity College for such financial aid as would enable it to have the same status as the National University in regard to endowment from the State. It should be stressed in such consideration that Trinity College is already heavily endowed; that it cannot cater for Catholics who form the vast majority in Ireland; that it is not bound by the Irish Universities Act of 1908, nor subject to the same limitations as the National University and its Colleges; that it is at present engaged in an unworthy form of academic competition with University College, Dublin; and that the National University, historically speaking, owes its origin to the insistence of Trinity College on its exclusively Protestant character.[75]

These matters were then brought before the Standing Committee of the Senate.[76]

Tierney also drew up a memorandum on the subject of the grant to Trinity College, a copy of which was sent to O'Rahilly for his comments on its suitability. Both presidents agreed that the document should not be circulated to the Senate, because the risk of its unauthorised publication would be too great. O'Rahilly advised against any official circulation, except privately to Bishop Browne of Galway. It could be read by Tierney to the Standing Committee and then forwarded to the Government. The President of UCC agreed with the memo but continued to warn Tierney against any invitation to the Government to change the 1908 Charters.[77]

Meetings of the Presidents' and Bishops' Liaison Committee (as it was coming to be called by the participants) in 1953 and 1954 heard the outcome of approaches made separately to the Government by the presidents and the bishops on the question of clinical appointments. This was settled on the basis of 'adequate representation'[78] for the colleges on interview boards, which was considered to protect the principle of autonomy. The provision of courses in general philosophy for non-clerical undergraduates was approved, as well as a new evening course at UCD leading to a special degree (BSocSc) where the emphasis would be on practical philosophy: psychology, ethics, and sociology.[79]

Others besides Michael Tierney were concerned about the increase in the subsidy to Trinity College. Bishop Browne of Galway, a strong and useful ally, since he was also on the Standing Committee of the NUI Senate, wrote to Tierney: 'I think it is important that the question of the increase in the subsidy to Trinity College should be dealt with, as Trinity College is now claiming the status and rights of a national university as is evident from its attempt to get Co. Council scholarships and to get a large Government grant.'[80]

The challenge from Trinity, and especially its mounting rivalry with UCD in the capital city, became a major issue in discussions of the Liaison Committee from the beginning of 1954. Tierney was only too willing to produce one of his many memos for the bishops outlining what he considered to be the grave threat to his college from TCD's recent policies. In his memo of 1952 replying to O'Rahilly's defence of the 1908 Act and Charters he pointed to the fact that the endowment of TCD out of current taxes had reached the figure of £100,000 per year. When it was remembered that, if recognised as a college for Protestants, Trinity College served about 7 per cent of the population, this figure was extremely generous compared with £440,000 for the remaining 93 per cent, and still more so when compared with £233,000 for Trinity's real rival, UCD, which had at least a thousand more students. And it would not have escaped notice that within the past few months an effort had begun to be made to procure for Trinity some of the indirect benefits of the Act of 1908, in the shape of county council scholarships.[81]

Given the growing competition from TCD and the chronic accommodation problems at UCD, Tierney was able to press the bishops for
consideration whether UCD, 'inheritor of the traditions of the Catholic
University of Ireland, is to be kept permanently in the weak position, as
against Trinity College, in which it was undoubtedly placed by the 1908
Act.'[82] When, therefore, the Government set up the Commission on Accommodation Needs of the Constituent Colleges of the National University of
Ireland, the hierarchy, responding to the promptings of Tierney, wrote to the
Taoiseach, Éamon de Valera, stating that, given the lack of adequate
university facilities, there was the serious danger that Catholic students might
be forced or drawn to Trinity College. The bishops repudiated the claim that
Trinity could be regarded as being on a par with the NUI as a university
acceptable to Catholics. Their letter also stated that the increase in the number
of students and in the complexity of what was now included under university
facilities demanded a proportionate increase in the grant to the NUI. As
university accommodation depended on academic needs, they requested—in
vain, as it turned out—that the commission should include some persons with
experience and special knowledge of academic needs.[83]

The usefulness of the Liaison Committee to the NUI colleges and to UCD in
particular soon became evident in the handling of a number of important
issues that arose during the fifties and sixties. In their dealings with the
Government the presidents of the colleges, without too much difficulty, were
able to enlist the support and influence of the hierarchy on such sensitive
matters as the medical schools and Trinity College, where the church leaders'
views coincided with those of the college presidents. But even on questions
that on the surface seemed to invite no direct involvement on the part of the
bishops—such as the Government's proposals in 1955 for the establishment
of an Agricultural Institute for the education of agricultural students, or a
later Government's proposal of a joint board to administer the Veterinary
College—the presidents got powerful support from their allies the bishops.

THE AGRICULTURAL INSTITUTE AND THE VETERINARY COLLEGE

The plans of James Dillon, Minister for Agriculture in the second inter-party
Government, for the reorganisation of higher agricultural education (two
years in a university college followed by two years in a single agricultural
institute) ran into strong opposition not only from the farmers' organisation
and the universities but also from the bishops—especially from Archbishop
Walsh of Tuam, Bishop Browne of Galway, and Bishop Lucey of Cork, all
three of whom were members of the Liaison Committee. Dr Walsh and Dr
Browne were also members of the Senate of the NUI and of the Governing

Body of UCG, while Dr Lucey was a member of the Governing Body of UCC.

Archbishop Walsh said he had no confidence in any institute established in Dublin to direct agricultural activities. Bishop Browne held that the institute would not be independent and that it was entirely wrong that the state should take over education at university level. And Bishop Lucey maintained that the proposals were in conflict with Catholic social teaching, since the proper function of the state was to help the university in the matter of agricultural education rather than edge it out with its own agencies controlled by the civil service.[84]

That the opposition to the Government's scheme was not restricted to a few outspoken members of the hierarchy but emanated from the whole body was confirmed in a letter to Éamon de Valera six months after he had become Taoiseach once more in 1957. The bishops wrote that the hierarchy regarded as most detrimental to Catholic interests the proposal to deprive the National University of its Faculties of Agriculture (in UCD) and Dairy Science (in UCC). They hoped that the Government would take cognisance of their representations, as they would feel it their duty to oppose.[85]

Faced with such opposition, the Government altered the proposals. Under the Agriculture (An Foras Talúntais) Act (1958), agricultural teaching was left to the universities, and An Foras Talúntais became, instead of a teaching college, a body for the co-ordination of research. And Tierney was pleased that what he called the attempt to deprive the NUI of its Faculties of Agriculture and Dairy Science had been unsuccessful.

Up to the end of the Second World War the Veterinary College was owned, controlled and staffed by the Department of Agriculture. Veterinary surgeons educated in the Veterinary College in Ballsbridge, Dublin, were examined and registered by the Royal College of Veterinary Surgeons in London. After the war it was decided in Britain to hand over the examining and registering functions of the Royal College to selected universities. The Government followed suit, and UCD since 1946 and TCD since 1954 became partly associated with the training and qualification for the profession, though the main part of the training continued to be provided by the Veterinary College, still controlled by the Department of Agriculture.

The attempt to place veterinary education in the proposed Agricultural Institute of 1955 met with successful opposition, including that from the veterinary profession, which was keen to strengthen the association with the university. After a year and a half of negotiations the Veterinary Council of Ireland (the body responsible for registering veterinary surgeons) failed to find a solution acceptable to both UCD and TCD. The matter was brought to a head at the end of 1958 by a visitation from the Royal College of Veterinary Medicine, which found the Irish system unsatisfactory.

Between 1958 and 1960 the Government made a number of proposals directly to the two university colleges. The first of these, proposed by the Minster for Agriculture in a paper of December 1958, intended reconstituting the Veterinary College as the Irish Veterinary Hospital, under the control of a joint board consisting of representatives of the two colleges, the Veterinary Council, and the Government. This was rejected by UCD. Dr Tierney specifically requested Bishop Lucey, the secretary of the Liaison Committee, to put the question of the future of the Veterinary College on the agenda for the meeting of 13 January 1959.[86]

Tierney was probably most immediately concerned with a scheme that placed Trinity College on a footing of equality of control with UCD, despite the fact, which he so often emphasised, that UCD supplied 80 to 90 per cent of the veterinary students. In preparing his arguments against the Government's scheme he consulted his friends Alfred O'Rahilly and Patrick McGilligan SC. Between them they produced a strong brief against the proposal. It was argued that the Government's scheme ran counter to the Charter of the NUI, which placed barriers in the way of conferring degrees on students who had not followed approved courses of study in a constituent or recognised college of the university and which prevented the colleges of the NUI from sharing examinations, teaching or appointments with other institutions. It was argued that Catholic undergraduates in veterinary science were to be transferred to the jurisdiction of the state, the Veterinary Council, and TCD, with a minority representation from UCD on the proposed Joint Board. This, it was maintained, raised grave religious and constitutional issues. According to article 42 of the Constitution,

> the State shall not oblige parents in violation of their conscience and lawful preference to send their children to schools established by the State, or to any particular type of school designated by the State ... The State shall ... when the public good requires it, provide other educational facilities or institutions with due regard, however, for the rights of parents, especially in the matter of religious and moral formation.

There was also the danger that if the state's scheme were granted without demur there would be no reason why the same policy should not be applied to other faculties—Agriculture, Engineering, Dentistry, and Medicine. Tierney accepted that 'we have thus no option except to appeal to religious authority, constitutional safeguards and public opinion. The issue raised, without discussion or consultation, involves the pastoral office of the bishops, the guarantees embodied in the constitution, the conscientious rights of parents and students.'[87]

As the Taoiseach was also Chancellor of the NUI, the stage was set for a head-on confrontation between de Valera and Tierney when the veterinary question was discussed by the Standing Committee of the NUI Senate on 13 February 1959. In a letter to Archbishop McQuaid the following day Tierney described how they had spent two hours 'in a vigorous discussion,' with the Chancellor in the chair. He regretted the 'great misfortune that the Bishop of Galway was absent.' He reported: 'The Chancellor said most emphatically that the Government had already come to a decision not to hand over the Veterinary College to one University. I said with equal emphasis that we would not accept the proposal for a Joint Board.'

At the end of the meeting Tierney undertook to try to produce a compromise that might permit the work of the Veterinary College to continue as it was while allowing for the impasse on both sides. He expressed his doubts to McQuaid, however, whether such a compromise was at all possible. He thought he would suggest that the Veterinary College, for administrative purposes, be put under independent management, with the teaching done by the two colleges. He promised to send a draft of his proposals to the archbishop.

He also informed Dr McQuaid that he had said at the Standing Committee that the hierarchy would be opposed to the joint board scheme, 'but this statement was brushed aside and the Chancellor indicated that he was prepared to face that situation and said that he thought he understood the Catholic point of view on the matter.'[88]

Early in March 1959 the Taoiseach's office put forward a second scheme. This left to each of the two colleges its own Faculty of Veterinary Medicine and the right of appointment of teaching staff, while placing the Veterinary College's premises and facilities under the management of a board. This second scheme was acceptable to the bishops, but not to UCD.

In the face of statements from the UCD authorities that the college might have to contemplate giving up veterinary teaching altogether, and of the threat from the British college of the withdrawal of recognition for Irish veterinary surgeons, negotiations between the Government, UCD and TCD were resumed. By mid-March 1959 a third scheme—which retained a Faculty of Veterinary Medicine in both UCD and TCD, established a quota for the intake of students, in the proportion of fifty for UCD and ten for TCD, and left the ownership, maintenance and management of the college with the Minister for Agriculture—was eventually acceptable to all parties. Tierney's success in resisting the plans of the Government regarding the Agricultural Institute and the Veterinary College was to some extent at least due to his manipulation of the influence of the hierarchy through the Liaison Committee.

MEMORANDUM ON TRINITY COLLEGE

Even while the bishops and the presidents of the NUI colleges were still anxiously discussing the veterinary question and the role TCD might have in the Veterinary College, the broader issue of TCD's place in higher education had once more come to the fore in the minds of the UCD authorities. The same meeting of the Liaison Committee in January 1959 that at Tierney's request discussed the future of the Veterinary College also heard from Tierney about what he called the 'American situation', namely the setting up of Trinity's American Council.[89] It was agreed that Tierney would prepare a draft memorandum on the issue. Eight closely typed pages long and written with the assistance of the registrar, Jeremiah Hogan, the memo was dated 29 January 1959.

It had been announced that in October 1958 the Board of Trinity College had appointed an American Council for the University of Dublin. Its purpose was to advance the interests of the college in America. It was a high-powered council, having as its chairman George Garrett, a former American ambassador to Ireland, and among its other members Frederick Boland, Ireland's permanent representative to the United Nations; William H. Taft III, also a former American ambassador to Ireland and then an assistant in the State Department; Arthur Hillis, Treasury adviser to the British mission to the United Nations; James McGurrin, president-general of the American Irish Historical Society; and Henry Lee Shattuck, former treasurer of Harvard University.

The chairman of the council spoke of Trinity entering a new era, in which the college would take a leading part in devising ways and means for Ireland to take its place politically and economically among the nations. He referred to the fact that young people from North and South were being educated together at Trinity, which, he felt, would surely sweep away some of the old suspicions and prejudices. Trinity too, he claimed, attracted hundreds of future leaders from all parts of the world. Its degrees ranked with those of Oxford and Cambridge. It had produced such statesmen as Burke, such churchmen as Berkeley, and such writers as Goldsmith and Swift. Trinity, he said, held a strategic place in Ireland's and the world's future, and it accepted its responsibility with zeal.[90]

These patriotic claims for Trinity, as if it were Ireland's national university, and the campaign in America for Irish-American money, were for Michael Tierney like a red rag to a bull. No doubt he was annoyed that an institution that, unlike the NUI, had its own sources of endowment and that had recently also been admitted to state funding had stolen a march on UCD in the arena of public relations and fund-raising in America. But it was the claims made on behalf of Trinity—academic and political—that really raised the hackles of the president of Ireland's largest university institution.

Since it was unlikely that citizens of the United States who were to be approached for funds understood the state of Irish university education, Tierney thought it desirable to present the case as fully as possible in his memo, entitled 'The Irish University Question'. Placing the question in its historical context, he said that Trinity 'was intended to be and remained for centuries one of the principal instruments of English control in Ireland.' It had also been for long a fairly effective proselytising institution. Its revenues had been drawn from the confiscated lands of Irish Catholic 'rebels'. To that day Trinity was a Protestant institution. The NUI and its colleges owed their existence to the refusal of Trinity to accept that a college for Catholics should be established side by side with Trinity in an enlarged and reformed University of Dublin. Catholics, making up 93 per cent of the population of the Republic, had never been satisfied with the constitution and character of Trinity College. Since 1946, when Trinity received its first annual grant, the state was in effect subsidising it in its effort to capture those Catholic students for whom up to 1908 it had refused to provide, thus depriving the NUI colleges of money that the state would otherwise be in a position to give them.

Trinity had no claim to the status of a national university for Ireland. Its true position was that of a unique remnant of a past educational and political establishment, isolated in the present by its own past decisions. Tierney described the *Irish Times* as the unofficial organ of Trinity College, engaged in an active campaign to hamper the development of UCD. Because of its greater number of students, UCD, not Trinity, was the principal university in the city and 'the real University of Dublin.' The great majority of the leading men in Irish politics, in the civil service and in the professions would be found among its graduates; without these the work of national recovery and rebuilding that had marked the last half century in Ireland would have been impossible. While its primary aim had been to serve the Irish people, it had always welcomed strangers and had expanded relations with foreign universities.

It was sometimes suggested that because UCD was in the main attended by Catholics it was therefore a sectarian institution, while Trinity was liberal. On the contrary, there had been far more non-Catholic professors and lecturers in UCD in the fifty years of its existence than there had been Catholic equivalents in Trinity College in over 350 years. Because of Trinity's sectarian character the authorities of the Catholic Church had always forbidden Catholics to attend that college.

Tierney's document ended by suggesting that UCD and the other colleges of the NUI had a greater claim on the generosity of American Catholics of Irish descent than an institution that had its origin in the Tudor conquest of Ireland and that still remained true to that origin.

Tierney's first draft was dated 26 January 1959. It was then submitted for criticism to the registrar, Jeremiah Hogan, whose comments and additions made the document more precise on some points but more sectarian on others. He elaborated on the advantages that Trinity, because of its constitution, its site and its magnificent buildings, enjoyed over UCD; on the state's neutrality and increasing subsidisation of Trinity; and on the decrease in the number of its Protestant students and in consequence its efforts to become a 'Protestant University for Irish Catholics'. Since wealth was still chiefly Protestant, argued Hogan, private benefactors either gave to Trinity or divided their donations among the colleges. He added a piece about there being an active campaign by Trinity, its supporters and the press to make difficulties for UCD and to hamper its legitimate development.

Though Tierney and Hogan were clearly of the same mind on most matters regarding Trinity, there was one revealing point on which they disagreed. Tierney's first draft had said of Trinity: 'The great men whom it undoubtedly produced in the past were all men of English origin and their greatness, except for the accident of their education in Dublin, is not part of Ireland's heritage but of England's.' This was vintage Irish-Ireland exclusiveness as preached by D. P. Moran of the *Leader,* or Daniel Corkery, or Tierney's own father-in-law, Eoin MacNeill. Tierney's philosophy had little time for the achievements of the eighteenth-century Anglo-Irish Ascendancy. In an essay in praise of Daniel O'Connell that he wrote for the O'Connell centenary in 1947 one can sense the relish with which he quoted from O'Connell's kinsman a description of the eighteenth-century Ascendancy as 'the rascally spawn of Cromwell'.[91]

But for Hogan, with his professional interest in Anglo-Irish literature, Tierney's stance was too extreme. He commented:

> No. The greatest of them—Burke—was as Irish as any of us; not certain yet—he perhaps did not know himself—whether the first Protestant was his father or grandfather. TCD in the eighteenth century was full of Catholics—parsons and lawyers in the making. I could not anyhow accept the sentence, because I am sure that the Sheridans and Burke and Swift and Goldsmith and dozens of others are part of our heritage.[92]

The offending sentence was deleted from the second draft; but Hogan had no objections to the retention of the sentence following it, which read: 'The Irish patriots educated in Trinity in the past became such not because of the prevailing spirit of the college but in spite of it.'

In his second draft, dated 29 January 1959, Tierney incorporated all Hogan's corrections and almost all his additional matter, and for the most part in Hogan's own words. But even Hogan admitted that in these suggested additions he had probably written too much.

What to do with the lengthy Tierney-Hogan draft memo was a problem. It was submitted to Archbishop McQuaid. In his covering letter Tierney admitted that neither he nor the registrar was at all certain 'that it is the kind of thing that is needed; and of course it is not clear how exactly such a document is to be used.'[93] He requested that after the archbishop had read over it he would discuss it with either the president or the registrar, or both, in person.

Going into so much historical detail, the memo was too long to have any immediate impact where it was intended: among Irish-Americans. It was a great deal longer than the report in the news bulletin of the American Council for the University of Dublin that had provoked it. In the event, no public use appears to have been made of this diatribe against Trinity College. However, much of its argument was incorporated in the memo 'The Two Universities in Dublin' that two years later (March 1961) was submitted by Tierney to the Commission on Higher Education.[94] It was, in any case, a clear indication of the feelings among the UCD authorities towards Trinity, feelings they shared with the bishops, and with Archbishop McQuaid in particular.

Michael Tierney had been the mainstay of the Liaison Committee, especially since the retirement of Alfred O'Rahilly as President of UCC in 1954. The last meeting of the committee that Tierney attended before his retirement was that of 7 January 1964. A few days before that meeting he had requested a preliminary word with Archbishop McQuaid. It appeared, he informed the archbishop, that the Commission on Higher Education was considering recommending that UCD become a full university. This, he said, raised the whole question of Trinity as a matter of urgency. 'We feel that we should be given the title of "University of Dublin", and this involves some change in our relations with T.C.D.'[95]

This was an adumbration of some kind of merger; and it was bound to raise questions about the episcopal ban on Trinity College. In either case it was an explosive issue and a fitting end to Michael Tierney's controversial presidency. It had put the bishops on their guard; but nothing more could be done until the commission had reported. By then Tierney's loyal friend and registrar, Jeremiah Hogan, was president; and although the Liaison Committee continued to meet at least down to 1968, the fire that one associated with Tierney had gone out of it. However, on 21 February 1968 Hogan sent copies of all papers arising from the discussion on the merger (which was being circulated to most of the staff of the college) to Archbishop McQuaid, Bishop Philbin, and Bishop Browne. The merger, therefore, was the last of the big issues with which the Liaison Committee concerned itself.

The removal of the hierarchy's ban on Catholic attendance at Trinity in

1970 also removed one of the principal reasons for the existence of the committee. It seems not to have been formally abolished by the late sixties but to have been allowed to drop into abeyance. Dr Thomas Murphy, Hogan's successor in 1972, never requested and was never asked to participate in any meeting of such a committee. The existence of the Liaison Committee had not been known among the professorial or other staff of the college.

And so a high-powered committee that had come silently and unheralded into existence in 1950 and had operated quite powerfully behind the scenes for almost twenty years slipped as silently and unnoticed back into oblivion. Yet these annual meetings involving four archbishops, three and even four bishops and three presidents of the NUI colleges took place publicly enough, during term time, almost invariably in 86 St Stephen's Green (except for a couple of occasions during the period 1950–54, when the venue was Archbishop's House in Drumcondra). The meetings in 86 took place, appropriately, in what was and still is known as the Bishops' Room.

Since leading ecclesiastics also foregathered annually in 86 on the occasion of the Mass at the opening of term, the arrival of the bishops for the Liaison Committee meeting hardly caused more than a glancing recognition from those passing in and out of 86, though they would have had no idea of the reason for their presence. In any case the lease of the old Catholic University houses to UCD had given the bishops certain rights related to the occupancy and use of the buildings, including the use of one room with reasonable access to it.

Since the Synod of Thurles in 1850 and down to the Irish Universities Act (1908), the bishops had played the leading role in demanding the establishment of a university suitable for Catholics. Once a compromise had been found with the setting up of the National University of Ireland and of University College, Dublin, as a constituent college under the 1908 Act, the public work of the bishops in this area was done. For decades after 1908 the bishops maintained a kindly, parental interest in the institution as UCD grew from strength to strength and consolidated its position in the forefront of the university life of the nation. Long after 1908 individual bishops served on the Senate of the NUI and on the Governing Bodies of the constituent colleges. The hierarchy, however, was not officially represented; and the bishops had no more rights or privileges than any other member nominated or elected to these bodies.

Then, during the period when John Charles McQuaid was Archbishop of Dublin and Michael Tierney was President of UCD, or more specifically from about 1950 until the late sixties, the bishops, on the invitation of the presidents of the NUI colleges, took a more active interest in the affairs of the colleges and of their relations with the state, and in the role of Trinity College. The Liaison Committee of the hierarchy and university college presidents, however, was an ad hoc body. It had not been set up or officially approved by the Senate of the NUI or by the Governing Bodies of the colleges. Its business had been conducted in private. It was a body of great power and influence; and although it might be an exaggeration to describe it as a secret committee, its existence, deliberations and decisions remained hidden from the majority of university people and from the general public.

By the nineteen-seventies, with a merger between UCD and TCD being publicly discussed and announced as Government policy and with the hierarchy's ban on Trinity College removed, UCD's links with the bishops— such as they were—came to an end, and the college became in reality what it had always been in law, an undenominational and even a secular institution.

THE MITRE AND THE GOWN

A very special relationship existed from the beginning between Archbishop John Charles McQuaid and Dr Michael Tierney. This was due in part to the fact that University College was situated in the archdiocese and for some purposes came under the spiritual jurisdiction of the archbishop; it was also partly due to the historical origins of UCD.

In the days of the Catholic University, personal relations between Archbishop Cullen and the first rector, John Henry Newman, may have been strained, but the constitutional connections between the archbishop, as Chancellor of the Catholic University and chairman of its episcopal committee of management, and the rector were of the closest kind. The first Chancellor of the NUI, from 1908 till his death in 1921, William Walsh, was also Archbishop of Dublin. Archbishop Walsh was also a benefactor to the college he had done so much to bring into existence.

For their part, successive presidents of UCD respectfully acknowledged their fealty to the Catholic Church and its chief local representative, the Archbishop of Dublin. This was readily accountable in the circumstances of the time. Before becoming President of UCD during the years 1908–1940, Denis Coffey, as professor of physiology and Dean of the Catholic University Medical School, had come even more directly under the control of the archbishop than did the Jesuit President of University College. The Archbishop of Dublin was chairman of the Board of Governors of the Medical School. The influence of the church did not suddenly end just because the Catholic University Medical School became the Medical Faculty of UCD.

Dr Coffey was a perfectly safe man from the hierarchy's point of view. As Dean of the Medical School he had been subject to the higher authority of the church, and he brought this apprenticeship with him into the presidency. His ethical stance could be trusted by both church and state, and while President of UCD he had also served on the Censorship Board during its most rigid decade of the nineteen-thirties.

Neither was the second president, Arthur Conway, one to rock the boat. He had served as registrar all during Coffey's long presidency and had only seven years, coinciding with the war and post-war years, at the end of his career in the office of president. In the days when Catholic newspapers were regarded as playing a very important role in what was called Catholic Action, Conway had been closely associated with the *Standard*.[96]

Given the unquestioned loyalty to the church, there was little danger of any clash between the college authorities and the archbishop. This was particularly true during the years 1921–1940, when Dr Byrne was archbishop. He showed no desire to interfere in the affairs of UCD, and this was in keeping with the popular view that he had not taken a vigorous hand in the administration of the archdiocese, especially since he had been in failing health for years.

One quality that his successor, the Holy Ghost father John Charles McQuaid, did not lack was administrative energy. His appointment as archbishop in November 1940 created a great stir of expectancy. When he presided at his first 'Red Mass' in University Church in October 1941, James Meenan noted that there was some speculation among academics beforehand about what he would deal with in his sermon, 'as he is expected to take a very direct interest in the working of the College.' However, Meenan reported, there were no signs of that in his sermon, 'which was short and very good and concerned with the love of God—the first time that I have ever heard any preacher at that ceremony talk of anything spiritual ... He is a very striking figure with a fine presence. He will either be a very great archbishop or he will inflict irreparable damage on the position of the Church in Ireland.'[97]

The worst fears of those who expected that McQuaid would involve himself directly in university matters began to be realised when he issued his Lenten regulations in February 1944 prohibiting Catholics from attending Trinity College. Reaction in UCD was reflected in the note of outrage recorded by James Meenan. He wrote in his diary:

18 Feb.   Consternation in College to-day. Aubrey Gwynn came in with the news that next Sunday's Lenten pastoral will make it a mortal sin for parents to send their sons to T.C.D. This absolutely appalling as an indication of what the man will do before he is finished. The T.C.D. aspect is bad enough—it is an example of exactly that kind of bigotry that we have always accused the North of and have prided ourselves that we were free from. But the U.C.D. outlook is far worse. Obviously the Archbishop wants to make T.C.D. a purely Protestant institution—then he will advance on us and make us into a Catholic University in which priests must necessarily rule and lay men will be a species of lay brother. This would be the most awful disaster imaginable—quite apart from the personal angle it would mean that no Irish Catholic would ever get a proper university education and it would certainly let loose a flood of anti-clericalism. This is another point that brings up the right of the Church to cut across what is after all national policy … Cannot help feeling that to-day is a definite land-mark in Irish history. For the first time the Church has done something that shocks the conscience of Irish Catholics. How can these people fail to learn from history? If this is to be the line of policy all Ireland will be anti-clerical in a generation. That will mean some bloody hopeless mess like Spain. God knows I am a poor Irishman and a very indifferent Catholic but this thing's eventual possibilities appal me.

20 Feb. … Rumours all too true. It is a mortal sin for a parent to send a child to T.C.D. or for a student to go there. This bad enough but he goes out of his way to say that U.C.D. is not a Catholic College. This bloody awful—it seems to mean that he will next try to get into the College and run it and eventually turn it into a Catholic College …

21 Feb. College still greatly agitated. Boylan who is Vicar General of the diocese in, and making it quite clear by inference that he was not consulted on the pastoral. Protestants in the Library up in the air but have found nothing that presages any action. Papers silent so far anyway. Would be best if nothing was said in public—the whole thing is one for action [sic] discreetly. Hope people like Kingsmill Moore will have the sense to keep their traps shut. Not sure that that doesn't go for Tierney on our side. Damn bad business.

24 Feb. Must put down the rhyme that is going around since last Sunday. I feel sure that it is not original but is an old one of Gogarty's—

> Your children may loot and pillage and shoot
> And rape and have carnal knowledge
> But however depraved
> Their souls will be saved
> If they don't go to Trinity College.

The 'striking figure with the fine presence' who had presided at his first 'Red Mass' in 1941 was being described by Meenan at the Mass of 1947 in a very different light. 'All my attention was taken by the Archbishop who looks more and more like something out of the Renaissance. One almost expected the celebrant to be poisoned by the sacramental wine. And I must admit there is something mean in his looks that I don't like …'[98]

That same October of 1947 another vigorous, if not autocratic, person, Michael Tierney, was elected President of UCD.

Given the assertive personalities of both archbishop and president, and the high sense of dignity that each man attached to his office, there might well have followed clashes between the ecclesiastical and the academic institutions that would rival, or at least reflect, those clashes between church and state that materialised during Archbishop McQuaid's career. But instead of being wary opponents, Tierney and McQuaid were to become staunch allies, to the benefit of each other's policies.

The new president accepted fully the teaching of the church on education. He also had a keen historical appreciation of how much the solution of the university question of the nineteenth century owed to the bishops. Where Michael Tierney and John Charles McQuaid met even more specifically on common ground was in the strong antipathy to Trinity College that they shared. The archbishop's condemnation of Trinity had to do with faith and morals; the president's objections were to the perceived trespassing of a rival college on UCD's territory regarding the university education of Catholics, financial claims on the Government and taxpayer, county council scholarships, and dentistry, agriculture and veterinary education. Though the archbishop and the president started out from a separate professional base, the conclusion they came to was the same: Trinity was regarded by both as alien. So strongly was this conviction shared that it provided much sympathy for each other's points of view over wide areas, made co-operation between them easy on several issues, and gave rise to a contact that came close to being an alliance.

Tierney's views on the dangers to the faith and morals of Catholics attending Trinity coincided with McQuaid's. As a loyal and obedient layman himself he would certainly expect and approve of full compliance with the archbishop's regulations. All of this had been stated both explicitly and implicitly in the two memos he wrote in 1951 and 1952 for the Liaison Committee of bishops and college presidents.[99] Bearing these in mind, who could be surprised if Archbishop McQuaid should feel himself invited to take a deep interest in developments generally within Tierney's UCD? One could hardly blame McQuaid entirely for any episcopal 'interference' in the affairs of UCD that might follow Tierney's memos.

In the memo entitled 'The Irish University Question' that Tierney, with the help of Jeremiah Hogan, drafted at the end of the nineteen-fifties[100] he wrote more strongly than ever in support of the hierarchy's ban on Trinity.[101]

> It is certainly the truth that the Irish bishops have at all times shown the greatest consideration for the educational exigencies of their people.
>
> We would suggest that it is highly unfair in the circumstances as they exist either to speak of an autocratic and unreasonable 'ban' on Trinity

College or to propagate the idea that this 'ban' may be arbitrarily remitted either in the present or in the future.[102]

In the first draft of this memo, the second sentence in the above extract was crossed out, and it was omitted in the second draft (29 January 1959). But the deletion as well as what remained did reveal that Michael Tierney personally endorsed and defended the ban, which in both drafts he declared to be 'strictly binding on the consciences of Catholics.'

'YOUR GRACE'S MOST OBEDIENT SERVANT'

It was perhaps symbolic of the gratitude that Tierney felt for the archbishop's stance that in his early years in office he subscribed his letters to McQuaid with the formula 'Your Grace's most obedient servant.' This, however, was less than the subservience it might seem to have implied.

Much of the correspondence between Tierney and the archbishop had to do with very ordinary matters relating to the appointment of the chaplains. The chaplains, or deans of residence, came and went from time to time, depending on the general needs and transfer of clergy in the many parishes of the diocese. Up to the mid-fifties the college authorities, as well as the archbishop, had indiscriminately and somewhat imprecisely written about the 'appointment' of the chaplains by the archbishop; then what might be detected as a gentle but firm note of independence occurred in the letters of Michael Tierney. 'I have today appointed Fr. Tuohy to act as Dean of Residence,' the archbishop informed the president in September 1955. In acknowledging this letter 'regarding the appointment of Fr. Tuohy,' Tierney replied: 'The College Statutes require that he be nominated by me for appointment by the Governing Body at its next meeting ...'[103] This may not have been what it sounds like—putting the archbishop in his place and asserting the legal authority of the Governing Body to make the appointment—for it was understood and fully accepted that the Governing Body would appoint only a cleric named by the archbishop.

The 'appointment' of the deans of residence therefore did not become an issue. But shortly thereafter the penny seems to have dropped, and from the late fifties onwards Dr McQuaid had become far more careful and precise in the language he used while communicating about changes in personnel. In July and August 1959, instead of 'appointing' he was now 'proposing' the names of two priests as assistants to Father Tuohy and was grateful for the president's acceptance of his 'proposal' that Father Tuohy be regarded officially as the senior chaplain.[104] A year later he was reminding Tierney that the latter had 'kindly agreed that another chaplain was needed at University College' and that 'you asked me to supply a name for the June meeting of the Governing Body.'

The president acknowledged the letter in which the archbishop had 'nominated' a chaplain.[105] From then onwards the word 'nominate' appears in all the archbishop's correspondence with Tierney relating to the change of chaplains;[106] and 'nominate' is the word that survived in the correspondence between the successors of McQuaid and those of Tierney.

Tierney had won a point: he had stood behind the Statutes, which had asserted the independence of the Governing Body in the appointment of chaplains of any denomination. And the archbishop had respected the independence of the college in this matter. The legalities having been observed and the territorial claims having been defined and accepted, clerical and lay authorities co-operated with mutual respect for the welfare of the students.

Nevertheless, from the start of his presidency Michael Tierney was very much aware that he was dealing not only with a very powerful archbishop but with one who also took seriously his claim to be Rector of the Catholic University. Each annual issue of the *Irish Catholic Directory* continued to remind the public that the rectorship was vested in Dr McQuaid. It might long have been little more than a legal fiction, a ghostly survival from the past; but, like many such fictions, what was important about it was not its lack of any substance in the practical world but what claims it could make through its symbolism. Within a church and a society where symbols were significant they could be more than ritualistic and could lead to very practical results. In its symbolic role the rectorship was analogous to the presidency of the Irish Republic, 'virtually established,' which had conferred great theoretical power on the IRB in the days before independence. Much, of course, would depend on the importance attached to the symbol, and in this case to the title of rector, by the holder of the office.

The Rector of the Catholic University was in evidence, if only in the background, in the correspondence during March and April 1950 between McQuaid and Tierney concerning the Luxeuil Conference in honour of St Columbanus. Dr McQuaid had been asked by the French government to secure three papers from Irish scholars to be delivered at the conference. Dr Mitchell of Maynooth had agreed to give one; the archbishop asked Dr Tierney to get one or more of his staff to provide the other papers. Professors John Ryan and Aubrey Gwynn consented. Father Gwynn informed Tierney that Dr Ludwig Bieler also hoped to read a paper, and Tierney, who thought it would be an honour to have as many scholars as possible from Ireland attend this prestigious conference, requested the Governing Body to provide travel subsistence for Bieler. On receiving this information from Tierney the archbishop replied: 'It is a matter of grave surprise to me to learn that Fr. Gwynn tells you Dr. Bieler is to read a paper at Luxeuil. I regret that I know nothing of such a paper, for it has been arranged independently of me.'[107] Tierney explained that Dr Bieler, like other scholars, received a circular from the French organising committee that contained a general invitation to scholars to propose papers, and Bieler's proposal had been accepted. The archbishop thanked Tierney for explaining the origin of Dr Bieler's proposed contribution to the conference and, characteristically, added no further comments or explanations on his own part.

The correspondence on the Luxeuil conference hints at Dr McQuaid in the role of rector of a Catholic university of whose jurisdiction UCD formed part; it also suggests the image of the headmaster he had once been in Blackrock College expecting, and receiving, an explanation for any behaviour going outside his precise regulations. The headmasterly attitude was one that would often recur in his dealings with UCD, and in this connection Michael Tierney (like Alfred O'Rahilly in another context) came to be treated as one of the headmaster's very bright boys, in whose talents he delighted but whose exuberance he wished to control. Michael Tierney learnt to tread very warily where the archbishop's interests were involved, and it must sometimes have seemed to him like walking on eggs trying not to offend episcopal sensibilities.

When it came to the centenary celebrations of the appointment of Newman as Rector of the Catholic University in 1851 and the delivery of Newman's lectures in 1852 on 'The idea of a university', and shortly afterwards the centenary celebrations of the opening in 1854 of the Catholic University, the full significance as well as touchiness of the archbishop as rector was borne in on the President of UCD quite vividly. Tierney informed the archbishop that a small UCD committee had been exploring the possibility of honouring the appointment of Newman.[108] He requested an interview to go into every aspect of the proposal. The archbishop, granting a time and place for the interview, replied: 'Your reference to a discussion of "every aspect of the proposal" makes me wish that you would do me the favour of stating in advance what are these aspects, for you will kindly realise that your letter, the first intimation received by me, has taken me by surprise.'[109] The archbishop's expression of 'surprise'—or, worse, 'grave surprise', as in the case of the Bieler lecture—was his mannered way of administering a reprimand to the over-independent or wayward head boy. Tierney found himself once again having to go into a patient explanation.

> The matter had only been discussed in UCD within the last few days ...That you should be somewhat taken by surprise by the proposal is indeed not strange. What I meant by discussing every aspect of the subject was simply that we should lay before you the general ideas which have emerged at our two committee meetings. It is my feeling, which I think everyone shares, that the whole character of any celebration we may decide upon will necessarily depend on what attitude Your Grace may feel it right to take ...[110]

If this sounds like abject appeasement we would do well to remember that it was taking place in the thick of the row over the Mother and Child Scheme and that Dr Noel Browne, the Minister for Health, had resigned and sensationally released to the newspapers on 12 April 1951 the flood of correspondence on the issue between the bishops and Government ministers. Tierney's first letter to McQuaid on the question of the Newman celebrations was written barely two weeks after the publication of this correspondence. Eighteen months later, when the details of the much bigger public celebrations of the opening of the Catholic University were being planned, the president's office informed the archbishop's secretariat that the UCD Centenary Committee agreed that nothing definitive could be decided until the archbishop's return to Ireland and requested that an appointment be arranged for the president to meet the archbishop to discuss the matter.[111]

In the event, the centenary celebrations were a triumph for Tierney's policy of exhibiting UCD as being in direct succession to Newman's Catholic University, and for the Archbishop of Dublin in his role as Rector of the Catholic University.[112] The price to be paid for the triumph was that the president was drawn ever closer into the sphere of influence of the archbishop.

The key to what some people referred to as 'interference' in UCD's affairs by the archbishop but what Tierney himself sincerely saw as genuine attempts to assist the college lay not in the opportunities provided by such connections as the chaplains or hostels or clerics on the academic staff, or Catholic University centenary celebrations, but, paradoxically, in the question of Trinity College. The stance taken by both McQuaid and Tierney in their opposition to Trinity possessed grave if indirect dangers that UCD might be lured further and further into the ecclesiastical web. For if the archbishop and the president were agreed that Catholics should be banned from Trinity, UCD would feel under pressure to cater for the increasing number of Catholics who did not possess the Matriculation requirements (especially in Irish) for entering UCD or who were being offered degree facilities in Trinity not available to them in UCD. This gave rise to much of what Tierney himself acknowledged as unhealthy and unseemly rivalry. UCD found itself having to sing the tune 'anything you can do, we can do better,' with the archbishop if not exactly calling the tune at least conducting the choir.

While UCD since its foundation had been making significant contributions to national life, Trinity College, like the Big House of the Anglo-Irish gentry, had retreated largely into a state of isolation. In its determination to break from the ghetto-like situation in which it had found itself, Trinity began offering attractive new courses. One of these, for example, was the diploma in public administration (1941). The lectures for this course, given mainly in the evening, attracted numbers of junior civil servants who had not previously had the opportunity of a university education, or who might have attended the cyclical BA evening degree course in UCD. To counteract Trinity's temptations for public servants and others, UCD found itself under pressure to provide alternative sanctuary.

Following a dinner party at the archbishop's home in Killiney to which were invited Michael Tierney, Jeremiah Hogan and Rev. Professor Horgan, the details of a draft circular on UCD's evening degrees were prepared.[113] Instead of the then BA (evening) course in a three-year cycle, continuous lectures in the first-year, second-year and third-year courses were made available. No longer could students wishing to attend Trinity claim that they would have to wait a couple of years for the beginning of a new UCD cycle.

The first draft circular did not contain enough information for the satisfaction of the archbishop's secretariat. An amended draft was sent from the president's office, which contained additional information about the UCD diploma in public administration (first introduced in 1942/43) and details of how it could be taken in conjunction with the BA (evening) during first and second year. The amended draft also outlined the syllabus and the fee. The president's secretary wrote to the archbishop's secretary: 'I hope that this version will suit your requirements, but if it is still not exactly what you want please do not hesitate to let me know and I shall alter it accordingly.'[114]

When it was agreed, two hundred copies of the circular were sent to Archbishop's House. Expressing Dr McQuaid's gratitude for the making available of the circular on evening degrees for 1952/53, his secretary informed Dr Tierney: 'It is my intention to send this circular to each applicant for permission to attend Evening lectures in T.C.D., suggesting at the same time that the applicant should consider taking the courses in U.C.D., since the arrangements at U.C.D. are so favourable and convenient.'[115]

Later the same year the registrar informed the archbishop's secretary that the Faculty of Commerce had agreed to recommend the offer of a first-year course for the BComm degree to be taken in the evenings.[116] Father Mangan, who looked after the applications of those who sought permission to attend Trinity, obtained from UCD the various calendars and syllabuses of courses so that he could check the statements of applicants for Trinity.[117]

Archbishop McQuaid was concerned not only with stating the general principle against Catholics attending Trinity College but with each individual Catholic applicant. He was very pleased when, as a result of his representations, the President of UCD was able to arrange for Marguerite Matthews, daughter of the American ambassador, to attend UCD. 'It would have been tragic had she too gone to Trinity College,' wrote the archbishop to the president.[118] 'Tragic' was the way this man, who chose his words very carefully, regarded the attendance of Catholics at Trinity. It might be said that the daughter of the American ambassador was a high-profile Catholic whose attendance at Trinity might have been interpreted as 'one in the eye' for the hierarchy; but the archbishop's office was equally anxious about the faith and morals of junior civil servants applying to take evening courses.

The arrangement that had been arrived at between UCD and the archbishop meant that the college was occasionally asked to waive or bend its regulations in favour of individuals who would otherwise go to Trinity. Typical of this kind of request was the letter from Father Mangan to the president in which he said that the archbishop would be grateful if UCD would allow three named students to attend the DPA, BComm and BA evening lectures even though they were late for registration. The three had applied for permission to attend Trinity College and the archbishop had refused to grant it, on the grounds that their reasons were insignificant. In this instance UCD replied that the three students would be accepted when they applied.[119]

Late registration was one matter, but to UCD's credit there were other areas where it remained unbending, despite the archbishop's representations. Father Mangan had hoped that a student whose mother wished her to go to a Catholic university would be accepted in UCD, as Trinity was prepared to accept her. It transpired that UCD had already informed her that her qualifications were not acceptable for Matriculation purposes. J. P. MacHale, who had consulted the president on the matter, replied to the archbishop's secretary in a vein that many would have recognised as vintage MacHale: 'If Trinity College decide to admit students with qualifications below university level, I am afraid there is nothing we can do about it.'[120]

This sort of problem arose from the fact that while the archbishop anathematised Catholic attendance at Trinity without his permission as a mortal sin, he was genuinely anxious to be merciful and kind to the would-be sinner. It seemed hard to him, he informed Dr Tierney, writing of a particular case (a Blackrock College boy of good intellectual calibre and achievement, selected for the Leinster Schools rugby team, whose father was sixty-seven), that he must go to Trinity because he was three days younger than the UCD age limit. Tierney stood firm, however, replying that concession on the age limit would involve both injustice to others and accusations of favouritism.[121]

But minor differences about the admission of individual students on whose behalf Dr McQuaid made representation did nothing to undermine the alliance between archbishop and president directed against Trinity as an appropriate college for Catholic students. On this issue they were at one. When in his conferring speech of October 1955 Tierney replied to the remarks of the Provost of Trinity College, Dr McConnell, about discrimination against Trinity,[122] Dr McQuaid in thanking Tierney for a copy of the address congratulated him on his answer 'to an unjust speech by the Provost of Trinity College.'[123]

The archbishop in turn kept Tierney informed on matters relating to Trinity. Referring to one of the Liaison Committee meetings, he wrote: 'You may remember that I gave warning at our meeting of my inability to find out yet with complete accuracy the list of Catholic and non-Catholic staff in Trinity College. I am working on the list and will give you a copy as soon as I can.'[124] He was not to know that Tierney himself was being asked to help in providing the information he was promised. The former President of UCC, by now Rev. Alfred O'Rahilly, who apparently was assisting the archbishop in drawing up the list, wrote to Tierney: 'The Archbishop wants absolute accuracy. Unfortunately I am doubtful about the religion of a number of people who might be Catholics. Could you please help me? Somebody in the Medical Faculty and another in the Faculty of Veterinary Science could, I am sure, give you the information.'[125]

The outcome of this investigation was published by O'Rahilly in *Studies* in the autumn of 1961. Taking the faculties of Arts, Science, and Medicine, he stated that 7.5 per cent of the professors and 20.6 per cent of all lecturers above the category of assistants were Catholics. This list was possibly being compiled for no more than statistical purposes, to support the argument about the non-suitability of Trinity for Catholics;[126] but any idea of an episcopal black-list would no doubt have seemed ominous to those whose names were on it.

One month after the archbishop's reference to this uncompleted list, his Lenten pastoral of 1960 dealt in more specific detail than ever before with the question of UCD and Trinity as institutions appropriate for the education of Catholics. In earlier pastorals UCD had been described as no more than 'sufficiently safe' for Catholics to attend; but the 1961 pastoral was eloquent in its praise of the college. 'Happily in this city, Catholic parents can find an Institution of higher learning that gives them the guarantees both of academic excellence and of Catholic inspiration ...University College, Dublin ... is the lawful heir to the Catholic University founded by the Irish bishops with the approval of the Holy See.'[127] The pastoral went on to say that there was one institution in our midst in respect of which for over a hundred years the bishops, with the full approval of the Holy See, had felt obliged to warn Catholic parents. It quoted the statute and the regulations attached to it and pointed to the contrast in attitudes between 'just-minded Protestants' and some allegedly ignorant and ambitious Catholics.

> It is significant that just-minded Protestants, and they are many, have seen at once, and have accepted, that this enactment is directed, not as an attack upon non-Catholics but as legislation binding in conscience on Catholics. Some Catholics could with advantage imitate the balanced attitude of those Protestants.
>
> Emotional reasoning and social involvements, not to say ambitions,

can prevent Catholics from loyally accepting, in obedience of mind and action, the legislation of the Bishops. In face of their ignorance and misunderstanding, it is necessary to point out that the Statute of the Hierarchy, with the calm honesty of a legislator, faces the fact that Trinity College, Dublin, as a non-Catholic University, has never been acceptable, and is not now acceptable to Catholics.[128]

The pastoral, however, stirred up some opposition in UCD. At a debate at the L&H on 'The sacrosanctity of the status quo', the auditor, Dermot Bouchier-Hayes, declared: 'We are not bound to accept the Lenten pastoral of his grace the Archbishop of Dublin on the subject of university education.' The arguments used in the pastoral were 'stupid and futile', and they as students were entitled to criticise them. 'We are entitled to say that the archbishop is wrong. I definitely say that he is wrong.'

The auditor was the only speaker to deal with the pastoral. Tom O'Rourke (a former auditor of the L&H, a well-known secondary teacher in Synge Street CBS, a part-time assistant in UCD's Department of Education and clerk of Convocation of the NUI), who was in the chair, defended the right of the archbishop to speak on university education and referred to 'the fundamental truth of religion in medicine, ethics, law and all other branches.'[129]

In a letter to the archbishop apologising for 'the disgraceful performance of the auditor,' Tierney explained:

> The college authorities are very sensible of the discredit such actions bring on the college, but are quite certain that the sentiments expressed represent only the tiniest minority of notoriety-seekers among the students. It is because of this element of notoriety that I have judged it best to take no disciplinary action against the student concerned. Such action would, I am convinced, do more harm than good all round ... Please accept my assurance of the utmost personal abhorrence of such conduct.[130]

Thanking Tierney for his letter, McQuaid replied: 'I was pained by the suffering that such ignorance must bring on you and the College authorities. To know the author of these remarks is to forgive them. May I say that I am glad that you have decided to take no disciplinary action.'[131]

Not only on the issue of Trinity but in other matters close to Tierney's heart—dentistry, relations with the Government, and Belfield, for example— he could count on the sympathy and support not only of Archbishop McQuaid but also of O'Rahilly. When the Secretary of the Department of Education, Tarlach Ó Raifeartaigh, returned from London with proposals regarding dentistry, Tierney confided in O'Rahilly: 'What disheartens us most is to find that all other parties have their interests considered at all times, except the college which is calmly told that it must continue to work under grave and unnecessary disabilities, although it is obviously the institution whose interests ought to be first considered.'[132] Tierney sent a copy of this letter to Archbishop McQuaid also.

O'Rahilly fully sympathised with Tierney's sense of frustration, agreeing that 'the Government is amazingly hostile to U.C.D. They have beaten us concerning the Dental School. I understand your present inability to make it a casus belli.'[133] On the question of Belfield, O'Rahilly, like the archbishop and many others, was prepared to congratulate Tierney and see it as one of his greatest achievements. On a visit to the site when the Science Building was in progress, he wrote: 'Yesterday I saw the buildings at Belfield. Amazing progress. But how terribly impersonal and Factory like! I know it is inevitable. You have a wonderful site. I do hope that your tenure will be prolonged to enable you to inaugurate a scheme which owes so much to you.'[134]

After Tierney's retirement in 1964 the close relationship that had been built up between him and the bishops, and especially with Archbishop McQuaid, continued under Jeremiah Hogan.

As soon as the Belfield building programme got under way, the archbishop made it abundantly clear that one of his principal concerns was that a church should be built in the college grounds. It was not until eight years after the archbishop had first raised the matter with Tierney that the Church of Our Lady Seat of Wisdom was built, the funds being supplied by the archbishop's businessman-friend Michael Devlin. On that occasion Hogan apologised to the archbishop, saying: 'We regretted the constitutional position which required that the church must be temporary and the site leased to Your Grace on very restricted terms.'[135] McQuaid's reply betrayed a certain frustration and annoyance and was also a reflection of the changing circumstances that resulted from the increasing criticism of the ban on Trinity and the debate on the merger.[136]

> You do see, I am happy to note, that for the Archbishop of Dublin it has been a desolating experience to be treated with penal-day attitudes. The situation has not been made more easy by the constant clamour of University College staff for co-operation with Trinity College and the unconditional reversal of the Hierarchy's legislation concerning Trinity College.
>
> It is for that staff and for the students whom they guide that, in spite of consistent disregard, I have provided a church.[137]

It was almost as if the archbishop had meant to convey that no staff and no body of students needed the church so badly. It was a far cry from the encomium lavished on UCD's staff in the Lenten pastoral of 1961. McQuaid's reference to himself in the third person, as the Archbishop of Dublin who was subjected to Penal Law attitudes, was a sure sign of his annoyance that his office was not being treated with the dignity it was due. And one wonders if he did not say to himself that none of this could have happened under Michael Tierney.

Hogan, however, was as careful as Tierney ever was to respect the archbishop's wishes and at the same time to regard him as a powerful ally. During the difficult merger debate he sent to the archbishop a copy of Donogh O'Malley's statement before the Governing Body, which gave the fullest account so far of the Government's intentions, and a copy of the president's own draft memo that he was about to present a week later to the Governing Body. He said he would keep the archbishop in touch with further developments.[138] True to his promise, he sent to McQuaid and also to Cardinal William Conway, Archbishop of Armagh, and to Bishop Browne and Bishop Philbin—all members of the Liaison Committee—all the papers arising from the discussions between UCD and Trinity on the merger.[139] Acknowledging these documents, the cardinal wrote to Hogan: 'I was very impressed with your exposition of the situation at our meeting last January' (the Liaison Committee meeting on 9 January 1968).[140]

As far as UCD was concerned, the hierarchy, through Dr Hogan, was kept fully informed of developments in the merger negotiations. The supply of all the relevant papers to the bishops for their information in February 1968, the opening of the church at Belfield in February 1969 and the announcement in June 1970 of the removal of the ban on Catholics attending Trinity College 'in view of the substantial agreement on basic issues that has been reached between the National University of Ireland and Trinity College' on the merger brought to an end not only the meetings of the Liaison Committee but also the correspondence with Dr McQuaid on all the great issues that had exercised the minds of president and archbishop since the nineteen-forties.

Four months after the removal of the ban, McQuaid wrote to the president: 'I am obliged to nominate a Dean of Residence for Catholic students at Trinity College, Dublin ...'[141] John Charles McQuaid had always prided himself on choosing his words very carefully; the phrase he chose on this occasion was no exception. It would seem to indicate that he had only reluctantly succumbed to circumstances and to pressure from the majority of the bishops on the issue of the removal of the ban.

In February 1972 Dr McQuaid retired from the archbishopric. When in April that same year Jeremiah Hogan retired as President of UCD, it was truly the end of an era.

Dr McQuaid's successor was Rev. Professor Dermot Ryan, who continued for a couple of years as acting professor in his department. Not since Dr Bernard in 1919 resigned as Church of Ireland Archbishop of Dublin to become Provost of Trinity College had there been so close a relationship between an episcopal throne and a university chair. The college took pride in having one of its professors made archbishop. Ironically coinciding with that occurrence, the official correspondence between archbishop and president declined dramatically—perhaps an instance of the maxim that 'the nearer the church, the further from God.' The frenetic communications between mitre and gown in the days of Archbishop McQuaid and Dr Tierney had become part of history. When Tomás Ó Fiaich became Archbishop of Armagh in 1977 the letters that passed between himself and Dr Tom Murphy began in both cases with 'Dear Tom.' For good or ill, the era when the President of UCD was 'Your Grace's most obedient servant' was now long past.

THE LONG SHADOW OF THE ARCHBISHOP

Certain faculties and departments had engaged the special attention of Archbishop McQuaid. One of these was Medicine. The teaching hospitals were a particularly sensitive point in the relationship between the college and the archbishop. Complicating the difficulties were the other interests that were involved: the state, which provided the finance; the nuns, who managed the hospitals; and the professional medical bodies, whose function it was to grant or withhold recognition for the doctors who were trained in these hospitals.

Curiously enough, the problems that arose in this area came more from the staunchly independent stand of the orders concerned, the Sisters of Charity (St Vincent's Hospital) and Sisters of Mercy (Mater Hospital). Their proper concern prolonged for three years the negotiations made necessary by policy changes following a report on the UCD Medical School by representatives of the American Medical Association. (Requirements laid down by the American medical authorities regarding the control of clinical training had to be satisfied before graduates of Irish medical schools might be recognised for appointments in the United States.)[142] At one stage the unfortunate Jeremiah Hogan, as acting president during the absence of Dr Tierney through illness, found himself the meat in the sandwich between Dr McQuaid and the formidable Mother Teresa Anthony, Mother-General of the Sisters of Charity, who had raised a question about the order's children's hospital in Temple Street, Dublin, directly with UCD rather than through the archbishop.

In the end, despite the Temple Street hiccup, clinical teaching in the Mater and St Vincent's was organised in such a way as to satisfy critical external professional opinion. It was agreed that there should be a professor of medicine and a professor of surgery in St Vincent's and in the Mater, both of whom would receive their appointment as professor by the Senate of the National University in accordance with the Statutes. These professors would have the general control and direction of the teaching in the hospitals. Medical teaching staff other than the professors would be appointed by a selection board consisting of three members nominated by the college and three by the hospital authority.

The report of the Commission on Higher Education recommended as a model for other schools of medicine this agreement that UCD had worked out with the teaching hospitals. Much of the credit for the successful outcome had to go to the lengthy and difficult work that the archbishop had put into securing the agreement.

Since under the 1908 legislation theology or divinity could not be financed by the state, philosophy became the discipline in which the teaching of the Catholic Church could be most assiduously promoted. In UCD, philosophy was divided between three foundation chairs: metaphysics, logic and psychology, and ethics and politics. The divisions as well as the content followed traditional Thomistic lines. Since the great majority of the students taking philosophy were seminarians, the archbishop took a keen and direct interest in developments. During most of Archbishop McQuaid's reign the three departments were controlled by Monsignor John Horgan (metaphysics, 1942–1971), Rev E. F. O'Doherty (logic and psychology, 1949–1983), and Rev. Conor Martin (ethics and politics, 1952–1980). Two other departments in the faculty, Education and Social Science, were also in the charge of priests: Rev. Seán Ó Catháin SJ and Rev. James Kavanagh, respectively.

A measure of the importance the archbishop attached to the social encyclicals was the establishment in 1950 of the Dublin Institute of Catholic Sociology. The director of the institute, Father James Kavanagh, a trained sociologist specialising in labour questions, was appointed an assistant in the Department of Ethics and Politics of UCD, teaching social science. In 1964 he was appointed a statutory lecturer and head of a new Department of Social Science; two years later he was appointed UCD's first professor of social science.

The evolution of this new department out of Ethics and Politics owed much to the interest and encouragement of the archbishop. Vivid examples of his direct interference can be seen in a letter he wrote to Tierney in 1960:

> I am acutely anxious about the very urgent necessity for developing the Politics department by the addition of a Georgetown or Fordham lecturer till an Irishman is properly trained ...
>
> Similarly, the Psychology department, which has succeeded so well,

The Salon in Newman House, plasterwork by Lafrancini Brothers.

Newman's University Church.

The Crest of the Catholic University.

The Kevin Barry window in the Council Chambers, Earlsfort Terrace.

An aspect of the Belfield campus.

A panel from the triptych by James Hanly depicting scenes of James Joyce's life in the College.

even in foreign circles, will need the addition of Dr. Bastable [Patrick Bastable, a specialist in Logic] in order to release Dr. O'Doherty for his Psychology work.

Monsignor Horgan undertook to explain to you my very grave anxiety in view of the Trinity developments.[143]

Dr McQuaid showed further concern for developments within the Psychology Department in 1966. He wrote to the president:

I wished to ask you if it could be arranged to establish on a proper Diploma basis a course for Career Guidance officers ... I am convinced that a Career Guidance service is gravely needed in our Secondary Schools, but that it ought to have University recognition. Mother M. Jordana, O.P. [secretary to the Diocesan Advisory Committee on Secondary Education], would be glad to meet you to discuss the proposal — But I envisage a wider scope than that of Secondary Education.

I have also asked Rev. Professor O'Doherty to hold himself at your disposal.[144]

This diploma in careers guidance was indeed established in the academic session 1967/68.

The fact that Monsignor Horgan was used — at least on some occasions — as official intermediary between the archbishop and the president conferred on him an influence beyond his own department or faculty that he knew well how to exploit. It was widely assumed that, within his own Department of Metaphysics, Thomism and the archbishop's interests would prevail. In a country where there was little tradition of lay Catholic philosophers, the Metaphysics Department since 1941 was staffed entirely by clergy until 1962, when a former seminarian who had completed his doctoral work in Louvain, Patrick Masterson, was appointed as an assistant.

Direct intervention by the archbishop in the affairs of the college was not always required, because Monsignor Horgan, the dean of the Faculty of Philosophy, was perceived by many to be the confidant and spokesman of Dr McQuaid. With piercing blue eyes and an inquisitive style of conversation, the 'Mons' was one of the few professors to chat to younger assistants in other departments. Having taken on himself the job of stoking the fire in the professors' room, he succeeded in stoking up much else besides. One of the most influential men in college politics, he was a member of the Senate of the NUI (1952–1972), elected by the graduate panel, largely as a result of the intensive canvassing he carried out among teachers in the schools run by religious. He was also a member of the Governing Body's Finance Committee.

The 'Mons', it was suspected, may not always have been acting on behalf of the archbishop, but his manner could convey the impression that he was looking after Dr McQuaid's interests and carrying out his business. While to some he appeared a genial and amusing college character, to others he was a machiavellian figure and a reminder of the Grand Inquisitor, injecting a sense of fear and conspiracy into the academic atmosphere.

The shadow of the archbishop, and Monsignor Horgan's invocation of that shadow, hung like an awesome cloud over some sensitive academic areas. The Department of Ethics and Politics, under a cautious but progressive Conor Martin, was keen to employ lay academics on its staff and develop the political science side of its functions. And one of its lecturers in the area of political philosophy, Rev. Fergal O'Connor OP, was highly respected by his students and, because of his contributions to the television 'Late Late Show', was generally regarded as a radical.

A striking example of how fear of the archbishop could operate within such a department is related by Professor Tom Garvin, who was a student of politics in the early sixties and an admirer of what the department was then attempting. He has related how John Whyte, soon after his appointment as the first lay lecturer in the department, began his research for his much-acclaimed book *Church and State in Modern Ireland.* The research included interviews with people who had been involved in the controversial Mother and Child affair of the early fifties. Whyte's professor, Father Martin, took him aside and informed him that he had heard on the clerical grapevine that Whyte had been asking questions about the role of the bishops in that affair. Possibly out of unnecessary fear of the archbishop (for Whyte had been quite pleased with his interview with McQuaid), the professor strongly advised (or, in Professor Garvin's term, 'forbade') Whyte from continuing with this work.[145] Shortly afterwards Whyte accepted a lectureship in Queen's University, Belfast.[146]

Garvin also recalls that as late as 1972 Fergal O'Connor begged him, then a young firebrand (as he describes himself), not to make a particular speech at the Faculty of Arts on the grounds that 'it would bring the archbishop down on us' and wreck the department that Conor Martin and Fergal O'Connor were trying to build.

The long shadow of the archbishop also extended to departments outside the Faculty of Philosophy. The History Department, with well-known professors such as Robert (Robin) Dudley Edwards and T. Desmond Williams, was looked on not only as one of the most progressive and successful departments in the college but also as one run by strongly independent-minded people. Yet they too felt constrained to recognise the hazards to be expected from an over-vigorous exercise of their independence. The choice of Father F. X.

Martin in 1963 to succeed Father Aubrey Gwynn in the chair of mediaeval history pleased the history professors, who had campaigned for him, but not Monsignor Horgan, whose favoured candidate was defeated. When vacancies arose shortly afterwards for lecturers in the rapidly expanding History Department, and Protestant candidates in several cases were highly commended, Dr Tierney warned that their appointment might be unwise: he recalled that history was among the subjects that the bishops had traditionally treated as within their purview, because of a supposed danger to the faith and morals of Catholic students unless they were taught by a Catholic professor. Interestingly, the president did not express agreement with this attitude but stressed only the hazard that it might be invoked, and therefore that it would be better in the circumstances not to appoint non-Catholics to permanent posts in History. If the archbishop's attention were drawn to the question, he argued, it could result in an undesirable situation in which the college would find itself having to fend off church interference in appointments to posts in other subjects as well. He was therefore against either seeking the archbishop's sanction (as Hogan advised) or letting the Protestant appointments proceed and inevitably run into difficulty when they came before the Finance Committee (as Hogan had warned would happen). The president did not have to remind the history professors that Monsignor Horgan was a member of the Finance Committee.

Notwithstanding the fact that they yielded pragmatically for a time to *force majeure,* signs of unease among the professors about the presidential ban on non-Catholic historians began to resurface in June 1965. Tierney had retired since the previous September, and Professor Martin had sent in a list of eleven names to the president, Dr Hogan, for submission to the Finance Committee in connection with the appointment of a replacement in Mediaeval History. Professor Martin admitted that the person recommended was not the one he would select in different circumstances. A majority of the history professors had not endorsed the appointment, and it seemed to them that 'the College authorities had simply taken the first named Catholic on the list,' who was below the standard normally accepted.[147]

What was seen as a breaking of ranks among the professors and the appointment of 'the first named Catholic on the list' acted as a catharsis. Suddenly no more was to be heard of this problem about the appointment of non-Catholic historians. Without any fuss, a non-Catholic was appointed in 1966 and another in 1968 to Modern History; and in that year two non-Catholics were also appointed to Mediaeval History, after which the question of a candidate's religion no longer arose.

Dr Tierney had retired in 1964, Monsignor Horgan in 1971, and Archbishop McQuaid in 1972. By the time John Whyte returned to UCD in 1983 as professor of politics, the era of clerical influence in UCD was long over and the atmosphere of fear had dissolved. His *Church and State in Modern Ireland,* first published in 1971, had contributed to the process of demystification.

It is difficult to understand now how in appointments to history in 1963–65 the question of the candidates' religion should have been so serious an issue. The president's ban on the appointment of non-Catholics in an undenominational institution could hardly have survived a legal challenge. And it has to be said that there is no evidence that the archbishop ever uttered a word against such appointments. Clearly what the president feared was the *possible* intervention of the archbishop, or the trouble that Monsignor Horgan might make. After all, the early Lenten pastorals of Dr McQuaid had described UCD as no more than 'sufficiently safe' for the faith and morals of Catholics. Tierney may well have feared that a number of non-Catholics on the staff of the History Department might have tipped the balance against UCD's 'sufficiently safe' status in the eyes of the archbishop. Nor did he wish to forfeit the high praise that the 1961 pastoral had lavished on the college.

The history professors probably had to take into account what would have been seen by them as the sinister role of Monsignor Horgan, whose attitude to the History Department since the battle over the chair of mediaeval history could not be regarded as friendly. The vaguest suspicion that John Charles McQuaid had preferred Monsignor Horgan's candidate for the chair of mediaeval history would be likely to make Father F. X. Martin and his brother, Father Conor Martin, tread warily in order to avoid causing any annoyance to the archbishop by the appointment of non-Catholics or the encouragement of publication in the sensitive area of recent church-state relations. As long as the professors of history could get qualified Catholics, their situation would have been somewhat similar to that of UCG, where the regulation was that a suitable candidate qualified also in Irish had to be appointed over a qualified candidate without Irish. Besides, the history professors were able to use the circumstances to argue for an improvement in the salaries of those appointed and for additional part-time and postgraduate assistance in the fulfilment of the department's teaching duties.

The archbishop's interest in UCD was not limited to areas related to the Faculties of Medicine and Philosophy. He had remained silent on History, but his concern with Agriculture was indicated in a congratulatory note he sent to Dr Tierney on learning of the purchase of the Lyons estate.[148]

When UCD instituted a new primary degree in law, the president sent the archbishop a copy of the draft recommendations for the new courses, 'in which perhaps you may be interested.' The principal change in the curriculum consisted of the addition of an introduction to philosophy as a subject to the first-year course; this would involve an hour a week on special ethics. It was also proposed to have canon law as part of the LLB courses, which Tierney hoped to discuss later with the archbishop. How interested McQuaid was is confirmed in his acknowledgment:

> I regard the proposals of very far-reaching usefulness ... The courses outlined will re-integrate the civil law with the corpus of European, Catholic philosophy which we had, in distinct measure, abandoned with the English jurists.[149] I congratulate you on the courage and foresight of the proposed changes and I assure you that it will be for me a privilege to co-operate with you in regard to Canon Law.[150]

The concern Dr McQuaid had shown with UCD in general gave Dr Tierney the opportunity to try to enlist the archbishop's support on behalf of UCD's Faculties of Engineering and Architecture. Canon Fitzpatrick, chairman of the City of Dublin Vocational Education Committee, attended the 1957 Vocational Congress in Bray as the archbishop's representative. The *Irish Times* reported him as saying there was a lack of co-operation between the universities and the higher branches of the vocational schools. He did not wish to say anything against the universities, but he thought it was from them that the scheme of co-operation should come. He would say to the universities not to be jealous; if certain work had to be done, either do it or let the vocational schools do it.

Tierney was furious, and in a letter to the archbishop he said it was obvious that when the canon said 'universities' he meant UCD; that his words would be read as meaning in some unspecified way that UCD had been negligent in its duty. He added that readers with some knowledge of the situation would recognise that the canon was referring to the long-continued attempts to establish in Kevin Street and Bolton Street schools of engineering and architecture to rival those of UCD. For over thirty years UCD had been refused the finance needed to keep its professional schools abreast of the times, while great sums of taxpayers' money had been spent in providing, through these vocational schools, a back-door entry to the professions. It would be necessary, said the president, for him to make a public reply to the canon's strictures, which he felt very grievously. He had a right to ask people of the canon's standing if they wished to make attacks on the college at least to do so by name and to be more specific about their reasons. 'We have enough enemies to deal with, without being sniped at by the higher clergy of the archdiocese of Dublin.'[151] Tierney made a rough draft of a letter on similar lines to Canon Fitzpatrick, but this was marked *Not sent*.

His letter to the archbishop was more typical of Tierney's fighting spirit than most of his correspondence with McQuaid. It was almost as good as implying that if he played ball with the archbishop he expected the archbishop to reciprocate, especially where the clergy of Dublin were concerned. Tierney took his role as defender of his college seriously, and he had no intention of letting the higher clergy off with what he perceived to be veiled attacks on UCD.

In an effort to smooth over troubled waters and to prevent the issue blowing up into a public row between his friends, the president and the canon, Dr McQuaid sent a conciliatory and, it would have to be said, masterly note to Tierney in which he said that he was quite unaware of the canon's speech.

> It is a matter of deep regret that his words should have been found by you to be cryptic and hurtful. You will not find it hard to accept my word that I should not wish to be either ambiguous or hurtful to University College, Dublin in view of my efforts to assist you and your work. If I had any observations to make you know I would not choose a public occasion on which to make any comments.
>
> My knowledge of Canon Fitzpatrick leads me to believe that he would not for any consideration damage University College, but I do know that he would speak without notes.
>
> I may not say what the President of University College ought to do in the circumstances, but I may be allowed to say that I hope no harm will result from a public reference to the Canon's words.
>
> I think I can guarantee that the matter will not become a public newspaper controversy, in so far as Canon Fitzpatrick is concerned.[152]

Tierney was mollified and took the hint that more harm than good might be done by publicly complaining about the canon's remarks.

Though Archbishop McQuaid's practical involvement in UCD extended further than that of any other Archbishop of Dublin, he also displayed genuine sympathy with the college and with the problems faced by its president. When the Dáil approved the move to Belfield, Dr McQuaid congratulated Tierney on the outcome of the debate and expressed his appreciation of the work done by him. He wrote: 'I thank you for the enormous work that you have put into securing for Catholics their fundamental rights.'[153]

When, a month later, the visitors' report on appointments in UCD reflected adversely on Tierney's policy and brought unwelcome public criticism of his administration, the archbishop was there to offer words of comfort. 'I very deeply regret what I have read these days about the Visitors' Report and I congratulate you on the dignity of your silence. When the dust of the misrepresentation has cleared it will be remembered what a vast work you have done for Catholic education.' And for one whose public image was that of a rather cold personality, his concluding gesture was that of a caring and warm individual: 'I should like to call to see you this evening at your home, if it were convenient. I could call after 8 p.m.'[154]

There were small practical ways in which the archbishop was also prepared to show his appreciation of the work done by the college, as on the occasion when he enclosed a cheque to add to the Birmingham Medal Fund in order that 'a more worthy medal may be awarded in memory of a man to whom the Catholic Medical School owes so much.'[155]

CONCLUSION

The letters in which John Charles McQuaid conveyed his ideas to Michael Tierney are written in his own neat handwriting. Remarkably, there are no mistakes, no corrections, no crossings out. They are brief, economical with words, always to the point; almost every sentence makes its own paragraph. His letters reflect the man's character: prudent, self-possessed, secretive, personally attentive to details, while presiding over a vast administration. For Dublin was easily the busiest diocese in Ireland; and given its size and the number of churches, parishes, priests and religious, schools and hospitals it encompassed, it must have been one of the busiest religious administrations in the world. Yet Dr McQuaid devoted a vast amount of personal attention to UCD.

Had he, as initially feared, 'interfered' in the college's affairs? If the answer is yes, it has also to be admitted that some good came of the evil of interference. 'Interfered', however, is probably too strong. Certainly, on the other hand, he had intervened. He had intervened between the Government and the college where his intervention had been requested on such matters as veterinary medicine, agriculture, and dentistry. He had intervened in UCD's interests, and at UCD's invitation, in the college's dealings with the nuns with regard to the teaching hospitals; and the arrangements that were come to between the Faculty of Medicine and the hospitals were held up as a model for other university colleges by the Commission on Higher Education. He had proposed or supported developments in physiotherapy, sociology, politics, psychology, career guidance, and law. To provide an alternative for students who might otherwise have gone to Trinity the archbishop had urged on the UCD authorities the provision of improved opportunities in the BA, BComm and DPA for evening students, thereby restoring the role in evening classes that Newman had envisaged for his university; and after Trinity had abandoned the evening degree, UCD increased its commitment to the evening student. He had made representations on behalf of individual applicants, but accepted UCD's regulations on admissions.

Much of his supposed interference arose out of the ban on Catholics attending Trinity. But in his attitude to that college he had the full sympathy and backing of Michael Tierney. Logically, because of their stand on Trinity, archbishop and president had to provide alternative facilities for Catholics at UCD. These included, on the archbishop's part, chaplains, hostels and a church as well as the release of many clerics of the archdiocese to serve for life in their scholarly careers. And on the president's part it involved co-operating with the archbishop's wishes. The archbishop's wishes were, if not quite commands, at least always treated with the utmost respect by Michael Tierney. Nor can it be denied that the president used the connection with the archbishop to the advantage of UCD. And throughout, both president and archbishop retained the dignity of their positions.

Co-operation between archbishop and president was intended for the mutual benefit of church and college; and there is no doubt that the college did in part owe its protection from Government interference and its development in a number of areas to the interest the archbishop had taken. The price to be paid by the college was the constant presence of the archbishop's shadow. His influence was so great that it was often supposed to exist in corners to which in fact it did not extend. Reforms proposed by the younger academics were sometimes rejected on the grounds that the Statutes would not permit them, or alternatively that they would not meet with the archbishop's approval. Disapproval by the archbishop carried by far the more sinister connotations.

UCD had in a very special sense been the creation of the Catholic hierarchy. Its ancestor, the university over which Newman presided, had been directly and unambiguously a Catholic institution. University College in St Stephen's Green had been managed and to a considerable extent staffed by the priests of the Society of Jesus. The 1908 Act and Charters had given UCD an independence of church and state, had established university autonomy and the right and opportunity to pursue academic freedom. Neither church nor state had control over the appointment of UCD's Governing Body, president, or professors — unlike the situation that had existed earlier in the Queen's Colleges, or in contemporary Germany or elsewhere on the Continent, where universities were more in the control of the state. Neither did they have any control over the curriculum: under the 1908 legislation the state did not insist, as would later be the case in the primary and secondary systems, on compulsory Irish; nor could the church insist on the teaching of Catholic theology or Catholic doctrine.

The 1908 legislation was a compromise between the two powerful forces of church and state. It left UCD in the position of being able to play one off against the other should the occasion arise where one seemed to be interfering with the college's autonomy. When it was felt, for example, that the merger might damage UCD in sensitive areas such as medicine, the UCD authorities were not beyond using the shield of the church against the state.

The university established in 1908 was by statute undenominational, in that all religious tests were forbidden. Nevertheless it was the bishops who had campaigned for an institution that would be acceptable to Catholics. It is to the credit of the bishops, however, that officially at least they were very careful to respect the integrity of UCD's autonomy. Given the particular circumstances of its origins, as well as the prevailing role of religion in contemporary Irish society, it was hardly surprising that until at least the nineteen-sixties the Catholic ethos prevailed in the nominally undenominational college. That this was bound to be so had been realised as early as 1889 by the Chief Secretary, Arthur Balfour, when he admitted that any new university established in Dublin could not be in practice undenominational.[156]

It was inevitable in the circumstances that there would be a big physical presence of priests in UCD in its first sixty years or so. It also followed that there would be a strong Catholic ethos among its staff and students, for the strength of Catholicism in the college was no more than a reflection of its overwhelming presence in society as a whole. Spreading out from the many churches and chapels, Catholicism infused the homes, schools, shops, offices and factories. It stalked the streets, filled the printed page and dominated the air waves of Ireland in the first half of the twentieth century; it was part of the atmosphere the country breathed. The Catechism was the one great formative influence. No symbolism, such as crucifixes in the lecture-halls and laboratories, was necessary to remind the college of its Catholic ethos, for, as well as being physically present in the priests on its staff and in the seminarians among its students, the church had also pervaded the intellectual, social and cultural climate of lay academics and students alike. The influence of the church in such circumstances would be great, but indirect.

It is not to be wondered at, therefore, that medicine and especially medical ethics, philosophy, politics, sociology, education, science, history and literature were all studied within the framework of the prevailing Catholicism. The certainties of religion and its formal ecclesiastical structures were as firmly established and as widely accepted as the laws of nature. Academics of John Marcus O'Sullivan's, Michael Tierney's or Jeremiah Hogan's generation had grown out of a period of struggle to win a university for Catholics. It was a period too that was still self-conscious about sectarian antipathies between the Catholic and Protestant churches in Ireland. For such men, and at such a time in our history, to behave as anything less than ardent Catholics would have cast them in the role of traitors to the cause. Educated lay Catholics were what the college was established to provide, and that is what the country got from UCD.

What may be surprising, however, is that nobody in UCD stepped out of line. So far as religion was concerned, there were amazingly no rebel intellectuals among the academics. This was not so much a reflection on the intellectualism of the academics as an indication of their conformity, and a measure of the strength and pervasiveness of Catholicism. There were none who were not Thomists among its philosophers. Publicly at any rate there were no free thinkers among its scientists, no Marxists among its historians, no socialists among its economists; and no breath of anti-clericalism such as one got in France or Italy ever rustled through its lecture-halls. No professor or lecturer who on taking office had signed the declaration not to make any statement or use any language disrespectful to the religious opinion of any student ever appears to have been complained of, much less reprimanded, under this section of the 1908 Act and Statutes.

In an era of authoritarianism and paternalism in education as well as in the church, academics, some perhaps concerned for what they had to lose, did not break rank. To do so would have required courage or foolhardiness, or eccentricity. In any case in the circumstances of the time the strong-minded were also Catholic Actionists of one kind or another. They not only accepted the church's dominant role in society but willingly and enthusiastically co-operated with it and promoted its apostolate. The McQuaid-Tierney relationship is only a striking example of the extent of the dominance of the ecclesiastical over the secular that an archbishop assumed; but it is equally revealing of how so strong-willed an intellectual as Michael Tierney fully accepted the subservience of the layman to the cleric. And Tierney's ambition to turn UCD into a publicly proclaimed and legally established Catholic university was highly indicative of a whole mental climate of the Ireland of his time.

Most academics in UCD would have considered such a move retrograde. In the tradition of John Dillon MP, they would have insisted on a lay-controlled university; or they would have opposed the change on the same grounds as Alfred O'Rahilly had done, believing that politicians and civil servants were not to be trusted with new university legislation. But much of the opposition would also have sprung from the conviction that the Tierney scheme would have been bad for the church as well as for the college. The Catholic ethos of the college was considered safest in its undenominational garb.

7

Acquiring Belfield

What has a better claim to the purest and fairest possessions of nature, than the seat of wisdom.

J. H. Newman, *Historical Sketches*, iii, 25.

THE FIRST SCHEME

The general election of February 1948 saw a change of Government, ending Fianna Fáil's sixteen consecutive years in office. In the first inter-party Government (February 1948 to June 1951) some of Michael Tierney's academic colleagues and former political associates and close friends held influential portfolios, notably John A. Costello as Taoiseach, Patrick McGilligan as Minister for Finance, James Dillon as Minister for Agriculture, and Richard Mulcahy as Minister for Education. He might now have expected an even more sympathetic ear from the Government than he had received from Éamon de Valera; this probably emboldened him to make a public statement about the desirability of moving from Earlsfort Terrace.

Referring to UCD's overcrowding and accommodation problems, Tierney told an *Irish Independent* representative on 14 August 1948, in what had all the indications of an official piece of public relations sponsored by the college authorities, that 'the only wholly satisfactory solution would be the erection of a completely new building on a site in or near the city. A "proper College" would require 200 acres of ground and its erection would cost about £2,000,000.' The airing of such views in a national newspaper served to prepare the public for the extent of the radical scheme that was to follow.

By 30 September 1948 Professor Joseph Downes had drawn up for the president the first of the Stillorgan Road schemes, on the assumption that the college could use Belfield and two adjoining properties as a site for the new buildings and recreation grounds. The area shown on his sketch is approximately 123 acres. Downes outlined the considerations that determined the layout of the plan, including the desirability of placing the buildings so that they would be reasonably remote from public roads; the assumption that no building be erected on the Merville site in case of delay in acquiring it; the grouping and orientation of the sports fields; the arrangement of the buildings, making Administration and the Library central and the heating station and other facilities remote; and a generous area of trees and parkland. Nearly all the buildings would be of four storeys, with basements in some. The plan was intended to indicate the dimensions and general possibilities of the site in relation to UCD's requirements; Downes recognised that if any future extensions were contemplated it would be necessary to acquire still more land.

In his seven years as professor of architecture (1943–1950), Joseph Downes had not only been involved in drawing up the plans for the several attempts to accommodate UCD on the Earlsfort Terrace and Iveagh Gardens site but also gave 'valuable service in an intensive study of the all-important question, whether the permanent buildings of the College might be sited at Earlsfort Terrace,' and he drew up the first plans for siting the buildings at Stillorgan Road. It was only proper to record, as the president's report stated in his obituary, that his investigations, which were thorough-going and costly, were done 'as a free gift to the College.'[1] After his retirement from the chair he continued to enjoy considerable consultancy practice. He was responsible for a wide range of design and construction, including churches, hospitals, schools, hotels, and industrial buildings. Among his major projects were the Aer Lingus offices at Dublin Airport; the Irish Life Assurance Company building at Mespil Road (ironically, in view of the fact that it was once hoped that his School of Architecture might be established there); more fittingly, because of its UCD connections, St Vincent's Hospital, Merrion Road; and, most appropriately of all, the Science Building at Belfield, the earliest of the great buildings in the new college.

Meanwhile a rearguard action had been conducted with the Minister for Finance, Patrick McGilligan (professor of constitutional law in UCD, then on leave of absence because of his Government position). A letter from McGilligan to Tierney dated 4 October 1948 carried a note of finality about it, insisting on the unsuitability of the proposed Iveagh Gardens site for a School of Architecture and the intention of the Office of Public Works to proceed with its plans for a civil service club on the site.[2] Tierney, of course, protested, telling the minister that the objections to an Architecture School on the site must apply equally to the civil service facility; but he was also quick to seize an advantage, adding in his reply:

> The whole episode constitutes an invincible argument in favour of the removal of the College to a much more commodious site than is afforded by the Iveagh Grounds, and I hope that when considering the Memorandum with which I supplied you this morning you will give due weight to these arguments.
>
> I may say that I am sending copies of the Memorandum and plan to

the Taoiseach, the Minister for Education, the Minister for Agriculture, and the Minister for External Affairs.[3]

The material Tierney submitted to the Taoiseach and ministers included the Stillorgan Road plan and the covering letter of Professor Downes, and a forceful memorandum on the siting and financing of University College. Copies of the memorandum were also sent to the Presidents of UCC and UCG, as Tierney felt they should be kept in touch with developments. The memorandum, given its length and its detail, had clearly been prepared before the Minister for Finance had written to inform Tierney of the final decision regarding the proposed School of Architecture at the rear of 82–85 St Stephen's Green and was presented to the Minister for Finance on the very day his letter was received.

The memo began by stating that it was necessary that a decision be taken very soon on the siting of the college buildings, for not only was the college being further cramped each year but, because of the rapid expansion of the city, it might soon have to take a site far less suitable and more expensive than could then be got. The idea of placing the new buildings in the Iveagh Grounds, the memo stated, had had pretty full consideration. The blocks would necessarily be high and close together, and little could be preserved of the park-like amenity of the Iveagh Grounds as they then were. The gravest objection, however, was that no further extension of the buildings would be possible, and they must be seriously obsolete or insufficient in a comparatively short time. It would therefore be very unwise to spend a large amount of public money on the Earlsfort Terrace site.

The college authorities has also considered whether they might acquire other ground near Earlsfort Terrace and had tried to buy such ground more than once, but without success. Any such addition must be a slow, uncertain and very expensive process. The uncertainty was even more serious than the slowness. Prudently, nothing could be built until the whole enlarged area was in the hands of the college.

In contrast, the choice of a large site on the edge of the city, such as Belfield, offered very great advantages. And here the memo incorporated some of those arguments that Downes had advanced, including the larger site's adaptability and the space it provided for further expansion. UCD then owned approximately 58 acres at Belfield; Ardmore would add to this almost 16 acres and Roebuck 50, giving Downes's total of approximately 124 acres. If Merville could be acquired it would add approximately 50 acres more. UCD, therefore, had the opportunity of possessing the most up-to-date buildings and equipment to be found anywhere. The memo recognised that there must be some loss in moving from the city centre, especially with regard to libraries and hospitals and to accessibility, but these losses must be balanced against the gains attached to a suburban site.

The memo then went into considerable detail about the estimates and financing of the proposed siting and equipping of the new college. It estimated the total outlay on site, buildings and equipment (assuming compensation for the old buildings in Merrion Street and Earlsfort Terrace) at about £3 million and suggested the allocation by the Government of a capital sum of £10 million, to be administered by a body of trustees working for and with the college.

Following the specific proposal in the memo that the Government add the Ardmore site to Belfield to form the nucleus of the new college, a news item appeared in the *Irish Independent* on 24 November 1948 that read: 'The building of a new broadcasting house on a 20 acre site recently purchased at Ardmore, Belfield, Stillorgan Road, is under consideration by the Government ...' Tierney was annoyed and reacted immediately, with three separate missives sent off on the same day to the Taoiseach, Minister for Finance, and Minister for Posts and Telegraphs. He reminded the Taoiseach of the memorandum that he had submitted, and he pointed out that UCD had already been refused permission to erect a School of Architecture at the back of 86 St Stephen's Green, while at the same time the Department of Finance intended to erect a club for civil servants at the back of Iveagh House at a cost of £70,000. This decision, in Tierney's view, had rendered it impossible for the college to develop reasonably in its present site, and he continued: 'If the situation arises that wherever the College proposes to establish itself, some Government Department gets in first, prospects for the College are going to be exceedingly poor.'[4]

In his letter to the Minister for Finance he left no doubt about who he thought had inspired the item in the *Irish Independent*. 'It would seem that the Secretary of the Department of Posts and Telegraphs [León Ó Broin] thinks that a little publicity might assist in propelling the Government towards a decision in favour of the Broadcasting House at Ardmore.'

Whether because of Tierney's importunities or not, no more was done about establishing the broadcasting centre at Ardmore. Then, on 2 June 1949, Montrose, a house and grounds outside Donnybrook a short distance from Belfield on the opposite side of the Stillorgan Road, was bought by Michael Tierney. It cost £21,000, including auctioneer's commission. Montrose and its twenty-three acres had come suddenly on the market following the death of its owner. Tierney reported to the Governing Body at its next meeting (14 June 1949) that he had had to proceed with the purchase without calling a meeting of the Governing Body but that he had obtained the views of the members of the Buildings Committee, who had agreed that the opportunity should not be lost. The committee had visited and inspected the house and grounds. A resolution that the committee be empowered to complete the purchase was passed unanimously by the Governing Body, which also formally approved the purchase. And the former president, Dr Arthur Conway, who was still a member of the Governing Body, congratulated the college on the acquisition of 'a very valuable property.' The president was of the opinion that the house might be used as a student hostel, though ultimately it was to become the RTE head office and broadcasting centre.[5] The purchase of Montrose ushered in the main phase of expansion at Stillorgan Road.

NEGOTIATIONS WITH THE GOVERNMENT

Formal discussions between members of the Government and representatives of the college regarding the site of UCD, which Tierney had been urging for some time, finally took place on 22 July 1949. The Government was represented by the Taoiseach and the Ministers for Agriculture, Finance, and External Affairs; UCD's representatives included the president, Professor Purcell and Senator Michael Hayes.

Tierney opened the discussion by stressing the building and space inadequacies experienced by UCD. He said that the best advice was that the college should be moved to a more suitable site, where all the schools would be together, on an area of at least two hundred acres; that he was accordingly asking the Government to help the college to acquire a suitable site and to build on the site chosen; and that the college authorities were keen to build around the Belfield site, suitably enlarged, but that unless action were taken fairly soon there was a danger that the land they would like to acquire adjoining Belfield would be acquired by others. If the Government was prepared to adopt this course the college would hand over to the Government the College of Science and Earlsfort Terrace buildings, retaining, however, 85 and 86 St Stephen's Green.

Tierney then gave a brief outline of how he perceived the move to Stillorgan Road. They would like to transfer the College of Science immediately; the Arts faculties would follow; the last faculty to be transferred would be Medicine. The travelling difficulties of the clerical students from Clonliffe and All Hallows 'could be easily overcome,' and he thought it should be possible to provide a number of hostels under the supervision of religious orders.

Purcell strongly supported the arguments for Stillorgan Road put forward by the president. The college already held 60 acres at Belfield and had just bought 22 acres at Montrose; and a site of 36 acres at Whiteoaks had now also come on the market. In reply to a question from the Government side he said that about 200 acres at a minimum would be required and that in general the cost of the land could be taken to be £1,000 per acre. While Professor Purcell was impressed by what he had seen of suburban Scandinavian colleges on his visit there with Professor Downes, Michael Tierney liked to refer to the

University of Nottingham, founded in 1948, which had then acquired 350 acres for its two thousand students. Nottingham, described as 'the first British University to engage a distinguished landscape architect,' with its open parkland 'commanding magnificent views ... over the flood plain of the river Trent and the city and castle of Nottingham,'[6] appealed to Tierney as a model for the future UCD.

During this discussion a question arose most unexpectedly and almost incidentally that twenty years later would be the biggest issue in university education. The minute of the meeting simply reads: 'The Taoiseach raised the question of Trinity College.' But from the reaction of Senator Hayes and Michael Tierney it was clear that Costello had raised the issue of some kind of merger or co-operation between the two Dublin colleges—anticipating the proposal of Donogh O'Malley when he too had to face the request for state funds for one of the colleges. The response of Senator Hayes was also to anticipate the kind of argument that would be advanced by the academics in the sixties against the merger. Hayes referred to Trinity's traditions and the desirability of retaining them. He thought Trinity should not be interfered with in any way, nor should any attempt be made to turn it into something like University College. While leaving Trinity its traditions, he thought UCD should be allowed to develop in its own way. There were about two thousand students in Trinity, some half of whom were from abroad, and of the remainder, five hundred were students who had failed to gain entry to UCD.

Tierney's response was to ask whether the authorities of the University of Dublin had ever been asked about their attitude to UCD. Trinity, he said, had a tradition as a Protestant college in a Catholic country. Any proposal for the amalgamation of the two colleges would operate to the disadvantage of University College. UCD had achieved a high standing; amalgamation with Trinity would only hamper its growth and alter the direction of its development. University College was a bigger clerical college than Maynooth, and its Medical School was unique. It was in fact a university masquerading as a college and was representative of all the Irish people.

Twenty years later, when the merger became a public proposal by the Government and a real possibility, Tierney would take the line that there was really room for only one university in Dublin.

Fascinating as was this first airing of the merger idea by the Government, it was then no more than a side issue in the general discussion between the Government and UCD. And the outcome of the meeting was that it was agreed that the most suitable site for the development of the college would be in the vicinity of Belfield; that the college authorities should continue to negotiate for the purchase of Whiteoaks, and that the Government would raise no objection. The Minister for Finance recalled that the University College authorities had already suggested that their building programme could be carried out for under £4 million; he did not see why £10 million as an endowment would be necessary; and he suggested that the president should revise the memorandum submitted the previous year and accompany it with a map indicating the college's proposals for building at Belfield.[7]

The revised memo submitted by Tierney on 29 July 1949 went into considerable financial detail, along grounds that had already been indicated in the earlier memo and at the meeting with the ministers. It elaborated on the stages by which it was proposed to proceed to a master plan for the development of the Belfield vicinity site.

These negotiations made no commitment to provide UCD with the £10 million endowment requested as one possible means of making funds available for the projected Belfield scheme. On the other hand, neither did they raise any objections to UCD's determination to carry out its plans to acquire the lands necessary for such a development. In the circumstances, UCD could be excused for thinking that a moral commitment had been made; and the college proceeded to buy the neighbouring estates when they came on the market.

The acquisition of Montrose was followed some four months later by the purchase in October 1949 of Whiteoaks, which was closer to the Belfield site. Whiteoaks had been built about 1840 and was perhaps the most villa-like of all the houses bought by UCD in the vicinity. It had a Greek Revival façade and a central porch with Doric columns and stucco pilasters. It had been the home of Dr T. O. Graham since about 1939. In the middle of the nineteenth century Richard Seymour Guinness, the head of the banking firm of Guinness Mahon, who left Dublin in 1860 to open a branch in London, had lived in it. Joseph Hone, a director of the Bank of Ireland and the father of Evie Hone, the stained-glass artist, had owned the property at least from 1889 until his death about 1909. She and her sister stayed on until about 1913 or 1914, when Evie Hone was twenty-two or twenty-three. The house was originally known as Roebuck Grove, which became confusing, because there were other Roebuck Groves in the area, and Dr Graham had changed the name to Whiteoaks.[8]

On 25 October 1949 the president reported to the Governing Body the purchase of Whiteoaks, comprising, according to the title deeds, almost thirty-four acres, for £30,000 (exclusive of auctioneer's fees and other expenses). At a later meeting of the Governing Body (20 December) the Buildings Committee was empowered to complete the purchase.

Under an indenture made on 26 February 1953 the college permitted the president to use Whiteoaks, which by now was renamed University Lodge, as an official residence. When Michael Tierney took up residence it was looked upon as 'an act of faith in the future.'[9]

By 1950, therefore, with Montrose and Whiteoaks, UCD had added another 57 acres to Belfield, bringing its total to approximately 115 acres. It was now moving steadily towards the minimum of 200 acres that the college representatives, in discussions with the Government in July 1949, had said would be required for the successful implementation of the Stillorgan Road project. The Government appeared to be going along with the idea, for a committee comprising the Taoiseach and the Ministers for Education, Finance, Defence and Health was established in April 1950 to consider and report on a long-term policy with regard to (*a*) the co-ordination of existing institutions providing university education and providing training for the medical profession, (*b*) the terms on which financial assistance by the state to such institutions should in future be provided, and (*c*) the question of financial assistance by the state towards the solution of the problem of accommodation in UCD.[10]

On the question of higher education UCD had clearly become a matter of priority for the Government. And the terms of reference for the Government committee anticipated in broad outline some of the major issues involved in the merger discussions seventeen years later.

At a meeting of the Buildings Committee in June 1950 the president reported that he had been approached by a firm of auctioneers who were sole agents for the disposal of Merville, the property of Colonel Hume-Dudgeon.[11] This property, adjoining Belfield at the Foster Avenue end, amounted to about sixty acres, and its possible acquisition was immediately recognised as the most valuable step that the college could take. The price asked for the sixty acres and thirty-room house, 'something over £100,000,' was considered high. A deputation from the Buildings Committee—Professors Purcell and Hogan of Engineering and Senator Michael Hearne (a very knowledgeable local authority representative who played an important role in the acquisition of Belfield)—met Colonel Hume-Dudgeon on 12 June. Hume-Dudgeon explained that he had been approached by various builders wanting to take small parcels of his land for development. He would continue to refuse such requests, and while he was not keen to dispose of the property immediately, he would give the college first option. Meanwhile his wife was to be given the opportunity to look over the Montrose property, which might be transferred in part payment for Merville.[12]

Friendly relations between Dr Tierney and the seller resulted from the negotiations. When the sale was completed, Colonel Hume-Dudgeon in a gracious letter to the president wrote: 'I like to feel it is going to help the youth of the country.'[13] He enclosed a copy of a letter of 1 September 1893 from a Mr Bradshaw, who had sold Merville to the Hume-Dudgeon family, arranging for the orange trees and wild ducks to be left to the new owners, and a motto from Psalm 127: 'Except the Lord build the House they labour in vain that build it.' He regretted that he no longer had the orange trees to give, as they had ceased to exist some years earlier. He also enclosed a note on Merville, dated 28 October 1825, which described it as 'the delightful villa of Lord Downes ... unquestionably one of the best kept places in the empire ... here, in the proper season, may be seen the best collection of spring flowers in the kingdom ... there is a small American ground where are the best private collection of bog plants we know of in the vicinity of Dublin.' Dr Tierney described these enclosures as 'exceedingly interesting' and said they would be carefully preserved.[14]

Merville, the largest house of the future Belfield site, had been built about 1750 and was early Georgian in style. The house and the road alongside the estate, Foster Avenue, are said to have been built by Anthony Foster MP (1705–1778), appointed Chief Baron of the Exchequer in 1765. He had a great interest in agriculture and a reputation as an improver and was one of the founders of the Royal Dublin Society. His second wife, a Burgh, is credited with selecting the site for Merville. On his death Merville passed to his son, John Foster, who opposed the Act of Union and was the last Speaker of the Irish House of Commons. The house was sold in the seventeen-eighties to Thomas Lighton, who also sat in the Irish House of Commons in the nineties and voted against the Union. After his death in 1805 Merville was bought by William Downes, Chief Justice of the King's Bench.

Following almost a year of confidential negotiation, it was reported to the Governing Body on 8 May 1951 that Colonel Hume-Dudgeon was prepared to sell Merville to the college for £100,000, and the detailed conditions of sale were outlined in a letter from his solicitors. Vacant possession would be available within two years of the date of execution of the contract. In fact it was not until September 1953 that UCD gained possession.

The president stressed that both parties wished to treat the matter as confidential. He said that they could spend a long time looking for anything as advantageous. The price was not small, but, as Senator Hearne had pointed out, the value of the land in the area was increasing daily. If the purchase were not made they might have to go further from the city. The verbal sanction of the minister, he reported, had been received. In reply to a question whether any thought had been given to the consequences of removal from the city, the president said that the question had been fully considered by the previous Governing Body but that of course before any action could be taken there must be further discussion and decision. Buying the land, as Professor Purcell pointed out, in no way committed them to build. Formal acceptance of the offer was unanimously approved.

Not only was Merville the largest of the estates acquired by the college in the area but the resolution to purchase it was decisive in determining the move. At a special meeting of the Governing Body on 6 November 1951, Professor Purcell gave a summary of the accommodation and building problems since 1909 and of the efforts that had been made to keep the college on a central site. Since he was convinced that this was no longer possible, the siting of the new college at Stillorgan Road was the obvious solution. Senator Hearne proposed 'that the Governing Body is of opinion that the best interests of University College, Dublin, require that the new University College buildings be erected on the lands owned by the College at Stillorgan.' Professor Purcell seconded this historic resolution, and it was adopted unanimously by the Governing Body.

BUILDINGS COMMITTEE RECONSTITUTED

Following this decision, Dr Tierney determined that appropriate action should at once be taken to put it into effect. He presented a memorandum to the Governing Body at its meeting of 29 January 1952 in which he suggested that they fully examine the nature, size and architectural character of the proposed buildings, and their cost. To do this he proposed that the Buildings Committee be reconstituted by the addition of other members of the Governing Body. At this time the committee had consisted of seven members: the three officers, president, registrar, and secretary; Senator Hearne, a Government nominee; the two professors of engineering, Purcell and Hogan; and the professor of architecture, Desmond FitzGerald.

Tierney decided that the most appropriate place for the professor of architecture was on an Advisory Architects' Board; he then added six others to the Buildings Committee, making a total of twelve. He also proposed that Professor Purcell be appointed chairman; that the committee meet regularly and more often than in the past; that it appoint an Architects' Board to advise it; that the assistant secretary, J. P. MacHale, be appointed secretary to the Buildings Committee; that the president receive all its papers; and that it make regular progress reports to the Governing Body.

The chairman of the committee, Professor Purcell, had long been a colleague of Michael Tierney's on the Governing Body. After forty-five years he retired in 1953 from the chair of civil engineering (though he continued to serve on the Governing Body), leaving the faculty he had done so much to build up in a flourishing state. Tierney's long tribute to Purcell concluded with the words: 'In a fairly varied experience of public and academic life, there has been no person with whom collaboration through the years has given me greater pleasure or greater pride.'[15]

Purcell's 'powerful and attractive personality', his humour and energy stood him in great stead as chairman of the Buildings Committee from 1952 until the early sixties, while Tierney was still president, and as the college's chief negotiator for many of the Stillorgan Road sites. Pierce Purcell well merited the description 'one of the great men of the College ... the creator of our Engineering School, one of the chief makers of the new University College Dublin at Belfield.'[16] He had served on the Governing Body of UCD, as the president said, 'for almost all of its sixty years,'[17] or, more precisely, from February 1916 until his death at the age of eighty-six in January 1968, having attended his last meeting of the Governing Body in June 1967. This would probably have made him the longest-serving member ever of the Governing Body.

Michael Hearne was a member of Longford County Council who used connections with the building industry to good purpose in helping to acquire the property around the Belfield nucleus and in the planning of the Science Building. Michael Hogan (professor of mechanical engineering 1939–1954, professor of civil engineering 1954–1968) also joined in negotiating the sites and drew up many of the technical reports on accommodation needs. J. P. MacHale (secretary and bursar 1954–1987) owed much of the power he came to possess in the college from the experience he gained in working closely with these colleagues. Others who served on the Buildings Committee during the fifties and early sixties included Jeremiah Hogan (Michael Hogan's brother, registrar 1952–1964, president 1964–1972), T. S. Wheeler (professor of chemistry 1945–1962), Monsignor J. D. Horgan (professor of metaphysics 1942–1971) and Michael Hayes (professor of Modern Irish 1951–59).

When the reconstituted Buildings Committee met on 12 February 1952, Senator Hearne was elected vice-chairman, and it was decided to meet fortnightly for the present. It was agreed as the first essential to obtain from the head of each department a schedule setting out space requirements for up to four thousand students. Professor Michael Hogan made himself available for consultation to anyone who might require his assistance. It was also agreed to have consultations with the University of Birmingham, the University of Edinburgh, or other universities that might have faced similar problems. Preliminary consideration was given to the appointment of an Advisory Architects' Board.

The enlarged and reconstituted Buildings Committee now had the task of spearheading the Stillorgan Road project. Much of its practical work devolved on the hard core of Purcell, Hearne, Hogan, and MacHale, with the president always in control of general policy and consulted on all major decisions. Indeed, though Dr Tierney was not present at the five meetings of the Buildings Committee held between February and July 1952, he was invariably present at, and sometimes chaired, all meetings of the committee from October 1952 onwards.

ACCUMULATING THE PROPERTY

After Michael Tierney's presidency, the Finance Committee was considered the key committee to which members of the Governing Body scrambled to get elected. During Tierney's regime the powerhouse of the Governing Body was the Buildings Committee, which was essentially hand-picked; all its members, in varying degrees, were president's men.

The work done by the Buildings Committee, especially between 1952 and 1965, was among the most important ever undertaken by any committee in the history of the college. It was concerned with buying enough land in the Stillorgan Road area on which to build the new college; drawing up the professional plans for the erection of the various buildings; planning the detailed schedules of departmental and faculty accommodation requirements; persuading the Government to agree to the transfer and to provide the necessary substantial finance; and keeping public opinion satisfied at least to the extent of restraining it from influencing the politicians and Government against the Belfield idea.

All these tasks had to be tackled more or less simultaneously. For the sake of clarity, however, it is perhaps as well to sketch briefly the accumulation of the properties that were eventually to become the Belfield campus. It is in its own sphere a remarkable story; and for the person with a sense of history the act of gradual acquisition and consolidation of some dozen contiguous estates is modestly reminiscent of the growth and expansion of the frontiers of one of the great empires of the past, or akin in its overtones and in its own small way to the unification of Germany or Italy in the age of nationalism.

Before the reconstitution of the Buildings Committee in January 1952, the most recent acquisition had been the large house and sixty acres of the Merville estate. The first report of the Advisory Architects' Board (October 1952) recommended Merville, rather than Belfield, as the site for the proposed new buildings. The board held to this recommendation, despite the acquisition the next year of Woodview, a late-Georgian house (*c.* 1820) with 18½ acres and access to the Stillorgan Road by a carriage drive, and the purchase in 1954 of 42 acres, called Byrne's Fields, linking the Belfield and Whiteoaks properties. While the Woodview lands had been acquired for £700 an acre, Byrne's Fields cost £1,000 an acre. This was twice as much as UCD had hoped to pay, but competition was now growing for land in the area: the Beech Hill housing estate and Browne and Nolan's (now Smurfit's) and other factories had been built or were being built on adjacent property. Without Byrne's Fields, University Lodge would have remained cut off from the main college site. With the addition of Byrne's Fields the college, according to the Buildings Committee, had now acquired a block of 228 acres, thus reaching the objective specified at the beginning of the decade for the full implementation of the new building scheme.[18]

Simultaneously with the negotiations for Byrne's Fields, transactions were being conducted for buying Belgrove. This house and its seventeen acres were strategically very valuable to UCD, wedged as they were between the Woodview and Belfield properties, fronting onto the Stillorgan Road and providing wider access to the Woodview lands should that area be chosen for the new buildings. Transactions for the acquisition of Belgrove began in July 1953. Professor Purcell was told that the owner, Mr Pearson, was eighty-three years old and difficult to deal with, but in fact he proved willing to sell on terms permitting him to continue his nursery business for his lifetime.[19] He received £19,250 for his interest in Belgrove, and the freehold was bought from F. A. Richards for £4,500. Belgrove, a mock-Tudor building, was demolished in 1973 when the Stillorgan Road became a dual carriageway.

The purchase of Belgrove shifted the centre of gravity away from Merville and a little closer to the city. Astride what was afterwards to become the main access route from the Stillorgan Road, Belgrove was placed almost centrally between the north and south limits of the whole site. The Advisory Architects' Board in its fourth report (20 November 1954) favoured a Belgrove plan for the new buildings in place of the original Merville plan. It was three-quarters of a mile nearer the city; it would allow the buildings to be at once more dispersed and more centrally placed in relation to the whole property; it afforded space for expansion in more than one direction; and a clinical institute, then a possibility, could be planned convenient to the Medical School and nearer than Merville to St Vincent's Hospital, Merrion Road. Tierney's own strong preference was for the Belgrove plan, and it was adopted unanimously by the Buildings Committee on 31 January 1955 and recommended to the Government for approval.

Further back from the Stillorgan Road than either Belgrove or Belfield was Ardmore, the mid-Georgian house on sixteen acres that had been acquired by the Department of Posts and Telegraphs as a potential head office for Radio Éireann. In 1951 the Secretary of the Department of Posts and Telegraphs, León Ó Broin, had approached Tierney with a proposal to exchange Montrose for Ardmore—the purchase price of the two properties had been approximately the same (£23,000). Protracted and difficult negotiations about the lease with the Montrose landlord, the Pembroke Estate, delayed the conclusion of the deal until Ardmore became part of the imminent college site in 1957.

Early in 1958, Thornfield, on 5½ acres on the Donnybrook side of University Lodge and facing Montrose, came on the market. Doubts about the wisdom of acquiring it were expressed at the Buildings Committee, on the grounds that UCD now had enough land and that its purchase might look bad at a time when the Commission on Accommodation Needs was still sitting. But the settled policy was to buy additional land if it was available at a reasonable price. It was decided to notify the Taoiseach of UCD's intention and to seek his approval for its purchase. The ubiquitous Purcell, Hogan and Hearne were authorised to advise the Taoiseach and negotiate for the property. By April 1958 Thornfield was bought, for £4,500. By 1959, when the Government's commission had examined the accommodation needs of UCD and recommended that the college be transferred to Stillorgan Road, UCD had acquired a site there of 250 acres.

Meanwhile, because of the continued pressure on space in Earlsfort Terrace and Merrion Street, it was decided to assign the houses at Stillorgan Road to various college departments. A sub-committee of the Buildings Committee under the chairmanship of Michael Hogan recommended that Industrial Microbiology be housed in Ardmore; Biochemistry and Pharmacology agreed to move to Merville; the Overseas Archives and the Laboratory of the Logic and Psychology Department were moved to Belgrove; and Woodview received Research into Clinical Medicine and Surgery, now the Department of Medicine and Therapeutics.

DEPARTMENTS OF FINANCE AND EDUCATION

In his memo to the Governing Body of 29 February 1952, Tierney had stated that the first duty of the Buildings Committee should be to appoint an Architects' Board to advise on the very important technical questions that would begin to arise almost immediately. Senator Hearne suggested that the board should consist of the professor of architecture, Desmond FitzGerald; the former professor, Joseph Downes; and Raymond McGrath, chief architect of the Office of Public Works, who had wide experience in the maintenance and running of large public buildings. This was formally approved; but though McGrath was willing to act, difficulties had arisen in view of his official position. The Taoiseach phoned Tierney to say that he had discussed the suggestion with the Minister for Finance (Seán MacEntee), who said it was not possible to make the services of the principal architect of the OPW available to UCD. De Valera and Tierney agreed that although it would be some time before any buildings would be erected, it would be desirable, since the state was expected to provide the funds, to have some arrangements for consultation between representatives of the departments concerned and representatives of the college. Departmental representatives might include the principal architect of the OPW as well as officers of the Departments of Finance and Education, though they would not be empowered to commit the Government to any particular proposal.

The Taoiseach also said that because of the financial situation the erection of buildings could proceed piecemeal. He also said, in reply to a strong complaint from Tierney (in a letter of 1 December 1951), that the submission of proposals concerning expenditure on university education would be better sent in the first instance to the Minister for Education, rather than to the Minister for Finance, as the former was more likely to be sympathetic. Tierney, however, had always believed that university education should be a matter for the head of the Government and the Minister for Finance and should not get lost in the Department of Education, which was primarily concerned with the administration of the schools system.[20]

This role of the Department of Education in matters of university education had arisen with a letter (16 November 1951) from O. J. Redmond of the Department of Finance to the Registrar of the NUI, in which it was stated that the Department of Education was responsible under the Ministers and Secretaries Act (1924) for university education. Tierney, as Vice-Chancellor of the NUI, responded that he was astonished at the letter, in view of the fact that the Department of Finance itself had consistently dealt with grants for the endowment of universities ever since the foundation of the state. He pointed out that there was no officer or section in the Department of Education to deal with university matters. In the past the Minister for Education had repeatedly repudiated any responsibility for universities and had never taken any more than the most formal part in any discussion with the universities. He suggested that the Ministers and Secretaries Act was misinterpreted in the letter from Finance, and at any rate there was no doubt whatever about what the practice had been. The Department of Finance had taken over from the British Treasury in Ireland, and the Treasury in Britain still administered university endowments.[21]

Despite Tierney's strong opposition, however, de Valera had sided with the proposal to link the universities with the Department of Education. A year later, by the time UCD had submitted its new buildings plan to the Government, Tierney had agreed that the Department of Education as well as Finance should be involved in the projected consultations with UCD, and, ironically, he was to find Education more sympathetic than Finance to UCD's proposed move.

When UCD was not able to avail itself of the services of Raymond McGrath, Professor Michael Hogan was sent to Britain to make inquiries about a suitable substitute and he recommended Professor Gordon Stephenson, professor of civic design at the University of Liverpool (who later took up an appointment in Australia and was replaced by Professor Robert Matthew of the University of Edinburgh). Stephenson was appointed chairman of the Advisory Architects' Board from 1 August 1952.

The board set to work immediately and submitted its first report by the middle of October. This report considered the relative merits of the Belfield and Merville sites and decided in favour of the latter, and gave its reasons for the general disposition of the buildings and the practical and aesthetic considerations that should be borne in mind. The report envisaged a construction period of perhaps twelve to fourteen years, at a total capital cost of £5,812,000, having taken into account the schedules of accommodation prepared for the various departments. It included a sketch drawing showing the general positioning of buildings on the Merville site. The report and sketch were approved by the Buildings Committee on 22 October 1952 and sent to the Government with an accompanying memorandum.

The memorandum claimed that the position with regard to accommodation had been gradually worsening. In the Faculties of Science and Engineering — 'an essential part of any programme of industrial development' — one very bad effect of the overcrowding had been to render it almost impossible to conduct research in the laboratories. Though there had been some slight fluctuations in the number of students in UCD because of various economic and war conditions, the trend had been steadily upwards until 1946/47, when the total became more or less stable at between 3,000 and 3,200. This had been achieved by restrictions on the entry of students from overseas, limitation of numbers in Medicine, a rise in the standard for entrance to Engineering, and elimination of students who had not passed their examinations within a definite period.[22] Space had been found for new developments only by shuffling existing activities, but any further possibilities in that direction had been pretty well exhausted.

The plan now presented to the Government provided for 3,500 to 4,000 students, with a good deal more postgraduate and research work being done than was possible in the old buildings. The memorandum stated that it was proposed to start with the transfer of Science and Engineering. The removal of Physics from Earlsfort Terrace would begin the alleviation there. Architecture too should be moved early, because the accommodation at Earlsfort Terrace was 'so highly unsuitable.' The Library, Arts and Administration would follow in due course. Hostels would also have to receive consideration. It was noted that out of 3,500 students, about 1,500 were already provided for, either in religious houses or in their homes. This left a balance of 2,000, and assuming that about half would require hostel accommodation, the proposal was to provide ten to twelve hostels in units of 80 to 100 students. These would be constructed on separate adjoining sites.

Éamon de Valera, having recently celebrated his seventieth birthday, was in Utrecht undergoing what turned out to be six operations for detached retina. Tierney, when submitting the architects' report, sketch plan, estimate of costs and memorandum to the secretary to the Government, also enclosed copies to be transmitted, if thought fit, to the Taoiseach. He also suggested that an early opportunity be made available for a conference between representatives of the Government and a deputation from the Buildings Committee to discuss the proposals and estimates.[23]

In the absence of the Taoiseach, to whom copies of the documents were sent, the documents were submitted to the Tánaiste, Frank Aiken, who in turn directed them to the Department of Education. The Secretary of the Government also informed the Departments of Education and Finance that, at the wish of the Taoiseach, arrangements were to be made for consultation between these two departments and UCD.

It was at this point, while de Valera was undergoing his operations in the Netherlands, that the first signs of opposition and trouble for the Stillorgan Road plan emerged from the Department of Finance. Despite repeated urgings by de Valera, both from Utrecht and following his return home (virtually blind) at Christmas 1952, the Minister for Finance, Seán MacEntee, and his department dragged their feet. Their attitude was alarmingly illustrated in a minute from the Secretary of the Department of Finance, J. J. McElligott, to the Secretary of the Department of Education. The minister found it 'difficult to enter into even preliminary consultations on this matter.'[24] In the minister's opinion, overcrowding could be dealt with by raising fees and standards and by seeking more accommodation in the St Stephen's Green area. Policy on higher education generally needed to be considered, including the requirements of UCC, UCG, Trinity College, the College of Surgeons, and so on. Possible co-ordination of activities should be considered. Also, should more resources not be devoted to technical education than to the universities? It seemed to MacEntee that there should be a comprehensive inquiry by a representative committee as a necessary preliminary to taking any decisions on the UCD proposal.

Much of this argument against the Stillorgan Road project anticipated the criticism that would gradually emerge in the newspapers, in the Dáil, in the Graduates' Association, and finally in a pamphlet published by Tuairim, a political discussion group. And UCD would have the opportunity of publicly providing the counter-arguments. It is perhaps just as well that this was an inter-departmental minute and not a public statement, for otherwise Michael Tierney would have suffered something like an apoplectic outburst.

One can almost feel the shock waves that went through the Department of Education, even though its response was cushioned in civil service language. The Secretary of the Department of Education, Micheál Breathnach, wrote to the Secretary of the Department of the Taoiseach saying that he was directed by the minister to enclose a copy of the Finance Department's minute for the Taoiseach's consideration. Particular attention was drawn to the sentence that said that the Minister for Finance found it difficult to enter into even preliminary consultations on the Stillorgan Road scheme, and to the sentence that referred to a comprehensive inquiry by a representative committee before any decisions were taken on the UCD proposal.[25]

Meanwhile, blissfully unaware of these inter-departmental communications, Michael Tierney in a letter to the Taoiseach requested an advance of £200,000 to cover the cost of acquisition of sites so far. This figure was arrived at from a deposit of £10,000 on Merville, with a further £90,000 outstanding that UCD was contracted to pay by August 1953. The college had already incurred a liability of £56,000, borrowed from the bank, for the purchase of Montrose and Whiteoaks. 'These borrowings were verbally sanctioned by the then Minister for Finance [McGilligan].' To the figure of £156,000 for three sites there had to be added rates, rents, and maintenance, which brought the figure to £175,000. Tierney added that, as other properties were likely to be available within the near future whose purchase would provide the college with a site sufficient for the new buildings and hostels in contemplation, the Buildings Committee felt that the time had come when the Government might reasonably be asked for a capital endowment of the order of £200,000.[26]

De Valera took up the matter quickly with Tierney and Purcell on the one hand and the Ministers for Finance and Education (Seán Moylan) on the other hand, with the result that Tarlach Ó Raifeartaigh, then Assistant Secretary of the Department of Education, wrote to Tierney informing him that the Minister for Finance would be prepared to consider providing the money in the next budget, on condition that it be understood that such provision not be regarded as committing the Government in any way to any attitude of approval of the college's proposals for new buildings or any action in respect thereof, and, secondly, that the college would undertake (by way of a Governing Body resolution) not to overdraw on the bank at any time in the future by more than £35,000 without the prior consent in writing of the Minister for Finance.[27]

RESISTANCE TO THE TRANSFER

In his budget speech on 6 May 1953, the Minister for Finance stated that the grant of £200,000 would be made to University College, Dublin, 'towards the cost of certain properties at Stillorgan which are the nucleus of new university buildings.'

It would not be true to say that all hell broke loose on the release of this information: on the contrary, there would have been virtually a total public silence had not the *Irish Independent* one week later, on 13 May 1953, begun a protest against the Stillorgan Road site idea, which began slowly enough but which from time to time over the next seven years became stormy and bitter. During that seven years the very formidable opposition to the Belfield project would include—in varying degrees of intensity and for a variety of reasons— the *Irish Independent*, *Irish Times*, and *Sunday Press*, the Minister for Finance and his department, members of the Dáil and Seanad from all parties, certain professors in UCC and UCD, Tuairim, individuals prominently associated with the NUI Graduates' Association and Convocation, and individuals in the correspondence columns of the newspapers.

Referring to the grant promised in the budget speech, the editorial in the *Irish Independent* said that the public would await with concern further information; 'if it means that some unknown authority has committed the country to Stillorgan as the site of new university buildings then there is every reason to protest.' Many of the arguments against Belfield that would afterwards emerge were foreshadowed by this editorial. It said that there were grave doubts about the wisdom of planting a university building in a suburb that showed every sign of being surrounded by private residences within a very few years. The selection of the site was a decision that should be taken only after the most searching inquiry and deliberation. It asked whether the university should be a residential institution. It raised the question of the present system of higher education, with its overlapping and multiplicity of professional schools in Dublin. Neither the Government nor the university authorities had any right to decide the matter before the taxpayer was satisfied that the right cause was being pursued. It concluded: 'In our view this is eminently a subject for a comprehensive public enquiry to decide the future of university education in this country and on that basis to proceed to the scarcely less serious decision as to the most suitable place—possibly far removed from Dublin—for the central buildings.'[28]

The editorial aroused no public response. Five months later, however, on 12 October 1953, the *Irish Independent* returned to the topic with an editorial headed 'The new university'. It repeated in stronger terms the charge of secret dealings and ended with a challenge and an incitement to protest: 'Possibly the unknown persons who are endeavouring to present the community with a *fait accompli* have not yet gone so far that they may not be restrained. If the people raise their voices they may compel the Government and the bureaucrats to observe the rules of democracy.'[29]

The gravity of the *Irish Independent's* charge prompted an immediate response from the President of UCD, in which he emphatically denied that the cause of higher education was served by the suggestion that either the Department of Finance or the President and Governing Body of UCD were acting 'arrogantly or behind a veil of secrecy.' Such secrecy as had been observed in the purchases had been nothing more than the ordinary prudence called for in the conduct of either public or private business. The editor replied by stating that the president's letter 'bore out our worst fears,' since it revealed that UCD had decided that a new building should be erected without reference to the National University and before any inquiry into higher education had taken place.[30]

These and further exchanges alerted the politicians. When, therefore, the Acting Minister for Finance, Frank Aiken, introduced the vote on the supplementary estimate to provide £200,000 for UCD, a good deal of opposition from members of all parties was voiced in the Dáil. Apart from Aiken, of the nine TDs who made speeches on the vote, eight spoke strongly against the proposal. It was alleged that the estimate was being steamrolled through the Dáil.

The opponents of the project in the Dáil concentrated their fire on the question of the site of the proposed new university buildings. Several alternatives to Stillorgan Road—depending on the constituency interests of the speaker—were put forward; Athlone, Mullingar, Birr, Donabate (County Dublin) and Wexford were all offered in turn as in keeping with the Government's policy of decentralisation. When Portrane (County Dublin) was flippantly mentioned as a possible site, a TD with St Ita's (Mental) Hospital in mind retorted: 'There's one there already.'

Pressure from within the political parties and from individual TDs might conceivably undermine the whole scheme. But threatening as this was in itself, the response from the Acting Minister for Finance was even more alarming for the UCD authorities; and what the coalition Government had seemed to sanction could now be swept away by the Fianna Fáil Government, with the support of some Fine Gael and Labour Party members of the Dáil.

Aiken assured the protesting deputies that the token estimate for £200,000 'in no way commits this Dáil to any scheme of building at Stillorgan, or elsewhere for the National University. The Government have not approved of any scheme of building at Stillorgan or elsewhere.' He agreed with all the deputies who had said that the matter was a big one and should be thoroughly examined, and he knew that the Government intended to do so. Questioned by some of the objectors, he said that the purchase of the land was not made with Government approval, and that as far as he was aware the Government had not been consulted by UCD, which borrowed the money and made the purchase on its own responsibility. Before the money was provided for new buildings that might cost six or twelve million pounds, the question remained open to the Dáil and the Government to consider. The £200,000 in the estimate was simply putting UCD in funds to repay the loan for the purchase of lands.[31]

The *Irish Independent* now felt justified in returning to the attack.[32] It observed that the American medical experts in their report on UCD referred to plans that were being made for the new University College, and they could not have invented this information. But an even more urgent question was, who spoke for the Government? Seven months earlier Seán MacEntee, Minister for Finance, said that the Stillorgan lands were being bought as 'the nucleus of the new university buildings.' Aiken, the acting minister, was now saying that the Government had not approved of any scheme, for Stillorgan or elsewhere.

The public and the Dáil deputies, as well as the *Irish Independent*, may have been mystified; but UCD's position was clear, at least to its Governing Body and Buildings Committee. The decision had been taken by the Governing Body to build in the vicinity of Belfield; plans had been drawn up and submitted to the Government; and—largely on the insistence of the Taoiseach—representatives of UCD and the Departments of Finance and Education were examining the proposal closely. But within UCD it was realised that the criticisms in the Dáil, and especially the statements made by Aiken, were, to say the least, not very helpful.

Professor Patrick McGilligan, never one to duck a major political row, which this showed all the appearances of becoming, attacked Aiken for attempting to propagate the idea that the UCD authorities had acted on their own responsibility and had not consulted the Government or been given Government approval. He explained that when he was minister he had arranged with the President of UCD to submit to the Government the plan for the proposed new buildings. He had provided UCD with enough money to clear its overdraft; he had removed the restrictions on UCD running into an overdraft without approval from the Department of Finance, to encourage UCD to get money in order to purchase Merville; and he had promised to bring the matter before the Dáil for its approval. Negotiations taking place between UCD and the Department of Post and Telegraphs for the exchange of Montrose for Ardmore also meant that another Government department was aware of the plan. The Governing Body, before which the Stillorgan Road plans had been discussed, had among its members nominees of the Government and eight representatives of the General Council of County Councils. He asked how, in the face of all that he had recounted, anybody could say that UCD had acted on its own responsibility and that the Government had not been consulted. In view of the fact that a full statement of all that was planned had been before the Government for many months, he suggested that the phrases used by the Acting Minister for Finance were misleading.

McGilligan, however, did not stop at putting the record straight but used the opportunity for party-political purposes. He insinuated that the Fianna Fáil Government had been antagonistic to the college.[33] He alleged that in all its term in office from 1932 to 1948 Fianna Fáil had done nothing for UCD, and contrasted this neglect with the favours that the coalition Government had begun to bestow. Angry words flew between McGilligan and the Taoiseach when de Valera wanted to know what demands of UCD the Government had turned down and accused McGilligan of making allegations that were completely false.[34]

By contrast with McGilligan, that other staunch defender of UCD, Michael Hayes, speaking earlier on the estimates in Seanad Éireann and before it had been discussed in the Dáil, thanked the Government for taking steps to remedy the difficulties with regard to space in UCD. He acknowledged that over a long period, and in consultation with various ministers and more than one Government, consideration had been given to what could be done. He pointed out the urgent need for a better building for UCD, which, he claimed, from the point of view of catering for Irish nationals, was at least as big as all other university institutions in the Republic. He paid tribute to the President of UCD, to Professors Purcell and Hogan of the Engineering School and to 'a member of the Governing Body who is a member of this house and sits on the Government benches [Senator Hearne]' for the great work they had done to achieve the current stage of UCD's development with regard to building. The purchase of a site by these people had been done in the only way of conducting such a business, by private treaty and negotiation, not after a public discussion in which the minister announced he was going to buy land in a particular place for the college. Indirectly he answered the criticisms that had been made by the *Irish Independent* and anticipated those that were to emerge in the Dáil. He responded that the notion that the college could be built from scratch in some part of the country was not sound, because, among other reasons, of the need of the Medical School to be near hospitals.[35]

The Taoiseach, in condemning what he termed the partisan spirit Mr McGilligan had introduced, hoped that when the question of building the college at Stillorgan Road came before the Dáil for final decision all sides would approach it from the point of view of the national interest and not in any party spirit.

In view of the use that Tuairim made of a later remark by de Valera to support their argument against the move to Belfield,[36] it should be stressed that what he said in the Dáil during this debate in December 1953 showed him, on the contrary, to be a supporter over a long period of a suburban site. Though he was not in office at the time, he had been pleased to read a newspaper report that Montrose had been bought by the college. He felt too that the college was quite right in acquiring Merville. When he returned to office he had expected to find, at least in the records of the Department of Finance, Government sanction for the expense incurred in the acquisition of this property; but he was adamant that there were no records of prior consultation.[37] The actual signing for Merville, he rightly surmised, had been done about the time of the change of Government. He insisted that in future the procedure would have to be put right and that the university's autonomy could not extend to the point of incurring debt that the Government then had to meet without prior sanction.[38]

Having made it clear that he could not say anything in defence of the procedure that had been adopted before his Government's return to office, he emphasised that he, for one, was 'completely satisfied that the University College authorities acted well and prudently in acquiring these properties.' If another site could be suggested and it was decided that a more suitable site was available, the properties already acquired could be readily sold, as they were well worth the money that was being paid for them. All sides should approach the matter 'with the idea of doing what is best for University College, and thereby doing the best for the nation.'[39]

But by the end of 1953 the Stillorgan Road project was in grave danger of becoming a political football. It had been stated by the Acting Minister for Finance that the Government had not been consulted and had not given its sanction to the purchase of Merville; and, according to the Taoiseach, there was no record of any sanction for the purchase in the Department of Finance. Both the Acting Minister and the Taoiseach had assured the Dáil that the Government was in no way committed to providing buildings on the lands acquired by UCD, and it was accepted that such a serious matter would have to be considered by the Dáil.

If these aspects alone had been emphasised, the UCD authorities would have had every reason to feel uncomfortable. The emphasis on these points, to the extent that they were intended to embarrass McGilligan, the former Minister for Finance, were party-political. McGilligan's reaction too had injected into the debate a substantial quantity of party spirit. That he had given only verbal sanction to UCD to proceed with the purchase of Merville, and at a time when the Government to which he belonged was leaving office, helped to inflame the partisan atmosphere that was threatening to engulf the project. However, the references by McGilligan to the memoranda and plans submitted to the Government by UCD, and by de Valera to the negotiations on these plans taking place between the Departments of Finance and Education and UCD, were an acknowledgment that UCD had certainly not left successive Governments uninformed about its intentions.

The debate, moreover, gave de Valera the opportunity to act the role of statesman appealing to the 'national interest' above party spirit. If all his own remarks were not above the party-political, the general thrust of his speech displayed a great amount of sympathy with UCD's accommodation difficulties and even with the Stillorgan Road plan.

THE INTER-DEPARTMENTAL COMMITTEE

While UCD's building plans were thus receiving their first public airing in the Dáil, the work of the inter-departmental committee formed to conduct the discussions between Finance, Education and UCD, as directed by de Valera, was proceeding quietly and efficiently, away from the public gaze. The key figure on the Government side was Tarlach Ó Raifeartaigh, Assistant

Secretary of the Department of Education. By April 1953 he was requesting from UCD, on behalf of the Minister for Education, a vast amount of statistical and other information in order to facilitate further consideration of the Stillorgan Road plan. The information sought for certain specified years dealt with such matters as the number of Dublin students whose home residence was north or south of the Liffey; the distribution of students according to province; the number of foreign students; the total fees payable in respect of each faculty; provisions limiting entry; the likelihood of expansion in student numbers; the extent to which graduates from each faculty had obtained employment, either in Ireland or abroad; the average number of openings for graduates in the different professions; and an estimate of any additional expenses if the college were established at Stillorgan Road.[40]

Reports had also been received from the Advisory Architects' Board on that portion of the preliminary development works (ring road and water mains) that could be proceeded with in advance of any decision on the final siting of the buildings. UCD urged this matter on the Government at a meeting on 6 August 1953 between a deputation from the Buildings Committee and the Taoiseach, the Minister for Education (Moylan), and Ó Raifeartaigh. The Taoiseach declared that he and the Minister for Education were in favour of the proposal to transfer UCD to Stillorgan Road but that the Government must first be satisfied. It was agreed that the inter-departmental committee would examine the whole question, taking into account the detailed information supplied by UCD in response to the request of the Department of Education, and that the Minister for Education would then bring a memorandum on the matter before the Government.

De Valera agreed that the scheme of buildings should form an architectural unit, and that they would not be at odd, unrelated levels. He said he did not like high buildings and hoped they would not exceed three storeys in height, that some at least of the buildings would have a view of the sea, and that no extensive bulldozing would be required. He also wanted to be assured that the question of having the buildings as close to town as possible had been considered. Pending a Government decision, no expenditure could be incurred on site works.

The Taoiseach took the opportunity to press for an issue close to his own heart. In what had about it more than a hint of a *quid pro quo,* he asked the college authorities to do their very best for Irish, and mentioned that some deputies might aver that the college was negligent in this matter. Dr Tierney replied that the college had received a good deal of unfair criticism on this score and that for his part he was doing his best and was prepared to do anything that he would consider would further the cause of Irish.

The UCD deputation was so encouraged by the Taoiseach's approach to the Stillorgan Road project that the Buildings Committee agreed that

Professor Purcell would carry out the preliminary civil engineering survey of the site so as to be ready to begin the new buildings if and when Government approval was given.[41]

The inter-departmental committee that examined the proposed move to Stillorgan Road consisted of Tarlach Ó Raifeartaigh (Department of Education), Mr J. Mooney (Department of Finance), and Raymond McGrath (Office of Public of Works). Ó Raifeartaigh was the driving force. By early September 1953 he had prepared the first draft of the report, which included a fair amount of information he had collected beyond that already supplied by the college. This was submitted to his colleagues as a basis for discussion. McGrath had been thinking of the college being primarily the hostels, with classrooms and other facilities as adjuncts. While Ó Raifeartaigh agreed that this would be the ideal, he pointed out that the hostels were very much at the hypothetical stage, and they could hardly base a recommendation on such an ideal, as it would throw the whole project back on itself; and in any case the state, he hoped, was not going to be asked to provide the hostels. He asked McGrath whether it would be a serious commitment if the chief architect were to discuss the matter with Dr Tierney, who wished to discuss the whole layout with him.

A second report followed, and early in the new year (on 15 January 1954) what Ó Raifeartaigh hoped would be the final report was presented to the Minister for Education. The report acknowledged that the proposal created something of a dilemma. On the one hand it called for a large capital expenditure, and on the other it seemed clear that if it was not implemented the present arrangement involving the use of temporary structures, over-crowding and lack of space for equipment and research in faculties vital to the country's welfare must continue. The direct consequence of this would be to limit the number of students to the present figure and to bring about a certain degree of stagnation in the faculties most affected—Engineering and Science—thus rendering the college to some extent impotent to play the very important part in the national life that was expected of it.

In conclusion, the committee stated that they might add that their examination of the problem had been confined to the needs of the college in so far as these related to its utilitarian function. They had not regarded it as within the scope of their inquiry to advert to the importance of ensuring that the leading national university institution, on which the country must largely rely for a significant contribution to the advancement of learning and culture in accordance with our traditions, should find a home befitting its high purpose and enabling it to discharge adequately and with dignity its great responsibilities. But that consideration must nonetheless present itself in any final review of the issue. Michael Tierney himself could hardly have put the case for UCD more strongly.

In a memo from the Department of Education that had been prepared for submission with the report to the Government it was stated that the Minister for Education had considered the report; that he was satisfied that there was no reasonable alternative to the transfer to the Stillorgan Road site; and that he therefore requested Government approval in principle for the proposal. The minister, on the advice of the inter-departmental committee, recommended completion of the project within twenty years and recommended that he be authorised to inform the college that, given normal costs, the Government hoped that it would be possible to finance the transfer in such a way that it would be completed within that period. He also recommended to the Government a suggestion of the committee that the project be financed out of a National Development Fund.[42]

A note with a copy of this memo that was submitted to the Department of the Taoiseach indicated that the agreement of the Minister for Finance to its submission to the Government had been sought on 24 February 1954. The Department of the Taoiseach, in a fourteen-page memo of July 1955, said it was not aware of any subsequent development regarding the submission, and that it had never been presented to the Government.[43] The explanation for the report not being considered by the Government is undoubtedly connected with the failing fortunes of the Government itself. De Valera's Government of 1951–54 was a minority one, whose existence depended on retaining the support of the substantial number of independents elected in May 1951. It has been said that 'the cabinet of 1951–54 has strong claims to be the worst de Valera government.'[44] The deflationary campaign of MacEntee, the Minister for Finance, and his identification with austerity had the full support of Joseph Brennan, Governor of the Central Bank, and McElligott, Secretary of the Department of Finance, who was relieved not to have to contend with the audacity of McGilligan—'McElligott's intellectual superior.' Economists have since described the policy as misguided and have referred to 'the stagnation of the whole economy.'[45]

In these circumstances, and as the Government, losing the support of the independents, began to crumble, the Minister and Department of Finance were not likely to support the Department of Education and what deserves to be called the Ó Raifeartaigh Report, on account of the large expenditure that would have to be committed to the Stillorgan Road scheme.

OPPOSITION FROM CORK

The return to office of John A. Costello at the head of the second inter-party Government (June 1954 to February 1957) could only have raised expectations in UCD. It was true that McGilligan, then in failing health, was not again Minister for Finance but had been given the office of Attorney-General. Despite the continuing poor economic situation, it was to be expected that the

UCD authorities would begin to exert increased pressure on their friends in the Government for a favourable decision on the proposed new buildings.

The new Government took office just as UCD reached the high point of its celebrations during July 1954 of the centenary of the Catholic University. Tierney, as we have seen, in a sophisticated piece of public relations had successfully linked Newman's Catholic University with the proposed new buildings at Stillorgan Road. The new Taoiseach, John A. Costello, stated publicly in proposing a toast to UCD during those celebrations that he hoped the new college would be worthy of the nation. The force of this statement was the simple assumption by the Taoiseach that the building of the new college on the Stillorgan Road site was firmly sanctioned: his statement had none of the hesitancy of Frank Aiken's remarks in the Dáil six months earlier when he said that the project had yet to be approved by the Government.

The sheer success of all the centenary hyperbole and of UCD's propaganda resulted in ripples of anxiety elsewhere within the National University. The most significant of these apprehensions were expressed in the article in the autumn 1954 number of the *University Review* written by the UCC professors Gwynn and Hogan. This article, as we have seen, gave rise to one of the most bitter divisions ever experienced in the Senate of the National University. From the standpoint of Michael Tierney, the criticism of UCD's building objectives from within UCD itself and the sister colleges of the NUI was intolerable enough, but worse, it raised the prospect of inciting public and political opposition to the Stillorgan Road project and perhaps of scuttling the whole scheme. Nor did he have long to wait for the criticisms to be repeated in the newspapers.

The *Irish Times* on 16 November 1954 drew attention to the *University Review* article and the supposed hazard of a dissolution of the NUI. The *Sunday Independent* on 21 November referred to disagreements within UCD over the Stillorgan Road project as well as between the NUI colleges. James Meenan wrote in his diary: 'The *Sunday Independent* featured the tension between the Colleges in its habitually ignorant way. As sure as God Paddy Bourke[46] wrote on it tonight in his usual style asking for investigation and for decentralization etc. Didn't see a proof but I feel in my bones that he did.'[47]

But the real storm broke with the newspaper reports of a lecture given in UCC by Professor Denis Gwynn on Sunday 28 November 1954. Gwynn's lecture, nominally on 'Newman's University and the Queen's Colleges', was used as the occasion for repeating, if anything in stronger and more direct language, the apprehensions expressed in the *University Review* article at the prospect of 'the vast building programme' for UCD: 'they involved a demand for a vast financial outlay which must reduce the amount available for the other colleges.' And if Gwynn's words were not clear enough to its readers, the *Irish Independent's* report of his lecture was headed 'UCD building plan opposed'.

This was precisely the sort of campaign that the authorities in UCD did not want and that UCD men like James Meenan feared. Fortunately, the president himself did not become embroiled in what was shaping up to be a nasty inter-collegiate row in the press. The replies from UCD to Gwynn and the *Irish Independent* came instead from Thomas Nevin (professor of experimental physics), Patrick Donovan (supervisor of examinations), and Michael Hayes (professor of Modern Irish). Nevin forecast (correctly) that the future of the NUI federal system would not be settled in that generation and should not divert attention from what really mattered: the provision of proper and adequate accommodation in Dublin for more than half our 26-County students. 'Since the foundation of the Irish State no great public buildings have been erected in our capital city. The project to erect on a beautiful site on the Stillorgan Road, overlooking Dublin Bay, a group of University buildings is one of vision and imagination, a symbol of belief in the future of our country and reminder of our position in the world of learning in the dark ages.'[48]

Both Donovan and Hayes denied that any statement, official or unofficial, had been issued from UCD suggesting that it wished to break away from the NUI. And the letters from all three UCD academics rejected the suggestion that the provision of sorely needed buildings for the students of UCD was a threat to the continued existence of UCC or to the claim of that college for a fair share of public expenditure on university education. It was an inferiority complex and a poor tribute to Cork to suggest that it would go into decline unless supported by UCD. Hayes added: 'Certainly, an interchange of speeches from College to College will not strengthen the National University of Ireland, nor increase the grant from public funds to any of the Colleges.'

The report of Gwynn's lecture in the *Irish Times* was headed 'UCD's claim to Newman challenged'. What was keenly resented in UCD about Gwynn's remarks on UCD's claims to Newman was the fact that Gwynn, himself a distinguished graduate of the college, had taken an active part in the centenary celebrations as a guest of the college and had introduced Herbert Butterfield for an honorary degree, and that he was the brother of Aubrey Gwynn SJ, one of the college's most respected scholars, who had displayed in his own writings his great pride in the threads linking Newman's university with the Jesuit college and with UCD.

It has to be said that the President of UCC, Henry St John Atkins, played his part in trying to smooth the ruffled feathers in UCD. He wrote to the newspapers to state that it should be understood by the public that Professor Gwynn spoke for himself and not for UCC, and added: 'As regards the claims of University College Dublin for increased financial assistance and for new buildings, it is not for University College Cork to intervene beyond expressing sympathy with the efforts of one of our sister colleges to solve its urgent requirements.'[49]

A letter the following day from Gwynn confirmed that the opinions he had expressed were entirely his own responsibility. In a more conciliatory spirit than his lecture, his letter said that he was in complete agreement with the President of UCC that it was not for UCC to intervene beyond expressing sympathy with the efforts of the sister college to solve its urgent requirements. He and many of his colleagues in UCC were graduates of UCD and would not wish 'to hamper in any way the progress of U.C.D.' With regard to his references to the desire in UCD to break away from the NUI and to increased building grants for UCD affecting the financial claims of Cork, he merely said (perhaps rather lamely, in the eyes of his UCD controversialists) that his remarks were made in a wider context, on which he did not elaborate.[50]

Taken together, the brief letters of Gwynn and of the President of UCC should have been regarded as a gracious withdrawal of any criticisms in Cork, and by Gwynn in particular, of the Stillorgan Road project. A longer letter from James Hogan, however, was much more argumentative. Hogan maintained that the article in the *University Review* was 'strictly confined to a discussion of the merits of the federal system' and that the discussion had arisen directly out of comments by Tierney and Williams in *Struggle with Fortune*. He vehemently denied that the article was an attack on UCD's attempts to get finances for its building project. Academics in Cork, he declared, were in full sympathy with Tierney's plans for the development of UCD—'but, of course, with the proviso that the federal structure of the University should be preserved beyond doubt or qualification.'[51] So, while the welfare of the university was to be beyond qualification, that of UCD had a proviso attached. This was not very reassuring to UCD; and again it was the juxtaposition of the two issues, the federal system and UCD's development, that was the root of the unease between representatives of the two colleges.

Gwynn's lecture, as reported in the newspapers, had been even more specific in its criticisms of the financial aspects of the plans for UCD than the article he had jointly written with Hogan. Hogan's reasoning in his letter may have been too subtle for the majority of his readers. Certainly the bulk of the editorials, reports and letters in the press concentrated almost entirely on the issue of the Stillorgan Road buildings. Tierney was anything but mollified by Hogan's defence of the *University Review* article, and it goes a long way towards explaining his determination at the Senate meeting a few days later to cut the NUI grant to the Graduates' Association. The barrister Vincent Grogan and the UCD lecturer Eileen MacCarvill, in replies to Professor Hogan, reminded him that the dissolution of the NUI about which he was so alarmed could not take place without due notice to the public, without an amendment to the Constitution (because of the university seats in the Seanad), and without legislation in the Oireachtas to replace the Act and

Charters of 1908. But these two letters were practically the only ones in which reference was made to the issue that Hogan had claimed to be the sole concern of the article in the *University Review*.

As the letters to the papers ran into their second week, the controversy was never going to be confined to academics or the issues they were debating. Some of the non-academic literary gladiators entered the arena professedly regretting the development of 'a public newspaper wrangle between various members of the academic staffs of the constituent colleges of the National University of Ireland';[52] but clearly many welcomed the opportunity to air their own opinions, extend the debate beyond the immediate issues, and settle old scores. One correspondent said it was as well the present controversy had come about, because 'there are a lot of aspects of life in College which could bear closer investigation—not the least being the lack of democracy in the authorities' treatment of students and graduates. A weft of placemanship and jobbery exists, based upon the peculiar Redmondite politics of some in control.'[53]

Among the better-known non-university names who participated were Uinseann Mac Eoin, Alasdair Mac Cába and the Earl of Wicklow. Lord Wicklow was to have been chairman of that notorious meeting of the L&H a few years earlier that was to have debated the Communist Manifesto and that Tierney had banned. He asserted that the necessary space for completing the Earlsfort Terrace building was still vacant at the back of the college (this, as we have seen, was considered by the college to be no longer adequate). The proposed site on the Stillorgan Road, apart from the 'unjustifiable expense', he regarded as being too far out for the students.[54]

Mac Eoin, an architect, argued that a university should not be sited outside the city but instead should take part in the civic and national life to the full and should not be 'incubated and cloistered in semi-novitiate style', 'upon the Stillorgan Road'. He also objected to the expense of buying land for the proposed new university 'at a highly inflated price.'[55]

Mac Cába, a founder and managing director of the Educational Building Society, wrote that nobody would object to UCD meeting its needs but asked why this could not be done in the immediate neighbourhood of Earlsfort Terrace, when they could build up as well as out. He said that the UCD professors were evidently perturbed that there had been 'even a suspicion of mystery about their grandiose plans for expansion in Dublin.' Adding fuel to the fire, he continued: 'The resources that should be at the disposal of the nation for purely educational purposes are to be squandered on a project that has for its primary aim the creation of a rival in size and pretentiousness to Trinity College.'[56]

Michael Tierney's temper would not have been sweetened by the variety of charges and innuendo tossed about in the course of this newspaper controversy. To his opponents he appeared to be as tyrannical as those fascist regimes of the nineteen-thirties that he was supposed to admire. He was seen by some critics to be an over-enthusiastic Catholic; but there was no doubt in the minds of critics and admirers alike that he had an imperial vision of what the largest college of the NUI should be. His Belfield project—now much advanced, as far as the acquisition of the necessary land and the examination of the plans by the state were concerned—was under severe attack from all sides and from within and without the NUI. The president could only have felt that all the bats in the belfry were beating at his window.

The authorities in UCD did not at all welcome this unfavourable publicity generated in the newspaper wrangle. Michael Tierney's unease would have been further increased if he had been aware that the Taoiseach's office had kept a fairly comprehensive file of the editorials, reports and letters to the editor covering the controversy. The Taoiseach himself, however, in effect brought this phase of the public argument to an end. He used the opportunity of the annual dinner of the Christian Brothers' College Past Pupils' Union in Cork to damp down the dispute. Speaking to an audience that included the President of UCC and the Lord Mayor of Cork, he assured the public that the Government had no intention of interfering with the federal nature of the university system and said it would be a bad thing for the country if such a thing were to happen. 'There is no threat implied to University College, Cork,' he asserted, in an attempt to remove fears that had sparked off the recent controversy. He gave the further assurance that whatever might be done for the needs of UCD would in no way prejudice the rights of the other colleges but, on the contrary, probably ensure further benefits for them.[57]

The Stillorgan Road project, of course, did not go away: it merely subsided temporarily from the pages of the newspapers. Six months later the *Irish Independent* returned to the subject. It ventured once more to ask for information about the plans. The public were aware that UCD had been 'buying land on a vast scale'; it was accepted that the college authorities proposed to erect 'palatial buildings' to replace the inadequate premises in Earlsfort Terrace; but not one word about this came from the college nor from the late or present Government, one or other of which must at some stage have authorised the college to go ahead with the scheme, which must involve the taxpayers in an expenditure of several million pounds. The *Irish Independent* believed that any scheme to provide the money for new premises would not commend itself to the community until there had been a thorough inquiry by a commission into the whole future fabric of higher education 'and also into the selection of the most desirable site, whether in Dublin or outside Dublin.'[58]

Two months later the *Irish Independent* once again repeated many of the same charges and demands. This time it was able to report: 'At last the

President of UCD has lifted a little corner of the veil. He has publicly stated that "through sympathetic considerations from successive Governments," U.C.D. has been "enabled to purchase an estate on which the College may be properly housed." When did this happen? Why was the decision kept secret?' The editorial concluded that 'the whole thing is more than disquieting.'[59]

This drew a response from the Secretary of UCD, J. P. MacHale, who referred to the grant of £200,000 that had been provided in the supplementary estimate introduced by Frank Aiken in December 1953. But this response did not satisfy the *Irish Independent,* for when it renewed its campaign it accused the college spokesman of a lack of candour in not reporting that when Aiken introduced the grant he had specifically stated that the token estimate in no way committed the Dáil to any scheme of building at Stillorgan or elsewhere and that he had agreed that the whole matter should be thoroughly examined before the Dáil decided to provide the money for a new university.[60]

MEMO OF THE DEPARTMENT OF THE TAOISEACH

Meanwhile the Taoiseach's office, having kept itself fully informed of the controversy that had blown up, made a thorough examination of the whole history of the project. In its fourteen-page memo dated 21 July 1955 the department detailed the developments since 1948, noting among many other matters that from an early stage members of the Government were informally aware of the policy of the college authorities to provide a site for new build-ings in the Stillorgan area, and that, on de Valera's initiative, consultations on building plans had been opened between representatives of Government departments and UCD. The memo went on to pose the crucial question, how far had the state been committed to approval of the proceedings of the college authorities, or to the grant of financial assistance? On the one hand it noted that in 1952 and 1953 the Minister for Finance had serious misgivings about the whole matter, and it had been clearly stated by the Government, and accepted by UCD, that neither the grant of £200,000 nor the inter-departmental negotiations committed the state to acceptance in principle of the Stillorgan Road proposals. On the other hand, the officials in the Department of the Taoiseach noted that UCD had been requested to submit comprehensive plans; that the college authorities had received a great deal of encouragement in private and in public from leading politicians on both sides, in and out of office; and that Mr de Valera had informed the college representatives that he and the Minister for Education favoured the proposal for new buildings, while also emphasising that Government approval would be necessary. The memo concluded that in general the UCD authorities had fairly substantial grounds for expecting that Government approval would eventually be given to their proposals for new buildings at Stillorgan Road and for the transfer to that site, and that the money required for these purposes would be provided by the state.[61]

The implications of this memo were considerable. It seemed to establish a moral commitment that was thereafter to pervade and restrict the thinking of John A. Costello's Government with regard to the project. The Taoiseach sent a copy of his department's memo to the Minister for Finance, and he also discussed with Professor Purcell estimates of the maximum expenditure for the new building scheme.

Meanwhile the situation in UCD had been deteriorating rapidly, and Tierney responded by putting further pressure on the Taoiseach. He reminded him that it was nearly a year since UCD had applied for an increase (of £90,000) in the annual grant in order to do its work efficiently. The cost of living index had risen by several points; demands for increases in wages by the staff were urgent; rapid developments had taken place in certain professional departments, especially in Medicine and Dentistry; and there was a danger that if the system were not brought up to date, recognition accorded to graduates in Britain might be summarily refused. He referred to the urgent question of adequate buildings for the college. Previously, priority had been given to Science, Engineering, and Architecture, but now it must be the Medical and Dental School. He pressed for an early interview with the Taoiseach and, when this was not forthcoming, waxed even more indignant, saying that the college was facing one of the most desperate crises in its whole history.

Some concessions on salaries were granted, and the Minister for Education (Richard Mulcahy) was persuaded by the force of argument in favour of the college. The Government decided (on 15 June 1956) to approve in principle the transfer to Stillorgan Road; but it was also agreed that UCD would have to take its place in the queue of demands on the limited resources available for capital expenditure.

A memo from the Department of Education was revised, mainly to emphasise that no expenses were to be incurred pending clarification of the position regarding the availability of resources, due regard being given to the requirements of directly productive capital works and of urgent capital works of a social character. The amendments had all the wordy caution characteristic of the Department of Finance.

After further observations by Finance and Education, the Government meeting of 28 June 1956 authorised the Minister for Education to proceed along the lines of the revised memo, and a draft statement on the proposed transfer was prepared in the form of an announcement that might be made in the Dáil, probably in connection with the estimate for universities for 1956/57.[62]

By now, however, the country's economy was in further difficulties, and the Minister for Finance (Gerard Sweetman) had increased the austerity measures;

MacBride was on the point of withdrawing his party's support, and the Government was on its last legs. Tierney's patience was also exhausted. His increasing frustration with the Government was registered in the addresses he gave at successive conferring ceremonies. That of 16 July 1955 had been relatively moderate. Though he warned that if UCD's resources were allowed to fall any further it 'would be accounted as a very serious blemish on the historical reputation of our contemporary governmental authorities,' he went on to acknowledge that the appeals of UCD had 'received sympathetic consideration from successive Governments,' and it had been enabled 'to purchase an estate upon which our College may in the future be properly and worthily housed.'[63] A year later, on 14 July 1956, his address was much more focused and hard-hitting. In the modern world, he said, university education had long ceased to be the luxury of a small class: it had become a stringent necessity for the prosperity of the nation as a whole. But, unfortunately, it seemed to be excessively difficult to persuade the Irish people and their political leaders that the same sort of effort that was being made for the provision of higher education in other countries was also a first necessity of public policy in Ireland. The 'appallingly difficult,' 'disgraceful' and 'meagre' conditions in which UCD's Schools of Engineering, Architecture, Medicine and Dentistry had to work were 'the product of decades of neglect and procrastination.'

By the next conferring, on 3 November 1956, the president was envisaging the distinct possibility that UCD's medical graduates might be refused recognition in Britain and its dependencies, thus dissipating all the work done for Catholic medical education in Ireland since the days of Newman—a subtle reminder to the politicians of the interest taken in medicine by the hierarchy, whose opposition to the Mother and Child Scheme had brought down the first inter-party Government only a few years earlier. This was Tierney wielding the crosier over the heads of the second inter-party Government. With regard to the new buildings needed, the president insisted that the Republic had the distinction of lagging behind countries like Nigeria, Venezuela and Mexico, not to speak of Britain and Northern Ireland, in the provision of resources to universities—and all these countries had been faced with economic difficulties proportionately quite as great as any that had faced us. But their governments had been enlightened enough to realise that without well-endowed universities no country could claim a high place among civilised communities. 'It took just over fifty years to induce a foreign government to recognise that the Irish people must be given their own University. It is beginning to look as if it will take much longer to persuade a native government that without decent and adequate buildings and equipment, a sufficient staff and a reasonable endowment, a university may well become a liability rather than an asset.'

The conferring ceremonies had provided him with a public platform. And, if he did not invent it, he was the first president of UCD to employ consistently the conferring address for this purpose. There was the brief, almost dismissive routine introductory sentence or two of congratulation for the graduates ranged in the seats in front of him; the rest of the speech was addressed to a wider audience outside the college and devoted to the problems that faced the college (and with Dr Tierney the problems of the college were always closely integrated with the problems facing the country). All his addresses in 1955/56 were quoted extensively in the press and were intended to be read by the politicians, the clergy and the public, whom he hoped to use as a weapon to spur the Government into concessions to UCD. They were a deliberate exercise in shaping public opinion. The conferring speech was the lay equivalent of the contemporary Confirmation sermon, used effectively by some of the strong-minded bishops to make pronouncements on current national questions. Much of what Tierney said on these occasions had an episcopal—if not indeed *ex cathedra*—tone and manner about it.

Tierney's sharpness of tongue, outspokenness and impatience on behalf of his college had never shown to better advantage than in his laceration of the inter-party Government for its tardiness with regard to financing the move to Belfield. It was perhaps just as well that the Government had already committed itself in principle to the transfer before Tierney's latest attack at the conferring on 3 November 1956. Another group of individuals in power might have so resented his reprimand that they would change their minds about the project; but Tierney must have known his men, for before the end of the month—on 20 November—the Government decided that £20,000 would be allocated for site clearance at Belfield.[64] Another interpretation of this outcome might be that the Government had come slowly and reluctantly to recognise the candour and good sense, the ring of truth and the persuasiveness of Tierney's presentation of the critical building needs of the college. As far as effectiveness goes, said John Henry Newman, even false views of things have more influence and inspire more respect than no views at all.[65] None could deny that Michael Tierney held strong views. He was the last of the Roman consuls before administration by committee came to hold sway in UCD. Without his tenacity and the steel in the fibre of his character, Belfield might never have materialised.

De Valera's last Government and the Belfield project

A sum of £20,000 allocated for site clearance was UCD's share of the £1 million provided by the Government at its meeting of 9 November 1956 for the relief of unemployment and announced by the Taoiseach during the two by-election campaigns then in progress. It was not to be taken as going beyond the approval in principle already given. The college was reminded of the strict conditions then imposed and was asked to submit for examination by the inter-departmental committee set up in 1953 the revised layout and plans and the estimate of costs of what was known then as the Belgrove Plan.[66]

The second inter-party Government was dissolved in February 1957. Within two months of the formation of Éamon de Valera's last Government (March 1957 to June 1959), Michael Tierney, in correspondence followed by a meeting (24 May 1957), was pressuring the Taoiseach for Government action on the new buildings. Seán Moylan, who had proved sympathetic to UCD, was no longer Minister for Education, but his successor, Jack Lynch, was also seen to be not unsympathetic. The more hostile, or at least more difficult, Seán MacEntee had been switched from Finance to Health and his place in Finance taken by Jim Ryan. After further discussions, the Department of Education prepared yet another memo (18 June 1957) for the Government, which confirmed that the Department of Education was still running very strongly with the idea of the transfer. It requested that the Government reaffirm the decision previously taken agreeing to the transfer in principle; that the agreement should carry the implication that the finances (£20,000) would be provided to allow for the necessary architectural planning and the beginning of urgent site work; and that accordingly the Government introduce a supplementary estimate that would give the Dáil the opportunity of discussing the matter fully. In a reference to observations made by the Department of Finance it was asserted that the Minister for Education did not consider that a commission of inquiry could do any more than draw attention to facts already known, and that there ought to be no question of proceeding on the basis that there might be a subsequent decision to retain indefinitely part of the college at Earlsfort Terrace. Regarding the suggestion that there be an international competition for the design of the new college, or that architects of world repute be engaged as consultants, the memo pointed out that the latter course had already been adopted in appointing the chairman of the Advisory Architects' Board.

This was all very much in step with the line advocated by the UCD authorities themselves, and so far everything seemed hopeful. Then came a bombshell from, of all places, the Department of Health. Seán MacEntee might have changed his department but had not changed his opposition to the proposed Belfield move. His observations on the Minister for Education's memo included many of the points that had been raised by different commentators during the recent controversy. Once more he estimated the likely cost at a much higher level (£10 or £11 million) than the UCD figures accepted by the inter-departmental committee. Once more he asked whether the potential of the Earlsfort Terrace and St Stephen's Green area had been fully examined. Expanding on the idea of a commission of inquiry, as proposed by the Minister for Finance, he thought that planning should be under a committee representing Finance, Education and the UCD Governing Body in order to curb internal angling for advantage between the various faculty and professorial interests. He supported his colleague's argument for holding an international competition for the design of the new buildings if they were to go ahead. He concluded on an old hobby-horse, suggesting that it might be better to devote a greater part of any future university expenditure to Cork and Galway: the Government, after all, was committed to decentralisation.[67]

The Department of Finance strongly welcomed this analysis, yielding now to the proposal for a commission of inquiry that might deal not only with Belfield but also with other aspects of university education.[68] The result was in effect an alliance of two of the most influential and respected people in the Government, two founder-members of Fianna Fáil, Jim Ryan and Seán MacEntee. Their opposition within the Government was the neophyte Jack Lynch, who would require the full backing of de Valera if his Department of Education was going to have its way. But when the Government met on 6 August 1957 to consider the question, circumstances did not favour the proposals made by the Department of Education. The Taoiseach reported that he had had conversations with the Presidents of UCC and UCG about the needs of their colleges, concerning which proposals had already been submitted to the Department of Education. He emphasised that the needs of UCG and UCC would need to be taken into account before a decision could be taken on UCD. The general feeling was that a commission should be set up to examine the accommodation needs of the three NUI colleges, the terms of reference and personnel of which would be discussed by the Taoiseach with the Minister for Education.[69] De Valera then informed the college that doubts had arisen regarding the merits of the transfer proposals. He said that a commission might be necessary, but its purpose would be to bring matters to a head and not to delay a decision.

Tierney sought an immediate meeting before such a commission might be appointed. In the meeting that followed between the Taoiseach, the Ministers for Education and Finance and the President and Registrar of UCD on 12 August 1957, the Government representatives explained the reasons for the inquiry. The Taoiseach opened the meeting somewhat tentatively by reporting that the general impression of the ministers was that it was desirable, before coming to a final decision, that some kind of committee of inquiry or commission be set up to inquire into the accommodation needs of all three colleges of the NUI and especially to look at the question whether UCD should be transferred or should remain in Earlsfort Terrace. It was vintage de Valera, with all the subtlety of the qualifying phrase for which he had become famous. He elaborated on certain aspects of the problem that members of the Government desired to have considered. Among these were questions of finance: if a large capital sum were given to UCD, would there be a shortage for other colleges and a curtailment of the annual grants for all? Could expansion be met more conveniently and cheaply at Earlsfort Terrace? Were we attempting something on the Ardmore/Belfield site too great for our means? Could a small committee of inquiry be found that would examine these and other aspects of the matter and report with speed?

Against this *volte face* by de Valera, supported by his Minister for Finance and also by the Minister for Education, who now fell in with the general Government view in favour of a commission, the president and registrar could not prevail. The most that Tierney could get was an assurance from the Taoiseach that there was no question of the appointing of a commission involving delay, that the Government's aim was to have it report 'this side of Christmas.' Its purpose would be to say what plans would best suit the convenience of the students; what would be the cheapest way in which to give effect to these plans; and whether such plans could be implemented on a gradual basis, and if so in what order.[70]

De Valera's attitude to the Belfield proposals was quite interesting. From all he had said in previous meetings with Tierney he had seemed personally to be strongly in favour of the transfer. As recently as May 1957 he had assured Tierney that the latter's option for the transfer since 1949 had been the right one and that there was a clear case for a new site. Now, in August 1957, he had gone along with those Government colleagues who wanted the whole matter of the transfer re-examined and even the question of UCD's staying put at Earlsfort Terrace reopened. It could be said in extenuation of his apparent change of mind that he had bowed to pressure from within the Government, that financial circumstances had deteriorated, and that the effects of any huge capital commitment to UCD would have to be considered in the context of the possible impact on the needs of Cork and Galway.

The manner in which he announced his change of attitude is perhaps even more interesting. The minute of the Government meeting merely stated that 'the general feeling' was in favour of the establishment of a commission: it did not state that this had been the firm decision of the Government. And de Valera's letter informing UCD of the outcome had been couched in language less than definitive: it said that a commission might be necessary. Yet the Government had already agreed that the Taoiseach and the Minister for Education would discuss the terms of reference and the personnel of the proposed commission; and in notes that passed between the Taoiseach's office, the Department of Education and the Minister for Health these matters were discussed in detail even before de Valera had informed UCD that the commission might be necessary. (In deliberating on the names of people to serve on the commission, and its terms of reference, the Minister for Health continued his active role with detailed suggestions.) So, arising from the Government meeting of 6 August and the communications between ministers immediately afterwards, the obvious intention of the Government was to set up a commission of inquiry. Yet when the Taoiseach and the Ministers for Finance and Education later met the President and Registrar of UCD on 12 August, de Valera introduced the subject once again in rather tentative language, saying no more than that the general impression of ministers was that a commission was 'desirable' before coming to a final decision. It was as if de Valera in all of this wished to spare the UCD authorities the pain of telling them bluntly that he had had at least a change of attitude if not of heart and that a commission was already decided on, which at best would postpone any decision on Belfield for the unspecified duration of its deliberations. The commission also provided a golden opportunity for those who opposed the move.

On 15 August 1957, three days after this meeting and following further consultations between the Taoiseach and the Ministers for Finance and Education, the terms of reference of the commission were completed: 'To enquire into the accommodation needs of the constituent colleges of the National University of Ireland and to advise as to how, in the present circumstances, these needs can best be met.' Tierney had lost this particular round, and the decision to establish the commission must have been for him particularly disheartening.

It was the end of September before the membership was announced. Tierney assured the Department of Education that the commission would have the full co-operation of UCD, and he threw himself once more into preparing the case for Belfield with all his accustomed energy and urgent persuasiveness.

The Commission on Accommodation Needs

The Commission on Accommodation Needs of the Constituent Colleges of the National University of Ireland consisted of nine people. Its chairman was Mr Justice Cearbhall Ó Dálaigh. Of the other eight members, four were company directors: J. J. Davy of the stockbrokers' firm; Séamus Fitzgerald, president of Cork Chamber of Commerce; Stephen O'Mara; and Aodhogán O'Rahilly. Of the remainder, George Lee was a former Galway County Engineer; Joseph Wrenne was a former Cork County Manager; John Ernest Hanna was a former Assistant Secretary in the Department of Finance; and Seán Mac Giollarnáth was a solicitor and a former district justice.

It was a group of hard-headed businessmen, not likely to spend taxpayers' money foolishly. Tierney, if he were not so convinced of the righteousness of his cause, had every reason to be apprehensive about the outcome. He may well have influenced a letter sent to the Taoiseach by the Bishops of Raphoe and Achonry, secretaries to the hierarchy, which denounced any diminution of the NUI, such as the current proposals to deprive it of the Faculties of Agriculture and Dairy Science, and regretted the failure to include on the commission any person professionally acquainted with academic needs.[71] By contrast, the opponents of the Belfield project, led by the *Irish Independent,* welcomed the appointment of the commission.

The person who had become identified most prominently with opposition to Belfield in favour of Earlsfort Terrace, and who had called for a commission to examine the issue, was Senator Roger McHugh, a lecturer in English at UCD and a member of the Governing Body. He was also closely associated with the *University Review,* organ of the Graduates' Association, and was regarded as one of the central figures in the opposition to Tierney. Following the announcement that fees were to be substantially increased because of the shortfall in the annual Government grant, McHugh had commented in the *Irish Times* (21 March 1957) that an alternative to the increase in fees was for the college to abandon the Belfield project, to which no Government was yet openly committed and which consequently seemed both uncertain and expensive, and that there was much to be said for remaining and expanding in the city.

This had provoked a wordy controversy in the *Irish Times,* which continued into April. The redoubtable Thomas Nevin (professor of physics) argued cogently for the Tierney line. McHugh was supported by Dr Lorna Reynolds (Department of English), the novelist Kate O'Brien, and Frank Winder, the chairman of Tuairim.[72] There can be no doubt that some of the points made during this controversy influenced the Minister for Health and perhaps other members of the Government when a couple of months later they were exchanging memos on the question of Belfield. And copies of some of the letters from this newspaper controversy were retained in the Department of the Taoiseach.

McHugh welcomed the establishment of the commission, availed himself of the opportunity to make representations to it, and attended before it to elaborate his views. He was in fact the only person not representing an organisation or university department to make a submission. It was he in particular who presented the brief vigorously for the retention of UCD at Earlsfort Terrace, asserting that the college in its urban setting and the city itself exercised a reciprocal influence on each other.

The members of the commission visited universities and other institutions in Ireland, England, and Denmark, observed at first hand the grossly overcrowded conditions in UCD, and considered in exhaustive detail the possibility of expansion in the Earlsfort Terrace area. The outcome of these investigations, they said in their report, was that everything they had heard about the experience of other universities with problems similar to those of

UCD, together with the advice they received, 'has indicated to us that the right solution of the Dublin problem—and the only final solution for it—is to transfer the College, the entire College, to a new site of adequate size.'[73] Furthermore, since the site should be 'big enough to prevent the recurrence of this problem in 25 to 50 years,' the report concluded: 'The 250 acre site which the College authorities have already acquired at Stillorgan Road is such a site and we have little doubt that it would not now be possible to find a site as suitable.'[74] This site, it said, was big enough to provide for every likely extension and development. There was space too for the erection of halls of residence or hostels; and some residential accommodation was generally considered a desirable feature of university life.

Among its other recommendations was one that endorsed a suggestion made by the Ministers for Finance and Health, that the planning and design of the new college buildings should be the subject of an open architectural competition with an international board of assessors.[75]

The section of the report dealing with UCD was signed subject to a reservation by one member of the commission, Aodhogán O'Rahilly. In March 1958 O'Rahilly had submitted his resignation, on the grounds that the minister's ruling on the question whether it was within the terms of reference of the commission to consider the integration of UCD and TCD had been interpreted by his fellow-members as precluding them from considering that possibility. In O'Rahilly's opinion there was no other solution, and consequently his continuing to act on the commission would serve no purpose. He believed that, had they been free to advise on integration, the minister would have got unanimous advice that before any new building was done every possible effort and pressure should be used to work out a *modus vivendi* between the two colleges. He claimed it was a reasonable, rational and logical solution that would save the exchequer thousands of pounds annually; it would be a hopeful portent that some day, in some way, a solution of partition might be found by good will and reasonableness; and it would eradicate the sectarian atmosphere at Earlsfort Terrace.

These points he elaborated in a memo he submitted with his letter of resignation.[76] Apparently he was persuaded to withdraw his resignation, for he continued to serve on the commission and outlined his views in favour of a merger between UCD and TCD in a reservation to the report. In this reservation O'Rahilly stated that if one started from the premise that the only university that the majority of young people could attend was UCD, and that a sum of between £5 and £10 million could be made available, the conclusion was logical that it was better to build on the Donnybrook [*sic*] site than to attempt to acquire the additional sites in the vicinity of Earlsfort Terrace. But he did not accept this premise. He pointed to the position of university education in Dublin, where UCD was 'utterly overcrowded' while Trinity was 'struggling to keep open by taking in foreign students.' He would solve the space requirements by amalgamation and rationalisation and said he could imagine the Trinity buildings housing Arts, Commerce, and Law, Merrion Street accommodating Science, and Earlsfort Terrace accommodating Medicine, Engineering, and Architecture. Extension to Earlsfort Terrace could be made gradually by acquiring property towards the canal, and Trinity could be expanded by acquiring property along Pearse Street and Westland Row (which is precisely what Trinity has done in recent years). 'We would then have a university in the centre of the city in a location probably unsurpassed in Europe.' The partition of academic life in Dublin was of our own making and could be removed by Government decision.[77]

O'Rahilly's reservation added much fuel to the debate that followed publication of the report. His case for the integration of UCD and Trinity College touched on all sorts of cultural, social and political questions that Ireland was about to face in the nineteen-sixties; and undoubtedly it made a major contribution to the promotion of the merger proposal in 1967.

Shortly after O'Rahilly's memo to the minister suggesting the amalgamation of the two university colleges in Dublin, and before the publication of his reservation, Professor John O'Meara, in a wide-ranging lecture on education in Ireland, also argued that some union between UCD and Trinity would be of both financial and political benefit; that it would be advantageous from the point of view of prestige; that the idea should not be dismissed lightly; and that future plans should take account of it.[78]

O'Rahilly's arguments helped to underline the need for a commission on university education generally—one that was not restricted to the chronic issue of accommodation but rather one that would embrace questions such as the amalgamation of the two Dublin colleges. The publication of this proposal in an official report enhanced the status of an idea that in recent years had been floating only vaguely about in academic and newspaper circles. The Commission on University Education was indeed established in 1960; but the question of the merger of Trinity College and UCD took another seven years before it emerged as a real possibility with strong Government backing.

The report of the Commission on Accommodation Needs was presented to both houses of the Oireachtas on 2 June 1959. On the same date a statement issued by the Government Information Bureau said that the Government had especially considered the commission's recommendations in regard to new buildings urgently needed for University College, Dublin, and had agreed in principle, subject to the approval of Dáil Éireann, that the college should be transferred gradually to a site in the college's grounds on the Stillorgan Road.[79]

The publication of the report, and its acceptance by the Government, represented a watershed in the history of UCD. Its recommendations were in essence a vindication of ten years of planning and struggle on the part of the UCD authorities and of its president in particular. For Michael Tierney it was the triumphant end to the 'struggle with fortune' that Newman had predicted and that had thwarted the development and institutional viability of UCD's illustrious predecessors, the Catholic University and the Jesuit college. The problem of a dignified physical presence that had faced successive leaders of Catholic university education for over a century was apparently about to be solved.

The report was welcomed in the college with a sense of relief and optimism. 'By far the most important event of the year' was how Dr Tierney described the publication of the report in his conferring address in July 1959. 'Those of us who have been actively concerned with the difficult problem of College buildings have been highly gratified to find that the members of the Commission have agreed emphatically with what has been our own view for the last ten years.'[80]

The brochure *University College Dublin and its Building Plans,* which the college issued later in the year, was also infused with the same triumphal note. Drafted by Jeremiah Hogan, the brochure had the benefit of suggestions and emendations provided by others in Tierney's circle of advisers.

Opposition to the commission's recommendation in favour of the transfer of UCD to Stillorgan Road had been spearheaded in Aodhogán O'Rahilly's reservation to the report, and the opposition was continued in the outspoken newspaper comment by Professor John O'Meara, in which he supported the views of O'Rahilly.[81] When *University College Dublin and its Building Plans* was being drafted, a whole section was devoted to answering the criticism and counter-proposals of O'Rahilly and O'Meara. Indeed Michael Tierney wrote a rejoinder that bordered on the offensive. One of O'Meara's suggestions was that there should be co-ordination within the National University, since a small and poor country did not need three Departments of Chemistry and Engineering within the National University alone. Tierney wrote: 'If he really believes this to be practical politics he should confine himself to the elucidation of Porphyry.' (O'Meara had published a book on Porphyry's philosophy that year.) O'Meara had referred to Trinity as 'a national heritage of great prestige,' which was being foolishly rejected. Tierney commented that he would find that there were a great many people in Ireland still who did not 'want any part of it and would contentedly leave it to its real owners.' Tierney also accused O'Meara of 'careless use of his texts.'[82]

Tierney's reply to O'Meara does not appear to have been published, but its arguments were incorporated at length in an early draft of *University College Dublin and its Building Plans.* When the draft was submitted to others, the draftsman, Jeremiah Hogan, received sound advice, especially from the professor of chemistry, T. S. Wheeler. Wheeler found himself at variance with the polemical, non-academic tone of certain sections. His idea of a brochure was a factual document stating UCD's present position and what they hoped to achieve; he had no missionary wish to convert anyone to his view. He then suggested that the brochure drop all loaded words like 'Ascendancy'; that 'Catholic' and 'Protestant' be used as little as possible; that references to Trinity College, complimentary or otherwise, be cut to a minimum; that any criticism of the Government be removed ('Let us not, until after the meal, bite the hand we hope will feed us'); that *ad hominem* arguments be eliminated; and that those who criticised the commission were not necessarily 'irresponsible' or 'hostile'.

Wheeler also suggested that one critic (who was not named but who clearly was O'Meara) was given too much prominence. Whether he was aware of its origins or not, he disagreed strongly with a paragraph that had come directly from Tierney's unpublished reply to O'Meara. Wheeler wrote: 'I regret I shall not live to see a University of Dublin with two constituent colleges, T.C.D. and U.C.D. The alternatives given are not, in my opinion, exhaustive. It is, however, impossible in the present climate of opinion to contemplate any union with T.C.D. and there is no point in discussing it. I doubt if more than a few lines are necessary.'[83]

Wheeler's advice, supported by that of others, had the desired effect. It was decided that the brochure should attack no-one but should furnish arguments in favour of what had now been decided; that gratitude should be expressed to the Governments that had allowed UCD to buy the land for building the new college; that all reference to hostile critics be omitted: their arguments might be examined but nothing said about the arguers. The polemical sentences were edited out, and the whole section in the draft that had dealt with the criticisms of O'Rahilly and O'Meara were reduced to a single footnote, which was the essence of moderation.

> Since the publication of the Report, the suggestion has been made that University College need not move out of town, and need not spend so much money on building, if it were joined, in some fashion not precisely defined, with Trinity College. It is certainly possible that an advantageous arrangement may at some time be made between the two university institutions in Dublin. But in this many interests would be concerned, and the negotiations must be too lengthy for our urgent space needs to await their conclusion. Anyhow, no arrangement short of a complete fusion could have a bearing on that problem. Further, even if anything so unlikely were to happen, the problem would be little altered. The buildings of T.C.D. are small and old, and they are pretty full of students. Nor would T.C.D.'s vacant space suffice for buildings on our scale; its whole area, built and unbuilt, is only equal to the area

within the ring-road of the Belgrove lay-out, which the Commissioners consider to be too cramped.

As published, the UCD brochure outlined the story of the efforts since 1850 to provide an acceptable university education and proper university buildings for the emerging Irish nation. It proudly quoted Newman: 'The old names of the Irish race are mounting up into status and power ... We consider the Catholic University to be the event of the day in this gradual majestic resurrection of the nation and its religion.' The same kind of pietas infused the references to the second phase of the Catholic University's existence, when the Arts and Science Departments were placed under the management of the Jesuits and given the now long-familiar name of University College, Dublin. In competition with the Queen's Colleges of Belfast, Cork and Galway, the brochure pointed out, University College carried off the great majority of the Royal University prizes; and this part of the college history became known to the world at large through the name of one of its professors, the poet Gerard Manley Hopkins, and of one of its students, James Joyce.

In the section covering the third phase of the history of the institution as a constituent college of the National University of Ireland (1909–1959) it was asserted: 'The College is not an institution which has outgrown buildings that were at one time adequate, but one which, properly speaking, has never been built at all.'

University College Dublin and its Building Plans incorporated a narrative that had often been told before, but this time the happy ending was always in sight, and the mood of the storyteller was ebullient throughout. In the section dealing with the report of the Commission on Accommodation Needs it stated: 'It was fortunate that they refused to take our conclusion on trust and went over the whole problem independently and thoroughly, because this means that an all-important question has been absolutely and finally settled.' The brochure ended in the same optimistic and celebratory vein: 'The favourable *Report* of the Commission has come just in time; and we may congratulate ourselves on having in readiness the excellent site which, if we had not acquired it before building was a practical proposition, we very certainly could not obtain now.'

A final point is worth noting. While the drafts were being discussed, a pencilled note asked: 'Which name for the entire site or campus? Donnybrook—Stillorgan—Belfield—Belgrove?' In a later draft of the brochure, wherever 'Stillorgan Road' was used in reference to the location it was altered to read 'Belfield'. And in the published version a footnote was added: 'The Belfield estate was bought in 1934, to provide playing fields. As Belfield has a rather long association with the college, and as it was the nucleus to which the other properties were added, its name seems to be the one best fitted to apply to the whole campus. In these pages Belfield is used in this wider sense.' The informal name 'Belfield' was thus given semi-official recognition, and thereafter entered common parlance.

The Government's attention had been concentrated on the drastic overcrowding of UCD in its existing buildings, not only by the report of the commission but also by the costly expedients to which it found itself giving sanction. Throughout the fifties a policy of physical expansion, renovation and adaptation had been pursued in the Earlsfort Terrace and Merrion Street premises. The transfer of certain departments to the vacant houses on the Stillorgan Road properties allowed for reshuffling in Earlsfort Terrace. The dilapidated buildings of the Royal University at the back of Earlsfort Terrace were converted into temporary accommodation. The Aula Maxima of the Royal University was reconditioned in 1950 and used for examinations and conferrings. Beside it the 'Pillar Hall', which was being used for storage, and Convocation Hall, which was being used as a studio for Architecture, were converted into the Library, with its Denis J. Coffey Hall, Eugene O'Curry Hall, J. H. Newman Room, and George Sigerson Room. Library seating was thereby nearly doubled. The space formerly occupied by the library in the old building and in the Council Chambers of the new building was released for other purposes. Architecture, formerly scattered here and there, could now be concentrated in more suitable premises in that part of the old building vacated by the Library; and the Council Chambers became three sizable lecture-rooms, with seating for about 350.

In 1958 an additional floor was put into the Chemistry Laboratory, thereby doubling its floor area. The following year more work of this nature provided some extra space, in all two new laboratories and a lecture-room for Chemistry. The total cost of the improvisations of the fifties was about £150,000, much of which was borne by the state.[84] It was realised that something more permanent and more suitable would be a better investment than these makeshift expedients.[85]

Despite these improvisations, the Commission on Accommodation Needs was convinced that if the provision of basic facilities for undergraduates were poor, those for research were worse.

> We saw enough of research facilities in English and Danish Universities in the sciences to say that in this field the University lags a long way behind. In our opinion—and for economic not less than for academic reasons—members of university staffs and post-graduate students will have to be afforded opportunities for research, and accommodation provided for it. More than ever the standards of today are international standards.[86]

Notwithstanding all the improvisations in Earlsfort Terrace and Merrion Street, accommodation needs remained critical, especially in the Faculty of Science, where the intake of entrants, static for years, more than doubled in the four years 1954/55 to 1958/59. It was accepted by the Minister for Education and others that this faculty was facing 'breaking point' or a situation of 'complete breakdown'.[87] In these circumstances the college authorities had urged that the required accommodation for Science should form part of a completed Belfield scheme, and they requested permission to employ an architect for this purpose. The Government's response was to establish an inter-departmental committee to consider the needs of the Science Faculty in consultation with representatives of UCD.

In these consultations the UCD representatives urged that any building, whether at Earlsfort Terrace or Belfield, should not be temporary — a temporary structure would cost almost as much as a permanent one. They argued instead for a permanent building at Belfield and said that it would not be feasible to submit the design for competition, given the delay that would be involved and the need for consultation between client and architect. They urged that the whole Science Building be designed and that a portion be built as soon as possible, into which research students and senior classes from Physics and Chemistry could be transferred. These submissions were acceptable to the inter-departmental committee and incorporated in its report. The cost of the proposed building at Belfield was estimated at £250,000. The state's contribution was to be a maximum of £150,000, and UCD was to provide the balance.[88]

The Minister for Education was on the point of recommending the acceptance of this report to the Government when the most comprehensive case yet for the retention of UCD in the city came in a pamphlet published by Tuairim. This pamphlet and its favourable public reception caused the government to hesitate over the whole Belfield scheme.

Tuairim was founded in 1954, its objective being 'to encourage young people to formulate by means of study and discussion, informed opinions on Irish problems, and to influence by means of lectures, writings and speeches, the opinion of the public.'[89] By 1962 it had nine branches and had published nine pamphlets. Recent graduates were among its most active members, and some had been active participants in college societies.

Tuairim's pamphlet *University College Dublin and the Future* was the work of a research group organised by its Dublin branch. It provided a close examination of the report of the Commission on Accommodation Needs. The conclusion was that the proposed move to Stillorgan Road was 'highly undesirable and entirely unnecessary.'[90] Tuairim maintained that the commission had interpreted its terms of reference too narrowly by not taking into account the wider problem of the existence of plans for the development and co-ordination of other third-level institutions. It strongly supported the case that in the whole area from St Stephen's Green to College Green the city had 'a cultural and educational complex' of unique value. This area included UCD, Trinity College, the College of Surgeons, the College of Physicians, the Dental Hospital, the College of Art, the Folklore Commission, the Irish Manuscripts Commission, the National Gallery, the National Library, the National Museum, the Central Catholic Library, the Institute for Advanced Studies, a number of schools and university hostels, the premises of several professional bodies, and a long list of Government departments and other state agencies. Tuairim claimed that to remove UCD from its urban site 'would result in great losses to the College itself and to the city.'

This was perhaps the most attractive aspect of the case against the move to Stillorgan Road. It focused attention on the fact that it was not just an argument about buildings, or even of a move from one site to another; it was not just a controversy between the governing 'clique' at UCD and an internal college opposition to that administration: it also had much to do with public aesthetics, with public culture, with the thesis that a new UCD in the Earlsfort Terrace area would be culturally, socially and intellectually the best contribution UCD could make to the capital city. It was a point that was pressed strongly by Tuairim and by individuals such as Roger McHugh. Kate O'Brien had written that a university should not 'build itself a tiny little new city all its own, behind some high bushes in a suburban field';[91] it should be instead a part, an awkward but valued and honoured part, of a city's growth and of all its life.

The Tuairim pamphlet received influential public support. The *Irish Times* (8 January 1960) described it as 'a convincing document' and suggested that the decision to transfer to Belfield had been made on insufficient grounds. It called on the Government to act quickly to enable a co-ordinated plan of development to be formulated for UCD and other institutions in place of the 'costly' and, it seemed, 'unnecessary' Belfield project.

Whether known to Tuairim or not, the Minister for Health, Seán MacEntee, as well as civil servants in his former Department of Finance, still had misgivings about the Belfield project. And since the Government had so far announced only acceptance in principle of the transfer, and the Dáil had yet to give its approval, Tuairim must have felt there was still time to influence the outcome.

Hot on the heels of the appearance of UCD's brochure, reported in the *Irish Press* of 19 December 1959, Frank Winder, chairman of the Tuairim research group, sent advance copies of the pamphlet to the Taoiseach, Seán Lemass, and all Government ministers on 21 December 1959, saying it would be published in the new year. On the same day and the following day, UCD sent copies of its brochure to all ministers and parliamentary secretaries and early in the new year to all members of the Oireachtas. The choice facing the legislators had become clear: whether to proceed with a Stillorgan Road site, as recommended by the Commission on Accommodation Needs, or accept Tuairim's proposal for developing the urban site around Earlsfort Terrace. One thing was certain: because of the chronic accommodation problem, there was no time for indecision.

The Taoiseach requested the Department of Education to examine Tuairim's pamphlet and to produce a memorandum for his consideration. A month later the Department of Education replied in a lengthy analysis.

Once again it was to be the same Department of Education that earlier Michael Tierney had been so anxious to keep out of university affairs that came to his support. In response to the Taoiseach's request, the department's officials, presumably again led by Tarlach Ó Raifeartaigh, provided a detailed, acute, point-by-point rejoinder. Tuairim, it said, tended to sidestep or ignore the difficulties that a city development might provoke. From the point of view of cost, a city development might well prove more expensive than the Stillorgan Road project. Tuairim's solution involved the compulsory acquisition of industrial, commercial, educational and domestic properties in the area stretching from St Stephen's' Green to the Grand Canal bounded by Harcourt Street, Charlemont Street, Earlsfort Terrace, and Harcourt Terrace. Its approach to this matter was uninformed and unsound. Educational and cultural interests could not be regarded as having an over-riding claim to the area in the face of claims of equal weight that could be advanced by administrative, commercial and industrial interests. As regards Tuairim's case for an educational and cultural complex, the Department of Education's commentary pointed out that all the institutions specified had a separate and distinct life of their own, which in no way depended on the proximity of UCD, and that contact at undergraduate level with these institutions was on the whole slight and occasional.

To the suggestion that UCD and Trinity College might share accommodation and equipment the department replied that it was not simply a matter of physical adjacency: there were more complex issues of control of facilities, financing their provision and the organisation of courses in the two colleges so as to make co-operation possible. The limitation of numbers by raising standards and fees, as proposed by Tuairim, would create other problems and would affect UCC, UCG and Trinity and be unfair to a large number of students.

Six days after supplying the Taoiseach with his department's examination of the Tuairim pamphlet, the Minister for Education, Dr Patrick Hillery, recommended to the Government the acceptance of the inter-departmental committee's report on a Science Building at Belfield.[92] He also announced his intention of seeking the Dáil's approval for the Government's decision to transfer UCD to Stillorgan Road. He informed the Government further that he proposed to establish a commission to inquire into and make recommendations on higher education generally. These proposals were approved, and the Government authorised Hillery to inform UCD that, subject to the approval of the Dáil of the proposed transfer, the Government was prepared to authorise the college to erect part of the new Science Block in Belfield, and that the building be so sited that it could be integrated with a complete scheme of university buildings in any layout eventually chosen.

THE DÁIL APPROVES

With the Government's blessing, Dr Hillery brought the whole Belfield issue before the Dáil on 23 March 1960 with a supplementary estimate for a token amount of £10. He took the opportunity to deliver a fairly comprehensive overview of the history of UCD's accommodation problems and the solutions that had been proposed.

It was a long speech and of a quality rarely heard in Dáil Éireann in relation to university education. It gave clear evidence of the importance his department officials attached to the move to Belfield. He came down strongly in favour of the recommendations of the Commission on Accommodation Needs and declared that 'there was no reasonable alternative to the transfer of University College, Dublin, to the Belfield site.'[93] His speech was in essence a manifesto on behalf of the Belfield project. The possibility of some kind of integration or amalgamation of UCD and Trinity was rejected. He opposed it, he said, because the state must not oblige parents in violation of their conscience to send their children to any particular school designated by the state.[94] (Seven years later, when announcing a merger between the two colleges, Donogh O'Malley as Minister for Education was not to feel himself restricted by this interpretation of the Constitution.)

Congratulating the minister on his 'comprehensive contribution of a character not usually associated with a supplementary estimate of £10,' James Dillon, leader of the opposition, acknowledged that Dr Hillery had delivered a 'justifiable marathon'.[95] A couple of speakers said how envious they were of a minister who had found himself in a position to take a decision that could be of the greatest consequence to the country. Hillery was highly complimented for his speech. It provoked other valuable or interesting contributions — notably from James Dillon, Patrick McGilligan, Noel Browne, Vivion de Valera and Donogh O'Malley in the Dáil and from Michael Hayes and Owen Sheehy Skeffington in the Seanad. Following the example set by Dr Hillery, a few of the better speeches attempted to place the UCD issue in its historical perspective. Pride in UCD's tradition was pronounced in the contributions made by Dillon and McGilligan; de Valera, a science graduate, was particularly well briefed in the problems of the Faculty of Science.

Earlsfort Terrace and Merrion Street had strong associations with the battle for a suitable premises for the college, and many who had spent their student years there had fond attachments to these places. Yet in spite of nostalgia the transfer to Belfield won the approval of those who felt that the move must be the harbinger of an even brighter future for the college, whose traditions and vitality and pride in its origins were taken as a guarantee of further progress.

By the time the Dáil came to discuss the move, many deputies appeared to have accepted the position as a *fait accompli*—and that very phrase was used by a number of them in the course of the debate. Several on both sides of the Dáil and in the Seanad praised Tuairim for its public-spiritedness, its 'disinterested zeal', its objective analysis, and the considerable trouble that a voluntary body had taken with the question.

Donogh O'Malley of Fianna Fáil, P. Byrne of Fine Gael and the independents Noel Browne and Jack McQuillan, as well as Senator Anthony Barry, spoke in favour of some kind of merger between the two Dublin colleges, thus supporting the point made by Aodhogán O'Rahilly in his reservation to the commission's report and by Roger McHugh and John O'Meara of UCD. But on the main issue of the transfer to Belfield, the Government was supported officially by Fine Gael and the Labour Party. In the end, only Noel Browne asked to be recorded as opposed to the move.

It was not until nine months after the Dáil's approval that the Seanad had the opportunity to discuss Belfield, on a motion that stated 'that Seanad Éireann disapproves of the proposal to transfer University College, Dublin, from its existing site at Earlsfort Terrace ...' The motion went on to say that the cost involved in the transfer could be more usefully expended in expansion and improvement at Earlsfort Terrace and in UCC and UCG and in the provision of new constituent colleges at other centres. Senators from Cork were most prominent in supporting the motion (Professor Patrick Quinlan of UCC, however, congratulated the Government on accepting the commission's report). Tributes were again paid to the case made by Tuairim, which was praised as a fine example of intelligent citizenship. The possibility of a merger with Trinity College was also raised; but it was generally conceded that the decision to transfer was a *fait accompli*.

The case for Belfield was put by the Minister, by Professor Michael Hayes and Dr John O'Donovan of UCD and by Owen Sheehy Skeffington of Trinity. Something of the frustration felt in UCD was expressed by Hayes when he described the attitude of those opposing Belfield as 'postpone, postpone, postpone; let us have considerations; let us have commissions; let us have competitions; let us have anything except buildings for UCD.'[96]

Sheehy Skeffington's fair-minded and generous comments must have come as a pleasant surprise, for, as was well known, he did not by any means approve of all the actions of the UCD authorities. He was convinced, he said, that the official brochure got out by UCD presented a sound 'and indeed unanswerable case.'[97] While he wished to be associated with the tribute paid to the Tuairim pamphlet, he disagreed with its conclusions. It made the mistake, he said, of thinking that the university population in Dublin could be kept at its present figure, and it failed to see that growth was essential. He stressed the speed at which Dublin was growing, which was bound to increase the number of university students. 'There is no doubt in my mind that a great deal of imagination and foresight has been shown by the authorities of University College, Dublin, down the years since they first thought of this scheme at Belfield.'[98] This was praise indeed from a most unexpected quarter. No doubt remembering his own brushes with the UCD authorities, Sheehy Skeffington concluded: 'I should like to believe that if and when the transfer is made of UCD from its existing site out to Belfield, there will be not merely a broadening of acres but also a broadening of minds.'[99]

The proposer of the Seanad motion felt that if left to a free vote it would have been defeated. He was satisfied the discussion had served a useful purpose, and so begged leave to withdraw it.

The Dáil's approval of the transfer of UCD to Belfield was passed on 31 March 1960. The following day Archbishop McQuaid wrote to the Taoiseach, Seán Lemass, thanking him for the Government's decision. He said it had given to Catholics an assurance of their right to higher education, and he added: 'It is a decision that is historic in a sense that, I fear, few persons realise.'[100] Lemass assured the archbishop that the knowledge that this project had his approval was 'an encouragement and a source of strength to the Government.'[101]

The archbishop's comment was very much in keeping with Patrick McGilligan's view when he said during the Dáil debate: 'There is definitely a new stage being reached as far as the Catholic University in this country is concerned.'[102] It was clear from the context that he saw Belfield as ensuring the continuing Catholic ethos of UCD. From the standpoint of the old guard, the fight for equal facilities for Catholics in university education was still successfully in progress.

In the aftermath of the Dáil vote a flood of congratulations acknowledged the role that had been played by Michael Tierney. A retired medical professor noted that there had been 'a great spate of adverse opinions,' which, he was afraid, would delay or spoil 'the far-seeing and progressive plan.' There had been great support from the staff, 'but', he added, 'the occasion must be regarded as your personal triumph.'[103] Professor James Dooge (civil engineering) congratulated Tierney 'on the successful outcome of a long and arduous campaign.'[104] Professor James Ruane (farm management) wrote: 'You must feel both relieved and proud that such a long and arduous task has been brought to such a very desirable conclusion.' And he wished the president many years 'to see the fruits of your foresight reach the harvest it so richly deserves.'[105] A professor in UCG wrote: 'It is a tremendous tribute to your vision and effort' and wished they had Tierney in charge of UCG.[106]

It was left to Professor Robin Dudley Edwards to compose what must have been to Tierney the most satisfying eulogy of his role. Edwards wrote: 'Thinking over the whole thing it seems very clear that, a half-century hence, you will have become immortal as the second founder of U.C.D.—if, for once, the historian can attempt to prophesy!'[107] And indeed UCD as it exists today is as much a product of Tierney's vision as of Newman's. Like a Roman emperor, he had presided over his imperial conquests. Belfield stands today as a monument to Michael Tierney's vision.

8

Confronting the President

THE VISITATION

The meeting of the Governing Body in June 1959 that received the report of the Commission on Accommodation Needs, together with the Government's approval in principle of the move to Belfield, had before it correspondence from John Kenny, an assistant in the Faculty of Law (later to be a Supreme Court judge), concerning the propriety of certain types of appointment made by the Governing Body. It stated that, unless the practice were changed, Kenny proposed to petition the Government to appoint a visitor to decide the matter. By a remarkable irony, this coincidence of items on the agenda ensured that the same meeting witnessed both the greatest triumph of Tierney's policy and an intimation of what would turn out to be his most humiliating defeat.

UCD had been accustomed for years to promote a number of non-statutory staff originally engaged as 'junior assistants' or 'assistants' to posts as 'assistant lecturers' or 'college lecturers', such promotion qualifying them for an increase in salary and giving them the academic prestige of the title 'lecturer', which otherwise could be obtained only as an NUI appointment involving a complicated and time-consuming process of application and canvassing.

The university and college charters made no provision for such appointments by the colleges; neither did they forbid them. Whether or not they were legal was therefore a moot point. In raising it, Kenny and those who agreed with him argued that such lectureships should not be created until they were given a statutory basis, removing the possibility of random appointments at the whim of the Governing Body, without competition and open to improper patronage—in theory also leaving the appointees liable to dismissal on the same whim with which they had been appointed.

On the other side of the case it was stressed by Dr Tierney and Professor Hogan, supported by the greater number of Governing Body members, that UCD had outgrown the small institution in which the literal application of a charter was adequate to meet its staffing requirements; that the system gave the college the flexibility and means to respond to needs as they arose; that appointments were never made except on the recommendation of the professor in the department concerned; and that by providing an attractive career path they facilitated the engagement of new staff from abroad to revitalise the intellectual life and reputation of the college. The Governing Body rejected Kenny's demand and, on the president's recommendation, refused even to seek legal advice, though urged to do so by two members, Mr Justice Brian Walsh[1] and Máirín Uí Dhálaigh.

In the event, the Government set up a board of visitors, consisting of three judges: George Murnaghan—replacing the first choice, Kevin Dixon, who had died—and Thomas Teevan of the High Court, with Michael Binchy of the Circuit Court. Having heard submissions, the board found that college lecturers and assistant lecturers were not assistants of the kind that UCD was empowered to appoint and remove under the college Charter. The Government responded by securing the passing of the University College, Dublin, Act (1960), which in effect legitimised the appointments already made and permitted similar appointments for a limited period. It also announced that a Commission on Higher Education would be established, which, among other matters, would make recommendations with regard to university appointments.

A bald reciting of the facts at issue and the manner in which they were settled, however, does not begin to describe the extent of the bitterness unleashed by this affair. It had in fact begun in 1956, when it had been proposed (on the initiative of Professor George O'Brien) that Dr Roy Geary, the renowned Director of the Central Statistics Office, should be appointed college professor of econometrics on his impending resignation from his civil service position. Opposition to the creation of this post had been raised variously in the Governing Body and the Academic Council by Professor E. J. Conway (founder and chairman of the Graduates' Association of the NUI, whose *University Review* had carried the article that so annoyed Tierney), Professor John O'Meara (Latin), Dr Roger McHugh (English) and Dr Lorna Reynolds (English). Ranged against them were, among others, the president, the registrar, James Meenan (political economy), Professor Aubrey Gwynn (history) and Senator Michael Hayes (Irish). The college authorities prevailed. Though Dr Geary, in the circumstances, did not take up the chair, battle had been joined.

The dissidents equipped themselves with legal opinions to sustain their allegation that college lecturer and assistant lecturer appointments were illegal and continued to press their case, carrying it at one point into the NUI Senate, where they received cautious encouragement from Professor James Hogan of UCC (and *University Review*) and the President of UCC, Henry St John Atkins. Bishop Browne of Galway, on the other hand, sided with Tierney, whose view again carried the day.

The visitation brought this rumbling discontent to a head. Submissions against the practice of the college authorities were made by John Kenny and Professor Séamus Henchy of the Law Faculty, Professor O'Meara and Dr McHugh. The college practice was defended by its counsel, Professor Patrick McGilligan (law), the registrar, the secretary and bursar, Professor Wheeler (science), Professor Michael Hogan (engineering), Professor Thomas Nevin (physics) and Senator Hayes.

The visitors were clearly impressed by the criticisms they heard, as can be gauged from the tone and content of their report. It not only decided the issue of legality but also rebuked the Governing Body for failing to seek legal advice when the question had first been raised; it denounced what it saw as a breach of duty by the president in leaving many statutory lectureships unfilled; and it added that if the Charter was outmoded, the college should have petitioned the Government to amend it rather than take the law into its own hands.

The report deeply offended the president. It did indeed seem to be poor recompense for the great expansion in the numbers of junior staff appointed during the Tierney years, especially the post-war influx of young scholars from British universities. These recruits included many who would later hold important academic posts outside Ireland: H. F. Kearney, J. B. Morrall, J. A. Watt (history); Donald Nichol, James Shiel, Peter Walsh (classics). Others, including Neil Porter (physics), David Brown (chemistry) and Ann McKenna (psychology) were to stay on at UCD, to the great benefit of the college. There was also a sprinkling of refugees from the war-torn Continent: Ludwig Bieler (classics and palaeography) from Vienna, Sidney Ehler (history and law) from Prague. Through all of these, new courses were on offer and fresh enthusiasms opened windows to the world outside after the claustrophobic atmosphere of the war years. Irish postgraduates, once more able to spend time in foreign universities, were returning to the college as junior staff. And a first batch of new professors—T. Desmond Williams, John O'Meara, J. J. Tierney—also back from foreign universities were replacing the foundation holders of chairs. Against such an achievement, to be denigrated for a mere dispute over nomenclature (as the appointments argument appeared to the president and his closest confidants) was understandable cause for deeply felt anger.

The response by the college authorities to the visitors' report, on the other hand, shed unintended light on the frustration and indignation inspiring their critics. In a long confidential memo to the Minister for Education they firmly put the blame for the controversy on a small but determined minority in the Governing Body who had allegedly been casting about for a long time for a weapon with which to attack the president and the majority.[2] It named the Graduates' Association and elements in UCC and UCG, 'which had their own reasons for opposing UCD.' The legal point raised in the petition for a visitation had been seen 'as a means of scoring a victory over the President.' UCC had had a college professorship and a number of college lectureships, which were changed into university posts, 'plainly as a move in the campaign.' The memo went on to complain about what it saw as the bias against the UCD authorities displayed throughout by the visitors, and in particular by the chairman (Mr Justice Murnaghan). From the outset he had acted 'rather as counsel for the prosecution than as an impartial witness'; at one stage the registrar had had to request that the college be treated with something of the same respect it accorded to the visitors. In the view of the college, what the board had been called on to do was not to discuss college policy, or the 'reasons' for college lectureships, or the 'meritorious basis' of academic appointments—for which it had no competence, though all of which were nonetheless adversely commented on—but simply the law relating to the Charters. Not surprisingly, the memo asserted, the consequence was a report that was 'ill-informed, biased and misconceived.'

The memo ranged widely, but it continued in the same general self-exculpatory vein. There was little room in Michael Tierney's scheme of things for acknowledging the genuine interest in the college's welfare underlying the attitude of his critics. His single-minded pursuit of the college's best interest, as he saw it, inclined him to suspect malice where there was at root only difference of opinion. In this, it should be said, he was not alone. His most stalwart supporters—Hayes, McGilligan, Hogan, and, on such an issue, the retired O'Rahilly of Cork—all shared the suspicion felt by those who had borne the heat of the day through most of the university's history towards latecomers, younger in the main and often beneficiaries of what their elders had achieved, whose disputatious activities seemed to serve no purpose other than undermining the hard-won gains and continuing work for the college by its veteran administrators. Naturally, the longer it lasted the more this paternalism exasperated the would-be reformers, who wanted to contribute out of their own vision to the evolution of UCD. They resented what struck them as autocratic decision-making by a clique that had no exclusive right to determine the direction of development. In the president's benevolent despotism they increasingly perceived the despotism rather than the benevolence.

This confrontation over what were essentially academic perceptions was now translated to the least appropriate forum, the parliamentary debates in Dáil and Seanad on the successive stages of the University College, Dublin, Bill, to validate the disputed appointments. Predictably, for Deputy Noel Browne, then allied with Deputy Jack McQuillan in the National Progressive Democratic Party, Michael Tierney represented a conservative clerico-political establishment that supposedly held the country in its grip and obstructed all social progress, as it had obstructed Browne's Mother and Child Scheme ten years before. Both Browne and McQuillan accordingly felt free to abandon restraint.[3] The visitors' report, said Browne, was 'a most damning indictment,' which showed the UCD Governing Body to be 'dominated by an autocrat and dictator.' McQuillan claimed the Governing Body had been manipulated by the president, his 'yes-men' and henchmen, among whom he named Jeremiah and Michael Hogan, Hayes and Purcell. Charges of corruption, blackmail and a 'reign of terror' in which junior staff were unable to exercise their right to freedom of expression followed in the speeches of the two deputies, with references to the hazards said to await staff members who opposed the move to Belfield.

It was an extraordinarily intemperate performance, virtually unprecedented for the vehemence of its attack under parliamentary privilege on people outside the Dáil who could defend themselves or the president only in letters to the newspapers and articles in journals—which duly followed from T. S. Wheeler, J. P. MacHale, J. J. Hogan, Rev. Alfred O'Rahilly, and others, all of which served to focus considerable public attention on the controversy.

Back in the Dáil the leader of Fine Gael and of the opposition, James Dillon, said he was 'appalled at the irresponsible, reckless malice of those who sought to denigrate and slander' a distinguished scholar and public servant. McGilligan in the Dáil[4] and Hayes in the Seanad[5] spoke vigorously also in defence of the college administration and its appointment practices, referred to the 'dissident minority' in UCD, and criticised the visitors, who had produced, according to Hayes (quoting O'Rahilly), a report containing 'irrelevancies, inaccuracies and insinuations.' This denunciation of the visitors was tactically a mistake. A number of deputies and senators, though anxious to dissociate themselves from the sentiments of Browne and McQuillan, could not concur in abusing the three judges. Most notably, Senator Owen Sheehy Skeffington, who had generously (in view of Tierney's ban on his proposed participation in an L&H debate) shown appreciation of the dilemma facing UCD in the matter of appointments, protested against Hayes's 'grossly improper' remarks about judges doing their duty.

Also repudiated by some of the parliamentarians was an implication in the speeches of Dillon and McGilligan, as well as a speech by Patrick Quinlan (a UCC professor) in the Seanad, that the attacks on the college authorities came from the tradition of those who had always been opposed to a Catholic university. There was a difference between UCD and the Catholic Church, said Donogh O'Malley—one of the new breed in Fianna Fáil who would be heard from again on the subject of universities: the President of UCD was not entitled to speak *ex cathedra*. O'Malley also wondered who was going to meet the costs of the visitation, bearing in mind that a county manager who exceeded his powers could be surcharged; to which an opposition deputy responded by asking whether he was suggesting that the Chancellor (Éamon de Valera) be surcharged.

Richie Ryan of Fine Gael, Brian Lenihan and Eoin Ryan of Fianna Fáil and other younger members of the Oireachtas managed in the parliamentary debates to avoid personalities while defending the judges and in several cases suggesting that more evidence of freedom of expression would be welcome from UCD. Signs were accumulating of discomfiture with the self-righteousness of the old guard—who in its turn could take some satisfaction from the widespread disavowal of vituperation. And on that note, with the joint support of Fianna Fáil and Fine Gael, the Bill was passed.

In the same few weeks a crowded two-day meeting of Convocation, the assembly of NUI graduates, confirmed the signs of the times by 'noting with regret,' on a vote of 355 to 55, 'the violation of the rule of law in the University revealed by the Report of the recently-appointed Board of Visitors.' It also passed a resolution, by 246 votes to 101, with 94 abstentions, censuring 'the present administration of UCD for the disrepute which its recent activities have brought upon the College.' An attempt by Professor Robin Dudley Edwards to encourage the foundation of an independent graduates' body, to be called the Friends of UCD, was ruled out of order.[6]

The University College, Dublin, Act (1960) duly became law but also the focus of a legal wrangle over its interpretation. This was not finally settled until a meeting of the Governing Body on 16 October 1962 (whose attendance included those old Tierney rivals McHugh, O'Meara, Brian Walsh and Máirín Uí Dhálaigh) resolved unanimously, in line with a letter from the Secretary of the Department of Education, 'that, in the session 1962–3 Assistants (I) shall, for administrative purposes, be deemed to be College Lecturers and that Assistants (II) shall, for administrative purposes, be deemed to be Assistant Lecturers.' The resolution deeming graded assistants to be college and assistant lecturers was subsequently passed annually by the Governing Body and marked the end of the controversy over the nomenclature to be applied to non-statutory staff.

The row that had created such a public fuss and much anxious turmoil within the college thus ended in anti-climax. To many it would seem in retrospect to have been a storm in a teacup. Assistants grade I, II and III were appointed with that title for the session 1963/64; but for 1964/65 and thereafter they were designated in the minutes of the Governing Body as college lecturers, assistant lecturers, and assistants. It was further agreed by the Governing Body (on 12 March 1963) that college lecturers with ten years' service, at least five of which were as college lecturer, be appointed to the age of sixty-five. It was then only a matter of time before the Academic Staff Association came to an agreement in 1970 with the Governing Body that a contract to the age of sixty-five after a probationary period be offered to all grades of the junior staff.

ASSESSING THE CONTROVERSY

Michael Tierney and the UCD officers in their confidential memo to the minister, as well as Patrick McGilligan in the Dáil and Michael Hayes in the Seanad, had claimed that the visitation controversy had arisen from the existence of a small group opposed especially to the president and that this group, having failed to get the support of faculties, Academic Council, Governing Body or Senate, then applied a legal magnifying glass to Charters and Statutes, not because they were anxious that these should be rigidly observed but because they desired to thwart and hamper the authorities of UCD. Whatever truth there may have been in the claim that this was the match that started the flame, it had become totally irrelevant once the public controversy had assumed such proportions. As Sheehy Skeffington said, Senator Hayes could not really ask people to believe that the whole report and the conclusive vote in Convocation were the result of some 'fiendishly clever, appallingly hostile little group of people.' If one were to judge by the majority of speakers in the Dáil and Seanad, and by the comment in Convocation and in the press, UCD, through its spokesmen, had come across not so much as being upright and beyond reproach and sinned against as having itself sinned and been self-righteous when called to account. The argument that the whole unpleasant controversy was begun by the personal hostilities of a small disruptive faction within the college carried little conviction with the public, and held little interest outside UCD.

Similarly, it was claimed by officers of the college and their allies that the proper business of the visitation was only a trivial matter of titles—whether 'assistants' could be called 'lecturers'. There is a sense in which this was in fact true. But if this simple matter were the single issue at stake it would not have merited much public attention.

Trivial though it may have appeared in the strict legal interpretation of the Charter, it soon acquired mammoth proportions. Immediately on the publication of the report of the visitation, the public was shocked and disquiet was aroused by the allegation of the 'violation of the rule of law' by, of all people, the university authorities. The situation in which appointments to the teaching staff of the largest educational establishment in the country could be so readily questioned was, in the words of the *Irish Times* editorial of 30 April 1960, 'to say the least of it, unhappy.'

Apart from the validity of the appointments there was the method and tenure of these appointments, which raised massive questions of academic freedom and charges of tyranny, patronage and corruption in high places. It would be tragic, said *Hibernia* (3 June 1960), if members of the UCD staff were afraid to voice critical views because of the insecurity of their tenure. And it reported that graduates present at the meeting of Convocation were worried 'by an apparent intolerance of criticism on the part of the UCD authorities.' It was high time, said *Hibernia* in an earlier issue, for the authorities in UCD to learn that academic freedom cuts both ways: 'it means freedom for the University to go its own way free from State intervention in ordinary matters, though substantially supported by the State. But within the College it should also mean toleration of divergent views of College policy and freedom for the academic staff from the least hint of a threat of penalisation.'[7]

One effect of the unseemly row between the college authorities and the group of academics who had opposed them remained difficult to measure but crucially important for all that. It had often been asserted in the heat of battle that the authorities, by their behaviour in flouting the law and not adhering strictly to the Charter in the matter of appointments, by their bitter attack on and charges of partiality against the judicial visitors, by their arrogant defence of the indefensible and by their attempts to prevent freedom of discussion in the university had set a very bad example for the students under their care. In reply it was alleged that the whole public odium to which UCD had been subjected had been stirred up by a cabal among a very small group of academics who in their bitter opposition to the president, for a variety of personal and other reasons, were determined to find some means of defeating him, irrespective of the great damage their action did to the college and its reputation and without any thought for the unsettling effects their example would have on the students.

The philosophical observer might well be excused for apportioning the blame equally between two groups of strong-willed people who, determined to have their own way, gave little consideration to the reputation of the college and the welfare of its students and who, if it had not been for their strong dislike of each other, would never have been blinded to the primary interests of the college, which both camps—it need hardly be said—not only professed but sincerely promoted according to their lights. Because of their inflexibility, the protagonists were unable to employ the politician's knack of disguising retreat as advance.

Tierney's opponents had got their visitation and had won the verdict. On the other hand, the Government had endorsed the Governing Body system of non-statutory appointments by legalising it. Both sides therefore could claim to have won. In each case, however, it was a Pyrrhic victory; and the college was the real loser. This was widely assumed and repeatedly stated by critics and defenders alike. However, any loss suffered by the college was hard to quantify concretely. The cynic could be excused for pointing out that if measured statistically the dramatic growth in student numbers most emphatically had not been curbed. Great as everybody said they were in 1960, they had doubled again by 1970. Nor had staff recruitment been adversely affected.

What was alleged to have suffered, however, was that abstract thing, the college's reputation. Certainly UCD had got a bad press. It was also true that when the call went out at the meeting of Convocation for the formation of an association of Friends of UCD there were no apparent takers, and the proposal was still-born.

Indeed in this area the UCD authorities had had an unhappy experience. The NUI Graduates' Association in the nineteen-fifties, and graduates in organisations such as Tuairim, Gael-Linn, An Comhchaidreamh and Convocation, had all been highly critical of the Tierney regime. The UCD authorities could hardly be blamed therefore for their deep mistrust of such graduate bodies, or for seeming none too eager to encourage the establishment of a graduates' association. Besides, Dr Tierney had always held that to set up a graduates' group even for the purposes of fund-raising was in effect to let the Government off the hook with regard to performing its duty to finance university education. The graduates, for their part, were not exactly enthusiastic about concepts of loyalty to the college. Had it not been for the camaraderie fostered in the flourishing student societies and sports clubs, any sense of loyalty would have been very thin indeed. It would be another twenty years after the visitation controversy before the time would be ripe for the establishment of a UCD Alumni Association.

One of the most surprising aspects of the controversy was the great public interest that had been shown in the affairs of UCD. As the largest constituent of the National University, UCD had been instituted in response to the agitation and aspirations of Catholic and nationalist opinion of the early twentieth century. Over the intervening half century it had continued to be sensitive to these political and religious attitudes, simultaneously helping to inform and direct the changes that were taking place in public opinion and faithfully reflecting those developments. The public debate over the visitors' report and the University College, Dublin, Bill was one such moment when the intersection between the college and the nation was vividly illustrated. Sheehy Skeffington was only reflecting the views of many other commentators when he said that his first and foremost reason for speaking on the Bill was that the matter was one of public interest, and that the universities were in a situation of public trust.

Nothing illustrated and underlined more dramatically the fact that UCD was looked upon as the premier university institution in the country than this widespread critical interest in the conduct of its affairs. Staff, students, graduates, Convocation, the Dáil, Seanad and national newspapers and journals were all eager to comment and advise on how best the college should be run. Trinity College, by comparison, was not subject to anything like the same kind of democratic control, scrutiny, or comment. And neither Cork nor Galway could have evoked the same degree of national interest, for they were then still provincial by comparison with UCD. Its standing as a national institution was also attested to in the public's subconscious, for, as Michael Hayes said, one of the commonest pieces of confusion among public and graduates alike, and especially in the sports arena, was the labelling of UCD as 'the National'. The college could not live up to its own desired position as the leading national university institution and expect a public that was proud of its possession not to take an active interest in its well-being. Despite some hard things that had been said, the dispute had revealed a healthy awareness that UCD should be a national concern.

The controversy was a traumatic experience for the college. It had divided the staff into two bitterly opposed factions and had created questions of personal allegiances and great anxiety for the majority who were committed to neither camp. For those who sought to mediate, the difficulty was, as Professor Robin Dudley Edwards confided to his diary, how to make any proposal 'without appearing like a rat deserting a sinking ship and without joining the grievance-ridden critics.'[8] And while James Meenan was irritated by the attack in the Dáil and readily conceded that Tierney had his own difficulties within UCD, he confessed to being 'more and more annoyed with Tierney's knack' of creating fresh difficulties for himself by choosing the occasion of the visitation row to have a fight with the L&H by banning its inaugural meeting.[9] He added: 'One resents this constant dragging of the College into the news and always over some piece of stupidity.'[10]

While senior staff were faced with problems of allegiances, and students found that the L&H inaugural was banned, a sense of insecurity hung over the junior staff, who were the ones most affected by the University College, Dublin, Bill and its interpretation. 'This is a bloody mess' was Meenan's comment, as it appeared to him that the junior staff were in revolt.[11] Morale within the college had suffered seriously.

The controversy had also proved a huge distraction from academic pursuits. A commentary in the *Leader* on 18 June 1960 hoped that there would be no more washing of dirty linen in public and that academic peace would reign once more within UCD. It called also for 'a powerful example of unashamed intellectuality.' What was wanted from our universities, and sorely needed, was the advancement and diffusion of knowledge through research and scholarly publications, not news of personal controversies and factions. And it called for a gigantic movement of scholarly inspiration where dedication, arduous and total, to the essential task would dissolve lesser difficulties. 'When we hear of learning and truth as the sacred cause which absorbs them we shall know that there is an end to the distressing news that has saddened all of us in recent times.' From London in July, Professor Dudley Edwards noted: 'After the stress of UCD politics, and the emergence of fairly clear evidence that sweet reason will in future be the ostentatious policy, one can look forward to creative work once more ...'[12]

The college had endured other losses as a result of the controversy. Because of the legal issues raised by those who claimed that the college was acting *ultra vires,* Roy Geary had not accepted the college professorship of econometrics. Those in college who had supported the visitation in the first instance might well respond to the charge that their action had prevented such developments by claiming that what had been gained was 'public respect for Law, the maintenance of the University's authority in the Colleges, and freedom of opinion within the College.'[13] And these, it may be conceded, were 'matters of the greatest consequence,'[14] however abstract they may have appeared to the college lecturers and assistant lecturers at the centre of the row. In the matter of any practical improvement in their situation, the junior staff were no worse but scarcely any better off as a result of the University College, Dublin, Act.

As far as the protagonists were concerned, there were no winners here either. The administrators had been publicly humiliated, and some of the mud thrown at Dr Tierney stuck. The president had clearly been through a period of great stress, and the question was asked widely throughout college whether he was on the point of resigning. Diarists like Meenan and Edwards, though they also raised the question, felt that, through great courage or blind stubbornness, it was not in Tierney's character to do so. It had been speculated that an outsider like Cearbhall Ó Dálaigh might have replaced Tierney in the event of his resignation.

Professor O'Meara was later to feel that for his part in the affair he had been made to suffer in a number of petty ways. Nor did the affair improve his chances of being again a member of the Governing Body, or being elected dean, or of succeeding Tierney in the presidency four years later. Perhaps it was just as well that John Kenny, who had been praised extensively in Dáil Éireann for his courage in bringing the petition forward, was made a judge shortly afterwards; otherwise his career in UCD was likely to have been as frustrated as O'Meara's.

It is interesting that the people behind the request for a visitation were graduates of UCD; the three judges on the board of visitors were graduates of the university; many of the critics in the Dáil and Seanad (such as Richie

Ryan, Brian Lenihan, and Eoin Ryan), as well as those in Convocation, were graduates of UCD. So too was the minister who introduced the University College, Dublin, Bill. At one level all of this only emphasised the dominance of UCD's graduates in the life of the nation. At another level, the fact that the leading critics were UCD graduates emphasised the fact that the college, through its graduates, had come of age and was no longer psychologically insecure or defensive. This was indicative of the generation gap that existed between those who were born before and after independence, those who had experienced the struggle to establish the National University and those who were secure in its consolidation. On the one hand there were those like McGilligan and Dillon in the Dáil, or Quinlan in the Seanad, who saw in some of UCD's critics an attempt to undermine the Catholic university system that had been so laboriously achieved after so long a struggle; this point cut no ice with those younger graduates of UCD who agreed with Sheehy Skeffington's dismissal of McGilligan's references to those who were 'traditionally opposed to higher education for Irish Catholics' as 'balderdash'.

The younger graduates were no longer concerned with the alleged besmirching of the Catholic University and had matured enough to be critical of the manner in which they perceived their alma mater was being run. It would be far too simplistic, therefore, to speculate that the visitation controversy was some kind of subliminal struggle between the devotees of the Catholic University and of the National University. There was, however, a germ of truth in the speculation, since the older concept of a Catholic ethos for the college was being gradually replaced, or at least losing its force to a more secular one.

In other ways also the visitation controversy reflected a society that was changing. Michael Tierney, like John Charles McQuaid, represented an Ireland that had existed at least up to the end of the nineteen-fifties. It was a society in which for the great majority the hierarchy represented God, and the church was dominant and infallible. Authority and obedience were laws of God and Nature. But underneath the surface the structures of society were quaking, and the old certitudes were showing signs of crumbling. As it happened, people who perhaps in their own way were equally autocratic and wilful became the voices of the undercurrents seeking change. A Noel Browne (a Catholic graduate of Trinity College), a John O'Meara (a former Jesuit seminarian), a Roger McHugh (an old Republican)—each in his very different way spoke for the disaffected with an abundance of contemporary liberalism in their words but not without traces of that same arrogance and authoritarianism to which they, as the voices of dissent, had raised objection.

The visitation controversy acted in some ways as a catalyst. It aroused in the public an interest in university affairs greater than any since the agitation that preceded the establishment of the NUI in 1908. It encouraged public opinion to welcome the Commission on Higher Education. The experience deepened the resolve of the UCD administration to seek independent university status. It conditioned Government ministers to think of interference in university structures and organisation without consulting the universities. And it helped a later Minister for Education come to the decision to announce unilaterally a proposal for the merger of UCD and Trinity.

The controversy of 1960 set the stage, if not directly the agenda, for the most agitated decade in university education. All the major issues in third-level education during the sixties—the commission, the merger, the 'Gentle Revolution' of the students—might well have arisen had there never been a visitation and the subsequent controversy. But they would have taken place in a very different atmosphere and in a different spirit. The visitation, far from being trivial, left a major imprint on the university and affected some of the wider issues of the sixties, such as the role the university was expected to play in changing the structure of society.

TIERNEY, THE L&H, AND STUDENT CRITICS

The relationship between Dr Tierney and the L&H was a stormy one, occasionally reaching even gale force, as during the row over the banning of the debate on the Communist Manifesto in 1949. A more prolonged storm occurred during the years 1959–1961, coinciding with Tierney's visitation troubles, which were not altogether unconnected with the behaviour of the L&H. In this brief but hectic period the L&H provided what amounted to an open forum for students to articulate the grievances they felt they had with the Tierney administration. The society became in effect the spearhead of the attack on the president by his student critics.

Some of its officers and members were deeply involved in a whole series of wrangles with Dr Tierney. As will be seen, it was they who instigated the Palles Library complaint; they attempted to change the constitution of the L&H in order to remove the president as president of the society *ex officio*; they joined in the criticism of his most cherished policy, the move to Belfield; they clashed with the authorities over the disciplining of a student and the subsequent banning of the inaugural meetings of two college societies; they gave vigorous backing to Convocation's censure of the UCD administration; and they eagerly solicited participation in the affairs of the L&H by those members of the academic staff who had been most closely associated with the visitation. None of this was calculated to lead to easier relations between the L&H and the college administrators.

The law library of Chief Baron Palles, consisting of 2,169 books, had been bought by Dr Walsh, Archbishop of Dublin, and transferred to UCD under a deed of trust in 1920. The deed provided that UCD would give this library a special and suitable place in the college and keep and maintain it distinct from all other books, and that the books would be embossed with a distinctive stamp bearing the words *Chief Baron Palles Library, UCD.*

The immense pressure on space in the years before the move to Belfield had forced the college into all sorts of makeshift arrangements. During 1958/59 the Library reconstruction plan involved the transfer of the History Library and the Law Library, formerly housed in the Council Chambers, to new premises, named O'Curry Hall and Coffey Hall.[15] Because of these accommodation difficulties the Palles Law Library was dispersed. The books in use were kept together in the stacks at the back of O'Curry Hall; those less frequently used were kept in the stock room underneath the hall; the law reports and other volumes rarely required were kept in bookcases in the Great Hall.

Early in 1959 the Commissioners of Charitable Donations and Bequests received a complaint from three law students that the terms of the trust under which the Palles Library had been donated to the college were being violated by this dispersal. The college solicitor applied to the commissioners to vary the terms of the trust; if this were not possible the president wished to abandon the trust and return the books to the legal representative of the late Archbishop Walsh. The commissioners made no decision on the application but referred the matter to the Attorney-General.

The Attorney-General asked for a meeting with college representatives to see whether proceedings might be avoided. As a result of a meeting with the secretary of the college, the Attorney-General expressed his satisfaction with the temporary arrangements. The complainants then protested to the Governing Body that the unity of the Palles Library, guaranteed by the terms of the deed of trust, had 'completely disappeared,' that these arrangements were 'a gross violation of the Deed of Trust,' and that if steps were not taken to rectify the breach of trust the matter would be referred to the courts.[16]

The Governing Body set up a sub-committee of three (Judge Walsh, James Meenan, and the secretary) to interview the Attorney-General and the commissioners in order to expedite the settlement of the matter. At first the sub-committee had recommended that the Palles Library be rehoused on a raised balcony at the end of O'Curry Hall. The Librarian, Ellen Power, was unwilling to do this, on the grounds that she required the space for office purposes and that she considered the floor would not be strong enough to support the weight of the books. Though the professor of architecture advised that the floor would support the volumes if carefully arranged, Power had her way. The outcome was that it was decided to keep all the books belonging to the trust in glass bookcases at the side of O'Curry Hall. The books would be accessible to students through the normal procedure of filling up a docket.

Legal advice confirmed that this would be sufficient to satisfy the terms of the trust.

The three students who had been the complainants—Michael Hogan, Dermot Bouchier-Hayes, and Aidan Browne—were also active members of the L&H. Bouchier-Hayes was auditor from May 1960 to May 1961, and he and Browne appeared to have had something of a partnership in operation at meetings of the L&H. The Palles Library row, which had started early in 1959 and only ended in December 1960, was in a certain sense the student parallel to the visitation. In both cases it was claimed that the college authorities had not kept within the legal obligations imposed on them. Just as members of the academic staff found a legal spearhead to use against the president in the visitation, so did these students in the L&H use the Palles Library affair. In their arguments with the authorities, the threat of legal action was to be their ultimate weapon.

In October 1959 Bouchier-Hayes and Browne conducted a campaign in the L&H to remove Dr Tierney as president of the society *ex officio*. When Bouchier-Hayes first called on Tierney to resign, the minutes of the meeting recorded that 'this effort was abortive.'[17] At the next ordinary meeting of the society Charles Lysaght 'talked somewhat irrelevantly about a person called Tierney and some law books called the Palles bequest. He saw some rather esoteric relations between the two.'[18] Then, at the request of twelve members, an extraordinary meeting was called to change an article in the constitution to read that the president of the society 'shall be elected in the same manner as the vice-presidents.' Speaking to this motion, which was introduced by his friend Browne, Bouchier-Hayes, in the words of the record secretary, presented 'an awful indictment of Dr Tierney.'

The motion was considered by some not to be in the best interests of the society, and because of the uproar the auditor adjourned the extraordinary meeting for a week.[19] When the motion was put at the adjourned meeting the voting—fifteen for, twelve against, and two abstentions—was not enough to change the constitution, and the motion was lost.[20]

A short time later the L&H opposed Dr Tierney on a matter that was very close to his heart: the Belfield project. First (on 21 November 1959) the society debated the motion 'that Belfield is beyond the Pale.' At a subsequent meeting the motion 'that this house welcomes the Tuairim memorandum concerning Belfield' was carried 'by an overwhelming majority.' Bouchier-Hayes and Browne spoke at both meetings.[21]

During the spring and early summer of 1960 the adverse publicity for Tierney resulting from the report of the visitors, and the subsequent motion of censure by Convocation, provided his L&H critics with ample opportunity for further attacks on his regime. Only a few days after he had been elected auditor of the L&H, Bouchier-Hayes called at the office of the secretary on 2 June 1960 and requested permission to inspect the Statutes. He explained to MacHale that he wished to inform himself on several points in them, as he intended making a speech that night at the meeting of Convocation (the meeting that would pass a vote of censure on the college administration). The secretary informed him that he was not entitled to inspect the Statutes, that inspection was a concession to be granted or refused by the college authorities. Bouchier-Hayes argued that he had a legal right to inspect them, since on entering the college he had signed an undertaking to be bound by the Statutes and since a printed regulation for students in the Calendar required him to observe them. He assumed therefore that the secretary was acting in 'a completely capricious manner' and beyond his true authority; he therefore requested the Governing Body, in a letter dated 2 June 1960, to instruct the secretary to make the Statutes available to him.[22]

MacHale referred this letter to the college solicitor, who advised that a graduate or student was entitled to have made known to him the Statutes of the college only in so far as they affected him. It was proposed to excerpt these sections and to make them available to any student who wished to inspect them, and Bouchier-Hayes was advised to this effect. Bouchier-Hayes did not inspect the extracts but gave notice that he had instructed his solicitor — Michael Hogan, his friend and ally in the Palles Library complaint, who at the meeting of Convocation on 2 June 1960 had pressed the motion of censure on the administration of UCD — to take legal action within one week unless all Statutes were made available to him. In the event, no legal action materialised; but the role that some members and former members of the L&H played in Convocation's censure of his administration did nothing to endear the society to the president.

STUDENT DISCIPLINE

Peter Donnelly, a third-year arts student and successful speaker at debates of the L&H, was also the editor of an SRC publication, the *Student*, in whose issue of February–March 1960 there appeared a short story written by himself. 'The Tyres of Life' described the scene in a transport café frequented only by long-distance drivers and a couple of prostitutes. One of these drivers, deaf and dumb and a loner, followed a teasing fifteen-year-old girl out of the café; she led him into an alleyway, where he strangled her. There were no pornographic details in the sparse narrative, and to a later generation the story might seem innocuous enough; but in the moral atmosphere of 1960 a story for a Catholic Irish student readership that so much as mentioned 'whores', nude calendars, a sexy smile, dirty laughter, a waitress who looked as if she were hiding a barrel under her dress (with the hint that her employer might have made her pregnant) and a sex crime in an alleyway was altogether too daring.

The committee of discipline that investigated the matter consisted of the president, the registrar, the dean of arts, and the dean of residence. The president, as a backbench TD, had played a critical role in the discussions that gave rise to the Censorship of Publications Act (1929); and, as a senator, he had also been deeply involved in the censorship debates in the Seanad in the early forties. He was always more concerned with pornographic newspapers and periodicals than with the banning of books. The registrar, Jeremiah Hogan, was himself a member of the Censorship Appeals Board (1954–1967). The dean of arts was J. J. Tierney, and the dean of residence was Father Patrick Tuohy. The composition of the committee was quite normal. Nobody commented on the interests and experience of Tierney and Hogan in censorship, or on the presence of a priest: this too was natural enough for the UCD of 1960.

The committee interviewed Donnelly on 11 March 1960 and decided that he should be excluded from all the premises of the college until the end of term (25 March); on receiving from the student an apology and an undertaking not to write again in any student publication of the college it would consider whether he be permitted to attend the following term and enter for the BA examination.[23] The Academic Council later confirmed the decision.

On 12 March the L&H discussed the suspension of Donnelly and set up a sub-committee of young law graduates—Hugh O'Flaherty (later a Supreme Court judge), Peter Nugent (later, when a Benedictine, headmaster of Glenstal), Richard Johnson (later a High Court judge), Dermot Bouchier-Hayes, and the auditor, Brian McSwiney—to inquire into the suspension and to submit a recommendation to an extraordinary meeting of the society. Dermot Ryan, a former auditor who chaired the meeting, suggested informing the press, the Council of Civil Liberties, and Tuairim—all of them to be reckoned among Michael Tierney's enemies.[24]

When the report of this sub-committee was being discussed, Bouchier-Hayes said that the facts of the case provided material for a successful legal action (this was at least his third proposal of legal action against the college in two years). Richard Johnson claimed they were dealing with illogical people. Having outlined the developments that resulted in the penalties imposed on the student, the L&H sub-committee in its report submitted that the action of the committee of discipline purporting to pass sentence three days before the meeting of the Academic Council was irregular and improper. It also held that the penalty imposed was onerous, unreasonable, and unfair, having regard to the implied threat of permanent expulsion if the student did not apologise and undertake never to write again for undergraduate publications. The report

Over-crowding in Earlsfort Terrace in the late 1950s.

The Gentle Revolution: John Feeney addresses students in the Great Hall.
(*The Irish Times*)

'The Minister for Education presents Dr Michael Tierney with a shoehorn to enable him to get another four or five hundred students into UCD.'

Cartoons from *Dublin Opinion* in the late 1950s.

'We may have to abandon our first Chemistry course — somebody broke the beaker.'

JOD.

Pierce Purcell, Professor of Civil Engineering (1909–53), one of the people foremost in the acquisition of the Belfield property.

Some of the properties acquired for the Belfield project: Woodview, (*above*), Whiteoaks (now University Lodge) (*left*). Next page (*from top*) Belfield House, Ardmore and Merville.

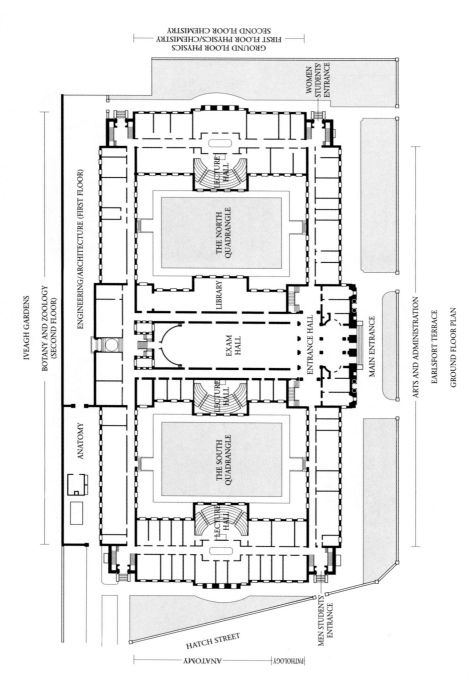

The intended development of Earlsfort Terrace (simplified) as designed by R.M. Butler, 1912.

GROUND FLOOR PHYSICS
FIRST FLOOR PHYSICS/CHEMISTRY
SECOND FLOOR CHEMISTRY

WOMEN STUDENTS' ENTRANCE

IVEAGH GARDENS

BOTANY AND ZOOLOGY (SECOND FLOOR)

ENGINEERING/ARCHITECTURE (FIRST FLOOR)

THE NORTH QUADRANGLE

LECTURE HALL

LIBRARY

EXAM HALL

ENTRANCE HALL

MAIN ENTRANCE

ARTS AND ADMINISTRATION

EARLSFORT TERRACE

GROUND FLOOR PLAN

ANATOMY

LECTURE HALL

THE SOUTH QUADRANGLE

LECTURE HALL

MEN STUDENTS' ENTRANCE

HATCH STREET

ANATOMY

PATHOLOGY

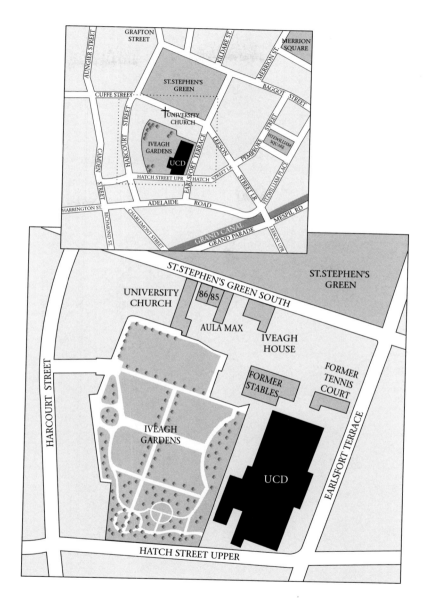

In the 1940s UCD had hoped to extend into some of the property which Lord Iveagh had donated to the State.

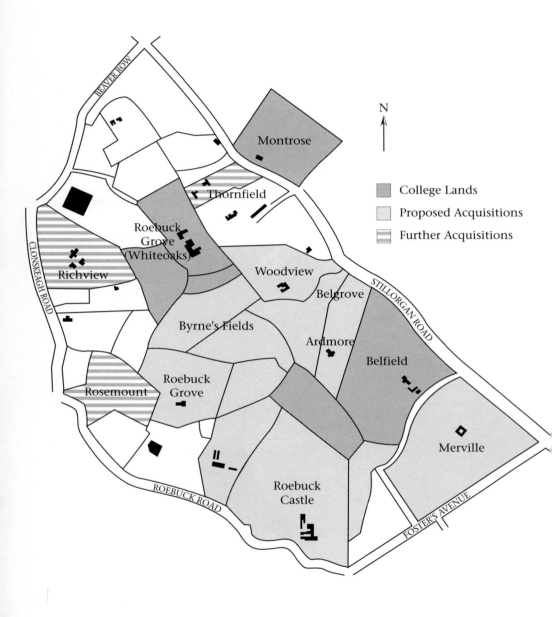

N

College Lands

Proposed Acquisitions

Further Acquisitions

Montrose

Thornfield

Roebuck Grove (Whiteoaks)

Richview

Woodview

Belgrove

Byrne's Fields

Ardmore

Belfield

Rosemount

Roebuck Grove

Merville

Roebuck Castle

BEAVER ROW

CLONSKEAGH ROAD

STILLORGAN ROAD

ROEBUCK ROAD

FOSTER'S AVENUE

In 1949 Michael Tierney sent this map to the Taoiseach indicating the properties already in the possession of the College and those which it was hoped to acquire. Montrose was exchanged for Ardmore in 1957.

then recommended that the following resolution be passed:

> That this Society approves of the findings of the special sub-committee. It deeply regrets the action of all concerned in the suspension of a member of this Society. It is deeply disturbed at the procedure adopted in suspending the member. It further regrets the summary manner in which a matter of such great importance to the individual concerned was disposed of by the Academic Council. It is deeply concerned at the severity of the sentence imposed upon the member, having regard to all the circumstances of the case.[25]

The report was adopted by twelve votes, with one abstention. Though it was by no means a well-attended meeting, at least when the vote was taken the resolution still amounted to a censuring of the Academic Council by the L&H.

This was not to be tolerated by the college authorities. A statement from the registrar's office said that, because the L&H purported to censure a disciplinary action by the Academic Council, permission to hold its inaugural meeting in the current session was being withheld. Permission for the inaugural meeting of the English Literary Society was being withheld for the same reason. The newspaper reporting the 'banning' of the two inaugurals also stated that the suspended student had since apologised and was now back in college.[26]

The L&H responded to the prohibition of its inaugural by calling an extraordinary meeting of former auditors outside the college, in a hotel. Fourteen former auditors attended this meeting and decided to send a deputation to the college authorities. But they were unsuccessful.

The auditor reported to the next meeting of the L&H that he had been informed that if the society passed any resolutions on the matter, certain consequences would follow. He pointed out that the inaugural was 'prohibited', not 'banned'. This nice distinction was presumably meant to convey that the college's withholding of permission was to be interpreted as a penalty for insubordination in not accepting the ruling of a committee of discipline: it was not to be seen as the banning of the topic or of the invited speakers. The subject chosen for the auditor's inaugural paper was 'Samuel Beckett'. According to his widow, Owen Sheehy Skeffington was invited to be a guest speaker, and she claimed that the inaugural was banned because of this.[27] It is understandable, in view of the banning of the Communist Manifesto debate in 1949, that Sheehy Skeffington might have assumed that he was, for a second time, the cause of a ban on an L&H meeting, but there is no evidence whatever, either from student or college sources, that the prohibition arose for any reason other than the issue of discipline.

The auditor told the meeting that he had decided not to hold the inaugural. Various suggestions were then made from the floor: that the inaugural address be printed, at the expense of the society; or that it be read in the guise of a lecture outside the college. Others thought that acts of defiance at this stage would be foolish, that they should not jeopardise the chances of future students having the benefit of the L&H, and that they should back down with dignity and live to fight another day.

Richard Johnson repeated a point he had made at a meeting two months earlier, that the society was 'fighting against a power that knew no reason' and that they should take decisive and vigorous action to strike while the iron was red. The report of Johnson's speech continued: 'He gave us an ultimatum to live in Hell or University College, Dublin, with Michael Tierney at its head: the answer for the former was almost unanimous.' Johnson's view was supported by a former active member of the society, Séamus Sorohan (later a prominent senior counsel). He referred to 'the cruel burden under which the Society at present and in the past has had to labour owing to certain well-marked tendencies of the present "Authority".' Sorohan differed with the auditor's decision not to hold the inaugural.

One former auditor, trying to get the meeting to view the immediate issue in perspective, said that friction with the college authorities was 'an annual blister' and that it would be imprudent to mount their high horse.

All this talk about caution, moderation and prudence was very unlike the speeches that would be made only nine years later in 1969 by the Students for Democratic Action, marking the two generations of students a whole world apart. An old radical favourite with the L&H, a former auditor himself, Professor Robin Dudley Edwards, 'seemed to agree with the stand taken by the Auditor.' More surprisingly, Bouchier-Hayes also supported this stand, saying 'it would be disastrous to be headstrong under the present circumstances.'

The auditor responded to the debate by explaining in detail the reasons for his decision 'in a speech charged with reason, eloquence, virility and unselfishness,' and convinced his audience that his decision was a difficult one but made with the good of the society at heart and in accordance with his declaration to uphold the traditions of the society. The minutes reported that the house burst into an avalanche of applause.

If it seemed that the society was being made to eat humble pie, the bitter taste was in large measure relieved by a number of resolutions that were passed at an otherwise tense meeting. One motion introduced by Bouchier-Hayes 'in a moving and passionate tone' stated with heavy irony that the members wished to record their appreciation of Dr Tierney's outstanding service, especially to the society. Without his constant help, continued the motion, the society could not have coped with the phenomenal increase in recent years in the membership. Aidan Browne, 'with a depth of sincerity rarely seen,' besought the society to pass the motion introduced by his friend.

It was carried by a large majority. A second motion also introduced by Bouchier-Hayes, 'that Dr Tierney is the greatest thing in College,' was also passed by a large majority. The meeting concluded with the auditor declaring the motion listed for public debate, 'that little men cast long shadows when the sun is sinking,' to be carried unanimously.[28]

Dr Tierney's most vociferous and articulate critics in the L&H were recent law graduates, some of whom, though no longer students, continued to play an active role in the society's affairs. To deal with them the Academic Council on 22 June 1960 approved the following addition to the regulations for students: 'In order to be eligible for membership or office in a College Society, students must be in attendance at courses for Degrees or post-graduate Diplomas during the tenure of such membership or office. A student whose attendance or progress is very unsatisfactory, may, after warning, be required to retire from his course at any time during the session.'[29]

These changes in the General Regulations were approved by the Governing Body,[30] which, on the president's proposal, also appointed a sub-committee to report on the position of the L&H. Apparently unhappy about the finances of the society, the Governing Body's report specified certain conditions: the subscription to be raised from three shillings to five shillings, and the appointment of a senior treasurer (a former auditor, Tom O'Rourke). The report also suggested that visiting and inaugural speakers should be approved—subject to appeal by the society to the president—by a committee of three former auditors of at least seven years' standing, one of them to be the senior treasurer *ex officio*, one to be nominated by the president, and one to be nominated by the society.

The auditor elected for the session May 1960 to May 1961, Dermot Bouchier-Hayes BCL, who had been for some time a thorn in Tierney's side, interpreted the new regulation and the conditions laid down in the report as an attempt by the college to clip his wings and those of the society. He wrote to the president: 'It was suggested that because of this amended regulation I and some members of the Committee were ineligible to hold office, and that certain members of the Society were ineligible to be members.'[31] He asked for the president's views of the matter. The secretary replied: 'It is not the intention of the College to apply the Regulation which you mention to officers of College Societies who were elected prior to the introduction of the Regulation, and who hold office for part of 1960/61. This was explained by the President at the time that the Regulation was introduced.'[32]

Legal advice once again was taken by the auditor on this correspondence. John Kenny SC—the hero of those opposed to Tierney and shortly to be Mr Justice Kenny—assured the society that the regulations could not be enforced against the society in future. Already, at the end of October and the beginning of November, the auditor had supported the proposal of his friend Browne 'that Mr John Kenny, MA, LLB, is a fit and proper person to be a vice-president of the Society.' It had been carried by 44 to 2, with 2 abstentions. One week later he was elected by 37 votes to 3, with 2 abstentions.

The following week Professor O'Meara was in the chair for the debate on a motion 'that the search for truth has ceased to concern the Irish universities.' Peter Donnelly, the student who had been suspended for his short story, scored highest of the fourteen speakers. By making a fuss of Kenny, by inviting O'Meara to chair a debate, and by providing a platform for Donnelly, the L&H could be seen to be thumbing its nose at Michael Tierney. The honouring of Kenny in particular must have been something in the nature of a red rag to a bull. From then until the end of the session, relations between the president and the society deteriorated to their lowest point ever.[33]

In early 1961 boisterous partying and brawling in a flat used for a time in Leeson Street by the L&H was reported in the press (a member who had been present at a party, Maeve Binchy, asked at the subsequent meeting of the L&H whether the society was running a disorderly house!).[34] A sub-committee of the Governing Body looked into the matter, only to find that the rooms had not been leased in the name of the society, that no funds had been expended on the rent, and that the tenancy had since been terminated by the landlord. The auditor then switched to the attack and held that the regulation requiring officers and members of the society to be students of the college was not legally enforceable and that it had not come before the Academic Council and been passed by the Governing Body in a way similar to a Statute. The auditor was wrong, in that the regulation had indeed come from the Academic Council to the Governing Body, and all the rules in the General Regulations had been passed in the same way. The Governing Body referred the auditor's argument to the Academic Council as a matter of discipline.[35]

A special meeting of the Academic Council was called by the president to consider what disciplinary action should be taken with regard to the L&H Society. He explained that for some time past a sub-committee of the Governing Body had been investigating the affairs of the society, which had shown a tendency for several years to regard itself as independent of college discipline. The auditor had questioned the legality of the rule relating to membership of college societies. Notwithstanding the rule, the auditor had accepted as a candidate for election as auditor a person who was not a registered student (this was probably the auditor's friend and ally Aidan Browne). The constitution of the L&H had provided for appeal to the president from the decision of the auditor; a short while previously, however, the president had been informed that the society had held a special general meeting that had altered the constitution so as to deprive the president of this right. He proposed, therefore, that the proper course to follow was to suspend the society until further notice, and that a sub-committee of the Academic Council (Professors Nevin, Murphy, J. J. Tierney, and Wheeler) be appointed to inquire into the rules and working of the L&H. Two of Tierney's opponents in the visitation, Dr McHugh and Professor Henchy, proposed an amendment that the matter be postponed until a further meeting and that in the meantime legal advice be taken. This amendment was lost on a vote by two against twenty-two, which was the same vote that carried the president's motion.[36]

The removal of the president from the constitution of the L&H had been the culmination of a campaign that had proved abortive when introduced by Bouchier-Hayes and Browne in October and November 1959. The campaign was now reopened more persistently during the auditorship of Bouchier-Hayes. At first he proposed changing an article in the constitution that referred to the President's Gold Medal and substituting the name Society's Gold Medal. He told a meeting of the society that he found the word 'president' 'objectionable, vulgar and obscene.' He argued that 'as the President had declined to pay for the medal and had refused to take the chair at society inaugurals and generally speaking had been anything but a friend to the society ... his name be no longer connected with the medal.' The motion, which was extended to exclude the president altogether from this article of the constitution, was passed unanimously.[37] The final shot in the auditor's campaign against the president was the amending of the constitution to delete the word 'President' and substitute the words 'vice-president of the Society's choosing.'

In the course of the debate the regulation making non-students ineligible for membership was condemned. It was claimed also that the president was non-functional and that the Governing Body was the most 'irrational group of human beans [sic!]' conceivable. The change of the constitution was carried overwhelmingly.[38] 1960/61 had indeed been, in the words of the records secretary, 'an epic session'.

The long summer break between the last meeting of the old session (13 May) and the first meeting of the new session (21 October) allowed for a much-needed cooling off. The sub-committee of the Academic Council met the new auditor (Desmond Green) and reported that they had been impressed 'by his seriousness and his desire to co-operate with the College authorities.'[39] When the society held its next recorded meeting, on 21 October 1961, the auditor, in reply to questions, stated that no conditions had been attached to the society's readmission to the Physics Theatre. Clearly, however, under a new dispensation the L&H had pulled back from the brink. A more normal relationship between the society and the authorities was then resumed. And the laurels that the L&H had earned in 1959 by winning the Observer Mace competition for university debating teams with Owen Dudley Edwards and the Nigerian Godfrey Agbin were to be repeated in 1964 when Anthony Clare and Patrick Cosgrave represented the society. The history of the L&H in the fifties and sixties, as these honours showed, was by no means one of interminable rows with Michael Tierney.

It might be said that Tierney's temporary difficulties with the L&H and his occasional problems with student publications were to a certain extent of his own making, or at least not unrelated to his forceful personality. His deep involvement in politics from the nineteen-twenties to the forties, and his participation in party propaganda and publications, had probably sharpened the natural partisanship of his intellect and dulled the more judicial and calming aspects of the scholar's mind. He had engaged in controversy in the Dáil and Seanad on such explosive issues as censorship and had argued in the journals with people such as Seán Ó Faoláin on Irish culture and O'Connellite democracy and with others on nationalism and the role of Irish in education. It was said of him:

> In most of his dealings he showed himself to be a shrewd countryman, who enjoyed bargaining, manoeuvring, manipulating. He would have been in his element on a fair day at Ballinasloe, in his native County Galway. While he had great natural charm, he could browbeat as well as cajole and persuade. He was a man in a hurry, trying to catch up on the centuries of educational neglect of the mass of the Irish people, in the sphere of higher education, by successive British governments. To cross his path in these circumstances was to invite trouble. He was impatient and even brusque at times with staff, and more often so with students. He aroused opposition but more often evoked admiration and deep loyalty.[40]

He did not take lightly to what he considered indiscipline on the part of students. Discipline in his book, and in the Catholic Ireland of his era, was a virtue. In about 1940 he had compared the discipline of UCD students favourably with that of students of Trinity College. Indiscipline on the part of UCD students was letting the side down. But in the nineteen-sixties old moulds were being broken and Irish society, like the rest of the Western world, was changing perceptibly. America had elected an articulate and comparatively young president, John Kennedy, who had launched the 'New Frontier'. What his political style symbolised for youth all over the world was widely and enthusiastically welcomed. Chairman Mao was leading China into what was called the 'Great Leap Forward'. The British Prime Minister, Harold Macmillan, was telling the 'affluent society' in Britain, 'You've never had it so good,' and the 'wind of change' was how he described the wave of freedom that was sweeping through Africa as Nigeria, Tanzania, Zambia and the Congo became independent.

In Ireland de Valera had at last been replaced by Lemass as Taoiseach in June 1959, and a few months later Richard Mulcahy retired from the leadership of Fine Gael. The retirement of the old Civil War antagonists seemed to open up new vistas in the Kennedy era of youthful leadership and helped to undermine the position of the old guard in UCD—Tierney, McGilligan, Hayes—all of whom were the near-contemporaries of de Valera and Mulcahy and, like them, had contributed to the emergence and building of the new state nearly forty years earlier. Lemass began to lead the country into Whitaker's Programme for Economic Expansion and towards an economic 'mini-miracle'. In women's fashions what was called 'the rising hem and plunging neckline' betokened a more daring attitude to social mores. Phrases of the time from a changing Britain were an indication that similar urges were beginning to affect Ireland. 'Wind of change' was a term that had been used on a couple of occasions by Owen Sheehy Skeffington in the Seanad during the debate on the visitation. In referring to the Tierney regime he and John O'Meara had both employed the contemporary term 'establishment', with all its derogatory connotations.

The students of UCD reflected something of all these changes and aspirations. One of the motions proposed for debate in the L&H session of 1959/60 was 'that we have never had it so good.' That was one aspect of the brave new world that beckoned to them. It would therefore have seemed to some that Michael Tierney was a dinosaur from the age of de Valera and Mulcahy. Some thirty years later one could meet eminent graduates who would still recall their criticisms of the Tierney administration. They thought it amazing that he could still have acted in so illiberal a way in the nineteen-sixties; and to have been involved in a confrontation with him was almost a guarantee that a student was to become prominent in his career in the future. It is not surprising, therefore, that another motion in the session of 1959/60 proclaimed 'that we will look back in anger at UCD.'[41]

Tierney, however, stirred strong feelings of loyalty as well as of hostility and opposition. One is impressed by the number of those among the then junior staff who acknowledged a debt of gratitude to him for his personal interest in their welfare and encouragement in their careers. Tierney's old friend and collaborator over many years and his successor in the presidency, Jeremiah Hogan, in a very honest assessment acknowledged not only his great virtues but also his weaknesses. He stated that Tierney's ability, energy, academic standing and above all courage were all beyond dispute.

Some, however, not altogether without reason, thought him not only energetic and courageous but rash, inclined to speak too strongly and to take up extreme or challenging positions ... He did some things directly that should have been done after consultation and through an impersonal machinery—or not done at all ... He learned patience, though it was never of the wary and inexhaustible kind, disarming opposition, that one associates with D. J. Coffey ... Tierney like Coffey was full of humanity and kindness, and he was much more sociable and less aloof than his great predecessor. He was also much more articulate, which had great advantages but occasional disadvantages too.[42]

BALANCING CRITICISM WITH ACHIEVEMENT

All the criticisms and troubles of the Tierney regime have to be balanced against the substantial achievements and the strides the college was also making in these years. Tierney's commitment to and interest in Irish studies led to the establishment of a flourishing Department and Archive of Irish Folklore. Before his presidency, faculty meetings had been relatively few, brief and insignificant; Tierney presided over all faculty meetings and thus came to have a sympathetic insight into all the academic business and problems of the college. He extended the conferring ceremony by introducing the conferring speech, by which he brought to the notice of graduates, parents and the public the problems of the college. He used it to criticise the Government or to defend the college whenever he felt criticism or defence was needed. He was an effective publicist and had a keen sense of ceremonial for the historic occasion in celebrating important dates in the history of the college, such as the centenaries of Newman's lectures (1952) and of the Catholic University (1954) and the fiftieth anniversary of the NUI (1959).

His presidency saw great developments throughout the college. In Medicine the college and the teaching hospitals were more closely linked, and he insisted on improved standards and facilities for Dentistry. Engineering was extended into separate specialist departments. Courses in Commerce and Law were improved. Agriculture acquired the 1,300-acre Lyons Estate. The Veterinary College was fully incorporated into UCD. Science was given priority in the move to Belfield.

In the physical order, Belfield will of course remain Michael Tierney's greatest monument and fully entitle him to be called UCD's second founder. Student numbers rose from just over three thousand when Tierney was appointed in 1946/47 to almost seven thousand in 1963/64, the year he retired. Staff numbers also increased dramatically, and Tierney took a personal interest in improving staff grades, salaries and incremental scales, pensions, marriage and family allowances, and widows' pensions.

To the academic with the best interests of UCD at heart who had found himself caught in the middle of a war between a strong-willed administration and an equally determined opposition it must have seemed that it was the college's reputation that was being sacrificed. But despite all the din of battle on the surface, solid and even brilliant achievement was taking place in the classrooms and laboratories of individual departments.

In the very thick of the public controversy about the college lectureships, testimony to the real achievements of the college came from a qualified commentator, 'insulated from the emotive factors of being personally involved.' Dr Peter Walsh had been an assistant in classics in UCD (1952–59) and had held a college lectureship for two years before accepting a lectureship in classics at the University of Edinburgh.[43] He was a keen observer and, as an active participant in UCD, peculiarly well placed to assess the situation in the college. He had given tangible evidence of his value as a teacher and researcher during his time in UCD. He was a member of John O'Meara's department and one of that new breed of academic staff from abroad whom Tierney warmly welcomed to the college.

He was by no means uncritical of the college and its administration, but he saw that the fundamental cause of UCD's difficulties lay in the fact that 'within a single generation, a small institute of a few hundred undergraduates had emerged as Ireland's premier university in a technological age.' He realised that it was not only the buildings that had failed to keep pace. The close administration of the thirties, in which every staff appointment and all student activities were closely scrutinised by the president, had also been largely retained into the sixties. He pointed out that staff generally had no rooms, so that effective guidance of students at an individual level barely existed. Nor had academics the facilities of a staff-room in the Library in which to work. He held that greater responsibility in the working of the college should be delegated to the junior staff. No other university in Ireland or Britain received 'such meagre support, both from public funds and from private endowments.' One reason for this in his view was 'a lack of awareness of its achievements, and a destructive scepticism about its stature.'

Yet, he maintained, if compared with universities of similar size elsewhere, the results were by no means unfavourable to UCD. One of the most heartening changes had been the expansion of the Faculty of Agriculture. In the thirty or so years of its existence student numbers had increased from 20 to 332. Almost all these graduates found employment in Ireland. The criticisms that were made of Medicine by the representatives of the American Medical Association in 1953 mentioned inadequate staffing in all departments, lack of control over appointments in teaching hospitals, methods of clinical teaching, and inadequacies in the Pathology Department. Considerable progress had been made with these problems. New departments had been created in Social and Preventive Medicine, Pharmacology, and Microbiology. Arrangements had been drawn up with the teaching hospitals that gave the Governing Body tighter control over medical appointments. When, in 1959, the New York Board of Regents sent representatives to examine Irish medical schools, favourable comment was made on the great improvements since 1953. NUI graduates now compared very favourably with their British and American counterparts, and the UCD Medical School 'is being built up into what is probably the best in Ireland.'

Dealing with the Faculty of Science, Walsh claimed that in Professors Nolan, Nevin and Conway the college had three men of international reputation. Under Professor Wheeler the Department of Chemistry 'produces a great volume of published work.' In UCD more was being achieved in science than in Scottish, Welsh or many Continental universities. The position in UCC and UCG was not so advanced; nor did Trinity College aspire to the same eminence in the scientific field.

The standards in some Arts departments left much to be desired. It was no accident, however, that the History Department was outstanding. In its book purchases and in the recruitment of non-Irish as well as Irish teachers, said Walsh, History had shown an enlightened example to others.[44] What was needed above all was a systematic and constructive interest, and the fostering of pride in UCD's prestige.

Tierney had seemed to thrive on battle. Besides, his dream of bringing Belfield to fruition had kept him going. The strong autocratic tendencies that opponents complained of were the very qualities that ensured his survival under attack, and the success of his Belfield project.

9

Rethinking UCD

THE COMMISSION ON HIGHER EDUCATION

As early as about 1940, looking back over the thirty years since the establishment of the NUI, Michael Tierney had advocated the setting up of a commission to inquire into the whole area of university education. Throughout the nineteen-fifties the calls for such an inquiry had been increasing; by the late fifties a well-organised campaign for the establishment of a university college in Limerick had added to the need for such an inquiry.

A Council of Education, established in 1950, had already been looking into primary and secondary education. It had published its report on the function and curriculum of the primary school in 1954; it then began examining the post-primary level, and its report on the secondary school curriculum was eventually published in 1962. During the visitation controversy the Minister for Education, Dr Patrick Hillery, had spoken on a number of occasions of the intention to appoint a commission on higher education. The one thing that protagonists on both sides agreed on was the need for just such a commission. So, in 1960, when Dr Hillery eventually appointed the Commission on Higher Education, the announcement was widely and enthusiastically welcomed.

At a meeting of the Government on 16 August 1960 the commission's terms of reference were readily agreed. These were:

> To inquire into and to make recommendations in relation to university, professional, technological and higher education generally with special reference to the following:
>
> (a) the general organization and administration of education at these levels;
>
> (b) the nature and extent of the provision to be made for such education;

(c) the machinery for the making of academic and administrative appointments to the staffs of the universities and university colleges; and

(d) the provision of courses of higher education through Irish.

Only one amendment had been made in the wording of the terms of reference as submitted by the Department of Education. In its original form, paragraph (b) above had continued: 'having regard particularly to the avoiding, wherever possible, of duplication.' The Taoiseach did not appreciate the need to include these words. The avoidance of unnecessary duplication, he said, was obviously desirable and would be so seen by the commission; he doubted, therefore, the necessity of giving it the prominence of a special mention, for the words might be interpreted as implying some suggestion about the amalgamation of the University of Dublin and the NUI, or of ruling out consideration of a college in Limerick.[1]

Agreement on the membership proved to be more difficult, and consideration of this was postponed to the next meeting of the Government, on 23 August.

The importance of the question had already exercised many minds. Professor T. Desmond Williams of UCD urged the Taoiseach to secure the services of Herbert Butterfield, Vice-Chancellor of the University of Cambridge and Master of Peterhouse, who had close personal experience of the NUI, Trinity College and Queen's University, Belfast, stretching over the years and had many friends in these institutions (not least his former postgraduate student T. Desmond Williams). Others stressed the need for individual disciplines to have a voice—agriculture and economics in particular. Though civil servants were to be excluded, the minister agreed that the retired secretary of a Government department could be appointed.

The Minister for Health, Seán MacEntee, wrote to Dr Hillery to warn against the danger that Catholic Church interests would dominate the commission unless there was adequate representation of science, industrial economics, and 'the emancipated element among the National graduates.' Of UCD personnel he recommended Frank Winder (a Tuairim activist), Patrick Lynch, and Garret FitzGerald.[2] Hillery replied that he favoured a selection 'on broad lines' but wanted only one person associated with each college; and in any case the practical experience of people in charge of industrial enterprises was 'worth a ton of theory.' The sciences, he thought, would be well represented, but he was personally keen to have Professor Theo Moody of Trinity College, both as a Northerner and as historian of Queen's University, 'undoubtedly by far the best living authority on Irish universities.'[3]

After revisions and additions, a commission of twenty-eight people was eventually nominated, under the chairmanship of Mr Justice Cearbhall Ó Dálaigh of the Supreme Court. The membership included such well-known figures from public life as C. S. Andrews, Chairman of CIE; Lieutenant-General M. J. Costello, General Manager of the Irish Sugar Company; Phyllis Uí Cheallaigh; Dr Juan Greene, President of the NFA; Joseph Griffin, Managing Director of the Irish Glass Bottle Company; Dr J. J. McElligott, Governor of the Central Bank and former Secretary of the Department of Finance; Dr Tom Walsh, Director of An Foras Talúntais; and Martin Cranley, Principal of Kevin Street College of Science and Technology. Among the clergymen on the commission were William Conway, Auxiliary Bishop of Armagh (who resigned in February 1964 following his elevation to the archbishopric), William Philbin, Bishop of Clonfert, and Richard Gordon Perdue, Church of Ireland Bishop of Cork, Cloyne, and Ross. Outside expertise was represented by two distinguished scholars, Professor Herbert Butterfield of the University of Cambridge and Professor Charles Carter, professor of political economy in the University of Manchester.

The universities and colleges were not specifically represented, but distinguished academics were appointed because of their personal standing in higher education: Professor T. W. (Theo) Moody of Trinity College, Professor James Mitchell, Registrar of UCG, Professor J. J. McHenry of UCC, and Professor Edward Keenan, Dean of Medicine in UCD (who died in 1962 and was replaced by Eoin O'Malley of UCD). The membership also included a sprinkling of teachers from primary, secondary and vocational schools.

The members of the commission represented the humanities, the sciences, and many facets of public life. As Dr Hillery reminded them on the occasion of their first meeting (8 November 1960), though several commissions before 1908 had examined the problem of higher education this was the first that was accountable directly and primarily to an independent Irish state.

The distinguished status of the individual members was matched only by the breadth and intensity of the work the commission carried out over the next six years. It held 48 plenary meetings (most of them two-day sittings) and 55 meetings to take oral evidence; there were 21 meetings of working parties or study groups and 77 of the drafting consultative committee; and there were 77 visits to educational institutions, in Ireland and abroad. Not since the Dublin Commission had visited universities in Britain in 1908–09 had there been anything approaching this concentrated study of third-level institutions. The Commission on Higher Education, however, far outdistanced the Dublin Commission by the sheer breadth of the investigation, with visits to many institutions not only in Britain but also in several Continental countries—Belgium, Denmark, Finland, Germany, the Netherlands, Sweden, and Switzerland—together with written information from these and from countries further afield, including the United States and South Africa.

The total number of people and bodies that made written submissions was 245, and 154 witnesses gave oral evidence. The written submissions amounted to approximately 1.1 million words and the oral evidence to an estimated 1.6 million words. The summary of the report and the two volumes of the report proper amounted to 425,000 words. In all, it was a massive piece of work resulting in an impressive report.

Various individuals and bodies within UCD availed themselves of the opportunity to co-operate eagerly with the commission. At first sight it may seem strange that the Governing Body did not itself make any submission. Dr Tierney told the members that he had carefully considered this matter and had come to the conclusion that it would not be possible for the Governing Body as such to make representations to the commission.[4] Instead he had informed the chairman of the commission that 'the Governing Body has decided that I should give evidence on behalf of the College, with such assistance as I may require.'[5] This may appear only too characteristic of the paternalistic way in which the college was allegedly run; but that there was no intention of restricting any submissions from UCD became clear in the rest of Tierney's letter. Not only did he say that he would like to be accompanied to the oral sessions by the registrar and secretary, who could give certain information in greater detail, but he took it that individual members of the Governing Body who might wish to make their own representations would be allowed to do so. He added that it would be advisable also to hear evidence from the heads of the professional and technological faculties and from extern examiners.

True, when the Dean of the Faculty of Veterinary Medicine enclosed for the president a copy of an addendum to the submission that had by then been made to the commission, he added: 'subject of course to your having no objection.'[6] Others (including two members of the staff of the UCD Dental School) requested the opportunity to discuss their memoranda with the president before submitting them to the commission. On the other hand, a copy of the report of the Academic Staff Association (which had been formed at a meeting on 12 December 1960, partly with the immediate intention of representing the views of the staff to the commission) was simply forwarded to the president with the comment that it was probably too long for anyone to read![7] And on an issue such as the breaking up of the federal system in the NUI and the creation of independent universities, the Academic Staff Association (which then numbered 203 members) took the opposite view to that advocated by the president.

At the outset a misunderstanding arose between the chairman of the commission and the President of UCD. Tierney had supposed that oral evidence would be given first, with written submissions in support to follow. Ó Dálaigh wanted written submissions first, to be clarified and elaborated in subsequent oral hearings.[8] Tierney yielded in response to diplomatic urging by a friend of long standing, Professor Aubrey Gwynn SJ, whose judgment he greatly respected. Gwynn, for his part, had been recruited by Dr Tarlach Ó Raifeartaigh, now Secretary of the Department of Education, to persuade Tierney 'that it might be wiser to meet the wishes of the Chairman of the Commission.'[9] The episode was an interesting example of the surgical delicacy needed to prise Michael Tierney out of a preconception.

The commission provided the opportunity to reflect on UCD's experience of fifty years in the NUI system, to take stock of its circumstances, and to outline its vision of the future.[10] Inevitably this involved questions about its relationship not only with UCC and UCG but also with Trinity College. Dr Tierney accordingly submitted five memoranda:

(1) The Two Universities in Dublin
(2) The Autonomy and Legal Position of UCD
(3) UCD and the National University
(4) The Finances of UCD
(5) Professional and Technical Education.

All but number 4, which was prepared by J. P. MacHale, secretary and bursar, were written by Tierney himself, with typical clarity and punch, well illustrated by his comments on professional and technical education. The possibility, then looming, that diplomas equivalent to university degrees might be awarded to engineering and architecture students at colleges of the City of Dublin Vocational Education Committee he regarded as a device for providing 'cheap back-doors into remunerative practice' at the expense of the Dublin ratepayers.[11] On the other hand he had no objections to the legal and medical professional bodies giving practical training to students educated by the universities in theory and fundamental principles—a distinction of the clear-cut kind that Michael Tierney could always make, with his masterful command of reasoning. (The commission was to agree with him on this, but not on his disapproval of degree-status courses in colleges of technology.)

On Trinity College, in his first memorandum and in his oral evidence he repeated much of what he had been arguing for years, as well as points more recently raised to contradict comments by the Provost of Trinity College, Dr A. J. McConnell. Trinity was a Protestant college, Tierney insisted, the greater number of whose students came from outside the Republic. UCD had had in fifty years far more non-Catholics on its staff and Governing Body than Trinity had had Catholics in 350 years. Its then claim to be a national institution was unwarranted propaganda directed at Irish-Americans, while its fund-raising efforts in Britain stressed its character as an outpost of British culture. It was unacceptable that it could be a better university for Irish Catholics than the institution set up expressly for their benefit. Its attempts to lure them were putting unjust pressure on UCD to provide evening diploma courses, which it could ill afford to do and which were tending to lower standards, for example by accepting for higher degrees NUI graduates not qualified to undertake such studies at UCD. The call to have local authority scholarships tenable at Trinity was an assault on a modest system of indirect endowment intended to benefit the colleges of the NUI.

Tierney's trenchant comments on Trinity could be understood in the light of the grinding uphill climb to achieve completion of the fair deal for the national majority that he might consider still a long way from being delivered: he had to make his case, after all, from within the crammed, crowded, crumbling Earlsfort Terrace, where he was increasingly assailed by critics from within and without. There was much truth in what he said, however harshly he said it, and this was acknowledged not only from likely quarters— Archbishop McQuaid, M. J. Costello, the Catholic Headmasters' Association—but, remarkably, in articles in English newspapers, the *Observer* (11 March 1962) and the *Times* (22 May 1962). (In the *Times,* Trinity was described as one of 'John Bull's outposts,' a playground 'where wealthy English students pass their time in comfortable idleness.')

More significantly, Professor T. Desmond Williams, wrote to Tierney: 'An important person on the Commission told me yesterday that the UCD President's performance before the Commission was commanding, masterly, full of ease and genial, to the point of making others seem very small indeed.'[12] Those who knew Desmond Williams would readily agree that to him by far the most important person on the commission was his old supervisor and friend, the Vice-Chancellor of the University of Cambridge, Herbert Butterfield.

There was much that was valid in Tierney's argument; but it was not the whole picture. What he missed, or misunderstood, was how the complexion of Trinity had been changing since 1945 and more recently at an accelerated pace under Dr McConnell. Student numbers were being increased, the proportion of foreign students was being reduced; younger people were being introduced to the top administrative posts in what has been described as a 'palace revolution', and these were determined that Trinity College should play a role in Irish society. Among those spearheading the new emphasis was the widely respected professor of modern history, T. W. Moody, whose writings on Thomas Davis might be described as the first full blast of nationalism emanating from Trinity since the establishment of the Irish state. Another graphic signal of change was the appointment in 1956 of Máirtín Ó Cadhain, author of the celebrated novel *Cré na Cille,* as lecturer in Modern Irish. These and other developments enabled the provost, in his oral evidence, to assert that the college was 'very anxious to integrate itself into the national life' and that it was 'an Irish institution' with 'an Irish atmosphere.' Relations with UCC, UCG and Maynooth were 'excellent', as were relations between corresponding departments in Trinity and UCD. 'Unfortunately,' he said, 'relations are not nearly as good at the top.' He regretted the ban on Catholic attendance: 'I do not want Trinity College to be regarded as a Protestant institution for Protestant students; I want it to be a university for all Irishmen.'[13]

This fitted in well not only with the prevailing Davis-type nationalism (by contrast with the O'Connellite version favoured by Tierney) but also with the state's attitude towards Trinity College. Governments committed to ending partition were anxious to show that the Protestant minority and its institutions would have no need to fear discrimination in a united Ireland. Already, since 1947, an annual grant was being made to Trinity College; and it did the college no harm that McConnell was a friend of de Valera (their friendship was said to be based on a common interest in solving mathematical problems). Dr Ó Raifeartaigh, as Secretary of the Department of Education, assured the commission that the state had no particular attitude to Trinity more than towards any other university college; and his minister told the Dáil that each of the four university colleges had its own appropriate part to play in the building of the nation.[14]

The commission was to reflect considerable sympathy with this view, readily accepting the wish of Trinity College to integrate itself into the life of the country, recognising its honourable place in the history of European learning and its liberal tradition as a valuable part of the Irish inheritance. It therefore set itself against making any recommendation that might undermine the status of Trinity College—as it might have been led to do if it followed the logic of further submissions by Dr Tierney, with which it found itself basically in agreement. These were the submissions on the legal position of UCD and its relations with the other colleges in the NUI federal system.

Pointing out that UCD had grown to be as big as Trinity College, UCC and UCD together, and that so large a college in Britain would long ago have been made a university in its own right, Tierney argued against its continued involvement in the NUI. A cumbersome constitution and the duplication of administrative work made for friction between the colleges. The inability of UCD to institute its own professorships was ludicrous when Queen's in Belfast could do so even though it was only half the size of the Dublin college. The NUI system of appointments to chairs was complicated and inappropriate. The uniformity of standards, allegedly achieved through the engagement of common extern examiners, was of necessity more honoured in the breach than in the observance. The procedure known as visitation was antiquated and had been applied to the college in an unfair and publicly embarrassing manner. In short, the NUI should be disbanded and each college raised to full university status; or at the least UCD should be so raised and given the autonomy without which it could not function as it should.

It was a cogent argument. It clearly impressed the commission, which in its report was to reject the case made by UCG, UCC and the Academic Staff Association of UCD for the continuance of federation: it recommended instead the chartering of all the colleges as separate universities. But Michael Tierney's case went further. Contrary to what would afterwards be reported, he did not advise that Trinity College should be closed down; but he did stress what he considered the wasteful anomaly of two universities in Dublin. This he emphasised also in his comments on technical and professional education, where the division of one veterinary college between two universities went some distance towards making his argument for him. Ideally, he thought that UCD and Trinity College should be brought together in a new University of Dublin, 'located at Belfield'; and to the writer of the *Observer* article 'he speculated about Trinity providing the liberal arts and the divinity faculties for a combined university.' At any such plan the commission baulked. On the one hand, it would undermine Trinity in precisely the way against which the commission had set its face; on the other hand, it found that all the arguments that had convinced it of the need to release UCD from federation were scarcely less strong when considering whether it should be tied to another.

The commission therefore recommended decisively that the NUI be dissolved and its three constituent colleges be established as separate and independent universities. But it concluded, equally decisively: 'Our recommendations leave two universities in Dublin.' It was not to be the last word on the possibility of a Dublin merger.

THE MERGER

The question came dramatically to a head shortly after the commission published its report on 22 March 1967. Michael Tierney was already three years into his retirement, having been succeeded as President of UCD by his friend and supporter Dr Jeremiah Hogan. It was Hogan who had called a special meeting of the Governing Body for the afternoon of 18 April to consider the commission's report. No other business was to be taken.

Dr Hogan had intended to put forward a paper that might express the general response of the Governing Body to the summary report recommending the dissolution of the NUI and the establishment of UCD as an independent university. That morning, however, he had been called at short notice to meet the Minister for Education, Donogh O'Malley. The minister informed him that a decision had been taken by the Government that there was to be one university in Dublin, with two constituent colleges, UCD and

Trinity. He said that Hogan would receive from him by 2:30 p.m. a copy of the statement he would make to the press in the afternoon.

Ten minutes before the start of the Governing Body meeting the president received the minister's statement; and since he had not yet read it himself he asked the secretary to read it to the meeting.

The statement began by saying that everyone, the minister thought, would agree that 'the university situation in Dublin is far from being satisfactory.' In the capital city of a small country there were to all intents and purposes two separate university institutions, each going its own way, without any sharing by them of scarce national resources. The state, he said, could not be expected to continue 'to subsidise any avoidable duplication of university services.' The Government was already inescapably committed to high expenditure with regard to UCD's move to Belfield. In addition, Trinity College was now seeking a grant of almost £2½ million for new buildings (including £812,000 for a new Engineering Building and £740,000 for the first of two Arts Blocks). He reprimanded Trinity for the decision to expand in buildings and in numbers at a time when it still had over 1,200 non-Irish students, out of a total of 3,327. Though strongly in favour of a leavening of non-Irish students, he considered that it was unhealthy that there should be any large block of them, especially from a country (Britain) that was already developed.

He recognised that 'our present university set-up is a legacy of history — and history is a stubborn wrestler.' Because of the competing claims of the two Dublin colleges he had come to the conclusion that the solution to the problem in Dublin was 'a joining of forces with a view to the obviating of all unnecessary duplication.' He had formally brought the matter before the Government in December 1966, with a view to exploring 'how best to rationalise the university position in Dublin.' Despite the urgency, the Government decided to await the views of the commission. But now that the minister himself had seen the larger part of the report proper (before publication) he was not prepared to accept the commission's recommendation that the two colleges should continue as entirely independent entities. The public interest demanded the establishment of a formal relationship between the two institutions, and the Government had authorised him to proceed on the lines of his proposals of December 1966. These proposals were framed on the basis of there being 'one University of Dublin, to contain two colleges, each complementary to the other.'

The minister stated that the moment of announcing this decision was not without its solemnity. 'It marks the end of an era in the long story of university education in Ireland and also, it seems to me, in the history of the country itself.' Glancing back over the famous names associated with Trinity

College, O'Malley wrote: 'Trinity is not going to pass away. It will merely be taking the final step across the threshold of that mansion to which it properly belongs, the Irish nation.' He could not help thinking that it was 'a pity that when in 1908 an opportunity occurred for Trinity to enter the new university complex which was then being established here, she was guilty of what might be termed the Great Refusal.'[15] The present moment, he felt, was a most auspicious one for a reversal of the 1908 decision. Clearly it was time to try to rationalise the position whereby, for instance, the state had to pay UCD £160,000 annually and Trinity £86,000 towards the support of two distinct veterinary faculties, producing about forty-five and ten graduates, respectively. Would it not be well if these two faculties could be merged in a single institution?

Finally, he explained that the new University of Dublin would not be 'neutral' denominationally but 'multi-denominational'. There would be provision for both Catholic and Protestant schools of divinity and theology.

Despite the length of the minister's statement, it is important to emphasise that only the bare principle had been stated: one university and two colleges, complementary to each other. The statement was remarkably short on detail about how this was to be implemented. The minister frankly admitted that he had treated largely of the economic reasons behind this decision. His promise of providing multi-denominational schools of divinity and theology in place of non-denominational neutrality was a clever appeal for the support of the bishops and for their reconsideration of the ban on Catholics attending Trinity.

To the public and to the two colleges concerned, the announcement of the joining of UCD and Trinity College in one University of Dublin was a bombshell. But every bit as surprising in its own way was the Governing Body's amazingly rapid answer, on the same day, to a very complex question. It issued a text in which it agreed with the minister that 'the existence of two teaching universities in Dublin is the cause of much wasteful duplication and that it is necessary to bring this to an end.' But it went radically further than the minister's proposal of one university and two colleges and declared that 'the benefits sought by the Minister would be best achieved by a complete unification of the two institutions.'

This, at first sight, seems remarkable, since the UCD authorities had for some time been pressing for independent university status for the college. The Commission on Higher Education, accepting the force of these arguments as presented by Michael Tierney, had proposed just such independence for UCD as one of its central recommendations. Here now was the spectacle of UCD, which had recently argued for independence and had received the blessing of the commission's recommendation in favour of that independence, proposing, quite consciously and emphatically, its own extinction.

The apparent *volte face* merits close examination. Even more remarkable was the fact that the President of UCD, Jeremiah Hogan, had prepared for the special meeting of the Governing Body (before receiving notice of the minister's announcement) a statement in favour of the complete unification of UCD and Trinity College. The statement he had prepared in response to the presentation and summary report of the commission was re-drafted at the Governing Body meeting in the light of the minister's statement. But essentially the original draft prepared by the president and the re-drafting done at the Governing Body meeting were identical from the viewpoint of the ideas expressed, with only the wording adapted to the new circumstances.

The original statement said that the considerable changes in the structures of UCD and Trinity College recommended by the commission would cause much disturbance in the working of the institutions concerned, without 'any promise of the advantages which might accrue from a more thorough and radical procedure.' It went on to criticise the commission's report along lines that had emerged in some of the reservations (those of Costello and McElligott in particular) and in the newspapers, saying: 'Though aware that the existence of two teaching universities in Dublin is the cause of much costly duplication, the Commission proposes no effective remedy for this. It is plain however that if the duplication continues it must become increasingly harmful to both institutions and to the country. Public criticism of the recommendations has already settled on this point.'[16]

A long-standing complaint of Michael Tierney's then surfaced in a reference to Trinity's use of the title University of Dublin. The commission's recommendation, said Hogan's text, had not made available to UCD in its proposed university status 'a proper and natural title corresponding to those which will be assumed at once by the new universities in Cork and Galway.' It would seem in fact that Tierney before his retirement,[17] and certainly Jeremiah Hogan and others since then, had been considering a new relationship with Trinity College and the University of Dublin. In an article in *Studies* on the minister's merger proposals the Secretary and Bursar of UCD, J. P. MacHale, referring to the apparent rapidity with which UCD responded to the minister, argued that it had to be remembered that the report of the commission had been awaited for six years; that there was widespread disappointment when no concrete proposals for the rationalisation of the university situation in Dublin had been included in the report; and that 'during all this time the problem of university education in Dublin, and its possible solution, was very much in the minds of individual members of the Governing Body and many of them had decided that anything short of complete unification would not be a long-term solution.'[18]

To those who worked closely with Hogan the solution he advocated in his statement to the Governing Body came, therefore, as no surprise.

We believe that the time has come when the Dublin university question, now more than a century old, should be finally settled by the foundation of a new University of Dublin, in which the separate identity of the two existing institutions would completely disappear, and which would pool all their resources, intellectual, material, and financial, under a single authority. We believe that this can be done with good will on all sides and without injustice to anyone, and that it would be productive of very great benefits to higher education and to all the interests of the country.

He concluded by saying that UCD, as the largest university institution in the Republic, was prepared 'to do everything possible towards this end.'[19]

In support of his own solution, Dr Hogan was able to argue that the federal link between the two Dublin colleges now proposed had been considered and rejected by the Commission on Higher Education. It was also claimed that every federal university in Britain had been defederalised. The Governing Body's re-draft of the president's statement significantly omitted his criticism of the commission for not facing up to the problems created by the existence of the two university institutions in Dublin, and for leaving the proposed independent UCD nameless. During the discussion on the president's draft the point was made that the Governing Body's statement should be 'framed towards securing co-operation.' No doubt it was for this reason, and to avoid reminding Trinity College of what could be a very sensitive issue, namely the danger of the smaller unit being swallowed up by the larger, that all references to UCD being by far the biggest university institution in the country were also omitted. Otherwise the press statement from the Governing Body was essentially the same as the original draft prepared by Dr Hogan.

Of the twenty-seven people present at this meeting of the Governing Body, only four voted against issuing any policy statement. They would have acknowledged the minister's announcement and merely said that the Governing Body, when it had an adequate opportunity of considering it, would issue a statement. Mr Justice Walsh, who urged this procedure most strongly, argued that they could scarcely be expected in one afternoon to assent to a proposal either by the minister or by the college that the college, as they knew it, should cease to exist. When the motion not to issue a statement was defeated, only three voted against the statement as re-drafted by the president.

INITIAL REACTION

The celebratory note with which the public greeted the minister's announcement was epitomised in the headline in the *Irish Times* on 19 April 1967: 'TCD and UCD to be united: O'Malley announces wedding plans.' A briefing of political and educational journalists by the minister revealed something more of the Government's objectives than had been contained in the 3,000-word official statement. This had emphasised the economic benefits of the proposed union of the two colleges. In talking to the correspondents about the statement, the minister implied that the Government's objectives were political or social as much as economic. The proposal, he said, would put an end to 'a most insidious form of partition on our own doorstep' — the present division between Trinity College and UCD. He added that he had 'neither sought nor obtained' from the Catholic hierarchy any agreement that the ban on Catholic students attending Trinity would be removed. Ominously, from the point of view of the unitary solution for which UCD's Governing Body had opted, he said that the total fusion of the two existing institutions would be 'an appallingly bad decision' and that each of them would run the risk of losing its separate identity. In the words of the *Irish Times* correspondent, the minister appeared to be in 'a cheerful, confident, shoot-first-and-ask-questions-afterwards mood.'

The newspapers also carried the full text of the statement issued by the Governing Body of UCD and the personal statement of the Provost of Trinity College. The provost said that for many years Trinity had expressed a desire for closer co-operation with other university institutions and that the college would look at the minister's plans with the utmost sympathy. They would be anxious, however, that the great traditions of Trinity and of UCD would continue, and he was glad to see that the minister proposed that they should be preserved. Anyone reading closely the statements of the Governing Body and the provost could detect serious differences in emphasis and foresee huge problems ahead.

The public enthusiasm for the principle of a single University of Dublin showed how dramatically the atmosphere of receptiveness had evolved during the previous decade. In March 1958 Professor John O'Meara of UCD in a public lecture had suggested a union of UCD and Trinity College,[20] but the suggestion had been firmly rejected by the then Catholic primate, Cardinal John D'Alton, who saw it as 'an attempt at a union of incompatibles.'[21] Since then Dr Tierney had insisted to the Commission on Higher Education that the most important matter it had to consider was the question of the two colleges in Dublin. More recently another UCD professor, Denis Donoghue, speaking to Trinity College Elizabethan Society in January 1967, had said he could think of 'no more welcome development in university education than that Trinity and UCD should be united.'[22] It was known also that Dr David Thornley of Trinity College, active as honorary secretary of the Irish Federation of University Teachers, was sympathetic to the idea.

This kind of thinking among academics had clearly influenced the political parties. Fine Gael, in its educational policy statement of 28 November 1966, was already on record as calling for 'a close co-ordination of university facilities in Dublin.' Notwithstanding the contrary opinion of the Commission on Higher Education, the O'Malley proposal had issued from a Fianna Fáil Government. It was warmly approved by the Labour Party leader, Brendan Corish.[23] And a joint statement from the Students' Representative Councils of Trinity College and UCD had welcomed the move towards rationalisation.

More surprising, perhaps, was the favourable response from episcopal quarters. Bishop Lucey of Cork said that 'the amalgamation of the two universities will put an end to a lot of historical troubles.'[24] Cardinal Conway thought the plan 'contained a number of good ideas and ... could mark a positive step towards a rationalisation of the situation in all its aspects.'[25] The tone of these remarks gave grounds for believing that the ban on Trinity might well be reconsidered in the light of the proposed new University of Dublin, a move that would sit well with the new spirit of ecumenism generated by the Second Vatican Council.

The editorial in the *Irish Times* of 19 April 1967, while strongly commending the proposal, expressed worry over the statement of the Governing Body of UCD. 'Unification into one college could only be seen by TCD as a complete take-over by Earlsfort Terrace.' Within a week (on 26 April) the paper's Trinity correspondent was reporting the development of a siege mentality among staff and students, while the UCD correspondent simultaneously recorded considerable understanding of Trinity's fears on the part of many UCD staff.

These fears could be detected in the statement from the Board of Trinity College eight days after the minister's announcement. It welcomed the idea of 'a single University of Dublin with constituent colleges' but stressed that 'the traditions of scholarship associated with the names of Trinity College and of University College' had to be continued in the new situation. This emphasis on the continuity of the colleges and their traditions was the very opposite of the view of UCD's Governing Body, which had proposed that 'the separate identity of the two existing institutions would completely disappear.'[26]

Of course much of the problem relating to emphasis and interpretation lay in the wording of the minister's announcement. There was to be 'one University of Dublin, to contain two colleges, each complementary to the other.' The UCD authorities chose to interpret this statement as tending logically towards one University of Dublin with two colleges—each doing very different work. This interpretation seemed to be implied in such phrases as the 'complementary allocation' of the faculties and the 'coalescence' of staff, the 'obviating of all unnecessary duplication,' the need to 'rationalise the university position in Dublin,' and the economies to be expected from the elimination of 'competing claims.' Some understood UCD's interpretation of the minister's words to mean the 'rather harsh dichotomy' between the work to be undertaken in each college.[27] Other and apparently quite contradictory phrases in the minister's announcement—such as 'there will still be some overlapping,' 'Trinity is not going to pass away,' 'the two Colleges would be founded on the two existing institutions,' and 'in the matter of the identity of each College the feeling of the existing authorities will be given the utmost weight'—provided some solace for Trinity.

The ambiguities only reflected the complexities and difficulties involved in any attempt to merge two colleges with proud and different traditions under one strong university authority established on a democratic basis like that of UCD's Governing Body, with two subsidiary authorities similarly constituted for the governance of each college. There was an inherent contradiction in the minister's proposal. He could not have a new, powerful University of Dublin with two colleges that were 'complementary' to each other and at the same time retain in any real position of strength the two very different traditions. In the circumstances, a single university and two colleges was almost a contradiction in terms. It was possible, of course, for the minister and the Government to leap either in the direction of the UCD or of the Trinity interpretation. As a matter of fact, however, he had little choice. Trinity College, much more than UCD, had to be wooed and assuaged: the Trinity authorities were being told that they would have to share their University of Dublin with their old rivals; they were going to lose their privilege of self-perpetuating government and be opened up to more democratic forms, with the possible addition of Government appointees and public representatives; they were informed that they could no longer expect state subsidies for the large number of non-Irish students, or building grants for avoidable duplication of university services. Furthermore, the political parties (Fianna Fáil, the Labour Party and, eventually, Fine Gael, after initially wavering towards the UCD line), determined to show their tolerance of minorities, were eager to declare their concern that Trinity's wishes and traditions should be respected. As the political correspondent of the *Irish Times* reported (21 April 1967), 'there is a keen interest among many deputies in preserving Trinity as "a bastion of radicalism", fearlessness and an island where even the most unorthodox views can be expressed and heard with a Liberal calm.' This paper was certainly following its traditional line of safeguarding Trinity's interests.

Apart from all the reporting and commentary on the minister's statement in the daily and Sunday newspapers, the merger provoked possibly the first really serious, informed and widespread debate in the media on the university question since 1908. In what became a long-running story, every national newspaper and journal had worthwhile things to say in editorials and commissioned articles. During one week alone in May, for example, the *Irish*

Independent published a series of four commissioned articles by academics.

From the beginning of the controversy the contributions by UCD academics revealed wide divisions within the college. The anonymous 'National University correspondent' in the *Sunday Independent* (23 April 1967), Garret FitzGerald in the *Irish Times* (26 April 1967), Maurice Kennedy at an Academic Staff Association seminar (13 May 1967) and John O'Meara in the *Irish Independent* (15 May 1967) were all, in different ways, opposed to the Governing Body's proposal. And, not surprisingly, Michael Tierney in the *Irish Ecclesiastical Record* (May 1967) supported the Governing Body's recommendation: after all, he was probably, with his friends Hogan and MacHale, its inspiration. As the 'National University correspondent' stressed, the choice lay between the minister's one university with two colleges and the Governing Body's one university with one college.

O'Meara, on the other hand, came out positively in favour of the idea that each college in the university would contain among its students a cross-section of all faculties. It all added up, he wrote, 'to continued teaching of both Arts and Sciences in both UCD and TCD.'[28] Professor Maurice Kennedy (later Registrar of UCD) in his paper to the ASA, though strongly critical of Government intervention, was equally positive in favour of the two-college solution. 'I suggest that we should try to formulate with TCD tolerable proposals for a University of Dublin with two colleges maintaining their individuality and traditions by means of strong governing bodies, that is to say, governing bodies with considerable powers.'[29]

The most comprehensive public consideration of the minister's statement was published in *Studies* (summer 1967), which carried a total of fifteen articles devoted to the issue. J. P. MacHale and Basil Chubb (professor of political science in Trinity College) both declared that they expressed only their own personal views, but there was no doubt that each elaborated on the official statements that had been issued by the Governing Body of UCD and the Board of Trinity College, respectively.

Interestingly, perhaps the most useful recognition of Trinity's anxieties came from two of the UCD contributors to the symposium. Professor Eoin O'Malley wrote that a rough-and-ready summary of MacHale's case was that UCD 'take over the whole show.'[30] Denis Donoghue claimed that a most encouraging sign was that many of the teachers in both colleges, especially the younger ones, 'do not want to see Trinity absorbed by University College. They do not think it likely, on the other hand, that UCD will be absorbed by Trinity.'[31] Thornley, in his role as honorary secretary of IFUT and for other reasons, had many contacts with the academics referred to by Donoghue. In urging the minister to 'set his face firmly against this total merger' Thornley advised him that, 'notwithstanding the statement of the UCD Governing Body, he is supported here by substantial numbers of the staff of UCD.'[32]

The debate within UCD

Meanwhile, inside UCD there began the prolonged and detailed consideration of the merger proposal that was to involve every section of the academic staff. When the Governing Body next met, on 9 May 1967, the president, noting that the Governing Body's statement had been described as 'a take-over bid', said that on the whole he thought it had been seen as it had been intended: as an offer by the college to give up everything if a really satisfactory solution of the university problem in Dublin could be obtained.

The president, the registrar (Dr Thomas Murphy), the secretary, Professor Thomas Nevin and Professor James Meenan were appointed by the Governing Body as UCD's team for any negotiations with the Minister for Education and Trinity College that might ensue. The three college officers met the minister on 11 May 1967 in the hope of learning more precisely what his ideas and his immediate practical proposals were. As for the Governing Body's own initial proposals, Professor Nevin later put it: 'The Minister made it clear that the Government was not prepared to accept one integrated university, that there would have to be one University and two colleges, each separate legal entities with, in general terms, each faculty on one campus or the other.'[33]

When a report of the meeting with the minister was made to the Governing Body on 1 June 1967 it was further stated that the university was to be strong and the colleges weak. The university, it was understood, would control all teaching and research and the buildings then owned by the colleges. Its governing authority would be composed of, say, ten representatives from each of the existing colleges and ten Government representatives. There would be only one of each faculty. The colleges would administer the hostels, restaurants, clubs, and societies. At the interview the minister had requested each college to prepare a memorandum, and also expressed the wish to meet members of the Governing Body of UCD and the Board of Trinity College so as to elaborate his proposals.

At the same meeting on 1 June the minister gave an address to the Governing Body, which he also read to the Board of Trinity College on 7 June. He said that the Government had given the fullest consideration to the two possible solutions—total assimilation of the two colleges or his own plan—and that it had decided firmly on the latter. While he acknowledged that the former solution had the attraction of simplicity, it would also entail the loss of identity for the colleges, which would be a throwing away of traditions whose disappearance the nation could not afford. Where the UCD officers understood from the minister's first announcement and from the interview they had had with him that 'complementary' colleges meant the allocation of whole faculties to one or other institution, the minister's address to the Governing Body showed that he was less rigid than their interpretation on this issue. His description of the new university now carried the additional significant phrase 'as far as possible.' It now read: 'two colleges as far as possible complementary but without the loss of identity of either ...' And while he stated that the university would decide in which college particular faculties might be based, he also added that a certain duplication might be necessary, in the light of numbers and accommodation. Neither college would be allowed to become the 'Oxford of Ireland' with the other as the 'red-brick university'. Each college would have 'a good spread of disciplines,' and 'teaching in some subjects at all levels' would be given in both. Due regard would have to be given to the views of the existing colleges, but 'at first sight' the larger faculties of Arts and Science might be assigned to UCD and the smaller professional faculties—Medicine, Dentistry, Veterinary Medicine, Agriculture, Law, Architecture, Commerce, and Business Management— could go to Trinity. But how exactly 'the Faculties would merge' was a matter for detailed working out through the 'fullest consultation'. He requested that the matter be approached in a big-hearted way, on the basis that there would no longer be a question of 'we' and 'they', but that both sides cast their eyes ahead to a position in which they would think only of 'we of the University of Dublin.'

A couple of weeks after the minister's address (22 June 1967) the Governing Body met to consider a draft memorandum, rapidly prepared by the president (with the assistance of the other officers and Professor Nevin). All, he said, were agreed on the creation of a single university; but the preservation of the colleges in considerable strength was now insisted on by the minister. The draft was an attempt to find a middle way between the unitary university and two colleges that otherwise would really be two separate universities; it was based on the strict division of departments and faculties between the two colleges, so that they would be complementary to each other in the sense of each being in sole possession of a faculty that the other lacked. The resultant fusion of staff within each faculty would be the real unification process on which the single university would be based.

The president's scheme was opposed by other members of the Governing Body—notably Patrick Lynch, Garret FitzGerald, and John O'Donnell (chemical engineering), with Máirín Uí Dhálaigh (wife of Mr Justice Cearbhall Ó Dálaigh) and Bryan Alton backing them. They argued in favour of Arts and Science being retained in both colleges, to preserve the identity and character of their traditions. They wanted a balanced academic organism and pointed to the danger of the two institutions becoming polarised, one into a liberal arts college and the other into a technical institute, if the existing colleges were dismembered along rigid faculty lines. James Meenan, observing that the minister's proposal was less drastic than they had originally thought, also expressed reservations about division along strict faculty lines, since he believed that this would be a loss of true academic character.

A further meeting of the Governing Body on 29 June 1967 revealed so much division of opinion regarding the draft memorandum that the matter had to be postponed until October. In the meantime the president proposed holding discussions with the faculties and with the junior staff. But tension was growing. Two members of the Governing Body, T. Desmond Williams and John O'Donnell, agreed reluctantly to withdraw a motion they had intended putting to a meeting of the Academic Staff Association that Dr Hogan was to address.[34] This would have supported the Governing Body dissidents by declaring that each college should retain a wide range of faculties, especially the principal arts and science subjects.

When the president spoke to the professors and junior staff after the summer holiday there was an element of stage-management: the same motion, sponsored by the president, was proposed at eight separate meetings. It said that the professorial staff were 'prepared to explore the principle of unified Departments and Faculties in one college or the other.' Only in the small Law Faculty was it not carried. But in Arts a second motion was also passed, that 'the Faculty further resolves to investigate other possible solutions to the University Question.' Both Arts resolutions were carried unanimously at a meeting of the Academic Council on 20 October, but at the Governing Body on 31 October a consolidated version of the Academic Council resolutions, proposed by O'Meara and seconded by Meenan, passed by a vote of only fifteen to nine—possibly because by then it was seen that skilful management on the part of the president and his team had put him in a position to tell the minister that UCD was prepared to negotiate on the basis of unified faculties, even though this contradicted the view publicly expressed by many of UCD's leading academics.

Dr Garret FitzGerald in his autobiography has related how a certain group of nine (no doubt dubbed a 'clique' by those not included) used to gather in his house before meetings of the Governing Body with a view to concerting tactics.[35] Among them were Desmond Williams and John O'Donnell; three of the Government appointees, Dr Éamon de Valera, Mr Justice Brian Walsh, and Máirín Uí Dhálaigh; and Patrick Lynch and Bryan Alton, who had been elected with FitzGerald from the graduate panel on a 'reform' platform. This list identifies eight of the nine who voted against the president's resolution in the Governing Body; they were also the eight who signed the so-called minority report, which they transmitted to the minister. Dr FitzGerald in his autobiography says: 'This action was denounced as disloyal. We were told that there simply could not be such a thing as a minority report from the Governing Body: that only the majority view could be expressed.'[36] The minutes of the Governing Body, however, record that the president did not think there need be any objection to such a proceeding, since the minister had said that he would like to know the views of minorities. It is true that the president objected to the use of the term 'minority report', on the grounds that the Governing Body was not a commission set up by the Government to report to a minister but rather a statutory body to govern the college, and that those who voted against any particular resolution had to accept the decision of the Governing Body as a whole.[37]

NEGOTIATIONS WITH TRINITY COLLEGE

The UCD and Trinity negotiators entered into a series of meetings, beginning on 10 November 1967 and continuing until 17 February, which were presided over by the minister's appointee, Dr Tarlach Ó Raifeartaigh.

The UCD representatives put forward the principle of united faculties and departments, to be in one college or the other. The Trinity College representatives responded that the minister was prepared to allow duplication where it was unavoidable, and emphasised the preservation of the identity of their institution, which, they said, required a wide range of subjects. They wished to work on 'areas of study' and not on the principle of faculties.

The first Trinity College plan, on this basis, was circulated at the meeting of 9 December 1967. It suggested a division that would assign nine subject groups—history, geography, Irish, English, French, economics, business studies, mathematics, and statistics—to each college, to be taught to equal numbers of students. All other subject groups would be assigned solely to one college or the other.

The UCD response to this first Trinity plan was to see it as incompatible with the Government decision and to quote all those references in the minister's two papers (the statement of 18 April and the June address to the Governing Body of UCD and the Board of Trinity College) to division along faculty lines, including his own suggestion about which faculties might be assigned to each. It argued that the Trinity memorandum reduced the decision to an emphasis on the two colleges retaining their identity.

The UCD negotiators drafted a memorandum, submitted on 8 January 1968, that examined critically the Trinity plan and claimed that it split science from top to bottom and restricted the choice in combining subjects for the BA. The memo outlined UCD's own plan, which followed the minister's suggested allocation along faculty lines: UCD to be allocated arts, science, agriculture, engineering and architecture, and Trinity to be allocated medicine, dentistry, veterinary medicine, law, commerce and social science. Service teaching required for these faculties in arts subjects was not seen to present a serious problem. Beyond this, however, the UCD plan also conceded a limited exception to the principle of single faculties in allowing for a small range of arts teaching to be done in Trinity—for example in social science (which was part of the Arts Faculty in UCD), and perhaps in some other arts group—provided the general principles of the merger were accepted and any duplication kept small. The fusion and transfer of staff along faculty lines was seen by UCD to be fundamental and the very essence of the merger. The Governing Body's initial proposal of one university with one college had been dropped, at the minister's insistence; but in proposing a division along strict faculty lines it could be said that the UCD negotiators had not really moved off the original Governing Body scheme. It was largely the old concept in more acceptable garb—perhaps, even, the old wolf in sheep's clothing.

The greatest sacrifice UCD was being asked to make, as its negotiators stated in their memorandum, was that of a full university with all its faculties at Belfield. 'The case for a complete university on a single adequate site was made with unanswerable force by the Commission on Accommodation Needs, 1958.' Having its faculties in several different places, UCD was keenly aware of the disadvantages of such separation. In its comments on the Trinity plan for two colleges equal in numbers, the UCD memorandum maintained that such equality was 'surely more than the present capacity ... and perhaps beyond the potentiality' of the College Green site.[38]

The Trinity representatives said that no solution would be acceptable that did not provide for substantial arts teaching in and by their college. They also reported that in an expert survey prepared by Professor Myles Wright of the University of Liverpool their site had been found to be adequate for a multiple-faculty university of at least six thousand students.

The UCD representatives accepted an invitation to visit Trinity College and have the development plans explained to them. As a result of this visit the president, in a letter to the chairman of the negotiations, suggested the possibility of placing the whole of arts alone at Trinity College.[39] This proposal, together with Trinity plan II and UCD's comments on it, were considered at subsequent meetings, where the UCD representatives said that if any other faculty were added to arts in Trinity it should be law rather than social science. In putting forward this solution the UCD negotiators said they now thought it the best and most permanent. Arts and law in the old and monumental buildings, and the newer faculties on larger and out-of-town sites, they argued, was now almost the norm where universities had to be divided.

Trinity plan II qualified and altered in some respects the college's first plan, but it remained staunchly opposed to the UCD 'faculties' proposal. The Trinity representatives concurred with the IFUT report of September 1967 and quoted from it, saying that 'each College should contain an adequate range of Arts, Science and professional subjects, without which it would not be possible for either College to provide the nucleus of a real academic community or to retain what is valuable in its identity and traditions.'[40] From this principle Trinity College did not budge. Neither did UCD budge from its own position regarding whole-faculty transfer. The UCD representatives criticised Trinity plan II on the grounds that the presence of even a limited arts or science faculty in whichever college must make the whole arrangement unstable, because it would be argued that without some subjects a faculty would be incomplete and there would inevitably be an urge to duplicate.

Arising out of this impasse it was agreed at meetings on 8 and 17 February that the UCD and Trinity plans, together with seven other documents relating to the negotiations, should be referred to both colleges for consideration.

While the negotiations at official level between the two colleges were running into difficulties, opposition to the idea of any kind of merger had been hardening during the summer among the academics of both UCD and Trinity. Indications of this opposition had already appeared at the ASA seminar held in Belfield on 13 May 1967. There Dr Eoin O'Malley had argued that the commission's recommendation of four independent universities following defederation of the NUI represented the most natural evolution from the present position. At the same seminar the most firmly entrenched conservative view was aired in a paper by Professor Maurice Kennedy. He paid tribute to the 1908 arrangement, which, he said, had allowed the work of higher education to be carried on without stress. He found it frightening to think how the commission, a body appointed by the Government, could so easily be bypassed. He was worried that rationalisation might be decided on behind closed doors in the civil service, and he was disheartened 'to see such ready acquiescence by academics and indeed by the general public' to proposals whose details were not known.

Following a general meeting of the Academic Staff Association on 27 June 1967 a sub-committee was appointed to consider the merger proposals. A report based on the work of this sub-committee was considered at two further general meetings (30 November and 8 December 1967), and a memorandum was ready for presentation to the minister and the Governing Body dated 22 January 1968. This stated that the ASA was 'in no way committed to the view that the best solution to the university problem in Dublin is offered by the establishment of one university with two colleges.' Taking the minister's proposal as a working hypothesis, the memo's principal recommendation was that at least major arts and science subjects should be retained in both colleges. This was approved by a large majority of the ASA. Apart from this, it recommended that the professional schools should be merged and each school be established in one or other college, and that collaboration at undergraduate level and organisation at postgraduate level should be ensured. These were approved without dissent.

Clearly there was strong opposition within the ASA to the idea of a merger with Trinity College; but if the minister's proposal was going to be imposed it could be inferred that the ASA inclined more towards the Trinity plan than towards that of the Governing Body. This was also the line that had been adopted in the IFUT report of September 1967.

So matters stood in February 1968 when the UCD and Trinity plans, together with the documents that had emanated from the negotiations, were referred to the various academic bodies within the colleges.[41]

While these documents were being considered during the first half of March 1968, the hardening of the opposition to the merger became more apparent. The Faculty of Arts voted overwhelmingly (27 to 6) against all the merger proposals put before it. Perhaps rather surprisingly, in view of the ASA memo, it voted 33 to 0 against the Trinity plan. The smallest faculty, Law, also voted against the proposals. The Faculties of Engineering, Medicine and Science all used the same formula, resolving that 'the Faculty regrets that neither of the plans would give UCD what it has long worked and hoped for—a complete University on a single site.'[42] Since, however, they had been asked by the Government to consider the merger, they preferred the UCD to the Trinity plan. Commerce believed that it should be sited with Arts, otherwise it too preferred the UCD plan, as did Veterinary Medicine and Agriculture. At a meeting of college lecturers and assistant lecturers, who were not members of the faculties, a clear majority voted against both plans and, if they had to accept one, favoured the UCD scheme. By the time the junior staff had voted it was known that the Trinity College staff were also opposed to both plans.

At the Academic Council, 25 voted that neither plan was acceptable, 31 voted for a merger, and there were 4 abstentions. If the choice were only between the UCD and Trinity plans the voting was 37 to 0 for UCD; but the fact that there were 23 abstentions in that vote indicated a fairly determined opposition to any merger. Finally, when the Governing Body met on 19 March 1968 the voting showed that sixteen preferred the UCD plan and none the Trinity plan, and the nine who abstained had it recorded that they regarded neither plan as acceptable.

Though the president tried to make much of the fact that the UCD plan was overwhelmingly preferred to that of Trinity, the writing was on the wall as far as the merger was concerned.[43] On the day the Governing Body met to consider the reports from the various college bodies on the merger plans the first item of business was a vote of condolence with the widow and family of Donogh O'Malley. The author of the merger had died; it remained for his successor, Brian Lenihan, to ensure that the merger had not died with him.

THE LENIHAN SCHEME

In March 1968 the Governing Body (with one abstention) had authorised its representatives to resume negotiations on the terms of the original brief. Nothing further happened, however, until 5 July 1968, when the president was called to the Department of Education and given a copy of what became known, after its publication in the press the following day, as the sixth of July plan or the Lenihan plan. It stated that the Government had decided in principle to accept certain of the basic recommendations of the Commission on Higher Education: (1) that the National University of Ireland be dissolved and that University College, Cork, and University College, Galway, be constituted as separate universities, and (2) that a permanent authority be established to deal with the financial and organisational problems of higher education. Referring to the 'decision to join University College, Dublin, and Trinity College in a reconstituted University of Dublin,' the statement said that the Government had examined fully 'the final proposals' of the Governing Bodies of the two colleges, together with the various other proposals submitted, and had decided that the most suitable allocation of faculties would be as follows: arts and science, including mathematics and statistics, to be provided in both colleges; the main centre for experimental sciences (i.e. physical sciences) to be UCD and for the biological sciences to be Trinity College; law, medicine, veterinary medicine, dentistry, pharmacy and physiotherapy to be based entirely in Trinity College; engineering, architecture, commerce, social science and agriculture to be based in UCD. It was envisaged that St Patrick's College, Maynooth, as an associate college, would be in a position to play the fullest part in the teaching of theology.[44]

The reaction from UCD differed dramatically from that which had greeted the O'Malley scheme a year earlier. The Lenihan scheme from first to last was met with angry, determined hostility. Throughout July special meetings of various faculties considered the minister's statement. Medicine, Engineering and Architecture, Science, Arts and Law all registered their disapproval of the new proposals, as did the president in a conferring address on 16 July, when he said that in place of the new university promised by O'Malley there was now to be a 'reconstituted University of Dublin'. The Academic Staff Association issued a statement on 19 July reiterating its position that it was in no way committed to the view that the establishment of one university was the answer to the problem in Dublin. The interests of higher education in Ireland, it said, 'will best be served by four independent and closely co-operating universities.'

Lenihan went ahead the following month to set up the Higher Education Authority, as recommended by the commission, and said that its interim assignment would be to advise him on the legislation required to implement the decisions announced on 6 July—i.e. the Lenihan 'merger' plan. This sparked an acrimonious correspondence between the President of UCD and the minister, with Hogan complaining that UCD's views were being disregarded and Lenihan asserting that 'the Government's decision to have one university in Dublin is a final one.' The president responded by labelling the Lenihan scheme 'a pure and simple diktat' that abandoned 'the vital complementary principle' in various ways, including the provision for Faculties of Arts and Science in both colleges. The new plan, he claimed, was essentially what had been sought by the Board of Trinity College in its statement of 4 May 1968. The minister held to his position and advised the president to concentrate on placing before the HEA any views he might have on the form that legislation might take.

All this correspondence, together with the resolutions of the faculties, was considered by the Academic Council on 11 October 1968. It declared that it could not see in the minister's plan of 6 July 'a workable basis for a single university. The Council notes that a strong preference has developed among the teaching staff for four independent co-operating universities. The Council believes that, unless a satisfactory solution on the basis of one university in Dublin can even now be put forward, the four universities plan is that which will best serve the interests of higher education in Ireland.'

It could be said that the resolution of the Academic Council represented a synthesis of two schools of thought, one that considered four independent universities (two in Dublin, one each in Cork and Galway) to be the best solution and another that thought this second-best to a satisfactory scheme of a single university in Dublin based on the principle of complementarity. This was, as Professor Meenan said, as near to a unanimous decision as could ever be got, and the motion was passed unanimously by the Governing Body.

The resolution looked, perhaps, in two directions. But with this formula, which consolidated opinion in college on the one hand and was cleverly tactical on the other, the UCD negotiators were going to make contact with the HEA and give it the college's view of the unacceptable July scheme.

The Lenihan scheme had had the result of healing the divisions within the Governing Body, or at least of uniting in opposition to the scheme the two camps that had emerged. To an overwhelming extent, the rest of the college was also united in opposition, and there was mounting resistance among the teaching staff in Trinity to any form of merger. That the opposition was not confined to UCD is evident from a statement signed by 467 members of the teaching staff of the NUI colleges and Trinity College that was published in the newspapers on 21 September 1968. The signatories said that they felt it their duty to express their conviction that the development of higher education could best be served by a system of four or more co-operating universities. The Academic Staff Association on 4 November 1968 urged the minister to amend the terms of reference of the Higher Education Authority so as to provide for consideration of the reorganisation of university education on this basis.

By now the Government's enterprise in announcing the creation of one University of Dublin was slipping from its grasp, and the initiative was being resumed by the universities. There was the increasing conviction in the Governing Body that the Government would not force its decision on a college that stood four-square against the proposed allocation of faculties. There was the growing confidence among the negotiators that the HEA would not recommend to the minister a scheme, or any part of a scheme, that they were convinced was not viable or, on balance, was likely to be more damaging than beneficial to higher education.

With all this backing and encouragement, Dr Hogan and his team of negotiators enthusiastically accepted the minister's challenge. They kept up the momentum against the Lenihan scheme and brought the battle into the HEA. What personally equipped Hogan most of all for this battle was the patience that he exhibited in abundance at all his meetings and his capacity for the hard work involved in the writing of several memoranda.

FURTHER NEGOTIATIONS

The UCD negotiating team met the HEA on 13 November 1968. (D. K. O'Donovan, Dean of the Faculty of Medicine, had replaced the registrar, Dr Thomas Murphy, who had been appointed to the HEA, as had Patrick Lynch, another member of the Governing Body.) It emerged at this meeting that the HEA was not sure whether it was confined to considering the mode of implementation of the July plan or whether it could listen to arguments on the merits of the plan and the possibility of its being replaced. A letter of 15 November 1968 from the president seeking clarification on this point elicited a cleverly ambiguous reply from the chairman of the HEA, Dr Ó Raifeartaigh.[45] It stated succinctly that the HEA was working on its interim assignment: the formulation of legislative proposals on the basis of the Government's decision of 6 July; but it was also very happy to understand that it could look forward to further discussions with UCD.

This reply was interpreted as meaning that the UCD team would be free to discuss the whole question. It was welcomed by the president, because he thought that convincing the authority was one of the best possibilities before them. The authority continued its work on the assumption that there was to be one University of Dublin, with two colleges. The UCD negotiators, while being prepared to discuss the more specific questions related to the legislative measure required (for it was still assumed that some new institutions would be created), were also critically discussing the merits of the Government's proposal.

While these meetings between UCD and the HEA were taking place, Dr

Hogan turned to the Senate of the NUI for assistance in UCD's hour of need. Remarkably, the NUI, which it was proposed to abolish, had not been involved at all up to this point in any discussions about the merger. Following Dr Hogan's initiative it agreed that 'the Senate of the National University has an obligation to make its attitude known with regard to the changes proposed in the university system and should have the right to have its views fully considered by the Government.'[46]

At the request of the NUI a meeting took place on 6 February 1969 between a deputation from its Senate and the Taoiseach, Jack Lynch, who was accompanied by the Minister for Education, Brian Lenihan. The deputation argued that the NUI should not be dissolved until all the constituent colleges were satisfied with the arrangements made for them, and that the proposals for UCD in the July plan were the main obstacle to the supercession of the university by any new institution. Dr Michael D. McCarthy, the President of UCC, said he favoured a complete union of the two Dublin colleges but that what was now proposed was unworkable. The Taoiseach replied (according to the report given to the Governing Body on 29 April 1969 by Dr Hogan) that a complete merger was 'politically impossible, as it would be held to be unfair to Trinity College.' Lynch admitted that a strong case had been made to the HEA by the UCD deputation but confirmed that the HEA was not free to widen the terms laid down by the Government, and he asked the deputation not to press him on the point.

The President of UCD was full of appreciation for 'the extremely loyal help' that had been given to UCD by the presidents and professors of UCC and UCG on this deputation: 'they had put the case for Dublin as well as its own representatives could have done and probably all the more effectively.' This was undoubtedly one of those occasions when being a constituent of the NUI was of advantage to UCD and served as an antidote to the irritable restrictions that were felt to be imposed by the federal system. The Taoiseach had received the deputation 'in a very open and friendly way.' The president wrote to him on 1 April: 'Your open and sympathetic attitude gave me great hope.' The result of the meeting was interpreted as strengthening the negotiating position of the college with the HEA.

The NUI representatives met the HEA on 27 May 1969 and repeated the case they had already put to the Taoiseach. This was one of those meetings that began with tough words being spoken on both sides and, after the exchanges had cooled down, ended in a more amicable manner. The Presidents of UCC and UCG spoke 'very forcibly' on behalf of UCD. There was 'strong resistance' among members of the HEA to the points outlined by the NUI delegation. In the view of the President of UCD, as reported to the Governing Body, a majority opinion was forming in the authority that was threatening to all university institutions in the country: they thought of the universities as mere channels for funds, not as institutions with an independent existence that had to be recognised and respected.[47]

The chairman of the authority complained that the attitude of UCD had been negative. The college representatives made it clear that they could not agree to the proposed merger. This looked like stalemate. Patrick Lynch confirmed that members of the HEA were using the July plan as a working hypothesis but were free to recommend alternative proposals if such were put forward. It was then that one of the professors from Cork (possibly Patrick Quinlan) drew attention to the fact that the commission had envisaged not only four universities but also co-operation between them. The question therefore was really one for all prospective universities, and it was suggested that the issue should be discussed by representatives of UCC, UCG, UCD, and Trinity College. All the NUI representatives and all the members of the HEA agreed to this. The authority had said that it was necessary that the question of the ban on Trinity should be resolved. The President of UCD saw some prospect of success in establishing four similarly constituted universities, with public representation in all four. The chairman of the HEA confirmed that if, from the proposed discussions between the NUI colleges and Trinity, some proposal emerged that was more satisfactory to all institutions concerned than the July plan, this would be acceptable to the authority. It was felt that the proposed four-college discussions would put the whole issue in a much more sensible and less heated context.

Following a resolution at the July meeting of the Senate, the NUI, with the good will of the HEA, took the initiative in issuing an invitation to the Provost of Trinity College to discuss the possibility of 'an agreed alternative' to the Government proposals of 6 July 1968. The resulting correspondence between the Registrar of the NUI and the Provost of Trinity College did not give the President of UCD much cause for optimism. There were three points, Hogan reported to the Governing Body on 21 November 1969, on which the provost's latest reply 'was as negative as it could be.' Firstly, Trinity rejected the idea of an outside chairman for the discussions, on the grounds that this would give the proceedings too much status and formality. Dr Hogan interpreted this to mean that Trinity did not want a successful outcome. Secondly, it seemed to him that the provost had ruled out any negotiations on the possibility of similar constitutions for the two colleges. In Hogan's view, close co-operation demanded that there be equal rights and privileges based on similar constitutions; UCD would not be prepared to allow any of its faculties to be moved to an institution that would modernise its constitution only as it itself wished. Thirdly, with regard to the distribution of faculties, it appeared that Trinity was not prepared to have any discussion on the July 1968 plan.

The long series of meetings already held between the two colleges did not suggest that agreement would ever be reached, the provost wrote, and he saw little point in going over the same ground fifteen months after the Government announcement. Understandably, therefore, the President of UCD felt that there were no grounds on which negotiations could start.

When Dr Hogan discussed the matter with friends of UCD in the Senate of the NUI it was thought that it would be better for the university not to be seen as the party that would not agree to negotiate but rather to begin talks even though progress might not be made. This line was accepted on 18 December 1969 by a meeting of the Governing Body, which was fully aware of the narrow ground on which negotiation was possible.

It was in this not very hopeful mood that the representatives of the NUI and Trinity College met under the chairmanship of Dr McCarthy, President of UCC, on 9 January 1970 and agreed to reconvene for another meeting. There followed over the next couple of months a number of intensive meetings, whose confidentiality was preserved throughout. In April 1970 the document that became known as the NUI-TCD agreement was ready for consideration.[48]

THE NUI-TRINITY AGREEMENT

The essence of the NUI-Trinity agreement was that there should be four independent universities, with broadly similar constitutions, and a Conference of Irish Universities with representatives from each institution, which should seek to foster co-operation between them.[49] The agreement then proceeded to outline certain modifications in the 6 July 1968 allocation of faculties. It accepted the Government's plan that the present range of subjects in arts and science would continue to be taught in the two Dublin institutions, with Trinity as the main centre for the biological sciences and UCD for the physical sciences. It accepted also the Government's plan for having veterinary medicine and dentistry in Trinity and commerce, social science, agriculture and architecture in UCD. Pharmacy, which the Government had assigned to Trinity, could go to whichever college the Irish Pharmaceutical Society might wish.

Adjustments, however, were made with regard to the Government's plan, which had so incensed UCD, of assigning all of medicine and law to Trinity. The HEA-NUI agreement recommended that there be two independent, co-operating pre-clinical schools in Dublin, with the aim of qualifying equal numbers of students per year for admission to the clinical courses. There should be a joint university clinical school operating in three hospital centres, and a joint co-ordinating body. With regard to law it was agreed that Trinity should become the main centre of legal studies but that some provision for the teaching of law subjects for a wider arts degree would be needed in UCD.

To balance these concessions to UCD in medicine and law it was proposed to modify the Government plan to place all of engineering in UCD by allowing two Schools of Engineering in Dublin: UCD to provide detailed courses in civil, agricultural, mechanical, electrical and chemical engineering and Trinity to give a non-specialised course designed to provide a basic education in engineering science during the first three years, with a restricted range of options during the final year.

In summary, the Government plan of 6 July 1968 allocated subjects to the proposed University of Dublin as follows:

UCD	*Trinity*
Arts; science; engineering; commerce; social science; agriculture; architecture	Arts; science; medicine; law; veterinary medicine; dentistry; pharmacy; physiotherapy

The NUI-Trinity plan of April 1970 allocated subjects to the proposed independent universities as follows:

UCD	*Trinity*
Arts; science; engineering; medicine (pre-clinical); some law subjects in arts; commerce; social science; agriculture; architecture	Arts; science; engineering; medicine (pre-clinical); law; veterinary medicine; dentistry

UCD and Trinity would have a joint university Clinical School of Medicine.

The NUI-Trinity agreement was considered and approved by both the Senate of the NUI and the Board of Trinity College on 23 April 1970. That afternoon it received preliminary consideration at the Governing Body, and it was sent for consideration during the following week to the various faculties, the Academic Council, the non-statutory staff, the SRC, and the staff-student committees. There was wide general acceptance of the proposals throughout the college bodies. Both the Academic Council and the Governing Body, in accepting the agreement, regretted the loss to UCD of veterinary medicine and law. The president summed up the general feeling in the college when he described the agreement as an improvement whereby UCD would not lose as much as under the Government's July 1968 plan but would still lose more than Trinity. But now, at least, UCD staff would be transferring to a Trinity College with a constitution similar to that of UCD. He stated that as much had been gained as possible; to have held out further would have led to a breakdown in negotiations.

It had been ten years since the Government appointed a commission to make recommendations on the future of higher education. It was over three years since the preliminary report had been published and since Donogh

O'Malley's announcement of the merger. Summing up the three-year merger discussions, the president told the Governing Body on 5 May 1970 that the purpose of the Government had been (*a*) to bring Trinity College finally 'over the threshold of the Irish nation' and (*b*) to save money. He believed that the NUI-Trinity agreement had achieved these two objectives. There was a note of finality (too optimistic, as it turned out) about the president's remarks as he thanked all involved in the long negotiations. He asserted that they had 'cleared a way for the College where there had seemed to be an insuperable barrier.'

Yet Dr Hogan's claims and the grounds of his optimism were to an extent justified. The fact that the NUI and Trinity College had come to an agreement to the effect that certain professional courses were to be available only in Trinity, or under joint control in the case of clinical medicine, and that Trinity's constitution was to be made broadly similar to that of the NUI colleges created a new set of circumstances in which the ban on Catholics attending Trinity became an anachronism. Two months after the NUI-Trinity agreement, on 25 June 1970, the Catholic hierarchy announced:

> Some hope of a change that would make this constitution [of Trinity College] acceptable to the Catholic conscience was provided by the announcement of a proposed merger—as it was called—of Trinity College and University College, Dublin. This announcement enabled the bishops to reconsider the attitude that might be adopted to a new Trinity College. In consequence, the aptness of the existing statute has been examined on more than one occasion recently by the bishops.
>
> In view of the substantial agreement on basic issues that has been reached between the National University of Ireland and Trinity College, the hierarchy has decided to seek approval from the Holy See for the repeal of statute 287 of the plenary synod.[50]

The O'Malley merger announcement had made the bishops reconsider the ban; the NUI-Trinity agreement had clinched the issue for them. The removal of the ban was therefore one of the most dramatic and most significant consequences of the whole merger affair.

After a delay described as almost like waiting for Godot, the HEA published its *Report on University Reorganisation* in July 1972, by which time Dr Hogan had retired and had been succeeded as President of UCD by Dr Tom Murphy (who had been much involved with the merger question as Dean of Medicine, Registrar and, more recently, a member of the HEA). The report sided substantially with the NUI-Trinity agreement because of 'fundamentally altered circumstances' since 1967: the ecclesiastical ban on Trinity

College had been withdrawn; the proportion of non-Irish students at Trinity had been reduced to 10 per cent; and an agreement on the amalgamation of a number of faculties had been reached. It doubted, however, that the proposed Conference of Irish Universities, involving all the university colleges in the Republic, could effectively implement the redistribution of faculties in Dublin, and to that end it recommended the establishment of a statutory Conjoint Board.

Observations on the HEA report were sought by the Government. During the long delay, however, feeling within UCD had hardened against the proposed allocation of faculties and even against the idea of merger. If there was a single breaking-point, that rock of destruction, as far as UCD was concerned, was probably medicine. Dr Murphy was sympathetic to the merger; but his colleagues in Medicine who were more closely associated with the teaching hospitals were less favourable to the practical details of the merger plan. With all their considerable influence they now advised the president against accepting the proposals in the HEA report.

The historical background to the HEA report was depicted by Paddy FitzGerald, professor of surgery at St Vincent's Hospital, in a memo sent to the president and others, as the intertwining 'with true Celtic artistry' of three tales. The first of these was O'Malley's scheme—a 'simple, naïve, generous and impulsive sketch.' This was followed by Lenihan's 'fiat' of 6 July 1968. Neither of these versions having proved palatable to the colleges, there followed 'a tale of solemn brokerage.' The wise men of Cork and Galway then joined the debate and, 'under conditions of decent obscurity,' consulted colleagues of the two Dublin colleges. In order that the impossible might become practical, tokens were exchanged with grave deliberation. In this exercise, faculties were 'moved like pawns in the opening gambit of a major chess game, little attention being paid to the fact that they are not pawns at all, but most complex and delicately balanced organisms.' The Faculty of Medicine was relegated to Trinity College on the erroneous pretext that this would place it nearer to the hospitals; but this, wrote Professor FitzGerald, was fallacious, because the *clinical* part of medicine must be in the hospitals, where the clinicians work. The pre-clinical school must be within a university college, while the administrative centre—which is what the authors of the HEA report, he supposed, might mean by the term 'faculty'—could be anywhere convenient. The siting of faculties seemed to him to be more the work of men unfamiliar with the difficulties, however anxious to solve them.[51]

Still sharper representation came from another highly respected medical professor, D. K. O'Donovan, Dean of the Faculty of Medicine and professor of medicine at St Vincent's Hospital, in a confidential letter to the president at his home address. He reminded Dr Murphy: 'Your position as the President of UCD is one of enormous historical responsibility for this country.' And he continued:

> The HEA Report is designed to beat University College down to the level of a second-rate institution ... University College will lose Law, Dentistry, Veterinary Medicine and in the Arts School will acquire quantity whilst quality will go to the attractive Library of TCD ... We are finally left with a rump of a University which boggles the imagination as to what it could be called. It is certainly not Newman because it is not Catholic. It is not National because it has no Gaelic affiliations. This is not a very pleasant prospect for the first President of the new university.[52]

Meetings followed between representatives of UCD and Trinity College towards the end of the year to see what degree of agreement could be reached on the HEA report in relation to medicine. The president reported to the Medical Faculty that the Trinity representatives had stated that unless UCD was prepared to stand by the NUI-Trinity agreement there was no point in having any further talks.[53] The real sticking-point now was the attitude of the hospitals: St Vincent's and Mater doctors did not want St James's to become the base of the clinical medical school, with all the advanced facilities that would entail.

The 'Representations of University College, Dublin, on the Higher Education Authority Report on University Reorganization' were ready for submission to the Minister for Education on 30 January 1973 after the matter had been considered by all the college bodies. While the college reaffirmed its approval of the distribution of faculties and subjects in the NUI-Trinity agreement of April 1970, it pointed out that the proposals in that agreement derived from the Government plan of 6 July 1968 for a single University of Dublin. This plan contained allocations that 'are in part not only contrary to our interests as an individual university institution, to our campus development and to our present and future role in higher education, but also detrimental to the best interests of higher education in the country generally.' Furthermore, the college did not agree with the interpretation the HEA placed on the NUI-Trinity agreement in relation to certain faculties, and these were spelt out.

Present at the special meeting of the Governing Body on 25 January 1973 that agreed to this submission to the minister was Richard Burke TD, one of eight public representatives elected to the Governing Body in January 1970 from the General Council of County Councils. Observations on the HEA report were still being received when the Fianna Fáil Government fell and was replaced by the coalition of Fine Gael and the Labour Party led by Liam Cosgrave in March 1973. Richard Burke became Minister for Education, and

awaiting him on his desk were the submissions on the HEA report—
including the one from the UCD Governing Body to which, as a member, he
had assented.

Some people in UCD had always looked enviously at Trinity College
because its Board was composed entirely of Trinity academics, whereas the
UCD Governing Body had quite a high proportion of public representatives.
Some advantages, however, were attached to the UCD structure, not least of
which was the fact that these public representatives carried considerable
political influence. The fact that Dick Burke was not only a graduate of UCD
but had been a member of its Governing Body since 1970 might now be
expected to count for something in UCD's favour. He was joined in
Cosgrave's Government by another and very vocal member of the Governing
Body and of UCD's teaching staff, Dr Garret FitzGerald, who was appointed
Minister for Foreign Affairs. Here, possibly, were friends in court.

The Governing Body on 15 May 1973 decided that the college officers
should seek an interview with the minister to ascertain the intentions of the
new Government with regard to the previous Government's decision of 6 July
1968 and the alternative known as the NUI-TCD agreement, or whether the
Government regarded the matter as open. It was stated that if the present
Government did not consider itself bound by the decisions of its predecessor,
the UCD negotiators would feel free to reopen discussions. At the subsequent
meeting on 3 July 1973 it was stated that 'the Minister is agreeable to consider
any representations which University College, Dublin, may wish to make
regarding the allocation of Faculties as between University College, Dublin,
and Trinity College, Dublin.'

A memorandum of 18 October 1973 to the minister from the Governing
Body summarised UCD's position. It pointed out: 'We must stress that the
NUI/TCD Agreement was negotiated under the threat of the implementation
of the Government plan of 6 July. Thus the allocation of faculties contained in
the Agreement did not arise from negotiations carried out in complete
freedom, but were from the UCD point of view the lesser of two evils.' The
memorandum agreed that some rationalisation was necessary and therefore
did not ask for any changes in the faculty distribution of the NUI-Trinity
agreement, except with regard to medicine, law, science, and veterinary
medicine. It went on to set out in detail the reallocation of these faculties that
it thought desirable.

Trinity's comments (dated 11 January 1974) were sharp. The Board
pointed out that the new proposals from UCD were a departure from the
agreement negotiated between Trinity College and the NUI with regard to
subject distribution. It considered it essential that further rounds of indecisive
debate should not take place. 'An equitably balanced allocation' was how the
Board of Trinity College described the NUI-Trinity agreement; the new

proposals in the UCD memorandum were now seeking unilateral advantage for UCD, the Board asserted, which proceeded instead to defend the allocations that had been made to Trinity College.

The form of democracy imposed by the 1908 Act and Charter had accustomed UCD people to the methods of electioneering and canvassing. The presidency, the registrarship, deanship, membership of the Governing Body and Senate, academic appointments and promotions were determined by successful canvass and election. The lobbying of politicians, including Government ministers, was therefore nothing unusual for the UCD authorities, and it was an activity in which they possessed some expertise. The coalition Government was not a particularly difficult one for UCD to persuade to its way of thinking. Fine Gael politicians accounted for a majority of the Government, and UCD still had very strong ties with that party. Apart from the fact that two members of the Government were members of UCD's Governing Body at the time of their appointment, a number of UCD people were friendly with the Taoiseach, Liam Cosgrave, and other members of his Government. Tom Murphy's reserves of affability were particularly useful in these circumstances. These connections, along with lobbying expertise and UCD's well-reasoned memorandum, won the college a sympathetic hearing and decisions with which it could be satisfied.

THE BURKE STATEMENT

The Minister for Education, Richard Burke, issued a statement on 16 December 1974 announcing the Government's decisions. There should be three universities: UCD, Trinity College, and the NUI, comprising UCC and UCG. St Patrick's College, Maynooth, was to have the option of becoming a constituent college of any one of the three universities. The National Institutes of Higher Education in Limerick and Dublin were to be established as recognised university colleges, with the capacity to evolve into constituent colleges or autonomous degree-awarding institutions. A Conjoint Board was to be established to co-ordinate the two Dublin universities and to ensure the rational use of resources and mobility of staff and students between them; and a Conference of Irish Universities was to be established.

The redistribution of faculties in Dublin made in the Burke statement pleased the authorities in UCD as much as it displeased their opposite numbers in Trinity. In this latest reallocation, law was not to be united in Trinity but was to continue in both colleges; veterinary medicine was to go to UCD instead of Trinity; there was to be a joint Science Faculty; the joint Clinical Medicine School would operate from three hospitals (St James's, St Vincent's, and the Mater) and would be under the direction of the Conjoint Board; dentistry and pharmacy were to be in Trinity alone. Business studies, social science, agriculture and architecture were to be in UCD alone. Arts and pre-clinical medicine would be provided in both. Engineering was assigned to UCD and engineering science to Trinity, but without capital investment. Each university Senate would consist of thirty-five members.

The reception given to the Burke statement in UCD was one of relief and pleasure. Dr Murphy, after outlining briefly the UCD interpretation of the history of the merger proposals, acknowledged that the Burke statement had improved considerably the position of UCD, most notably with the retention of law and veterinary medicine. The Governing Body decided not to concern itself for the moment with other institutions but to confine itself to the decision that UCD was to be an independent university.

For some considerable time all concerned with higher education had been urging the need for a decision by the Government. The Governing Body was pleased that a decision had now been made, and it issued a statement to that effect, which also said: 'University College, Dublin, welcomes the decision that it is to be given the status of an independent autonomous university. We trust that arrangements which will ultimately be made for our sister Colleges in Cork and Galway will prove acceptable to them.'[54]

It was now Trinity's turn to reject the Government's decisions as 'quite unacceptable', in the words of the new provost. One of the earliest tasks for F. S. L. (Leland) Lyons, the noted historian, who had succeeded McConnell in October 1974, was to issue a statement highly critical of the Burke statement and its departures from the NUI-Trinity agreement and the 1972 HEA report. In his opposition, he had the strong support of the Board and staff.

The heads of the colleges were also dissatisfied with aspects of the Burke scheme relating to the proposed Conjoint Board, the status of UCC and UCG, and what was regarded as further intrusion in the internal affairs of the universities. As a result, only parts of the Burke scheme were brought into operation. And the great merger plan that Donogh O'Malley had announced in April 1967 was now, after seven years of hectic negotiations and vast quantities of memoranda, allowed to fizzle out and disappear off the Government's agenda.

What by way of merger had been achieved? Since law was to be retained in UCD, similar arguments could be used to justify the retention of business studies and social science in Trinity. The Faculties of Science were also left undisturbed in both colleges. The only changes that took place were that veterinary medicine went to UCD and pharmacy and dentistry went to Trinity. The creation of a single School of Dentistry, allocated to Trinity College, was smoothly achieved. The arrangements for veterinary medicine and pharmacy involved more complicated procedures but eventually took effect as intended.

Business studies and social studies were to provide the last of the many altercations sparked off by the merger proposal. This argument went on for more than a year and concluded only in May 1978, when the Governing Body of UCD reluctantly accepted the decision of the Minister for Education in a new Fianna Fáil Government, John Wilson, that business studies and social studies should continue to be provided in both UCD and Trinity.

What had begun, from the point of view of the UCD authorities, as a magnanimous gesture (more comprehensive in its scope than even Donogh O'Malley's) to create a single University of Dublin ended more than a decade later with UCD complaining that it had given up pharmacy to Trinity College on the understanding that it was to receive in return both business and social studies and with Trinity determined to hold on to these disciplines. And as far as the School of Pharmacy was concerned the irony was that more than twenty years later it was still housed in its old premises in Shrewsbury Road and not, as had been expected, on a college site; and the Dental Hospital had not vacated Lincoln Place, nor Veterinary Medicine its premises in Ballsbridge.

CONCLUSION

To borrow Donogh O'Malley's phrase, employed in his initial announcement, his merger had been caught in the web of history. A merger of kinds had indeed been on and off the agenda since Gladstone's University Bill of 1873. And following him, Bryce, Dunraven and even Carson had in ways anticipated O'Malley. It had been very much favoured in the pronouncements of Archbishop Walsh between the eighteen-eighties and 1908. One could say that it was in the nineteen-fifties and sixties in a sense a UCD idea, inherited from Archbishop Walsh and strongly advocated in different guises by prominent UCD men like Michael Tierney, Jeremiah Hogan, John O'Meara, and Denis Donoghue. It was taken up by Donogh O'Malley and the secretary of his department, Tarlach Ó Raifeartaigh, and by the Government; and O'Malley ran enthusiastically with the ball. It was seen as solving with one deft stroke the great twin problems of financing the modern university and removing the socio-religious shackle of the Catholic hierarchy's ban on Trinity College. The Government, through Brian Lenihan, and no doubt for its own political ends, bent over backwards to accommodate Trinity's feelings. But this had the result of arousing the hostility of UCD to the whole scheme, and the Lenihan plan floundered on the groundswell of UCD opposition.

Neither UCD nor Trinity College had been quite ready for a single new University of Dublin in which both traditions were to be merged. It was the wrong time, because relations between the colleges' authorities were at a low ebb, rivalries and mutual suspicions were rife, and it was too early to propose amalgamating the two institutions in the manner suggested by the Government.

The *Irish Times* on 28 April 1964 carried a headline, 'UCD/TCD not to be amalgamated?' This was an indication that, while the Commission on Higher Education was still sitting, there had been some expectation of a recommendation in favour of amalgamation. So strongly indeed had two non-academic members of the commission felt that, in their reservations, M. J. Costello had argued for a single University of Dublin and J. J. McElligott had written in favour of making some division of university education between UCD and Trinity College. The commission had taken into account the size of the two colleges, their very different traditions, and the argument that a new federation was unlikely to succeed where the commission was recommending that the old one of the NUI should be discarded. So, having examined the option of a merger, the commission by a large majority had decided firmly against it. In view of the difficulties that emerged when the several attempts were made to work out the details of merging the two colleges, it could be argued that the commission had shown its wisdom in rejecting merger as the solution.

The problem of the costly duplication that the merger was intended to deal with came to some extent under the control of the HEA. And the problem associated with the ban on Catholics attending Trinity College disappeared with its removal by the hierarchy in 1970. The ending of the ban and Trinity's subsequent full acceptance as an Irish institution was the one solid, if indirect, result of all the time that had been spent on the merger. The twin objectives of the proposal, therefore, no longer obtained. With the continuing expansion of UCD and Trinity College and the emergence of three university institutions in Dublin, following the establishment in Glasnevin of what was to become Dublin City University, it became far too late to talk of merger.

So the two colleges survived, no longer regarded as Protestant and Catholic. The irony is that thirty years later the secularist ethos predominates in both, making it almost impossible to distinguish one from the other sociologically, especially now that the majority of students in both colleges come from the Irish Catholic background.

10

The Gentle Revolution
'A short frolic on the world stage'

Bliss was it in that dawn to be alive,
But to be young was very heaven!

I t was an age of protest. The nineteen-sixties saw the civil rights campaigns in America led by Martin Luther King and others; civil rights protests in places like Northern Ireland; opposition to apartheid in South Africa; the Campaign for Nuclear Disarmament arising from a worldwide fear of nuclear extinction; the protests against the war in Viet Nam, the saturation-bombing of a small Asian country by the most powerful Western state; and protests by 'drop-outs', 'hippies' and 'angry young men' against the injustices and rampant materialism of the 'affluent society'.

In all these various protests, students played a prominent part, and a wave of student unrest erupted in universities all over the world. The post-war 'baby boom' had become particularly noticeable by the late sixties in the universities. In one generation in France the number of students rose from 50,000 to 600,000. In UCD the student population had expanded from a little over 2,000 in 1939 to over 10,000 in 1969. And they were crowded mainly into the half-completed building in Earlsfort Terrace that—had it ever been finished—was intended for 1,000.

By the mid-sixties American universities were becoming hotbeds of agitation. The University of California at Berkeley, with its 27,500 students, hosted the first of the big student protests, and the effects were felt across America and beyond. In the first six months of 1968 more than 220 major demonstrations took place in American colleges. The organisation that did most to channel student unrest in the various colleges was 'Students for a Democratic Society', a radical movement dedicated to the rejection of capitalist society that was to have many imitators elsewhere, including 'Students for Democratic Action' in UCD.

Columbia University, New York, witnessed one of the toughest confrontations. One raid by police on the buildings occupied by students led to the arrest of more than seven hundred and the treatment of a hundred in hospital; seventy-three students were suspended, the president resigned, and many of the staff moved elsewhere. Every self-respecting student body had to have its protest. Student leaders became household names, chieftains of discontent: Rudi Dutschke in Berlin, Daniel Cohn-Bendit ('Danny the Red') in Paris, Tariq Ali in London. Nineteen of the thirty-three Italian state universities were affected. 'We shall fight, we shall win, Paris, London, Rome, Berlin!'

Student revolt reached its climax in Paris in May 1969. Rioting spread from the Sorbonne to the rest of the city and then all over France. Hundreds were wounded in street fighting. The question was asked: were we witnessing the beginnings of a movement that would in time reshape society in a manner comparable to the great French and Russian revolutions? Universities were especially vulnerable. Fewer than a hundred determined students could disrupt the work of an entire college. The example, the excitement, the publicity, the temptation were too great to be resisted.

Everything that would happen in UCD in the revolt of 1968–69 had just happened on a more terrifying and radical scale in Berkeley, New York, or Paris. Dublin of course had its own particular underlying causes for the disturbance. The Minister for Education had had an unsettling effect on the university with his dramatic announcement of a merger between UCD and Trinity College. Students were involved in this debate and their opinion given a weight never previously enjoyed. Overcrowding in Earlsfort Terrace was chronic; library conditions in particular were a major source of trouble. Staff grievances were freely aired: approximately 65 per cent (the so-called junior staff) were on one-year contracts. Communications within the college were considered to be almost non-existent; and the administrative structures established for a college of five hundred students in 1909 were totally inadequate for the rapidly changing conditions of a mass university. Student unrest could flourish in such an atmosphere.

The Second Vatican Council (1962–65) affected the mood of Catholics everywhere in the nineteen-sixties. It produced a great stirring, *aggiornamento* and renewal certainly, and the liberalisation of Catholic thinking; but it also provoked much questioning of established practices and beliefs. Rebel theologians like Father Charles Davis had many followers, as had the so-called New Left Church movement. The controversies within the church contributed to the mood of the time and coloured the opinions of a number of staff and students in UCD, and the case against *Humanae Vitae,* the encyclical on birth control, was argued in *University Gazette* (issue 34, 1968).

Student unrest in other parts of the world, more immediately the 'Paris insurrection' of May 1968, produced its first reverberations in Dublin in that same month when a small group of Maoist students in Trinity College demonstrated against the King and Queen of the Belgians, then on a state visit to Ireland. Scuffles with the gardaí and a sensationalised press report of the incident resulted in a protest march on Independent Newspapers and Pearse Street Garda station. Some left-wing UCD students (including Basil Millar, Ruairí Quinn, Una Claffey and John Feeney) arranged a march of solidarity with Trinity. According to fellow-students in the UCD Pax Romana Society, these UCD marchers were given a poor reception by the Maoists, but some of them, getting a taste for radical action, and not to be outdone by Trinity, formed Students for Democratic Action.

The SDA was at first, in the late spring or early summer of 1968, an amorphous group consisting of certain left-wing activists from the religious societies (the Student Christian Movement and Logos—whose auditor in 1967/68 was John Feeney), from the political societies (the University Branch of the Labour Party, the Republican Club and the Political Studies Society— of which the auditor in 1967/68 was Basil Millar and the correspondence secretary Una Claffey), and the magazine *Campus*. Among them too were a few who were considered to be romantic anarchists. All through the summer holiday they met sporadically in Newman House and, as John Feeney later wrote, 'studied the latest revolutionary pamphlets from abroad ... We were living in a state of sustained, permanent excitement transfixed by the prospect of the next term.'[1] Within the group, according to Feeney,

> Basil Millar, an Economics graduate and Labour [Party] member, was undoubtedly our spiritual leader. He strode around with evident purpose written on his face, bedecked in sunglasses and Guevarrist beard and moustache, carrying his revolutionary literature and utensils in a gigantic Vietcong bag. In one way his leadership was determined by his intellectual brilliance ... Basil seemed to know most about Trotskyism and his manner seemed to prefigure and embody the times that were coming.[2]

Believing itself to be both genuinely democratic and messianic, the SDA consciously rejected any forms of bureaucratic organisation. It had no list of members and no executive. A chairman was elected for a week at a time, and his only function was to arrange that week's meetings. It was clear, however, that certain individuals dominated and carried much influence with their colleagues. Their declared aim was 'to involve students in activities inside and outside the university designed to promote radical change.'

RUMBLINGS OF REVOLT

One of the warning signs of unrest in Earlsfort Terrace concerned library opening hours and overcrowding. In June 1968 medical students had staged a sit-in in the Medical Library, demanding that it be kept open during the summer months. Similar protests were held over opening hours and conditions in the Arts Library in June 1968 and the following October. The librarian, Ellen Power, and the college authorities seem to have endeavoured to meet student demands for improved facilities and longer opening hours where practicable.

There were slight rumblings even in the new college in Belfield. In October a sit-in was being threatened in the Science Building unless improved library hours were negotiated. Students in the third-year chemistry class decided not to submit to compulsory lecture attendance and rearranged their seating plan in lecture theatres to frustrate roll-call. Also, in the Science Building only one common-room had been provided for students, which had become a female preserve, generally occupied by nuns. A desegregation 'coup' took place quietly and without incident, after which the common-room was then said to house both sexes comfortably.

But the overcrowded conditions of what was to be for a majority of students the last two years of UCD's home at Earlsfort Terrace presented a much greater hazard of general conflagration.[3] Earlsfort Terrace was the real powder keg.

A potential trouble-spot was the projected staff-student committees, the formation of which had been recommended by the Commission on Higher Education.[4] A plan for such committees was accepted by the faculties, the Academic Council and the Governing Body at the beginning of the new term in October. They were to be broadly grouped and set up at department level in the case of the larger faculties of Arts and Science and at faculty level in the case of the smaller faculties. Students would be in a majority generally of two to one. The committees' functions would be 'to discuss Faculty and Depart-mental matters as they affect students and if necessary make recommendations to the appropriate authorities.'

The staff-student committees were regarded by some as a radical change, aimed at giving students a greater say in the running of the college. They were, at the very least, listening-posts that could pass on to departments and faculties the grievances and suggestions of students in the different stages of their courses. On the other hand, they were restricted by the Act, Charter and Statutes under which the college operated, so that any official student involvement in the decision-making bodies—faculties, Academic Council and Governing Body—was prohibited. While the President of the SRC welcomed these committees as a move in the right direction, he said that the students' objective was participation and not simply representation.[5] The more sceptical or more extreme students described the proposals as a 'fob-off by a few very clever academics to make a pretence of student participation' in the running of the college.

The approval of the establishment of the staff-student committees and the election to which they gave rise helped unwittingly to increase the political tempo throughout UCD. At the conferring ceremony in the Great Hall in Earlsfort Terrace on 31 October 1968 a group of students—thirty or, in another report, forty—protested against the staff-student committees with placards that read *Participation—not consultation* and *Democracy—not bureaucracy*. A spokesman for the protesters who, according to one newspaper, declined to be named but in another was named as Ruairí Quinn, a fifth-year architecture student and chairman of the University Branch of the Labour Party, said that the staff-student committees would serve no useful purpose: all they offered was the right to be heard, but this was not good enough and fell far short of what was required.[6] A classical stage in the anatomy of revolution was being reached: the moment when the old regime, relaxing its rigid hold, takes its first nervous liberalising steps, and the revolutionaries react by disdainfully rejecting the concession, believing they have the regime on the run.

Determined not to be marginalised by the SDA or pushed aside as irrelevant by the increasing pace of events, the SRC asked for the use of the Great Hall for a 'teach-in' on another burning issue: the merger. This was refused—on trivial grounds, according to the students. The reasons given, according to *Campus* (6 November 1968), were that the acoustics were poor; that the presence of non-UCD students would lead to disorderly behaviour and damage; and that the hall was required for use by the Library. The SRC decided to ignore the refusal, and students occupied the Great Hall at lunchtime on Friday 8 November 'as a peaceful assertion of their rights.'

About two thousand students were involved, most of whom, reported the 'UCD correspondent' of the *Irish Times* (13 November 1968), 'were doing little more than obviously enjoying the fickle spotlight of public attention' and some of whom 'had little else to do during a lunch-hour when rain hammered off the grey parapets of the College.' The correspondent also suggested that the student community was open to being 'misrepresented by an embryonic extremist element in College numbering about 12 students,' and that the thunder of the SRC had been stolen in the same way that it had been stolen on the question of staff-student committees and in the same way that plans were being made to steal it in a protest march on the grants issue.[7] He described it as a 'take-over of the take-over' by minority pressure groups in college, which he identified as the Republican Club, the Labour Party, the SCM and *Campus*.

On Friday 15 November 'over 3,000 students from Dublin's two university colleges crowded into the Great Hall' to hear a panel of speakers discuss the merger,[8] despite the refusal by the authorities to grant permission for the use of the hall. Among the staff members who spoke was Senator Garret FitzGerald, 'who was welcomed as the only member of the Governing Body to attend.' These academics could be perceived as having joined the students in defying the authorities. Other speakers included Senator Owen Sheehy Skeffington (once banned by Michael Tierney) and Tommy Murtagh of Trinity College. Among the students who spoke were Howard Kinlay, President of the Union of Students in Ireland, and Ruairí Quinn. Though speakers kept mainly to the question of the merger, and all of them to a greater or lesser degree stated their opposition to the Lenihan scheme, the note of defiance of the UCD authorities was also strongly in evidence. This was underlined in a short speech of support for the students from Hugh MacDiarmid, the Scottish poet, who was on a visit to Ireland. 'Whatever your aims are,' he said, 'you cannot make a worse mess of it than your elders have' (*Irish Times,* 16 November 1968); and his advice was 'to go as far as the most extreme speaker' (*Campus,* 20 November 1968). At least two of the junior staff who spoke at the teach-in (Hilary Jenkins and Denys Turner) were later to be suspected of being involved in the student revolution.

There were very different reactions to this second teach-in. Gus Martin of the English Department was quoted as describing it as 'one of the most impressive gatherings in UCD' (*Campus,* 20 November 1968). Basil Miller of the SDA said this second meeting brought the debate backwards from the previous week, 'Garret FitzGerald managing in his wet blanket way to defuse the debate completely,' and that it was 'all in all a shambles' (*Campus,* 4 December 1968).

On Monday the librarian, Ellen Power, declared library service suspended until the hall was cleaned, despite the fact that the SRC had tidied it on the Saturday morning to the satisfaction of the building superintendent. The head porter, Paddy Keogh, had exclaimed that he had never in his life seen the place look so clean (*Campus,* 20 November 1968).

A few days later the president in a statement to the Governing Body revealed the sense of shock and disbelief that senior administrators and academic staff experienced when they were first accosted by 'student power'. Dr Hogan told the Governing Body that discipline had become a big problem everywhere and that the theory of student power had definitely arrived in Ireland. According to this idea, he explained, a university was not a place where young people came to learn under the discipline of those who taught them: it was now looked on rather as the special world of young people, which they should rule. It appeared that they, at least as much as anyone else, should settle what they were to learn, the academic standards, and the content of courses. The number of students seriously and deeply accepting this doctrine he believed to be small, but they were a minority fanatically devoted to it. Matters had recently come to a head over the use of the Great Hall. He explained why its use had been refused: it seemed very dangerous, he said, to crowd into it any number beyond 1,500, because of the hazards of fire and panic. Besides, the hall was in use as a reading-room for the Library. The same meeting of the Governing Body noted as 'read' a motion passed by the L&H, 'that this house calls on the Governing Body of UCD to remove Mr MacHale from his position as Secretary of the College.'

Following these events, and perhaps realising they were in the driving-seat if only they dared provide the leadership, the SDA issued what they called an 'Interim Statement of Principle' (25 November 1968) over the name of Owen Sweeney, 'Ad Hoc Chairman' (who was described by his colleague John Feeney as 'flamboyant' and a 'romantic anarchist'). The document was intended as a basis for further discussion and invited those interested to contact the SDA. It asserted that the basic aim of the SDA was the abolition of 'the present elitist system of education in Ireland,' so that the university could serve the interests of the people as a whole. This would involve widespread and frequent contact between students and workers, with the workers coming to the university for mass teach-ins and smaller discussion and action groups and the students taking up causes to serve the people. In the meantime the SDA offered to provide a framework within which any student could work for the democratisation of education and society. They pledged to support 'progressive actions' on the part of the SRC, USI or any other body and to initiate and co-ordinate such action. The SDA would act as 'the dynamic for radical change within the university and as the counterpart for similar activity outside the university.'

Greater financial provision for students was announced by the Government, to take effect from 1968. The USI complained that the grants were inadequate and that the scheme excluded students already in higher education and those who had qualified for entry before 1968 but who, for financial reasons, were then unable to enter higher education. It threatened direct and militant action, which would include the disruption of the normal course of college life for three or four hours a day, and announced a student protest march to the Dáil for Tuesday 19 November.

Newspaper reports put the number of students who participated in the march at between three and four thousand; student reports put the figure at four or five thousand. The march was supported by the SRC, SDA, University Branch of the Labour Party, and others in UCD. But while it was an impressive street demonstration it had nothing concrete to show for all its noise and bluster, beyond the decision that all lectures should be cancelled the following Friday. However much the ASA and the trade unions might approve of the policy of the USI to enable everyone to avail himself or herself of higher education, the expected support from these bodies had not materialised, because they had not been notified of the students' plans.

The Minister for Education said that 'to accede to these demands would add to the already heavy tax burden on the community and particularly those tax-payers who would in no way benefit in relation to their own families.'

A tremendous sense of deflation, even betrayal, set in among the most active of the UCD students. The boycott of lectures that the USI had planned for Friday 22 November fell through because of lack of organisation or support. And *Campus* (4 December 1968) asked in a two-page headline, 'The "Revolution": what's happened?' It went on to say that just when it suddenly seemed that UCD was about to become 'a dynamic, thinking, real university,' all had collapsed. What had seemed like the beginning of a concerted assertion of student rights had degenerated into disarray. Student leaders had been continually calling for student participation; students had been 'roused from their sheer bloody indifference' and were then 'abandoned' after 'one futile gesture.' *Campus* complained that the lack of a clear, co-ordinated and controlled plan of action by the USI, SRC and SDA had resulted in a fiasco for what appeared to have been the best thing in student life in recent years. 'Whatever has happened must not happen again.'

In this state of animated disillusionment, the SDA seized the moment, accused the 'bureaucratic' organisations—the USI and SRC—of having sold out on the campaign, of cancelling the boycott of lectures, and of having shown themselves totally unable to give any leadership or achieve anything concrete by mass action. About a thousand students, it was claimed, realised this and on the evening of the march held a further mass meeting in the Great Hall under the auspices of the SDA and decided to go ahead with independent action and discussion.

The first public action of the SDA, according to Feeney (*Irish Times*, 3 February 1971), was the USI grants march to the Dáil. The SDA, marching at the head of the UCD contingent, had planned a confrontation with the gardaí, in the hope of radicalising the students. When this did not materialise, because only a few gardaí were present, the SDA, on their way back, decided spontaneously to occupy the Great Hall in Earlsfort Terrace and protest at the 'sell-out'. 'We started a Ho Chi Minh trot around the Green, burst into the Great Hall, hustled out the studying students and standing on the Librarian's desk we harangued a mass meeting. This raised our morale enormously and we redoubled our efforts holding longer daily meetings on every conceivable topic and harangued the students in the Main Hall weekly.' This first experience of the successful mass meeting, the force of numbers and defiance of the authorities whetted their appetite for more.

Immediately inside the main entrance in Earlsfort Terrace was the Main Hall, with the porters' office on the right and the administration's general office on the left. The Main Hall connected two narrow corridors or wings. The corridor on the right just beyond the porters' office contained the board-room, the professors' room, the staff room, and others. The one on the left, beyond the general office, housed the offices of the president, the registrar, and the secretary. In direct line from the main entrance to the college and only a few steps across the Main Hall was the Great Hall, which could comfortably house 1,500 to 2,000 and was used for conferrings, freshers' week, and other large functions.

The Main Hall, in contrast, was not nearly so spacious, nor had it ever been intended as a venue for meetings. It was, however, a favourite congregating place for generations of UCD students. As such it has found a place in literature. Flann O'Brien in *At Swim-Two-Birds* described it as it was in the early thirties, when student numbers were still only a small fraction of the 1969 figures.

> The College is outwardly a rectangular plain building with a fine porch where the midday sun pours down in summer from the Donnybrook direction, heating the steps for the comfort of the students. The hallway inside is composed of large black and white squares arranged in the orthodox chessboard pattern, and the surrounding walls, done in an unpretentious cream wash, bear three rough smudges caused by the heels, buttocks and shoulders of the students.
>
> The hall was crowded by students, some of them disporting themselves in a quiet civil manner. Modest girls bearing books filed in and out in the channels formed by the groups of boys. There was a hum of converse and much bustle and activity. A liveried attendant came out of a small office in the wall and pealed a shrill bell. This caused some dispersal, many of the boys extinguishing their cigarettes by manual manipulation and going up a circular stairway to the lecture-halls in a brave, arrogant way, some stopping on the stairs to call back to those still below a message of facetious or obscene import.[9]

During term the Main Hall always tended to be overcrowded. For any group wishing to disrupt the routine administration of the college, it was strategically the nerve-centre.

Here, on the morning of Wednesday 27 November, the SDA held an impromptu mass meeting.[10] For about two-and-a half hours a number of students spoke on the 'lack of democracy' in the college, the non-representation of various sections of the community, and the problems in departments and faculties. The ad hoc chairman, Kevin Myers, was instructed by the college's assistant secretary, Vincent Kelly, to call off the meeting. Myers replied that he had no right to do so, as it had been called by thirty people, and by acclamation the authorities' instruction was disregarded. The intervention by the authorities was referred to in *Confrontation* (2 December 1968) as an attempt to suppress freedom of speech and as being on the same level as the refusal by the 'totally arbitrary holders of power' to give recognition to the Republican Club. The SDA demanded that recognition be given to this club and affirmed its intention of taking action to achieve it.

The SDA issued the first number of *Confrontation* on 2 December 1968, and it continued to appear at irregular intervals at least up to March 1969. In presentation it could hardly compare with *Campus*. The latter, with its printed newspaper format and its photographs, was as well produced as contemporary newspapers; the quality of writing in the editorials and in many of the articles was in fact often of a higher standard than was attained in the Dublin dailies. Conor Brady (later editor of the *Irish Times*) was editor in 1968, and Gerald Barry (later an RTE political editor), Kevin Myers and John Feeney were already displaying considerable promise as future professional journalists, following in the tradition of standards that had been set by Henry Kelly, Christina Murphy and others in 1966 and 1967, just before the student revolt. By contrast, *Confrontation* was a varying number of inelegant photocopied sheets stapled together and full of typing errors. Its writing, while done by some of the same people (including Myers, Feeney, and Millar), suffered from an overdose of earnest revolutionary statements similar to the type of 'internationalist jargon' allegedly remarked upon by Henry Kelly when he came to do a report for the *Irish Times* on the occupation.[11] But for all its crudity and jargon it could also be lively, controversial and influential, and its surviving copies still faintly smell of the smoke of battle as they were rushed from the rebels' quarters into the hands of students in the Main Hall.

General dissatisfaction among students and some of the studio staff in the school of architecture had been increasing since the early months of 1968. This had to do with professorial control, the content of the courses, and fears about the continued recognition of the degree in Britain. The issue of the staff-student committees provided a focus for the architects' protest. Meetings organised jointly by the SRC and the Architectural Society were held on 28 and 30 October to consider the matter. Then, a month later, from 3:30 p.m. on 29 November to 10 p.m. on 30 November, the students occupied part of the Earlsfort Terrace building. The occupation was, as the report of the Academic Council later admitted, 'well organised and carefully controlled.' During the occupation the students produced a programme for the temporary housing of Dublin's homeless and a document on education—'both of more practical value than a year's lectures,' claimed *Campus* (4 December 1968). Only a restructuring could bring about a school sensitive to changing requirements, according to the students. The structure envisaged was one in which all interests in the school—students, studio and lecturing staff, and administrators—participated in the decisions affecting educational policy. To this end the students demanded a committee of equal staff and student membership whose decisions would be effective in running the school.

The architects' occupation was widely acclaimed as another example of the success of 'direct action' when other representations had failed. The SDA had played no part in it but praised it as a model of direct action.

BLOCKADE OF THE ACADEMIC COUNCIL

For several years a student society, the Republican Club, had been seeking recognition from the Academic Council but without success, because it failed to meet the criteria for recognition as a branch of a registered political party. In a letter to the registrar (4 December 1968) the SRC asked that the Republican Club be given recognition; it stated that four motions were passed at the Students' Council over the course of the year urging the Academic Council to give recognition. The latest motion on the subject had been passed unanimously.

The recognition of clubs and societies was on the agenda of the meeting of the Academic Council called for 12 December 1968, and once again the Republican Club's application was included in the list. The president was absent because of illness, and the chair was taken by Rev. Professor Frank Shaw SJ. The minutes of the Academic Council reported tersely: 'During the entire meeting of the Academic Council a group of students describing themselves as Students for Democratic Action assembled in the hall outside the Boardroom door and held a meeting which caused considerable disturbance. At 5.30 p.m. the Chairman with the unanimous approval of the Council decided to adjourn the meeting as it was no longer possible to transact the business of the meeting.'

The chairman regarded it as a case of very serious and dangerous disorder. In his report to the president (16 December 1968) he said that the din, increasing all the time, began soon after the start of the meeting and lasted for nearly three hours. The door and windows were beset by students, who carried banners demanding recognition for the Republican Club. From about 4:30 onwards, he said, it was not possible to leave or enter the room. At times the clamour was so great that it seemed that the meeting could not continue. The Academic Council agreed to complete the more urgent business and then adjourned, because of the noise and the attempt to interfere with the council. The chairman wrote:

> I did not realize how bad the affair was until finally we were allowed to leave the room. The din was unbelievable; and at this time the demonstrators had worked themselves up to an hysterical frenzy. With

savage hostility from a distance of some six inches, they screamed and screeched into our faces. Undoubtedly this was the mood of irresponsible violence, and I reckon it fortunate that in fact no physical violence was used.[12]

A meeting organised by the SDA in the Main Hall had been designed to coincide with that of the Academic Council. The Academic Council committee of inquiry later reported, and an SDA press statement confirmed, that the students then staged a sit-down outside the door of the board-room and prevented members from leaving until a favourable decision had been taken on the Republican Club or a deputation from the students was received. Some of the council managed to leave by the door and were abused while doing so; 'those physically able', said the press statement, 'were forced to leave by the window.'

The registrar—who, as *Confrontation* admitted (16 December 1968), was reportedly in favour of recognition of the Republican Club—urged the students to disband and said that a decision on the club could not be taken until the Academic Council met again. Members had refused to conduct business under threats and intimidation. The students, who were reported as numbering more than four hundred, then decided that the Academic Council did not deserve recognition by them. History students among the SDA may well have remembered that at the start of the French Revolution the Third Estate had withdrawn itself from the Estates-General meeting at Versailles, constituted itself the National Assembly, and, in the tennis court, vowed not to disperse until a new national constitution was drafted. The SDA-led group likewise declared itself to be the real Academic Council, and overwhelmingly recognised the Republican Club.

Confrontation claimed (16 December 1968) that during the blockade Professor Denis Donoghue 'forced his way out, deliberately standing on a girl student's shin.' The SDA issued a warning to 'people like Professor Donoghue, who use violence against students, that in any future action of this kind retaliation in the same form will occur.' Otherwise the SDA were greatly amused by the spectacle of disruption they had caused. A piece in *Confrontation* entitled 'Palsied frolics au fenêtre' and signed 'Kamaroy' (written by Kevin Myers, according to John Feeney) played on the gerontocratic theme. The article referred to the Academic Council as 'the confluence of decrepitude,' 'possessed of a corporate befuddlement,' 'an association of dotage,' 'in the grip of hoary, toothless senility.' Such a council was 'genetically incapable of grasping the concept of democracy—for which they will normally substitute words like "Mob".' The tone of its meetings tended to be 'one of somnolent indulgence, alleviated only by the clack of false teeth and the flash of a moistened pate.' On the occasion of the blockade, the Academic Council had undertaken 'physical exercises of a peculiarly fenestral nature.' To show each other and all the world what a stern gathering of sturdy souls these 'elderly irrelevances' were, 'calves were bared, teeth removed and last, grimly defiant glances were made before wobbly limb was guided by rheumy eye, down, down to the depths below.' The article ended with another reminder of the French Revolution. 'Knit one, pearl [*sic*] one, mes jolies tricoteuses. History students among the besiegers, and there were many among them, could well have been forgiven had they felt that they were being presented with a dramatic re-enactment of an episode which their text-books referred to as "the defenestration of Prague".' 'This magnificent piece of satire' was described by John Feeney as 'the best piece of prose to come from the Gentle Revolution' (*Irish Times*, 3 February 1971).

For the chairman of the meeting, Professor Shaw, it was a 'patently undemocratic attempt to solve an issue, not by reasoned discussion, but by threats, by physical force and by the conventional weapons of the bully.' While Father Shaw accepted that the SRC had no part in the disorder, he asked the President of the SRC whether the SRC proposed to take any action to ensure that matters it referred to the Academic Council might be discussed on their merits and 'without the misguided intervention of a noisy minority who would seem to favour government by decibels.' The 'democrats', he said, 'screamed and thumped and sang' for their cause.

> The singing was one of the gems of this melodramatic spectacle. With bone-crunching predictability and with a heartening absence of sophistication, shades of Birmingham, Alabama, were evoked by a moving rendering of 'We shall overcome.' This was a victory celebration. The demonstrators, with the naïveté of the folktale and the nursery, had 'turned themselves' into the Academic Council and had forthwith granted the recognition about which so much lung tissue had been stretched in the preceding three hours. It is a pity nobody thought of this earlier.[13]

The question of the recognition of a college society was a routine and comparatively minor matter. But in the explosive circumstances of the student agitation the issue provided a rallying-point that allowed the SDA to take the initiative. The immediate question was quickly resolved. At the resumed meeting of the Academic Council, on 6 January, the rules relating to clubs and societies were reconsidered, and recognition was granted to the Republican Club. It was assumed in the club's favour that it had nothing to do with the disturbance on the occasion of the previous meeting of the Academic Council. The perception among students, however, was that where the SRC had failed over eighteen months to obtain recognition for the club, the SDA by its direct action had succeeded. In a referendum on 4 March the students by a large majority passed a vote of no confidence in the SRC.

The last day of term was 18 December 1968. The meeting of the Governing Body that was to take place on the seventeenth was postponed until the nineteenth, 'owing to the indisposition of the President,' according to the minutes of the Governing Body (19 December); but according to the draft minutes, which were amended in a number of significant details, the president had explained to the Governing Body that the change of date was 'partly so that the Governing Body should not be in danger of being treated in the same fashion' (as the Academic Council). Meetings of the Governing Body and the Academic Council, he said, might even have to be held in Belfield—a sort of government in exile! If trouble recurred, the board-room in Earlsfort Terrace was 'too much in the midst of the students and at the mercy of interference.' Advice on how to proceed against the offending students, ranging from the very tough to the cautious, was offered to the president by several members of the Governing Body. It was agreed that at the conferring on 11 January the president would refer to the incident of the blockade and make it clear what the penalty for such conduct would be in the future.

In his conferring address, Dr Hogan referred to the doctrine of 'student power', which, he warned, if pushed to the full 'would destroy the universities of the world as we know them.' Referring to the blockade of the Academic Council and the threat of physical violence against a professor, he added: 'I wish to say that in future any student taking part in such a demonstration incurs the risk of permanent expulsion from the College.' The newspaper reports, and some student bodies, read much more into the president's words than he had said: 'a threat of expulsion ... against students participating in expressions of "student power"' (*Evening Press,* 11 January 1969); 'participation in future marches proclaiming "student power" ... would be met with permanent expulsion' (*Sunday Independent,* 12 January 1969); 'any student ... who takes part in ... "student power" demonstrations will ... run the risk of expulsion' (*Irish Press,* 13 January 1969); 'Professor J. J. Hogan ... has warned that students participating in future marches proclaiming "student power" ... incurred the risk of permanent expulsion' (*Irish Independent,* 13 January 1969).

It was quite inaccurate to report that the president had threatened expulsion for participating in marches or demonstrations or other expressions of 'student power'. He had been quite specific about the recurrence of any incident like the siege of the board-room during the meeting of the Academic Council. Unfortunately, the juxtaposition of his condemnation of 'mob rule' in general and this particular incident in UCD left his speech open to misinterpretation and to the charge that he was opposed to freedom of speech and of assembly. And this was the interpretation that the newspapers and student activists chose to give to his words.

On the afternoon of the conferring the USI at its annual congress in

Galway, on the initiative of the UCD delegation, condemned the speech by Dr Hogan as an attack on free speech. During private business at a meeting of the L&H 'a motion condemning President Hogan's recent conferring speech threatening expulsion of students who take part in future protests, and promising action if students were discriminated against in this way, was proposed and passed by a large majority.'[14]

The SDA swam with the tide and issued a statement to the press replying to the president's expulsion threat. The statement greatly exaggerated what Hogan had said by alleging that he had threatened that any students who participated in demonstrations 'would be expelled forthwith.' The SDA condemned 'in the strongest terms this threat to the democratic right of students to express their dissatisfaction with the university and society.' And the group availed itself of the opportunity to proclaim that it wished to democratise universities so that they might serve the Irish people and not 'the system which economically and socially represses them.'

There was a danger, said an editorial in the *Irish Press* (13 January 1969), that some of the more volatile elements among the students would take the president's words as a direct challenge and reply with some action that would leave him with no option but to expel them, with resultant upheaval among the rest of the hitherto unaffected students. Alec Newman in the *Irish Times* (14 January 1969) felt that the president's comments served only to emphasise the rigid stand taken in that establishment over the years against any kind of student liberalism and that they perpetuated 'the image of UCD, so sedulously fostered under Presidents Coffey and Tierney, as a bulwark of conservatism, a forcing-bed of undergraduate orthodoxy.' In extensive comments on television on the controversial expulsion threat one member of a panel (Vincent Grogan) thought Dr Hogan was foolish to have said what he did (*Irish Press*, 16 January 1969). And the President of the SRC (Eddie O'Connor) admitted that the SDA had a more advanced political consciousness than most students; but this, he said, was shared by many on the SRC.

A meeting organised by the SDA in the Physics Theatre on Wednesday 15 January 1969, attended by 350 students, called on Dr Hogan to explain to a general assembly of students and staff his threat of expulsion. One member of the SDA said: 'We want the university reconstituted. We want the students and staff to run it—not Professor Hogan and an academic clique.' *Campus* added its voice to the denunciation of the president's conferring speech and described UCD as 'a grotesque parody of democratic institutions.'[15]

Meanwhile the SDA's enthusiasm was being fuelled by events outside the college. In support of the Dublin Housing Action Committee it joined in marches, street-blockings and sit-downs and in demonstrations outside

Mountjoy Jail and at the Department of Justice, where it was joined by two members of the UCD staff, Denys Turner (ethics and politics) and Patrick Masterson (metaphysics): Turner was briefly arrested but later explained that he had been present only as an observer. The SDA also acted in solidarity with the Young Socialists and the left-wing People's Democracy movement in making a protest to the British Embassy about RUC behaviour and picketing the Mansion House during the celebration of the fiftieth anniversary of the First Dáil, whose Democratic Programme, it alleged, was flouted by the Dublin housing crisis.

THE LIBRARY ISSUE

After these town-and-gown experiences, with all the attendant exhilaration of press, radio and television coverage, and after several scuffles with the gardaí, a confrontation with the UCD authorities was not an intimidating but rather an exciting prospect for the SDA. All that was needed was an issue large enough to unite the more moderate behind them. Such an issue presented itself in the arrangements to be made for the transfer of students and libraries to Belfield.

When the final roof slab of the Arts-Commerce-Law Building was completed in October 1968 it had seemed assured that the transfer of these three faculties would take place at the opening of the 1969/70 session. It was intended to use some of the space in this building as a temporary library. As staff and students became aware that the Library would not be functioning to coincide with the transfer of teaching to Belfield, unease began to spread. A great deal of uncertainty and many rumours surrounded the timing and the nature of the move. During the first term of 1969/70 the Librarian, Ellen Power, explained to a Department of Social Science staff-student committee that, until the Library was completed, makeshift arrangements would be necessary. The books most urgently required for first-year and general students would be stored in Belfield, with temporary reading facilities in the Arts Building; honours students and postgraduates would have to get their books from the Library in Earlsfort Terrace.

The SRC organised an action committee to look into the problem. They considered the possibility of preventing the move until proper library facilities were available or, alternatively, obtaining a temporary library by way of prefabricated buildings. A number of college societies passed resolutions disapproving of the move in the absence of library facilities. The president's statement at the conferring on 11 January 1969 that the portion of the Library that they had permission to build (phase 1) had cost more than estimated, and his hope that the Government would provide the difference and so avoid the delay that any redesigning would entail, added to the general unease. Resolutions passed by the Faculty of Arts and by the ASA also reflected the growing concern about the Library and any leap in the dark. This deepening anxiety on the part of students and staff was understandable, given the shortage of reading places, when over 80 per cent of students lived either at home or in lodgings, and given also that the high failure rate was the cause of much adverse publicity. These matters and the many doubts and questions that surrounded them were kept before the students during December and January in the pages of *Campus* and *Confrontation.*

On the night the Minister for Education was shouted down in Trinity College and had left through a window, the authorities in UCD were trying to explain to a mass meeting in the college that library facilities would be provided in Belfield in the next session. The task of the college officers had not been made any easier by a newspaper report a few days earlier (*Irish Independent,* 20 February 1969) of a meeting between the SRC and the Minister for Education. At this meeting the minister had informed the SRC that the Students' Union building (which had been a will-o'-the-wisp ever since 1909) should be constructed by August 1971, and that the £350,000 promised by the Government for that purpose a year earlier would be made available. He had also assured the students that they would be given one-third representation on the Academic Councils and Governing Bodies. And the minister had also said that while phase 1 of the Library would not now be complete until September 1970, approval had been given for phase 2.

This report incensed the President of UCD. In tones almost as angry as those he had used in his earlier letters to the minister over the announcement of Lenihan's merger plans, he complained that the president of the college ought to have been informed of the Government's decision regarding the Library at least as soon as anybody else in the college, especially since the minister had not been able to give a delegation of college officers definite information on this very point at their meeting only ten days earlier. The president's feeling of being placed at a disadvantage was all the greater in view of the fact that the better-informed SRC had prepared its big 'teach-in' on the whole question of the move to Belfield, to which the president and his colleagues were invited.

The president, registrar, secretary, Professor Michael Hogan (Chairman of the Buildings Committee) and librarian attended the teach-in. The purpose of the meeting was diversely understood. The college officers regarded it as an occasion on which to give the most up-to-date and accurate information about the move to Belfield. Some students looked on it as an opportunity to impugn the authorities and denounce the system. As the officers attempted to give details about the move, extremist students surrounded all the microphones placed around the hall, made revolutionary speeches about the rights of students to a voice in the decisions of the college, and prevented the moderates from speaking. Several speeches and replies could not be heard.

The meeting deteriorated, and the college officers were subjected to verbal abuse.

The intention of the SDA was to reveal a rift between the officers and the students. The officers had arranged to attend from 8 to 10:15; when they left at 10:30, this was reported in some papers as a 'walk-out'.

THE OCCUPATION

After a mass meeting organised by the SDA at lunchtime on the following day (Wednesday 26 February) attended by about 150 students, it was resolved that there should be no move to Belfield until full library facilities were available; that the Governing Body should be abolished; that a fifty-fifty staff-student committee should be set up to govern the college; and that students present should at once occupy the administration offices.

The occupying SDA force numbered at first about 40, but later that night over 140 were present, of whom about 60 spent the night in the administration wing. The registrar reckoned that the UCD students were augmented by ten or twelve from Trinity College; and twenty students from Bolton Street College of Technology arrived on Thursday evening and joined the occupation. The first reaction of the general student body was that of onlookers' curiosity. Medical students, finding their usual route through the corridor blocked and mindful of impending examinations, grew irritable, and 'a few incidents bordered on violence.' Commerce students repudiated the occupation and collected almost 450 signatures. Extensive discussions took place in the Main Hall.

Photocopiers, typewriters and a great quantity of college stationery were commandeered by the occupiers. Notices declaring *You are now entering the liberated zone* and cartoons depicting college officers in an unflattering light were posted on doors and walls. But no serious damage was done to property, and no member of the staff was threatened with assault.

The secretary of the college met the students and repeatedly asked them to leave. When he tried to discover the motive for the occupation he was answered with complaints against society in general, which the SDA said they wished to overturn, beginning with the college. Two gardaí—not summoned by the college authorities—arrived on Wednesday afternoon. The SDA claimed that they had been called by students opposed to the occupation; others suspected that the call had been made by one of the occupiers. MacHale requested them to leave.

The SDA felt greatly stimulated by the two-day occupation. A writer in *Confrontation* (4 March 1969) described the 'unique atmosphere' in which students for the first time were thinking, talking and acting together; college had never been 'so alive and so free'; the occupation was an assertion that the university was a place where people discuss and work together, free from the shackles of tradition and dogma. The SDA were convinced that the occupied university created a real academic community and that the occupation was 'the first hint that it is possible to create a new kind of university—radically different from the present one.'

On Thursday morning the occupiers were not pleased with the press reports and thought the *Irish Independent* excelled itself in distortion. As the day progressed they were gladdened by evidence of increased support from the moderates, especially whenever the registrar or secretary attempted to take the names of the occupiers by demanding their students' cards.

That evening, while a cleaning committee was left in the 'liberated zone', the majority of the occupiers attended the teach-in in the Great Hall, called by the SRC to discuss the occupation. At least 1,500 students were estimated to be present, though the number was variously reported as 2,000 or even 3,000. After a number of speeches, including five by members of the staff ('four of whom were sympathetic, one hostile,' according to *Confrontation*), a resolution was passed supporting the occupation. The meeting, however, called on the occupying students to end the occupation for the moment, in order to join with the SRC in demanding

(*a*) that the Governing Body be reformed so as to delegate power to joint committees of staff and students democratically elected;

(*b*) that a joint staff-student committee make all decisions pertinent to the move to Belfield; and that no decision should be made without adequate consultation with the whole body of staff and students whose directions would be obeyed;

(*c*) that no student should be victimized for the occupation.

The meeting then agreed to reconvene on the following Wednesday (5 March) to consider direct action on the basis of the response of the authorities to these demands. The occupiers voted to vacate the administration offices after final cleaning-up was done.

As the move to Belfield and the library facilities had been a major issue in the disturbance, MacHale issued a detailed factual statement of the position. This was published in the newspapers on Monday 3 March and distributed to students throughout the college. It made the point that the Governing Body had requested the Government to build, at the same time as the Arts Building, sections (if not the whole) of a library, a restaurant and a Students' Union building. Since these had not materialised, the statement also pointed out that the Buildings Committee of the Governing Body was consulting a staff committee since December, and a sub-committee of the SRC since January, on the possible solutions to the problems of the move.

When the Governing Body met the following day it endorsed the MacHale press statement and issued its own briefer statement to the press, radio, and television. It was also distributed throughout the college. It said that before the final decision on the move to Belfield was taken, joint discussions would be held with the Buildings Committee, the Committee of the Faculty of Arts, the Committee of the ASA, and the Belfield Committee of the SRC. On the SRC demands that had emanated from the teach-in on 27 February the Governing Body showed itself to be in a fighting and determined mood. 'The Governing Body has a legal obligation which can only be altered by Act of the Oireachtas, to carry out all the affairs of the College. It intends to continue to do so, and will not yield to intimidation. The Governing Body is prepared to meet the SRC at any time.' The Governing Body also welcomed the setting up of a committee of the Academic Council on the previous day to establish the facts about the recent disturbances.

The gulf between the SDA and the Governing Body seemed to be unbridgeable. A generation gap separated the students of the sixties, who wanted a new kind of university in a new kind of society, from the college authorities, who had learnt to conduct the business of the institution in the very different atmosphere that had prevailed during the first fifty years of its existence. The president's shock at the students' revolt was revealed in his comments at the special meeting of the Governing Body on 4 March called to consider the occupation. He said that the whole idea of revolt was something new in the college and had done great damage to its idealism. The students one met at the usual student activities, society meetings, sports fixtures and dances, he said, seemed hardly aware of what was going on. (On that point the SDA would have agreed. But the SDA attitude would have been very different, seeing nothing to be complacent about in student activity that restricted itself to social events.) The president went on to say that the growth of the revolutionary group 'of about 120 well-trained extremist students had been carefully concealed.' At an inaugural meeting of the L&H in the Michaelmas term, at which he had presided, he had heard, he said, 'definite communist sentiments expressed and applauded from a considerable part of the meeting.'

The resumed mass meeting to consider the response of the Governing Body to the demands that had been made was due to take place on Wednesday 5 March in the Great Hall. Given the collision course that the SDA and Governing Body seemed to be travelling, many among the academic staff were actively engaged in trying to defuse the situation. On the day the Governing Body met, the ASA issued a statement recognising that the college was facing a period of rapid change and development and that in just such a time the greatest temptation lay for extremism in innovation or in reaction. It urged restraint and moderation, and added that the ASA appreciated the need for the development of suitable means for the proper expression of genuine student concern.

There was the feeling among ASA members, who had already experienced deep involvement in the merger debate, that they should act as the voice of moderation in what appeared to be the confrontational attitudes of the SDA and the authorities. The junior academic staff in particular had their own grievances about their exclusion from participation in departmental and faculty decisions. It seemed odd to them that while demands for student participation in the government of the college might yet be conceded, the claims of the junior academic staff were being ignored.

The view of some among the junior staff was that recent disturbances could be traced to what was looked upon as the autocratic system of the past and to the tardiness with which that system was giving way to reform that would allow wider participation. It was felt that some junior staff were even pleased at the embarrassment and inconvenience the occupation caused to the authorities. These junior staff were sympathetic at least to the extent of understanding the students' frustration that had led to the occupation. Most if not all staff members had no desire to see a reoccupation. On the other hand, there were those who did not wish to see the momentum for reform lost; and it was these who now moved to the centre of the stage.

The week between the two mass meetings of 27 February and 5 March was one of intense activity. Resolutions, all related in one way or another to the occupation and its aftermath, were passed by the L&H (1 March), the Academic Council (3 March), the Governing Body (4 March), and the ASA (4 March). A great deal of effort was engaged in by individual staff members and groups to defuse the situation. Garret FitzGerald was involved in seeing that the meeting on 5 March would be chaired by a moderate (John Maguire) and that it would be run in such a way as to prevent the SDA from gaining control.

A group of the junior staff met on the night of 4 March in a private house in Ailesbury Road to consider the situation. This group, later referred to by the Academic Council's committee of inquiry as the 'Secret Group of Twelve', favoured the idea that the mass meeting should be channelled towards a policy of holding seminars on the future role of the university. Bernard Jensen from Copenhagen, a tutor in the History Department, was reported to have been the chief proposer of the idea.

Relatively moderate counsels were asserting themselves within the SDA also. On the afternoon of the scheduled meeting of 5 March the SDA decided by a majority vote not to reoccupy the administration wing. It was felt that a second occupation would not have the same dramatic impact as the first, and that the SDA would lose support from students if the medical exams due to take place the following week were impeded, or if the college had to be closed, as was being widely assumed would happen. It was felt that the authorities would use the opportunity of reoccupation to wrong-foot the SDA.

Here was the old battle of the two extremes in this confrontation: the SDA and the college authorities, each trying to outmanoeuvre the other by not driving the large body of moderate students into the opposite camp.

At the meeting in the Great Hall the seminar idea, as opposed to reoccupation, was carried by the great majority. The motion stated:

> That normal academic activities in College be suspended from 9 a.m. tomorrow, Thursday, 6 March 1969, for the purpose of discussing:
> (a) the institutional structures of UCD and the values and attitudes which give rise to them, and
> (b) the function of the university in the context of the needs and interests of the Irish people.

Subsequently described as a face-saving operation for the SDA to get them off the hook, the proposed plan involved holding, over the following days, mass seminars during the normal lecture periods. This would imply a theoretical, or 'in the mind', occupation of the college. From this point, the influence of the SDA began to wane. That evening in Garret FitzGerald's house a group of more moderate students and three staff members met to discuss how the seminar idea might work. The following morning a steering committee of staff and students was elected to oversee the seminars. The SDA fared badly in these elections.

Guidelines from the steering committee recommended that a vote be taken to establish whether the majority wished to hold a seminar or a lecture, and that the results of this vote should be conveyed to the relevant lecturer. The seminars began rather slowly, as there had been little or no organisation. Some staff co-operated; others refused to suspend their lectures. No instruction on this point had yet been issued by the authorities.

A number of staff members sympathetic to the seminars issued a statement on Friday 7 March, signed by nine professors and over sixty of the junior staff. Senator FitzGerald, who was its principal sponsor, drafted the statement, which was amended on the advice of others. It declared: 'Something quite unique is happening in UCD at the moment. To describe it as a student revolt is to misunderstand it totally.' Many students and staff members had suddenly found themselves in an emotional climate in which barriers to communication between them had been removed, which had given rise to a great and potentially fruitful debate. It recognised that not all staff members or students wished to participate in the exercise, and that it might fail to produce conclusions of value; but by participating and trying to help, members of the staff were minimising the risk.

The Social Science Department (with Rev. Professor James Kavanagh as head and Rev. Conor Ward as one of the senior members) held a departmental meeting that reached a consensus that normal lecture time be devoted to contributing to the better structuring of institutions and the university community. Professor Phyllis Clinch told a meeting of students in Belfield that she and her Botany Department were willing, if the students so wished, to cancel lectures in favour of discussion. The English Department achieved a compromise through allowing classes other than lectures to be devoted to discussion on the nature of the university. Professor Conor Martin gave freedom to his lecturers in the Department of Politics and Ethics to use their classes as they saw fit.

A considerable amount of concern, however, was expressed about the obligation to maintain the scheduled classes. Professor John Kelly, Dean of the Faculty of Law (and later a colleague of Garret FitzGerald in Government), listed defects in the structures and said there was a case for discussion with the students, but he told his own students that in view of the professional nature of his subject he had an obligation to give his lectures; that it would be a breach of duty not to do so; that he would continue to give lectures until he was physically stopped; and that he was ashamed that some staff members were aiding and abetting the agitators by giving them such blatant support. A university substantially run by students and 'student-orientated' junior staff, he said, would not be worth studying in.[16]

The divisions in the ranks of the academics that were created by the student revolt were neatly illustrated in the reaction of three well-known UCD clerics. Father Desmond Connell (later Archbishop of Dublin) formally complained to the registrar that when he arrived at the Physics Theatre at noon on Thursday 6 March to give his lecture he had found the theatre occupied by history students and lecturers, who were holding a meeting. The registrar wrote to Rev. Professor F. X. Martin of the History Department for an explanation and received a reply stating that Father Martin was not aware of the incident, that he had inquired into the matter, and that one of the history lecturers had apologised to Father Connell. While Father Connell had tried without success to give his lecture, and Father Martin was blithely unaware that lecturers in his own department were holding a meeting with the students, Rev. Professor James Kavanagh (later an auxiliary bishop of Dublin) had decided in his Department of Social Science to hold seminars with the students.

In this three-way split between prominent clerics one has not only a characterisation of three strong personalities but also an encapsulation of the trauma for individuals that was brought to a head by the student agitation. It did not make for easy relations among colleagues. Reaction ranged the whole gamut from near-support for the SDA and full-blooded participation in the 'teach-ins' to downright opposition. Some would have looked on their more enthusiastic colleagues as bandwagoning, or as being motivated by their discontent with their lot in college, and would have resented as offensively patronising the remarks of a junior colleague who advised the students in one of the teach-ins that older members of the staff who had built up a system over forty years must be 'treated with patience, forbearance and firmness.' The staff members who participated saw it as a great awakening, an intellectual excitement, a sign of the real vitality of the university, and an opportunity to convert rhetorical release into effective thinking, constructive vision, progressive action and fundamental change. All the superlatives were applied, while the newspapers supplied the headlines and the pictures.

A statement from the President of the Union of Students in Ireland, Ciarán McKeown, circulated at the meeting of Thursday night (6 March) caught the feverish mood of the participants.

> [The]USI welcomes the great awakening of UCD and looks forward to the spectacle of UCD students and staff deciding with vision, maturity and determination the kind of optimum college they would like to have. At last the biggest college in the country has asserted itself and we call on the other colleges to assess their position now ... We call on all academic staff and governing bodies to approach this gentle revolution with the same spirit.

And the term 'gentle revolution' stuck.

At the end of the second day of seminars (Friday 7 March) a mass meeting was held. The SDA proposed that the seminars continue indefinitely, but the majority decided to end them the following day (examinations were to take place in the Great Hall on Monday) and decided that a committee would collate the reports from the various group discussions and present them at another mass meeting, on Wednesday 12 March. Another SDA proposal for the formation of a student-worker alliance and for visits to factories to inform workers of their ideas was also defeated. The SDA walked out, and their members resigned from the steering committee. Outmanoeuvred by the moderates and by the more professional debaters and L&H types, who had the active support of many of the staff, the SDA was becoming increasingly marginalised.

In response to all this flurry of activity the president showed the relief of the administrators when he reported to the Governing Body on 11 March 1969 that there had been no repetition of the invasion of offices. The 'violent action', as he called the occupation, had released a much larger movement among a more numerous body of students. These, he said, had not been prepared to follow the 'violent leaders' all the way, but in abandoning their classes for the seminars they had in fact followed them to that extent. Some lecturers, while not participating themselves, had permitted classes to hold these discussions. Some members of the staff had joined in the discussions. He had been thinking a lot about what had happened, the embattled and harassed president said, and it was clear that it was not something that would easily pass by and be forgotten. This was taken by Senator FitzGerald to be a threat of victimisation, which greatly depressed him.[17]

Some county councillors on the Governing Body raised the matter of a member of the Governing Body (FitzGerald) addressing the students and telling them that he was prepared to introduce a Private Member's Bill in Seanad Éireann for the reform of the Governing Body. The president said it was natural that many members of the Governing Body had been offended by this proposal. He thought it strange that anyone who had attended the previous special meeting of the Governing Body, which had issued unanimously a statement with regard to the students' demands of the previous week, should attend a mass meeting of students and offer as a member of Seanad Éireann to bring in a Bill to change the Governing Body in accordance with their wishes. This seemed to undermine the authority of the body of which he was a member.

Senator FitzGerald explained that he and other members of the staff had been concerned lest the mass meeting of 5 March end in serious disorder. They took steps to try to ensure that this would not happen. They arranged that they would have a chairman who would conduct the business in an orderly fashion. It seemed to him important to point out that the Governing Body had not got power, even if it wished, to respond to the demands made by the students. Change could only be effected by changing the law. He had spoken of the possibility of altering the Governing Body with a view to relieving tension at the mass meeting. As a result the meeting had ended with the heavy defeat of the SDA. It was with a view to achieving this that he had intervened.

FitzGerald's explanation only confirmed what spokespersons of the SDA specifically warned students against: the deliberate defusing of the movement's revolutionary momentum by a moderate majority led by the staff. As Kevin Myers wrote,

> what had begun as an occupation by scruffy, anarchic, long-haired students emerged in the clear light of a liberal day as a basically respectable and staff-controlled movement with aims specifically defined within the university ... Once the staff began to assert themselves in the seminars, thereby giving support to the naturally conservative part of the UCD students, the original motives of the occupiers were lost.[18]

Two of FitzGerald's friends supported him. Professor Patrick Lynch said he thought that Senator FitzGerald had spoken to the mass meeting as a member of the staff, not as a member of the Governing Body, and that his offer had had a calming effect. Professor O'Donnell agreed. But six other academics on the Governing Body spoke of the seriousness of the situation and of the importance of maintaining order in the college.

The president said that the Governing Body could, if asked to do so, recommend changes; but any sensible legislation would be unlikely to depart essentially from the pattern settled in 1908. This conservative line did not reflect how the students and some staff members were thinking. It was hardly compatible with suggestions made by two Ministers for Education, O'Malley and Lenihan, regarding the composition of Governing Bodies. On the question of student representation on the Governing Body, Dr Hogan believed that the best students were often not interested in seeking election to student bodies; that it took a considerable time, which students had not got, to become a useful member of the Governing Body; and that they could certainly not be regarded as delegates taking their instruction from, and reporting back to, the student body. Government nominees and local authority representatives took part in the work of the Governing Body as individuals and did not report back to anyone. These remarks were yet another indication of the unbridgeable gap between the thinking of the authorities and of the students.

It was unanimously agreed by the Governing Body that the registrar should send a directive to all heads of department that members of the staff, unless prevented, should give their lectures and classes according to schedule; discussion on other matters could be held at other times. It was decided that this directive would be made public. So, apart from the hiccup over Garret FitzGerald's participation in the mass meeting, the Governing Body maintained a united and firm line throughout.

The mass meeting of Wednesday 12 March, the last day of term, was presented with the amalgamated report of the collating committee based on the work of the seminars. The SDA charged that the staff had taken control in order to defuse the revolutionary impulse, and argued for the resumption of the seminars.[19] The majority, however, voted to accept the report as a basis for negotiation with the ASA, and arrangements were made to elect four student negotiators.[20] The SDA walked out in disgust, singing 'The International'.

After all the 'spring fever' of the Hilary term, from January to mid-March 1969, things began to cool for a while. Disillusioned with the turn of events inside the college, the SDA returned to the streets, concerning itself with the affairs of society beyond Earlsfort Terrace. Between 17 and 22 April the SDA occupied the premises of G. A. Brittain Ltd in solidarity with the car workers, occupied the British embassy in solidarity with the people of Northern Ireland, and demonstrated outside Dáil Éireann. Up to mid-May, and with the examinations approaching, the atmosphere inside the college was described as 'politically dormant at the moment.'[21] It was as if all the detailed and complex constitution-making during the seminars and mass meetings at the end of term had proved confusingly boring to the bulk of the student body and had drained them of whatever remained of enthusiasm for structural change. Activity had provided catharsis.

THE ACADEMIC COUNCIL COMMITTEE OF INQUIRY

The committee of inquiry appointed by the Academic Council on 3 March 1969 had as its terms of reference 'to establish the facts about the recent disturbances in the College, to meet the teaching staff and the Students' Representative Council, and to report back to the Academic Council.' It was composed of twelve professors.[22] It contained no junior staff and no students. Professor Robin Dudley Edwards was elected chairman and Professor Michael McCormac secretary.

The committee decided to engage in 'the fullest possible consultation' with the administration, staff and students as a matter of urgency. It considered about sixty written submissions, heard oral evidence from over thirty individuals or groups, and met in twenty-four private sessions during March, April and early May.

After decades of teaching Irish history and of editing the scholarly *Irish Historical Studies,* Professor Dudley Edwards, one of the college's characters, played out his role as chairman of the tribunal with gusto. His colleagues admired how this new responsibility infused 'Dudley' (as he was called by staff and students alike) with a new lease of life. His two months in charge of the committee of inquiry refreshed and stimulated him more effectively than any sabbatical in foreign academies might have done. With his flowing locks and scholarly presence and with his secretarial assistant, seconded from the registrar's office, by his side, he was a visible reminder to all of the seriousness of the investigation the college had undertaken.

Given the international context of student revolt, and the rumours and suspicions that surrounded the events in UCD, it was not surprising that the committee showed a determination to get to the bottom of any possible conspiracy there might have been between the radical students and those members of the junior staff who were suspected of having given them ammunition and support. The committee concerned itself with such questions as: What was the SDA? Was there, as some observers asserted, an external element to the unrest? And had its members been trained abroad in student radicalism? The fact that some members had attended a course dealing with 'student power' in the London School of Economics or were on delegations to international student conferences, or that Bernard Jensen, tutor in history, had contacts with student revolution in Copenhagen before his arrival in UCD and that Michael Chesnutt (English Department) had spent part of the year in Copenhagen, aroused suspicions of external conspiracy. Questions were in the air about how and from where the SDA was financed for its travel and publications.

The conspiracy theory exercised the mind of the chairman to a considerable extent in his first draft of his report. This was especially so in his references to 'the secret group of 12 or more staff conspirators' who had met in Ailesbury Road, where, apparently, the idea of the staff-student seminars, instead of a second occupation, had been promoted. Among those who should be the subject of particular scrutiny were Michael Chesnutt and Bernard Jensen, and Hugh Gough and Brian Sommers (both of the History Department). Dudley Edwards suspected that there were others who were not present at the meeting in Ailesbury Road but who were among the more astute sympathisers and who had begun to sense the need to stay under cover. And here, he said, 'he would very tentatively put forward the names of Professor F. X. Martin and an assistant in his own Department—Donal McCartney.' On the other hand, though Garret FitzGerald and Professor P. K. Lynch took an active interest in the occupation, to the extent of talking to the occupiers, Professor Dudley Edwards knew of no evidence suggesting that they were accessories. But a reference by one SDA activist to a lecture given by Professor John O'Meara in April 1968 was enough for him to play with the idea that Professor O'Meara might well have been an accessory before the fact.

All Dudley Edwards's guess-work had to be taken against his well-known propensity to stir up trouble for his colleagues. Questions would have to be addressed, he said, to Denys Turner and Philip Pettit (both of the Department of Ethics and Politics), who were alleged to be in Opus Dei. According to Professor Dudley Edwards, the Catholic element in the student revolution should be stressed, because this was not obvious to those who were obsessed with the idea that it had an exclusively communist origin.

Nothing better revealed Dudley Edwards's character and his determination to get to the bottom of any alleged conspiracy than another document that he submitted to his committee. This was marked *Confidential* and headed 'Secret statement of Chairman on alleged staff secret XII revolutionaries. March 1969'.[23] What followed had all the ingredients of a spy mystery set in Kim Philby's Cambridge of the nineteen-thirties. It explained: 'On Sunday, March 23, in response to a telephone enquiry, a non-statutory colleague in Arts, to be denoted hereinafter as C.O'D., agreed that he had heard of a conspiracy in the disturbances under investigation. He included the following persons as being, by hearsay evidence, involved in varying degrees (to whom I prefix numbers).' He then listed the twelve and their departments, to each of whom he gave a number.

His informant had been invited by No. 3 (Michael Chesnutt) to attend a meeting on the evening of 4 March at the premises of Mrs Woods, an

American living at Ailesbury Road—a rather exclusive suburb in Dublin 4 and an incongruous meeting-place for 'revolutionaries' (if not the perfect cover). Mrs Woods, he explained, helped to run the Catholic organisation Grille and was interested in the student revolution. The mystery continued. 'Her husband is usually on the premises but concentrates on T.V. A key to the premises is held by No. 6 above [Hilary Jenkins] ... No. 3 expected about 20 to attend to advise on the best way to support his efforts after he had been virtually rejected in his radical policy at the preceding meeting of ASA.' Dudley Edwards's informant 'was told later by No. 5 [Hugh Gough], partly verified subsequently by No. 6,' that the attendance was only twelve; and as this number also attended the next meeting, the group came to be known as 'the XII'. Professor Dudley Edwards added that the term 'revolutionaries' was to be construed very loosely. He said it was to be noted that of the 'XII', eight came from outside the Republic, seven were connected with the Department of History, and all were of the Faculty of Arts.

It was alleged that No. 7 (Bernard Jensen) proposed the radical alternative to the occupation of the administrative offices, namely the taking over of the college for seminars. No. 2 (Diethelm Brüggemann) did state that Nos. 5 and 10 (Brian Sommers) favoured reoccupation and that for this No. 10 was attacked by No. 3. Views on the role of No. 7 were described by No. 1 (Sister Benvenuta) as part of a witch hunt.

The document concluded by stating that Nos. 5 and 7 had influenced No. 1 to participate in the television programme after her speech in the Great Hall on the morning of 6 March.

Mystery, appropriately enough, still surrounds the identity of Dudley Edwards's informant. Though the initials C.O'D. are supposedly those of 'a non-statutory colleague in Arts', a search of the staff lists reveals nobody with these initials. Dudley Edwards's involvement as a judge in the *Sunday Independent* crosswords may have encouraged him to bequeath this puzzle to posterity. C.O'D. was no doubt a clever ruse on his part, one worthy of his daughter Ruth, who enjoys writing detective mysteries.

However, by the time all submissions were received and considered by the committee, including those from most of the 'Secret XII', and after wiser counsels (or less intuitive ones, as the case may be) prevailed, all mention of the Secret XII was dropped from the final report, and the college community was spared the public hanging of esteemed colleagues and teachers. The Department of History, in particular, would have been decimated.

Despite the aura of conspiracy that, in the minds of some, hung over the events of February and March, the committee of inquiry established for itself a certain credibility and even won the confidence of staff and students. It was accepted that it was not a committee of discipline but a committee 'to establish the facts about the recent disturbances.' And this proved attractive to those who had grievances to air or a case to make for reform, or who wished to justify stances they had taken.

University, a bulletin put out by members of the staff, the first number of which appeared early in February 1969 and the second in March, was looked upon by the more conservative as contributing to the revolutionary fervour. Most of the articles, as an early draft of the committee of inquiry's report pointed out, rebuked the authorities specifically for their handling of the move of the Arts Library to Belfield. These articles also called for reform of the governing structures, better communications within the college, and the participation of staff and students in decision-making. These were all areas where student and staff demands coincided. The feeling that there were grave problems in the way that UCD was being run was by no means restricted to a few radicals but extended to many academics.

A great deal of emphasis from staff and students alike was placed on poor communications. Professor Dunning claimed that on six different occasions he had put forward a proposal for a university gazette. And he made the telling point that Newman, even with a much smaller college, had understood this need and that one of his first projects had been the publishing of the *Catholic University Gazette.*[24]

A number of members of the junior staff shared the students' hostility to the college administrators. The three at the top (president, registrar and secretary) were the special targets of strongly worded criticism. It was alleged by their harshest critics in *University,* and repeated in the submissions, that the troika took upon themselves the entire negotiation with the Government and the making of decisions affecting the whole university community. They were accused of ramming policies down the throats of academics and of being unable to comprehend what it was the institution stood for. It was said that they had imposed a 'stifling authoritarianism', had shown little interest in the students, treated both junior staff members and students as children, and possessed a 'paternalistic mentality'. They were described as a 'bureaucratic junta of dubious legality and competence' and as a small clique that had assumed powers of the kind formerly arrogated to themselves by the British and had also assumed the lofty imperial style of government. (This was from an English member of the staff who would otherwise be described as among the mildest of men.)

The chairman of the inquiry in his draft report described the general tone of *University* as being 'an endorsement of the occupation.' In the submissions made by the 'radicals', however, no member of the staff condoned the occupation. On the other hand, in comments made by a few members of the staff there was a readiness to excuse or explain the occupation. It was argued that the rationale of the students' action had to be understood as aiming a blow at the system and creating a sense of involvement for the majority: that 'occupation' was the equivalent of their form of 'communication'. R. B. Walsh wrote in *University* that the 'occupiers' should be treated as parties to a critical dispute rather than as offenders against college discipline—however monstrous this might seem to those in authority.

So, while many of the junior staff shared the grievances of the students on such issues as the lack of information, the structures, and the Library, most were anxious to deny that they had fomented the disturbances, to distance themselves from any taint of participation in the demonstrations and sit-ins, and to show themselves as really the defusers of a revolutionary situation. It was stated that staff members who took part in the mass meeting exercised a moderating influence. All those involved in these events, argued Garret FitzGerald on his own and their behalf, were acting with constructive intent; and the suspicions attached to some of them, though at first shared by him, were groundless.

The occupying students had indeed found some comfort in the more extreme remarks by members of the staff. In their final statement from the 'liberated zone' (on college stationery) they went so far as to assert that some of the junior staff supported the occupation on the stated demands, and thanked them for their solidarity. It was only to be expected that at least the leaders among the occupiers would have read the first number of *University*, which had appeared before the occupation had occurred, and would have welcomed its angry views on the Library's move to Belfield and on the lack of communication.

Apart from *University,* there was evidence in the submissions that some SDA members had also read, and used selectively to their advantage, reports of speeches by senior staff members. In a lengthy submission by one of the SDA's propagandists, D. Ó Brolcháin, reference was made to a lecture given by Professor John O'Meara at a Pax Romana study conference in April 1968 in which he referred to the failure of academics to use their academic freedom. He quoted also from an address by Professor John Kelly to the effect that the Governing Body had made serious mistakes—the biggest being to support Donogh O'Malley's idea of one University of Dublin. A letter to the *Sunday Independent* (1 December 1968) by Dr Geoffrey Hand (Faculty of Law) on the merger controversy, in which he wrote that 'if it does nothing else, it will bring a desperately needed wind of change,' was also used. It was asserted that in anybody's terms UCD was nowhere near the 'imaginative force' that Professor Denis Donoghue had called for. Professor Ivor Browne's comment regarding a society that was 'steadily ripping people apart' was mentioned as well.

These expressions of opinion by senior staff members were in their own way felt sincerely by the students. And it mattered little to the SDA that the material culled from the professors' statements was employed tendentiously, or that John Kelly and Denis Donoghue were also among the most outspoken critics of the student extremists. They were, for SDA purposes, a good stick with which to beat the authorities and an argument with which to justify their revolt. When the quotations from the staff were added to other references in Ó Brolcháin's submission to the report of the Kenny Visitation and the report of the Commission on Higher Education, what was revealed was a fairly impressive reading-list pointing to an intellectual liveliness on the part of the more involved students. One has also to allow for the fact that some at least among the SDA had some acquaintance with the theories of popular philosophers of the student revolt, including Marcuse—a fierce critic of contemporary consumer society, in which people had no say in decisions.

On the wider issue of the structures of government the claim was made by staff critics that no-one thought the existing structure satisfactory. Conservatives among the staff had always taken the line that any tampering with the Act and Charters of 1908 would only open the flood-gates to Government and civil service interference with the university. SDA statements, describing the Governing Body as 'a repressive rigid hierarchy of power,' said that for its incompetence it should be dismissed by its masters and that it disregarded completely the interests and opinions of students.

The oral evidence given to the committee of inquiry only confirmed the general lines of what had already emerged in the documents. What a member of the committee (Professor Donoghue) referred to as a serious sort of left-right split among the academics towards the disturbances clearly did exist; yet this polarisation hardly did justice to the variety of positions strung between the extremes. The Chairman of the ASA (Professor Brendan Coakley) thought the committee should find out where the SDA got its money. Another member of the staff (Father John Moore) wondered whether they had been trained. A member of the ASA committee (Art Cosgrove) described the SDA as subscribing to 'a very negative philosophy that indicated a tinge of anarchy.'

Another ASA committee member (Paddy O'Flynn) referred to the 'fair grievances' of the students. He added that staff had sympathy with the aims but not with the actions of the students, and that the moderates had taken over as a result of a lot of hard work on the part of the staff. Garret FitzGerald admitted that it took the SDA to produce an explosion, and that he had urged his students to assert themselves and balance the SDA.

Among the so-called 'Secret XII' sympathisers, Sister Benvenuta claimed that a number of staff members who may have given out radical ideas were singularly subdued during the occupation and had remained in their homes during the week of the great debate. Hilary Jenkins stated that many of the staff, because of their youth, were in close contact with the students and that it was a real problem for the over-35s to deal with a generation they did not understand. Bernard Jensen in his evidence felt that the presence of a number of clergymen on the staff heightened the paternalistic atmosphere of UCD. Denys Turner felt that he himself turned more towards the students than towards the senior staff.

Some academics did little to hide their opinion of certain leading members of the SDA. Professor Patrick Lynch knew a number of them because they were in his tutorials and had been influenced by the books of Herbert Marcuse and others on their reading-list. Paddy Masterson noted that a book the SDA were reading was *The Run Away World* by Edmund Leach and that, 'as far as he could judge, the SDA were very intelligent and many are very highly strung.'

Father Michael Nolan referred to the arrogance of Kevin Myers in his speech at the teach-in on the Library. Even John Feeney was shortly afterwards to admit that '[the] SDA, like nearly every left-wing student group, suffered from an unbearable arrogance,' especially in so far as they felt 'they knew more about how to succeed than others who had tried and failed.'[25] MacHale, who during this teach-in had been personally abused by an SDA speaker, told the committee of inquiry that he thought Kevin Myers was 'the most unpleasant little pup he had met in a long time.' This was not the opinion of Myers held by some who worked in the occupied offices. One of these who had first-hand experience of the occupation of her office and who witnessed his concern about the nature of the operation said of him: 'Kevin was very polite and very gallant.'[26]

Those aspects of SDA philosophy that were most firmly rooted in their minds were revealed in cross-examination before the committee of inquiry. It was agreed that their ideology contained elements of Marxism and socialism but that basically the whole thing was Christian. They strongly denied affiliation with any external subversive organisation and said that they were not financed by Moscow. Any training they got was in the slums while working for the Dublin Housing Action Committee and in the Library of UCD. (By this they meant that their grievances had sprung from library conditions and not from any radicalism they might have gleaned from the books contained therein!) They rejected eastern European communism, saying it was not a democratic but an imposed system. Cuba, on the other hand, appealed to a number of their leading spokesmen. The Cubans they saw as an oppressed people trying to create some sort of society that would reflect human values. Cuba was an example of democracy in action, and they approved of the team work that was done there. The only point of contact the SDA said they had with the People's Democracy (mainly composed of Queen's University students) was that they were both left-wing. They claimed that the SDA was essentially non-violent, that they never extended violence against any individual. To speak of violence against property, however, was for them a misuse of terms. They respected people, not property. If destroying a thing was going to help people, then they would do so. Some laws become obsolete; certain formalities in college were obsolete; you had to break a law to change these obsolete formalities. They realised that the sit-in in the administration offices was outside the framework of the law.

'Property is theft' was the most famous aphorism of the nineteenth-century socialist Proudhon. In keeping with left-wing notions that property was the god of capitalism, the SDA held that all college property belonged to the students. During the occupation, when they used college stationery and college photocopiers to issue their statements, they did so on the principle that 'college' by definition included students.[27] They told one of the administration staff who was protective of the typewriter in her office that it belonged to them. On the other hand, unlike their American counterparts, who broke into government offices and burned conscription papers, the SDA put up notices on files in the administration offices that read *Do not touch!* (They displayed indeed a fastidiousness reminiscent of William Smith O'Brien's leadership during the 1848 rebellion when he ordered the rebels who might wish to cut down trees for a barricade to get the permission of the landlord first.) The students returned an orange that had been stolen from one woman's desk. A cardigan and shoes that had gone missing from another office were eventually recovered by their owner. And when it was discovered that an umbrella was missing from the offices, Kevin Myers went to see the owner and offered the £1 that was stated to be its value, which was accepted. When the umbrella was found in the porter's office three days later, the £1 was returned. There are those who would hold that revolutionaries should be made of sterner stuff.

The occupation had not set out to do anything in particular, apart from raising questions about the whole university issue and increasing the awareness of otherwise apathetic students. They insisted that the question that should be asked was not what was going to happen to students who had stepped out of line by the sit-in but what had caused it. The question was, had the students got problems?

The reason for the occupation was two-fold. They believed (*a*) that the existing university was not an academic community and (*b*) that the university did not serve the needs of the people. The SDA held that it was important for graduates to come out of the university into society with a social conscience.[28] They were opposed to the 'processing' of students, whereby they ended up in safe jobs in international corporations. They rejected the idea of people emerging from university with degrees but who were also narrow-minded and unaware of society and its problems. One of them put the question to the professors on the committee of inquiry: 'Are you content to maintain UCD on the same level as the old London commerce schools that even Newman criticised?'

Students involved with the SDA asserted that on the whole they had little contact with the staff. They had hoped that members of the staff would have gone to SDA meetings, but this had not happened. Some SDA members had been in touch with their lecturers, but this had not been general or institutionalised. They did not want more dialogue with the staff: in fact they spoke of a coalition between the junior staff and the skilled debaters such as those from the L&H that had defused the momentum for radical change. There were others disillusioned by the outcome who regarded the defusing as an effort inspired by Garret FitzGerald and his Fine Gael friends among the moderate students.

The SDA had little time for the moderates and for the role they had played. It became apparent that rather than replacing the system, the moderates were happy enough just to improve the existing capitalist university. The report of the collating committee that emerged was, according to Myers, 'uniformly conservative and singularly uninspiring'[29] and, according to Feeney, 'illiterate and futile.'[30] It was change for change's sake, but it had really offered nothing to change the university or society.

Apart from opposition from the moderates, the SDA felt that the Belfield students had been organised against them on the argument that Earlsfort Terrace was dictating to Belfield. There was an engaging openness in their recognition of the fact that a more comfortable existence in Belfield would not be in the interests of the SDA's ideology, for they admitted that the better the conditions, the worse for the SDA.

THE REPORT OF THE COMMITTEE OF INQUIRY

Having sifted through all the evidence that was laid before it, the committee of inquiry issued its report. This outlined the events culminating in the occupation; gave a detailed account of the occupation itself and the subsequent events; examined the part played by members of the teaching staff; suggested underlying causes of the disturbance; and submitted recommendations to the Academic Council.

In its analysis of the underlying causes the report began by stating that student unrest had been part of a general malaise in society that increasingly challenged the authority of church, state, and family. In Ireland much of the recent controversy in the media about the place of the university in society had been stimulated by the dramatic announcement of the intended merger with Trinity College and its unsettling effects. A picture had emerged of apparent contrast between a vigorous young minister and a venerable commission that had deliberated for over seven years. The media and two successive Ministers for Education had involved the students in this debate from the beginning. It seemed that Lenihan had met representatives of the students more often than he met the college authorities, thus flattering student influence.

The report pointed out that whereas in the United States and France students had protested that university-state relations were much too close, UCD by contrast had been superficially denounced as living in an ivory tower. The element of truth in the denunciation, however, was that the college should have made greater efforts to explain its role in higher education, that its centralised administrative arrangements were obviously inadequate for the rapidly changing conditions of a modern mass university, and that the administration, therefore, tended to appear remote to the mass of students and some members of staff. The very poor physical conditions obtaining in Earlsfort Terrace, and library conditions in particular, were a major source of trouble. Staff dissatisfaction with the Library and differences with the administration filtered through to the students. Some staff also felt that their views regarding departmental matters were not heeded. The committee was convinced that some complaints on this score were justified.

Though not a disciplinary body, the committee had to face the issue of general discipline within the college. It considered that the recent disturbances culminating in the occupation constituted a serious breach of discipline and a major infringement of the undertaking to observe the regulations that every student signed on entering the college. For the future the committee recommended that the undertaking should be specifically signed by each student each year.

The only reservation to the report was expressed by Professor Denis Donoghue, who proposed that every student who was identified by an officer of the college as having taken part in any recent disturbance should be presented with a form undertaking to obey the rules. If the student signed the undertaking, no further action should be taken; any student refusing to sign should be expelled.

On the question of participation by students in the running of the college, the committee recommended that the representative status of the SRC should be acknowledged (otherwise the mass meeting might take its place). It also recommended that the President of the SRC and one other member should be invited to attend meetings of the Governing Body.

With regard to the junior staff (about 65 per cent of the total), the committee recommended the granting of security of tenure. It acknowledged with approval the fact that proposals were being considered for the extension of faculty membership to non-statutory staff. And it added that the college should consider establishing as soon as possible a further number of statutory lectureships, that heads of departments should hold regular departmental meetings, and that the office of dean should rotate.[31]

Turning from student and staff problems to the more general aspects of college affairs, the committee was clearly impressed by the constant emphasis on the inadequacy of external and internal communication. Consequently it recommended the appointment of a full-time public relations officer and the publication of an internal monthly gazette. It emphasised that the college's financial requirements must be stated promptly and forcefully to the Government and noted that the college had sometimes been diffident in these matters and had too readily allowed UCD to take the blame for defects that arose from inadequacy of Government financing.

Finally, on a somewhat vaguer note, the committee of inquiry recommended that the college should institute a long-term research investigation into student revolt as part of the malaise of society and so contribute to the solution of a general problem. Staff members could be seconded from a variety of academic disciplines for this purpose. The committee recommended setting up a small sub-committee of the Academic Council to report on its feasibility and on possible sources for the finance required. A sub-committee of seven members of the Academic Council was subsequently established and charged with the task of investigating the project.

On the major issue of constitutional change in structures, the committee took the line that UCD could hardly be isolated from the general proposals for change in the other university institutions in Ireland. It was taken for granted that structures, so much part of the merger debate, would be considered by the Higher Education Authority.

A report as prudent and as safe as this was bound to win for the twelve members of the committee of inquiry many compliments from their fellow-professors on the Academic Council. It was discussed over four meetings of the Academic Council during May and June, and its recommendations received the council's approval.

By establishing the committee of inquiry in the first place the Academic Council had shown that it did not dismiss the students' demands out of hand: it had shown a willingness to consider the 'causes' of their revolt. The recommendation of the committee in favour of an interdisciplinary research investigation into such issues as the emergence of new forces in society, the breakdown of the old social divisions, the changing role of the individual in society and of university institutions in relation to the community within which they were established and the changing role of youth in the academic environment further indicated that the impulses of the committee of inquiry were genuine in trying to understand what had happened in the university.

The Academic Council and its committee had also diverted the Governing Body from insisting on any immediate hard-line disciplinary action. The committee found itself positioned between the administration and those moderates and liberals who favoured reform.

SEQUEL TO THE REPORT

A special meeting of the Academic Council was called to consider the report on Saturday 17 May. But before it had done this the situation had changed dramatically.

The *Irish Press* that morning published a summary of the section of the report dealing with discipline. The Academic Council protested at the premature publication; but worse was to follow. The Sunday papers sensationalised the story, with much reference to students' surprise and anger over what so far they knew only from the newspaper reports. A 'storm', and even a fresh revolution, was forecast.

The horrified committee of inquiry issued a statement saying that the published material was taken out of context; but, predictably, the student radicals reverted to form. Mass meetings took place, and a further overnight occupation of the administration wing. The Academic Council responded with a disciplinary committee, which the SDA duly denounced. But the college year was ending, examinations loomed, and the student body showed little inclination to rally to the radicals.

Nine students were summoned to appear before the disciplinary committee. The charges were found to be proved in respect of six. The committee recommended that no punishment be imposed in the present case but that formal notice be sent from the Academic Council to each of them. It read: 'If, in the future, you are found guilty of any offence against discipline and good order involving the disruption of teaching, research or administration in the College, you will expose yourself to permanent exclusion from the College.'

If the student disturbances in UCD had been accurately labelled the 'Gentle Revolution' it would have to be admitted that the disciplinary action was correspondingly gentle—no more than a showing of the yellow card to the offending six.

AFTERMATH

The summer of 1969 provided the necessary cooling-off period. Some of the more dynamic among the student radicals got their degrees and did not return to college. Kevin Myers got first-class honours in history and slid naturally into journalism. Garret FitzGerald was elected to the Dáil, ultimately to become Taoiseach. And something like normality returned to UCD. The president, secretary and registrar returned to the routine business of college administration; the junior staff radicals concentrated on packing their bags in preparation for the move to Belfield; the commerce students moved into Belfield; and the giddy minds of the history students busied themselves once more with foreign wars and battles long ago.

Like old soldiers, the SDA didn't die. It simply faded away, many of its members into those very capitalist establishments they had once hoped to overthrow. Less than thirty years later the '68–'69 generation had itself come to power: some were in Government; some became advisers to the Government; some joined state bodies; and some became prominent in the media, moulding public opinion. This must have been the surest and the saddest sign for the idealists among them: that not only had they in the days of 'student power' been defeated but that many of their rebel colleagues had gone over to the enemy. In their philosophy of protest against the affluent sixties they had complained that the university was no more than a big impersonal conveyor-belt carrying the graduate willy-nilly into the service of capitalism, the oppressive state, the professions and big business, without any regard for the humanising and personal factors or for the ideal of participatory democracy or concern for the social and political evils in society that were the results of capitalism. In contrast, a later generation of students liked to feel sure that a university degree was in fact conveying them towards the certainty of a job after graduation.

Meanwhile, after deliberation over four meetings, the Academic Council adopted the report of the committee of inquiry 'without commitment to any particular recommendation in it.' [32] Nine specific recommendations arising from the report were made to the Governing Body. Not only was there nothing remotely radical in these but they could be said to be in some respects a watered-down version of those proposals in the report that were already sufficiently conservative. The so-called annual declaration of obedience, which had been picked on and inflated by the newspapers and had been the cause of all the furore, was quietly dropped and figured no further in discussions at the Academic Council or the Governing Body. The recommendation on discipline went no further than to state that the registrar should examine the rules generally, obtain copies of the rules of other universities, and report back to the Academic Council in the autumn. Although this seemed innocuous enough, nothing further appeared before the Academic Council on the matter.

What was thought by some members of the committee of inquiry to be the report's most far-reaching and significant recommendation was the establishment of the multi-departmental research project on the nature of student revolt. The Academic Council committee that was appointed to report on its feasibility advised that the college should not undertake the project on the scale suggested, as it would be very costly and time-consuming. The report also drew attention to the fact that a student was engaged on a thesis for the MSocSc degree on student movements, which, if awarded, would be available in the Library.[33] Reducing the long-term multi-departmental research project to the level of an MSocSc thesis (however worthy) was perhaps the most eloquent illustration (however unconscious) of what the Academic Council committee really thought of the committee of inquiry's grand design.

The only recommendations from the Academic Council to the Governing Body that were acted upon had to do with public relations, the SRC, and the non-statutory staff. The recommendation that a whole-time information officer be appointed was something that had already found favour with the authorities. Captain Charles O'Rourke was appointed to the post, to start on 2 March 1970. Details concerning the circulation of a gazette were left until after the information officer had taken up office. The first number of *UCD News* was published in October 1970 and continued thereafter at regular intervals.

The Academic Council recommended that the Governing Body set up a committee under Judge Charles Conroy to report on the structure and functions of the SRC, with particular reference to whether any changes were necessary in the method of election of representatives. The Governing Body agreed, and the committee was named in December 1969. An interim report six months later recommended an additional levy of £2 on each student for the Students' Union building. The Governing Body decided to impose this levy for the session 1971/72. And it was not until 1975 that the new constitution was eventually agreed, following a referendum among students to change the name from Students' Representative Council to Students' Union and after an election for the presidency and committee of the union had already taken place.

There were three recommendations from the Academic Council regarding academic staff. The council accepted that, instead of the annual contract that was still being offered to all assistants and assistant lecturers, they should be given instead security of tenure. The Finance Committee recommended to the Governing Body (20 April 1971) that from October 1971 contracts of appointment to the age of sixty-five be offered to all present and future full-time members of the non-statutory academic staff, on condition that they should have served a probationary period and that they should have been recommended by the head of their department. It could hardly be argued that the contract for non-statutory staff had been solely a result of the recommendation of the committee of inquiry and its acceptance by the Academic Council. The demand had long been urged, and the Academic Staff

Association had played a decisive role. The most that could be said for the recommendation of the committee and its endorsement by the Academic Council was that it had given weight to the demand and had probably speeded up the process.

The second recommendation concerning the academic staff was the extending of faculty membership to non-statutory staff, who made up something between 65 and 70 per cent of the total number of academics. A decision by the Governing Body to offer contracts, from October 1971, to the age of sixty-five to all non-statutory staff meant that under existing provisions all college lecturers now automatically became members of the faculties. The addition of full-time assistant lecturers to the appropriate faculties in December 1982 greatly extended the membership of the faculties. The membership of the Faculty of Arts hugely increased, as the following table illustrates.

	Total	Professors	Statutory lecturers	College lecturers	Assistant lecturers
1970/71	48	39	5	4	—
1972/73	83	40	3	40	—
1974/75	99	38	17	44	—
1983/84	209	48	47	94	20

The circumstances of the junior staff were further enhanced by the establishment of a large number of additional statutory lectureships (thirty-two) in February 1971.

The result of these changes was not only greater security and greater participation in decision-making for the junior staff but also a certain shift in the balance of power. An obvious sign of this was that non-professorial deans began to be elected to the larger faculties from the nineteen-seventies.

The third recommendation on academic staff was that staff numbers should be considerably increased, especially in those departments where shortages were most pressing. This was put in motion by the Governing Body on 20 June 1969; implementation would be dependent on the necessary finance being available. In June 1970, when submitting estimated requirements for the years 1971 to 1974 to the Department of Education, the secretary said that from October 1970 the college hoped to have recruited about forty additional staff members and requested funds for an additional eighty per year for the following three years, beginning in October 1971, in order to improve the staff-student ratio.

In the mid-fifties the ratio of full-time staff to students had stood at approximately 1:15. It deteriorated seriously in the years preceding the student revolt; in 1968/69 it was 1:20. (The actual ratio was far worse than these figures suggest, because the part-time evening students in arts and commerce—1,742 in 1969/70—were not included. Neither were students in medicine, veterinary medicine, agriculture and architecture beyond first year. It was calculated that the real ratio in commerce was 1:146.) The HEA had set a target of 1:12, which would be reached by UCD in 1973 if the additional forty were added in 1970 and the additional eighty per year were added during the following three years. After 1973/74 an increase of twenty-five staff members per year would be required to stabilise the staff-student ratio at 1:12. This was the ideal.

In the event, the number of new staff who took up duty in October 1970 was a respectable thirty. But on 22 June 1971, because of the serious financial situation, the Governing Body decided, among other things, that no additional staff should be employed beyond the twelve to which the college was already committed. The average number of new staff who had been appointed over the four years 1967–1970 was thirty per year. By 1970/71 the staff-student ratio was 1:19. The college revised its estimates in the light of the adverse financial circumstances and claimed that an increase of forty per year for the three years 1972/73 to 1974/75 should be regarded as the minimum in order to achieve the more moderate ratio of 1:15.[34]

RESULTS OF THE GENTLE REVOLUTION

What had been the results of the Gentle Revolution? Clearly, the attempt of the SDA to overthrow capitalism and to effect a transformation of society outside college had failed utterly. Part of the problem was that the student movement left no permanent party or organisation behind. 1968, despite the high hopes of radicals everywhere, turned out to be no 1848 or anything remotely like the French, Russian or Cuban revolutions.

Within college the grand objective had been to change its structures so that student power would govern; or at least student participation would ensure a say at all levels of decision-making. But the structural reforms sought even by the moderates (spurred into action by the SDA) were not achieved; and the structures designed by the 1908 Act and Charters survived at least down to the Universities Act (1997). A token student nominated by the Government to a 34-member Governing Body was not what even the moderates had planned or two Ministers for Education had promised. Like the merger, it was a case of the mountain groaning in labour and a ridiculous little mouse being born. At the end of all the demonstration and disruption it is hard to see what the students, in practical terms, had gained from the Gentle Revolution. The very useful staff-student committees, which seem to have been a response by UCD to student troubles in Paris and elsewhere, were already in train before the occupations and demonstrations.

It might be argued that the only gainers from the student revolt were, ironically, the junior staff. But even these gains had been on the way as a result of ASA negotiations; and the most that could be claimed for the student revolt was that it possibly helped to hasten these concessions. But this could have provided only cold comfort to the SDA, which felt betrayed by the junior staff. So, however strongly one might disagree with what was then the Kevin Myers philosophy, one would have to endorse the Myers verdict on the Gentle Revolution: 'Gentle it was. Revolution it was not.'

Whatever achievements were made were largely of the abstract kind. Of course students who participated in the revolt got a giant kick out of the circus atmosphere of the demonstrations and sit-ins. John Feeney was honest enough to acknowledge that much of what went on in the name of the revolution was also great fun. It provided an escape from routine study. There was also among the occupiers the sense of camaraderie, of communal participation, and idealistic endeavour. And there was the sheer delight in the exercise of power, based on great numbers. In an age of publicity-seeking, vast coverage by the press, radio and television was assured. And protest feeds on publicity. There was too all the excitement, and perhaps fame, of participating in what promised to be a worldwide and historic revolution. 'Maybe if we work on it,' wrote a young Kevin Myers as early as November 1968, 'we'll manage a short frolic on the world stage.'

The student protests of the sixties were part of the growing-pains of a society in transition and one in which youth were demanding to be acknowledged. Authoritarianism, and even respect for authority as it had been known up to the sixties, was being shaken off and consigned to the past. In its place was being asserted a more open society and a healthy freedom — sometimes exaggerated into permissiveness. The flood of protests in the sixties, together with the sheer increase in student numbers and the teeming thousands in universities throughout the world, had helped to create a new social and political force: student power. 'Youth', as Eric Hobsbawm said, 'emerged as a recognisable group, and not merely as a period of transition between childhood and adult life.'[35]

Before the student hurricane of the late sixties had blown itself out completely, the winds affected the agricultural students in Glasnevin in the new academic year during November and December 1969, the philosophy students in February and March 1970, the architecture students in March, and the Republican Club also in March. None of these protests achieved the significance of the occupations of February or May 1969; and support for them was largely restricted to the students directly concerned. Also, the point where the authorities could be shocked had already been passed during the 1968/69 session, rendering future student disturbances less alarming.

By the autumn of 1970, almost everywhere the student movement had run its course. This turning of the tide affected UCD. There were also local conditions that helped the ebbing of the revolt. One of the most powerful of these was the move to Belfield. Here the spacious physical and architectural environment (without any obvious congregating point, such as the Main Hall or Great Hall had afforded in Earlsfort Terrace) seemed to be designed precisely to defeat the idea of the mass meeting. The first students in the Arts Building, removed from the overcrowding of Earlsfort Terrace to a 300-acre site, were like fish out of water, or intellectual dissidents banished to a concrete jungle.

The naming by the Governing Body of the three floors in the new restaurant in Belfield after three UCD men — Thomas MacDonagh, Kevin Barry, and Frank Flood, who had been executed in the fight for independence — was rejected by the Students' Council; they substituted the names of Connolly, Marx, and Lenin. Nothing illustrated more dramatically the gulf between the two generations. The fact that neither set of names stuck or caused any controversy was itself a clear indication that the battles of the sixties were over and the Gentle Revolution had been consigned to history.

11

Building Belfield

Unless the Lord build the house they labour in vain who build it

Psalm 126 [127]

1960–1975

At the time of the Dáil's approval of the transfer to Belfield (March 1960) it was agreed that part of the Science Building should be erected immediately. The significant increase in student enrolment in October 1960 made it clear, however, that the provision of only part of the block would be quite inadequate to deal with the additional numbers. By the time the Seanad debated the move (January 1961) the Government, after representations from UCD, had agreed in principle to the immediate construction of the entire Science Building.

Preliminary work began on the site almost immediately, and the cutting of the first sod took place on 7 June 1962. The national significance of the event was illustrated by the presence of President de Valera, the Taoiseach, Seán Lemass, and Archbishop McQuaid.

The architect of the Science Building was Professor Joseph Downes, and the builders were McInerney Brothers, who had submitted the lowest tender, at £1.94 million. It consisted of three wings—one for chemistry, one for physics, and one for biology—eventually linked to a central block of lecture theatres by glass corridors forming covered bridges. The formal opening of this, the first of the new buildings, took place on 24 September 1964, coinciding with Michael Tierney's retirement. His work was now done.

Because of the crisis in science it had been agreed to proceed with this building without architectural competition. The Government, however, laid down the condition that a competition, adjudicated by an international board of assessors, would be necessary before proceeding with the remainder of the buildings.[1] Competitors were required to take into account the Science Building then under construction, harmonising it into the general layout. It was also agreed that the design of one building should be coupled with the competition, and Arts and Administration were selected as being the most suitable.

The board of assessors consisted of six people, three being architects of international standing from abroad. Over five hundred registered for the competition. When it closed, in June 1964, 105 entries had been received from over twenty countries. A young Polish architect, Andrzej Wejchert, was the winner. The assessors were particularly impressed by the fact that 'the various buildings are arranged at either side of a pedestrian mall,' producing a sense of spaciousness.

In the late sixties and early seventies, planning and building continued with great energy. One by one massive constructions began to appear as the suburban university took shape; but no mere summary of the buildings as they appeared can give any idea of the number of meetings, the hours of discussions, the estimates of costs, the quantities of detail about floor areas, the haggling between college authorities and civil servants and between college officers and academics of the individual faculties—all of this demanding intensive attention while the planning and construction of the several buildings was in progress.

The transfer of Science had been relatively smooth, especially when compared with the difficulties that arose in connection with the Arts-Commerce-Law Building. The three faculties wanted 160,00 square feet, as against the 120,000 planned. A compromise of 140,000 was agreed, but only after the Government's insistence that the staff and collections of the Folklore Commission be accommodated in the building.[2] Another compromise had to be arrived at over temporary library arrangements (a sensitive issue, with complaints coming from the SRC and the Academic Staff Association, not to mention the possibility of exploitation by student agitators).[3]

The architect of the Arts-Commerce-Law Building was Wejchert, and the builders were J. Sisk and Sons. The final roof slab and the shell of the Arts Building were completed by October 1968. (The fact that demonstrations by the general body of students in UCD had not yet begun gives the lie to the subsequent speculation that the new college was designed in the way it was so as to avoid the creation of convenient meeting-places for protesters, such as the Great Hall and the Main Hall in Earlsfort Terrace had provided.) The Arts-Commerce-Law Building was finished two years later, and the official opening by President de Valera took place on 29 September 1970. According to the press reports, scuffles between gardaí, security men and Maoists took place as the Taoiseach arrived. The protesting Maoists were believed not to be UCD students.

The work of the Commerce Faculty, day and evening, had already been transferred in October 1969, with a temporary library and restaurant provided in the building. The dean of the faculty, Professor James Meenan, reflected the feelings of many when he noted in his diary that he had an interesting walk around the new building 'and it looks as if it could really be a new start.'4 A few months later, on 'a lovely evening', he could hear the Angelus ringing from Mount Anville or Mount Merrion, and from his office in the college he saw people playing tennis. 'This is the kind of peace and contentment that I love about the place.'5 But he felt it might not altogether last once the Arts Faculty was also in occupation.

His doubts became darker when it was proposed to provide in the basement a temporary reading-room for the arts students. 'It won't do to put the students down in a basement' to read. This would be 'an appalling start to life in the new building and asking for trouble ... This is the kind of thing that makes one wonder if the College can ever become a good place.'6 By the following year the inconveniences of the move had receded, and the professor's delight in the new college had reasserted itself. He described another lovely spring day: 'Belfield looked enchanting and it is so heartening to think of what it will look like when the buildings are finished and the grass and shrubs and trees begin to grow. They are deeply fortunate indeed to be young in such a place. We should produce good people indeed in future years ...'7

Later that summer he was still reporting that the college 'looks grand just now,' not only because of the trees and the flowers but also because the students were taking full advantage of the playing-fields and coming out to spend their time there.8 He was also greatly pleased by the social amenities provided in the new Arts Building. He described the common-room bar as 'an attractive place ... which always seems to me to be a very civilised and encouraging place ... The College in these things at least gets better every year.'9

Meanwhile the question of providing a church in the college grounds had been raised. The Irish Universities Act (1908) precluded the use of public money for the provision or maintenance of a church. The Governing Body, having received the legal opinion of Kevin Liston SC, agreed to the leasing of up to one acre to the archbishop for a temporary building. Though he found the terms of the lease restrictive, the archbishop accepted this proposal and provided the church, with financial assistance from a businessman.10

Phase 1 of the Restaurant was opened at the same time as the official opening of the Arts-Commerce-Law Building. The architect was Robin Walker, a graduate of UCD School of Architecture. The Administration Building (designed by Wejchert) was ready for use in 1972; and the first registration of students took place in October that year. Also completed in 1972 was the remarkable water tower, 180 feet high and with a capacity of 150,000 gallons. The architect again was Wejchert, and the builders were John Paul Construction Ltd. The water tower was acclaimed as a remarkable feat of design and construction. Like a massive torch of learning seen for miles around, it stood as a symbol affirming the presence of UCD to the surrounding area.

Phase 1 of the Library was also in operation by the autumn of 1972. The architect was Hardie Glover, of a Scottish firm that specialised in the design of university libraries. The bank (designed by Wejchert) was completed in 1973. In the early seventies also arrangements were made to erect the magnetic observatory, formerly sited in the Fellows' Garden of Trinity College. The observatory was designed by Frederick Darley and built for Trinity in 1838. This observatory is itself rarely observed by the public, tucked away as it is in a remote corner of the grounds, near where Roebuck Grove once stood. Whenever it was not entirely forgotten about the college had difficulties in finding any practical use for it; yet it stands as a testimonial to the fact that the old sectarian hostilities between UCD and Trinity College had at last been buried.

1975–1995

The rest of the college buildings took longer to complete. During this phase, involving the acquisition of additional land and negotiations on the construction of the later buildings, the secretary, J. P. MacHale, and the buildings officer, Pat O'Beirne, together with successive presidents, did trojan work in carrying on in this respect the tradition of Professors Pierce Purcell and Michael Hogan.

Throughout the seventies and eighties, however, the constant complaint was that funds were not forthcoming, and many delays were experienced. It was an era of massive state borrowing, deficit budgeting, and successive economic crises. Because of the shortage of public money the college was pressured into increasing fees, reducing staff numbers, leaving vacant posts unfilled—and deferring some of its building projects.

Agriculture—still based at Albert College, Glasnevin, despite the finding by the Commission on Accommodation Needs (1959) that this was inadequate and that the separation of agriculture students from the rest of UCD was inappropriate—submitted a request in July 1961 for a building of 64,650 square feet at Belfield, to cost £740,000. In the same breath, as it were, Professor James Ruane of the Agriculture Faculty's Department of Farm Management detailed the need for a new farm on which to teach applied subjects further away from the expanding city than Glasnevin. The related Department of Horticulture also wanted new accommodation. It was to take nearly thirty years of elaborate negotiations before these various requirements were finally met, though the purchase in 1962 of the Lyons estate of 1300 acres at Celbridge, for £100,000, provided early relief for the problems of Farm Management.

By the time the dust settled in the early nineties, Horticulture's field

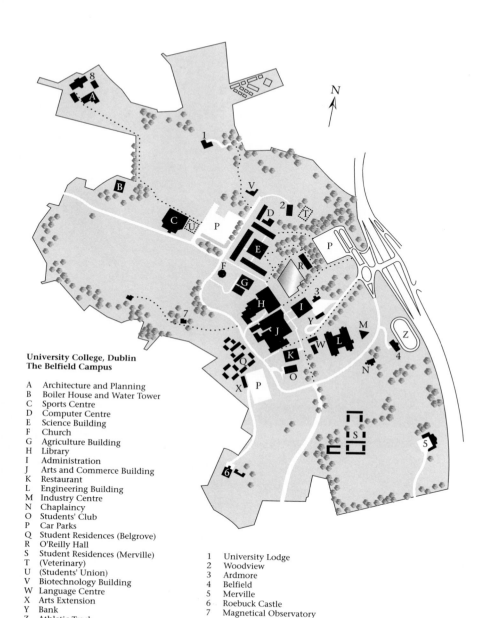

**University College, Dublin
The Belfield Campus**

A   Architecture and Planning
B   Boiler House and Water Tower
C   Sports Centre
D   Computer Centre
E   Science Building
F   Church
G   Agriculture Building
H   Library
I   Administration
J   Arts and Commerce Building
K   Restaurant
L   Engineering Building
M   Industry Centre
N   Chaplaincy
O   Students' Club
P   Car Parks
Q   Student Residences (Belgrove)
R   O'Reilly Hall
S   Student Residences (Merville)
T   (Veterinary)
U   (Students' Union)
V   Biotechnology Building
W   Language Centre
X   Arts Extension
Y   Bank
Z   Athletic Track

1   University Lodge
2   Woodview
3   Ardmore
4   Belfield
5   Merville
6   Roebuck Castle
7   Magnetical Observatory
8   Richview

The modern campus.

Thomas Murphy, President of UCD
(1972–85)

Patrick Masterson, President of UCD
(1986–93)

Art Cosgrove, President of UCD
(1994–)

Paddy Keogh, Head Porter, who served the College for more than 50 years, with Michael Tierney on the occasion of the turning of the first sod at Belfield, 1962.

The pedestrian mall

The Library

Biotechnology Building

O'Reilly Hall

The
Agriculture
Building

University
Industry Centre

Relaxing from study

The Michael Smurfit Graduate School of Business formerly Carysfort College

Caroline Hussey,
Registrar of UCD (1994–)

At work in the Library

Lecturing in the Arts
Building

'The Age of Freedom' by Rowan Gillespie

Detail from 'Pangur Bán' by Imogen Stuart

'James Joyce' by J. McCaul

'The Pillow Talk' by Louis le Brocquy

facilities were established at Thornfield and Rosemount, while Farm Management was housed on about 570 acres which was what was left of the Lyons estate after 580 acres and the mansion house, which had once belonged to Lord Cloncurry, friend of Edward Fitzgerald and Daniel O'Connell, had been sold off in 1990. General teaching and laboratory work had been transferred in 1979 to a handsome Agriculture Building at Belfield (designed by Patrick Rooney and built by John Paul and Company), financed by the Department of Agriculture and the World Bank. The move from Glasnevin was seen as a historic moment when, for the first time, the students and staff of Agriculture joined those in Science, Arts, Commerce and Law on the one site, which by then also had the Library, Restaurant, Administration Building, sports fields, and church.

Another of the buildings that involved prolonged discussion and delay was Engineering. The removal of Science from Merrion Street and of other faculties from Earlsfort Terrace brought temporary relief to Engineering. But the Government's concern, for security reasons (following the UVF bombs in Dublin in late 1972), to get possession of the College of Science, and the momentum of the transfer of the college generally, stimulated preparations by the School of Engineering. Planning for the new building was in its early stages in 1973/74; the aim was to start construction in 1977. In March 1975 a board of assessors selected the architect, Ronnie Tallon of Scott Tallon and Walker, from about 140 applicants. A schedule of accommodation was prepared by Professor Seán de Courcy and submitted to the Higher Education Authority.

The construction of the Engineering Building, however, had to be suspended, at the request of the Government, for financial reasons. For similar reasons there were delays in other building projects. The Minister for Education then agreed to examine a proposal to proceed with the Engineering project in stages. Phase 1 of the building was finally fitted out for occupation in 1989. Two departments—Civil Engineering and Agricultural and Food Engineering—had still to be housed in Earlsfort Terrace, and the Governing Body was to press for the completion of phase 2. But this had not yet materialised by the late nineties. The energy crisis of the mid-seventies had left its mark on the Engineering Building, its smooth surfaces and modest, economical windows, despite the bulk of the structure, contrasting with the huge windows and horizontal lines of the Agriculture, Arts, Library, Restaurant and Administration blocks.

Phase 2 of the Library had also been delayed. Phase 1 had been in partial operation since 1972. Before any part of the Library was ready for service a considerable section of the lower and ground floors of the Arts Building had been given over during the transitional period for use as a temporary library. Similarly, student facilities and a bookshop had continued to be housed in

Arts, taking up precious space. The college proposed to the HEA during 1974/75 enclosing the 'undercroft' or basement of the new Library to accommodate the book-stacks then in Earlsfort Terrace and the student facilities and bookshop then in the Arts Building. The proposal was accepted, and the work on the Library infill was completed in August 1978. Approval for phase 2 was given during 1981/82, and it was due for completion first in December 1985, then a year later. Fitting and furnishing eventually took place in 1987, and the Science and Agriculture Libraries were transferred to what now became the Main Library.

Other buildings experienced similar delay. Approval had been received during 1973/74 to proceed with the design of the Sports Centre. Because of lack of funds UCD was asked in the mid-seventies to defer this building. The work eventually began in July 1978; when it was completed at the end of 1980 it consisted of two main game halls, six squash courts, two handball alleys, and various committee-rooms, changing-rooms and a refreshment area. The administrative personnel for all sports activities were also housed in this centre.

Given the cut-backs in Government spending consequent on the economic depression, these delays were only to be expected. Some proposed buildings, however, were placed on the long finger, and a few seemed to have been totally abandoned. Newman had laid great stress on the idea that students living in colleges, halls or hostels was an essential part of university life. One of the great criticisms of the Irish Universities Act (1908) was that no money was made available for the building of residences. This deficiency was only partially dealt with by the provision of a number of hostels by religious orders. From the start of the Belfield project it was hoped to have hostels established around the periphery of the college. These were sketched into the architect's original site layout of 1964, and kept under review during the late sixties. Developers' proposals to build a student block were examined, and a hostels sub-committee of the Governing Body was established to do a feasibility study in 1970/71. Nothing further was achieved until work began during 1987/88 on the conversion of the north wing of Roebuck Castle (acquired in 1985) to provide residential accommodation for students for the first time in the history of UCD (October 1989).

Further student residences were envisaged, for which the Taoiseach, Charles Haughey, had laid the foundation stone in May 1989. The first of these 'student villages', in full use from October 1990, formed part of a self-financing project planned by a sub-committee of the President's Development Council. The second was formally opened in March 1992. Roebuck Hall, Belgrove Residence and Merville Residence, as they were named, provided accommodation for about 1,300 students. It was the realisation of a long-cherished aspiration. The apartments were designed by Burke-Kennedy,

Doyle and partners. They were built by Pierse Contracting Ltd at no cost to the college or the state, as the developers had the management of the complex.

An Aula Maxima had been scheduled for construction at the same time as the Arts and Administration Buildings. Alongside Administration it was to form part of the core of the college site. Its construction, however, was postponed for financial reasons. A Students' Theatre included in the original plans had also been dropped. Meanwhile the Dramatic Society, formerly based in Newman House, had been given some accommodation in the lower ground floor of the Arts Building in 1972/73. The possibility was then considered of 'combining the functions of the Aula Maxima and Student Theatre within one building.' 'Such a Hall', wrote Wejchert, 'would make a great impact on the cultural life of not only the Campus, but the whole community.'[11] Both the Aula Maxima and Students' Theatre, however, disappeared silently from the evolving scheme, not to resurface in any serious planning until O'Reilly Hall came on the scene.

In October 1992 the college announced the largest gift (£2 million) it had yet received. This was a personal donation by one of its graduates, Dr A. J. O'Reilly, for the construction of a Great Hall. The design was by the architects Scott Tallon Walker. O'Reilly Hall was to be used for formal college events, large conferences, and arts-related activities. This was seen as continuing the tradition of the original Aula Maxima in Newman House and the Great Hall in Earlsfort Terrace, which had since been restructured as the National Concert Hall.

The Students' Theatre, however, never materialised in its own separate building, despite its proud history. Stemming from that most famous of college societies, the L&H, 'Dramsoc' has had its periods of glory as the nursery of some distinguished acting and play-writing talent. In its first flush of success, in the late twenties and early thirties, it had Cyril Cusack, Mervyn Wall and Roger McHugh. In the early fifties one of its leading lights was the future American film and television actor Carroll O'Connor. By the mid-fifties there were Mairín O'Farrell and Lelia Doolan. In the late fifties the UCD thespians included Frank Kelly, Fergus and Rosaleen Linehan, Des Keogh and Pat Laffan; Jim Sheridan and Neil Jordan were involved in the 1960s. In the seventies there were Dermot Morgan and Gerry Stembridge, Lorcan Crannitch, Frank McGuinness and later Marina Carr.

From the very earliest days of Earlsfort Terrace there had been talk of the need for a Students' Building, or a Students' Union, as it was then called; and a proper Students' Building was to have been a significant feature of the new college. A committee of students, graduates and staff under the chairmanship of Judge Charles Conroy submitted a report in the mid-sixties on the requirements of the Students' Building in the light of practice in other countries. During one of Donogh O'Malley's last visits to a society meeting in the college, the president had told him that the Students' Union building would be more immediately urgent than hostels.[12]

Subsequently the president formally requested the erection of the first stage of the Students' Union building, containing offices, meeting-rooms, a lounge and other amenities and costing about £350,000. Notwithstanding a favourable response,[13] however, a delay in the construction of the Library prevented progress. A temporary beer and wine bar near the Restaurant, intended to be a limited social centre, soon acquired the reputation of serving more beer than any public house in Dublin. During 1972/73 the HEA informed the college that, because of other commitments, funds for a students' building would not be available before 1978 at the earliest.

Financial constraints were still delaying developments in 1981/82, but by 1985 it had been possible to complete a new building (designed by Freddie Fitzpatrick), named the Students' Club, to accommodate the bar and pool tables and to be the nucleus of a future Students' Union building.

Student officers had brought up the question of a Students' Union building from time to time. These officers, however, were replaced annually, and what were seen to be urgent student issues changed even more rapidly, so that there was never for long any persistent demand for a building from those for whom it was intended. As a consequence, the Students' Union building suffered regular deferral. Early in 1997 it was announced that the Governing Body had recently approved a proposal for the development of a Student Centre in the new college. This was intended to complement the student services and facilities already provided by the many clubs, societies and student representative bodies. Work on the construction was planned to begin in late 1997. The architects for the project were Murray Ó Laoire, and the project was being undertaken through UCD's Development Office.

A swimming-pool was also on all the original plans. When, however, the Sports Centre received approval in 1973/74 it was stated that it was not possible to provide the swimming-pool at that time. It too was abandoned and did not resurface in serious negotiations until about 1987, when a national Olympic swimming-pool was the subject of discussions between the college and the Irish Amateur Swimming Association. While the college was prepared to provide the site free of charge, it was in no position to sustain any financial liabilities, especially since the estimated cost was £5 million and there would also be considerable operating expenses. The swimming-pool has yet to materialise.

On the other hand, buildings not in the original plans but registering the college's response to recent developments in science, business and language studies had to be added. Soon after the Science Faculty was fully functioning at Belfield a smaller temporary building in 1969 had to be designed as the Computer Centre. The Government's proposed total grant for 1969/70 included £100,000 for the Computer Centre, £75,000 less than the college had asked for.[14] An extension was completed in the spring of 1980, and a new building for the Department of Computer Science, larger than originally planned, was in use from March 1982.

The University Industry Centre, designed by Ronnie Tallon, was in use from the summer of 1985. This project had been made possible by successful fund-raising directed at industry and the engineering profession. A purpose-built dwelling with meeting-rooms for the deans of residence (financed by the archdiocese) came into use during 1988/89. The architect was Professor Cathal O'Neill of UCD's School of Architecture.

A Biotechnology Institute, which was to inaugurate the development of a school of life sciences engaged in interdisciplinary research, was completed in 1993. In the late nineties a building to include the Language Centre was completed, as was an Arts Extension Building; and plans for the remaining buildings—including Veterinary Medicine—were well in hand.

ACQUISITIONS, 1960–1985

While the buildings were being planned and erected, the college had continued to purchase properties alongside those already acquired.

Roebuck Grove, Clonskeagh—to be distinguished from Roebuck Grove, Donnybrook, which was renamed Whiteoaks and later University Lodge—had been bought in 1961. It consisted of 35 acres and a house (demolished in 1980) and cost £66,000, nearly twice what earlier properties had cost per acre, since prices in the area had greatly increased—largely, no doubt, because of the decision to move UCD. In 1971 the college bought another 13.4 acres contiguous to the Arts Building from the Little Sisters of the Poor, for which it paid £87,500; £71,347 of this came as compensation from Dublin City Council for land taken along Stillorgan Road during road-widening.

The Richview estate of 17.4 acres was added in 1980. The house, on the western boundary of the college along Clonskeagh Road, was a tall square block with classical doorcase and fanlight, built about 1790 for the Powell family. In 1887 it became the Masonic Orphan Boys' School, and it was extended by the addition of two tall gabled ranges. The cost was £2.1 million, provided by the Government in consideration of the college's agreement to vacate part of the Merrion Street buildings. Richview was adapted by Professor Cathal O'Neill to become the home of the School of Architecture, the Department of Regional and Urban Planning, and the Department of Environmental Studies. Subsequently 6½ acres of the land at Richview was sold to the Department of Posts and Telegraphs.

The proceeds of the sale of the 6½ acres at Richview were used in 1981 to acquire the Rosemount property from the Woulfe-Flanagan family, consisting of a house and 13¾ acres further along Clonskeagh Road, near the present Clonskeagh entrance to the college and adjoining the Roebuck part of the grounds. The house was demolished in 1985. In 1985 an additional 11 acres on the Roebuck boundary was bought from the Little Sisters of the Poor.

Roebuck Castle and lands were acquired in 1986. The buildings and the 10 acres attached cost £620,000. The college authorities were reprimanded for not getting approval in advance from the HEA; it was explained, however, that the money came out of college funds and that the property would be made to pay for itself. This was done by letting some of it and by charging a full commercial fee for a postgraduate diploma in accountancy.[15] Roebuck Castle dated back to the early years of the Norman Conquest. It came into the possession of the Westby family in 1856 and was bought by the Little Sisters of the Poor in 1943, who used it as an old people's home. UCD developed it to provide the first residential accommodation in the college as well as rooms for the postgraduate diploma course, temporary accommodation for the deans of residence, and an examination centre. Its large assembly hall, formerly the church, was used for the first honorary conferring ceremony to be held here, in July 1987. Research units, financed by the IDA for industrial and technical projects, were also housed in Roebuck.

The Michael Smurfit Graduate School of Business was also established in the renovated Roebuck Castle until it was transferred in 1990/91 to the recently bought Blackrock site, formerly Carysfort Training College, and the Faculty of Law moved to the accommodation vacated at Roebuck. When Carysfort first came on the market UCD had decided against it, partly on the grounds that the £6½ million being asked was much more than the planned Roebuck development for the Business School. Carysfort was acquired instead by a businessman for housing development. Some seven months later the building and its nineteen acres were bought by UCD for £8 million, which the Government of Charles Haughey provided for this purpose. UCD provided £2 million of privately raised funds for renovation. The question whether the Government or UCD had made the first approach to the other gave rise to a public controversy.

Within the Commerce Faculty there was some criticism of the transfer to Blackrock, since college policy over the years had been the establishment of a centralised college at Belfield.[16]

By the end of the nineties Medicine and Veterinary Medicine were the only faculties without a new building. The Medical Faculty had retained its premises in Earlsfort Terrace, while in the houses acquired at Stillorgan Road, Microbiology continued to be housed in Ardmore, Medical Research and Surgery in Woodview, and Pharmacology and Biochemistry in Merville. The White Paper of December 1974, which in effect ended the seven-year merger controversy, stated that the sole school of veterinary medicine should be based in UCD. A site of four to six acres to the east of car park no. 5 was earmarked for this purpose, and a schedule of accommodation was submitted to the Department of Agriculture for approval. In the late nineties Veterinary Medicine was still in Ballsbridge, though fund-raising and building plans were in train for removal to Belfield.

While all the construction work was in progress, other developments were also transforming the site. A landscaping programme softened what at first appeared to students as a 'concrete jungle'. From a nursery near the Owenstown entrance, plants and shrubs were provided. The college's commitment to the development of its environment was indicated by the tree-planting ceremony that took place in 1973 when the president, Dr Thomas Murphy, was joined by his two immediate predecessors in planting an evergreen oak, a birch and a linden on the west side of the lake. An ash was also planted in memory of the recently deceased Professor Michael Hogan, former chairman of the Grounds Committee.

Simultaneous with the erection of buildings had been the development of sports grounds and pitches. During the fifties the Irish Athletic Championships had been dominated by UCD. It was afterwards felt that the lack of facilities had hampered the full development of the club. An all-weather athletic track at Belfield, near the main entrance to the college on the Stillorgan Road, was the result of a co-operative effort. The total cost was estimated at £160,000. The Department of Education, through the Irish Olympic Council, provided half the finance, and Dublin City Council and Dún Laoghaire Borough Council jointly provided the other half. This tartan track was the first of its kind in the country and was of the standard required for international athletic events. The formal opening took place on 14 June 1977. Many of the events of the European Special Olympic Games were held here in 1985.

An artificial lake added an air of tranquillity to the scene. Car parks, footpaths, a ring road and a bus terminus were provided. A new building for the college creche had been erected at Rosemount during 1985/86. Those who had criticised the buildings in their rawest state may have lacked the vision of the designers. As the site matured and responded to the skilled and sensitive landscaping of Liam Clifford and his team of groundsmen, it became what many visitors acknowledge to be one of the loveliest of modern university campuses in Europe.

The Belfield dream had been a long time evolving into reality. Thomas Davis, in the eighteen-forties, when looking forward to the establishment of a University of Ireland, had written: 'How glorious to see its peaceful towers among the slopes of the park or at the foot of the Dublin mountains and to know that there dwelt the greatest minds of Ireland labouring to make the universe clear and docile.'[17] Such a view and such a flourishing institution had often filled Newman's mind, finding expression in his silvery prose. Newman's successor (1861–1879), Dr Bartholomew Woodlock, had moved so far towards its realisation that the plans for the Catholic University buildings at Clonliffe West had been put on paper and the foundation stone laid in 1862. A successor to Woodlock (1883–1906), Monsignor Gerald Molloy, wrote about this dream in 1883: 'Gladly, indeed, would we see these various colleges [of the Catholic University] lifted up from their isolation, and planted together on some pleasant site, abounding in shady walks and green fields ... such a hope we fervently hope may one day be realised in fact ... It is well to keep ever a lofty conception in view.'[18] Belfield was the fulfilment of the dream that had haunted Catholic university authorities for over a hundred years.

THE CITY-CENTRE BUILDINGS

Once the Dáil agreed to the move to Belfield it became part of Government as well as college policy that Earlsfort Terrace and Merrion Street would revert to the state as a *quid pro quo* for the grants made to the college towards the purchase of sites and the erection of the new buildings.[19] The College of Science in Merrion Street, the most recently acquired of the three buildings, was the first to be selected for surrender.

The spill-over of the Northern troubles marked by bombings in Dublin between 1972 and 1974 ensured that the College of Science, as part of a complex that included Dáil Éireann and Government offices, became a secure building. The Government's anxiety resulted in a directive that Merrion Street should be vacated as soon as possible by the college.[20] But it was not until Architecture moved out from Earlsfort Terrace to Richview that two departments—Civil and Agricultural Engineering—could transfer from Merrion Street to the vacated space. Although over the years from 1972 much discussion and planning regarding the new Engineering Building at Belfield took place, phase 1 of this building was not ready for occupation until 1989. When eventually the College of Science had reverted to the Government, a good deal of money was expended on its restoration, to turn its façade into one of the architectural attractions of the city. Much of the former college itself became the offices of the Department of the Taoiseach.

The evacuation of Earlsfort Terrace has taken longer to accomplish, for it became home to the migratory departments from Merrion Street. From the fifties to the eighties the Terrace went through a period of perpetual adaptation as one department or function replaced another. When Arts, Commerce, Law, Administration and the Library moved out to Belfield, other college activities—expanding departments in Medicine, Architecture, and Engineering—had to compete for space with state institutions.

By July 1972 temporary storage space was requested in Earlsfort Terrace for the hard-pressed National Library. By May 1974 the future of the Great Hall as the National Concert Hall was under discussion; it was handed over to the OPW in June 1978. The last conferring to be held in the Great Hall was in the autumn of 1977. Its loss necessitated hiring additional accommodation in the RDS show halls in Ballsbridge for examinations. Sections of Medicine and of Engineering continued into the late nineties to share the Earlsfort Terrace building with the National Concert Hall.

The withdrawal of UCD from its urban setting had been strongly and articulately opposed on various cultural and social grounds. But even those who, for practical reasons, considered the move inevitable were concerned lest something in the college's tradition be lost in the transfer. According to Newman there would arise in the course of time in a university 'a self-perpetuating tradition, or a *genius loci,*' which 'haunts the home where it is born,' imbuing and forming the individuals who had been brought under its shadow.[21] One of the most elegant and evocative pleas on behalf of the *genius loci* and the preservation of UCD in its St Stephen's Green and Earlsfort Terrace setting had come from the pen of the novelist Kate O'Brien.[22] She wrote:

> Stephen's Green was very important in our student life ... A tradition and an atmosphere have been forming there. It has already its ghosts ... The steps of 86 have been worn down by many footsteps of the great, living and dead. Are we, in the name of plumbing and playing-fields, to abandon and forego the whole sad, valuable century since Newman was all but driven mad by us in Stephen's Green?[23]

With her keen sense of place and appreciation of Newman's concept of the *genius loci,* she concluded:

> So for the sake of its now well-formed tradition, for the hope of preserving that precious intangible influence ... I for one hope that, whatever extensions may have to be faced and wherever, U.C.D. will always spring from and flow back to 86 and Stephen's Green, and all that stretch, cold, rainy, windswept—round to Earlsfort Terrace. That bleak and characteristic piece of Dublin is peopled now by many figures and legends. And for better and for worse, it is U.C.D.[24]

A couple of years after the Government decision had been taken to approve the transfer to Belfield, and the contract for the Science Building had been signed, Kate O'Brien returned to the subject.[25] 'House-moving can stir a lively dust,' she wrote. 'All this healthy fussing out of U.C.D. to Belfield and the suburbs' reminded her of what was being left behind. She wrote nostalgically: 'From 82 to 86 is a small bit of pavement, a slice of dilapidated masonry. But in the last hundred years it has been crowded and worked upon; has suffered many histories. Ghosts walk about it often …'[26] In O'Brien's time (1916–19) the porch of 86, she remembered, 'was filled all day with lounging male geniuses': Eimar O'Duffy, Paddy McGilligan and 'that gloomy Platonist from the west, Michael Tierney.'[27]

Number 86, the birth-place of the Catholic University, had been immortalised by the ghost of the first Rector, John Henry Newman. When under Jesuit management it had received a re-dedication in immortality in scenes described in the writings of its most famous pupil, James Joyce, especially in *A Portrait of the Artist as a Young Man* and *Stephen Hero*. And now Kate O'Brien, one of the best-known novelists to come out of UCD in the early years of the NUI, had identified and confirmed 86 as the site of the *genius loci* of UCD and the heart and source of its tradition.

The college authorities felt called upon to answer those who feared the loss of a tradition. 'There need be no fear that the College will suffer in any way from its newness … The College is not a thing of yesterday … As for tradition, the College will still have behind it an unbroken academic history going back to Newman and the Catholic University—a history always looking to and preparing for such a fulfilment as now appears to be close at hand.'[28] It was true that plans had been drawn up and the foundation stone laid in 1862 for a new impressive Catholic University building in Drumcondra, and that half a century later the planned new building for University College at Earlsfort Terrace had never been completed. But by the time the decision to move to Belfield was approved, the traditions of the college around St Stephen's Green had been flourishing there for over a hundred years, and that *genius loci* that Newman had often spoken of as important for a university had established itself in the area.

It was because this was understood by the authorities that they declared that 'it is hoped that the historic houses on St Stephen's Green will always remain with the College …'[29] The St Stephen's Green houses were different from Earlsfort Terrace and Merrion Street, in that they were older and were the cradle of the college; and, unlike Earlsfort Terrace and Merrion Street, the OPW had no claim on them, since they were the property of the bishops, rented on long lease to UCD. But apart from any sentimental attachment there might be to Newman House, the college authorities on the eve of the move to Belfield stated that 'a town centre will be needed for the very important work of evening classes, for university extension classes etc.'[30]

Then, as the buildings in Belfield came to be occupied, one of the first acts of the new president, Dr Thomas Murphy, was to appoint a Newman House Committee. He wrote to the members of the committee on 19 October 1972: 'As a result of the move to Belfield, it has become necessary to consider the future of Newman House. I have therefore appointed this Committee to examine and report to me on possible ways of retaining Newman House as an integral part of the life of the College.'[31]

The eleven-member committee, having examined the costs and the use made of the house, recommended that

> in our opinion the College should not contemplate giving up '86' for the following reasons —
>
> i. Newman House has been for many years the only physical reminder of the College's link with the Catholic University of Ireland and with its first Rector;
> ii. it seems most desirable that the College should maintain a presence in the centre of the city;
> iii. there is now, and will long continue to be, a continuing need for accommodation of student activities in Newman House.

In the opinion of the committee, 'no place in the possession of the College has more dignity and tradition than Newman House.' For its further development the committee recommended reviving limited restaurant facilities, including a bar and a reading-room for staff and graduates, 'perhaps in Room 9 which was, in fact, used for this purpose years ago.'[32]

While student activities, staff dinners and other functions continued in Newman House, the suggestion that it might also become another university club in St Stephen's Green, where there were already two such clubs, did not materialise.[33] Then, in 1986, the ownership of numbers 85 and 86 (Newman House) and 84A (the Aula Maxima) were transferred by deed from the bishops to the college. With a grant from Bord Fáilte and under the patronage of Gallaher (Dublin) Ltd, a conservation and restoration project began in 1989/90 and was carried out during the early nineties to preserve for UCD and for posterity these important and beautiful Georgian buildings.

For a number of years after 1908 the college had been a relatively simple institution. The small number of students were lectured to and examined in the time-honoured way by an equally small number of professors and their assistants. All that was needed then were classrooms, blackboard and chalk, a few texts, a modest library, and a few simple laboratories for the professional and science subjects. The administrative staff was small, and secretarial assistance for professors was meagre.

The move to Belfield roughly coincided with the vast developments that were taking place in every aspect of university life. The extraordinary increase in student numbers demanded a corresponding increase in academic and support staff; and a variety of new disciplines and functions were added to the work of the institution. The expansion in the infrastructure of administrators, accountants, secretaries, personnel officers, information and development officers, security people and groundsmen, technicians and others altered the balance and changed the emphasis. From being primarily and simply a teaching institution UCD became a complex business organisation, striving to keep pace with the latest developments in the university world and responding to changes in society. For this purpose, shifts in emphasis and perspective became necessary, but always with the corollary that something good in the old balance between teaching and administration could be lost in the transition.

The 'business of a university', Newman had written, was 'to set forth the right standard, and to train according to it, and to help forward all students towards it according to their various capacities.'[34] In this educative process knowledge could be pursued for its own sake, the intellect would be disciplined, and a liberal or philosophical habit of mind formed. With the change that had taken place coinciding with the move to Belfield, Newman's phrase 'the business of a university' has taken on an additional meaning. Because of the thousands of people now involved, the variety and complexity of its functions, and the vast amount of money required for its operation, the modern university has become big business. There is, of course, a world of difference between the business of a university and the university as a business; yet these concepts have become interdependent and react intimately on each other—with consequences that can be both beneficial and deleterious. They are not exclusive: the successful running of the business side of the university can and should contribute to the essential business of the university. Despite the dangers, Newman's values need not be submerged in the modern institution.

The crippling effects of the lack of space, buildings and equipment had been the constant complaint of UCD during most of its existence. A university is more than bricks and mortar; yet the building of Belfield had been a priority in the business of UCD. The new college was seen as the remedy for much that was wanting. Belfield not only marked the beginning of a new phase in the history of the college but also presented fresh challenges and the express hope that it would be the fulfilment of Newman's vision of his university: 'It is a place which wins the admiration of the young by its celebrity, kindles the affections of the middle-aged by its beauty, and rivets the fidelity of the old by its associations.'[35]

Epilogue

*T*he uneasiness resulting from the visitation, and the excitement as well as apprehension that followed the setting up of the Commission on Higher Education, had focused the minds of academics on the need to band together in an Academic Staff Association, and this was formed in December 1960. Throughout the sixties and early seventies the ASA played a significant role in the affairs of the college. Open to every full-time member of the academic staff, it provided a forum for all when membership of the faculties was restricted to senior staff and when widely representative committees dealing with all aspects of college life had yet to become the norm. Meetings and sub-committees of the ASA provided opportunities not otherwise available to a scattered staff of about six hundred for fraternisation among members of the various faculties and allowed individuals to observe at close quarters the commitment of colleagues to the college and academic objectives.

In catering for the immediate interests of its members, the association established specialist study groups on salaries, promotion, tenure, pensions, contracts, and career structure. It organised common-room amenities and social events such as golf outings and tennis tournaments. Members were kept informed of all these activities through the *ASA Bulletin.* Apart from negotiations with the college authorities, discussions were held between representatives of the ASA and the students.

One of the association's earlier tasks was the preparation of a report submitted to the Commission on Higher Education in November 1961. A later ASA publication was a report on academic and administrative structure (October 1972). The sub-committee that drafted this report, it was claimed, devoted to it a total of 270 hours in meetings and consultation.

Among the ASA's most successful ventures was the annual seminar held in Greystones, County Wicklow, during the sixties and early seventies. These seminars gave impetus to the debate about the role of universities and the best way of organising and directing them. The proceedings were published as the series *Contemporary Developments in University Education.* The papers and discussions covered such varied matters as failure rates, departmental structures, the careers and appointments service, modern languages in the university, and universities in an integrated Europe. Belfield and the merger came within their purview, as, of course, did the Commission on Higher Education.

The panel that discussed the future role of UCD at a seminar in February 1972 consisted of six of the college's most prominent academics, who were considered possible candidates in the forthcoming vacancy for the presidency: Tom Murphy (registrar), John O'Donnell (engineering), James Dooge (engineering), Patrick Lynch (economics), Gerry Harrington (biochemistry), and Denis Donohue (English). Among the issues raised by the panellists were the question of having a planning unit or 'think-tank', as in industry, better relations with the community outside the college, and improved internal structures. The ASA, in agreement with the Commission on Higher Education, also pressed for a limited term of office for the presidency.

Dr Murphy, who was duly elected by the Senate of the NUI, held office from 1972 to 1985. He was the last president to be appointed without limitation of term until the age of seventy and was the first to administer the college from its new site. He was also the first president—and so far the only one—to have pursued for some years a career outside college: he had served as a medical officer with Bord na Móna, with Kildare County Council, and with the Department of Health. This experience helped prepare him for the duties he was to perform successively as professor (1955), Dean of the Faculty of Medicine (1962), registrar (1964) and president (1972–1985) during a hectic period that included the visitation, the merger, the student revolt, and the move to Belfield. At a time of great expansion in student numbers he was directly responsible, as registrar, for setting up the Admissions Office and introducing the points system for entrance to the universities. In the front line during the Gentle Revolution, he did much, with his cheerful, outgoing disposition, to defuse the situation and ensure that the revolution remained 'gentle'.

One important feature of Dr Murphy's presidency was the increased democratisation of decision-making: boards of assessors made recommendations on appointments; staff representatives served on committees that decided on promotion and tenure; headships of departments rotated; the office of dean changed more frequently; and full-time non-statutory staff became members of faculties. The work of the ASA, of which Dr Murphy had been a founder-member, could be seen to be bearing fruit.

During his thirteen years as president the number of students remained comparatively steady, at between nine and ten thousand, but the number of full professors (excluding those in Dentistry and Pharmacy, which were transferred to Trinity College) increased from 82 to 111; and prospects for promotion improved with the creation of about 120 additional statutory lectureships and some additional associate professorships. A number of the new chairs in the Faculty of Commerce were endowed by business interests— Irish Banks, Jefferson Smurfit, Esso, P. J. Carroll, and R. and A. Bailey—where a progressive dean, Professor Michael McCormac, had laid the foundations of a very successful business school.

Dr Murphy proved to be an excellent chairman, quick to grasp the mood of a meeting. A facilitator rather than an innovator, he had the ability to delegate and to inspire teamwork in his colleagues. Warm-hearted and blessed with a sense of humour, he was the most approachable of presidents, caring and anxious to listen. He had the ability to remember the first name of staff members—non-academic as well as academic—and treated all as important members of the university family.

Professor Patrick Masterson (philosophy of religion), who was elected president in January 1986, belonged to the generation of academics who began their teaching career in college when the ASA was already actively engaged in the problems of university life. He was the first president to be elected under provisions adopted in 1984 by the Governing Body that fixed the president's term at ten years or the age of sixty-five, whichever should come first. In politics this was the era of Charles Haughey and Albert Reynolds, and business was dominated by the millionaires Tony O'Reilly, Michael Smurfit and Tony Ryan—all of whom received honorary degrees from the university.

One of Dr Masterson's first decisions was to appoint a working party to produce a ten-year development plan for consideration by the college's various bodies. The objective was to achieve a college-wide consensus on the way ahead. It formulated a number of programmes for action. He simultaneously appointed a President's Development Council, mainly consisting of people prominent in business and other areas of public life. A Development Office was set up to engage in the fund-raising required for the implementation of the programmes envisaged in the plan. A notable outcome was the creation of a scheme of Newman Scholars, which provided mainly postdoctoral fellowships for a period of three years. This has attracted international as well as national researchers and brought new blood into the scholarly life of the college at a time of economic stringency when, because of Government restrictions on recruitment, academics were presenting an aging profile. The Development Plan had noted that only 9 per cent of the academic staff were below the age of thirty-five. The scheme coincided with a big increase in the number of postgraduate students as a result of support for applied research from international agencies and from industry.

Tax incentives enabled the President's Development Council to fulfil the long-standing ambition to build student residences in the college, which transformed Belfield into a more attractive environment for the students and gave it a degree of collegiate cohesion. The Graduate School of Business benefited from an endowment of £1½ million from the Smurfit Group and the acquisition of the extensive buildings of Carysfort College. The development of relations with graduates, the restoration of part of Newman House to its Georgian splendour, a Biotechnology Complex, television educational services produced by the Audio Visual Centre and proposals from staff for new courses—such as drama, film, and equality and women's studies— formed part of the development.

Dr Masterson relinquished the presidency in December 1993 after eight years in office to become principal of the European University Institute in Florence.

By now the college, like other third-level institutes, had become familiar with the jargon of big business, the language of the advertising industry, and the salesmanship of the supermarket. 'Unit costs', 'cost-effectiveness' and 'benchmarks' were only a few of the terms in common currency. The packaging and marketing of its services were considered essential. School-leavers were diligently sought after through open days and other promotions, and scholarships were offered as an inducement for those good at sporting activities. Americanisation was unmistakable: the age-old 'terms' of the academic year were replaced by 'semesterisation', and courses of study were subdivided into 'modules'. An 'alumni' network, also copied from American practice, was and is serviced by its own office, a special journal, and those regular visits to branches abroad that have become a feature of the president's functions. Research funding and new developments became more and more dependent on EU agencies, private industry and sponsorship.

Student numbers increased dramatically during the early nineties:

1985/86	10,177
1990/91	12,544
1992/93	15,016
1993/94	16,378

The student profile was also changing. In 1994/95 women made up 53 per cent of the student body. There was also a noticeable increase in the number of mature students. The expansion in the number of non-Irish students was reflected in the foreign languages being spoken in the college. EU schemes such as Erasmus brought students from the Continent; schemes such as the Junior Year Abroad and the Semester in Irish Studies catered for students from American universities; and respectable numbers from Asia and Africa confirmed UCD's international role.

In the early sixties students who were non-residents of Ireland—mainly from Britain and the Commonwealth—had amounted to over 7 per cent of the total. Following almost a doubling of UCD's student population during the sixties, pressure on space, and resultant restrictions on the intake of foreign students, the proportion of non-Irish full-time students dropped to 2.3 per cent in 1974/75 and only slowly began to move upwards again, as follows:

1961/62	7%
1964/65	7.5%
1969/70	3%
1974/75	2.3%
1979/80	2.5%
1984/85	3.2%
1994/95	4.4%

The 4.4 per cent in 1994/95 represented 616 full-time students from abroad.

A steady rise in the proportion of postgraduate students was also taking place. Excluding postgraduate diploma students (since so many of these were candidates for the higher diploma in education), the following table illustrates the development that was occurring:

1961/62	2.8%
1964/65	3.3%
1969/70	5.4%
1974/75	7%
1979/80	9.4%
1984/85	9.42%
1994/95	17.8%

If we include full-time postgraduate diploma students, the full-time degree and diploma postgraduates in UCD in 1994/95 amounted to 20 per cent of all full-time students. Of the total number of part-time students (2,343) during the same year, postgraduates (degree and diploma) constituted almost 40 per cent.

Professor Art Cosgrove was elected president in 1994. A graduate of Queen's University, Belfast, he was the first non-graduate of UCD (or its predecessor colleges in St Stephen's Green and Cecilia Street), and the first associate professor, to occupy the office. He had lectured in UCD's Department of Mediaeval History since the early sixties and served on the Governing Body for many years. Shortly after his election, Dr Caroline Hussey (industrial microbiology) was elected registrar for a period of ten years, the first woman to hold this office. When Professor Cosgrove took over the presidency a number of issues earmarked in the Development Plan had yet to be completed.

While these were under consideration, the Government introduced legislation that established the three constituent colleges of the NUI and St Patrick's College, Maynooth, as independent universities. Since Michael Tierney's time there had always been in UCD advocates of independent university status. The Commission on Higher Education recommended such independence in 1967; and after the proposals for the merger with Trinity College had failed, the Government in 1974 and again two years later reverted to the idea of university independence. Though elaborate plans for this eventuality were drawn up by the Governing Body, nothing had then come of the proposal. The argument continued intermittently in UCD over the next twenty years between those who favoured an independent status and those who preferred the federal status quo. During the eighties it appeared as if the federalists, especially in the Governing Body and Academic Council, were dominant.

Federalists in UCD as well as in Cork and Galway saw the NUI as a bulwark against the dangers of provincialism. They regarded the NUI as guaranteeing freedom from interference by local bodies in appointments and in framing curricula. Because it had existed for so long, a sense of loyalty to the NUI had grown up in the different colleges and had produced a bonding of collegiality and national pride.

There were those too who felt that Irish in the Matriculation could be best safeguarded in the Senate of the NUI, whereas an independent UCD in competition with Trinity might be strongly tempted to abandon the requirement. And there were always those in the colleges who regarded the Senate as a counterbalance and check on presidents and administrators who might be inclined to be autocratic. Finally, there was the ever-present fear among conservatives that if new legislation were brought in, and new Charters had to be drawn up, the politicians and civil servants would welcome the opportunity to gain greater state control and to interfere with those cherished principles of academic freedom and university autonomy.

When, however, Dublin City University was established as an independent institution (as well as Limerick University) in 1989, the balance in UCD moved once again in favour of independence, since UCD, the largest university institution in the city, was still a mere college, while Trinity College and Dublin City University held the superior title of university. Also, as university education grew more and more expensive, the Government had been encouraging colleges to look beyond Government funding and to seek development funds from private sources. In this connection, as in other areas, it was felt that the slow, bureaucratic mechanisms of the NUI hampered UCD, especially in competition with Trinity College, which could make its own quick decisions without reference to any federal body. It was in these circumstances that UCD urged in the NUI Senate that the NUI colleges should be made independent, and convinced the Senate to go along with the idea and request the Government to introduce the necessary legislation.

The purpose of the Universities Act (1997) was to establish the three constituent colleges of the National University of Ireland and St Patrick's College, Maynooth, as constituent universities of the NUI; to provide a revised composition for the governing authorities of the universities; and to provide structures for greater accountability and transparency in the affairs of universities. By this legislation the name of the college was changed to National University of Ireland, Dublin. (At the request of the college, the Minister for Education agreed to allow it to continue to use also the historical title University College, Dublin.)

Under the Act each university has a governing authority of not fewer than twenty and not more than forty members. Membership is to include representatives of the professorial, non-professorial and non-academic staff, the Students' Union, graduates, postgraduate students, the NUI, the General Council of County Councils, the Minister for Education, and organisations catering for employers, workers, the professions, business and the arts. The governing authority is also required to ensure that each sex is represented in accordance with a balance that may from time to time be established by the minister.

The Senate of the NUI is retained, but with greatly reduced powers. Its functions are restricted to determining the requirements for matriculation and recognising the degrees of the constituent universities as degrees also of the NUI. It loses its role in the appointment of presidents, professors and lecturers in the constituent universities. It might have been logical to abolish the NUI Senate altogether and devolve its functions on the universities. The Act, however, is very much a compromise between those who advocated outright independence and those who wished to retain some form of federalism.

The university of 1999 is in many respects quite different from the college of 1909. In size alone it now has over sixteen thousand students, where at first it had a little over five hundred. The expansion in its buildings, in the number of its academic and other staff and in the variety of courses and services offered has been equally impressive. The psychological changes have also been remarkable, for the mentalities of the men and women of 1909 belonged to a past where interests and objectives were very different from those of the present. Between 1909 and 1922 a strongly nationalist college had played a major role in revolutionary political developments. From 1922 the staff and graduates contributed significantly to the young state. A war of independence, a civil war, two world wars, an economic war and an infant state's struggle to maintain stability with many calls upon its purse had all conspired to restrict the ambitions of a proud but financially poor college.

The result was that the college of 1909 was still quite recognisable in the college of 1949.

True, by 1949 most of the original staff had died or retired, but they had been replaced in most instances by their own pupils. And the students were still participating in the traditions of the same societies and clubs, while in the student magazines they tried to emulate the achievements of *St Stephen's* and the *National Student.* Since the nineteen-thirties *Comhthrom Féinne* and its successors had placed more emphasis on literary endeavour than on the burning political issues that had preoccupied the pre-1922 student journals.

The fifties and sixties—the years of Michael Tierney's presidency and that of his successor, Jeremiah Hogan—ushered in a period of more rapid change. It was an era in which there were signs of great upheavals trying to happen, reflecting circumstances in the world and the country brought on by the new communications technology and the emergence of the global village. Radical and doubting forces seemed to be at war with, and undermining, the stabilising forces and certainties of the past. Nor was it a straightforward struggle between conservatives and radicals, for reforms—like the move to a bigger college in Belfield—begun by people in other respects considered conservatives created their own momentum and provided opportunities for the more radical students. And the process of questioning and re-examining engaged in by the Academic Staff Association during the sixties was conducted by academics who stood mainly within the established system.

Despite the pressures for change, strong forces of continuity had also been at work, so that in the end the institution that emerged had undergone development in response to changing times rather than any radical transformation. By the late nineties the college had become a university, yet it remained a federal institution still associated with Cork, Galway, and Maynooth. The democratic system of government enshrined in the legislation of 1908 was merely extended in the 1997 Act to bring it into line with recent democratic practices. The commitment to liberal as well as to utilitarian education, to 'red-brick' values as well as to the humanities, was still as much in evidence in the nineties as it was in the early days.

The political ethos had also evolved, and the college was no longer militantly nationalist in the pre-1922 sense. Though the founders of the Gaelic League, Hyde and MacNeill, along with many other active members of that organisation, had constituted a large proportion of the original academic staff, the college had long since lost its early enthusiasm for the revival. As in other matters, Michael Tierney had attracted more adverse comment than any other president for his outspoken criticism of the revivalist policies of the state and language organisations. In this he had the support of such UCD Irish scholars as Myles Dillon, Dan Binchy, Frank Shaw and Gerard Murphy. Ironically, Tierney was better informed and knew more about Irish culture than any other president. Genuine Irish scholarship, including Irish folklore, owed much to his active promotion.

The Catholic ethos had likewise changed with the times; clergy had disappeared from the governing authority and the Academic Council; chaplains restricted their services to a post-Vatican II role; the 'Red Mass' had given way to a low-key ecumenical service; deans of residence no longer inspected lodgings in the interests of the students' morals. Segregating the sexes in the UCD village residences was not an issue, for it all had moved a long way from what John Henry Newman had in mind for his halls of residence.

Tom Kettle, professor of the national economics of Ireland, wrote in 1910 that the first task of his generation was 'the recovery of old Ireland' and the second task would be 'the discovery of the new Europe,' for he held that in order to become deeply Irish, Ireland must become European. In his epigrammatic way he declared that 'in gaining her own soul Ireland will gain the whole world,' and he added that 'while a strong people has its own self for centre, it has the universe for circumference.'[1] The college founded in 1908 had played a central role in building up the nation. As we approach a new century, UCD, faithful to its twin mottoes—*Ad astra* ('to the stars') and *Cothrom Féinne* (the Fianna code of 'fair play')—and as a leading European university, has its part to play in the international arena.[2] What for John Henry Newman in 1854 was merely a vision has for us become reality: a prosperous country between two hemispheres and at the centre of the world, and in its capital city a flourishing university, the largest in Ireland.

Appendix 1

COLLEGE AND UNIVERSITY BODIES

Senate of the NUI   Manages and controls the affairs of the National University.

Governing Body (now Governing Authority)   Manages and controls the affairs of the constituent college (now university).

Academic Council   Responsible for the curriculum and for student discipline.

Faculties   Draft the regulations concerning degrees, courses, scholarships etc. within their own province.

Departments   Provide instruction in and contributed to the advancement of the studies within their scope.

Appendix 2

OFFICERS OF THE COLLEGE 1908–

Presidents

1908–1940	Denis J. Coffey
1940–1947	Arthur W. Conway
1947–1964	Michael Tierney
1964–1972	Jeremiah J. Hogan
1972–1985	Thomas Murphy
1986–1993	Patrick Masterson
1994–	Art Cosgrove

Registrars

1909–1940	Arthur W. Conway
1940–1952	John J. Nolan
1952–1964	Jeremiah J. Hogan
1964–1972	Thomas Murphy
1972–1974	*E. F. O'Doherty (Acting Registrar)*
1974–1983	Maurice Kennedy
1983–1986	Patrick Masterson
1986–1994	John J. Kelly
1994–	Caroline Hussey

Secretaries and Bursars

1909–1939	John W. Bacon
1939–1954	Augustine J. O'Connell
1954–1987	Joseph P. MacHale

Secretary

1987–	Gerard A. Wright

Bursar

1987–1998   Anthony J. Bennett

Librarians

1909–1917   David J. O'Donoghue
1917–1952   James J. O'Neill
1951–1973   Ellen Power
1973–1974   *Ellen Power (Acting Librarian)*
1974–1978   Henry J. Heaney
1978–   Sean Phillips

Appendix 3

SUMMARY OF MAJOR ACQUISITIONS FOR THE BELFIELD CAMPUS

1933 (21 Dec.)	Belfield House on 44 acres for £8,000.
1946	12 acres leased from Little Sisters of the Poor for £900 for playing fields.
[1948	Ardmore on 20 acres bought by government for a new broadcasting house]
1949 (2 June)	Montrose on 23 acres for £21,000 (incl. comm.).
1949 (Oct.)	Whiteoaks (University Lodge) on 34 acres for £30,000 (excl. of fees). Title signed in summer of 1950.
1951 (8 May)	Merville on 60 acres acquired for £100,000 (vacant possession to be handed over two years after execution of contract).
1953 (Sept.)	UCD gained possession of Merville.
1953 (Sept.)	Woodview on 18 acres for £22,000.
1954 (Oct.)	Byrne's Fields – 42 acres for £43,000.
1955	Belgrove on 7 acres for £23,750 (£19,250 to owner and £4,500 for freehold). The house was demolished in 1973.
1957	Montrose was exchanged with the Dept. of Posts and Telegraphs for Ardmore after negotiations which had begun in 1951.
1958 (April)	Thornfield on 5.5 acres for £4,500. This property has since been re-sold and the house demolished.
1961	Roebuck Grove on 35 acres for £66,000. The house was demolished in 1980.
1967	15 acres of the Roebuck Castle land for which £10,000 was paid for the freehold (the bulk of this land was first leased from the Little Sisters of the Poor for £900 in 1946).
1971	13.4 acres purchased from the Little Sisters of the Poor (Roebuck Castle) for £87,500.
1980–81	Richview (Masonic School) and 17.4 acres for £2.1 million.

1981	Rosemount (6.5 acres of the Richview land sold to Department of Posts and Telegraphs, the proceeds used to purchase Rosemount on 13.75 acres). The house was demolished in 1985.
1985	Additional 11 acres on Roebuck Castle estate from the Little Sisters of the Poor, for £800,000 (plus legal and valuers fees) funded by the sale of 13 acres along Foster's Avenue to Dublin County Council.
1986	Roebuck Castle on 10 acres for £620,000 (plus £15,000 for vacant possession of a dwelling house on the property).
1990	[Carysfort campus, Blackrock, on 19 acres for £8 million.]

Appendix 4

CHRONOLOGY OF BUILDING AT BELFIELD

1951 (6 Nov.)	Unanimous decision of the Governing Body that new University College buildings be erected on its lands at Stillorgan.
1959	Government Commission recommends that University College, Dublin should transfer to new campus at Belfield.
1960 (Mar.)	Dáil Éireann approves Commission's recommendation.
1962	Turning of the first sod (7 June) and work commences on the building of the Science block at Belfield.
1963 (Aug.)	Conditions for an International Architectural Competition for a layout plan and an Arts and Administration block at Belfield are issued.
1964 (24 Sept.)	Formal opening of new buildings for the Faculty of Science at Belfield. Announcement of the winning design, that of Polish architect Andrzej Wejchert, in the International Architectural Competition.
1968 (16 Oct.)	Final roof slab of the new building for the Faculties of Arts, Commerce and Law completed.
	Temporary computer centre erected.
1969	Faculty of Commerce transferred to Belfield.
	Temporary church, Our Lady Seat of Wisdom, opened.
1970	Faculties of Arts and Law (in part) moved to Belfield.
1970 (29 Sept.)	Official opening of Arts/Commerce/Law Building and of the Restaurant Building.
1970/1	Temporary beer and wine bar for students opened.
1972 (Mar./Apr.)	College offices move from Earlsfort Terrace to new Administration Building.
	Completion of the Water Tower.

1973 (8 Jan.)	Official opening of new Library Building (Phase I) which had been in operation since autumn 1972. Bank Building completed.
1976 (Nov.)	Work commenced on the new building for the Faculty of Agriculture.
1978 (July)	Work commenced on the Sports Centre. Students' Union and shops housed temporarily in Library infill.
1979	Faculty of Agriculture transferred from Glasnevin to new building.
1980	Richview Estate added to the campus and adapted for the Faculty of Architecture. Sports Centre completed. Opened 1981. Extension to Computer Centre built.
1982	New building for Department of Computer Science in use.
1985	Site work on Phase I of Engineering Building commenced. Roebuck Castle acquired, and adapted for teaching and other purposes. University Industry Centre completed. Students' Club opened.
1987	Phase II of the Library completed.
1988/9	Deans of Residence Building completed.
1989	Phase I of Engineering Building ready for occupation. Formal opening March 1990.
1989 (Oct.)	Student residential accommodation provided at Roebuck Castle.
1990	First student village (Belgrove) opened.
1992 (Mar.)	Second student village (Merville) formally opened.
1994	O'Reilly Hall opened. Biotechnology Building completed.
1996/7	Language Centre under construction.
1997	Student Centre proposal approved.

Notes

CHAPTER 1 (P. 1–24)

1. Walsh, *The Irish University Question*, 249–50.
2. Dónal Kerr, *Peel, Priests and Politics* (Oxford, 1982) 301, 311.
3. The fullest account of Newman's association with the Catholic University is by Fergal McGrath SJ in *Newman's University*. See also McRedmond, *Thrown Among Strangers*.
4. Newman to St John, 3 Oct. 1851 (LD, xiv, 377); also quoted by McGrath in *Newman's University*, 111.
5. *AW*, 282.
6. *AW*, 286.
7. *AW*, 288.
8. Minutes of Catholic University Committee, 15 Feb. 1853, UCDA.
9. 13 Feb. 1854 (*LD*, xvi, 43).
10. Newman to St John, 17 Feb. 1854 (*LD*, xvi, 48).
11. Newman to Flanagan, 26 Apr. 1856 (*LD*, xvii, 226).
12. W. Neville (ed.), *My Campaign in Ireland*, part I (privately printed), 65.
13. See above, pp 5–6.
14. A selection of extracts from his Dublin writings is to be found in McCartney and O'Loughlin, *Cardinal Newman*.
15. John Augustus O'Shea, Roundabout Recollections, vol. 2, 114, quoted by McGrath in *Newman's University*, 429.
16. Catholic University Register of Students (UCDA, CU5). This lists 1,196 entries; taking into account clerical errors and duplications, the correct number was probably 1,177.
17. *AW*, 298.
18. Newman to Moriarty, 15 Oct. 1861 (*LD*, xx, 58).
19. *Report on the conditions and circumstances of the Catholic University of Ireland, presented by a committee of the Senate, July 1859*, 4.
20. Newman, *Sermons Preached on Various Occasions*, 18.
21. 'Site of a University' in Newman, *Historical Sketches* (1891 edition), vol. 3, 31–2; also in Tierney, *University Sketches*, 30.
22. An excellent and most detailed account of his rectorship is to be found in Rigney, 'Bartholomew Woodlock and the Catholic University of Ireland'.
23. See illustration.

24. Dorrian to Woodlock, 28 Nov. 1866 (Woodlock Papers, quoted by Rigney, 'Bartholomew Woodlock and the Catholic University of Ireland', 230).

25. *Summary of contributions to the Catholic University of Ireland received from 15 May 1854 to 1 Oct. 1855*, 21.

26. Quoted by Rigney, 'Bartholomew Woodlock and the Catholic University of Ireland', 282.

27. Sullivan to Monsell, 15 May 1873 (quoted by Rigney, 'Bartholomew Woodlock and the Catholic University of Ireland', 367).

28. Newman, *Historical Sketches*, vol. 3, 58–9; Tierney, *University Sketches*, 55–6.

29. Newman to Woodlock, 4 Nov. 1874 (DDA, Woodlock Papers, quoted by Rigney, 'Bartholomew Woodlock and the Catholic University of Ireland', 57).

30. Tierney, *Struggle with Fortune*, 6.

31. See Society of Jesus, *A Page of Irish History*, 63–4, for the terms of this agreement.

32. For the history of University College under the Jesuits see especially Society of Jesus, *A Page of Irish History*, and Morrissey, *Towards a National University*.

33. Quoted by Morrissey, *Towards a National University*, 101.

34. Quoted by Morrissey, *Towards a National University*, 67.

35. Society of Jesus, *A Page of Irish History*, 87.

36. Quoted by Morrissey, *Towards a National University*, 69.

37. Society of Jesus, *A Page of Irish History*, 73, and Morrissey, *Towards a National University*, 83, give twenty-three as the vote for Hopkins, but the *Minutes of the Senate of the Royal University*, 30 Jan. 1884, 185–6, give the number as twenty-one.

38. See especially *The Irish University Question*, chap. 1.

39. *Royal Commission on University Education in Ireland, Appendix to the Third Report: Minutes of Evidence*, 360.

40. Society of Jesus, *A Page of Irish History*, 153.

41. *Hansard*, fourth series, vol. 177, 892 (4 July 1907).

42. See above, p. 15.

43. Edmund T. Whittaker, *Arthur William Conway, 1875–1950* (reprinted from *Obituary Notices of the Royal Society*, vol. 7, Nov. 1951, 330.

44. For the L&H see Meenan, *Centenary History of the Literary and Historical Society*.

CHAPTER 2 (P. 25–71)

1. *Royal Commission on University Education in Ireland, Final Report*, 37

2. *Royal Commission on Trinity College, Dublin, and the University of Dublin, Appendix to the Final Report: Minutes of Evidence and Documents*, iii.

3. Healy to Walsh, 8 June 1908 (P. J. Walsh, *William J. Walsh*, Dublin & Cork, 1928, 562).

4. See O'Dwyer, 'The University Bill', in *Irish Educational Review*, i, no. 8 (May 1908); and Finlay, 'Mr Birrell's University Bill', in *New Ireland Review*, xxix (June 1908).

5. *Hansard*, fourth series, vol. 193, 641 (25 July 1908).

6. P. J. Joyce, *John Healy, Archbishop of Tuam*, 165.

7. Dillon's seminal address under the auspices of the Catholic Graduates' Association was reported extensively in the *Freeman's Journal*, 9 Dec. 1904.

8. *An Claidheamh Soluis*, 30 Jan. 1904, quoted by Ó Buachalla, *A Significant Irish Educationalist*, 35. For Hyde's evidence see *Royal Commission on University Education in Ireland, Appendix to the Third Report: Minutes of Evidence*, 311–17, where the wording is 'the League desire that the popular element, either through itself and the county councils, or some other medium ...'

9. *An Claidheamh Soluis*, 6 Feb. 1904, quoted by Ó Buachalla, *A Significant Irish Educationalist*, 39.

10. *An Claidheamh Soluis*, 17 Dec. 1904.

11. Walsh to Birrell, 6 Jan. 1908 (DDA).

12. *Irish Times*, 20 May 1908.

13. *Hansard*, fourth series, vol. 193, 435–6 (23 July 1908).

14. Dillon, 'The origin and early history of the National University', in *University Review*, Part II, vol. I, no. 6. (Autumn, 1955), 20–1.

15. Murphy, *The College*, 205.

16. Mary Macken, *Studies*, no. 29 (June 1940), 176–86; John Marcus O'Sullivan, *Studies*, no. 34 (June 1945), 145–57.

17. William Doolin, 'The Catholic University School of Medicine (1855–1909)' in Tierney, *Struggle with Fortune*, 75–6.

18. J. J. Hogan, 'The work of Dr Coffey and Dr Conway' in Tierney, *Struggle with Fortune*, 95–6.

19. Dillon, 'The origin and early history of the National University', 21–2.

20. Tierney, *Struggle with Fortune*, 231–2.

21. J. H. Pollock, quoted by F. O. C. Meenan, *Cecilia Street*, 89.

22. Tierney, *Struggle with Fortune*, 232.

23. Tierney, *Struggle with Fortune*, 99.

24. J. J. Hogan in Tierney, *Struggle with Fortune*, 84.

25. *Report of the president, 1909/10*, 3.

26. A single student, whose school was given as Clonliffe, was registered for first medical.

27. See below, pp 168–70, for further details on the changing student profile.

28. Quoted by Tierney, *Struggle with Fortune*, 111.

29. O'Brien, 'UCD as I forget it', 7.

30. J. P. MacHale, 'The socio-economic background of students in Irish universities', *Studies,* no. 68 (autumn 1979), 213–1.

31. For Tierney's resentment of Trinity's attempts to persuade county councils to make their scholarships tenable at TCD see below, p. 191, 312.

32. Governing Body minutes, 29 May 1956.

33. *Commission on Higher Education, Presentation and Summary of Report,* 85–7.

34. *Calendar, 1980/81,* book II, 38.

35. Newman, *The Idea of a University,* discourse VI, 9.

36. For the history of this society see James Meenan, *Centenary History of the Literary and Historical Society.*

37. James Meenan, *Centenary History of the Literary and Historical Society,* viii.

38. James Meenan, *Centenary History of the Literary and Historical Society,* ix.

39. *St Stephen's,* vol. 2, no. 10 (Feb. 1906), 209–10.

40. Society of Jesus, *A Page of Irish History,* 286. The two friends published their essays together in a pamphlet.

41. Richard Ellman, *James Joyce* (Oxford University Press 1965), 100–1, quoting *Freeman's Journal,* 3 Feb. 1902.

42. Society of Jesus, *A Page of Irish History,* 549. William Dawson, himself a former contributor to *St Stephen's* and auditor of the L & H, wrote: 'Cruise O'Brien was the last editor of *St Stephen's* and involved it in the ruin which it was the sad lot of this modern Samson to bring upon College institutions with which he was associated' (*National Student,* ii, no. 2, new series (June 1931).

43. Eimar Ultan O'Duffy was born in Dublin in 1893 and educated at Stonyhurst College, Lancashire, and UCD, where he was a dental student 1911–17. He displayed a great interest in politics and literature, writing for and editing the *National Student* and speaking at the L&H. In 1920 he married the sister of Francis Cruise O'Brien. Novelist, playwright and poet, he died in 1935.

44. Eimar O'Duffy, *The Wasted Island,* 1919, 111.

45. Michael McGilligan was born in Derry in 1887, the older brother of Patrick McGilligan, and educated at Clongowes Wood College. He served in the Indian Civil Service, and was called to the Irish bar, where he became a senior counsel.

46. J. J. 'Ginger' O'Connell was born in 1887 and educated at Clongowes Wood College. He was a member of the General Staff of the pre-Truce IRA and later a general in the Free State army.

47. P. J. Little was born in 1884 and educated at Clongowes Wood College and became a journalist on nationalist publications. He was elected TD for Fianna Fáil 1927, Minister for Post and Telegraphs 1939–1948, and director of the Arts Council 1951.

48. James Meenan, *Centenary History of the Literary and Historical Society*, 90–4.
49. James Meenan, *Centenary History of the Literary and Historical Society*, 77–8.
50. *National Student*, vol. 1, no. 1 (May 1910), editorial.
51. *National Student*, vol. 1, no. 1 (May 1910), 'The Mission of the New University to the Nation', 7–9.
52. *National Student*, vol. 4, no. 11 (Nov. 1913).
53. *National Student*, new series, vol. 1, no. 1 (Mar. 1923).
54. Michael Tierney, 'A new departure', *Student*, vol. 1, no. 1 (Oct. 1954), 4–5.
55. See below, pp 295–6.
56. *Student* (Jan. 1961).
57. *St Stephen's*, new series, vol. 1, no. 1 (Trinity term, 1960), 3.
58. *St Stephen's*, Michaelmas term, 1960, 3.
59. *St Stephen's*, Hilary term 1962, 5.
60. *St Stephen's*, Hilary term [actually Michaelmas], 1962.
61. *St Stephen's*, 42–4.
62. *St Stephen's*, Trinity term, 1963, 4–5.
63. St. Stephen's, Michaelmas term, 1963, 8.
64. *St Stephen's*, Hilary term, 1967.
65. See below, chapter 10, 'The Student Revolt'.
66. Nuala O'Faolain, *Are You Somebody?* (Dublin 1996), 61.
67. *Campus*, 3 Nov. 1966.
68. *Campus*, 3 Nov. 1966.
69. McDowell and Webb, *Trinity College, Dublin*, 370.
70. Martin, *1916 and University College, Dublin*, 39.
71. James Meenan, *George O'Brien*, 30–1.
72. Newman, *Historical Sketches*, vol. 3, 81.
73. Newman, *Historical Sketches*, vol. 3, 81.
74. *Dublin Commission … Applications of Candidates*, 1909, vol. 1, 160.
75. McConnell, *Selected Papers of A. W. Conway*, 2–3.
76. McConnell, *Selected Papers of A. W. Conway*, 2–3.
77. McConnell, *Selected Papers of A. W. Conway*, preface.
78. *Dublin Commission … Applications of Candidates*, vol. 1, 46.
79. Gerard Murphy, 'Celtic Studies' in Tierney, *Struggle with Fortune*, 124.
80. McDowell and Webb, *Trinity College, Dublin*, 379, 550.
81. G. F. Mitchell, 'R. A. S. Macalister' in Ó Raifeartaigh, *The Royal Irish Academy*, 152.
82. G. F. Mitchell, 'R. A. S. Macalister' in Ó Raifeartaigh, *The Royal Irish Academy*, 152.
83. Martin and Byrne, *The Scholar Revolutionary*, 330–53.

CHAPTER 3 (P. 72–84)

1. Abbé Polin was a native of Alsace who came to Ireland after the Franco-German War and had been teaching modern languages at the Catholic University for about ten years when it was taken over by the Jesuits in 1883. He was appointed an examiner of the Royal University in 1882 and fellow in 1884. He died in 1889.

2. *Royal Commission on University Education in Ireland, Appendix to the Third Report: Minutes of Evidence,* 318.

3. *Royal Commission on Trinity College, Dublin, and the University of Dublin, Appendix to the Final Report: Minutes of Evidence and Documents,* 266.

4. *Royal Commission on Trinity College, Dublin, and the University of Dublin, Appendix to the Final Report: Minutes of Evidence and Documents,* 267. In *A Page of Irish History* (p. 468), in a section where the Jesuit editors acknowledge the assistance of Mary Hayden, it is inaccurately implied that Agnes O'Farrelly used the phrase about the cleavage being unfortunate; in fact it was said by her fellow-representative Miss Hanan, a Trinity graduate. It is perhaps amusing that the Jesuit editors in 1930 should draw attention to the unconscious pun. In case the reader missed it they rephrased it and put it in italic type as *a most unfortunate cleavage*; and in case one missed the italic they added in parentheses, 'italics ours.'

5. *Royal Commission on Trinity College, Dublin, and the University of Dublin, Final Report,* 27.

6. *Royal Commission on University Education in Ireland, Appendix to the First Report: Minutes of Evidence,* 91.

7. *Royal Commission on University Education in Ireland, Appendix to the First Report: Minutes of Evidence,* 77.

8. See Society of Jesus, *A Page of Irish History,* 470–1.

9. Hayden to Mother Patrick, 3 Feb. 1905 (quoted by E. Breathnach, 'A History of the Movement for Women's Higher Education in Dublin, 1860–1912', MA thesis, University College, Dublin, 1981, 130).

10. James Meenan, *Centenary History of the Literary and Historical Society,* 112.

11. Delany to Walsh, 8 Apr. 1908 (Lambert McKenna SJ, manuscript volume, National University, chap. 19, quoted by T. Morrissey, 'Some Jesuit Contributions to Irish Education', PhD thesis, University College, Dublin, 583).

12. *Royal Commission on University Education in Ireland, Final Report,* 49.

13. *Royal Commission on Trinity College, Dublin, and the University of Dublin, Appendix to the Final Report: Minutes of Evidence and Documents,* 406; see also evidence of Agnes O'Farrelly, 266.

14. Women Graduates' Association Papers (UCDA, 1/3 (4).
15. Women Graduates' Association Papers (UCDA, 1/3 (4).
16. NUI Charter, chap. 5. See also NUI Statute I, chap. 2; UCD Charter, chap. 5; UCD Statute I, chap. 3.
17. Mary Macken, 'Women in University College' in Tierney, *Struggle with Fortune*, 143–4.
18. *Royal Commission on University Education in Ireland, Appendix to the Third Report*, 360.
19. Mary Hayden, diary, 7 Dec. 1900 (NLI, MS, 16, 681).
20. Walsh to Birrell, 20 May 1908 (DDA).
21. *Hansard*, fourth series, vol. 187, 349 (31 Mar. 1908).
22. NUI Statute I, chap. 49; Statute LXXXVI, chap. 59.
23. Sacerdos, 'Mr Birrell's University Bill', *New Ireland Review*, no. 24 (June 1908), 214.
24. *Hansard*, fourth series, vol. 113, 471 (23 July 1908).
25. These statistics and calculations are based on the annual report of the president. For an account of some of the women in the college between 1909 and 1954 see Mary Macken, 'Women in the university and college: a struggle within a struggle' in Tierney, *Struggle with Fortune*, 142–65.

CHAPTER 4 (P. 85–111)

1. *Royal Commission on University Education in Ireland, Final Report*, 34.
2. *Royal Commission on Trinity College, Dublin, and the University of Dublin, Final Report*, 55.
3. Governing Body minutes, 26 Jan. 1911.
4. Governing Body minutes, 12 June 1911.
5. Dunbar Plunket Barton, who was a member of the Senate of the NUI, was educated at the University of Oxford, where he had been president of the Oxford Union, and was a judge of the Chancery Division of the High Court of Justice, Ireland. He had been professor of the law of property, King's Inns, unionist MP for Armagh 1891–1900, and Solicitor-General for Ireland 1898–1900. He also provided the college with the Dunbar Barton Law Prize (£10), which in 1912 was awarded to a student who later became Taoiseach, John A. Costello. Clearly Judge Barton had acted as mediator with Lord Iveagh in the interests of the college.
6. Mgr Gerard Molloy (1834–1906) had been professor of physics in the Catholic University during the eighteen-seventies and vice-rector; he was appointed one of the first senators of the Royal University and vice-chancellor but resigned in order to become a fellow. When the Catholic University was reorganised in the early eighties and the Stephen's Green College was handed over to the Jesuits, Mgr Molloy remained on as

professor of experimental physics (lecturing to outsiders rather than to students) while also becoming Rector of the Catholic University (1883–1906). His death in 1906, though genuinely regretted, helped the teaching of physics in the college, since his rooms and valuable instruments were placed at the disposal of the college. Fr James Healy (1824–1894) of Little Bray—where he served as administrator from 1867 to the year before his death, when he became parish priest of Ballybrack, Co. Dublin—was a well-known humorist and wit of his day. He was on close friendly terms with many leading contemporaries (see *Memoir* by W. J. Fitzpatrick). He outspokenly condemned the agrarian secret societies of the early eighteen-eighties, which, as he expressed it, no more minded shooting a man than shooting a crow.

7. Governing Body minutes, 28 Apr. 1921.
8. Governing Body minutes, 20 July 1920.
9. Governing Body minutes, 17 May 1921.
10. Some suspected that the unsightly paling that for a number of years was to detract from the architectural elegance of R. M. Butler's design was Dr Coffey's way of drawing attention to the unfinished state of his college.
11. Governing Body minutes, 21 Mar. 1922.
12. Governing Body minutes, 9 Aug. 1922.
13. *Irish Times,* 'Saturday Column', 2 Dec. 1989.
14. *Report of the president, 1916/17,* 35
15. *Report of the president, 1917/18,* 27.
16. Royal Commission on Trinity College, Dublin, and the University of Dublin, *Final Report,* 74.
17. *National Student,* vol. 4, no. 2 (Dec. 1913), 27.
18. *National Student,* vol. 4, no. 2 (Dec. 1913), 34–5.
19. Quoted by Martin, *1916 and University College, Dublin,* 17.
20. *National Student,* vol. 4, no. 2 (Dec. 1913), 28.
21. *National Student,* vol. 4, no. 2 (Dec. 1913), 27–9.
22. Martin, *1916 and University College, Dublin,* 21, 98.
23. Governing Body minutes, 23 Mar. 1915.
24. Governing Body minutes, 20 May and 16 June 1915.
25. Governing Body minutes, 10 Nov. 1914.
26. Governing Body minutes, 22 Dec. 1914.
27. For an account of the Medical School in the years of war see F. O. C. Meenan, *Cecilia Street,* 92–7.
28. Governing Body minutes, 22 Dec. 1914.
29. Governing Body minutes, 10 Mar. 1914, 9 Feb., 11 May and 26 Oct. 1915.
30. 'The War, TCD and University College', *National Student,* vol. 5, no. 1 (Nov. 1914), 1–3.
31. Martin, *1916 and University College, Dublin,* 22.

32. McDowell and Webb, *Trinity College, Dublin,* 420.

33. Memorandum of interview, 20 Nov. 1915 (quoted by León Ó Broin, *Dublin Castle and the 1916 Rising,* 59–60).

34. Governing Body minutes, 9 Feb. and 23 Mar. 1915.

35. Governing Body minutes, 18 Dec. 1917.

36. Governing Body minutes, 17 Dec. 1918, 26 Mar. and 26 June 1919, 23 Mar. 1920.

37. Governing Body minutes, 22 July 1919.

38. Governing Body minutes, 24 Oct. 1916.

39. Report of the president, 1917/18, 4.

40. Michael Hayes was later a minister of Dáil Éireann, Ceann Comhairle, and senator and professor of Modern Irish in UCD. Liam Ó Briain became professor of romance languages in UCG. Louise Gavan Duffy founded Scoil Bhríde while also acting as assistant in UCD's Education Department. Dr James Ryan later opposed the Treaty and served as Minister for Agriculture, Minister for Health and Minister for Finance in Fianna Fáil Governments. Maj.-Gen. Joseph Sweeney became Chief of Staff of the Defence Forces.

41. The title of an account of the rising by Charles Duff.

42. *Report of the president, 1915/16,* 4.

43. *National Student,* vol. 8, no. 1 (Dec. 1917), 1–2.

44. Governing Body minutes, 23 May, 20 July and 24 Oct. 1916, 3 July and 6 Nov. 1917, 23 Apr. and 17 Dec. 1918. See also Martin and Byrne, *The Scholar Revolutionary,* 387–90; Tierney, *Eoin MacNeill,* 245.

45. O'Brien, *My Ireland,* 111–12.

46. O'Brien, *My Ireland,* 112.

47. O'Brien, *My Ireland,* 114.

48. *National Student,* vol. 7, no. 1 (Dec. 1916), vol. 8, no. 4 (June 1917), vol. 8, no. 1 (Dec. 1917).

49. *National Student,* vol. 8, no. 3 (Dec. 1918), 5–8.

50. One of the famous Ryan sisters from Wexford and close friend of Seán Mac Diarmada, one of the executed 1916 leaders. She later married Richard Mulcahy. Her sister, Mary K. Ryan, who was in UCD's French Department, married Seán T. O'Kelly; after her death he married her sister Phyllis. Another sister was married to Denis McCullagh, president of the Supreme Council of the IRB in 1916. Their brother was Dr James Ryan.

51. Martin, *1916 and University College, Dublin,* 112.

52. *National Student,* vol. 8, no. 4 (Mar. 1919). The article was entitled 'Resurgamus'.

53. John Mowbray in James Meenan, *Centenary History of the Literary and Historical Society,* 174–5.

54. John Mowbray in James Meenan, *Centenary History of the Literary and Historical Society,* 174–5.

55. Celia Shaw diary (NLI, ms. 23409), Nov. 1920, 2–3.
56. John Farrell in James Meenan, *Centenary History of the Literary and Historical Society*, 171.
57. John Mowbray in James Meenan, *Centenary History of the Literary and Historical Society*, 176.
58. Celia Shaw diary (NLI, ms. 23409), Nov. 1920, 6.
59. Governing Body minutes, 4 Nov. 1920.
60. Celia Shaw diary (NLI, ms. 23409), 21 Nov. 1920, 9.
61. James Meenan, *Centenary History of the Literary and Historical Society*, 171.
62. Celia Shaw diary (NLI, ms. 23409), 17.
63. Celia Shaw diary (NLI, ms. 23409), 14 Feb. 1921, 17.
64. Governing Body minutes, 1 Mar. 1921.
65. Governing Body minutes, 1 Mar., 28 Apr., 26 July, 15 Nov. and 20 Dec. 1921.
66. Arthur Mitchell, *Revolutionary Government in Ireland: Dáil Éireann, 1919–22* (Dublin, 1995), 10, 110, 115, 252.
67. Governing Body minutes, 28 Apr. 1921.
68. James Meenan, *Centenary History of the Literary and Historical Society*, 175–6.
69. *Report of the president, 1920/21*, 30.
70. Governing Body minutes, 20 Dec. 1921.
71. Celia Shaw diary (NLI, ms. 23409), Dec. 1921–Jan. 1922, 21–6.
72. Governing Body minutes, 31 Oct. 1922.
73. Celia Shaw diary (NLI, ms. 23409), July 1922, 48–9.
74. *National Student*, new series, vol. 1, no. 1 (Mar. 1923).

CHAPTER 5 (P. 112–158)

1. *The National University Handbook, 1908–1932*, 63.
2. *Freeman's Journal*, 27 Mar. 1820.
3. Michael Taaffe, *Those Days Are Gone Away*, London: Hutchinson, 1959, 208.
4. Ó hÓgáin to the author, 26 June 1991.
5. De Valera to Conway, 26 Oct. 1940.
6. Buildings Committee minutes, 23 and 29 Sep. 1941; Governing Body minutes, 28 Oct. 1941.
7. Ó hÉigeartaigh to Department of Finance, 15 Jan. 1945; Conway to de Valera, 6 Sep. 1945; OPW to Department of Finance, 26 Sep. 1945 (NA, S13809A, 2–5); Buildings Committee minutes 22 Oct. 1952.
8. M. A. Hogan, 'Notes on the preparatory work required as a preliminary to the erection of new buildings for the College', 21 April 1947.
9. De Valera to Conway, 24 Apr. 1947; Buildings Committee minutes, 8 May 1947.

10. See below, p. 122.

11. Prof. Purcell's 'Statement' to the Governing Body, 6 Nov. 1951.

12. Tierney's later memo submitted to the Commission on Accommodation Needs of the Constituent Colleges of the National University of Ireland (1958) says that they learnt about Mespil House 'in the summer of 1945.' Prof. Purcell in his statement to the Governing Body (6 Nov. 1951) also states that they became aware 'in the autumn of 1945' that Mespil House and its 5½ acres had come on the market.

13. J. P. MacHale, *UCD News*, Feb. 1995.

14. Memo, 26 Jan. 1948 (NA, S13809A).

15. Report by Department of the Taoiseach, 21 July 1955 (NA, S13809B).

16. Downes to president, 16 Feb. 1948 (UCDA, PO2/50/2).

17. Obituary in *Report of the president 1967/68*, 81.

18. J. V. Downes, 'Proposed extension of buildings for University College, Dublin: some notes on the present position', 16 Feb. 1948.

19. McQuaid to Tierney, 22 Feb. 1948 (UCDA, PO/50/2).

20. Ó Raifeartaigh, *The Royal Irish Academy*, 85.

21. James Meenan, diary, 21 Jan. and 17 Feb. 1947.

22. O'Rahilly to Tierney, 3 Sep. 1947 (UCDA, Tierney Papers).

23. See James Meenan, diary, Sep.–Oct. 1947.

24. O'Donovan to Tierney, 15 Sep. 1947 (UCDA, Tierney Papers).

25. O'Rahilly to Tierney, 18 Oct. 1947 (UCDA, Tierney Papers).

26. Hogan to Tierney, n.d. (UCDA, Tierney Papers).

27. Ó Briain to Tierney, 23 Oct. 1947 (UCDA, Tierney Papers).

28. Ó Briain to Tierney, 23 Oct. 1947 (UCDA, Tierney Papers).

29. Ó Briain to Tierney, 23 Oct. 1947 (UCDA, Tierney Papers).

30. NUI Senate minutes, 30 Oct. 1947. An anecdote related by John V. Bourke (later registrar of the NUI) tells how Nolan and Barniville left the Senate room while the election was in progress and went downstairs to await the result. 'They were chatting outside the chief clerk's office when James J. Drumm came rushing down the stairs and into the chief clerk's room. In his excitement he did not notice Nolan or Barniville. He picked up the phone and dialled Tierney to be first to congratulate him on his appointment. Nolan, overhearing this, said to Barniville that Drumm had assured him that he was voting for him. Yes, said Barniville, he assured me of the same thing. That's how presidents are made.' (UCDA, John V. Bourke papers).

31. James Meenan, diary, 30 Oct. 1947.

32. Ó Briain to Tierney, 31 Oct. 1947.

33. Dillon to Tierney, 31 Oct. 1947.

34. Duignan to Tierney, 31 Oct. 1947.

35. Bourke to Tierney, 12 Nov. 1947.

36. For the messages of congratulation see UCDA, Tierney Papers, LA30, box 9.

37.   James Meenan, diary, 30 Oct. 1947.

38.   See below, pp 136–41.

39.   *Irish Independent,* 29 and 30 Nov., 1, 2 and 3 Dec. 1949.

40.   Statement by president to Governing Body, 1 Feb. 1949.

41.   L&H minutes, 15 Jan. 1949.

42.   Martin and McCarthy became judges; Connolly was the Attorney-General who resigned during the bizarre Macarthur affair in 1982.

43.   L&H minutes, 15 Jan. 1949. O'Connor, noted then for his histrionics at meetings of the L&H, had entered disguised as a priest and proceeded to bless the assembly. See Sheehy Skeffington, *Skeff,* 137, 254.

44.   *Irish Times,* 22 Jan. 1949.

45.   *Irish Times,* 22 Jan. 1949.

46.   Another correspondent, 'Post Graduate', agreed that few if any of the students would have supported the motion.

47.   Whyte, *Church and State in Modern Ireland,* 73, 163–5.

48.   The Earl of Wicklow replied that he did not believe Sheehy Skeffington was a communist: in fact he had recently been critical of communist policy. It was not fair to him to imply that he intended to act as the apostle of communism (*Irish Times,* 28 Jan. 1949). Lord Wicklow also had a point in stating that it was highly illogical to say that communism might be studied but not discussed in public.

49.   Noel Browne, *Against the Tide,* Dublin: Gill & Macmillan 1986, 110, 179–80.

50.   *Irish Times,* 24 Jan. 1949.

51.   Governing Body minutes, 1 Feb. 1949.

52.   As early as 1912, in the first number of *Studies,* which he then edited, Prof. Corcoran had launched his anti-Newman campaign; see *Studies,* no. 1 (Mar. 1912), 114–29.

53.   Tierney's *Tribute to Newman* coincided with the centenary of the reception of Newman into the Catholic Church and with the passing of the Queen's Colleges Bill—though neither of these events was mentioned as the occasion for the publication of the tribute.

54.   Tierney, *A Tribute to Newman,* 176. Roger McHugh (*Newman on University Education,* xxxiv–xxxv) also said that Newman's prose was 'more relaxed, more urbane in the pages of his historical essays than in the *Discourses.*'

55.   *University Review,* vol. 1, no. 2 (autumn 1954), 4.

56.   *University Review,* vol. 1, no. 2 (autumn 1954), 4.

57.   *University Review,* vol. 1, no. 2 (autumn 1954), 4.

58.   *Catholic University of Ireland, 1854: Centenary Celebrations, 18–23 July 1954,* 4.

59.   *Catholic University of Ireland, 1854: Centenary Celebrations, 18–23 July 1954,* 23–5.

60. *Catholic University of Ireland, 1854: Centenary Celebrations, 18–23 July 1954*, 21, 22.
61. *Irish Independent*, 20 July 1954.
62. *Irish Independent*, 23 July 1954.
63. *Irish Independent*, 23 July 1954.
64. *Struggle with Fortune*, 170.
65. *Struggle with Fortune*, 171.
66. *Struggle with Fortune*, 171.
67. *Struggle with Fortune*, 171.
68. *Struggle with Fortune*, 168.
69. Dillon to Tierney, 15 Nov. 1954. Dillon received five votes, McHenry seven and Atkins eighteen at the Senate, 28 Oct. 1954.
70. *University Review*, vol. 1, no. 2 (autumn 1954), 5.
71. *University Review*, vol. 1, no. 2 (autumn 1954), 4.
72. *University Review*, vol. 1, no. 2 (autumn 1954), 6.
73. *University Review*, vol. 1, no. 2 (autumn 1954), 5.
74. *University Review*, vol. 1, no. 2 (autumn 1954), 5.
75. *University Review*, vol. 1, no. 2 (autumn 1954), 5.
76. *University Review*, vol. 1, no. 2 (autumn 1954), 6.
77. *University Review*, vol. 1, no. 2 (autumn 1954), 6.
78. *University Review*, vol. 1, no. 2 (autumn 1954), 9.
79. *University Review*, vol. 1, no. 2 (autumn 1954), 5.
80. *University Review*, vol. 1, no. 2 (autumn 1954), 9.
81. *University Review*, vol. 1, no. 2 (autumn 1954), 7.
82. *University Review*, vol. 1, no. 2 (autumn 1954), 7.
83. *University Review*, vol. 1, no. 2 (autumn 1954), 8.
84. *Irish Independent*, 12, 14 and 16 Oct. 1953.
85. John O'Meara, 'Guardians of truth', *Irish University Review*, vol. 26, no. 1 (spring–summer 1996), 1–14.
86. NUI Senate minutes, 10 Dec. 1954.
87. Meenan to Tierney, 12 Dec. 1954 (UCDA, Tierney Papers, LA30/164).
88. James Meenan, diary, 10 Nov. 1954–13 Jan. 1955.

CHAPTER 6 (P. 159–226)

1. Quoted by Walsh, *The Irish University Question*, 196–7.
2. Walsh, *The Irish University Question*, 196–8.
3. Greek: Henry Browne SJ; English language and philology: George O'Neill SJ; education: Timothy Corcoran SJ; political economy: Thomas Finlay SJ; lectureship in pure mathematics: Michael F. Egan SJ.
4. Ethics and politics: Rev M. Cronin; logic and psychology: Rev. J. Shine; lectureship in eastern languages: Rev. P. Boylan.
5. *Royal Commission on University Education in Ireland, Appendix to the First Report: Minutes of Evidence*, 26.

6. 'Nothing, in our opinion, would be more fatal to the future of the University, than to approach its constitution in an anti-clerical spirit, which is absolutely alien to the whole character and disposition of our people.' See 'Statement of the Roman Catholic Hierarchy, June 1897', reprinted in *Royal Commission on University Education in Ireland, Appendix to the First Report: Minutes of Evidence*, 388.

7. *Royal Commission on University Education in Ireland, Appendix to the First Report: Minutes of Evidence*, 85.

8. Newman, 'Address from the Cui Bono Club of the Irish Catholic University', *My Campaign in Ireland*, 406.

9. The 'rules' referred to in the text were the guidelines operated by the officers of residence.

10. See above, p. 59.

11. 'Air of Christianity', *Comhthrom Féinne*, vol. 9, no. 3 (Dec. 1934), 1–2.

12. 'Pro Fide: its re-organisation', *Comhthrom Féinne*, vol. 9, no. 3 (Dec. 1934), 18.

13. Gwynn to Tierney, 20 Mar. 1936 (LA30/188).

14. Academic Council minutes, 26 Mar. 1936.

15. Kent and Brunicardi to Coffey, 29 Mar. 1936 (Academic Council minutes, 30 Mar. 1936).

16. Supplement to *National Student* (LA 30/188).

17. Academic Council minutes, 19 May and 13 June 1936. Pierce Kent qualified in medicine in 1938.

18. *National Student*, vol. 16, no. 3 (Sep. 1936).

19. Governing Body minutes, 7 July 1936.

20. Governing Body minutes, 12 Mar. 1935. See above, p. 117.

21. John Feeney, 'Recognition refused to Student Movement', *Campus*, vol. 2, no 2 (3 Nov. 1966). Pax Romana, the Catholic students' movement, was still active and strong in UCD at the time; but SCM planned more ecumenical activities.

22. *Campus*, vol. 2, no. 2 (3 Nov. 1966.).

23. The SCM Society was in fact listed in the official college calendars for the session 1967/68. For the following session, 1968/69, it linked up with Logos to become 'Logos Student Christian Movement Society'. During the next two sessions it disappeared from the calendars, since it was among those clubs and societies for which the list of officers was not submitted; it reappeared for 1971/72 as the 'Christian Movement (formerly Logos/SCM)'. It appeared under its original name, 'SCM Society', for 1973/74, and in 1974/75 it was described as 'Logos (SCM) Society'.

24. UCDA, PO5/63–72/3.

25. The number given in the *Report of the president* was 530.

26.   97.35 per cent is the precise figure according to the statistics supplied by M. Tierney to A. O'Rahilly, 28 August 1961 (PO3/63/13).

27.   James Meenan, diary, 20 Oct. 1940.

28.   *Irish Times,* 15 Oct. 1973.

29.   Counterpart deed of endowment, 3 Dec. 1912 (UCDA, Coffey Papers, 3/42).

30.   McQuaid to Tierney, 15 June 1959.

31.   Rev. Dermot Ryan, 'Theology in the proposed University of Dublin' in *The Proposed Merger with TCD,* papers read at a UCD seminar, 13 May 1967.

32.   For an account of this see Hartigan, 'The Catholic Laity of Dublin'.

33.   O'Sullivan, *Defending the Truth,* 4–5, 11–12, 15–16.

34.   *Irish Ecclesiastical Record,* vol. 57 (Jan.–June 1941).

35.   O'Sullivan, *Defending the Truth,* 12.

36.   *Seanad Debates,* vol. 27, col. 259–69, 3 Dec. 1942.

37.   But he opposed a campaign to restrict the importing of foreign newspapers by the imposition of a tariff, which would only benefit what he considered the incompetent Irish papers. He wrote: 'We have nothing to compare for intelligence and real value with the *Observer* and the *Sunday Times*' (*Studies,* no. 16 (Dec. 1927), 557).

38.   Censorship of Publications Act (1929), section 6 (3).

39.   *Derry Journal,* 5 Dec. 1928.

40.   See especially his articles 'The philosophy of sanity: Chesterton and Belloc', *Studies,* no. 11 (1922), 571–81 and 'The return of the Middle Ages', *Studies,* no. 14 (1925), 231–7.

41.   James Meenan, *George O'Brien,* 85. This sympathetic biography re-creates much of the flavour of UCD during O'Brien's time as an undergraduate and later during his professorship.

42.   *The Economic History of Ireland in the Eighteenth Century* (1918); *The Economic History of Ireland in the Seventeenth Century* (1919); *The Economic History of Ireland from the Union to the Famine* (1921).

43.   R. H. Tawney, *Religion and the Rise of Capitalism,* Harmondsworth (Middx): Penguin 1926 (Pelican, 1948), xv, 290.

44.   See especially 'An alternative to capitalism', *Studies,* no. 14 (Dec. 1925), and 'Religion and capitalism', *Studies,* no. 15 (June 1926), 217–29. This was the year in which O'Brien was appointed to the chair.

45.   James Meenan, *George O'Brien,* 163–4.

46.   D. A. Binchy, *Church and State in Fascist Italy,* Oxford: University Press, 1941, issued under the auspices of the Royal Institute of International Affairs.

47.   Dermot Keogh, *Ireland and Europe, 1919–1989,* Cork: Cork University Press 1990, 32.

48.   J. Anthony Gaughan, *Alfred O'Rahilly, Vol. 3: Controversialist,* part 1: 'Social reformer', 181.

49. Minutes of discussion prior to attendance of president, registrar and secretary at the Commission of Higher Education (19 and 20 Jan. 1962) held in Board Room, 17 Jan. 1962 (UCDA, PO box 105); *Report of Commission of Higher Education*, 662.

50. Academic Council minutes, 20 June 1946.

51. Roberts and Clarke, *The Story of the People's College*, 6, 9.

52. Academic Council minutes, 17 June 1948. The committee consisted of the president, registrar, Prof. O'Brien, Prof. Hogan, Prof. Shields, Canon O'Keefe, and Senator Hayes.

53. Roberts and Clarke, *The Story of the People's College*, 16.

54. Academic Council minutes, 11 Oct. 1948; Governing Body minutes, 14 Oct. 1948. When forty-two students had successfully completed the first two-year diploma in social and economic studies in UCD and wished to pursue further study, a course was so organised, and the Catholic Workers' College began its work in Sandford Lodge, Sandford Road, Dublin. In 1966 it was renamed the College of Industrial Relations, and in 1987 it became the National College of Industrial Relations. In 1998 it was again renamed, becoming the 'National College of Ireland'.

55. Governing Body minutes, 14 Dec. 1948. The course was advertised in the *Irish Independent* (3 Jan. 1949) as a college diploma in political, social and economic science. The *Report of the president* for 1948/49 (p. 29) described it as a college diploma in political and economic science. When the actual diploma was awarded, from 1951 onwards, it had become the extra-mural college diploma in social and economic studies.

56. For the information contained in these two paragraphs see the 'Report of the Director of Studies on the Initiation and First Term's Work ...' and 'Report of the Director of Studies on the Second Term's Work ...' (UCDA, Tierney Papers, box 5/131).

57. Newman, in his address to the evening students, 'Discipline of Mind', published in *The Idea of a University* (for the relevant extract see McCartney and O'Loughlin, *Cardinal Newman*, 124–5), spoke of his enthusiasm for the evening students: 'I thought of you before you thought of the University.' When 'wise and good men' asked him where he would get the students to fill the lecture-rooms of the projected Catholic University he answered: 'We will give lectures in the evening, we will fill our classes with the young men of Dublin.' He was convinced that the evening courses would not only be of benefit to those participating but would also bring honour and renown as well as literary, scientific and political advantage to Ireland. 'Much as I desire that this University should be of service to the young men of Dublin, I do not desire this benefit to you, simply for your own sakes. For your own sakes certainly I wish it, but not on your account only. Man is not born for himself alone, as the classical

moralist tells you. *You* are born for Ireland; and in your advancement Ireland is advanced;—in your advancement of what is good and what is true, in knowledge, in learning, in cultivation of mind, in enlightened attachment to your religion, in good name and respectability and social influence, I am contemplating the honour and renown, the literary and scientific aggrandisement, the increase of political power, of the Island of Saints.'

58. 'Course for Adult Catholic Workers', 8 July 1949, enclosed in a letter, Coyne to Tierney, 4 Aug. 1949 (UCDA, Tierney Papers, box 5).

59. Coyne to Tierney, 4 Aug. 1949 (UCDA, Tierney Papers, box 5).

60. Coyne to Tierney, 5 Aug. 1949 (UCDA, Tierney Papers, box 5).

61. Newman had also written in that lecture to the evening students: 'Gentlemen, the seat of this intellectual progress must necessarily be the great towns of Ireland.'

62. *Report of the president, 1952/53*, 42.

63. *Report of the president, 1950/51*, 37.

64. Governing Body minutes, 29 Nov. 1949.

65. *Report of the president, 1961/62*, 54.

66. Michael Tierney, 'The University Question after Thirty Years' (manuscript, UCDA, LA 30/207), 14–16. See also Tierney, *Struggle with Fortune*, 234, and 'Autonomy and Legal Position of the College' (memorandum no. 2, submitted to Commission on Higher Education), 11–12.

67. T. Desmond Williams, 'The college and the nation' in Tierney, *Struggle with Fortune*, 172–3.

68. Staunton to Tierney, 21 Oct. 1950 (UCDA, PO2/51/1).

69. Tierney to O'Rahilly, 4 Jan. 1951.

70. UCDA, PO7/2.

71. O'Rahilly's first response to Tierney's memo is dated 8 Jan. 1951; a copy is in UCDA (PO7/2). It was circulated at the meeting of bishops and college presidents on 17 January 1951. A copy of his second confidential memo (18 Apr. 1952), from which I have taken the above quotations, is in UCDA (PO7/3).

72. Tierney to Archbishop D'Alton, 12 Dec. 1951 (UCDA, PO2/51/1).

73. Tierney to de Brún, 25 Jan. 1951 (UCDA, PO2/51/52). For the Tierney and O'Rahilly memoranda and the minutes of the meeting see UCDA, PO7/2 and PO7/3.

74. Minutes of the meeting, 17 Jan. 1951 (UCDA, PO7/3).

75. Memorandum, 31 Jan. 1952 (UCDA, PO7/3).

76. O'Rahilly to Tierney, 4 Feb. 1952; Tierney to O'Rahilly, 5 Feb. 1952 (UCDA, PO2/52/65).

77. Tierney to O'Rahilly, 9 Feb. 1952; O'Rahilly to Tierney, 11 Feb. 1952 (UCDA, PO2/52/65).

78. One of the resolutions of the Catholic hierarchy of October 1885 read: 'That on Commissions or other public bodies appointed for educational purposes we claim, as a matter of justice, that the Catholic body should have a representation proportionate to their numbers; and that the Catholic representatives should be persons enjoying the confidence of the Catholic body.' See *Royal Commission on University Education in Ireland, Appendix to the First Report: Minutes of Evidence*, 384. A resolution of the hierarchy passed in July 1889 stated that their demands would be satisfied substantially '... (*c*) by securing to Catholics in the Senate or other supreme University Council, *an adequate number of representatives* enjoying the confidence of the Catholic body' [emphasis added].

79. Minutes of Liaison Committee of the Bishops and University College Presidents, 25 June 1953 (UCDA, PO2/54/2).

80. Browne to Tierney, 7 Jan. 1954 (UCDA, PO2/54/2).

81. 'Confidential Memorandum from the President of University College, Dublin', undated, p. 5, in reply to O'Rahilly's memo of 18 Apr. 1952. For both memos see UCDA, PO7/3.

82. 'Confidential Memorandum from the President of University College, Dublin', undated, p. 6 (UCDA, PO7/3).

83. William MacNeely (Bishop of Raphoe) and James Fergus (Bishop of Achonry) to the Taoiseach, 1 Oct. 1957 (SPO, S13809C).

84. Whyte, *Church and State in Modern Ireland,* 309–11.

85. William MacNeely (Bishop of Raphoe) and James Fergus (Bishop of Achonry) to the Taoiseach, 1 Oct. 1957 (SPO, S12809C).

86. Tierney to Lucey, 5 Jan. 1958 [actually 1959] (UCDA, PO 7/9.).

87. 'Notes on Government's Veterinary Proposal', undated.

88. Tierney to McQuaid, 14 Feb. 1959 (UCDA, PO2/59/2).

89. Tierney to McQuaid, 16 Jan. 1959 (UCDA, PO2/59/2).

90. *Report from Trinity College* (published by the American Council for the University of Dublin), vol. 1, no. 1 (Dec. 1958).

91. Michael Tierney (ed.), *Daniel O'Connell: Nine Centenary Essays,* Dublin: Browne and Nolan Ltd, 1948, 167–8.

92. Manuscript attached to draft of 'The Irish University Question' (UCDA, PO2/59/2). It will be noted in his comment on Burke that for Hogan as well as for Tierney, 'Irish' and 'Catholic' meant the same thing.

93. Tierney to McQuaid, 2 Feb. 1959 (UCDA, PO2/59/2).

94. See below, pp 311–12.

95. Tierney to McQuaid, 3 Jan. 1964 (UCDA, PO2/64/3).

96. Hartigan, 'The Catholic Laity of Dublin', 250. See above, p. 000.

97. James Meenan, diary, 19 Oct. 1941.

98. James Meenan, diary, 12 Oct. 1947.

99. See above, pp 185, 188–92.

100. See above, p. 196.

101. For a fuller discussion of the two drafts of this memo of 26 and 29 Jan. 1959 see above, pp 196–99.

102. Draft of 'The Irish University Question', 26 Jan. 1959 (UCDA, PO2/59/2), p. 6.

103. McQuaid to Tierney, 3 Sep. 1955; Tierney to McQuaid, 5 Sep. 1955(Ibid.).

104. McQuaid to Tierney, 16 July, 30 Aug. 1959(UCDA, PO2/59/2).

105. McQuaid to Tierney, 14 June 1960; Tierney to McQuaid, 15 June 1960 (UCDA, PO/60/3).

106. McQuaid to Tierney, 10, 29 July 1964; McQuaid to Hogan, 10 July 1965; 7 July 1967; 5 July 1968 (UCDA, PO2/64/3; PO2/65/3); PO2/67/2; PO2/68/2).

107. McQuaid to Tierney, 22 Apr. 1950 (UCDA, PO2/50/2).

108. Tierney to McQuaid, 27 Apr. 1951 (UCDA, PO51/5).

109. McQuaid to Tierney, 2 May 1951 (UCDA, PO2/51/5).

110. Tierney to McQuaid, 4 May 1951(UCDA, PO2/51/5).

111. President's secretary to Fr Liam Martin, archbishop's secretary, 2 June 1953 (UCDA, PO2/53/1).

112. On the Celebrations see above, pp 144–9.

113. McQuaid to Tierney, 17 July 1952 (UCDA, PO2/52/3).

114. President's secretary to Fr Mangan, 30 July 1952 (UCDA, PO2/52/3).

115. Mangan to Tierney, 1 Aug. 1952 (UCDA, PO2/52/3).

116. Hogan to Mangan, 24 Sep. 1952 (UCDA, PO2/52/3).

117. Mangan to O'Doherty (secretary to the president), 6 Aug. 1956 (UCDA, PO2/56/5).

118. McQuaid to Tierney, 10 July 1951 (UCDA, PO2/51/5).

119. Mangan to Tierney, 13 Nov. 1954.

120. MacHale to Mangan, 25 Aug. 1955 (UCDA, PO2/55/3).

121. Tierney to McQuaid, 9 Feb. 1963 (UCDA, PO2/63/2).

122. Report of Provost McConnell's speech in *Irish Independent*, 24 Oct. 1955.

123. McQuaid to Tierney, 8 Nov. 1955 (UCDA, PO2/55/3).

124. McQuaid to Tierney, 20 Jan. 1961 (UCDA, PO2/61/3).

125. O'Rahilly to Tierney, n.d. but replied to by Tierney on 4 Feb. 1961 (UCDA, PO3/63/13).

126. When dealing with the percentage of Catholics on the staff of Trinity College, O'Rahilly claimed that he was not really concerned with the private or public views of the staff concerning Catholicism: 'What we emphasise is that we are not going to submit to education of Catholic youth under such terms. If conditions were reversed, we should not expect Protestants to be satisfied with a university similarly dominated by Catholics' (*Studies*, no. 50 (autumn 1961), 249).

127. *Irish Independent*, 27 Feb. 1961.

128. Ibid.

129. Sunday Press 5 Mar. 1961; L&H minutes, 4 Mar. 1961.

130. Tierney to McQuaid, 9 Mar. 1961 (UCDA, PO2/61/3).

131. McQuaid to Tierney, 11 Mar. 1961 (UCDA, PO2/61/3).

132. Tierney to O'Rahilly, 10 May 1963 (UCDA, PO3/63/13).

133. O'Rahilly to Tierney, 3 Aug. 1963 (UCDA, PO3/63/13).

134. Ibid.

135. Hogan to McQuaid, 21 Feb. 1969 (UCDA, PO2/69/2).

136. See below, pp 314–37.

137. McQuaid to Hogan, 24 Feb. 1969 (UCDA, PO2/69/2).

138. Hogan to McQuaid, 16 June 1967 (UCDA, PO2/67/2).

139. Hogan to Conway, Browne, Philbin, and McQuaid, 21 Feb. 1968 (UCDA, PO2/68/1).

140. Conway to Hogan, 23 Feb. 1968 (UCDA, PO2/68/1).

141. McQuaid to Hogan, 26 Oct. 1970 (UCDA, PO2/70/1).

142. Dr Tierney reacted with indignation to the American report which excluded Irish medical schools while admitting British schools where clinical training was organised in precisely the same way (*Irish Independent,* 7 Nov. 1953). See also *University Review,* vol. 1, no. 1 (summer 1954), 'Background to the American Report on the Irish Medical Schools' by E. J. Conway and Patrick Fitzgerald.

143. McQuaid to Tierney, 23 Apr. 1960 (UCDA, PO2/60/3).

144. McQuaid to Hogan, 18 Jan. 1966 (UCDA, PO2/66/2).

145. 'The Strange Death of Clerical Politics in University College, Dublin, a Personal Memoir' (typescript).

146. John Whyte's widow has confirmed to the author that it was Prof. Martin's anxious attitude towards the research topic that decided Dr Whyte to move from UCD.

147. Minutes of the Board of History, 26 June 1965.

148. McQuaid to Tierney, 11 Apr. 1962 (UCDA, PO2/62/3) Like Tierney, he had opposed the original scheme for a teaching Institute of Agriculture outside of the University. See above, p. 192.

149. This comment by Dr McQuaid closely coincided with an obiter dictum by Mr Justice George Gavan Duffy in the then recent case of *In re Tilson, Infants* (1951, IR, 1 seq.). Referring to the Constitution, the judge said: 'Articles 41 and 42, redolent as they are of the great Papal Encyclicals in *pari materia* formulate first principles with conspicuous power and clarity … For religion, for marriage, for the family and the children, we have laid down our own foundations. Most of the resultant policy is both remote from British precedent and alien to the English way of life, and, when the powerful torch of transmarine legal authority is leashed across our path to show us the way we should go, the disconformity may point decisively another way.'

150. Tierney to McQuaid, 13 Jan. 1954; McQuaid to Tierney, 22 Jan. 1954 (UCDA, PO2/54/2).

151. Tierney to McQuaid, 18 June 1957 (UCDA, PO2/557/5).
152. McQuaid to Tierney, 19 June 1957 (UCDA, PO2/57/5).
153. McQuaid to Tierney, 4 Apr. 1960 (UCDA, PO2/60/3).
154. McQuaid to Tierney, 4 May 1960 (UCDA, PO2/60/3).
155. McQuaid to Tierney, 4 Dec. 1961 (UCDA, PO2/61/3).
156. See excerpt from Balfour's speech at Partick, Glasgow, on 2 Dec. 1889 in Walsh, *The Irish University Question*, 194–203.

CHAPTER 7 (P. 227–279)

1. *Report of the president, 1967/68*, 81–2.
2. McGilligan to Tierney, 4 Oct. 1948 (UCDA, Tierney Papers, box 3/45).
3. Tierney to McGilligan, 5 Oct. 1948 (UCDA, Tierney Papers, box 3/45).
4. Tierney to Taoiseach, 24 Nov. 1948 (UCDA, Tierney Papers, box 3/45).
5. It was especially appropriate for this, its ultimate use. In the nineteenth century Montrose had been a residence of the Jameson distilling family, one of whom, Annie Jameson, was the mother of Guglielmo Marconi, the inventor of radio.
6. *Manchester Guardian*, 21 Apr. 1955.
7. 'Discussion between members of the Government and representatives of UCD, at a meeting in the Council Chamber, Government Buildings, on Friday morning, 22 July 1949' (NA, S13809A).
8. Hume-Dudgeon to Tierney, 23 Feb. and 11 Apr. 1959 (UCDA, PO3/1959/5, file D).
9. *University College, Dublin, and its Building Plans*, 19.
10. Extract from Government minutes, 28 Apr. 1950 (NA, S13809A; also S14018 [B]).
11. Buildings Committee minutes, 9 June 1950.
12. Pierce Purcell, 'Memorandum to President re Negotiations for Purchase of "Merville", Stillorgan Rd', 15 June 1950 (UCDA, PO2/50/12).
13. Hume-Dudgeon to Tierney, 1 Oct. 1953 (UCDA, PO3/1953/16).
14. Tierney to Hume-Dudgeon, 9 Oct. 1953 (UCDA, PO3/1953/16).
15. *Report of the president, 1953/54*, 61–3.
16. *Report of the president, 1967/68*, 84.
17. Governing Body minutes, 30 Jan. 1968.
18. Buildings Committee minutes, 30 July 1953.
19. Memo from Prof. Purcell, Buildings Committee minutes, 30 July 1953.
20. Buildings Committee minutes, 12 Feb., 29 Apr., 22 July and 14 Oct. 1952; memo, Department of the Taoiseach, 27 Oct. 1952 (NA, S13809B).
21. Tierney to Redmond, 1 Dec. 1951 (UCDA, PO2/51/22.).
22. The last decision marked the death knell of a once-familiar UCD type, the 'chronic', a seemingly permanent student to be found in various faculties who never quite managed to complete his examinations, remained in college

through successive classes of his fellows (chronics were always male!), and was generally liked and treated as a kind of mascot.

23. Tierney to Moynihan, 30 Oct. 1952 (NA, S13809B).
24. McElligott to Secretary, Department of Education, 23 Jan. 1953 (NA, S13809B).
25. M. Breathnach, Department of Education, to Secretary, Department of the Taoiseach, 16 Feb. 1953 (NA, S13809B).
26. Tierney to Taoiseach, 9 Feb. 1953 (UCDA, PO7; also NA, S13089B).
27. Ó Raifeartaigh to Department of Finance and Department of the Taoiseach, 26 Feb. 1953 (NA, S13809B); Ó Raifeartaigh to Tierney, 11 Mar. 1953 (NA, S13809B; also Governing Body minutes, 12 Mar. 1953).
28. *Irish Independent*, 13 May 1953.
29. *Irish Independent*, 12 Oct. 1953.
30. *Irish Independent*, 14 Oct. 1953.
31. *Dáil Debates*, vol. 143, col. 1300–20, 1 Dec. 1953 .
32. *Irish Independent*, 4 Dec. 1953.
33. *Dáil Debates*, vol. 143, col. 2564–5, 15 Dec. 1953.
34. *Dáil Debates*, vol. 143, col. 2378–92, 15 Dec. 1953.
35. *Seanad Debates*, vol. 143, col. 123–38, 26 Nov. 1953.
36. Tuairim, *University College, Dublin, and the Future*, 11–12. This was a memorandum produced by a research group of the Dublin Branch of Tuairim.
37. This had been confirmed to the Department of the Taoiseach by the Department of Finance. See minute in Department of the Taoiseach (NA, S13809 B).
38. The debate also gave the Taoiseach the opportunity of stating the Government's position on the relationship between the universities and the Department of Education, the change in which had so exercised the mind of Michael Tierney.
39. *Dáil Debates*, vol. 143, col. 2752–8, 17 Dec. 1953.
40. Ó Raifeartaigh to Tierney, 15 Apr. 1953, (UCDA, PO7/7).
41. Irish Architectural Archive, Raymond McGrath Papers, box 2/14. Ó Raifeartaigh to McGrath, 17 Sep. 1953, enclosing note of the conference; minutes of Buildings Committee, 13 Oct. 1953.
42. Department of Education memo for Government, 2 Mar. 1954 (NA, S13809B).
43. Department of the Taoiseach memo on proposed transfer of UCD to Stillorgan Road site, 21 July 1955 (NA, S13809B).
44. Lee, *Ireland, 1912–1985*, 321.
45. Lee, *Ireland, 1912–1985*, 322, 312, 325.
46. Patrick Bourke SC, a graduate of UCC, was a leading member of the bar and also chief leader-writer of the *Irish Independent* (which was editorially

quite separate from the Sunday paper). Meenan at this time was also a leader-writer for the paper, engaged mainly to comment on economic matters.

47. James Meenan, diary, 21 Nov. 1954.
48. *Irish Independent,* 1 Dec. 1954.
49. *Irish Times* and *Irish Independent,* 2 Dec. 1954.
50. *Irish Times,* 3 Dec. 1954.
51. *Irish Times,* 3 Dec. 1954.
52. *Irish Times,* 4 Dec. 1954.
53. *Irish Times,* 6 Dec. 1954.
54. *Irish Times,* 7 Dec. 1954.
55. *Irish Times,* 6 Dec. 1954.
56. *Irish Times,* 7 Dec. 1954.
57. *Irish Independent,* 13 Dec. 1954; *Irish Press,* 13 Dec. 1954.
58. *Irish Independent,* 31 May 1955.
59. *Irish Independent,* 1 Aug. 1955.
60. *Irish Independent,* 13 Dec. 1955.
61. Memo of Department of the Taoiseach, 21 July 1955 (NA, S13809B).
62. Department of the Taoiseach, 15, 19, 21, 26 and 28 June and 4 July 1956 (NA, S13809C).
63. This was the sentence that the editorial in the *Irish Independent* of 1 August 1955, referred to above (p. 258), regarded as a slight lifting of the veil of secrecy surrounding the Stillorgan Road site.
64. Extract from Government minute, 20 Nov. 1956 (NA, S13809C).
65. Newman, *The Idea of a University,* preface (quoted by McCartney and O'Loughlin, *Cardinal Newman,* 47.
66. Draft of letter to Tierney from Secretary, Department of Education, 18 Dec. 1956 (NA, S13809C).
67. Observations by the Minister for Health on the memo regarding the proposed transfer that was circulated by the Minister for Education, 25 June 1957 (NA, S13809C).
68. Department of Finance's observations on the memo by the Minister for Health (NA, S13809C).
69. Minute of Government meeting, 6 Aug. 1957 (NA, S13809C).
70. Notes of discussion on 12 August 1957 between the Taoiseach, Ministers for Finance and Education and the President and Registrar of UCD (NA, S13809C).
71. William MacNeely, Bishop of Raphoe, and James Fergus, Bishop of Achonry, secretaries to the Irish hierarchy, to the Taoiseach, 1 Oct. 1957 (NA, S13809C).
72. *Irish Times,* 21, 25, 26, 28 and 30 Mar. and 1, 2, 3 and 6 Apr. 1957.
73. *Commission on Accommodation Needs, Report,* 34.

74. *Commission on Accommodation Needs, Report*, 35.

75. *Commission on Accommodation Needs, Report*, 45.

76. O'Rahilly to Lynch, 13 Mar. 1958 (NA, S13809C).

77. *Commission on Accommodation Needs, Report*, 47–8.

78. *Irish Times*, 28 Mar. 1958.

79. *Dáil Debates*, vol. 177, col. 643, 4 Nov. 1959.

80. *Irish Independent* and *Irish Times*, 17 July 1959; *Evening Herald*, 16 July 1959.

81. John O'Meara 'Why not combine Dublin's two universities?', *Irish Independent*, 30 July 1959.

82. Manuscript in Tierney's handwriting included with drafts for *University College, Dublin, and its Building Plans* in UCDA, J. J. Hogan Papers.

83. T. S. Wheeler to Hogan, 12 Aug. 1959, included with drafts for *University College, Dublin, and its Building Plans* in UCDA, J. J. Hogan Papers.

84. *University College, Dublin, and its Building Plans*, 20.

85. Correspondence in connection with the proposed intermediate floor in the chemistry laboratory in Merrion Street began with Tierney to de Valera, 30 Apr. 1958 (NA, S13809C), and the negotiations continued until the Taoiseach officially opened the new laboratory on 6 February 1959 (NA, S13809D). Reports of the speeches made on the occasion appeared in the *Irish Press* and *Irish Times*, 7 Feb. 1959.

86. *Commission on Accommodation Needs, Report*, 25.

87. *Dáil Debates*, vol. 180, col. 1397, 1406, 30 Mar. 1960; *Seanad Debates*, vol. 53, col. 968, 10 Jan. 1961.

88. Tierney to Secretary, Department of Education, 12 May 1959; Ó Raifeartaigh to Tierney, 2 June 1959; report of the inter-departmental committee, 13 Nov. 1959 (NA, S13809E).

89. Tuairim, *University College, Dublin, and the Future*, foreword.

90. Tuairim, *University College, Dublin, and the Future*, 57.

91. O'Brien, 'As to university life', 10.

92. Department of Education memo to Government, 22 Feb. 1960. (NA, S13809E).

93. *Dáil Debates*, vol. 180, col. 938, 23 Mar. 1960.

94. *Dáil Debates*, vol. 180, col. 940.

95. *Dáil Debates*, vol. 180, col. 955. Michael Tierney, thanking Dr Hillery for his speech, wrote: 'It is the most important public statement on university education since 1909' (Tierney to Hillery, 24 Mar. 1960).

96. *Seanad Debates*, vol. 53, col. 974, 10 Jan. 1961.

97. *Seanad Debates*, vol. 53, col. 950.

98. *Seanad Debates*, vol. 53, col. 953.

99. *Seanad Debates*, vol. 53, col. 954.

100. McQuaid to Lemass, 1 Apr. 1960 (NA, S13809E).

101. Lemass to McQuaid, 2 Apr. 1960 (NA, S13809E).
102. *Dáil Debates,* vol. 180, col. 1170, 24 Mar. 1970.
103. Thomas T. O'Farrell to Tierney, 1 Apr. 1960 (UCDA, PO2/59/48).
104. Dooge to Tierney, 31 Mar. 1960 (UCDA, PO2/59/48).
105. Ruane to Tierney, 1 Apr. 1960 (UCDA, PO2/59/48).
106. Frank Ford to president, 24 Mar. 1960 (UCDA, PO2/59/48).
107. Dudley Edwards to president, 25 Mar. 1960 (UCDA, PO2/59/48).

CHAPTER 8 (P. 280–306)

1. Walsh was congratulated on his elevation to the bench at the December 1959 meeting of the Governing Body.
2. 'Confidential for Minister for Education', 22 Apr. 1960 (UCDA, President's Office Papers, Department of Education file).
3. *Dáil Debates,* vol. 181, col. 302–418, 28 Apr. 1960.
4. *Dáil Debates,* vol. 181, col. 1090–118, 11 May 1960.
5. *Seanad Debates,* vol. 52, col. 1310–40, 1 June 1960.
6. Reports of these meetings of Convocation were published in the national newspapers of 25 May and 4 and 6 June 1960.
7. *Hibernia,* 6 May 1960.
8. R. Dudley. Edwards, diary, 2 May 1960 (UCDA, LA 22/45).
9. See below, p. 297.
10. James Meenan, diary, 28 Apr. 1960.
11. James Meenan, diary, 27 June 1960.
12. R. Dudley Edwards, diary, 1 July 1960 (UCDA, LA 22/45).
13. Letter signed 'Academicus' in *Hibernia,* 3 June 1960.
14. Letter signed 'Academicus' in *Hibernia,* 3 June 1960.
15. See above, p. 272.
16. Governing Body minutes, 28 June 1960.
17. L&H minutes, 17 Oct. 1959.
18. L&H minutes, 24 Oct. 1959.
19. L&H minutes, 31 Oct. 1959.
20. L&H minutes, 7 Nov. 1959.
21. L&H minutes, 21 Nov. 1959 and 16 Jan. 1960.
22. Governing Body minutes, 28 June 1960.
23. Academic Council minutes, 15 Mar. 1960, 'Report of the Committee of Discipline'.
24. L&H minutes, 12 Mar. 1960.
25. L&H minutes, 18 Mar. 1960.
26. *Irish Independent,* 29 Apr. 1960.
27. Sheehy Skeffington, *Skeff,* 202.
28. L&H minutes, 7 May 1960.
29. This was in addition to the famous rule no. 13, which had been introduced in the wake of the Communist Manifesto row in 1949. See above, p. 141.

30. Governing Body minutes, 28 June 1960.
31. Bouchier-Hayes to president, 14 Nov. 1960 (correspondence reported in L&H minutes, 15 Apr. 1961).
32. MacHale to Bouchier-Hayes, 15 Nov. 1960 (correspondence reported in L&H minutes, 15 Apr. 1961).
33. L&H minutes, 29 Oct. and 5 and 12 Nov. 1960.
34. L&H minutes, 11 Feb. 1961.
35. Governing Body minutes, 14 Mar. and 16 May 1961.
36. Academic Council minutes, 24 May 1961.
37. L&H minutes, 28 Jan., 3 Mar. 1961.
38. L&H minutes, 6 May 1961.
39. Academic Council minutes, 6 Oct. 1961.
40. F. X. Martin in Tierney, *Eoin MacNeill*, xiii.
41. L&H minutes, 28 Nov. 1959.
42. Jeremiah J. Hogan, 'Michael Tierney, 1894–1975', *Studies*, no. 65 (autumn 1976), 182–3.
43. He was later professor of Mediaeval Latin in Edinburgh and then professor of humanities, University of Glasgow.
44. P. G. Walsh, *Hibernia*, 27 May and 3 June 1960.

Chapter 9 (p. 307–344)

1. Lemass to Minister for Education, 13 Aug. 1960 (NA, S 16803A).
2. MacEntee to Hillery, 26 Aug. 1960. (NA, S 16803A).
3. Hillery to MacEntee, 29 Aug. 1960. (NA, S 16803A); Department of Education memo to Government, 12 Aug. 1960 (NA, S13809E).
4. Governing Body minutes, 29 Nov. 1960.
5. Tierney to Ó Dálaigh, 10 Dec. 1960 (UCDA, PO8/1960–67/6–7).
6. McGeady to Tierney, 5 July 1962 (UCDA, PO8/1960–67).
7. T. Desmond Williams (chairman of Academic Staff Association) to Tierney, 20 Nov. 1961 (UCDA, PO8/1960–67). At a general meeting of the ASA on 6 February 1961 an Executive Committee of eleven members was elected, with the power to co-opt a further three members. Eight belonged to the Faculty of Arts (three from History and one each from Mathematics, Irish, Logic and Psychology, Economics, and Classics), two from Medicine, and one each from Agriculture, Veterinary Medicine, Science (Chemistry), and Engineering. The report that the ASA made to the commission in November 1961 was prepared by the Executive Committee, which for this purpose held some sixty meetings, in addition to numerous meetings of sub-committees. In typescript it amounted to fifty-two pages.
8. Ó Dálaigh to Tierney, 13 Dec. 1960 (UCDA, PO8/1960–67).
9. Gwynn to Tierney, 28 Dec. 1960 (UCDA, PO8/1960–67).
10. The ASA in the introduction to its report to the commission said that 'social

institutions, particularly academic ones, must periodically carry out a self-examination' and also 'an examination of their relations with the community which they serve, and which maintains them,' in order to ensure that their functioning was adequate to meet the demands that were likely to be made on them.

11. Tierney, 'Professional and Technical Education', memorandum no. 5, 13–15.

12. Williams to Tierney, 25 Jan. 1962 (UCDA, PO2/62/51).

13. *Commission on Higher Education, Report*, vol. 1, 434–8.

14. *Commission on Higher Education, Report*, vol. 1, 439–40.

15. It had actually been so termed by Lord MacDonnell, former under-secretary at Dublin Castle, during the House of Lords debate on the Irish Universities Bill.

16. Governing Body minutes, 18 Apr. 1967.

17. Tierney to McQuaid, 3 Jan. 1964 (UCDA, PO2/64/3).

18. *Studies*, no. 56 (summer 1967), 122.

19. Governing Body minutes, 18 Apr. 1967.

20. *Irish Independent*, 29 Mar. 1958.

21. *Irish Independent*, 24 June 1958.

22. *Irish Times*, 1 Feb. 1967.

23. *Irish Times*, 19 Apr. 1967.

24. *Irish Times*, 19 Apr. 1967.

25. *Irish Times*, 22 Apr. 1967.

26. *Irish Times*, 27 Apr. 1967.

27. Education correspondent in *Irish Times*, 19 Apr. 1967.

28. *Irish Independent*, 15 May 1967.

29. Maurice Kennedy, '(4) The state and the university' in *The Proposed Merger with TCD, papers read at a seminar at UCD, 13 May 1967*, 21.

30. *Studies*, no. 56 (summer 1967), 122.

31. *Studies*, no. 56 (summer 1967), 161–2.

32. *Irish Independent*, 18 May 1967.

33. T. E. Nevin, 'Jeremiah Hogan and University College, Dublin', *Studies*, no. 74 (autumn 1985), 3.

34. Governing Body minutes, 29 June 1967.

35. FitzGerald, *All in a Life*, 57.

36. FitzGerald, *All in a Life*, 81–2.

37. Governing Body minutes, 28 Nov. 1967.

38. Memorandum for discussion with Trinity College representatives, 8 Jan. 1968 (UCDA, Merger 1/4.).

39. Hogan to Ó Raifeartaigh, 29 Jan. 1968.

40. Memorandum from Trinity College representatives, 29 Jan. 1968 (UCDA, Merger 1/4)/ The IFUT plan, because it supported duplication, was so severely criticised by the *Irish Press* in its editorial of 30 September 1967

that, according to Dr Hogan in a letter to the Minister for Education (17 Sep. 1968), some people thought the article was inspired by the Government.

41. James Meenan noted in his diary (29 Feb. 1968): 'G. Body was quite a good meeting all the better because Garret talked only about six times.'

42. Governing Body minutes, 19 Mar. 1968.

43. Later, in his memo to the HEA, 'The Case for University College, Dublin' (Apr. 1969), Dr Hogan admitted that there was in these meetings of March 1968 'more of opposition or reluctance,' arising partly, he supposed, from the fact that Trinity College had already declared against the plan. He calculated that half the 317 members of staff consulted had voted against any change but that 191 were prepared if necessary to accept the UCD scheme.

44. For the full statement see Higher Education Authority, *Report on University Reorganisation*, appendix II, 77–82.

45. Until earlier that year, Secretary of the Department of Education and chairman of the UCD-TCD negotiations (see above, p. 326).

46. NUI Senate minutes, 23 Oct. 1968.

47. Governing Body minutes, 29 May 1969.

48. For the full text of the NUI-TCD agreement see Higher Education Authority, *Report on University Reorganisation*, appendix III, 83–92.

49. Something like this conference had been proposed by the Commission on Higher Education. Dr Hogan said the conference would to some extent take the place of the National University, but with less power with regard to the individual universities (Governing Body minutes, 23 Apr. 1970).

50. *Irish Times*, 26 June 1970; F. McGrath, 'The University Question' in P. J. Corish (ed.), *A History of Irish Catholicism*, vol. 5, no. 6, 142; Whyte, *Church and State in Modern Ireland*, 343.

51. Patrick FitzGerald, 'Re HEA Report', 20 July 1972 (UCDA, PO 2/72/39).

52. D. K. O'Donovan to T. Murphy, 14 Nov. 1972 (UCDA, PO 2/72/49).

53. Faculty of Medicine minutes, 7 Dec. 1972 (UCDA, PO 2/72/49).

54. Governing Body minutes, 17 Dec. 1974.

CHAPTER 10 (P. 345–388)

1. John Feeney, 'Students in revolt', *Irish Times*, 3 Feb. 1971.

2. For a vigorous criticism of Feeney's interpretation see Basil Millar, *Irish Times*, 20 Feb. 1971.

3. *Commission on Higher Education, Report*, vol. 2, 812.

4. *Commission on Higher Education, Report*, vol. 2, 507, 813.

5. *Irish Press*, 11 Oct. 1968; *Irish Times*, 12 Oct. 1968.

6. *Evening Herald* and *Evening Press*, 31 Oct. 1968.

7. See below, pp 351–2.

8.   *Irish Times,* 16 Nov. 1968.

9.   *At Swim-Two-Birds* [first published 1939], Harmondsworth (Middx): Penguin 1967, 33–4.

10. The report of the Academic Council committee of inquiry (9 May 1969), p. 8, is wrong in its chronology of events when it states that 'the first occasion on which SDA committed a breach of discipline in the College was when its chairman called a meeting in the Main Hall on 27 October ...' The date of that meeting was 27 November. The error is based on a slip in *Confrontation,* which in the heat of battle printed 'Oct.' when clearly, even from editorial evidence in the paper, it should have been 'Nov.'

11. John Feeney in *Confrontation,* 4 Mar. 1969.

12. Frank Shaw SJ to Hogan, 16 Dec. 1968.

13. Frank Shaw SJ to Eddie O'Connor (president of SRC), 18 Dec. 1968.

14. L&H minutes, 11 Jan. 1969.

15. *Irish Press,* 16 Jan. 1969.

16. No doubt Prof. Kelly would have agreed with Raymond Aron's reprimand to his colleagues in the Sorbonne who had yielded to student pressure: 'A professor would have to be very ignorant indeed to be more ignorant than his students ...' (Raymond Aron, *The Elusive Revolution,* London, 1969, 53). See the report of John Kelly's address to the Blackrock Debating Society in the *Irish Independent,* 8 Mar. 1969. See also *Irish Press* and *Irish Times,* 7 Mar. 1969.

17. Evidence to Academic Council committee of inquiry, 20 Mar. 1969.

18. Pettit, *The Gentle Revolution,* 29, 30.

19. Kevin Myers in Pettit, *The Gentle Revolution,* 36.

20. The four elected were John Maguire, a tutor in politics, Dermot Gleeson, auditor of the L&H, Eddie O'Connor, outgoing president of the SRC, and Dónall Ó Riain, a final engineering student and SRC committee member.

21. *Campus,* 9 May 1969.

22. Ivor Browne (psychiatry), Denis Donoghue (English), Robin Dudley Edwards (history), P. Leahy (engineering), Michael McCormac (political economy), P. N. Meenan (medical microbiology), John O'Donnell (engineering), Rory O'Hanlon (law), Eva Philbin (chemistry), James Ruane (farm management), J. R. Timoney (mathematics), and T. Desmond Williams (history).

23. 'Secret Statement of Chairman on Alleged Secret XII Revolutionaries', Mar. 1969 (UCDA, R. Dudley Edwards Papers, LA 22/216 [87–8]).

24. Noone appreciated better than Newman the need for communication both within the institution and in its relations with the outside world. The first number of the *Catholic University Gazette* bears the date 1 June 1854, that is, five months before the Catholic University opened in November 1954. It began as a weekly production of eight pages, consisting of two parts, the first containing announcements, news, regulations, and proceedings of the

university, the second being articles by Newman himself on the nature and history of universities. From 8 March 1855 until it expired at the end of 1856 it was a monthly.

25. John Feeney, 'The arrogant magicians', *Irish Times,* 5 Feb. 1971.

26. It has to be said that any headaches Myers the student may have caused the UCD authorities of his day have been amply compensated for by Myers the journalist with the many good things he has written from time to time about his *alma mater.*

27. SCM members might have found an analogy in the Vatican Council's recent emphasis on the church as the people of God, that is, all believers.

28. This would also have coincided with Vatican II imperatives.

29. Pettit, *The Gentle Revolution,* 35.

30. Oral evidence to Academic Council committee of inquiry.

31. When, a few years later, one of the committee, Desmond Williams, did not retire from the deanship of arts after two terms of three years each (and was supported by the chairman of the committee of inquiry in so doing), he was challenged and defeated by the first non-professor to hold the post.

32. Academic Council minutes, 18 June 1969.

33. When the postgraduate student concerned submitted the thesis, she was advised to make certain alterations. She returned to America, the thesis was not re-submitted, and the award was not made.

34. Report of the president, 1970/71, 6, 11, 18, 19, 34, 42, 47, 48. This was the overall college ratio, computed on the new basis agreed by the HEA. (The Commerce Faculty was three times greater, with 1: 46.)

35. Eric J. Hobsbawm, *Industry and Empire: an economic history of Britain since 1750* (London, 1968), 250

Chapter 11 (p. 389–404)

1. Secretary of the Government to private secretary of Minister for Education, 20 Dec. 1960 (NA, S13809E).

2. *University College, Dublin: The Arts Building, Belfield,* 1970.

3. See above, p. 360.

4. James Meenan, diary, 27 Sep. 1969.

5. James Meenan, diary, 6 Mar. 1970.

6. James Meenan, diary, 13, 15 May 1970.

7. James Meenan, diary, 10 May 1971.

8. James Meenan, diary, 21 Aug. 1971.

9. James Meenan, diary, 25 Oct., 26 Nov. 1971.

10. See above, p. 213.

11. Andrzej Wejchert, Report and Development Plan (Nov. 1973, revised Mar. 1974), 8.

12. Governing Body minutes, 21 May 1968.

13. Ó Raifeartaigh to president, 9 May 1968.

14. Governing Body minutes, 29 Apr. 1969.
15. J. P. MacHale, *UCD News*, Feb. 1995, 10; Governing Body minutes, 18 Feb. 1986.
16. *Irish Times*, 24 Sep. 1991. 'The total cost of getting the project [Graduate Business School at Carysfort] up and running, including adaptation and equipment at Carysfort, will come to £11.7 million, of which UCD is contributing £2 million from funds raised in the private sector and the balance is being provided by the State. This arrangement was reached following discussions with Minister for Education Mary O'Rourke T.D.'—*UCD News*, Jan. 1991, p. 1.
17. Arthur Griffith (ed.), *Thomas Davis: The Thinker and Teacher*, Dublin, M. H. Gill and Son Ltd., 1914, 64–5.
18. Monsignor Molloy, 'The Catholic University', *Irish Ecclesiastical Record*, Feb. 1883, 135–6.
19. Memo (dated Dec. 1972) for Governing Body meeting of 23 Jan. 1973.
20. See memos on buildings (Dec. 1972), submitted to Governing Body meeting of 23 Jan. 1973.
21. Newman, *The Idea of a University*, discourse VI, 9 (quoted by McCartney and O'Loughlin, *Cardinal Newman*, 72).
22. O'Brien, 'As to university life', 3–11.
23. O'Brien, 'As to university life', 8.
24. O'Brien, 'As to university life', 11.
25. O'Brien, 'UCD as I forget it', 6–11.
26. O'Brien, 'UCD as I forget it', 6.
27. O'Brien, 'UCD as I forget it', 8.
28. *University College, Dublin, and its Building Plans*, 13.
29. *University College, Dublin, and its Building Plans*, 11.
30. *University College, Dublin, and its Building Plans*, 11.
31. Report of Newman House Committee (UCDA, PO2/73/5).
32. Report of Newman House Committee (UCDA, PO2/73/5).
33. But the basement of 86, for long a noisy, crowded and odoriferous students' canteen, was leased out to become one of the most highly regarded and exclusive restaurants in Dublin.
34. Newman, *The Idea of a University*, discourse VII, 1.
35. Newman, 'What is a university?', *University Sketches*, vol. 3, 16. An earlier version of this sentence was quoted by Michael Tierney in his speech at the cutting of the first sod for the new Science Building, 7 June 1962.

EPILOGUE (P. 405)

1. Thomas M. Kettle, *The Day's Burden*, (Dublin, 1937), xi–xii.
2. The design for the coat of arms and seal of the college was prepared by

George Sigerson (1836–1925), professor of zoology 1909–1923. He had been on the staff of the Catholic University Medical School since 1865 and was a distinguished figure in the scientific and literary life of the country.

Bibliography

1. *ARCHIVAL SOURCES*

(a) UCD Archives Department.

       Governing Body Minutes.

       Building Committee Minutes.

       Finance Committee Minutes.

       Academic Council Minutes.

       Faculty Minutes.

       President's Office Files.

       Registrar's Office Files.

       Secretary and Bursar's Office Files.

       Minute Book of the Committee of Statutory Officers 1944–46.

       Literary and Historical Society Minute Books.

       R. Dudley Edwards Papers.

       Michael Hayes Papers.

       Patrick McGilligan Papers.

       Eoin MacNeill Papers.

       James Meenan Papers.

       John Marcus O'Sullivan Papers.

       Michael Tierney Papers.

Catholic University of Ireland Records including:

       Catholic University Committee, draft minutes of meetings 9 Sept. 1850–16 Jan. 1856.

       Catholic University Committee, minutes of meetings 9 Sept. 1850–20 Feb. 1856.

       Episcopal Board of Catholic University, minutes of meetings 5 Aug. 1859–10 Sept. 1879.

       Council of the Faculty of Philosophy and Letters, minutes of meetings 26 June 1856–25 Jan. 1879.

       Catholic University Register of Students 1854–79.

       Building Fund Register 1862–66.

       Academic Council minutes.

       University Council minutes.

       School of Medicine Governing Body.

Albert Agricultural College Records.

Royal College of Science Records.

National University Women Graduates' Association Records.

(b) NUI Archives.

Minutes of Senate of National University of Ireland.

Minute Book of Convocation of the National University of Ireland.

Minutes of Senate of Royal University of Ireland.

Minutes of Standing Committee of Royal University of Ireland.

(c) Dublin Diocesan Archives.

Woodlock, Walsh, McQuaid papers.

(d) National Archives of Ireland.

Cabinet S Files.

(e) Irish Architectural Archive.

Raymond McGrath Papers.

2. *OFFICIAL GOVERNMENT PUBLICATIONS*

Commissions, Acts, Charters, Reports, Parliamentary debates.

Royal Commission on university education in Ireland. First Report; *Appendix to the First Report* (1901), H.C. [Cd 825–6]; *Second Report*; *Appendix to the Second Report* (1902) H.C. [Cd 899–900]; *Third Report*; *Appendix to the Third Report* (1902) H.C. [Cd 1228–9]; *Final Report*; and *Appendix to the Final Report* (1903) H.C. (Cd 1483–4]
[The 'Robertson Commission'].

Royal Commission on Trinity College, Dublin, and the University of Dublin. First Report; *Appendix to the First Report* ((1906), H.C. [Cd 3174, 3176]; *Final Report*; *Appendix to the Final Report* (1907), H.C. [Cd 3311–3312]
[The 'Fry Commission'].

Preliminary draft of the articles of a charter for the university to have its seat in Dublin (1908) H.C. [Cd 4041].

Revised draft of the articles of a charter for the university to have its seat in Dublin (1908) H.C. [Cd 4209].

Irish Universities Act, 1908. 8 Edw. VII, c 38, 1 Aug. 1908.

Report to accompany the statutes made by the Dublin Commissioners appointed under the Irish Universities Act 1908 (1909) H.C. [Cd 4726].

Irish Universities Act, 1908. Dublin Commission. University College, Dublin. Applications for Professorships, Lectureships and other Offices. Vol. I. Printed for the use of the Commissioners (Dublin, 1909; 1910).

Final Report of the Dublin Commissioners (1911) H.C. [5877].

Report of Commission on accommodation needs of the constituent colleges of the National University of Ireland [Pr 5089] [June 1959].

Commission on Higher Education 1960–1967: I Presentation and Summary of Report [Pr 9326] (Dublin, 1967).

Commission on Higher Education 1960–1967: II Report, vol. i chapters 1–19 [Pr 9389] (Dublin, 1967).

Higher Education Authority: First Report 1968/9.

Higher Education Authority: Report on University Organisation [Prl 2276] July 1972.

Higher Education Authority: Women Academics in Ireland (Dublin, 1987).

Report of the Board of Visitors to University College, Dublin (Dublin, 1960).

University College Dublin Act, 1960.

Universities Act, 1997 [No. 24 of 1997].

Hansard's Parliamentary Debates, fourth series.

Dáil Éireann Debates.

Seanad Éireann Debates.

3. *UNIVERSITY AND COLLEGE PUBLICATIONS*

Catholic University of Ireland Calendar 1855–1869 (Dublin, annually).

Catholic University of Ireland. Report of the Committee, and list of subscriptions (Dublin, 1852).

Summary of contributions to the Catholic University of Ireland received from 15 May 1854 to 1 Oct. 1855 (Dublin, 1855).

Report on the condition and circumstances of the Catholic University of Ireland presented by a Committee of Senate, July 1859 (Dublin, 1859).

Catholic University of Ireland 1854: Centenary Celebrations 18–23 July 1954 (1954).

Royal University of Ireland Calendar 1883–1909 (Dublin, annually).

National University of Ireland Calendar 1911– (Dublin, annually).

National University of Ireland. Act of Parliament, Charter and Statutes (Dublin, 1919).

National University of Ireland Statute LXXXVI [Pr 298] (Dublin, 1951).

The National University Handbook 1908–1932 (Dublin, 1932). Editor, Professor T. Corcoran, S.J.

The National University of Ireland. Summary of Progress 1932–1939 (Dublin, 1939).

University College Dublin Calendar 1909– (Dublin, annually).

Report of the President of University College Dublin 1909– (Dublin, annually).

University College, Dublin, Acts, Charter and Statutes 1–29 (Dublin, 1944).

University College, Dublin, Acts, Charter and Statutes 1–90.

Report of the Committee of Statutory Officers presented to the President, University College Dublin (28 January 1946).

University College Dublin and its Building Plans (1959).

University College Dublin Development Plan (June 1987).

University College Dublin Development Plan Phase 2 (Nov. 1991).

University College Dublin: Shaping a Vital Decade. (June 1991).

University College Dublin: Report on Internal Structures (March 1993).
University College Dublin: The Past the Present the Plans (1976).
Wejchert, Andrzej, *Report and Development Plan for Belfield Campus, University College, Dublin* (Nov. 1973, revised March 1974).
Albert Agricultural College: Centenary Souvenir 1838–1938 (UCD, 1938).
UCD News, 1970– .
UCD Alma Mater (a magazine for UCD alumni) 1993–96. continued as *UCD Connections* 1997– .
UCD Academic Staff Association Bulletin 1961–1974.
Academic Staff Association UCD. *Contemporary developments in University education: Report of a seminar* Nov. 1963 [Reports of papers and discussions at successive annual seminars of the ASA continued to be published over a number of years to 1972].
Academic Staff Association UCD. *Report on Academic–Administrative Structure* (Oct. 1972).
Report of the sub-committee on Academic-Administrative Structure (Oct. 1971).

4. STUDENT MAGAZINES

Among the longer lived were:
St Stephen's 1901–06; 1960–1977; 1986.
The National Student 1910–1921; new series 1923; 1930–35; continued irregularly as *National Student/Comhthrom Feinne* 1935–52; then as *National Student* 1952–53.
Comhthrom Féinne 1931–5 continued irregularly as *National Student/Comhthrom Féinne* 1935–52, appearing briefly as *Comhthrom Féinne* in a couple of issues in Irish in Feb. and March 1943.
The Student 1954–64.
University Gazette 1958–68.
Awake 1960s.
Campus 1960s.
Confrontation Dec. 1968–Mar. 1969.
College Tribune.
University Observer.

5. NEWSPAPERS AND JOURNALS

Atlantis Jan. 1858–Jan. 1870.
An Claidheamh Soluis.
Catholic Bulletin.
Catholic University Gazette 1854–56.
Crane Bag.
Freeman's Journal.
Hibernia.

Irish Ecclesiastical Record.

Irish Educational Review.

Irish Independent.

Irish Press.

Irish Times.

The Leader.

Lyceum 1887–94.

New Ireland Review 1894–1911.

Observer.

Spectator.

The Standard.

Studies 1912– .

Sunday Independent.

Sunday Press.

Third Degree.

The Times.

University: An ad hoc bulletin … issued by members of staff at University College Dublin [1969].

University Review 1954–68 continued as

Irish University Review, autumn 1970– .

6. SPECIAL STUDIES AND OTHER SECONDARY WORKS

Andrews, C. S., *Dublin Made Me* (Dublin, 1979).

A Page of Irish History: Story of University College Dublin 1883–1909. Compiled by Fathers of the Society of Jesus (Dublin, 1930).

Aron, Raymond, *The Elusive Revolution: Anatomy of Student Revolt*. Translated by G. Clough (London, 1969).

Binchy, D. A., *Osborn Bergin* (UCD, 1970).

Boland, John, *Irishman's Day: A Day in the Life of an Irish M.P.* (London, n.d.).

Bowman, John, '"The wolf in sheep's clothing": Richard Hayes's proposal for a new National Library of Ireland, 1959–60', in *Modern Irish Democracy*. Edited by Ronald J. Hill and Michael Marsh, pp 44–61.

Browne, Noel, *Against the Tide* (Dublin, 1986).

Clancy, Patrick, *Participation in Higher Education: A National Survey* (Dublin, Higher Education Authority, 1982).

Corcoran S.J., Timothy, 'Newman's ideals and Irish realities', in *Studies*, i, no. 1 (March 1912), 114–29.

   Newman's Theory of Liberal Education. Printed for academic use in the Department of Education, University College, Dublin (1929).

Corish, Patrick J., *Maynooth College 1795–1995* (Dublin, 1995).

Costello, Peter, and Van de Kamp, Peter, *Flann O'Brien: An Illustrated Biography* (London, 1987).

Curran, C. P., *Newman House and University Church* (Dublin, n.d.).
'Memories of University College, Dublin: The Jesuit tenure', in M. Tierney (ed.). *Struggle with Fortune*, pp. 221–30.

Delany S.J., William, *Irish University Education, Facts and Figures: A Plea for Fair Play* (London, 1904).

Dillon, Thomas, 'The origin and early history of the National University', part I, in *University Review*, 1, no. 5 (summer 1995), 43–51; part II, in *University Review*, i, no. 6 (autumn 1955), 12–28.

Doolin, William, 'The Catholic University School of Medicine (1855–1909)', in M. Tierney (ed.), *Struggle with Fortune*, pp. 61–79.

Ellman, Richard, *James Joyce* (Oxford, 1959).

Feeney, John, *John Charles McQuaid–The Man and the Mask* (Cork and Dublin, 1974).

Finlay, S.J., Peter. See Sacerdos below.

FitzGerald, Garrett, *All in a Life: An Autobiography* (Dublin, 1991).

Garvin, Tom, 'The Strange Death of Clerical Politics in University College, Dublin', in Irish University Review, xxviii, no. 2 (Autumn–Winter 1998), 308–14.

Gaughan, J. Anthony, *Alfred O'Rahilly I: Academic* (Dublin, 1986).
Alfred O'Rahilly III: Controversialist Part I: Social Reformer (Dublin, 1992).
Alfred O'Rahilly III: Controversialist Part II: Catholic Apologist (Dublin, 1993).
Newman's University Church: A History and Guide (Dublin, 1997).

Gwynn S. J., Aubrey, 'The Jesuit Fathers and University College', in M. Tierney (ed.), *Struggle with Fortune*, pp 19–50.

Gwynn, Denis, and Hogan, James, 'Some Afterthoughts on the Newman Centenary Celebrations', in *University Review*, i, no. 2 (autumn 1954), 3–9.

Hayden, Mary, and Sheehy Skeffington, Hanna, 'Women in University: a reply', in *Irish Educational Review*, i, no. 5 (Feb. 1908).
'Women in University: a further reply, Ibid. (April 1908).

Henchy, Seamus, 'The Visitor of the National University', in *University Review*, ii, no. 7, 16–24.

Hogan, J. J. 'Mary M. Macken: An Appreciation', in *Studies*, XXXIX (Sept. 1950), 315–18.
'The work of Dr Coffey and Dr Conway 1908–1947', in M. Tierney (ed.), *Struggle with Fortune* (Dublin, [1954]), pp. 81–102.
'The Newman heritage', in M. Tierney (ed.), *Struggle with Fortune* (Dublin, [1954]), pp. 213–21.
'Michael Tierney 1894–1975', in *Studies*, LXV (autumn 1976), 177–91.

Hogan, Mary J., *University College Dublin Women Graduates' Association 1902–1982* (n.d.)

Holland, C. H. (ed.), *Trinity College Dublin and the Idea of a University* (Dublin, 1991).

Joyce, James, *A Portrait of the Artist as a Young Man* (first published 1916). *Stephen Hero* (first published London, 1944).

Kane, Eileen, 'John Henry Newman's Catholic University Church in Dublin', in *Studies*, LXVI (summer/autumn 1977), 105–20.

Kennedy, David, *Towards a University* (Belfast, 1946).

Kerr, Donal, *Peel Priests and Politics: Sir Robert Peel's Administration and the Roman Catholic Church in Ireland, 1841–1846* (Oxford, 1982).

Larkin, Emmet, *The Making of the Roman Catholic Church in Ireland 1850–1860* (University of North Carolina Press, Chapel Hill, 1980). The later volumes of Larkin's monumental history of the Catholic Church in Ireland in the nineteenth century also contain many references to the Irish university question.

Lee, J. J., *Ireland 1912–1985: Politics and Society* (Cambridge, 1989).

Luce, J. V., *Trinity College Dublin: The First 400 Years* (Dublin, 1992).

Lyons, F. S. L., 'The minority problem in the 26 Counties', in Francis MacManus (ed.), *The Years of the Great Test* (Cork, 1967).

McCaffrey, Patricia, 'The Wyndham University Scheme 1903–4', in *Proceedings of the Irish Catholic Historical Committee 1968* (Dublin, 1969), pp. 27–47.

McCartney, Donal, and O'Loughlin, Thomas (eds.), *Cardinal Newman: The Catholic University* (Dublin, 1990).

McCartney, Donal, *The National University of Ireland and Eamon de Valera* (Dublin, 1983).

McConnell, Rev. James (ed.), *Selected Papers of Arthur William Conway* (Dublin, 1953).

McDonald, Walter, *Reminiscences of a Maynooth Professor* (Cork, 1967).

McDowell, R. B., and Webb, D. A., *Trinity College Dublin 1592–1952* (Cambridge, 1982).

McGrath S.J., Fergal, *Newman's University: Idea and Reality* (London, 1951). 'The University Question', in Patrick J. Corish (ed.), *A History of Irish Catholicism*, V, 6, pp. 84–142 (Dublin, 1971). *Newman in Dublin* (C.T.S.I.) pamphlet, Dublin, 1969).

MacHale, J. P., 'The socio-economic background of students in Irish universities', in *Studies*, LXVIII (autumn 1979), 213–21. 'The assembly of a campus', in *UCD News*, Feb. 1995, pp. 8–10.

McHugh, Roger (ed.), *Newman on University Education* (Dublin, 1944).

McKenna S. J., Lambert, 'The Catholic University of Ireland', in *Irish Ecclesiastical Record* fifth series, xxxi (1928), pp 225–45; 351–71; 482–90; 589–605.

MacLoughlin, P. J., 'Professor J. J. Nolan', in *Studies*, XLI (Sept. and Dec. 1952), 317–22.

MacNeill, Eoin, *Irish in the National University of Ireland* (Dublin, 1909).

McRedmond, Louis, *Thrown among Strangers: John Henry Newman in Ireland* (Dublin, 1990). *To the Greater Glory: a history of the Irish Jesuits* (Dublin, 1991).

Macken, Mary M., 'Dr Denis J. Coffey', in *Studies*, XXIX (June 1940), 117–86.
   'In Memoriam: Mary T. Hayden', in *Studies*, XXXI (Sept. 1942), 369–71.
   'John Marcus O'Sullivan', in *Studies*, XXXVII (March 1948), 1–6.
   'Women in the University and the College: A struggle within a struggle', in M.
   Tierney (ed.), *Struggle with Fortune* (Dublin, [1954]), pp. 142–65.
Martin, F. X. (ed.). *The Easter Rising 1916, and University College, Dublin*
   (Dublin, 1966).
Martin, F. X., and Byrne, F. J. (ed.), *The Scholar Revolutionary: Eoin MacNeill,*
   1867–1945, and the Making of the New Ireland (Shannon, 1973).
Maurice, Sir Frederick, *Haldane 1856–1915* (London, 1937).
Meenan, F. O. C., *Cecilia St: The Catholic University School of Medicine*
   1855–1931 (Dublin, 1987).
   'The Catholic University School of Medicine 1860–1880', in *Studies*, LXVI
   (summer/autumn 1977), pp. 135–44.
Meenan, James (ed.), *Centenary history of the Literary and Historical Society of*
   University College Dublin 1855–1955 (Tralee, [1956]).
   'The Student Body', in M. Tierney (ed.), *Struggle with Fortune*, pp. 103–20.
   George O'Brien: a Biographical Memoir (Dublin, 1980).
Meenan, Patrick N., *St Patrick's Blue and Saffron: a miscellany of UCD Sport*
   since 1895 (Dublin, 1997).
Miller, D. W., *Church, State and Nation in Ireland, 1898–1921* (Dublin, 1973).
Moody, T. W., *Thomas Davis 1814–45: a Centenary Address* (Dublin, 1945).
   'The Irish university question of the nineteenth century', in *History*, xlii, no.
   148, pp 90–109, (1958).
   and Beckett J. C., *Queen's Belfast 1845–1949* (2 vols., London, 1959).
Morrissey S.J., Thomas, *Towards a National University: William Delany S.J.,*
   1835–1924 (Dublin, 1983).
Murphy, Gerard, 'Celtic Studies in the University and the College', in M. Tierney
   (ed.), *Struggle with Fortune*, pp 121–41.
   'Osborn Joseph Bergin 1873–1950' , in *Studies*, xxxix, no. 156 (Dec. 1950),
   385–94.
Murphy, John A., *The College: a history of Queen's College/University College*
   Cork, 1845–1995 (Cork, 1995).
Newman, John Henry, *Historical Sketches* vol III: *Rise and Progress of*
   Universities (new edition, London, 1891). [Also known as *University Sketches*
   in numerous reprints.]
   My Campaign in Ireland: Catholic University Reports and Other Papers
   (printed for private circulation only, Aberdeen, 1896).
   Sermons Preached on Various Occasions (London, 1857; fifth edition 1881).
   The Idea of a University. Edited with introduction and notes by I. T. Ker
   (Oxford, 1976). [Another useful edition has been edited with an introduction
   and notes by Martin J. Svaglic (Indiana, 1982).]

Newman's Doctrine of University Education: Lectures Delivered in University College, Dublin on the Occasion of the Newman Centenary 1952 (Dublin, 1954). [The contributors were Michael Tierney, 'Newman's Doctrine of University Education'; Rt Rev. Mgr John D. Horgan, 'Newman on Faith and Reason'; Wm Doolin, 'Newman and his Medical School'; J. J. Hogan, Newman and Literature'; T. S. Wheeler, 'Newman and Science'.]

Nolan, J. J., 'Arthur W. Conway', in *Studies*, xxxix, no. 155 (Sept. 1950), 241–50.

O'Brien, Flann, *At Swim-Two-Birds* (London, 1939).

O'Brien, George, 'Prospect for the Future', in M. Tierney (ed.), *Struggle with Fortune*, pp. 193–211.

O'Brien, Kate, 'As to University Life', in *University Review*, i, no. 6 (autumn 1955), 3–11.

'U.C.D. As I forget it', in *University Review*, iii, no. 2, 6–11.

Ó Broin, Leon, *The Chief Secretary: Augustine Birrell in Ireland* (London, 1969).

Ó Buachalla, Séamas (ed.), *A Significant Irish Educationalist: the Educational Writings of P. H. Pearse* (Dublin and Cork, 1980).

O'Connor, Sean, *A Troubled Sky: Reflections on the Irish Educational Scene 1957–1968* (St. Patrick's College, Dublin, 1986).

O'Donovan, James L., 'Experimental Research in University College, Dublin', in *Studies*, X (March 1921), 109–22.

[O'Dwyer], Edward Thomas, Bishop of Limerick, 'The University Bill', in *Irish Educational Review*, i, no. 8 (May 1908), 453–63.

O'Faolain, Nuala, *Are You Somebody?* (Dublin, 1996).

O'Flynn, Grainne, 'Augustine Birrell and Archbishop William Walsh's influence on the founding of the National University of Ireland', in *Capuchin Annual*, 1976, pp 145–62.

O'Hickey, Rev. Michael, *An Irish University or else*—(Dublin, 1909).
The Nationalisation of Irish Education (a lecture delivered 14 Oct. 1902 under the auspices of the Central Branch of the Gaelic League. Gaelic League pamphlet no. 27).

Oldham, Alice, 'Women and the Irish University Question', in *New Ireland Review*, vi (Feb. 1897), 257–63.

O'Meara, John, 'Guardians of Truth', in *Irish University Review*, xxvi, no. 1 (spring/summer 1996), 1–14.
'Why not combine Dublin's two universities', in *Irish Independent*, 30 July 1959.

O'Rahilly, Alfred, 'The Irish University Question', in *Studies*, l, li (Autumn, Winter 1961; Spring, Summer 1962).

Ó Raifeartaigh, T. (ed.), *The Royal Irish Academy: a Bicentennial History 1785–1985* (Dublin, 1985).

O'Reilly, Séan and Rowan, Alistair, *University College Dublin* (Irish Heritage series, Dublin, 1990).

O'Shea, John Augustus, *Roundabout Recollections* (2 vols, London, 1892).

O'Sullivan, John Marcus, 'Dr Denis J. Coffey', in *Studies*, xxxiv (June 1945), 145–57.

Pelikan, Jaroslav, *The Idea of the University: a Re-examination* (Yale University Press, 1992).

Petitt, Philip (ed.), *The Gentle Revolution* (Dublin, 1969).

Report from Trinity College published by the American Council for Trinity College Dublin, i, no. 1 (Dec. 1958).

Roberts, Ruaidhrí, and Clarke, R. Dardis, *The Story of the People's College* (Dublin, 1986).

Sacerdos [Finlay S.J., Peter], 'Mr Birrell's University Bill', in *New Ireland Review*, xxix (June 1908), 210–20.

Semple, Patrick, 'The Royal University', in M. Tierney (ed.), *Struggle with Fortune*, pp. 51–60.

Sheridan, Niall, 'Brian, Flann and Myles (the Springtime of Genius)' in *Myles: Portraits of Brian O'Nolan*. Edited by Timothy O'Keeffe (London, 1973), pp. 32–53. Reprinted from *Irish Times*, 2 April 1966.

Skeffington, Andrée Sheehy, *Skeff: The Life of Owen Sheehy Skeffington 1909–1970* (Dublin, 1991).

Taaffe, Michael, *Those Days Are Gone Away*.

Tierney, Michael, *A Tribute to Newman: Essays on Aspects of his Life and Thought*. Edited by Michael Tierney (Dublin, 1945).

    University Sketches by John Henry Newman. Edited with Introduction and Notes by Michael Tierney (Dublin, [1952]).

    Struggle with Fortune. Edited by Michael Tierney (Dublin, 1954).

    'The struggle in retrospect', in *Struggle with Fortune*, pp 1–18.

    'The New College, 1908–1954', in *Struggle with Fortune*, pp 230–37.

    Daniel O'Connell: Nine Centenary Essays. Edited by Michael Tierney (Dublin, 1948).

    'Nationalism: a survey', in *Studies*, xxxiv (Dec. 1945), 474–82.

    'Thomas Davis: 1814–1845', in *Studies*, xxxiv (Sept. 1945), pp 300–310.

Tierney, Michael, *Eoin MacNeill: Scholar and Man of Action, 1867–1945*. Edited by F. X. Martin (Oxford, 1980).

Tuairim, *University College Dublin and the Future: a Memorandum from a Research Group of Tuairim, Dublin Branch* (1960). Tuairim 6 Pamphlet.

Vale, Mary, 'The origins of the Catholic University of Ireland', in *Irish Ecclesiastical Record*, lxxxii (1954), 1–16; 152–64; 226–41.

Walsh, P. J., *William J. Walsh, Archbishop of Dublin* (Dublin and Cork, 1928).

[Walsh, Wm. J.] *The Irish University Question: The Catholic Case: Selections from the Speeches and Writings of the Archbishop of Dublin* (Dublin, 1897).

Wheeler, Thomas S., 'Life and work of William K. Sullivan', in *Studies*, xxxiv (March 1945), 21–33.

'Sir Robert Kane: Life and Work', in *Studies*, xxxiii (June, Sept. 1944), 158–68; 316–30.

White, Norman, *Hopkins: A Literary Biography* (Clarendon Press, Oxford, 1992).

Whittaker, Edmund T., *Arthur William Conway 1875–1950*. Reprinted from *Obituary Notices of Fellows of the Royal Society*, vii, Nov. 1951.

Whyte, John, *Church and State in Modern Ireland 1923–1979* (second edition, Dublin, 1980).

Williams, T. D., 'The College and the Nation', in M. Tierney (ed.), *Struggle with Fortune*, pp 166–91.

7. WORKS OF REFERENCE

Boylan, Henry, *Dictionary of Irish Biography* (Dublin, 1988).

Dictionary of National Biography (London, 1908–).

Hickey, D. J., and Doherty, J. E., *A Dictionary of Irish History since 1800* (Dublin, 1980).

Irish Catholic Directory.

McRedmond, Louis (general editor), *Modern Irish Lives: Dictionary of 20th-century Irish Biography* (Dublin, 1996).

8. UNPUBLISHED THESES

Breathnach, Eileen, A history of the movement for women's higher education in Dublin, 1860–1912 (M.A., UCD 1981).

Finnegan, Belinda, The democratisation of higher education and the participation of university women in the labour force, 1920–1950 (M.A., UCD 1985).

Hartigan, Maurice, The Catholic Laity of Dublin 1920–1940 (Ph.D., Maynooth 1992).

Kiely, Jennifer Sarah, The development of the views of the Roman Catholic Hierarchy in the Irish University Question 1845–1908: Pursuit of Equality in Higher Education (M.A., UCD 1994).

Loze, Lara Suzanne, The Robertson Commission: Its achievement in contributing to the admittance of women to University Education in Ireland (M.A., UCD 1994).

Lydon, Peter, The Evolution of Belfield: the development of a university campus (B.A., UCD 1988).

Rigney, William J., Bartholomew Woodlock and the Catholic University of Ireland 1861–79 (Ph.D., UCD 1995).

The College magazines (including *UCD News*, *UCD Alma Mater*, *UCD Connections*) have published several valuable, brief contributions to various aspects of the history of the College. These are too numerous to list individually in the above select bibliography.

Index